The ART *and* SCIENCE *of* TRADING

Course Workbook

Detailed Examples & Further Reading

The ART *and* SCIENCE *of* TRADING

Course Workbook

Detailed Examples & Further Reading

Adam Grimes

Hunter Hudson Press, New York, New York
MMXVII

Published by Hunter Hudson Press, New York, NY.

This book is set in Garamond, using page proportions and layout principles derived from Medieval manuscripts and early book designs, codified in the work of J. A. van de Graaf.

ISBN-13: 978-1948101004

ISBN-10: 1948101009

Printed in the United States of America

10 9 8 7 6 5 4 3 2 1

To my readers:

Your support for my work has touched me.
Your dedication and perseverance have inspired me.
Your questions have challenged me, and I've learned so much from you.
I am honored to be a part of your journey.

Thank you

"It's what you learn after you know it all that counts."
– John Wooden

Contents

Forward (and how to use this book)

This is not a typical trading book. If you're going to use it most effectively, you need to know a few things about it.

What Is In This Book?

This book is a companion to the trading course, *The Art and Science of Trading*, available free of charge at MarketLife.com, and also to my first book, *The Art and Science of Technical Analysis: Market Structure, Price Action, and Trading Strategies* (2012). The content in this book fall in four broad categories:

- Exercises and "homework" for the trading course, available at MarketLife.com
- Collected blogs and other short pieces of writing relevant to each section and topic.
- More extensive studies in "whitepaper" format that provide a statistical foundation for this style of trading.
- A reading plan for The Art and Science of Technical Analysis.

A few thoughts on each of these:

Exercises for the Trading Course

One of the things that makes learning to trade difficult is that there has never been a solid curriculum to develop the skills of technical trading. This book includes exercises that have been shown to be effective over years of teaching and coaching traders: chartreading exercises that develop skills from reading inside individual bars to understanding large-scale moves of markets. The ways in which markets trend, and those trends come to an end, are examined in detail, as are other aspects of price action.

There are also some little gems hidden throughout this work: There's a full history of the Dow Jones Industrial Average in chart format, with performance summaries for each decade, and important geopolitical events marked on the charts. You literally hold in your hands the history of stock trading in North America. There are also charts that explore important and volatile situations in the market, as well as some charts that were specifically chosen to show conflicted and confusing technical patterns.

Effective trading requires much more than looking at chart patterns, and there's material here to help you craft an enduring and effective trading program: exercises aimed at developing a comprehensive trading and business plan, managing various aspects of trader psychology, keeping effective records, and doing statistical analysis and your own market research. Traders at any stage of development should find something of value here, and, for many traders, this information will lay a solid foundation for a lifetime of successful trading.

Developing traders often struggle with an insufficient perspective on market history. Time spent studying these historical examples, deeply, is time well spent. Do not focus too heavily on page count! Some of the most important work in this book occupies only one or two pages for each exercise.

Collected Blogs and Other Shorts

Over the past decade, I've blogged and written regularly in various formats. This book collects selected blog posts that will give insight on the topics covered. I have made an effort to retain the casual, informal tone of this format; these posts have been only lightly edited to fit into this book, and most posts feature the original graphics which, in some cases, were slightly lower production quality than what you might usually find in a book.

I admit to having some concerns about effectively republishing material I have already shared in another format. As this book started to take shape, those concerns faded because I saw how well the posts addressed the students' learning along the way. Also, one of the strengths of a blog is also its weakness—it's a living thing. Readers focus on current topics, and blog posts from years past are sometimes overlooked. Writing this book was a good opportunity to collect some of those older, historical blog posts and to connect them to overarching concepts.

Whitepapers

The whitepapers in Part II of the book have never been published in their entirety, though some of the information found its way into various presentations and blog posts I have done over the years. They give some good examples of ways in which we can apply quantitative techniques to market data. Hopefully, I've communicated some of the nuance involved with this work, and stressed the need for humility—we never have firm, final answers to most of our questions, and there's always another way to consider the problems involved. The last chapter in this section provides some solid examples of quantitative tendencies that support the style of trading in my first book and the online course.

There are several ways you can use the material in this book most effectively, depending on your experience and objectives.

How to Use this Book

Any book can be read cover to cover, and that might be a good way to familiarize yourself with the contents. After that first read through, there are several other ways you may best use this material:

As the Workbook to the Course

This is how this book started: as a collection of pdf documents and charts that were designed to extend the work in the course. If you are working through the online course, simply use the material in this book as your homework, working through each module consecutively.

If, for whatever reason, you do not have the course material, you can still do many of the homework exercises. Every effort has been made to make the explanations and descriptions as useful as possible without going into unnecessary and redundant detail. Some of these exercises may stand on their own better than others, but they will really shine when you work through them, as intended, with the online course.

The exercises and studies presented here are the result of many years of practical trading, teaching, thinking about markets, and feedback from readers and traders I have worked with. There are no "filler" or "throwaway" exercises—everything is important.

As a Study Guide for My First Book

You may also read my first book, *The Art and Science of Technical Analysis* (Wiley, 2012), with this book in hand, following the guided reading plan for that book. People who have read the book effectively generally read it more than once, take notes, and create exercises to help them understand the concepts. The online course was originally intended to be a companion to the book, to help people work through it in a structured fashion, and to make sure readers were getting the most out of it.

If you work through that book following the topically-ordered reading plan here, also take a look at the associated exercises; some of those exercises will appeal to you and will offer good opportunities to deepen your understanding of the material.

As a Stand-alone Reference

The whitepapers in Part II can be read by themselves, in the order in which they are presented. They will bring some challenges to some of the tools traditionally used by many technical traders. It is necessary to reiterate a point, here: the objective of these papers is not to disprove anything. In fact, it is not the nature of scientific inquiry to think in those terms. Rather, we are seeking evidence that these tools, which are purported to be very powerful, offer a statistical edge in the market.

These tools, in my studies, do not show an edge, but there could be many reasons for this. Perhaps the tests are flawed, perhaps the data was flawed, perhaps the methodology missed something important, or perhaps the tools do not have an edge. Regardless, these papers will give you some perspective on the problems of technical trading, and may suggest some new directions for your own investigations and research.

I hope you find this material interesting, useful, and fun. I have enjoyed writing it for you, and I wish you all possible success in your trading endeavors!

Adam Grimes
October 2017
New York, New York

Course Catalog

This is a list of modules and units from the online course, available at no charge from MarketLife.com.

I. Chartreading 101

Introduction
Basic Principles
Basic Chart Setup
Charts: Going Deeper
Reading Price Charts

II. Chartreading, Going Deeper

Pivots and Swings
Trends
Support and Resistance
Trading Ranges
The Problem of Randomness
Random Walks

III. Market Structure & Price Action

Trend and Range
Trend to Range and Back Again
Tools for Trends
Ends of Trends
The Two Forces
Market Cycles

IV. The Pullback

The Pullback
Expected Value
Where'd Your Charts Go?
Quantitative Techniques I
Record Keeping
Manual backtesting

V. The Anti

VI. The Failure Test

VII. The Breakout

VIII. Pattern Failures

IX. Practical Trading Psychology

Reading Plan for The Art and Science of Technical Analysis

Page numbers refer to *The Art and Science of Technical Analysis* by Adam Grimes, Wiley (2012)

I. Charts, chart setup, becoming a trader

1-8 (having an edge)
9-12 (basic chart setup)
22-30 (reading inside bars, charting by hand)
375-385 (becoming a trader)
399-408 (trading primer)
375-384 (becoming a trader)

II. Pivots and swings, support and resistance, basic patterns of trend and range

13-18 (two forces intro, pivots)
19-21 (basic swing patterns)
49-64 (trends)
97-120 (ranges)
78-84 & 93-96 (trend analysis)

III. More detail on trends and ranges, interfaces, the market cycle

85-92 (trendlines)
121-148 (between trends and ranges)
189-212 (indicators and tools for confirmation)
31-48 (market cycles and the four trades)

IV. Pullbacks and journaling

65-77 (pullback intro)
154-169 (pullback detail)
291-315 (pullback examples)
385 - 388 (journaling)

V. The Anti and cognitive biases

170-173 (the anti)
327-336 (anti examples)
353-359 (cognitive biases)
409-424 (deeper look at MACD and MA)

VI. Failure test and basic trading stats

VII. Breakouts, multiple timeframes, trade management

VIII. Risk

IX. Trader psychology

Acknowledgments

No creative work springs forth fully formed from a vacuum. It is the interactions with other thinkers that drive creativity, and this book, perhaps more than most, owes a lot to its readers. Over the years, your questions—whether they be simple, profound, or unanswerable, and your interactions with me—whether you were supportive, challenging, or downright angry—have driven me forward. People often wonder at the amount of free content I create, but I must honestly say I have probably benefited from this as much or more than anyone else.

Some other people contributed to this work in a very focused and direct way. Hannah Guerrero, our discussions, years ago, about teaching a complete beginner to trade provided the seed from which all of this course material grew. To Maria Tadros, thank you for unlimited proofreads on a very tight time schedule—in the end, you were a veritable ATM machine of ideas and valuable perspectives. Tom Hansbury, Peter Lawless, and Stewart Button, thank you for your critical thoughts and careful edits. Jose Palau helped me bridge the gap from experience to theory and back again; thank you!

To my wife, Betsy, thank you for being supportive, looking at multiple drafts of cover graphics that differed by a few millimeters, humoring me while we agonized over the virtues of color #0947D5 vs. #0945D4 (I exaggerate only slightly), and generally letting me disappear for days while writing this book!

To each of my readers, I owe a debt and many words of gratitude: thank you. You have helped create this work you now hold in your hands; I could not have done it without you.

Part the First

Chapter 1

Module 1–Chartreading 101

This module focuses on some important foundational concepts that are often overlooked. We begin with an investigation of what it means to have trading edge and why it matters. Our goal in all of this work is to focus on practical application, but to also supply enough theory to support the work and to make sure that the trader understands the "whys" as much as the "hows".

This module also includes a solid look into price charts. Too often, traders begin their work without truly understanding what the chart represents. Chart display choices are made based on vague visual appeal, similarity to something seen elsewhere, or a recommendation from a friend (who may or may not know what he is doing!) Thinking deeply about the chart also leads us to our next area of focus: chart stories.

I came up with the term "chart story" when I was working with beginning traders. When we think in these terms, we imagine that every aspect of every bar is important, and we try to understand the part every tiny detail plays in the developing story of the market. (We must acknowledge right away that this line of thinking is misleading because it does not respect the random variation in the market. Its value is only as a training tool to help build solid habits in chartreading.) This is one way to look at and to think about price charts, and it lays a solid foundation for developing market feel down the road.

The supplementary readings for this section also cover some thoughts on the process of learning to trade and why it can be so difficult. Simply put, we do not learn to trade at all—rather, we become traders. And that journey, richly rewarding as it may be, is long, challenging, and fraught with danger. The trader who understands this from the first steps is much better equipped to succeed.

Section 1: Chart Setup

You should begin to set up your charts, or, if you are an experienced trader, to rethink your existing chart set-up. While there's no right or wrong, it's probably a good idea to move toward simplicity and a focus on the chart itself (rather than on indicators.)

A common question is what my chart settings are. There's no need to duplicate exactly, but the charts in this section use:

- Modified Keltner Channels set 2.25 average true ranges around a 20 period exponential moving average.
- A modified MACD that uses simple instead of exponential moving averages, and the settings of 3-10-16 (with no histogram) for inputs.

For the developing trader, it's probably a good idea to use the same chart setup for all markets and timeframes. Of course, there may be reasons you want to use different indicators or setups on, say, monthly vs. 5 minute charts, but the purpose of these exercises is to train your eye to see the data in a consistent way.

Experiment and play with the options your charting package presents. Sometimes different color settings can be more pleasing to your eye, and it's also worth taking some time to look at the choices between candles and bars, spending more time on whichever you are less comfortable with.

Section 2: Chart Stories

This is an exercise that is designed to do a few specific things:

- To force you to slow down and to look at the details of the charts
- To get you to start thinking about the forces that might be behind the price formations
- To start thinking about emotional context in extreme situations
- To show you a handful of important historic moments in financial markets. (Not every chart in this sector is designed to that end; some are simply illustrations of interesting patterns.)
- To begin to awaken some sense of intuition and inductive learning.

For the purpose of this exercise, assume that every bar has a story; your job is to tell that story. Rather than worrying about being right or wrong, focus on the thought process and inductive nature of this analysis. There really are no wrong answers here, and you may even find value in doing these exercises more than once. Finding interesting examples on your own would be another way to extend the analysis.

If the chart has text, answer the question or do the specific analysis on the chart. If there is no text, then write a separate explanation for each labeled bar—in all cases, make sure that each bar designated with a label receives your attention and a text explanation.

Adequate explanations will usually be 2-6 sentences long and will focus on concepts such as:

- The position of the open and close within the day's range
- The position of the open and close relative to each other
- The range of the bar relative to previous bars
- Consider each bar both alone and in relation to previous bars
- Any "surprises" (This is a deliberately large category.)
- Action around any obvious support and resistance levels. (This is not an exercise in support and resistance, so do not focus on this aspect.)
- It may be useful to think in terms of large groups of buyers and sellers driving the market, and the battle between those groups.

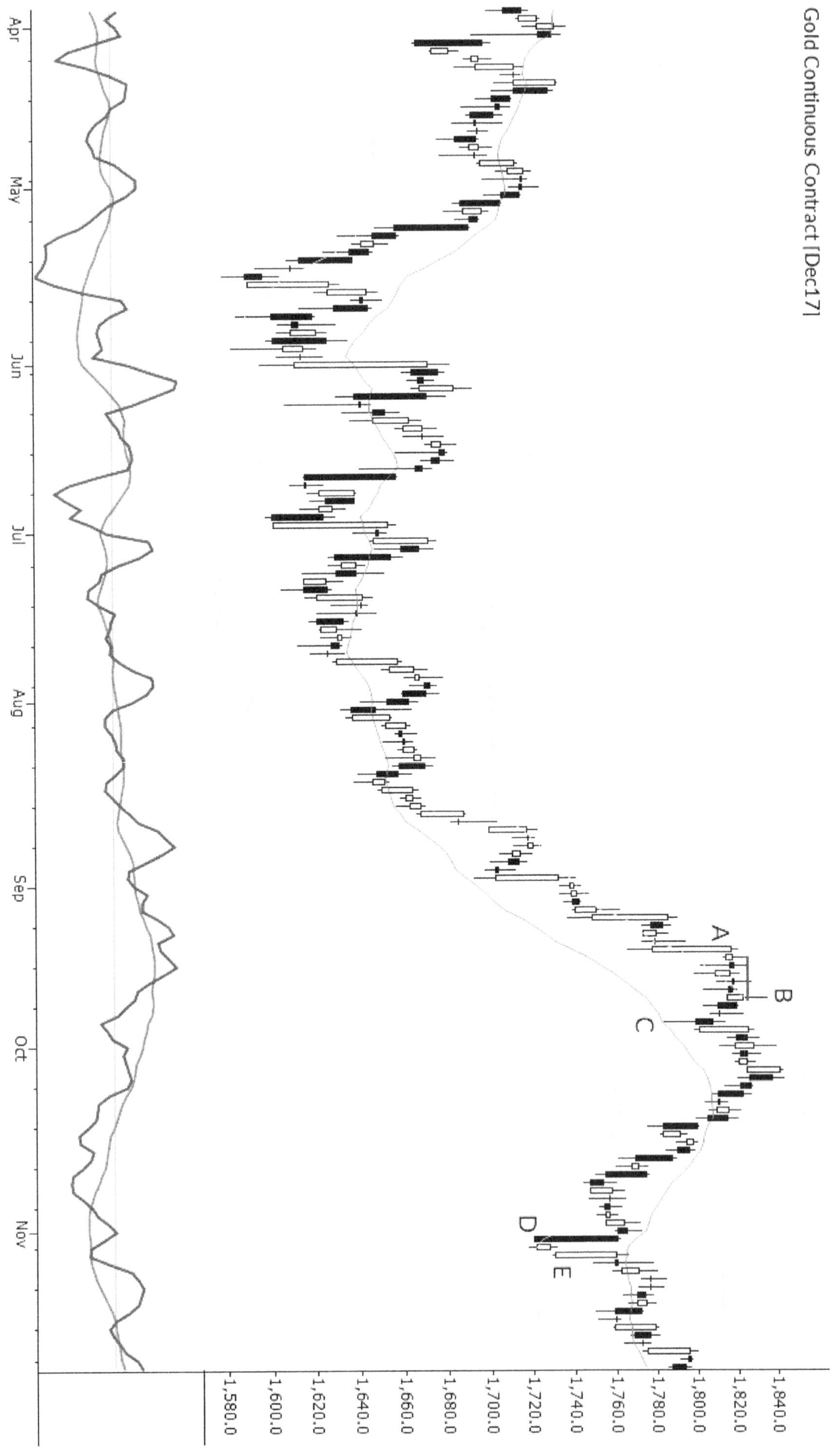
Gold Continuous Contract [Dec17]
A
B
C
D
E
Apr
May
Jun
Jul
Aug
Sep
Oct
Nov
1,580.0
1,600.0
1,620.0
1,640.0
1,660.0
1,680.0
1,700.0
1,720.0
1,740.0
1,760.0
1,780.0
1,800.0
1,820.0
1,840.0

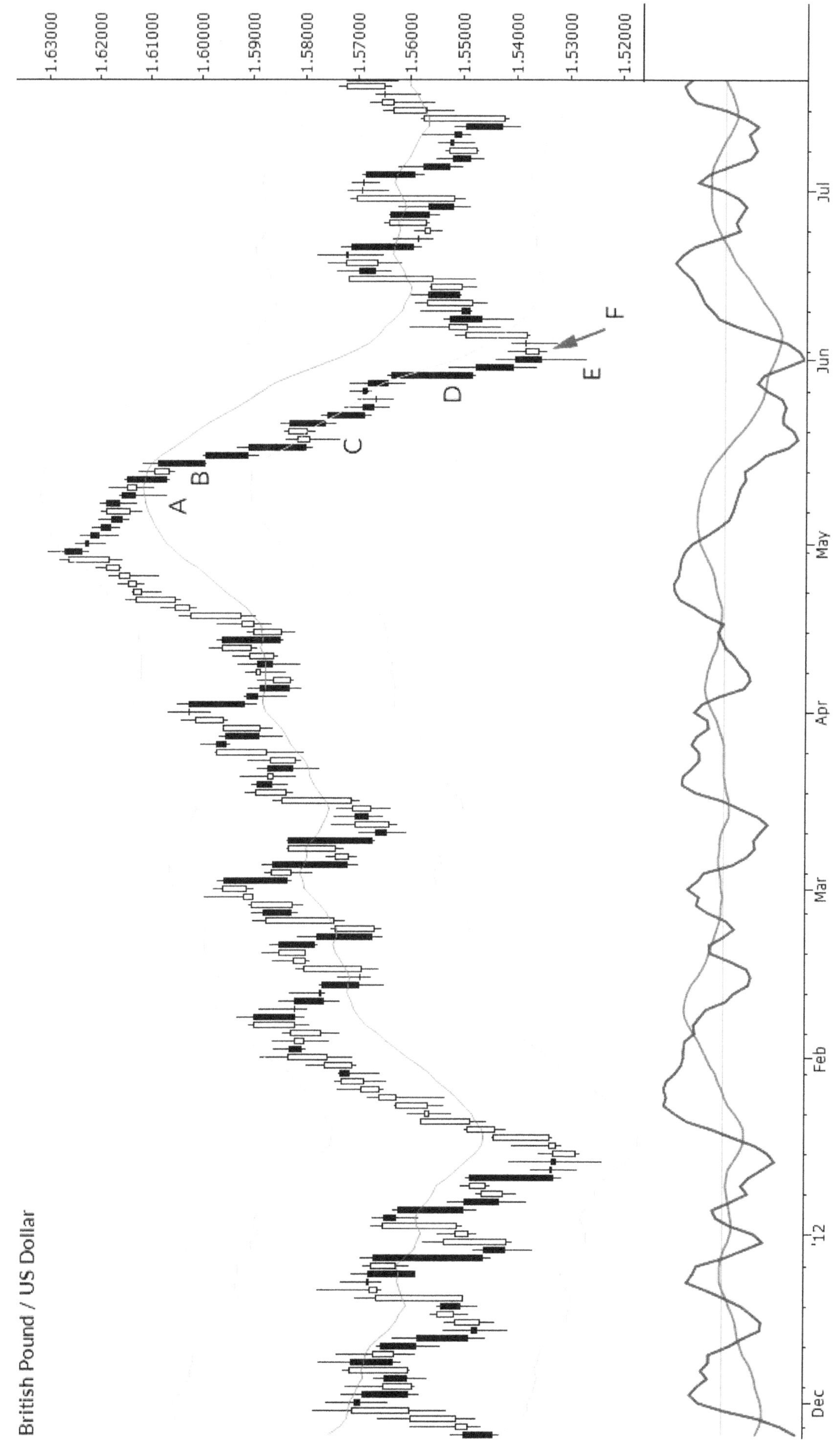
British Pound / US Dollar
1.63000
1.62000
1.61000
1.60000
1.59000
1.58000
1.57000
1.56000
1.55000
1.54000
1.53000
1.52000
Dec
'12
Feb
Mar
Apr
May
Jun
Jul
A
B
C
D
E
F

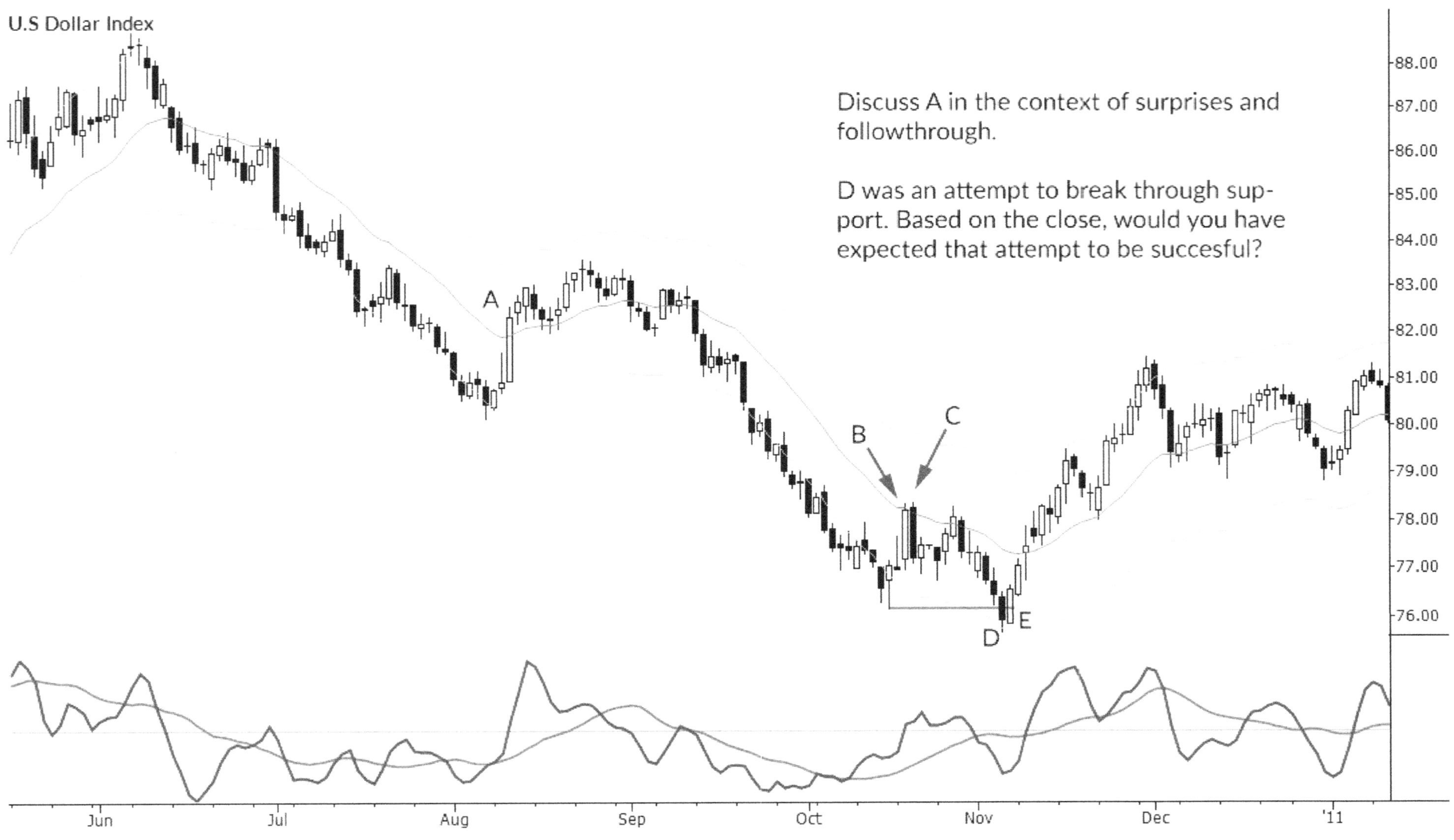
U.S Dollar Index
Discuss A in the context of surprises and followthrough.
D was an attempt to break through support. Based on the close, would you have expected that attempt to be succesful?
A
B
C
D
E
88.00
87.00
86.00
85.00
84.00
83.00
82.00
81.00
80.00
79.00
78.00
77.00
76.00
Jun
Jul
Aug
Sep
Oct
Nov
Dec
'11

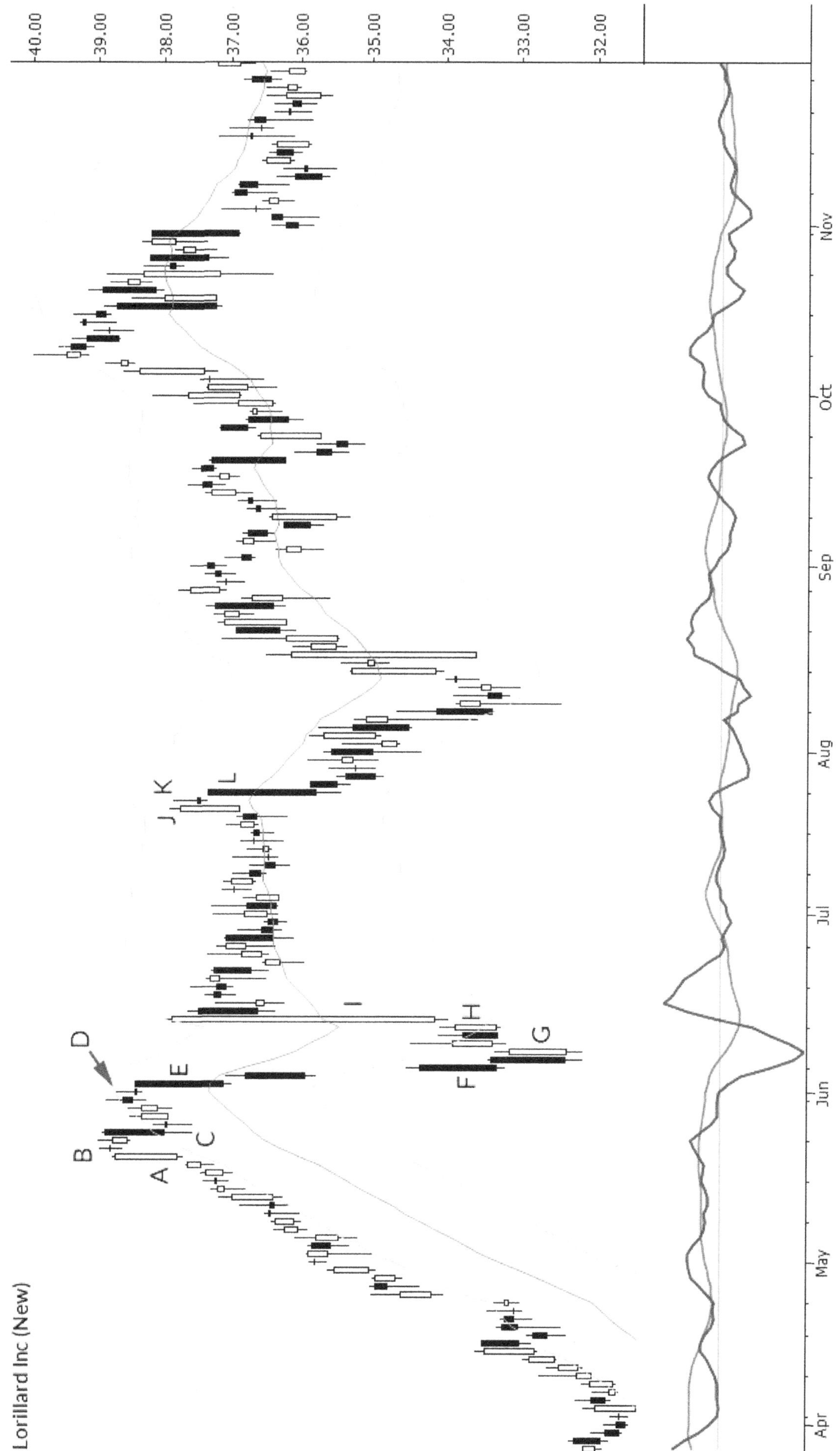
Lorillard Inc (New)
40.00
39.00
38.00
37.00
36.00
35.00
34.00
33.00
32.00
Apr
May
Jun
Jul
Aug
Sep
Oct
Nov
A
B
C
D
E
F
G
H
I
J
K
L

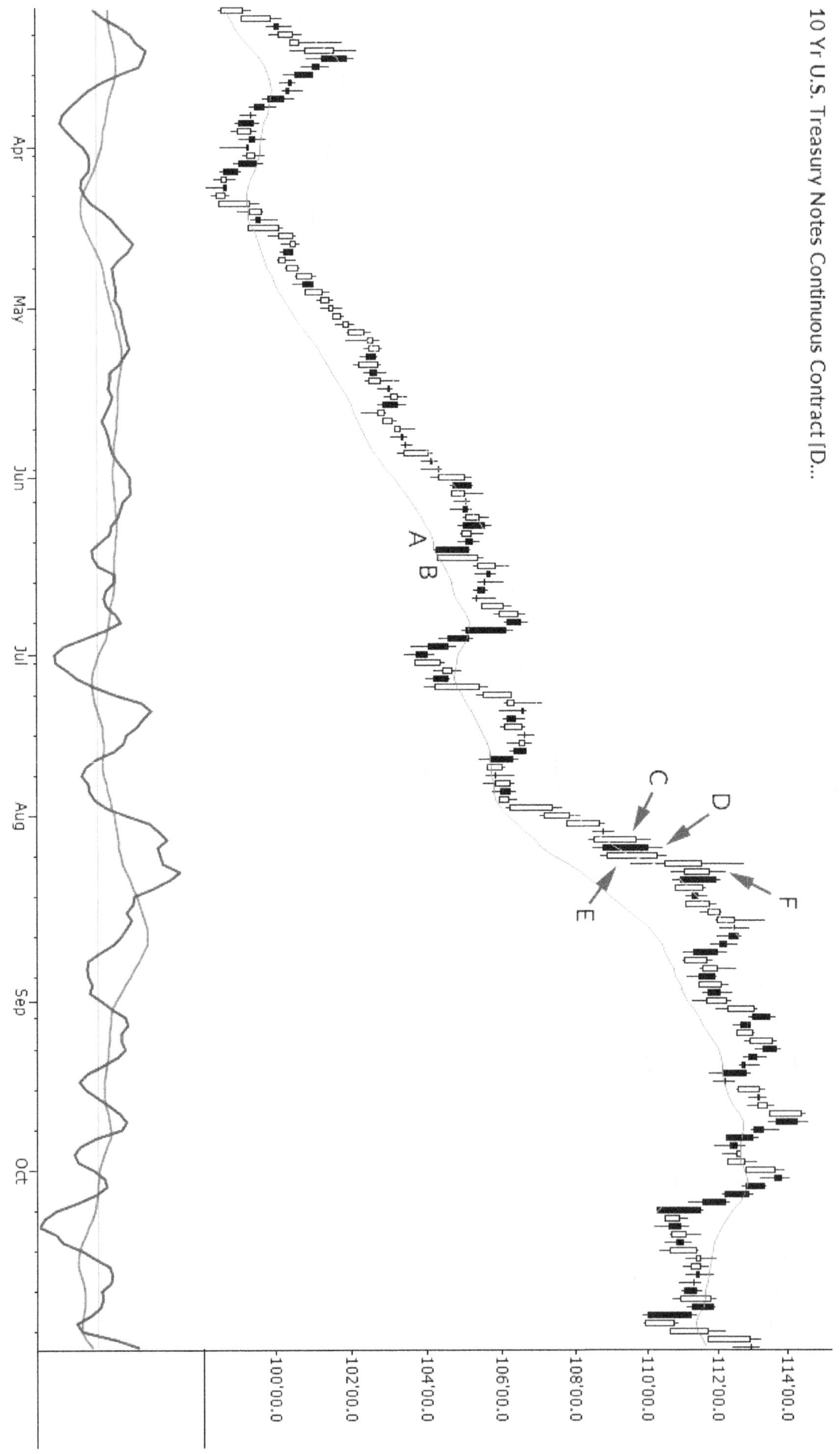
10 Yr U.S. Treasury Notes Continuous Contract [D...
A
B
C
D
E
F
Apr
May
Jun
Jul
Aug
Sep
Oct
100'00.0
102'00.0
104'00.0
106'00.0
108'00.0
110'00.0
112'00.0
114'00.0

Coca-Cola Co
40.00
39.00
38.00
37.00
36.00
35.00
34.00
Mar
Apr
May
Jun
Jul
Aug
Sep
Oct
A
B
C
D
E
F
This may have been a difficult chart to read in real time. With the benefit of hindsight, comment on this action. One of the key ideas is that "sometimes markets get ahead of themselves and need to pause." Comment on B, C, and D as broad ranges rather than individual bars. Comment on the other points as individual bars.

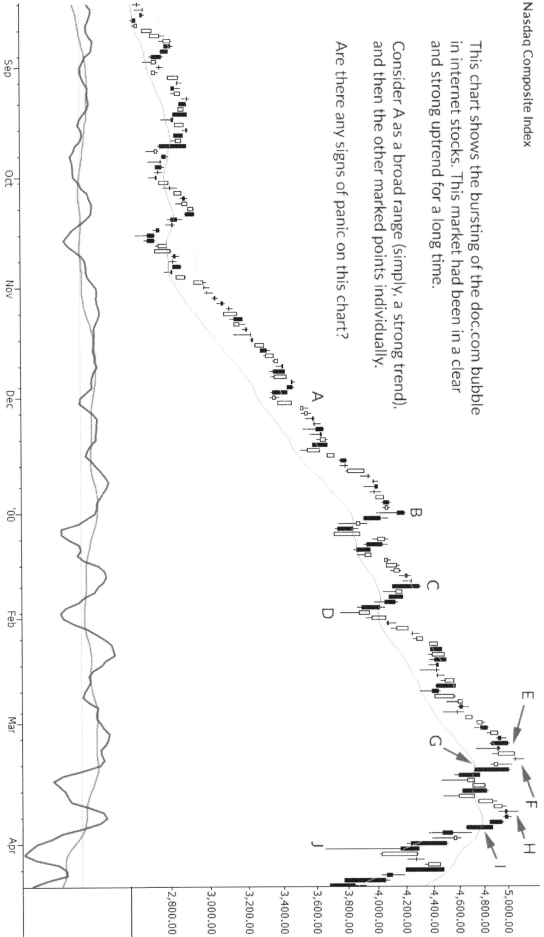

Nasdaq Composite Index
This chart shows the bursting of the doc.com bubble in internet stocks. This market had been in a clear and strong uptrend for a long time.
Consider A as a broad range (simply, a strong trend), and then the other marked points individually.
Are there any signs of panic on this chart?
A
B
C
D
E
F
G
H
I
J
5,000.00
4,800.00
4,600.00
4,400.00
4,200.00
4,000.00
3,800.00
3,600.00
3,400.00
3,200.00
3,000.00
2,800.00
Sep
Oct
Nov
Dec
'00
Feb
Mar
Apr

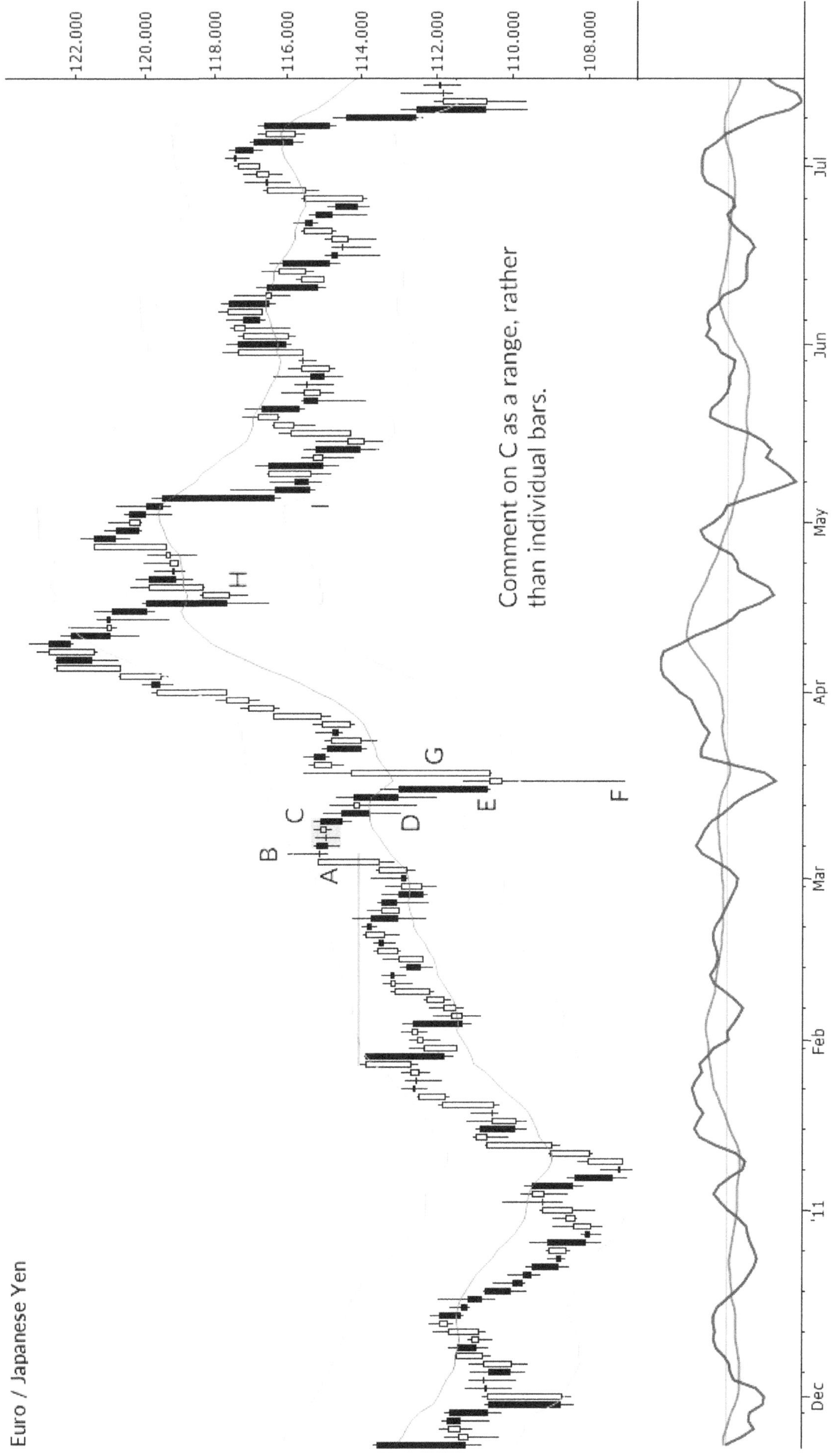
Euro / Japanese Yen
122.000
120.000
118.000
116.000
114.000
112.000
110.000
108.000
Dec
'11
Feb
Mar
Apr
May
Jun
Jul
A
B
C
D
E
F
G
H
Comment on C as a range, rather than individual bars.

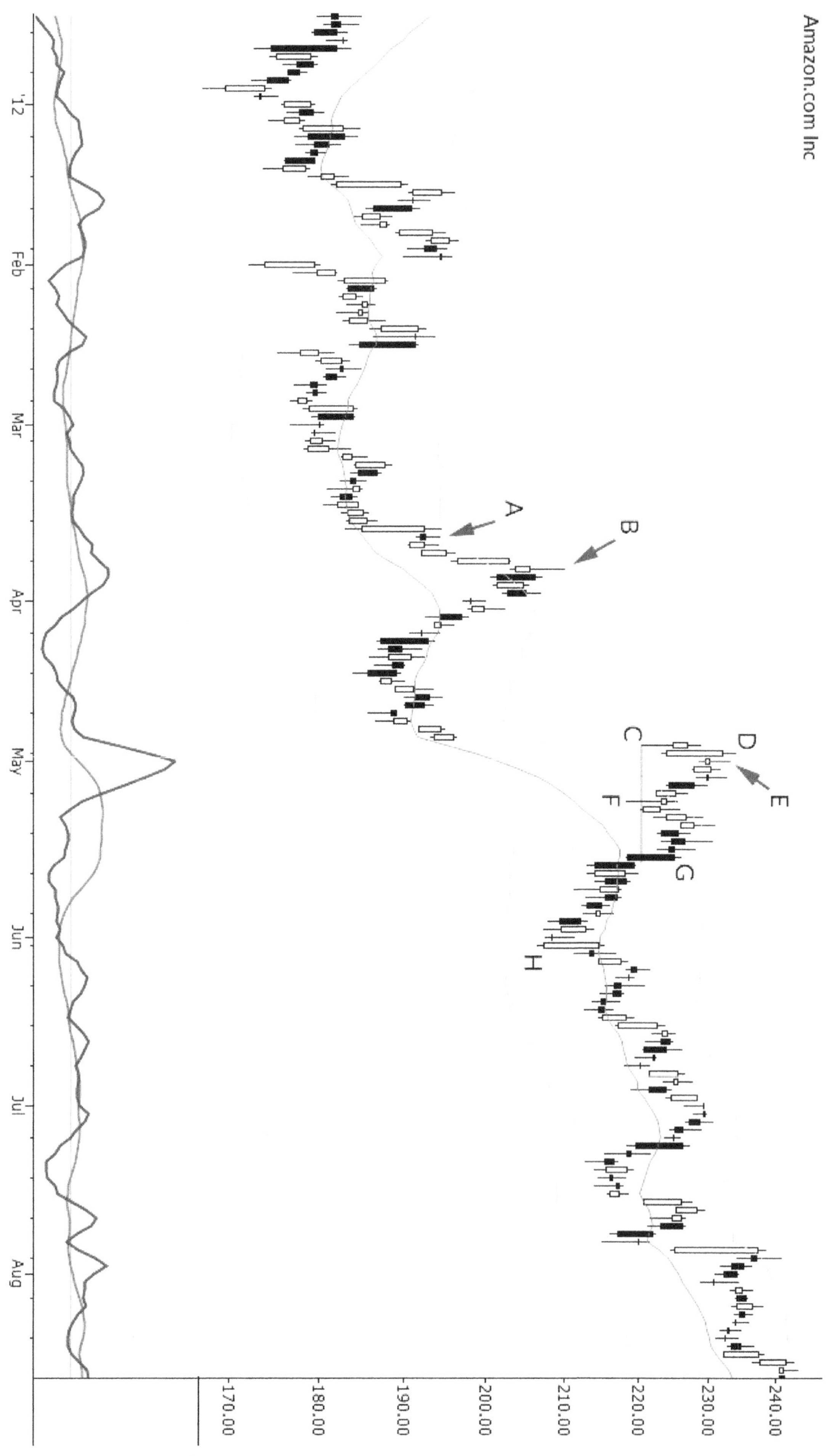
Amazon.com Inc
A
B
C
D
E
F
G
H
'12
Feb
Mar
Apr
May
Jun
Jul
Aug
170.00
180.00
190.00
200.00
210.00
220.00
230.00
240.00

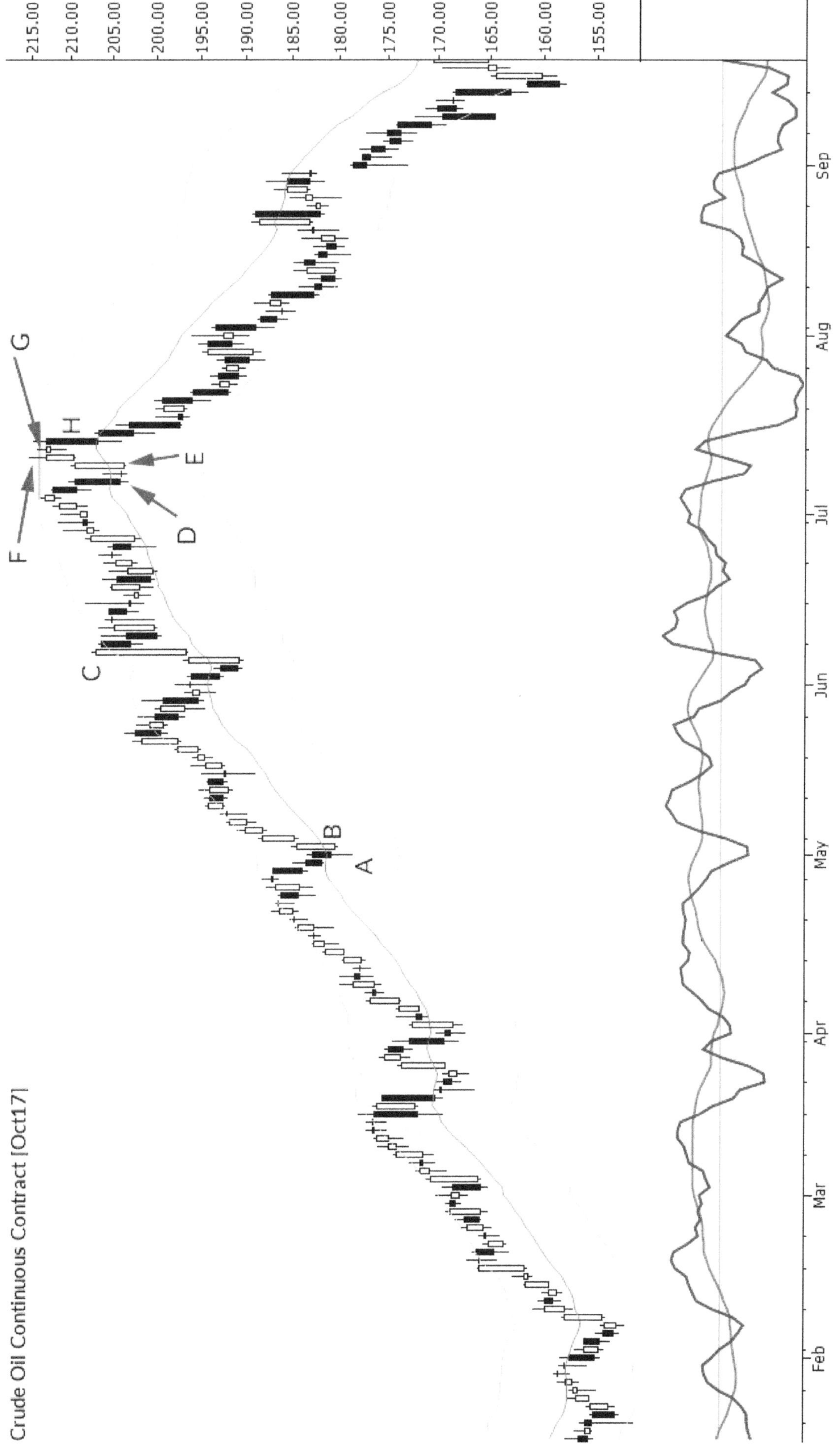
Crude Oil Continuous Contract [Oct17]
215.00
210.00
205.00
200.00
195.00
190.00
185.00
180.00
175.00
170.00
165.00
160.00
155.00
A
B
C
D
E
F
G
H
Feb
Mar
Apr
May
Jun
Jul
Aug
Sep

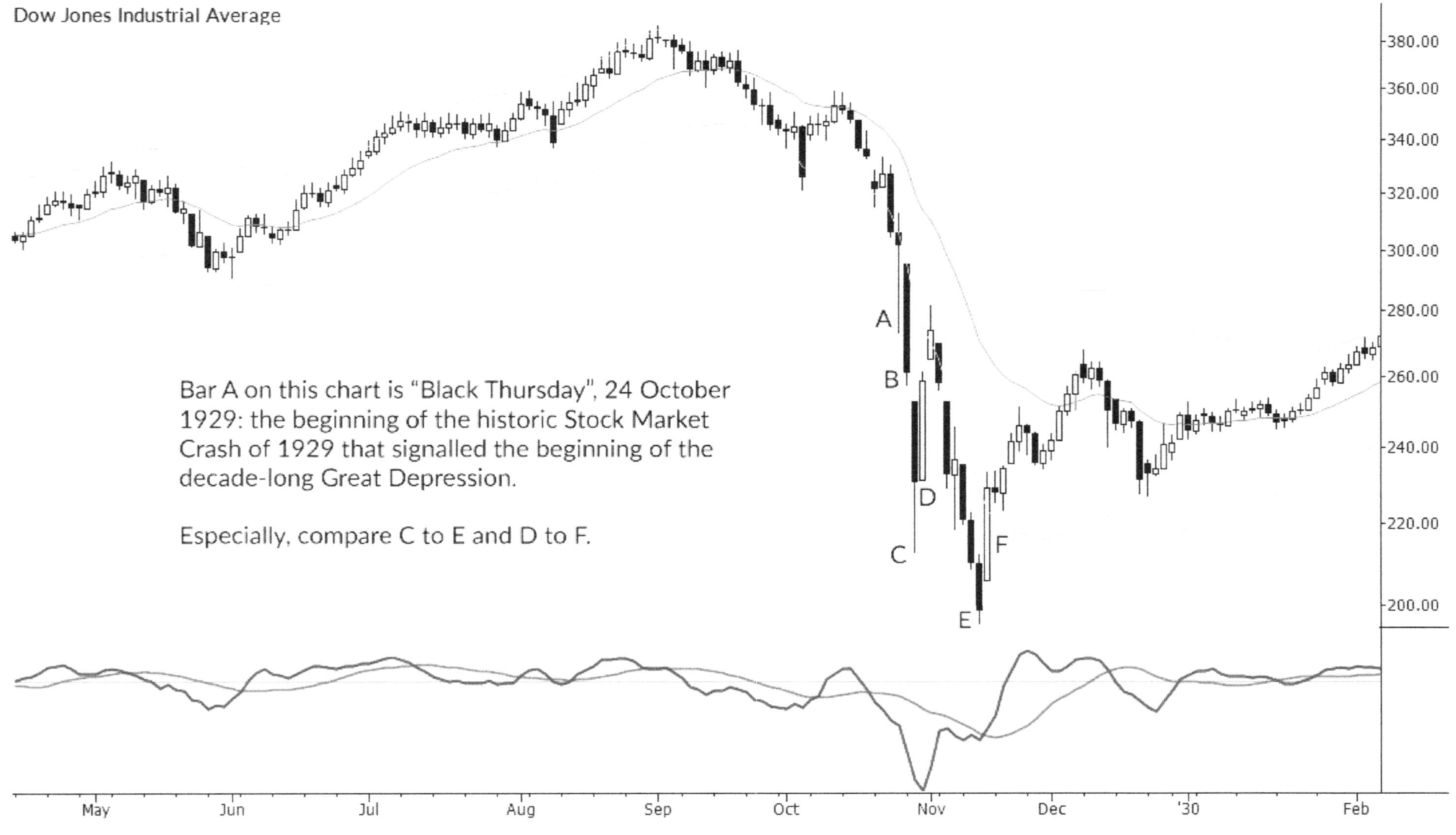
Dow Jones Industrial Average
Bar A on this chart is "Black Thursday", 24 October 1929: the beginning of the historic Stock Market Crash of 1929 that signalled the beginning of the decade-long Great Depression.
Especially, compare C to E and D to F.
A
B
C
D
E
F
380.00
360.00
340.00
320.00
300.00
280.00
260.00
240.00
220.00
200.00
May
Jun
Jul
Aug
Sep
Oct
Nov
Dec
'30
Feb

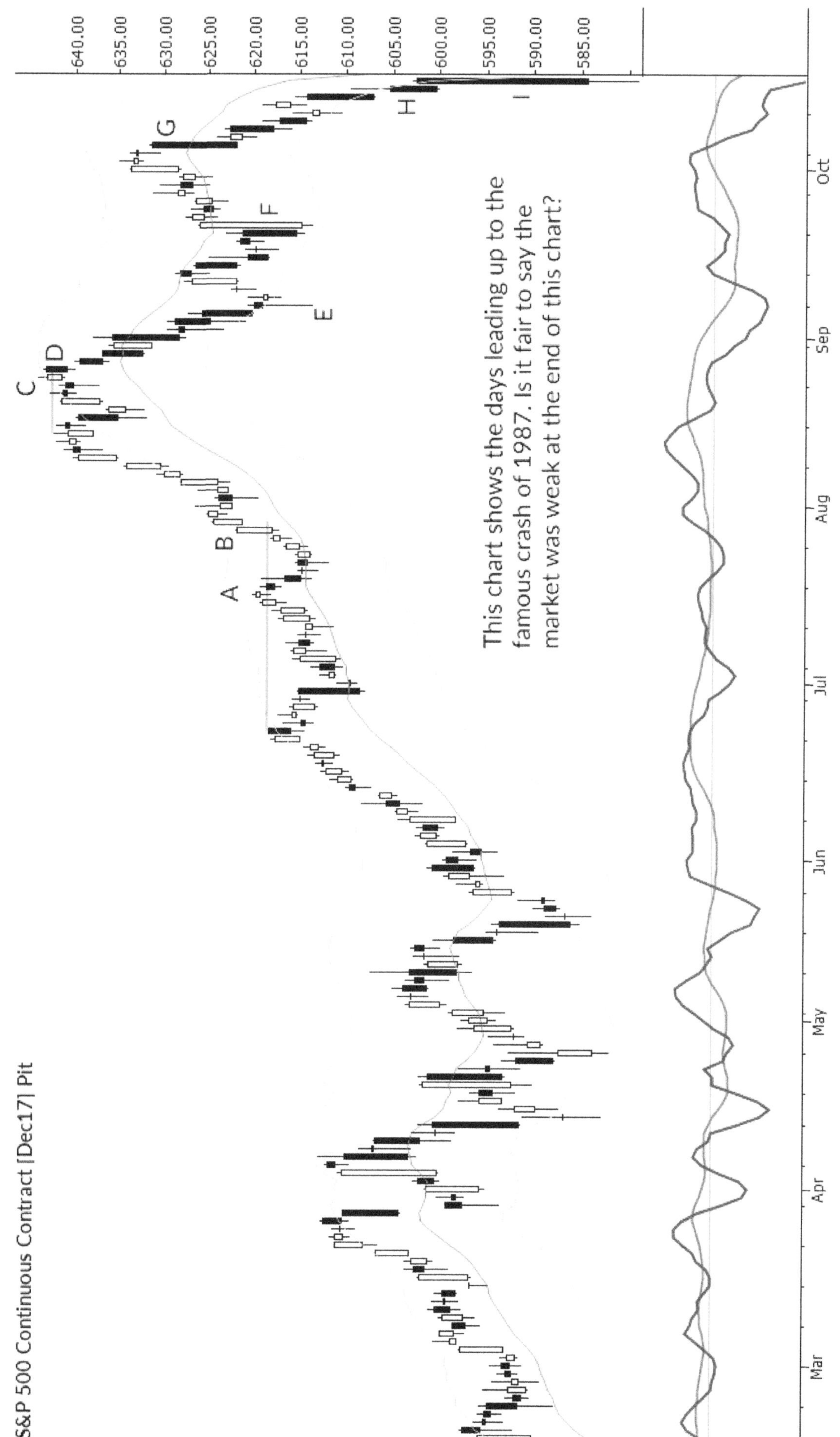
S&P 500 Continuous Contract [Dec17] Pit
This chart shows the days leading up to the
famous crash of 1987. Is it fair to say the
market was weak at the end of this chart?
A
B
C
D
E
F
G
H
I
640.00
635.00
630.00
625.00
620.00
615.00
610.00
605.00
600.00
595.00
590.00
585.00
Mar
Apr
May
Jun
Jul
Aug
Sep
Oct

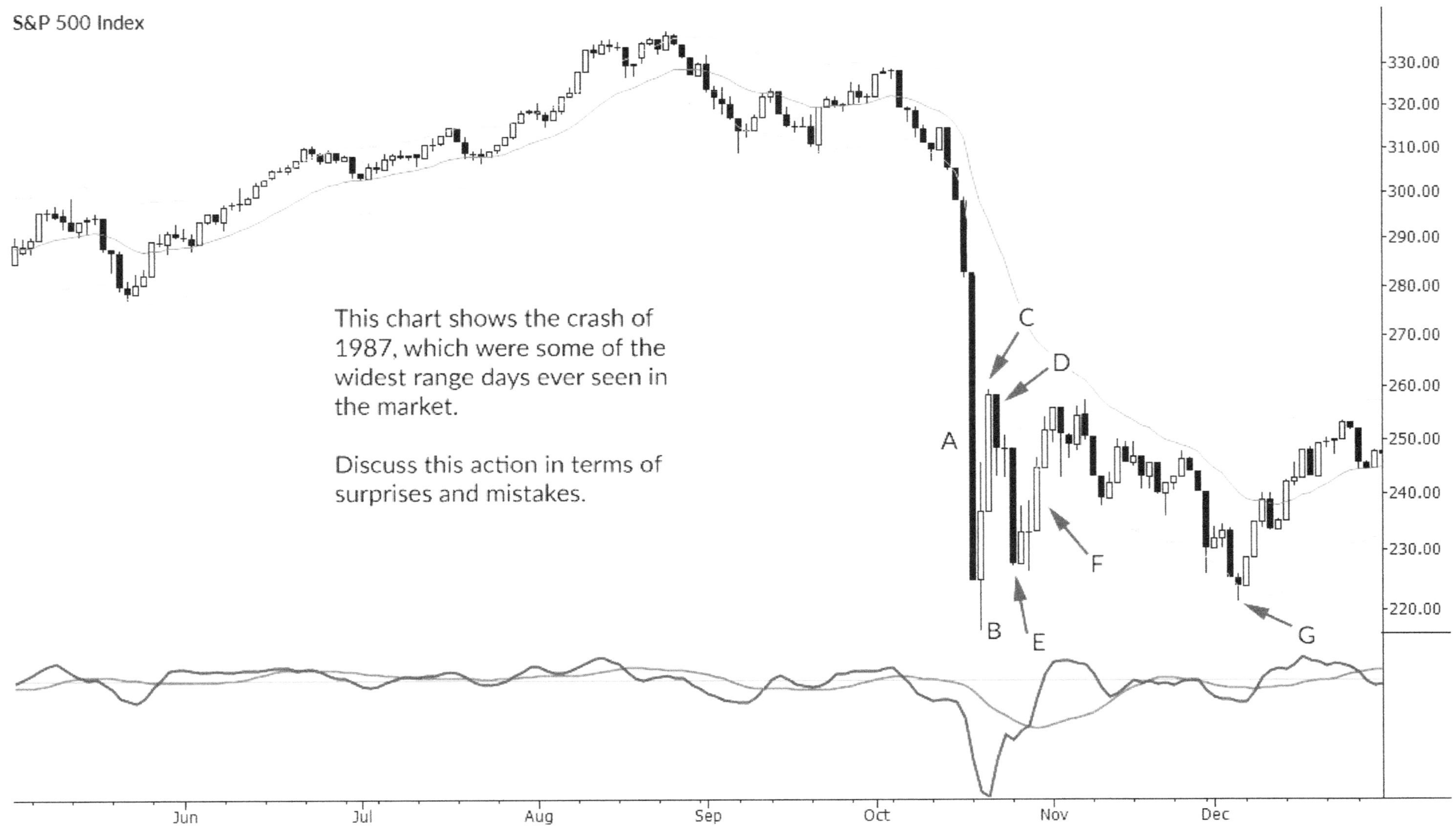
S&P 500 Index
This chart shows the crash of 1987, which were some of the widest range days ever seen in the market.
Discuss this action in terms of surprises and mistakes.
A
B
C
D
E
F
G
330.00
320.00
310.00
300.00
290.00
280.00
270.00
260.00
250.00
240.00
230.00
220.00
Jun
Jul
Aug
Sep
Oct
Nov
Dec

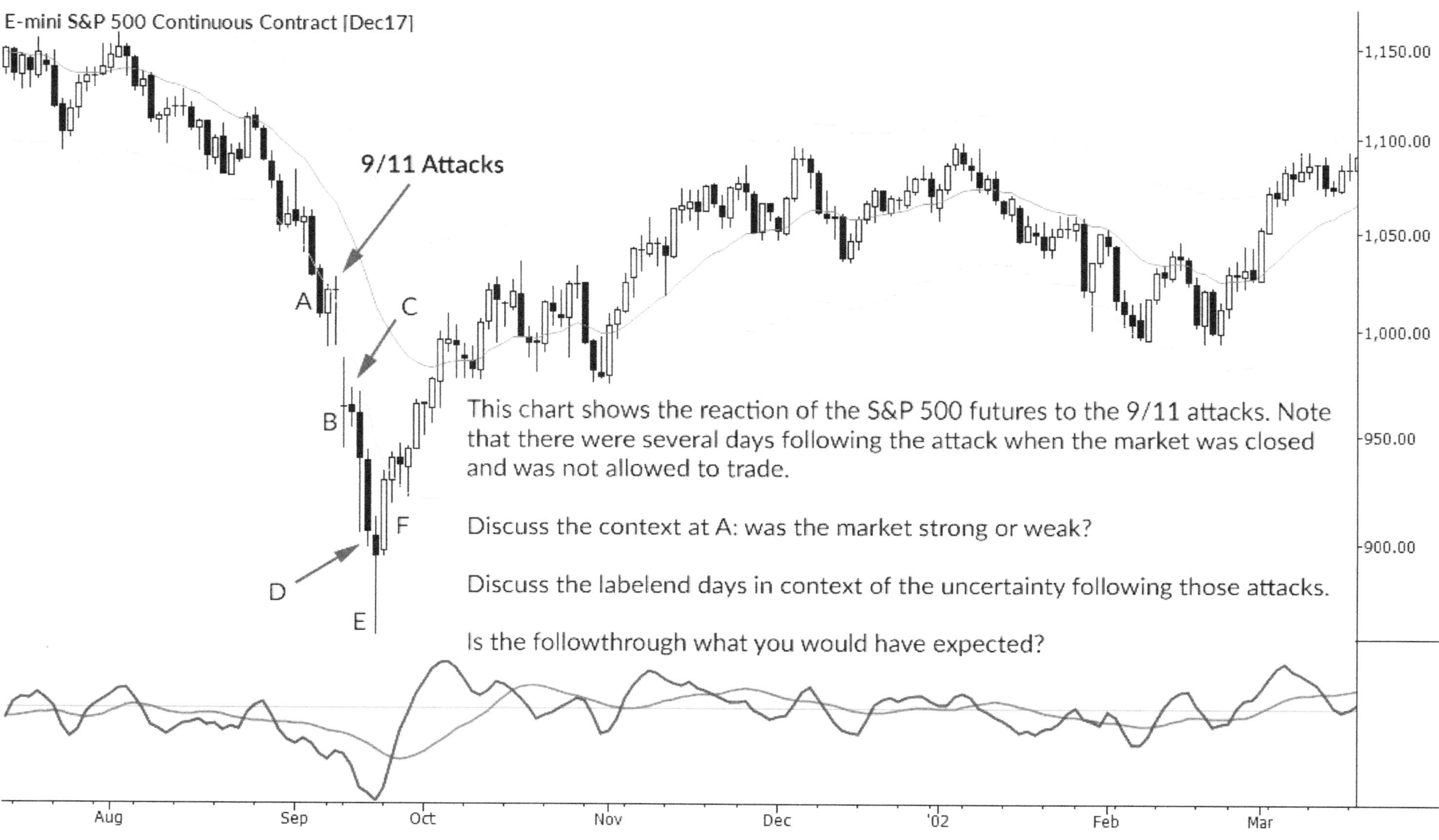
E-mini S&P 500 Continuous Contract [Dec17]
9/11 Attacks
A
B
C
D
E
F
This chart shows the reaction of the S&P 500 futures to the 9/11 attacks. Note that there were several days following the attack when the market was closed and was not allowed to trade.
Discuss the context at A: was the market strong or weak?
Discuss the labelend days in context of the uncertainty following those attacks.
Is the followthrough what you would have expected?
1,150.00
1,100.00
1,050.00
1,000.00
950.00
900.00
Aug
Sep
Oct
Nov
Dec
'02
Feb
Mar

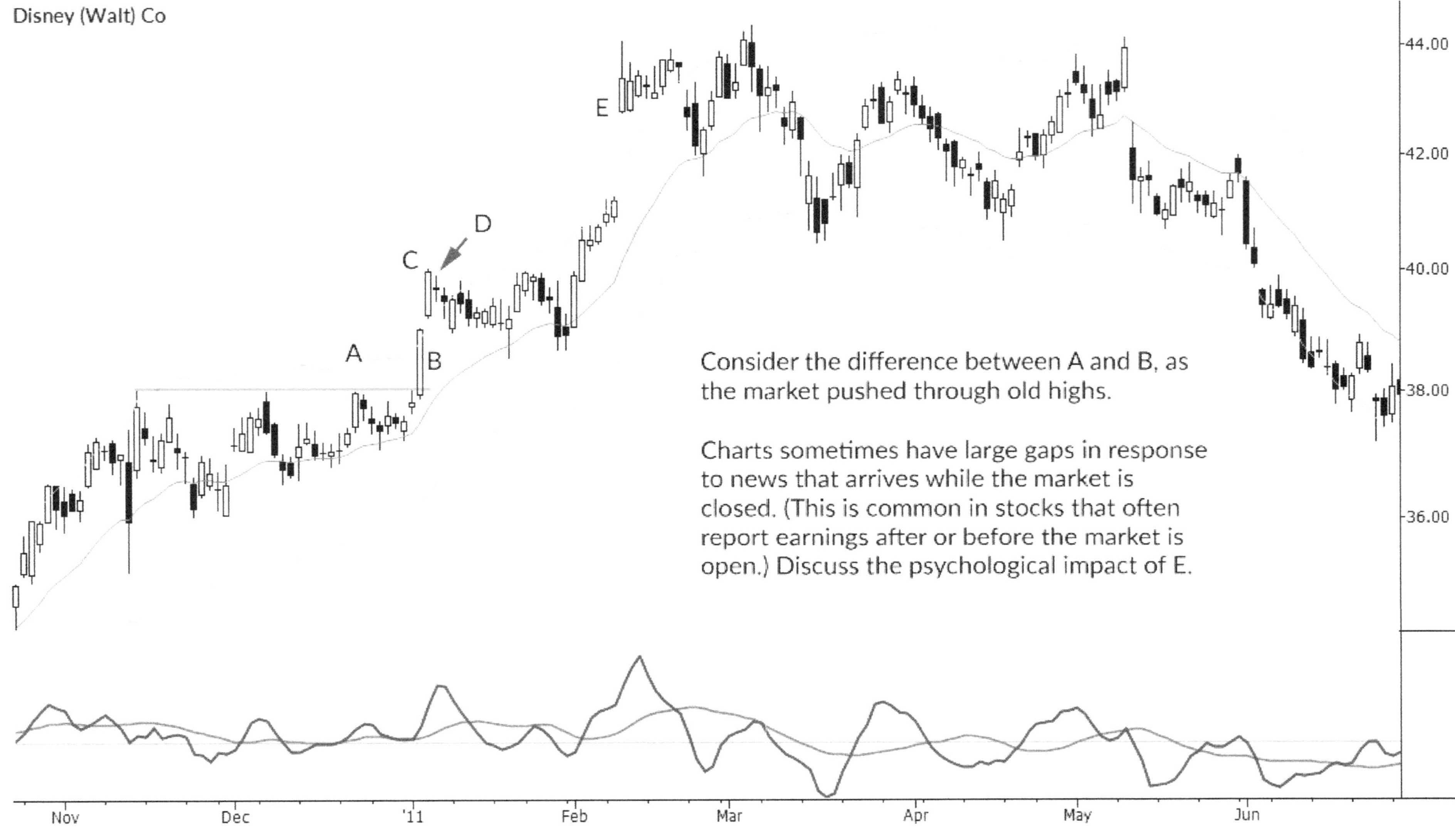
Disney (Walt) Co
A
B
C
D
E
Consider the difference between A and B, as the market pushed through old highs.
Charts sometimes have large gaps in response to news that arrives while the market is closed. (This is common in stocks that often report earnings after or before the market is open.) Discuss the psychological impact of E.
44.00
42.00
40.00
38.00
36.00
Nov
Dec
'11
Feb
Mar
Apr
May
Jun

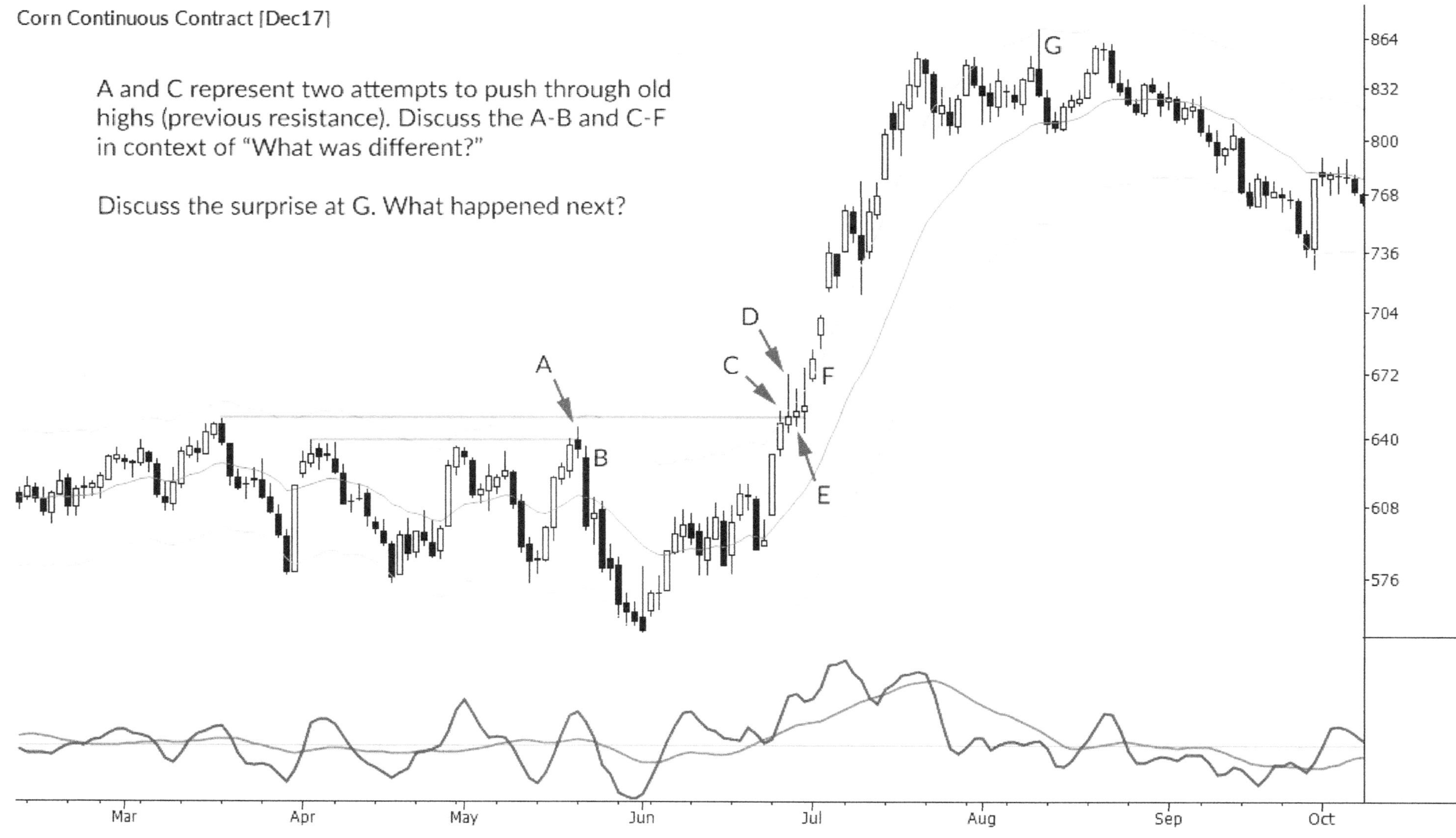
Corn Continuous Contract [Dec17]
A and C represent two attempts to push through old highs (previous resistance). Discuss the A-B and C-F in context of "What was different?"
Discuss the surprise at G. What happened next?
A
B
C
D
E
F
G
864
832
800
768
736
704
672
640
608
576
Mar
Apr
May
Jun
Jul
Aug
Sep
Oct

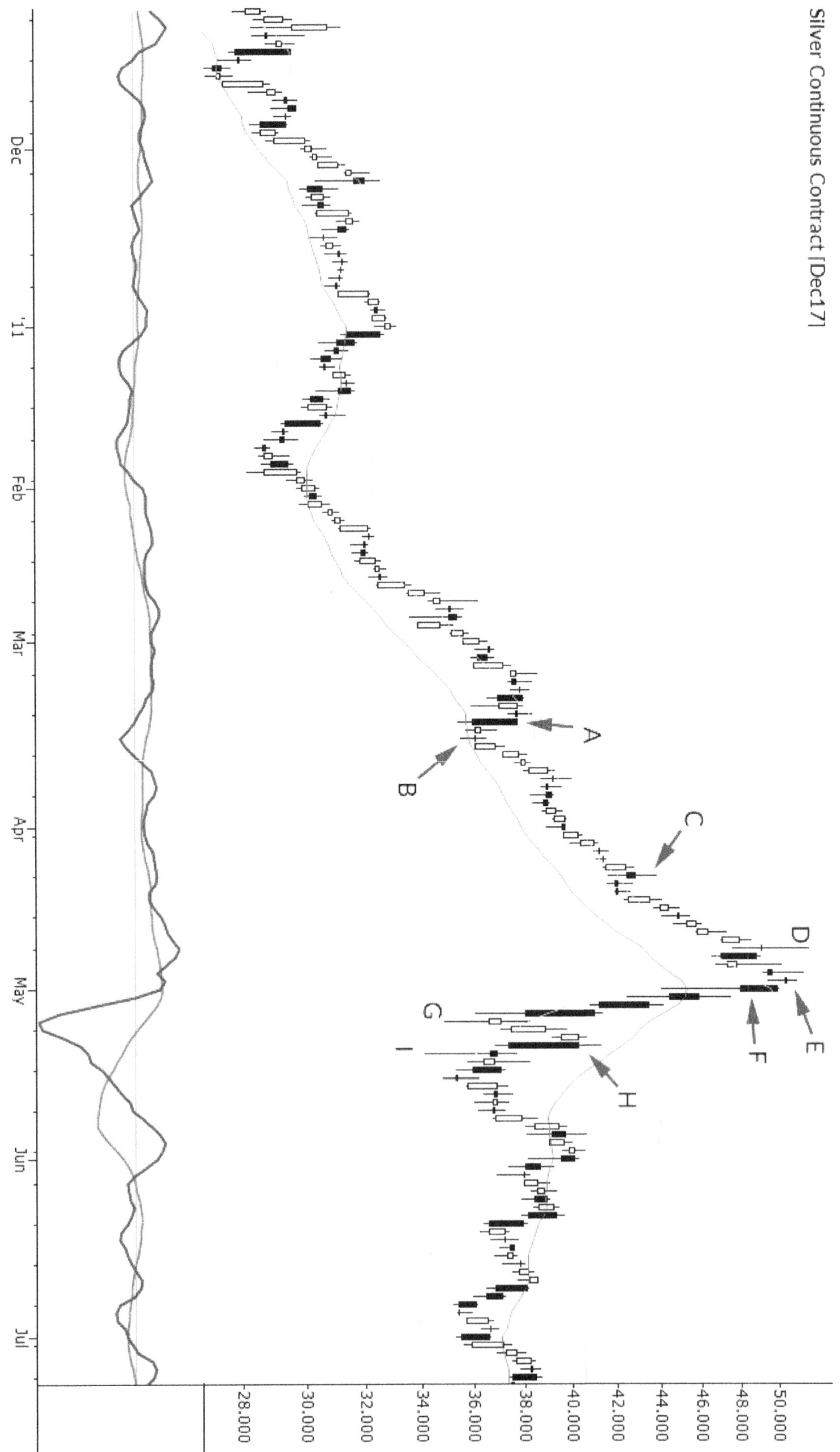
Silver Continuous Contract [Dec17]
A
B
C
D
E
F
G
H
I
Dec
'11
Feb
Mar
Apr
May
Jun
Jul
28.000
30.000
32.000
34.000
36.000
38.000
40.000
42.000
44.000
46.000
48.000
50.000

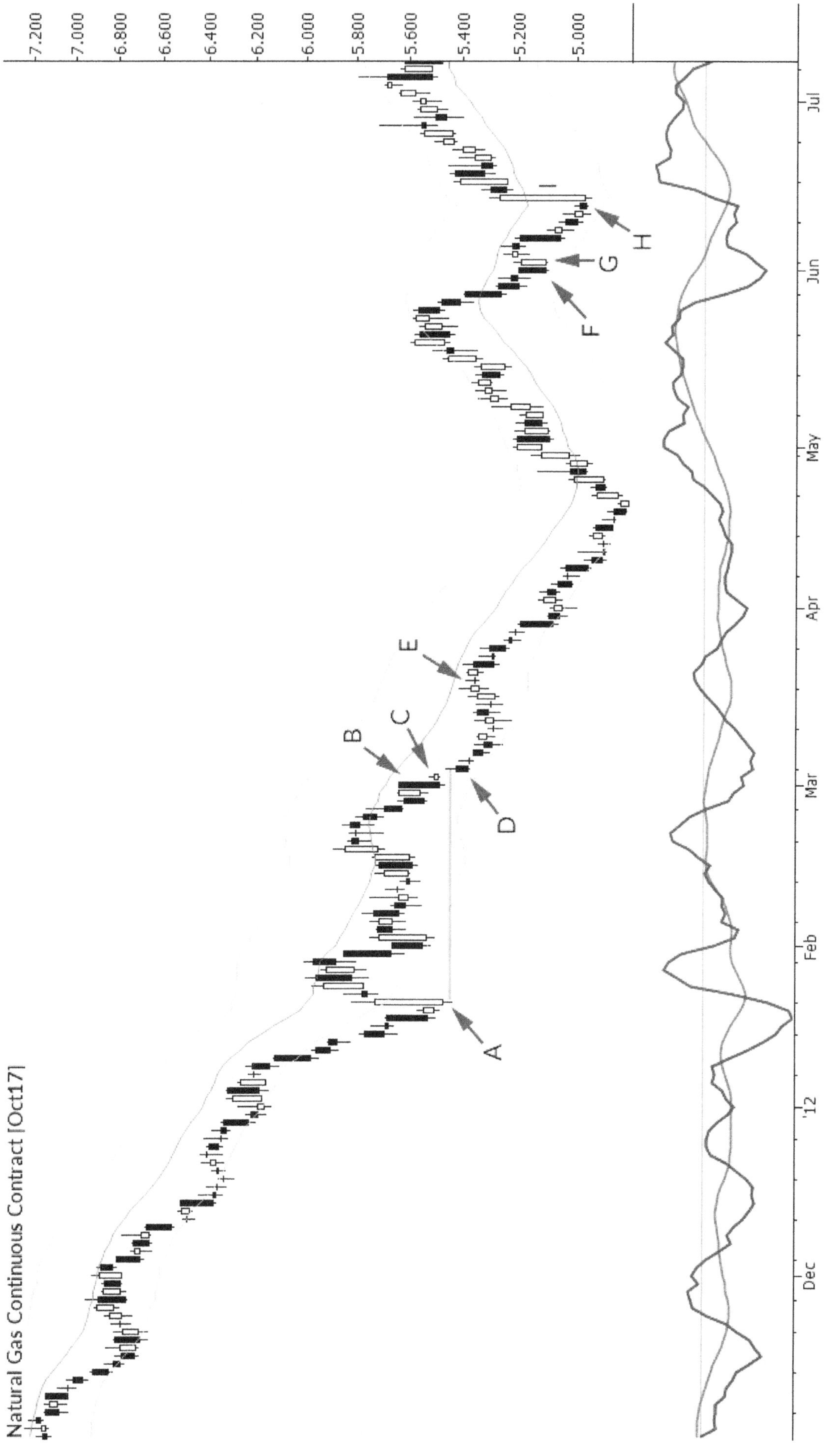
Natural Gas Continuous Contract [Oct17]
7.200
7.000
6.800
6.600
6.400
6.200
6.000
5.800
5.600
5.400
5.200
5.000
A
B
C
D
E
F
G
H
Dec
'12
Feb
Mar
Apr
May
Jun
Jul

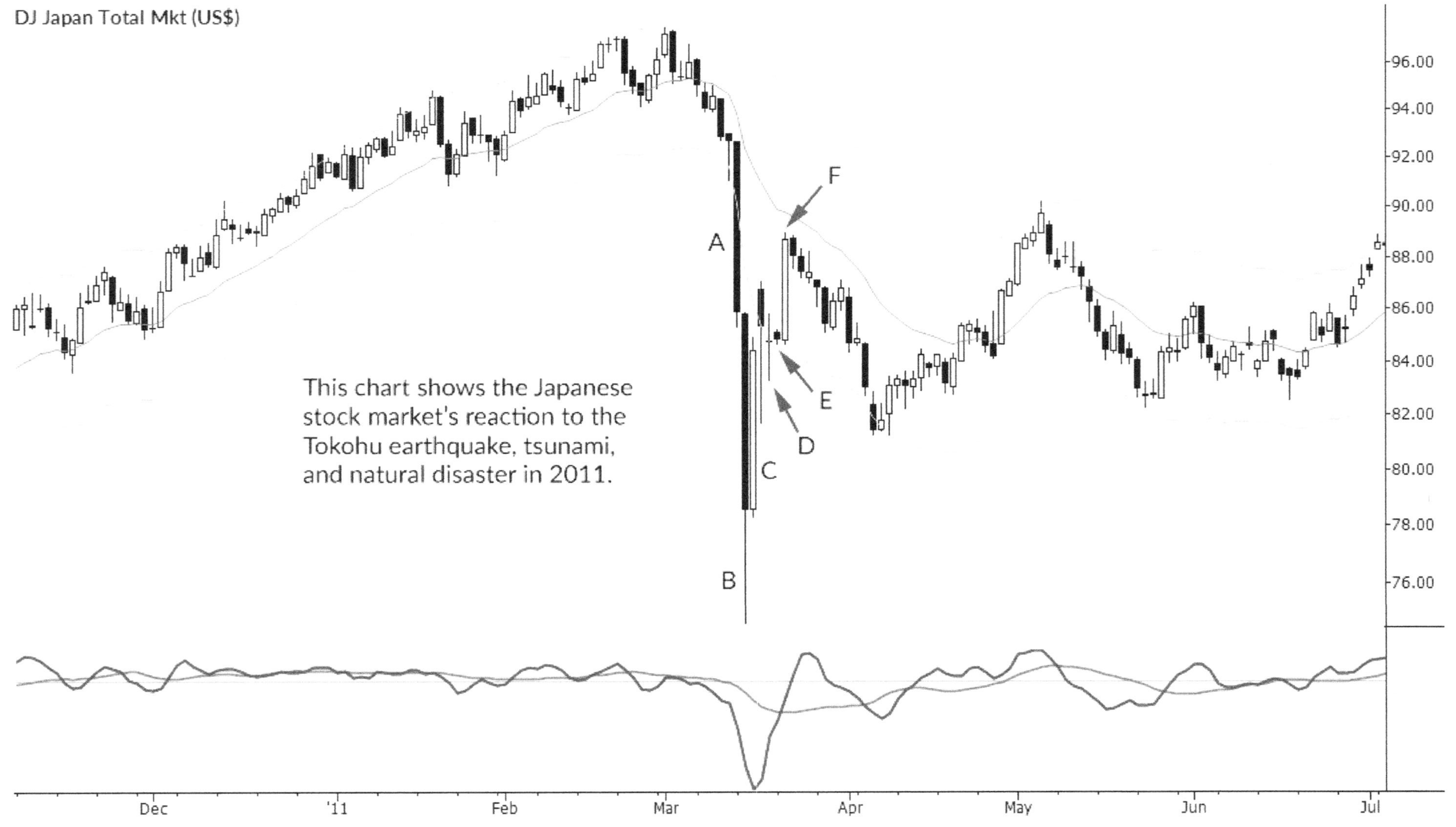
DJ Japan Total Mkt (US$)
This chart shows the Japanese stock market's reaction to the Tokohu earthquake, tsunami, and natural disaster in 2011.
A
B
C
D
E
F
96.00
94.00
92.00
90.00
88.00
86.00
84.00
82.00
80.00
78.00
76.00
Dec
'11
Feb
Mar
Apr
May
Jun
Jul

Section 3: Charting by Hand

There are several ways to do this exercise, and a few major benefits. The simplest is to simply write down closing prices for 3-5 markets you follow at the end of the day. If you are an intraday trader, you could record prices at regular intervals (e.g., every hour) throughout the day.

The next step up in complexity is to draw price charts. There are several ways to do this, depending on your time and artistic inclinations. Keeping bar charts is not too difficult, and candles also could be drawn by hand.

A swing chart (Kagi chart) or point and figure is an even better solution for many traders. In this style of charting, the X axis is not time. Rather, you drawn a line up until some reversal signal occurs, at which point you move forward one stop on the X axis and then start drawing a line down. You continue the line down until you get another reversal signal.

Here are some possibilities for reversal signals:

- A simple price movement. This is what point and figure charting uses, and you will have to figure out some appropriate value for the markets you follow. (For instance, if your reversal criteria is "the stock reverses $1 off a high or low", that's probably going to give you a very different number of flips for a $1 stock and a $500 stock.)
- Crossing a short-term moving average
- Some trend system like Parabolic Stop and Reverse
- Reversing a certain number of ATRs off a high or low (effectively the same as the Parabolic.)
- Market makes an N bar high or low

Don't get too caught up in the exact choice of flipping criteria, and don't make it too sophisticated or hard to calculate. Ideally, you want to see the reversals very easily, or have them marked somehow in your software (or in a spreadsheet.)

This should not be an extremely difficult task; a few minutes each day is enough, but much of the value comes from actually putting pencil (or pen) to paper.

Section 4: Readings

From the *The Art and Science of Technical Analysis: Market Structure, Price Action, and Trading Strategies* by Adam Grimes, Wiley, 2012:

Preface
1-8 (having an edge)
9-12 (basic chart setup)
22-30 (reading inside bars, charting by hand)
375-385 (becoming a trader)
399-408 (trading primer)
375-384 (becoming a trader)

The readings are not essential, but will help you get some deeper perspective on many of the issues discussed in this course.

On Becoming a Trader

The Trader's Journey: The Hero's Journey

I am a quantitative-discretionary trader. I have made it one of my life's goals to understand how financial markets move, to understand how to predict those movements, and to understand the limits of what can be predicted. Much of what I write focuses on these ideas and the reality of the marketplace, and I have often been very critical of much of traditional technical analysis and on trading methods that just don't work. Here, I want to focus on a different aspect of trading: on the journey that every trader must undergo, from rank beginner to experienced trader. Let's think about why that path is so long and hard, and maybe we can come away with some ideas to help bridge the gap between knowing and doing.

Understand the marketplace

First, we should spend a few moments thinking about how financial markets really work. There are many theories. On one level, we can easily understand that buyers and sellers meet and figure out what the market value for an asset is. We can also go another step further and see that rational buyers and sellers will quickly process any new information, and it should be reflected in those market prices pretty quickly and efficiently. (This is the lesson of the academic theory of market efficiency.) However, there is more going on here—psychology and human behavior play a pivotal role in the inner workings of markets.

Any decisions humans make are based on a combination of rational analysis and emotion—we can try to understand and control the contribution of emotions to the decision process, but we cannot eliminate it. A revolution in understanding comes when we realize that the financial markets are truly driven by these behavioral factors. As I wrote in my book, *The Art and Science of Technical Analysis*:

> *Part of the answer lies in the nature of the market itself. What we call "the market" is actually the end result of the interactions of thousands of traders across the gamut of size, holding period, and intent. Each trader is constantly trying to gain an advantage over the others; market behavior is the sum of all of this activity, reflecting both the rational analysis and the psychological reactions of all participants. This creates an environment that has basically evolved to encourage individual traders to make mistakes. That is an important point—the market is essentially designed to cause traders to do the wrong thing at the wrong time. The market turns our cognitive tools and psychological quirks against us, making us our own enemy in the marketplace. It is not so much that the market is against us; it is that the market sets us against ourselves.*

More and more people recognize the importance of these behavioral factors, both in academia and in practice. Working traders are often amazed to see themselves repeat the same, seemingly silly, mistakes over and over. We know that these behavioral and psychological factors drive prices, and we also know that prices can influence behavior. Because of this, many traders and writers have focused a lot of attention on trading psychology, but there might be another way to attack the problem.

"Trading psychology" might not be the answer

You are nervous about your entries, make impulsive trades, or just aren't having the success you want? The traditional answer is work on your psychology, visualize yourself succeeding, etc. Cynically, we could point out that, by focusing on psychology, developing traders can often ignore some critical issues. Consider some common reasons traders fail:

- **Not having a method that works.** You cannot escape the laws of probability, at least in the long run. If you don't have an edge in the market (and most methods do not), then you will lose.
- **Not being prepared for how long the learning curve can be.** For most traders, figure 3-5 years.
- **Being undercapitalized.** You can't learn to trade on a shoestring budget.

Unless these things are right, there can be no enduring success, and overemphasis on psychology may be emphasis on the wrong things. For instance, many psychologists trivialize the difficulty of finding a trading method that works, basically saying anything works as long as you are "properly aligned psychologically", when, in fact, it's hard to find a methodology that has an edge in the market. Working on our psychology may make us more relaxed and happier while we bleed money but it won't make us winners if we aren't doing what we need to win. A happy loser is still a loser.

Understanding the true nature of the market—that it is an environment that has evolved to encourage us to make mistakes—makes many of the traditional psychological problems fall into place. Cognitive biases, emotional decisions, fear and greed—these are all simply part of the market. That uncanny inclination you have to sell an asset in desperation at what turns out to be the absolute bottom of the decline, and to repeat a similar error over and over? It's not strange; it's actually those emotions, of all the traders and investors in the market, that create the bottom.

Understanding the nature of the market is a good start, but there still might be something we are missing about the process of becoming a trader. Maybe we misunderstand the journey.

Patterns to profits

There are patterns in markets. Much of my work has focused on finding patterns in prices that have predictive value, but there are also patterns in fundamental information, sentiment, etc.—and any of these patterns can be a source of a trading edge. This is why there are so many approaches to trading and so many different trading styles, but no matter how we trade or invest, we're really looking for these patterns. There are, however, a few problems with trading these patterns.

The most important issue is that these patterns offer only a slight edge. If we use the typical "fair coin" analogy, we might have patterns that show us when the coin is 55/45, instead of 50/50. Too many traders look for 80/20, and those types of edges simply do not exist on timeframes that human traders can trade.

This is an adjustment that most developing traders eventually must make: Yes, there are patterns, but they are slight. It is not easy to find them. It is not easy to trade them, and it is certainly not easy to trade them properly. Simply put, the game is much harder than most people would have you believe it is—the lights that guide our way on the metaphorical journey are not quite as bright as we might wish they were, nor is the path as clear as we'd hoped.

The problem of randomness

Humans are bad at dealing with randomness, as study after study has shown. Some of the things we do best, like pattern recognition, actually work against us in a highly random environment because our brains, finely-honed pattern recognition machines, will happily create patterns, even where none exist. This is a fundamental aspect of human cognition; it's a part of the way we think, and we cannot change it.

For developing traders, this creates many problems. The marketplace is highly competitive, and whatever edges we find are very small. This means that randomness will confound our results; we do not know if we lost money on a particular trade because we did something wrong, or simply because the (slightly weighted) coin happened to come up against us, purely due to chance. Even worse, we don't know if our big winning trades were the result of simply getting lucky, or that we did something right.

In this highly random environment, we must first act with consistency. This is why trading discipline is so important; you can't even begin to understand your results if you are doing something different every time. We also need tools to analyze and understand our results statistically. It's not enough to look at big winning trades, or even to study our losers. We have to understand how our edge works over a large sample size, and constantly remind ourselves that we are doing something that is difficult that goes very much against our instincts.

Why traders struggle

We've considered a number of things that make trading a real challenge, but there's more. Most traders discover that, even accounting for the size of the edge, trading is harder than it seems like it should be. Based on my personal experience, and my experience guiding, teaching, and mentoring hundreds of traders, I think there is another aspect of learning to trade that is often ignored. Many authors have correctly pointed out that trading is not really about knowledge. Though there is a lot of subtlety, most of the knowledge needed to trade could fit in a small book. There is a lot of thinking today about trading as a performance discipline, but this does not fix everything. I think I know the reason why: Trading is not about knowledge, and it's also not about skill. **If you want to trade, you must become a trader.** Successful trading is really about transformation, about making yourself into something that you were not before.

I think a useful model of transformation can be found in Joseph Campbell's work, which sees many of the stories told in human myth as variations of one single, great story. One of the most important aspects of this story is the Hero's Journey, which ties together human experience and narrative from religion to Greek epic poems to Disney movies—they are all different versions of this one story. Now, this is far more than a simple academic theory. In fact, one way Campbell suggested we might think about it is that these stories, even pure fiction, are "more true than factual stories" because they say something true about who and what we are as humans, and there is power in that truth.

The Hero's Journey

The Hero's Journey follows a path in which the aspirant begins in the normal everyday world, receives some kind of call to adventure, finds a mentor or guide, passes into an unknown mysterious world (there are often parallels with the Underworld here, or, in many cases, an actual journey underground), meets many challenges along the way, receives some kind of aid, and returns, victorious, to the everyday world with a boon—new powers to live in and to change that world. First, think through the basic pattern with the stories you may know: The Odyssey? Beowulf? Star Wars? The Lord of the Rings? Yes, all of the above (and many more) are basically the same story told in different ways.

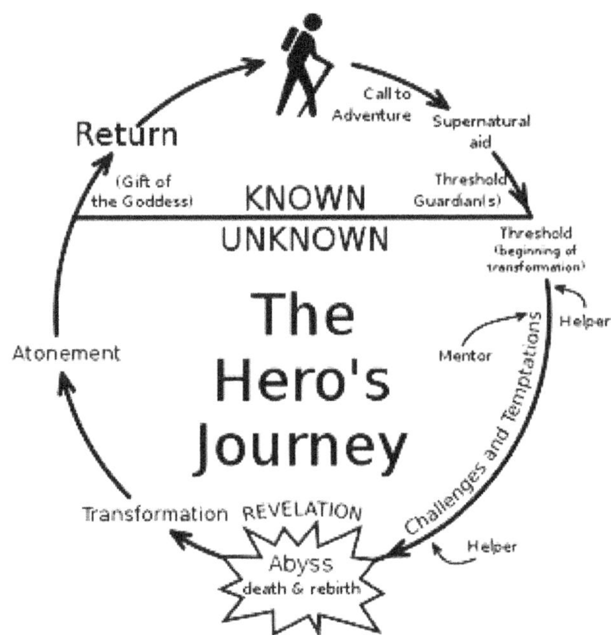

The trader's journey

I propose that there are also parallels here with the trader's experience. How many of us have trading histories that look something like this?

- **A grand call to adventure.** Who would not want to make a pile of money working from the comfort of your own computer screen?
- **Finding a mentor or a guide.** Good mentors matter! Few of us who have succeeded would have done so without some help.
- **Crossing over into an "unreal" world.** Markets are crazy. When we look deeply into markets, maybe we become a little crazy ourselves, and we certainly become disconnected from ordinary reality.
- **Facing dire challenges.** The emotional highs and lows of trading can be extreme. Is there a trader alive who hasn't been awake at 4am wondering if they can ever do this, why they ever tried in the first place, how they could be so stupid to make the same mistakes over and over, and what they were going to do tomorrow? (This is probably not the time to mention that we only write stories about the heroes that complete the journey! A lot of dragons feasted well, for a very long time.)
- **Failure somehow, almost miraculously, is transformed to success.**
- **We figure out how to incorporate** our trading activities into the everyday world, and discover that things probably weren't quite as exotic or difficult as we had thought.

See? Trading is not truly about learning patterns. It is not about learning some math. It is not about skill development, and it is not even about risk management. All of these things are important, but **the real work of trading is work on ourselves.**

Institutional shortcuts?

As an aside, one of the interesting questions you might ask is why this is not true for institutions. Certainly, when the banks had big prop desks, they did not hire traders and expect them to go through some mythical journey, not get eaten by a dragon, and eventually make money, right? How about prop firms today? Guys on the floor did not spend a lot of time thinking about transpersonal psychology. If learning to trade really is such a journey of transformation, there should be no shortcut. Does the story break down here?

It does not break down; the same idea and rules apply, even within an institutional framework. A few things to consider: the success rates, even in prop firms, are extremely low, often a fraction of a percent. There's no magic there. In a hedge fund or the old bank prop model, a trader would essentially be hired as an apprentice and spend a lot time watching experienced traders work before ever taking the reins themselves. This allowed learning to take place in a controlled and structured way, and many traders could make transitions to other roles if they discovered they were not cut out to manage risk. Furthermore, there are many types of trading, within the institutional framework, that are not quite the same thing. For instance, there are desks that hedge and lay off risk in derivative products. A trader doing a job like this (or working as a market maker) deals with risk in a different way than our fledgling discretionary trader—it's not quite the same task of conquering the market. In general, the institutional framework provides useful guides and constraints, and we can replicate some of these structures for the private trader.

Taking the journey

So, what are the lessons here and who are they for? I think these lessons primarily apply to the independent, self-directed trader who makes and is responsible for the consequences of her own decision. (A few points: this trader may (and probably should) work in a team, and we have not addressed funding. This trader may trade her own account, or she may trade clients' money; in either case, the key fact is that she is making the decisions.) There are probably also applications here for traders who are in the process of switching styles, or maybe even for institutional traders who are striking out on their own. (I saw many traders leave the floor and go through some variation of this journey, for better or worse. Sometimes the dragon wins.) So what are these lessons?

First, realize that learning to trade is a journey. It is a long and painful journey, and it will test you in ways you did not expect. Most people say that trading is the hardest thing they've ever done; in terms of constant second guessing and self doubt along the way, I could agree with that statement. Sometimes the journey is dark and the path is anything but clear. I don't tell you this to discourage you, but rather to prepare you. Many of the traders I have seen who have failed were actually doing just fine, but they maybe weren't prepared for how long and difficult the road was going to be.

Second, you must have a method that has an edge. You must have confidence in that method. With this workbook and the online course (MarketLife.com), you have a significant advantage; you will be exposed to patterns and ideas that have an edge, and will create the framework to craft your own trading style and approach. Above all, your studies here will emphasize the importance of doing your own testing and work to verify your edge. Get this wrong, and nothing good will happen in the end—you gotta have an edge.

Third, structure your experience. Work toward building a process that covers everything you need to do. Pay attention to your learning and your evaluation of your results, but also work on developing a process for trade selection, management, and review. Yes, create a trading plan and a business plan, but also work on fitting that into your life plan. It all has to work together.

Last, be open to the experience and to change. Trading is going to change you, and, as the Buddha said, much suffering comes from trying to hold on to impermanence. Don't fight the change. I think there is great value in practices such as journaling, introspection, meditation, and perhaps even letting some of your energy bleed over into a creative outlet. You may find new intellectual areas that interest you, and you definitely must be open to new experiences. You are going to grow and you are going to change, so do what you can to shepherd that growth, and, above all, don't be afraid of it.

I think this is a different perspective on the process of becoming a profitable trader, and the parallels with the Hero's Journey offer some exciting new avenues for thought and research. No matter how hard and long the journey, it is worthwhile. Find your path, and take those first steps—even the longest journey begins with that single, first step.

On Learning

The Rage to Master

Before I was a trader, I was a musician. In my career as a musician, I discovered the value of teaching—that I enjoyed teaching, I was good at it, and that teaching helped me refine my own skills and thinking. (The same is true of teaching trading; it's as good for the teacher as for the student!) One of the things that I struggled with most as a music teacher was why some students did so well while others, given the same effort and attention from the teacher, did not. Though this is obviously a complex question that will defy a "one size fits all" answer, I did see a common thread: The students who grew were passionate—in most cases, completely, totally obsessed. They loved music and it was a part of who they were. Without that passion, without obsession, success was average, at best.

I came to music relatively late in life (nearly 10 years old), but was able to make very rapid progress for many years. Once I became obsessed with mastering my instrument, I literally practiced 6-10 hours a day, every day. I carried printed music with me at all times and rehearsed in my head every chance I got. In nearly every class, I pretty much ignored the teacher and studied music as much as I could. Every spare minute, at recess or study halls I usually managed to work my way into a practice room instead of "wasting time" doing whatever "normal" kids did. I skipped school to practice, I read books about music, I listened constantly, and I rigged my instrument so that I could practice more or less silently, well into the wee hours of the night. I was, in no way, shape or form, a "well balanced" kid. I was completely consumed, completely obsessed with the drive to master my chosen craft, and I eventually became better than almost anyone else at what I did.

I was completely immersed in the process of learning and addicted to the flow experience. Incremental progress was as satisfying to me as any drug could have been—I took every failure as a challenge to get better. I was actually angry when I couldn't play something, and I channeled that anger into effort. Frankly, I didn't spend much time thinking about the possibility of failure. For one thing, I saw clearly that with proper focus and effort I could do pretty much anything. Challenges and milestones were clearly defined, and my teachers taught me how to break huge challenges down into manageable chunks. Any stubborn challenge was simply an obstacle to be conquered; the harder it was, the more it drew my attention until I won.

I wasn't until much later that I heard a term (first used by Ellen Winner) that captured the essence of what I experienced, and what I later saw reflected in my best students: the rage to master. People who have the rage to master are completely obsessed beyond any sense of balance, beyond any reason, with mastering their chosen craft. For these people, hard work usually doesn't seem like work. They are motivated by the end goal, yes, but perhaps even more so by the process of learning and the process of getting better. I had a major "ah ha" moment sitting on a plane, reading one of the first copies of Dr. Steenbarger's *Enhancing Trader Performance*, when he used that term—rage to master—to describe what he saw in the master traders he worked with.

Not everyone can, or should, approach financial markets with this degree of obsession. It is certainly possible to have fulfilling interactions with the market, enjoy the experience, and get something valuable out of it as a lifelong hobby. But, if you think you have made the commitment to really master this craft, I challenge you to ask yourself a difficult question. Do you have the passion to immerse yourself in markets and to become obsessed, probably beyond the point of balance and reason? Can you work on your path to trading mastery with that degree of focus? If so, are you prepared to maintain that level of intensity for the 3 to 4 years it will probably take you to achieve some mastery, perhaps without a lot of positive reinforcement along the way? If the answer to those questions is "no" or "I'm not sure", maybe ask yourself another question: how can you kindle that spark? How can you find the passion—the rage to master—within yourself?

Learning, Deeply and Well

We need a lot of skills to get through life. Even the basic day to day requirements can be daunting, and most people have specialized skills in certain field. To make things even more complicated, the world changes, sometimes it seems at an ever-faster pace, and we may need very different skills tomorrow than we do today. I think it's safe to say that the ability to learn—to be a lifetime learner—is the most important skill of all.

Learning as a skill

There's been some controversy recently: many pop science books and companies have focused on neuroplasticity, or the ability of the brain to rewire and change itself structurally. While this is true (and, I'm convinced, is a key part of learning and skill development), it's offset by some notable lawsuits and sanctions against companies that overreached with simplified and exaggerated claims of effectiveness.

Another difficult question is whether or not learning domain-specific skills have benefits that extend beyond the domain. A lot of research shows that studying chess, contrary to what we thought a few decades ago, doesn't make you smarter, more strategic, or better able to succeed in other fields; studying chess makes you a good chess player. There may be some carry-over, but many skills are frustratingly domain-specific.

One thing is clear: **learning is a skill.** It's probably the most important skill there is, because the world changes, and much of what we know becomes obsolete over the course of a lifetime. Learning new things can keep us engaged and vital as we grow older, and learning new skills helps us push back the horizon of our knowledge and limitations.

Developing the learning skill

We all learn differently, so there's no one way you must learn. Part of learning is understanding how you learn most effectively, and then structuring your work to take advantage of your strengths. (If you are the aural type, I've done podcasts on this subject that you might enjoy.)

Steps to learning

You have to be passionate. Sure, you can learn something you hate, but it's much easier if you love what you're doing. Consider what a chore it can be to take a class on a subject you don't care about with how easily you will learn something for a hobby or a game. (I had a friend who barely passed school and claimed he couldn't learn anything, but he was a veritable encyclopedia of baseball statistics and trivia going back to the beginning of the game.) Your passion for a subject might be instant or it may well grow over time.

Gather resources and information—**learn the basics.** It is becoming easier and easier in today's world to get information on any subject, but quality of information matters. In trading, there are probably ten bad websites and books for every good one, and it's hard, especially for the new learner, to sort out the quality of information. A good part of your early work will be in figuring out what these good sources of information are.

This gets easier as you understand the field a bit more. When you start out, you don't know anything, and don't, as the saying goes, even know what you don't know. You have no idea how large the field is, or what kind of skills experts have. As you start to learn just a little bit, the map fills in. There will still be some big fuzzy areas, but you'll get a pretty good sense of what you need to learn. That's the point of this early exploration: to map out your journey and to begin to build a plan.

Build or find a community. You'll also learn from the people learning around you. They will see things you don't, and they'll also make mistakes you don't. Discussion, give and take, and constructive disagreement will let you learn faster and deeper than you probably could by yourself. While you might lose interest on your own (this learning business can be hard!), having a group of people to learn with you can sustain you through the challenges and help you prioritize your learning.

It's also worth mentioning that **having a teacher, mentor, or coach can save you some time.** Your mileage may vary, but I've found that having a good teacher has helped me immeasurably as I've developed skills in different domains.

Make a plan and follow the plan. Once you get some background knowledge, you can begin to map out the field and see what you need to learn. Once you know what you need to learn, you can start thinking about how you will learn it.

As a general rule, a lot of learning comes from developing the skill of discrimination. Skill and understanding comes from knowing that "this thing is like this other thing and is different from that thing in these ways." You need to be exposed to many conditions and datapoints. Over time, you'll develop a bigger "reference set"; as you have more experiences you will be able to categorize new experiences better and faster, and understand smaller distinctions between different things.

Whatever you want to learn, this plan will serve you well: find something you love; gather enough resources to learn the basics (so you learn what you need to learn); find or make a community, possibly enlisting the help of someone who has the skills you want to develop; and then make a plan to learn and follow that plan.

Maintaining Motivation (Motivation as a Resource)

The New Year: resolutions are made, gym memberships bought, diet plans laid out, major projects are started—the whole time, everyone knowing that all these plans are doomed for failure. Why do we fail so consistently on these New Year's resolutions that it has become a cultural joke? Because we don't account for motivation.

Motivation is a resource

Motivation is a precious resource. With it, the sky's the limit—we can accomplish superhuman tasks and overcome nearly any obstacle. Without it, we sit on the sofa and watch daytime TV. Motivation is the essential fuel for action, and action is what separates those who achieve from everyone else.

It's too easy to blame failure on lack of followthrough and determination; it's too easy to say that we quit and gave up when we should have pressed on. In many cases, the failure to act is a symptom not a cause—a symptom of failed motivation. We need to focus attention on understanding and shepherding our finite, precious motivation.

In my experience, both the short and long-term views are important. When we talk about motivation, we usually think first of having a vision of success and knowing where we are going. Yes, this is important (perhaps essential), but I don't think it's enough. To maintain motivation, we also need to love the small stuff and respect the power of routine and habit.

Vision

Vision matters; without a good vision of where and how we want to end up, it's hard to get anywhere. A good vision is a shining beacon set somewhere in our future, and a powerful vision draws us to that place. A vision need not even be realistic or completely attainable to have power to shape our actions. A vision may be a moving target, and certainly may be subject to revision as we get feedback and refine our goals.

Though self-help books are filled with stories of people who set impossible visions and achieved them, this may not be the best plan. Imagine someone who sets a goal of being a pop music star and then sticks to that despite all evidence that this plan is not going to work out; this person probably let many opportunities for fulfilling and profitable career choices fall to the wayside, and will likely end up with an empty, unrealized dream—a fantasy. There's a careful balance here because it does make sense to have some giant dreams, but the dream itself is not the goal.

The Vision is the magnet that pulls us forward, so think carefully about where you want to put that magnet. All the wishful thinking in the world is not going to make your dreams come true. Walking toward that goal, taking the action of small steps—that's what works. Have a goal, and take action to get there.

The little things matter

Though dreams, vision boards, and big picture planning get most of the attention, it's the things you do that will actually move you toward that dream. Making these little things into habits is the key. Let me first paint the big picture:

- **Dream big.** Go ahead and dream bigger than you ever thought possible, and don't even worry about if it's achievable. Where do you want to go?
- **Think about how you'll get there.** Focus on the first steps. If we think about a physical path on a map, there are a lot of ways to get lost and a lot of wrong turns along the way. The middle and

end of the path may be complicated, but the first steps probably are not. Moving in one direction gets you closer to your goal. It doesn't have to be exactly right, and it doesn't have to be the path you'll follow for your whole trip, but just ask yourself in what direction do you need to go? What might those first steps look like?

- **Start to build habits around *doing things.*** Big changes are daunting, and when we think about how hard it is to accomplish something we might get discouraged. (You want to play that musical instrument? You can probably have some real skill in 5 years and maybe sound more or less like a pro in about 10 years.) So don't think about that big picture. Rather, think about the little things. Build small daily habits and routines that support your goal, and make sure that you are doing something, even very tiny "somethings", that move you in the direction you want to go.
- **Make a written plan.** I think putting your vision in writing, and changing that written plan as appropriate is a great idea. An even better idea is putting down, on paper, the three things you absolutely must get done today to move you toward your goal. Do that now. Do it every day for a few weeks and see what happens.

Motivation isn't magic

The key to maintaining motivation is working on both of these fronts. Have a big picture goal, a vision, a dream, of where you want to be. Without that, we're lost. But focus even more on the small tasks and things that will move you closer to that goal. Build them into habits and come to love the routine of those habits. When you love what you're doing, it's much easier to keep doing it. When you're doing the right things and loving them, you're going to be amazed at what you can accomplish.

The 10,000 Hour Rule is Bullsh*t

Have you ever heard someone say they are "working toward their 10,000 hours?" I'm sure everyone reading this has heard of the "10,000 hour rule": the idea, drawn from Malcolm Gladwell's bestselling book *Outliers*, that it takes 10,000 hours to become an expert in any field. There's a big problem with this: **the 10,000 number is not real.** It's made up. It is a carefully chosen fabrication intended to sell books, but it causes us to miss the things that are truly important—the things that will move us toward mastery.

It's a lie!

I think the 10,000 hours rule has been re-hashed enough that everyone knows it, but let's just cover the broad bases. In his book, Gladwell looked at some research that focused on German violin players. The research found that the "best violinists" accumulated significantly more hours of deliberate practice than did violinists who were to become music educators, noting that that group had to fulfill lower admission requirements.

After creating the 10,000 hour rule from this research, he then finds (or creates) other narrative examples of successful people, and backs into the magical 10,000 hour math. A reasonable extension of this rule, if it were true, would be that that natural talent or ability do not matter (or don't matter much), and, in fact, might not even exist—all that matters is what you work toward the 10,000 hours to mastery.

There are a few problems with this, but **the biggest problem is that it simply is not and never was true.** Gladwell did not conduct the research himself. Rather, he took the work done in this paper: *The Role of Deliberate Practice in the Acquisition of Expert Performance* (1993) by Anders Ericsson, Krampe, and Tesch-Romer and used that as the seed for a best-selling book. Gladwell is a great writer and knows how to craft a story, but that story does not reflect a solid understanding of the actual research.

For example, he cherry picked the 10,000 hours from the average of the elite groups' estimated lifetime practice at age 20. Had he picked another age, he wouldn't have come up with such a memorable number, (and probably wouldn't have sold many books!) At any rate, the 10,000 was an average, hiding a vast range between the high and low, and half of the violinists had not reached 10,000 hours by age twenty. Gladwell claimed conclusively that they all had; whether this was his misunderstanding of the research or a willful misrepresentation to strengthen his 10,000 hour narrative, we do not know. He then took this idea and extended it to other examples, fabricating a record for the Beatles and Bill Gates to explain their success in diverse fields as a product of 10,000 hours of "practice".

Too many people should have known better (particularly in the field of trading), but it's a very catchy idea that plays to our idea of the importance of passion and hard work. Pop culture seized on the idea, and it's become deeply entrenched. At the same time, people who *do* understand the issues have pushed back. The whole concept of 10,000 hours has been roundly criticized by scientists, perhaps none more so than Anders Ericsson himself, who has said that Gladwell simply didn't understand the research. Other writers have pointed out that mastery can be achieved in far less than 10,000 hours, and some people can never attain mastery, and that different fields require very different investments... the list of objections goes on. In the storm of controversy, Malcom Gladwell had this to say about the book:

> *Yes. There is a lot of confusion about the 10,000 rule that I talk about in Outliers. It doesn't apply to sports. And practice isn't a SUFFICIENT condition for success. I could play chess for 100 years and I'll never be a grandmaster. The point is simply that natural ability requires a huge investment of time in order to be made manifest. Unfortunately, sometimes complex ideas get oversimplified in translation.*

So there it is in a nutshell: complex ideas get oversimplified in translation.

Why we care

If we approach mastery with the idea that we need to push toward some mythical goal of 10,000 hours, we start thinking of ways to do just that. For reference, if you work a standard 40 hour work week and took no vacations during the year, you'd hit your 10,000 hours somewhere before year 5. On the other end of the scale, if you imagine a serious hobby at which you spend 10 hours a week (2 hours a day 5 days a week, or maybe 6 hours on the weekend with a sprinkling through the week—realistic for most serious hobbies), it would take you 20 years to reach 10,000 hours. Something you do only occasionally throughout the week? You probably wouldn't get there in a lifetime.

Now, here's our first clue that something might be wrong: how many people have logged far more than 10,000 hours in careers, but have not achieved "mastery" (whatever that means) in those fields? There are good reasons for that, and we'll get to those soon. But if you convince people that logging these hours is the key to success, a surprising number of people will start working toward that goal. Here are some specific things I've seen:

- Traders at a prop firm, probably laboring under the Puritanically-derived American "work ethic" that hard work should be miserable and require long hours, planning on getting to the desk early in the morning, sitting there all day, and staying until evening so they can work toward their 10,000 hours.
- There's a community (or was) of people learning self-taught piano playing who record their practice hours toward 10,000 hours.
- Well-meaning online communities of traders encouraging each other and saying they just gotta put in the screen time and log their 10,000 hours. Traders have always thought (wrongly) that learning to trade was just a matter of logging "screentime", but once the book came out some traders went nuts. I read a sad blog of a kid who graduated from college and passed on job offers so he could spend the next 3 years working toward his 10,000 hours... on a simulator.
- A community of online creative writers who set writing projects for themselves to work toward the goal of the mythical 10,000 hours...

You get the point. Pop science is a dangerous drug, but the messages resonate for a reason—because they are catchy and memorable—not because they are right.

What else matters

The discussion about the 10,000 hours cuts right to the heart of the nature/nurture divide. On one side, people say that genes and natural ability are all that matters, and the other side says that it's all training and anyone can learn to do anything. (If you want a shortcut to the truth, it's usually in the middle of any argument.) The 10,000 hours is all about hard work, but what else might matter? We now have some solid research that quantifies the effect hard work has on achievements in different fields. In the 2014 paper *Deliberate Practice and Performance in Music, Games, Sports, Education, and Professions: A Meta-Analysis*, authors Macnamara et al conclude:

> *Researchers proposed that individual differences in performance in such domains as music, sports, and games largely reflect individual differences in amount of deliberate practice.... This view is a frequent topic of popular science writing—but is it supported by empirical evidence? To answer this question, we conducted a meta-analysis covering all major domains in which deliberate practice has been investigated. We found that deliberate practice explained 26% of the variance in performance for games, 21% for music, 18% for sports, 4% for education, and less than 1% for professions. We conclude that deliberate practice is important, but not as important as has been argued.*

Deliberate practice

After I published a blog post on this topic, several of my readers raised the objection that I was oversimplifying Gladwell's book, and that he emphasized the importance of deliberate practice rather than just spending 10,000 hours doing something. Actually, it was the original research done by Anders Ericsson that emphasized deliberate practice, the research that Gladwell misrepresented and oversimplified. Here is what Ericsson himself has to say on the topic:

> *...Gladwell didn't distinguish between the type of practice that the musicians in our study did — a very specific sort of practice referred to as "deliberate practice" which involves constantly pushing oneself beyond one's comfort zone, following training activities designed by an expert to develop specific abilities, and using feedback to identify weaknesses and work on them — and any sort of activity that might be labeled "practice." For example, one of Gladwell's key examples of the ten-thousand-hour rule was the Beatles' exhausting schedule of performances in Hamburg between 1960 and 1964. According to Gladwell, they played some twelve hundred times, each performance lasting as much as eight hours, which would have summed up to nearly ten thousand hours. "Tune In," an exhaustive 2013 biography of the Beatles by Mark Lewisohn, calls this estimate into question and, after an extensive analysis, suggests that a more accurate total number is about eleven hundred hours of playing. So the Beatles became worldwide successes with far less than ten thousand hours of practice. More importantly, however, performing isn't the same thing as practice...an hour of playing in front of a crowd, where the focus is on delivering the best possible performance at the time, is not the same as an hour of focused, goal-driven practice that is designed to address certain weaknesses and make certain improvements — the sort of practice that was the key factor in explaining the abilities of the Berlin student violinists.*

So, yes, deliberate practice is important, and we should turn our attention there, rather than to the 10,000 hours. But what is it? In a nutshell, it's practice that challenges you; it's practice that pushes your limits. Deliberate practice may not be fun—in fact, if you're doing it right, you will have many failures—many times where you try to do something but are unable. This is a natural consequence of working at the edge of your ability, and it is uncomfortable.

An easy example might be to compare two piano players. One plays pieces of music he likes, sometimes plays in front of friends, and when he can play something pretty well, moves on to another piece he likes. He will stop to work on the parts that challenge him so he gets better, but he mostly enjoys playing things through from beginning to end.

Contrast that to the serious player who spends hours working on details, might work on a piece for weeks or months, and may spend days in which he does not play the piece in its entirety. If you were to listen to him practice, sometimes you couldn't even recognize the piece he's playing because he is playing very slowly, or is playing small sets of notes (sometimes as few as two or three) over and over in different ways.

One of these guys is not right and the other wrong; they are doing two almost completely different activities. The first person is playing casually, for fun. The second person has a different objective, and may not, on the surface, be having as much fun. The serious worker may end practice sessions dejected, and will begin again tomorrow by focusing on places he is likely to fail.

Passion matters

When we work in deliberate practice, we frequently face our limitations—we fail, over and over again. Though this is not fun, it can be profoundly rewarding. When we overcome obstacles, and someone working in deliberate practice certainly will, the emotional rewards are very sweet indeed.

Deliberate practice is not drudgery. In fact, I don't think you can do it without passion. Passion is a word that gets thrown around casually (especially by every business school student on a job interview. No... I don't think you are passionate about capitalizing operating expenses...), but it is the driving force behind the will to succeed. Unless you love something so much that it is a part of you, I don't think you can muster the constant work and struggle to work toward mastery. Without passion, you are doomed to be a hobbiest and mastery will ever elude you.

How to do deliberate practice

Deliberate practice is a mindset, and if you are working toward mastery, it will be a lifestyle. Let me share some ideas that will apply to a wide range of disciplines, then we will look at trading and financial markets, specifically:

- **Deliberate practice requires time and effort.** This is one of the true lessons of the 10,000 hours: it takes a lot of time and work to develop mastery. If you want to succeed at something at the highest level, assume that your path to mastery will be measured in years, or perhaps decades. You can expect to achieve some real competence and proficiency in most fields in perhaps 2-3 years, but there will be others where you are still building a foundation at 5 years. Your time commitment will be pretty much every day—on average, probably 5-6 days a week. You can take vacations and breaks—you'll likely find that doing so speeds your progress—but you will not get where you want to be working 2-3 days a week. It's ok to switch your focus once you get into something, but if you do decide to master a field, go into it with your eyes wide open: the days will turn into months will turn into years, and you will have thousands of hours invested in your mastery.
- **What you do matters.** You can't spend time just playing and exploring. You must work in deliberate practice. (Yes, this is a list about deliberate practice, but this point is so important it must be re-emphasized.) These thousands of hours you are putting in must be well-spent.
- **Understand the goals; evaluate your progress and get feedback.** This is one reason why you may get much better results working with a coach or teacher. When you're learning, you don't know what you don't know. Even when you are well along your path, having the outside perspective of a master teacher can speed your progress along. You may well create your own path, but you'll do that most effectively if you have a foundation of basic knowledge in the field. As you develop, you'll learn to tell good from bad, but even this must be taught at the beginning.

The beginner picking up the golf club probably feels equally awkward holding it correctly or incorrectly.

- **Break things into parts and parts of parts.** Watching a master do something, it often seems easy. Everything flows, but this ease is deceptive. What you're actually seeing is mastery of many little details, and some of these details may seem very boring. This is true of any discipline, and working toward mastery doesn't mean "doing really cool and hard stuff" as much as it means doing very basic things very well. One of the consistent reasons I've seen people fail in various pursuits is that they are unwilling to spend this time on the basics. They are too good, too proud, too "advanced"—and it is exactly this thinking that will doom us to mediocrity.
- **Failure is good.** Most people create their lives around the idea of avoiding failure. Failure is scary, and failure doesn't feel good. Someone working in deliberate practice will work toward failure and will cultivate practice techniques that assure failure. Now, there's abject catastrophic failure, which is a sign that we're reaching too far and can be harmful (and in some disciplines physically harmful), but good practice will *assure* thousands of small failures in a week. You might think of it like this: if you don't fail, you're not trying hard enough. Failure shows us where our "growing edges" are, and only by exploring those edges can we grow.
- **Repeat and repeat and repeat.** This almost goes without saying, but you're going to be repeating basic elements over and over. You're going to be learning something, relearning it, and then working on it long after you've mastered it. Once you think you've polished something, you'll begin to see imperfections and to see ways in which you can grow further. This might relate to part #4, but I've seen many people who are on a quest to accumulate as much knowledge as possible. They would rather have tons of superficial knowledge (e.g., reading hundreds of books on a subject) without really digging deeper. Mastery is both broad and deep. Going deep takes many repetitions, and then many more.
- If you do this right, **it's hard work.** But it's also incredibly satisfying. Even more important: it's the only way to get to mastery.

When Deliberate Practice Fails

Research can be confusing because answers are often unclear. We would like to think that science is black/white, true/false, but this is not at all the case: answers only come within the bounds of statistical uncertainty, researchers have motivations and perspectives that shape those answers, and many answers that appear to be solid defy replication. Errors in thinking can persist for decades. (We're seeing a good example of this now with the revision of thinking on low-fat "heart healthy" dietary guidelines that were supported mostly by research funded by sugar producers.)

Some of the best answers tend to come from meta-studies, which are large studies of other studies. A researcher doing this work has an eagle-eye perspective on a lot of data and different methodologies and can often create analytical techniques that compensate for the weaknesses and biases in some studies. No, there's still no certainty, but a good meta-study will often get us closer.

Brooke Macnamara, Hambrick, and Oswald published a substantial metastudy of the deliberate practice literature in 2014 (alas, to nowhere near the fanfare created by pop science bobbleheads over the "10,000 rule"): *Deliberate Practice and Performance in Music, Games, Sports, Education, and Professions: A Meta-Analysis.* That paper is worth your time to read, but here is the authors' conclusion, followed by one of the charts from the paper (emphasis mine):

> *Ericsson and his colleagues' (1993) deliberate-practice view has generated a great deal of interest in expert performance, but* ***their claim that individual differences in performance are largely accounted for by individual differences in amount of deliberate practice is not supported by the available empirical evidence.*** *An important goal for future research on expert performance is to draw on existing theories of individual differences to identify basic abilities and other individual difference factors that explain variance in performance and to estimate their importance as predictor variables relative to deliberate practice. Another important goal is to continue to investigate how and when task and situational factors such as task predictability moderate the impact of deliberate practice and other individual difference factors on performance. Research aimed at addressing these goals will shed new light on the underpinnings of expert performance.*

Things that matter

The conclusion of this paper was that **12% (that's the take-home number) of variation in performance was explained by deliberate practice,** across a wide range of situations and fields—twelve percent. That is not most, nearly all, or even a lot. It's some. It's probably important, maybe very important, but it's also clearly not, based on this study, the most important thing on which to focus.

I think one of the other key points is that deliberate practice seems to work best in highly predictable fields. You tell me, is learning to trade more like learning to play a Beethoven sonata on the piano—a task in which nearly every aspect is known and defined beforehand—or is it more like fighting forest fires? From the research above, we see that deliberate practice appears to fail in explaining peoples' success in professions (and, perhaps, in education), so this might not bode well for traders focusing on deliberate practice.

I think one of the problems with learning to trade is that there are no, true, "fundamentals" of trading. Before you object, let's consider fundamentals in other fields. In music, we have basic aspects of technique and theory. In knifemaking, we have fundamental techniques of moving hot metal, managing stresses in the piece, and controlling hardness. Every sport has a set of techniques that can, and must, be assimilated into muscle memory. In chess, we have the endgame, fundamental pieces of tactics and combinations, and patterns that occur, with variations, over and over.

Is trading the same? Though people have substituted things like booking screen time and doing silly keyboard drills, I would argue that the "fundamentals" of trading have been misunderstood. These are primarily psychological skills relating to performance under risk and pressure. There are ways to move toward mastery of this psychology—both from an emotion and intellectual perspective—but one of the critical factors is time. A beginning trader is a nervous, twitching mess every time he even thinks about putting on a trade. He swings between extremes of elation and depression with every tick. He can't see or think clearly (literally cannot because his brain is chemically compromised by the emotions of trading) while the market is moving.

If that trader does not blow himself up, after a few years he stops caring so much; he becomes desensitized to the movements of the market. The emotions naturally abate as he moves toward mastery. (An important linguistic note: English encourages the use of the gendered pronoun, so I realize I've written "he" throughout this explanation, but women, who account for a tiny percentage of traders, generally do this better and faster than men. More women should probably be traders because they seem to adapt to this world much quicker, in my experience, than do men!)

We need exposure to market patterns. We need education. We need to understand statistics, probability, cognitive bias, market microstructure and efficiency—all the things that explain why trading is hard, but we also need a lot exposure to the market and a lot of times at bat.

Discipline fails

We often think about discipline the wrong way. We tell traders they must be disciplined, and they fail to be disciplined. Why? It's not because these traders are stupid or that we are incompetent teachers—it's because we are asking the impossible. **Discipline is an outcome** as much as it is a goal. Discipline shows that a lot of things are working correctly in a trader's world, and that the trader has achieved some degree of mastery. To tell a developing trader to be disciplined is akin to handing someone a basketball for the first time, putting them on the free throw line, and telling them to sink 50 in a row.

Discipline is the outcome of the right mental framework, emotional skills (largely including the systematic desensitization to the stimuli of trading achieved over many years of exposure), and process. These things matter, and perhaps we don't focus on them enough.

What might matter most

One of the things that always bothered me about the 10,000 hours was that it did not line up well with my experience. When I started music, frankly, I was almost immediately "good". Though I started late (for a classical musician) I easily leapfrogged people who had been studying for years, and, perhaps even more important, I loved it—there was a virtuous circle in which I saw that I had skill, which reinforced my excitement and love for the field (passion), which led me to develop more skills. I can see a clear difference between the things that I have tried to do with moderate success and the fields in which I have achieved some significant degree of mastery. In the latter, I always had that "aha" moment at the beginning—some early successes, and an immediate attraction for the field.

When I had the experience of teaching a reasonably large body of music students, I saw some did much better than others, regardless of my effort as a teacher. In fact, because I was so aware of my potential failings, I think I worked harder with and for many mediocre students. Sometimes they sucked because they didn't care (not to mince words!), but that was not always the case. I saw several cases in which the students put in time, but just simply did not get the same improvement that someone else might have. I could also make the observation that passion again seemed to be a necessary, but not sufficient, precondition for success. Some of the less successful students loved what they were doing (and, I hope, will always find it to be a contribution to their life and happiness), but, without exception, every good to great student was on fire with the rage to master their discipline—success was only a road to the next challenge to be conquered.

I think this is harder in trading. Do you really love the process of trading, or are you focused on the financial success and the (very real) change it can make in your life? You don't have to love everything you do, and you might even need to fight the tendency for obsession that comes with passion, but I think your life will be best rewarded if you can bring some coherence. Trading is going to be hard, and it's going to take you at least a few years to have any measurable success. If you don't love it, you probably shouldn't be doing it—that's probably the most important thing of all. Life is short; if you don't love what you're doing, find something you do love.

On Charting

Charting by Hand

Though it is time consuming and is probably one of the oldest of the "old school" practices, I have found great value in keeping price charts by hand. In fact, it is the single most useful practice I know of to help a trader really learn how to read and understand price charts and to stay in the flow of the market.

When I started trading, I didn't use a chart service or a computer program. I was figuring everything out from scratch, and didn't even really know what kinds of chart services might have helped me or where to find them. Instead, I had a newspaper and graph paper and every day I would add one price bar to my charts for coffee, sugar, grains, meats and metal futures. I actually spent time in a library going back through old issues to find historical data to build older charts. This was incredibly time consuming, to say the least. After doing this for a while, I did eventually get a charting service, but I am sure those first few months of charting by hand laid the foundation for understanding the action behind the charts.

Several years later, I found myself struggling a bit as I made transitions to new products and new timeframes. One of the best suggestions I received was to take a step back and start keeping a five-minute swing chart of the S&P 500 futures by hand every day, and so it began. For the next year and a half, I graphed every single move of the market by hand. This required complete focus, and, most important, I had to be sitting at the desk every minute the market was open paying attention to prices on the screen. What began on a single piece of graph paper grew, after much taping and stapling, into a leviathan that coiled around the walls of my home office, and had cuts where the door was so it was possible to enter and exit the room. (It helps to have an understanding family if you are going to try a stunt like this!)

There are many ways to do this practice. You can skip the charts and simply write down prices at specified intervals. In other words, if you're a daytrader, maybe write down prices for 6 active stocks and the S&P 500 every 15 minutes throughout the day. Longer-term traders can write down end of day prices, maybe for major global stock indexes, bonds, gold, etc. Simply writing down prices has the benefit of pulling you away from charts. Many modern traders are probably too dependent on charts, and looking at raw prices forces you to think about the data differently. For most traders, this might be very uncomfortable at first. Try it and see—the less you like it, the more you probably need to do it, at least for a while.

You also can keep full charts by hand. The specifics of how to do this don't matter as much as having a consistent methodology for defining the swings. When I did this intraday, I was defining a swing as a move a certain percentage of intraday ATR off a swing high and low. So, for instance, once the market came off a high by a distance equal to 3 average bar ranges, I would draw a line on the chart and then wait for price to bounce three ranges off a low point to draw the next line. You can use a system like this, but there are many other options. It is just as useful to keep simple bar charts or point and figure charts.

Why in the world would anyone do this? Well, first of all, electronic charts may make life too easy. It's too easy to look at thousands of price bars a day on your screen and simply accept them for what they are, scanning for heads and shoulders or whatever pattern you want to give a shot this week. Pretty soon, your eyes just glaze over. Drawing lines by hand forces you to think about the buying and selling that is behind each move in the market. The act of picking up a pencil engages a different part of the brain and makes learning faster and more complete. This makes you pay attention. It is not enough that you are at your desk. You must really focus and be in the moment while you are trading. Keeping charts by hand encourages this state and enforces the kind of discipline needed for top-notch trading.

I am not saying this is the solution to all your trading problems, but I believe doing this taught me to read charts better than anything else I have done. At the very least, it's a different perspective on the learning process and market action—in this day and age you won't hear many other people tell you to sit down at your computer and break out the graph paper!

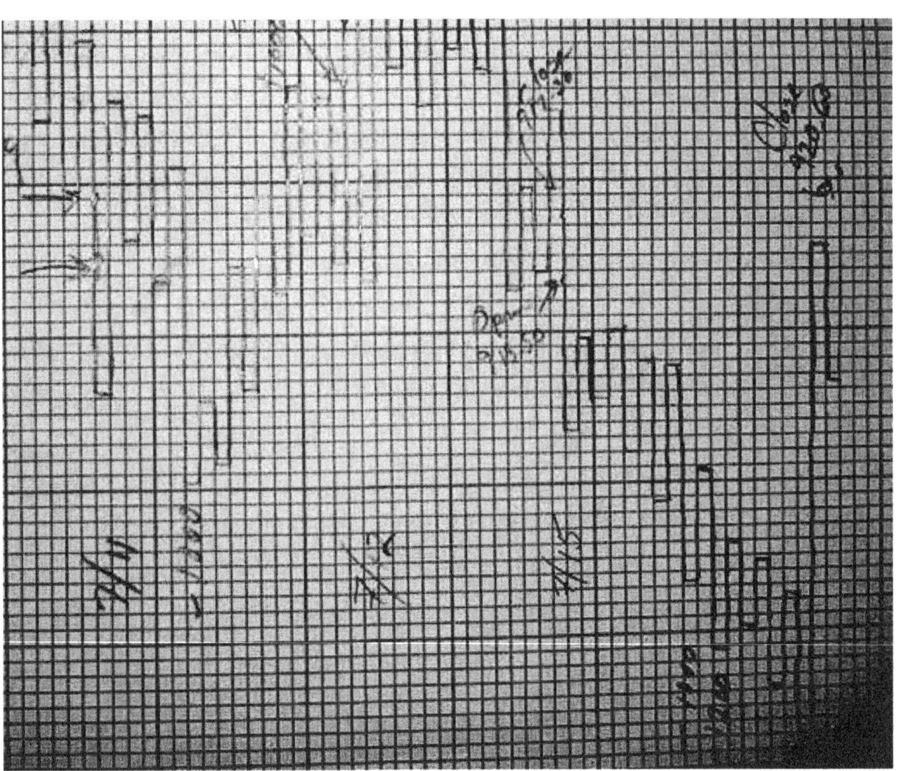

Trust Your Gut: The Power of Subjective Chartreading

Take a look at the two charts below. Don't overthink; these are not trick questions. What is your first impression of the best answer for each trade, assuming that you think the underlying trade ideas were solid? (Whether the idea is good or not is not the point—your placement of targets for market movements is the point.)

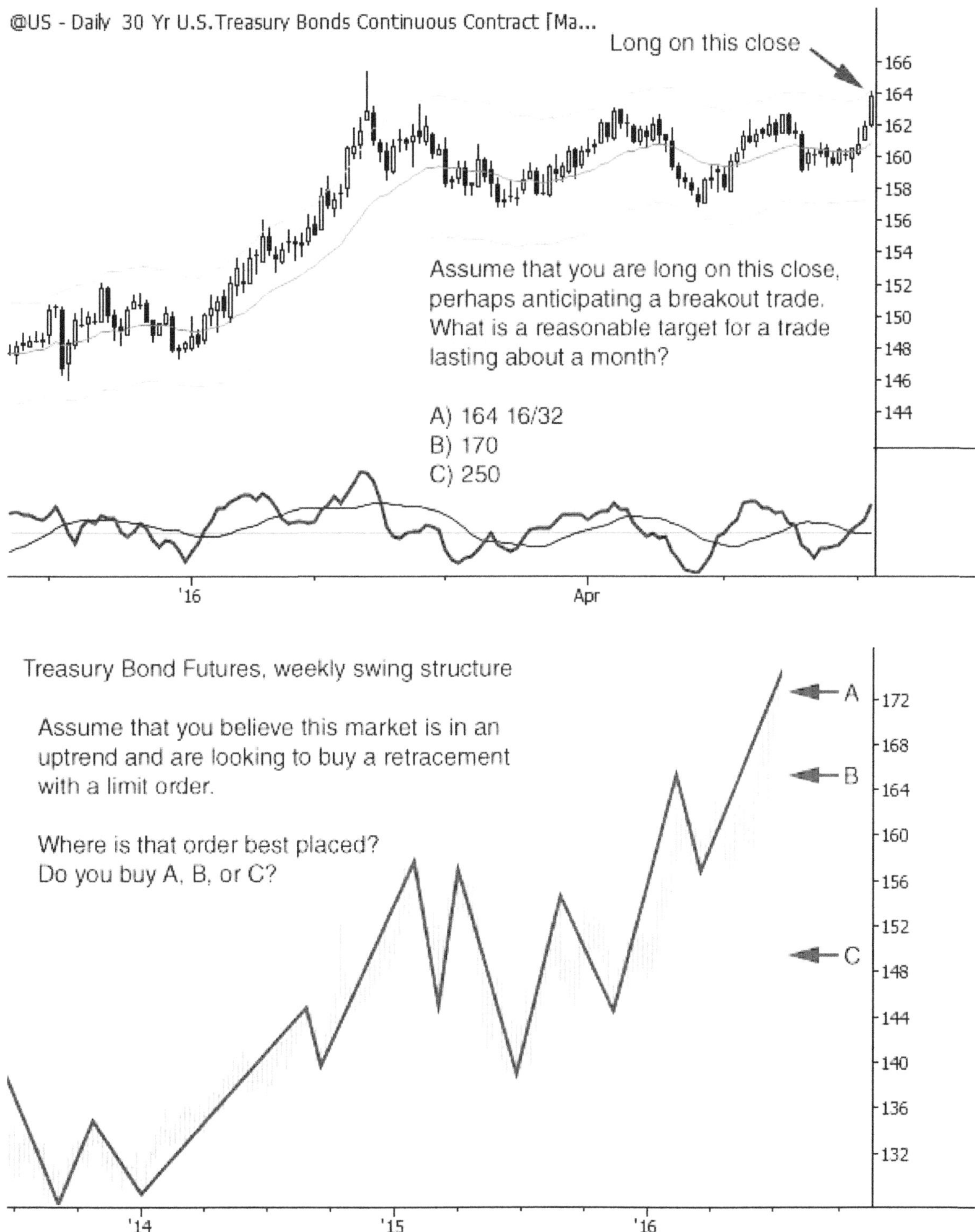
@US - Daily 30 Yr U.S.Treasury Bonds Continuous Contract [Ma...
Long on this close
166
164
162
160
158
156
154
152
150
148
146
144
Assume that you are long on this close, perhaps anticipating a breakout trade. What is a reasonable target for a trade lasting about a month?
A) 164 16/32
B) 170
C) 250
'16
Apr
Treasury Bond Futures, weekly swing structure
Assume that you believe this market is in an uptrend and are looking to buy a retracement with a limit order.
Where is that order best placed? Do you buy A, B, or C?
A
B
C
172
168
164
160
156
152
148
144
140
136
132
'14
'15
'16

What your answers say

I'm willing to bet that nearly everyone taking this quiz answered B) for both charts. In both cases, the middle value probably seemed most reasonable or felt right. Why is this?

I think the answer points to some sophisticated processing going on behind the scenes. When you look at a chart, you automatically make some assessment of volatility—you look at the size of the bars, of the swings, of the gaps, and get a good idea of "how much the thing usually moves." All of this may seem maddingly subjective to quantitative types, but subjectivity does not invalidate the analysis. In fact, embracing the wisdom of your subjective sense can unlock a deeper understanding of market action.

In the first chart above, the first profit target probably seemed almost stupidly close. When you looked at the third choice and realized how much space you'd have to add to get that number on the price axis, it probably looked "optimistic" to put it kindly. Note that I included a time element in the trade: I said to assume you were holding a trade for a month. Yes, given enough time we might eventually reach C, but it's not likely it will happen in a month—and, in trading, a solid understanding of "not likely" vs "likely" is the root of understanding probabilities in the market.

Measured move objectives

This is why the measured move objective works—it's simply a quick and dirty way to project what a reasonable move for a market might be, based on how the market has moved in the recent past. Of course, nothing is perfect: tomorrow's volatility can be much higher than today's and price can blow through your target or stop. Tomorrow's volatility might dry up, and we might drift sideways, basically never getting to the profit target. Or the trade can fail altogether. Though this simple tool isn't perfect, nothing is, and this simple tool will keep you aligned with the average volatility of the market.

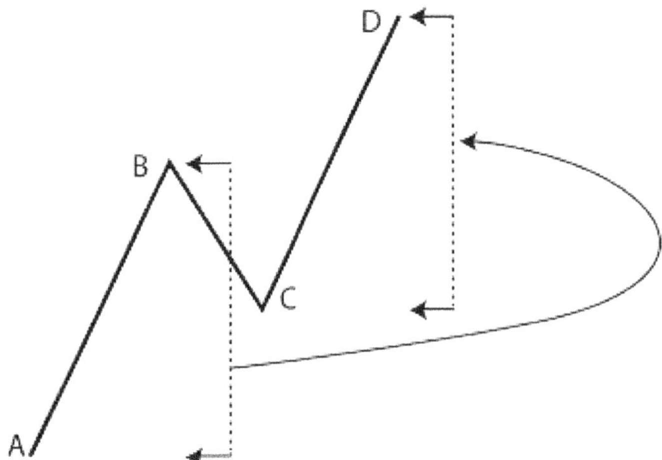

Buying pullbacks

If you take an objective look at retracements, you'll start to see something interesting. Retracements can "kinda stop anywhere" in the previous swing, but, on average, they retrace "about half, maybe a little more". In all my years of trading, I haven't found a more reliable rule than that, and it's also borne out in quantitative testing. The chart below shows the results of a test looking and hundreds of thousands of swings across all major asset classes, measuring the retracement as a percentage of the previous swing:

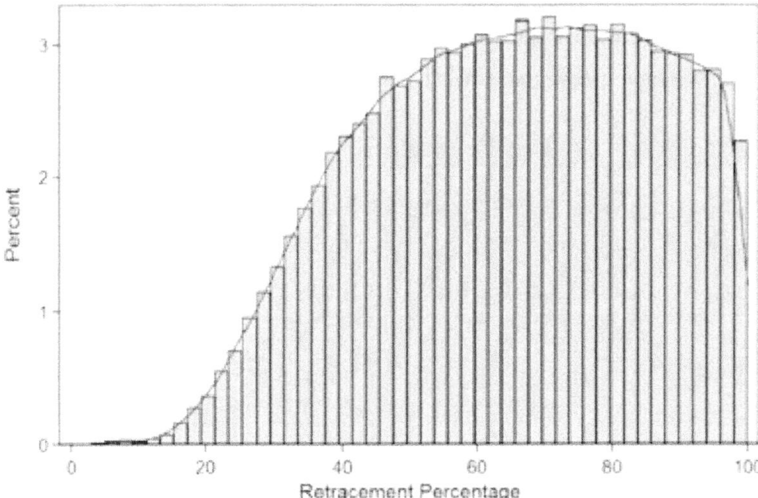

This chart shows swing retracements across the horizontal axis. (E.g., 60 means that the swing retraced 60% of the previous swing.) You can see that the peak is somewhere around 60%, with a very wide margin of error. (Technically, it's about 63% with a standard deviation of 21%.)

I'm also willing to bet that most of you thought the pullback around B), somewhere in the middle of the previous swing, was probably the best point to buy. Your simple guess here, again, hid a lot of wisdom and truth about how the market really moves. The interesting thing is that when I repeat experiments like this with different groups of traders, including people who are just starting out, the answers are the same. You did not make the choices you did based on years of experience of seeing thousands of patterns. You did not make these choices based on deep knowledge of how Treasury futures traded. Rather, you made the decision based on good, solid common sense—simply projecting the swings of the market forward in time and making some reasonable assumptions.

Good chartreading is a powerful heuristic. Though it might appear to be quick and sloppy, this "common sense" processing does many things that sophisticated quantitative models seek to imitate—at a glance, you can assess the volatility of a market and make some very educated guesses about where the market might travel in the future.

How to use this information

Why do we care about this? First, it should reassure you a bit about the power of your own analysis. Especially in a world where more and more computing power is brought to bear on financial markets, it's hard for some traders to have faith in the old Mark 1 Eyeball. Trust your eye, because there are some things it does very well.

However, the other lesson, to me, is to respect our limitations and the limitations of our methodology. If you use a calculated retracement ratio, just be aware that there's no magical power to the ratio. If you are buying at 61.8034% of the previous swing, that might be a little silly when the data says that anywhere between ~40% and ~80% is just about equally as likely. If you're setting a stop or a target to a precise point based on these levels, perhaps you should be willing to adapt to other information and be willing to make some adjustments as needed.

I suppose the irony is this: using the common Fib ratios probably do put you somewhere in the ballpark of what's right. So do pivot points and other levels, simply because they place lines somewhere in the reasonable expectations of market movements. You could do the same without them. To many traders, moving away from these levels is an important step in embracing the power of their own analysis, but, as long as our tools respect the volatility of the market and typical swings, we have powerful tools for managing risk and trades in markets.

Chapter 2

Module 2–Chartreading, Going Deeper

In this module, we start to understand how the market moves, but we do this first from a high-level perspective. In the last module, we focused on individual bars. Now, we turn our attention to how those bars relate to other bars, and encounter the first fundamental element of market structure: the pivot.

From pivots, we build swings. Swings outline the big-picture movements of the market, and reading swings is one of the key skills of effective chartreading. When we start looking at swings, we naturally see patterns emerge as the market moves from one price level to another. This brings us to the idea of trends, and we spend some time looking at the patterns of trends—how they move, and how they end.

There is a simple and logical progression here; from the ends of trends, we then investigate the areas in which the market is not trending and discover some of the patterns around trading ranges. Trading ranges are areas that seem to be controlled by support and resistance, and we next spend some time on the basic concepts behind support and resistance.

If there has been one failing in our work so far, it might be the assumption that the market is highly readable and highly deterministic. We have our first brush with the Efficient Markets Hypothesis (EMH), and consider the futility of trading if that hypothese were true. This is not all negativity, because the ways in which and reasons for which the EMH fail can point us toward profitable trading. We round out this module with the first of our more quantitative sections, looking at randomness, random walks, and how this factor profoundly influences all of our operations in the market.

Section 1: Pivot Analysis

This section has a number of charts to be labeled. For each chart, do the following:

1) Mark every first order (simple) pivot high and low. A pivot high is a bar with a higher high than both the preceding and following bar.

2) Mark every second order pivot high and low. Second order pivot highs are first order pivot highs preceded and followed by lower first order pivot highs.

For each chart, the answer key appears on the following page.

Take your time with these, and work only while you are engaged. When you start to tire and lose interest, take a break. There is no benefit to "cramming" this work and trying to do it in a short time. In fact, spreading it over a longer period of time will give your eyes and brain more time to adjust to seeing the data in this way.

US Dollar / Japanese Yen

Pivot chart example 1

SPDR S&P 500 ETF

Pivot chart example 2

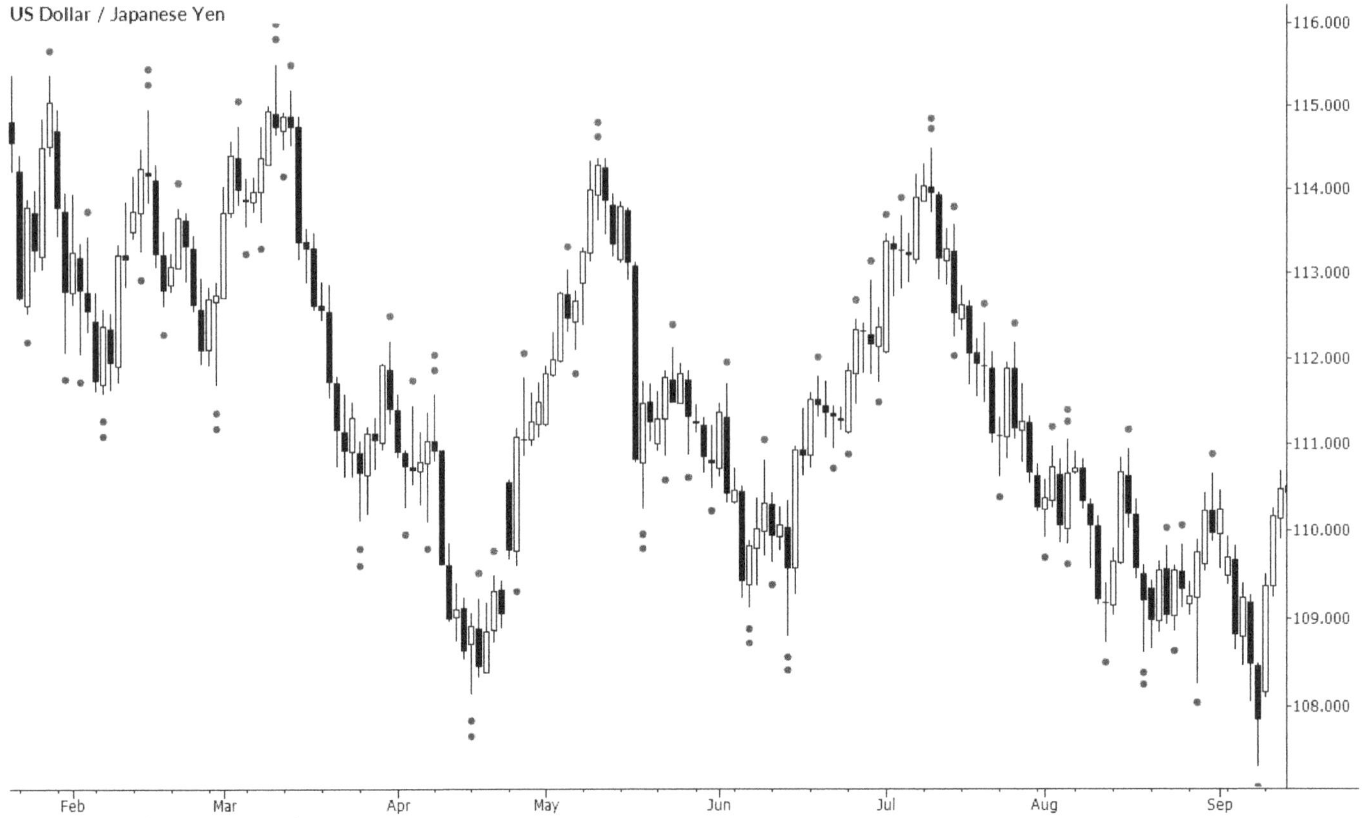

US Dollar / Japanese Yen

Pivot chart answer key 1

SPDR S&P 500 ETF

Pivot chart answer key 2

30 Yr U.S.Treasury Bonds Continuous Contract [De...

Pivot chart example 3

Gold Continuous Contract [Dec17]

Pivot chart example 4

30 Yr U.S.Treasury Bonds Continuous Contract [De...

Pivot chart answer key 3

Gold Continuous Contract [Dec17]

Pivot chart answer key 4

Apple Inc

160.00
155.00
150.00
145.00
140.00
135.00
130.00
125.00
120.00
Feb Mar Apr May Jun Jul Aug Sep

Pivot chart example 5

10 Yr U.S. Treasury Notes Continuous Contract [D...

127'16.0
127'00.0
126'16.0
126'00.0
125'16.0
125'00.0
124'16.0
124'00.0
123'16.0
123'00.0
122'16.0
Feb Mar Apr May Jun Jul Aug Sep

Pivot chart example 6

Apple Inc

165.00
160.00
155.00
150.00
145.00
140.00
135.00
130.00
125.00
120.00

Feb'17 Mar'17 Apr'17 May'17 Jun'17 Jul'17 Aug'17 Sep'17

Pivot chart answer key 5

10 Yr U.S. Treasury Notes Continuous Contract [D...

128'00.0
127'16.0
127'00.0
126'16.0
126'00.0
125'16.0
125'00.0
124'16.0
124'00.0
123'16.0
123'00.0
122'16.0

Feb Mar Apr May Jun Jul Aug Sep

Pivot chart answer key 6

Section 2: Swing Analysis

The first four charts in this example were drawn by hand, with a focus on the simple patterns of trend change. You will likely find these examples very easy because they play, nicely, by the rules.

The other charts in this section are drawn from real market action, covering a wide range of markets and timeframes from 1 minute to monthly. Apply the analysis strictly to these charts, and expect they will be harder. It is always possible to reduce these patterns to our simple rule set, but some of them may include some perplexing turns.

This is also the time to begin to consider both the value and limitations of this analysis. If you were to buy every time you marked an uptrend, and sell short every time you marked a downtrend, what would the results be? (It's not necessary to keep careful records; just consider it from a subjective perspective.) This is not a standalone trading methodology, but it does provide a solid foundation for a deeper understanding of market action.

The first chart is done as an illustration of how your analysis should look on the charts.

Use strict trend definitions:
UT = Higher High and Higher Low
DT = Lower High and Lower Low
R = "Range": any conditions other than UT or DT

You cannot go directly from UT to DT or vice versa. You must go through "R".

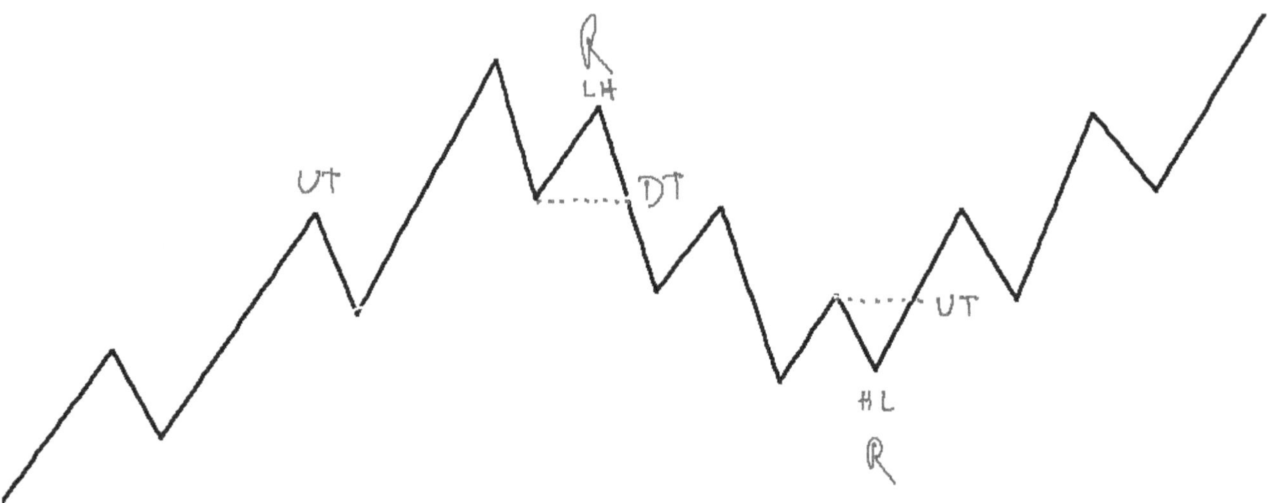

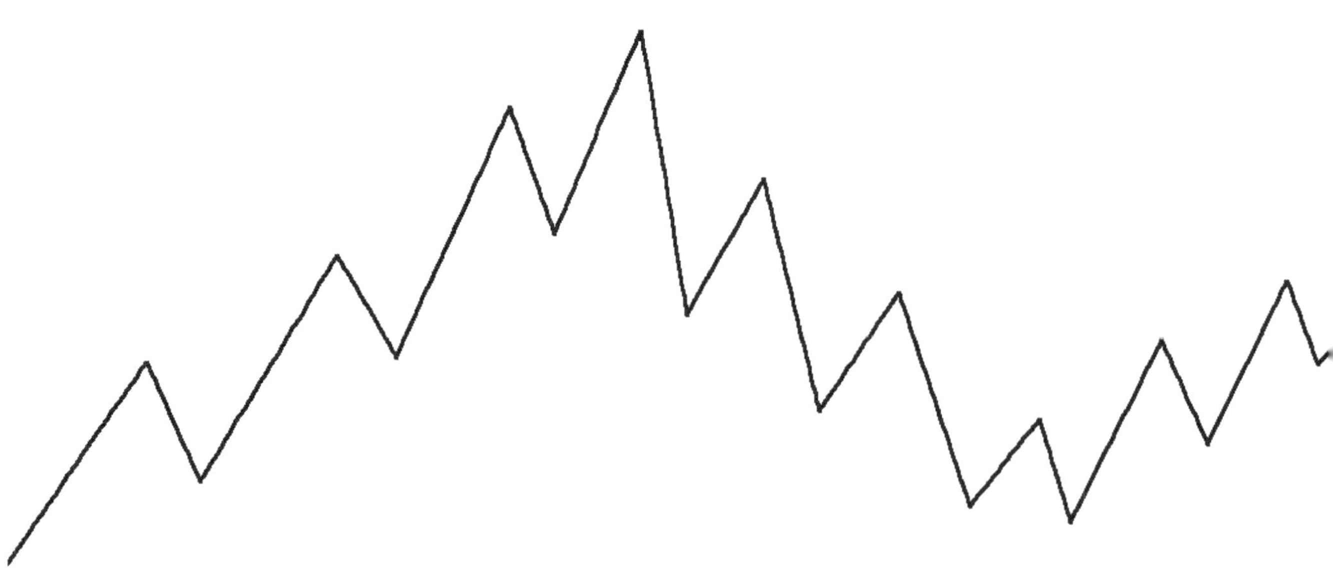

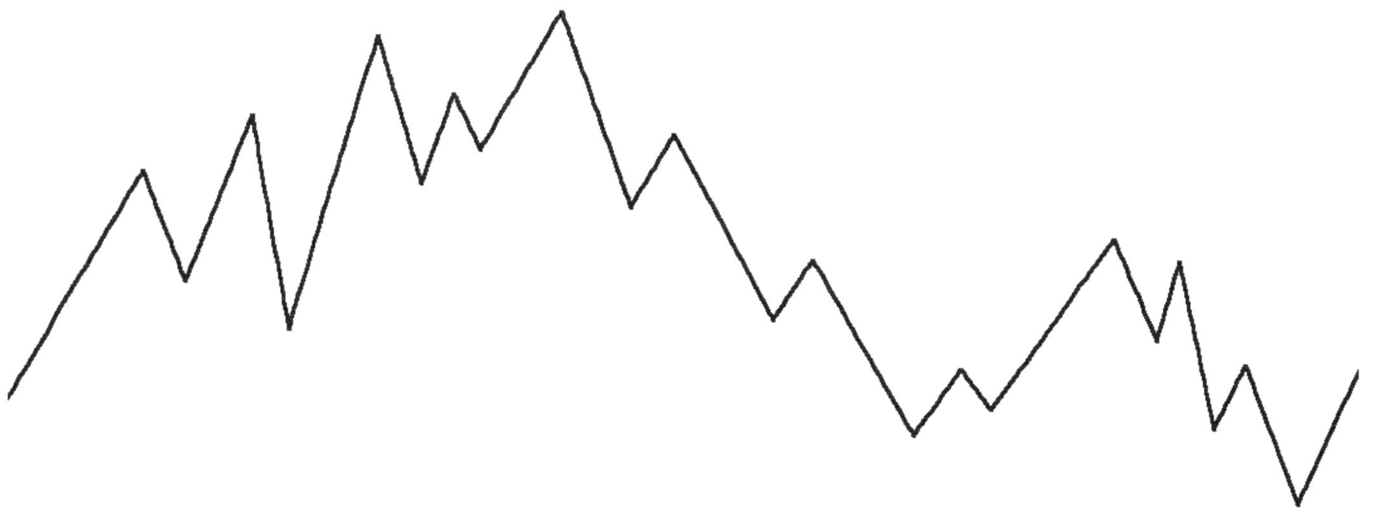

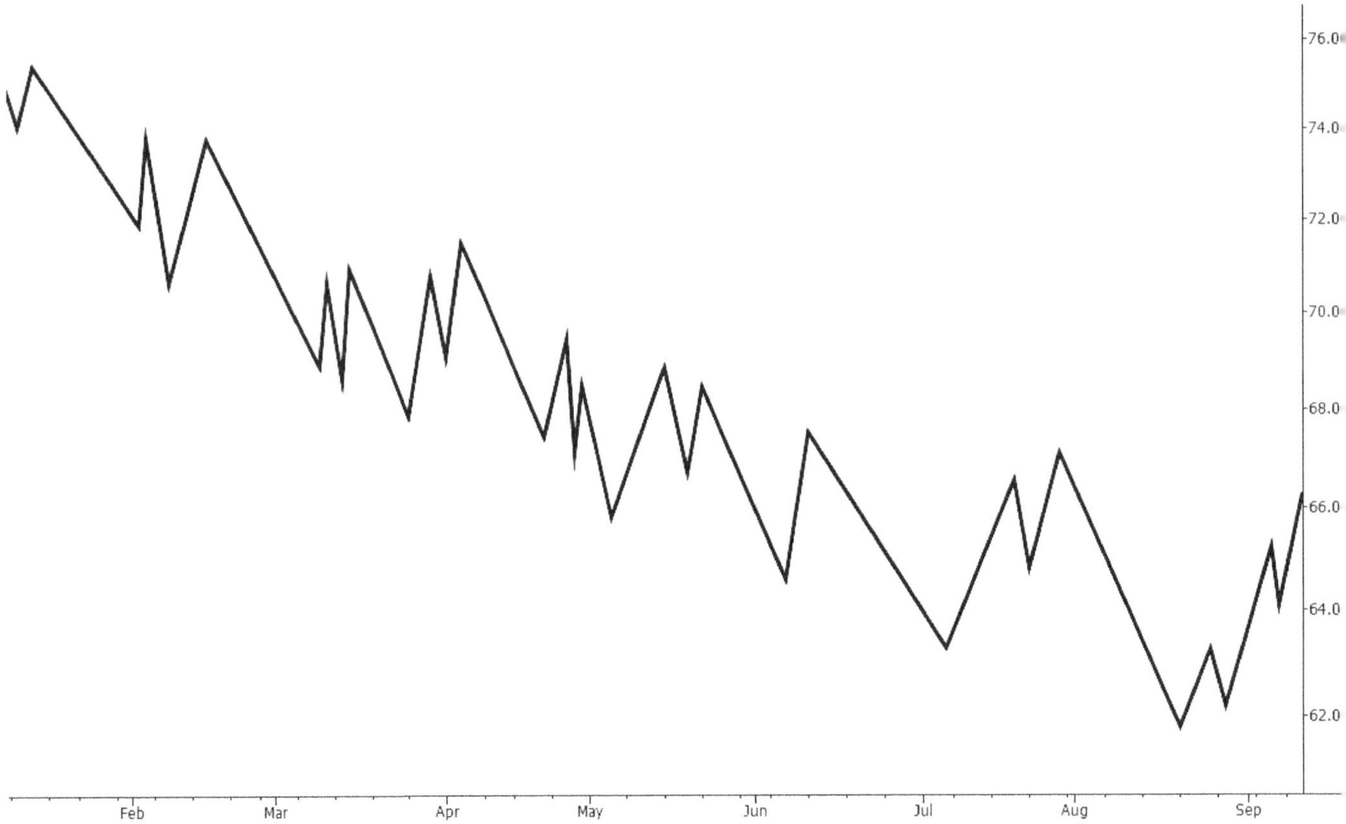
76.0
74.0
72.0
70.0
68.0
66.0
64.0
62.0
Feb
Mar
Apr
May
Jun
Jul
Aug
Sep

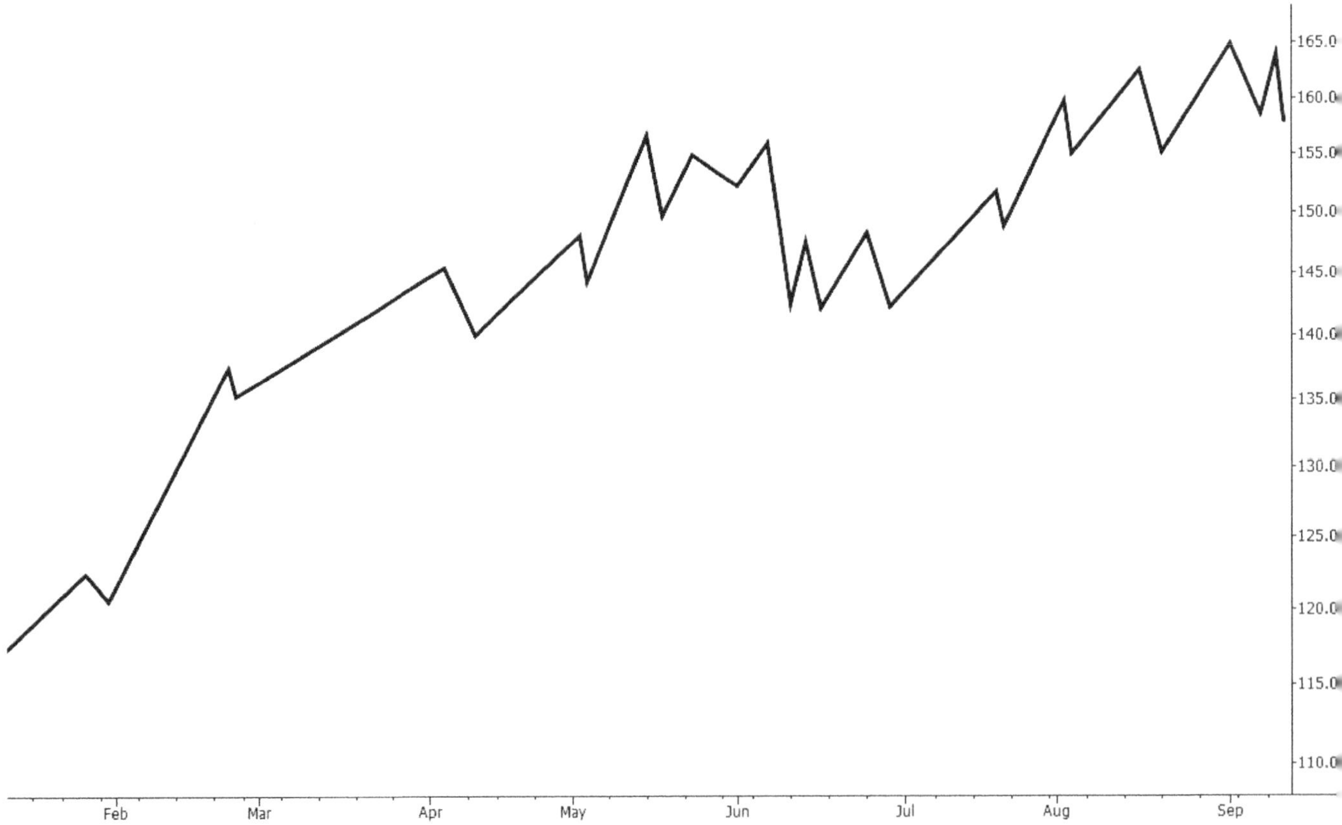
165.0
160.0
155.0
150.0
145.0
140.0
135.0
130.0
125.0
120.0
115.0
110.0
Feb
Mar
Apr
May
Jun
Jul
Aug
Sep

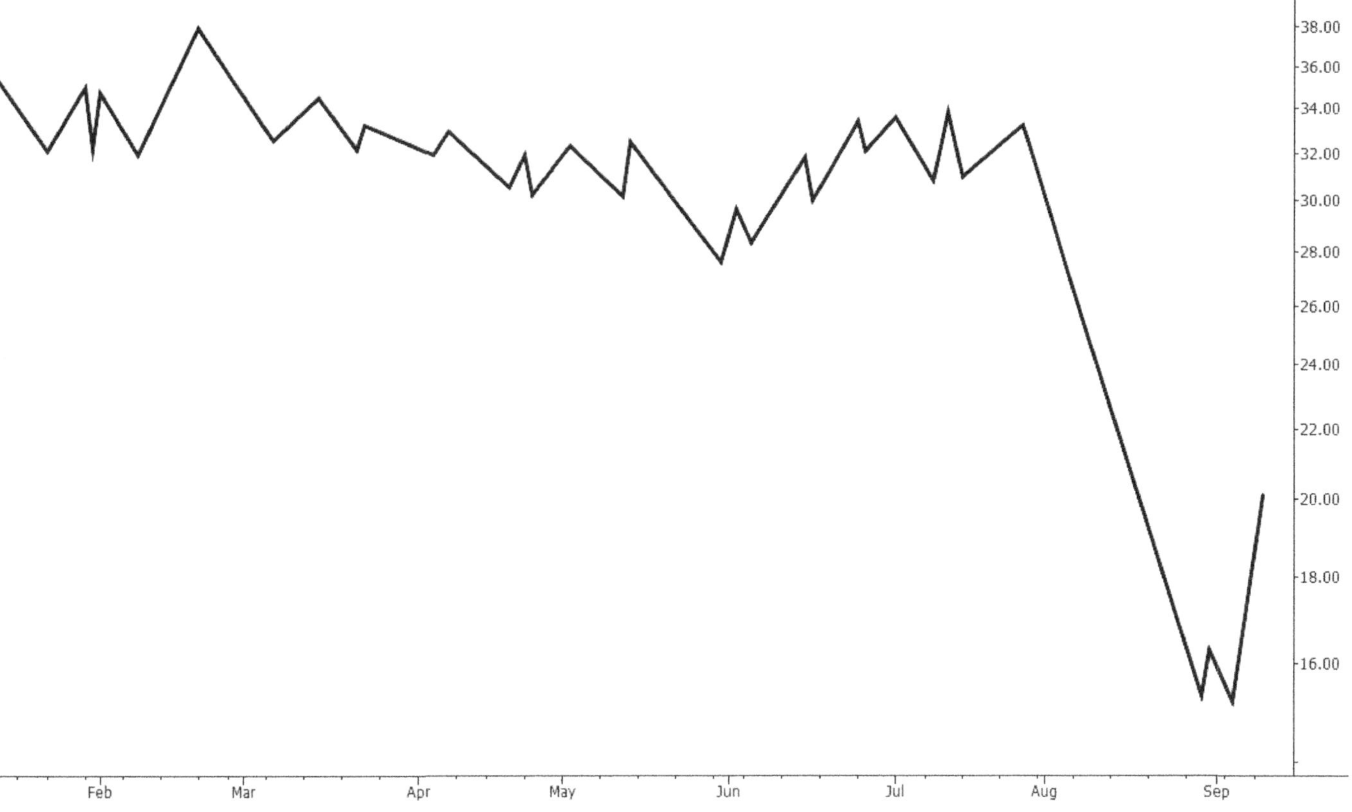
38.00
36.00
34.00
32.00
30.00
28.00
26.00
24.00
22.00
20.00
18.00
16.00
Feb
Mar
Apr
May
Jun
Jul
Aug
Sep

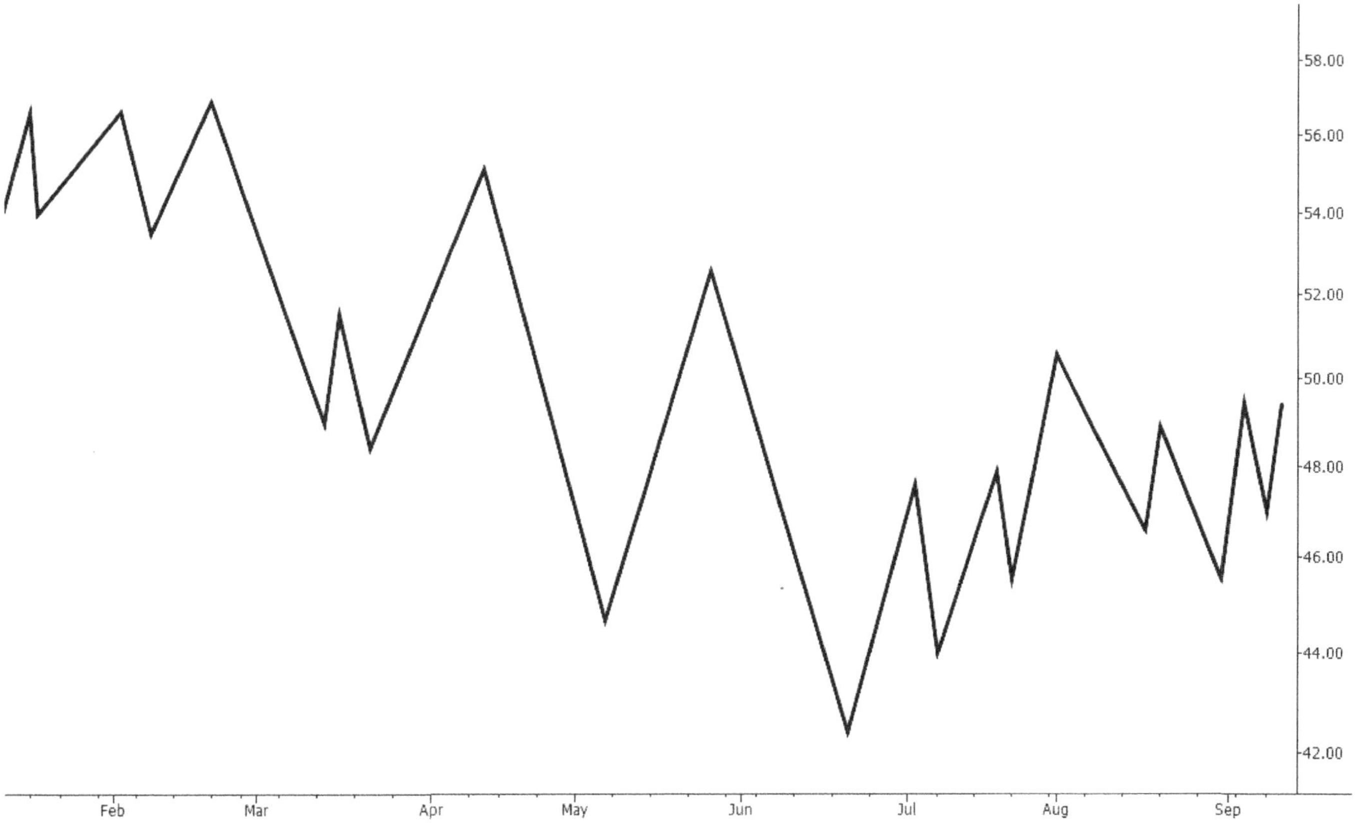

58.00
56.00
54.00
52.00
50.00
48.00
46.00
44.00
42.00
Feb
Mar
Apr
May
Jun
Jul
Aug
Sep

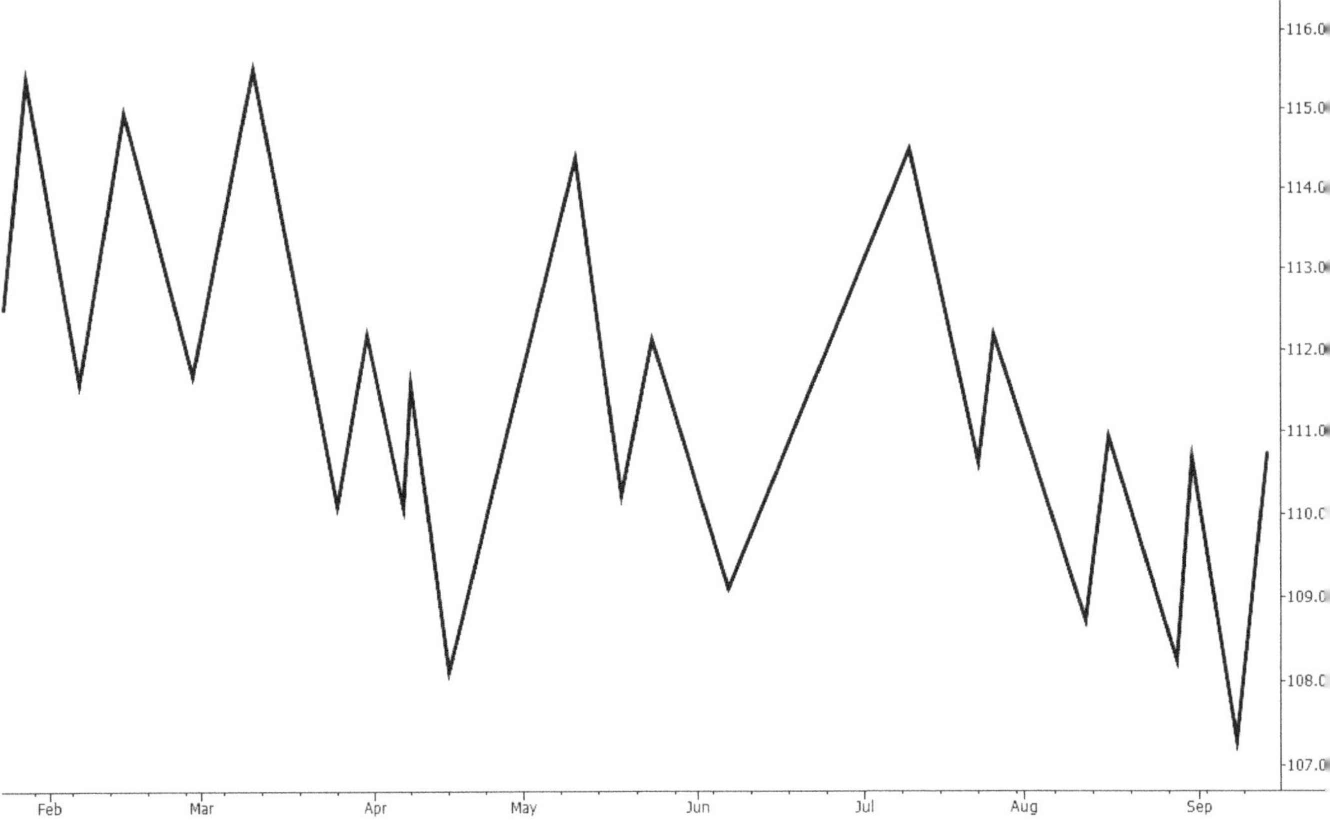
116.0
115.0
114.0
113.0
112.0
111.0
110.0
109.0
108.0
107.0
Feb
Mar
Apr
May
Jun
Jul
Aug
Sep

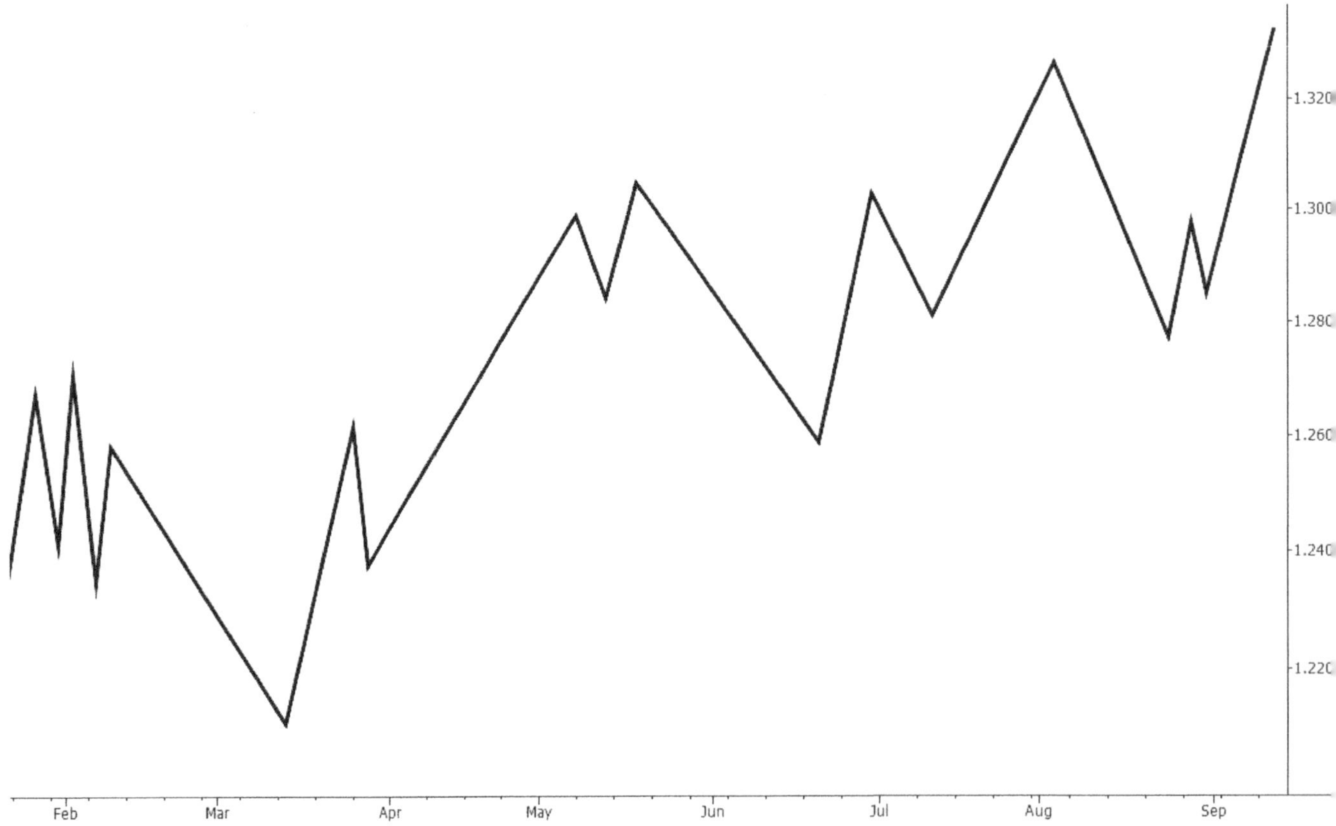

1.320
1.300
1.280
1.260
1.240
1.220
Feb
Mar
Apr
May
Jun
Jul
Aug
Sep

6,000.00
5,900.00
5,800.00
5,700.00
5,600.00
5,500.00
5,400.00
5,300.00
5,200.00
5,100.00
5,000.00
4,900.00
Feb
Mar
Apr
May
Jun
Jul
Aug
Sep

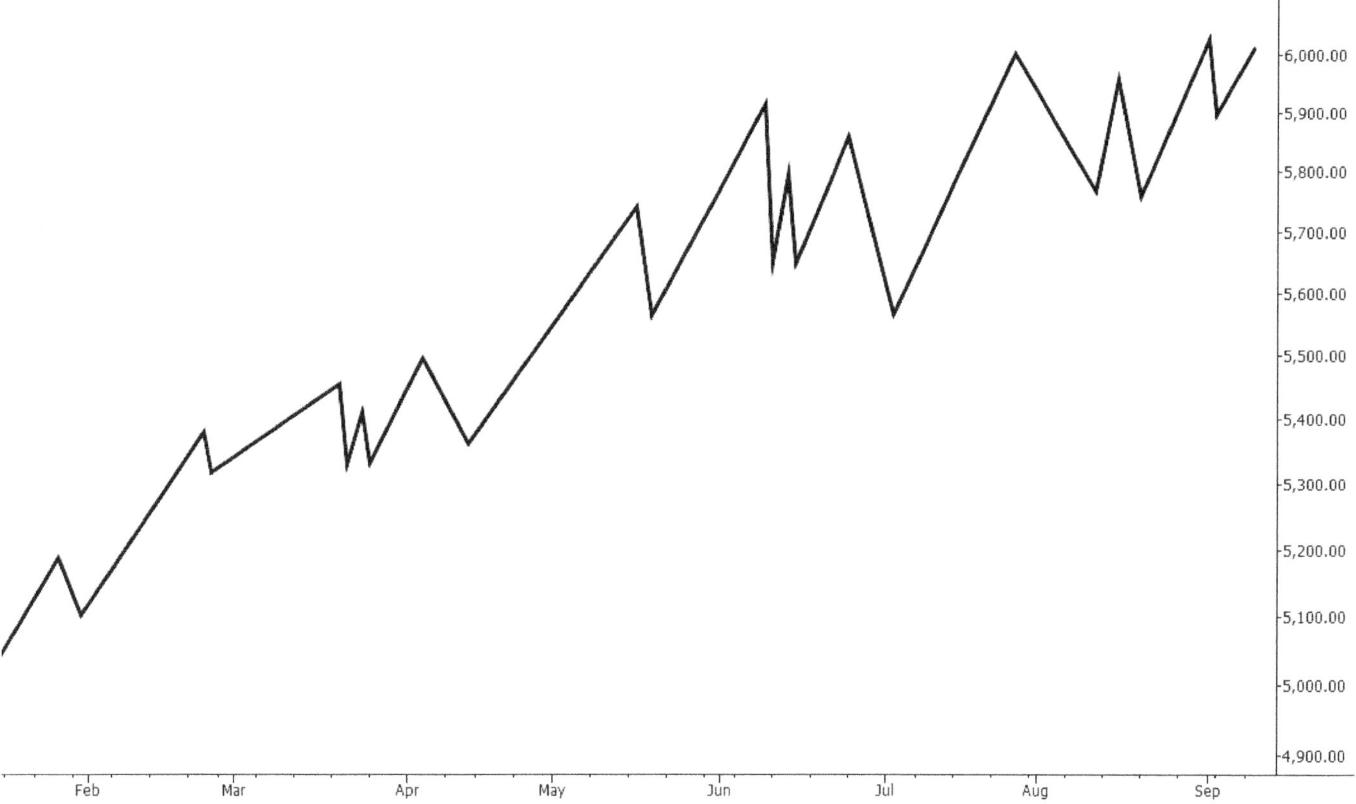

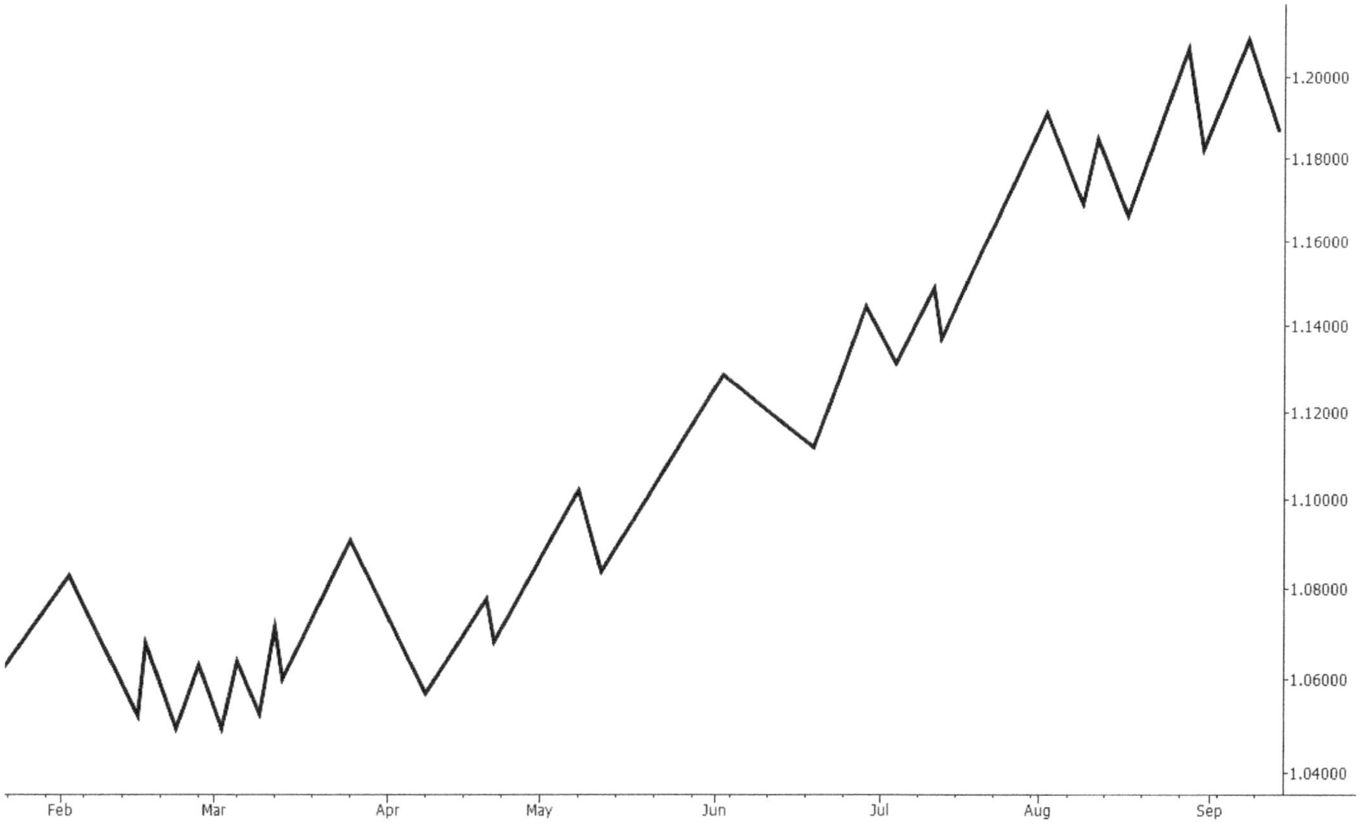

1.20000
1.18000
1.16000
1.14000
1.12000
1.10000
1.08000
1.06000
1.04000
Feb
Mar
Apr
May
Jun
Jul
Aug
Sep

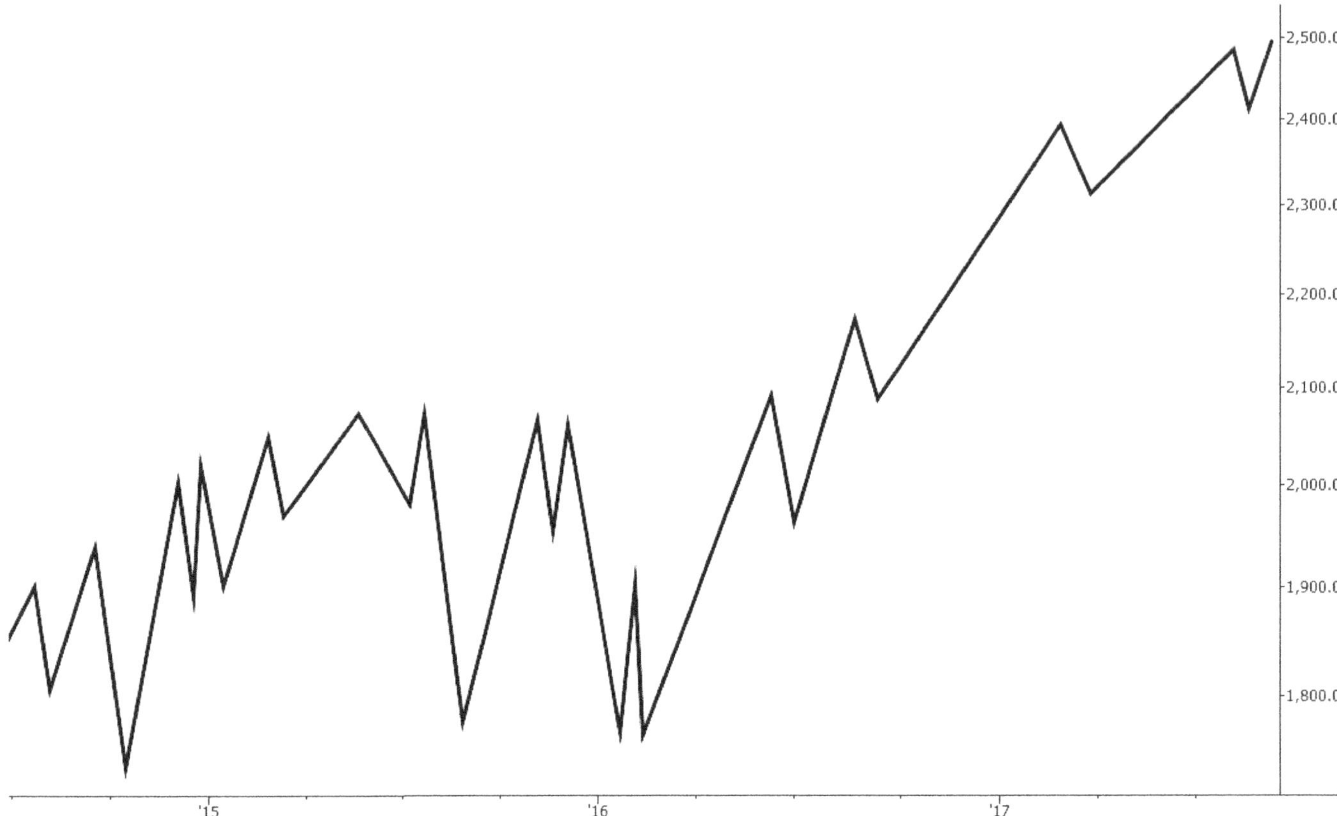
2,500.0
2,400.0
2,300.0
2,200.0
2,100.0
2,000.0
1,900.0
1,800.0
'15
'16
'17

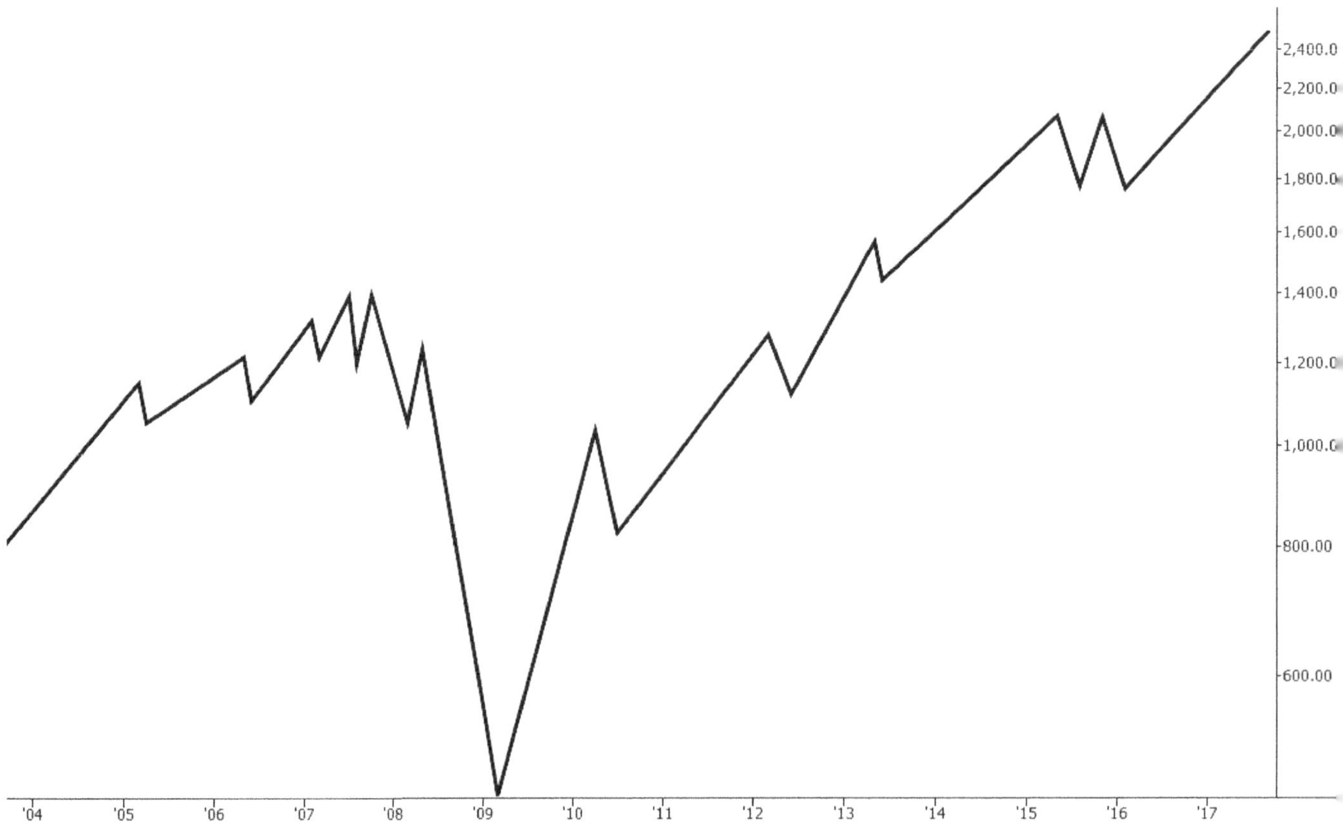

2,400.0
2,200.0
2,000.0
1,800.0
1,600.0
1,400.0
1,200.0
1,000.0
800.00
600.00
'04
'05
'06
'07
'08
'09
'10
'11
'12
'13
'14
'15
'16
'17

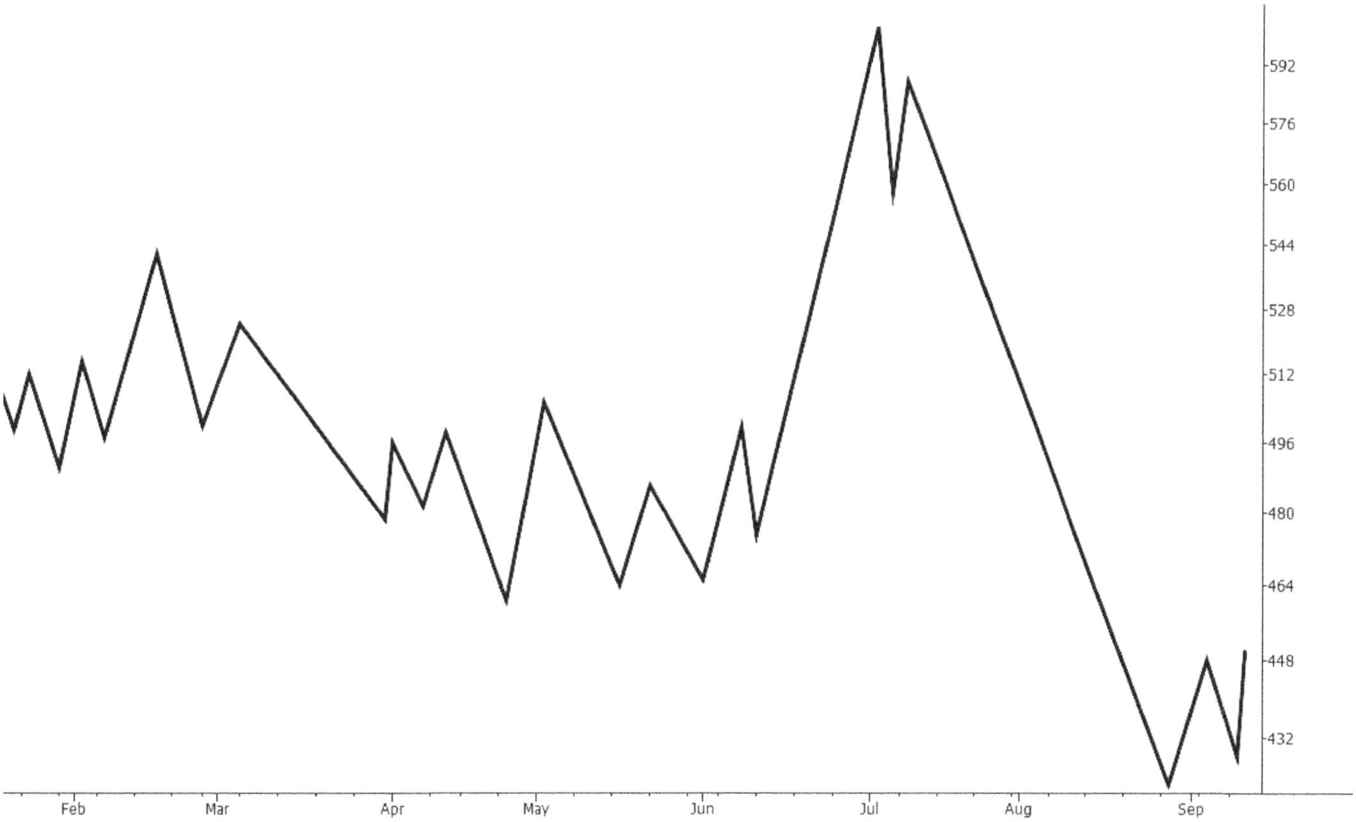
592
576
560
544
528
512
496
480
464
448
432
Feb
Mar
Apr
May
Jun
Jul
Aug
Sep

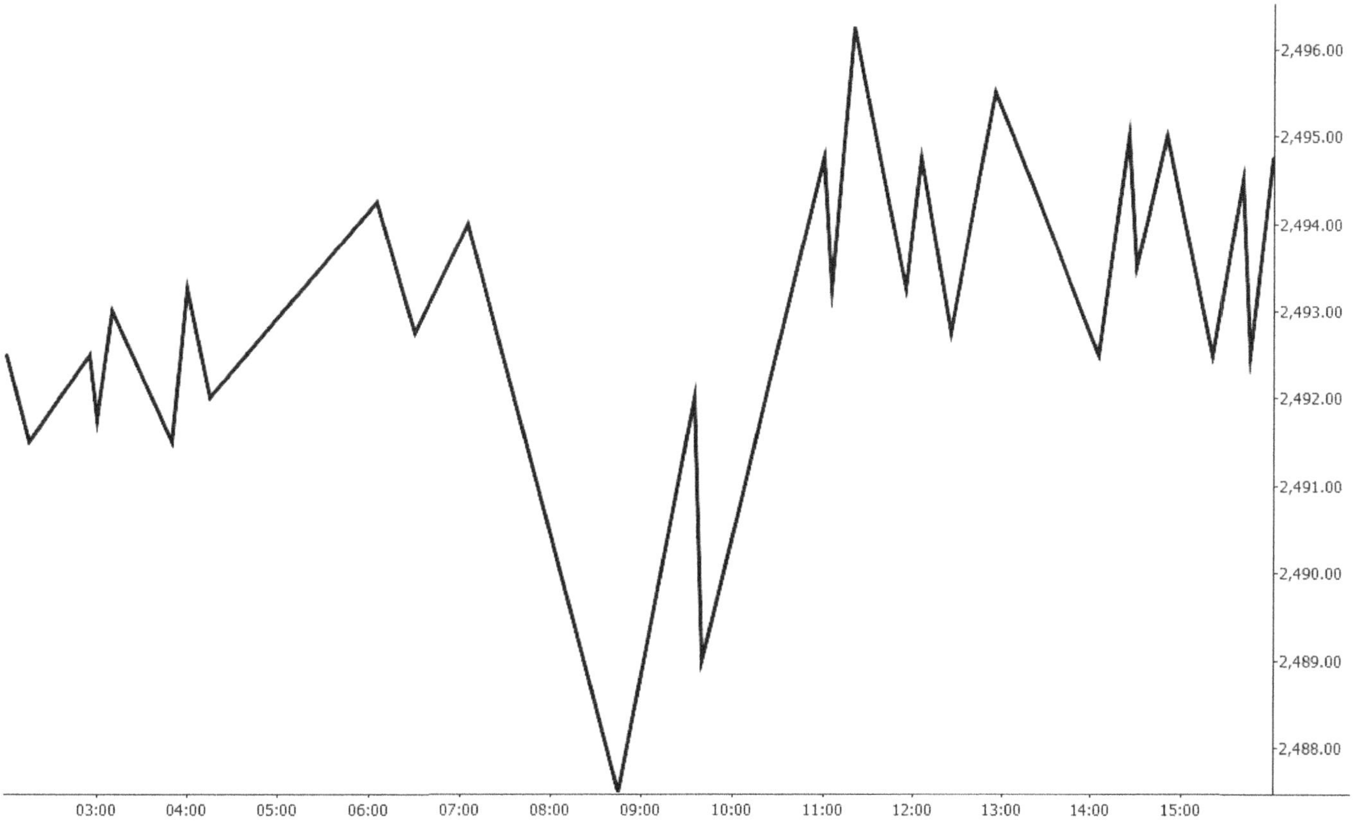
2,496.00
2,495.00
2,494.00
2,493.00
2,492.00
2,491.00
2,490.00
2,489.00
2,488.00
03:00
04:00
05:00
06:00
07:00
08:00
09:00
10:00
11:00
12:00
13:00
14:00
15:00

Section 3: Action around S&R and Ranges

The charts in this section each have specific points marked. In all cases, discuss:

- Action leading up to the touch of support or resistance (S/R)
- Action at the touch of S/R
- Action following the touch of S/R
- Any surprises or anything unusual. Use your chart story skills here.

In many cases, there are some additional specific questions about these areas.

This is still a backward-looking analysis, but you can begin to think about applying these tools in real time. In all cases, everything is clearer in hindsight, It may not have been possible to have made reliable predictions in every case but you would have been alerted to watch action around previous support or resistance.

E-mini S&P 500 Continuous Contract [Dec17]
(day session only)
A
B
C
D
E
F
G
H
The high and low of the day can provide important reference points for intraday action. Discuss action in this 15 minute chart of the S&P 500, considering the following points for each of the marked bars:
1: Is there price rejection?
2: Is this a multiple test of the same level?
3: Would you have expected the level to hold or break?
4: Would your expectation have been correct?
2,495.00
2,490.00
2,485.00
2,480.00
2,475.00
2,470.00
2,465.00
2,460.00
9/8
12:00
14:00
9/11
12:00
14:00
9/12
12:00
14:00
9/13
12:00
14:00
9/14
12:00
14:00

Sugar No. 11 Continuous Contract [Oct17]

A good example of a classic trading range. Discuss each of the points in A-E in context of the developing range.

F) and G) are simply action against support and resistance. What do you see that could give you insight into market dynamics here?

Euro / US Dollar
We are simply defining resistance here as the "highwater" mark of the trend, or the pivot high at the last trend extreme.
Discuss each of these levels in terms of expectations. In other words, based on the bar that engaged (broke or backed away from) resistance, would you have expected price to go higher? Would your expectations have been correct? What else might play into your thinking?
A
B
C
D
E
F
G
H
I
1.20000
1.18000
1.16000
1.14000
1.12000
1.10000
1.08000
1.06000
Apr
May
Jun
Jul
Aug
Sep

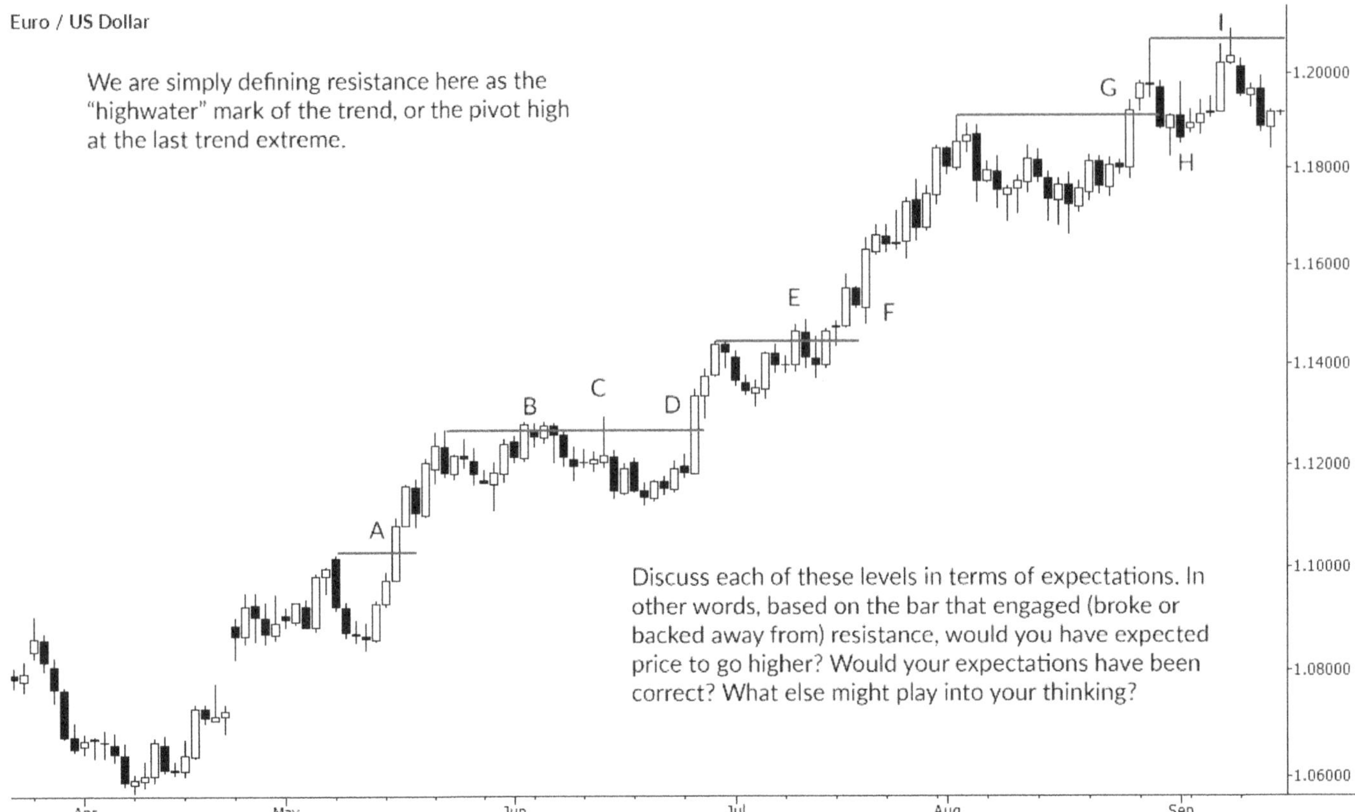

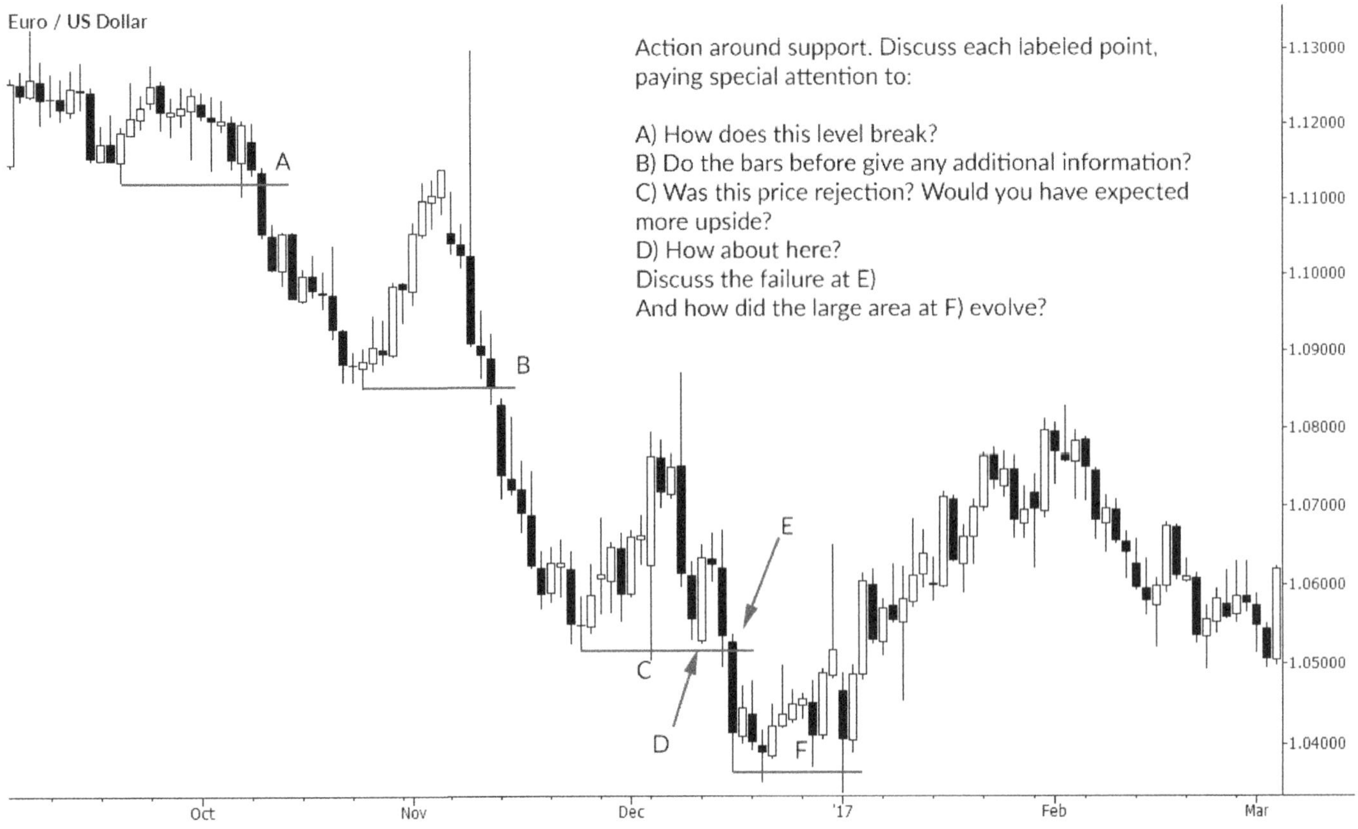

Euro / US Dollar
Action around support. Discuss each labeled point, paying special attention to:
A) How does this level break?
B) Do the bars before give any additional information?
C) Was this price rejection? Would you have expected more upside?
D) How about here?
Discuss the failure at E)
And how did the large area at F) evolve?
A
B
C
D
E
F
1.13000
1.12000
1.11000
1.10000
1.09000
1.08000
1.07000
1.06000
1.05000
1.04000
Oct
Nov
Dec
'17
Feb
Mar

30 Yr U.S.Treasury Bonds Continuous Contract [De...

Another exercise in reading the development of a trading range. As before, discuss all marked points, with the following specific questions.

B) Discuss these two bars in "chart story" and surprise context.
C) & E) Was this a test of resistance?
D) This is a large area with a few tests. What is going on here? Do we see price rejection?
F) How does the level finally break?

Perhaps the key point to be taken from this example is that textbook patterns are relevant, but real world examples can be rich and much more complex.

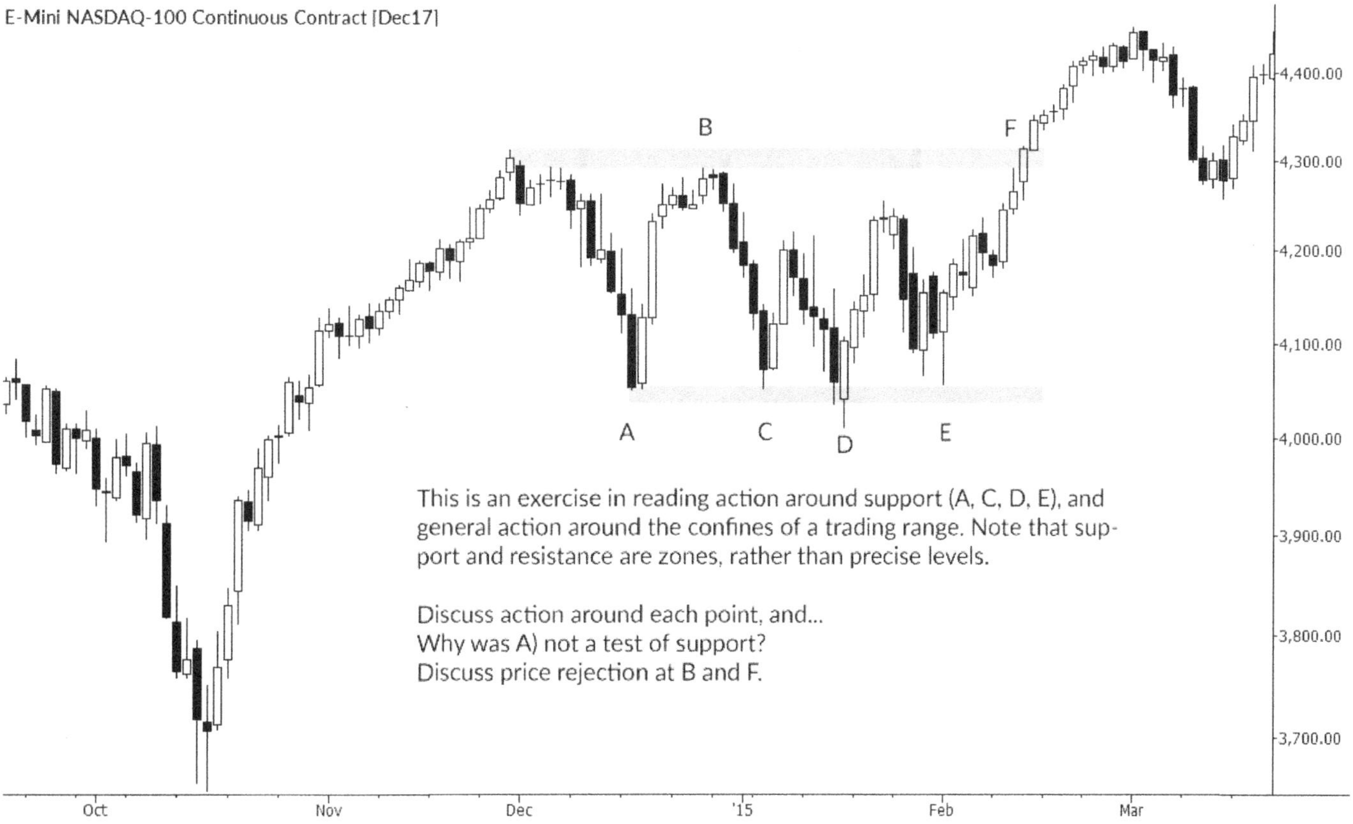

E-Mini NASDAQ-100 Continuous Contract [Dec17]

This is an exercise in reading action around support (A, C, D, E), and general action around the confines of a trading range. Note that support and resistance are zones, rather than precise levels.

Discuss action around each point, and...
Why was A) not a test of support?
Discuss price rejection at B and F.

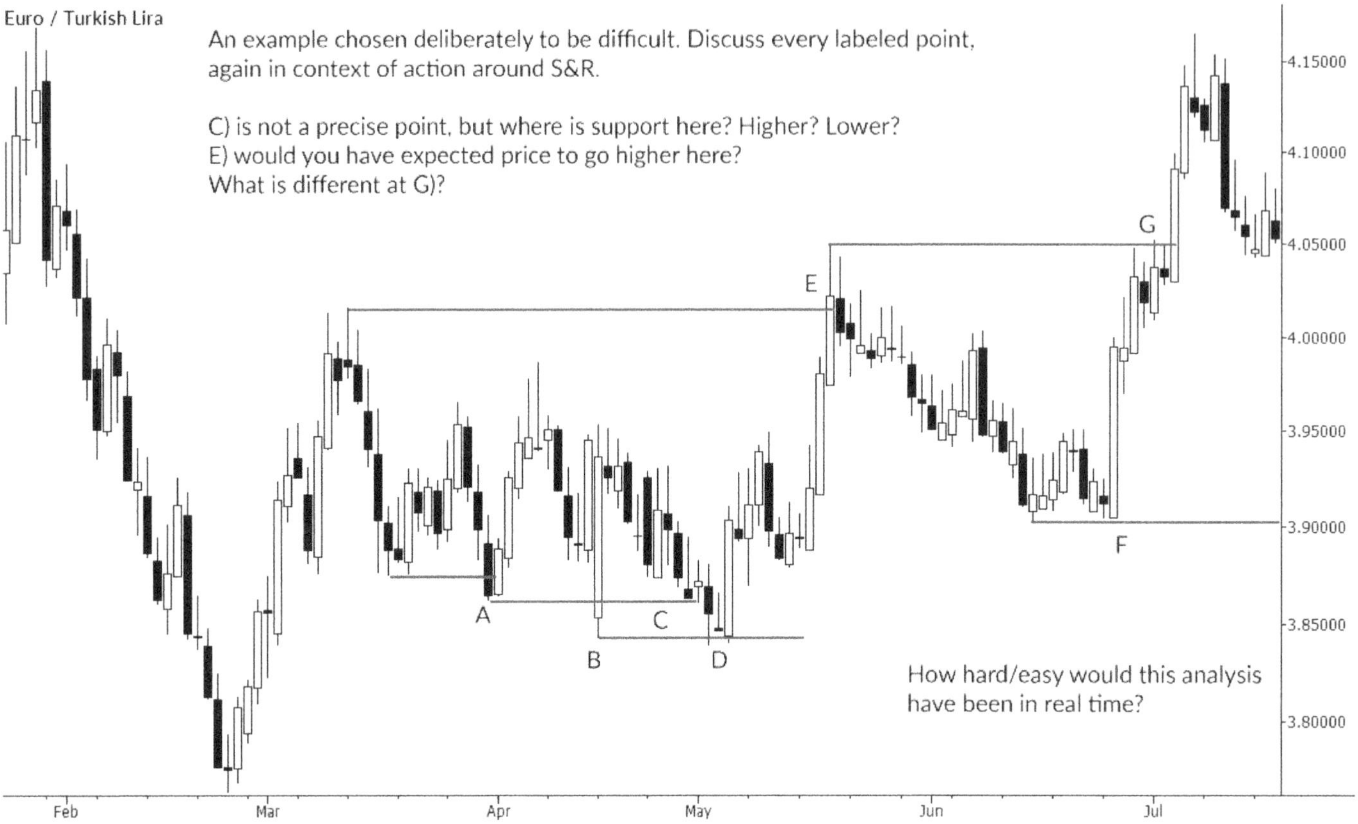

Euro / Turkish Lira
An example chosen deliberately to be difficult. Discuss every labeled point, again in context of action around S&R.
C) is not a precise point, but where is support here? Higher? Lower?
E) would you have expected price to go higher here?
What is different at G)?
How hard/easy would this analysis have been in real time?
A
B
C
D
E
F
G
4.15000
4.10000
4.05000
4.00000
3.95000
3.90000
3.85000
3.80000
Feb
Mar
Apr
May
Jun
Jul

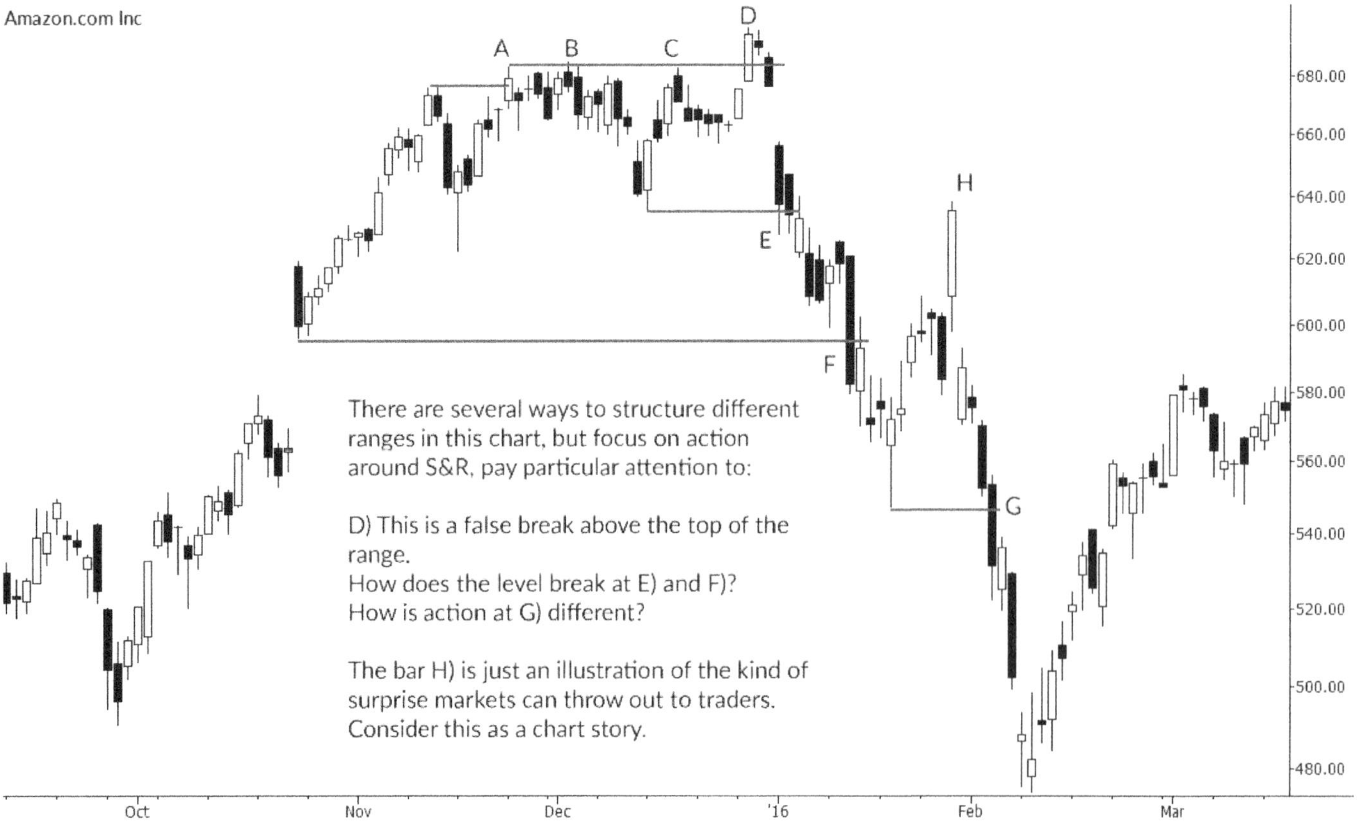

Amazon.com Inc
There are several ways to structure different ranges in this chart, but focus on action around S&R, pay particular attention to:
D) This is a false break above the top of the range.
How does the level break at E) and F)?
How is action at G) different?
The bar H) is just an illustration of the kind of surprise markets can throw out to traders. Consider this as a chart story.
A
B
C
D
E
F
G
H
680.00
660.00
640.00
620.00
600.00
580.00
560.00
540.00
520.00
500.00
480.00
Oct
Nov
Dec
'16
Feb
Mar

Natural Gas Continuous Contract [Oct17]

As before, discuss every labeled point, and also the following:

is B-C a downtrend or is range expanding lower? Would you have market support and differently?

What happened at F)? Would you have expected prices to go lower or back in the range?

Is the area around G) a test of support or is it too high? Should you redraw support higher here?

There are no definitive answers to many of these questions, but you should ask questions like this and think.

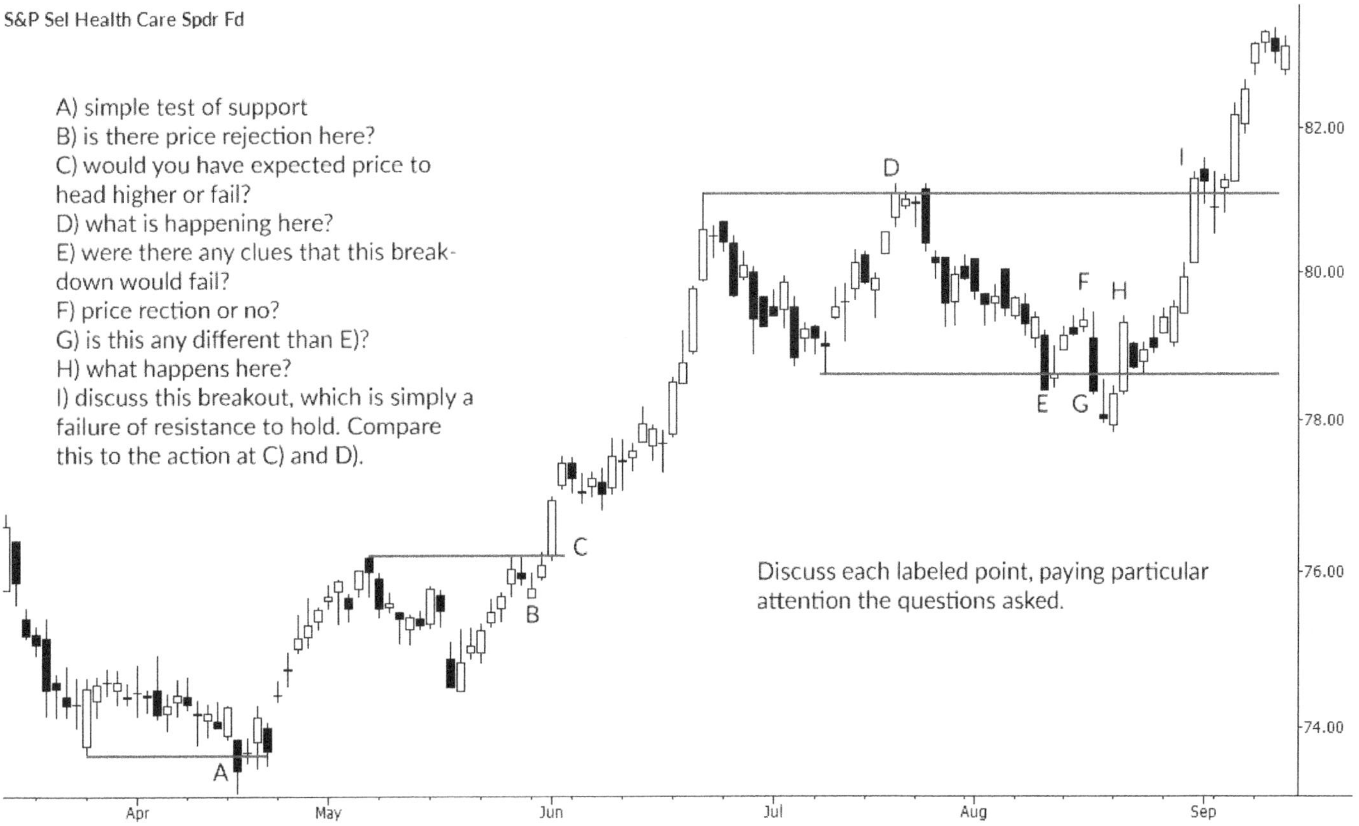

S&P Sel Health Care Spdr Fd

A) simple test of support
B) is there price rejection here?
C) would you have expected price to head higher or fail?
D) what is happening here?
E) were there any clues that this breakdown would fail?
F) price rection or no?
G) is this any different than E)?
H) what happens here?
I) discuss this breakout, which is simply a failure of resistance to hold. Compare this to the action at C) and D).

Discuss each labeled point, paying particular attention the questions asked.

Section 4: Chart Stories

This will be the last module in which we specifically do chart story work. You are not given specific examples here, but you should draw them from current market action.

This week, look at markets that you trade or wish to trade, and consider the action at interesting points in chart story context. Capture the charts, either in graphical format or hardcopy, and save them for consideration later.

Trust your intuition; the areas that draw your attention are exactly the areas on which you should focus.

Do not overdo this. It would be better to spend 3-5 minutes each day for two weeks than to try to do this for many hours in one day. Also, you will reach a point of diminishing returns. Doing a thousand of these will not make you a better trader, but doing 20 or 30 probably will.

Beginning with the next module, you should be starting to think more naturally in "chart story" format, every time you look at a chart. This has been a stylized exercise to make you look deeply into the chart, pay attention to the small details, and ask yourself what might be happening in terms of market dynamics.

Section 5: Charting by Hand

This is still a valuable exercise, and you should plan to continue it for the next few modules of the course. In the first module, we discussed the several ways you can do this exercise. The details are not important; it is far more important that you simply do it.

This should also not be a tremendous time suck—this is not a unique form of torture I have devised. A few minutes every day (but every day!) directed to drawing your charts, or a few minutes each hour if you are an intraday trader, will reward you with deep understanding of price action.

Section 6: Readings

From *The Art and Science of Technical Analysis: Market Structure, Price Action, and Trading Strategies* by Adam Grimes, Wiley, 2012:

13-18 (two forces intro, pivots)
19-21 (basic swing patterns)
49-64 (trends)
97-120 (ranges)
78-84 & 93-96 (trend analysis)

The readings from the book are a bit more extensive this week, and will expand on the specific formations of trends and trading ranges.

The Limitations of Knowledge

We Don't Know as Much as We Think We Do

We, all of us, tend to be overconfident and make too many assumptions. Consider this case: a few years ago, it seemed the TA landscape was swept with the idea of trading failed patterns. There was a lot of hype about trading patterns in which traders were trapped and had to panic out of positions, and you can still hear people talk about how reliable failed patterns (especially failed breakouts) are. But patterns are just patterns, failed or not. All we have, all we can possibly have, is a slight tilt in the probabilities, a suggestion that there may be a slight departure from randomness over the lifetime of any trade we put on.

One of the biggest mistakes we make is to assume that everyone sees the market like we do. Technicians are perhaps worse than most groups at this, and you can find many examples where people go through charts bar by bar explaining the presumed thought process of "traders" at each point. There are a few serious problems with this approach.

First, people execute trades for many reasons, and we can't possibly understand what motivates many of those trades. A good example is the options services that point out "unusual activity" in options—yes, perhaps there is value there rarely, but we are encouraged to draw overly simplistic conclusions. "Someone just bought a bazillion puts in AAPL. This is extremely bearish for the stock because it shows smart money is bearish." Well, maybe or maybe someone bought four bazillion shares and only hedged a bazillion with those long post; that's actually a very *bullish* position. Consider also if you see "someone" selling a lot of stock. Is that bearish? I don't know, and neither do you. Maybe someone is shorting, maybe they are taking profits, or maybe someone is just rebalancing a large portfolio. Oh, they are an insider you say? Perhaps that insider needs to buy a boat and so is raising cash. Who knows?

All of this leads to the market being much more random than we think. We need to check our assumptions. The crowd looking at patterns and making decisions based on patterns is probably a pretty small segment of the market. The levels you see on many of your charts are questionable. How are your charts back-adjusted (or are they)? Should they be? Is everyone making decisions around this tick looking at the same chart? Do they have the same motivations, limitations, and timeframe that you do? Even if they were looking at the same chart, would they make the same decisions or extract the same meaning? Of course not.

From this, we can easily draw the mistaken conclusion that "someone has to take the other side of your trade." A very basic understanding of market microstructure would tell you that's not true. When you push the button because a 5 minute range breaks out on your YM chart, the fact you are able to buy absolutely does not mean that someone is betting that the move is going to fail so they are shorting against you. People buy and sell for many reasons, at any point and at any time; the market is much bigger and much noisier than we expect.

The point of this is a gentle reminder to respect both the randomness of markets and the limits of our knowledge. To me, those epistemological questions are fascinating—what do we truly know about financial markets and human behavior? How do we know we know it? How do we know that knowledge is valid? Assumptions are dangerous because they lead to overconfidence, hubris, and potential ruin for a trader. Managing risk in financial markets takes flexibility, adaptability, and, above all, humility and respect.

On Trend Patterns

Reading Trend Strength Through Patterns

There are patterns in market prices that can point to trading opportunities and potential profits. This is one of the fundamental assumptions of technical/tactical trading (and can be verified by quantitative and statistical analysis.) Most people are familiar with the idea of finding patterns to set up trades, but these patterns have utility beyond trade entry and exit. In fact, a simple pattern can give us good insight into trend integrity and a very high level perspective on sentiment and market structure.

Some of the most useful trading patterns are variations of the pullback theme: trending markets move in alternating rounds of with-trend strength, interspersed with pullbacks or pauses against the trend that then break into further trend legs.

That's the theory, and it works like that often enough that you can build a complete trading program around this simple concept. We can take it a bit further by considering the strength and character of the move out of the pullback. (Yes, here we cross a line from what is clear and objective to something more subjective, but it's an assessment that can be made with a little experience—weeks instead of months to learn the concept and months, not years, to have a very good grasp on it.)

Take a look at the chart of the US dollar index below. The dollar index was in an uptrend for at least part of this chart, and I have marked points where the chart broke out of bullish consolidations with arrows. Consider the difference in character between the last three arrows and the rest of the chart:

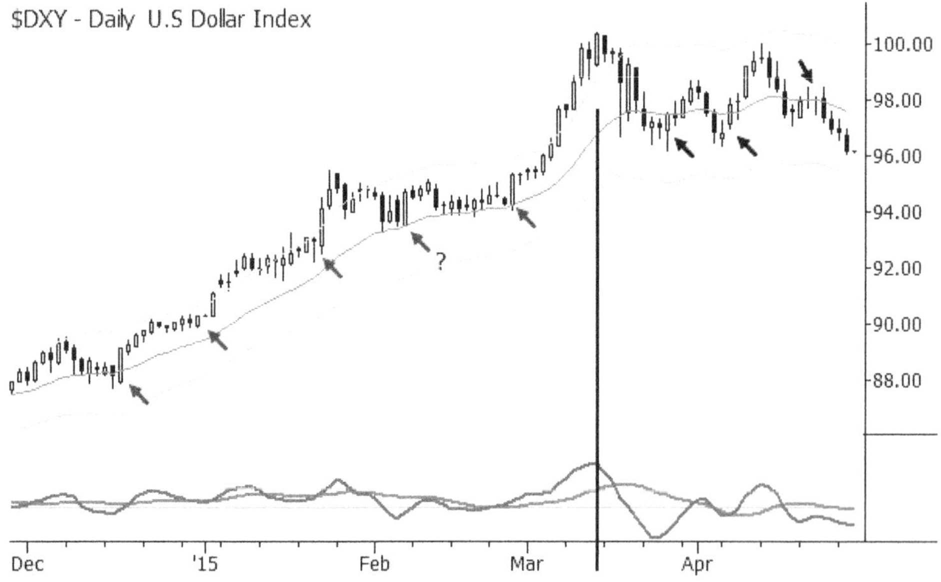

With one exception (marked "?") the moves before the vertical line had conviction; they quickly went to new highs, didn't pause very much, and made new trend legs that consolidated at higher levels. When we get to the right side of the chart, the attempted moves up failed pretty quickly. This alerts us that something has changed in the market—character has changed, maybe the market is entering a new regime, and maybe the long trades we would set up aren't as high probability as they would have been earlier on the chart.

Now, you might argue that this isn't useful because it is only history; of course the market was going up on the left side of the chart, so consolidations broke to the upside, and then it stopped going up, so consolidations had trouble breaking out. This is obvious and is to be expected. You would be right to make that argument, but there is one more thing to consider: this is not only history because we can also make these assessments in real time. We can judge the character of these breakouts and compare them against our mental map of what "should be" happening if the trend is intact. It's a subtle thing, but it's also an element of market analysis that can easily be learned.

So, give this a try. Pick a market you follow closely, and start watching the right edge of the chart. (Don't bother to go back and look at history because that is easy. This is an exercise that must be done as it unfolds.) When the market makes a pause or consolidation against the trend, watch the character of the move out of the consolidation. Compare it to previous moves, and think about what you should see if the trend is strong and intact. Spend a few weeks watching the market with this idea in mind—the subtle shift in attention to assessing the character of the extension out of the pullback is what will make the difference. In a few weeks, you may see the market with new eyes.

Volatility Clustering

There are many books showing randomly generated charts beside real charts, and most traders know, by now, that it is often very difficult to tell which charts are real and which are random. The conclusion that some people draw is that, since technical patterns appear on both real and randomly-generated charts, the entire idea of using price patterns to generate trading ideas is flawed—all forms of technical analysis are invalid. This conclusion is, itself, flawed on several fronts.

Randomly generated charts can be useful as a training tool, and understanding how real charts differ from those random charts points us toward some opportunities for profits. One of the most serious departures real charts show from simple random walks involves distribution of volatility throughout the chart. A random walk has no memory of what has happened in the past, and future steps are completely independent of past steps. However, we observe something very different in the actual data—large price changes are much more likely to be followed by more large changes, and small changes are more likely to follow small changes.

What is probably happening is that markets respond to new information with large price movements, and these high-volatility environments tend to last for a while after the initial shock. This is referred to in the literature as the persistence of volatility shocks and gives rise to the phenomenon of volatility clustering. The charts below show the absolute value of the standard deviations of daily changes for several years of daily returns in a few different markets with only daily changes > |2.0 stdevs| shown. It might be a bit difficult to see from visual inspection, but these large spikes are not dispersed through the data set randomly—they tend to cluster in specific spots and time periods and tend to follow previous spikes.

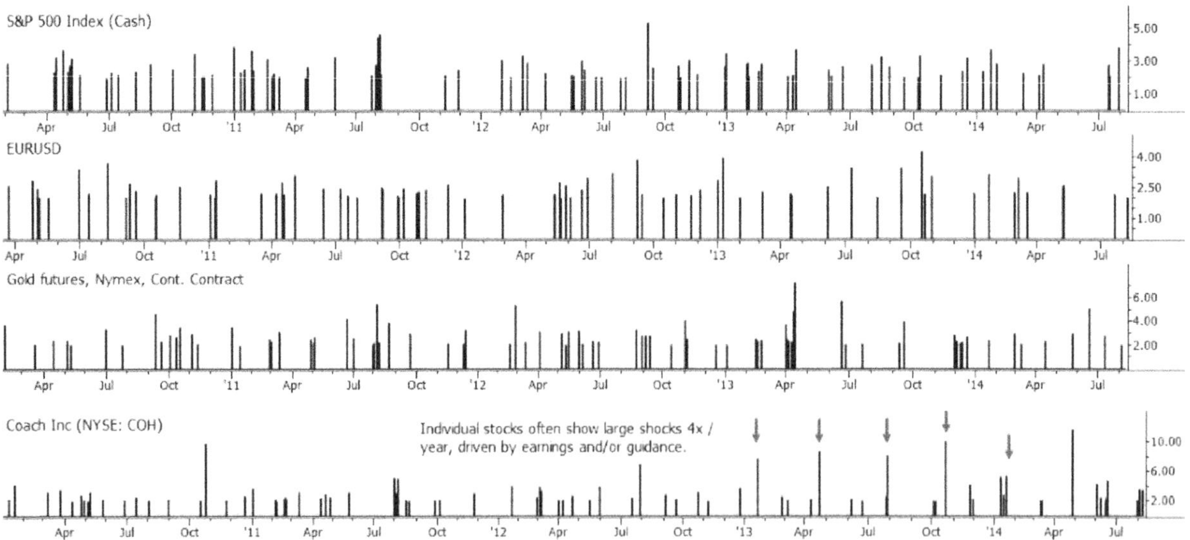

What we see here is autocorrelation of volatility (essentially, how volatility is correlated with itself). Even if price changes themselves were random and unpredictable, we can make some predictions about the magnitude (absolute value) of the next price change based on recent changes. Though this type of price action is a severe violation of random walk models (which, by definition, have no memory of previous steps), do not assume that it is an opportunity for easy profits. There is still a lot of random noise, and educated market participants are also aware of this tendency for volatility clustering (even if individual investors sometimes are not); derivatives tend to be priced accordingly so, as always, there is no free lunch.

There are important practical implications of an autocorrelated volatility environment—for instance, the tendency for large directional moves to follow other large price movements—but it is worth mentioning here that there are also academic models that capture this element of market behavior quite well. Autoregressive conditional heteroskedasticity (ARCH), generalized ARCH (GARCH), and exponential GARCH (EGARCH) are time series models that allow us to deal with the issue of varying levels of volatility across different time periods. A simple random walk model has no memory of the past, but ARCH-family models are aware of recent volatility conditions. (Though not strictly correct, a good way to think of these models is that they model price paths that are a combination of a random walk with another component added in. This other component is a series of error components (also called residuals) that are themselves randomly generated, but with a process that sets the volatility of the residuals based on recent history. The assumption is that information comes to the market in a random fashion with unpredictable timing, and that these information shocks decay with time. The effect is not unlike throwing a large stone in a pond and watching the waves slowly decay in size.) If this topic interests you, Campell, Lo, and MacKinlay (1996) and Tsay (2005) are standard references.

From a practical standpoint, volatility clustering is important for everyone to understand: certainly, options traders must understand it (the options market already understands and (largely) prices for this effect, so you should too!) But active directional traders, portfolio managers, and risk managers also need to be aware of this tendency. When a market has a volatile shock, what is the best bet? That, in some way, shape or form, more volatility is around the corner—do not expect a quick return to quiet markets.

An important caveat is that this kind of volatility is non-directional. A market can make a big move up, and then have a period of volatility that is up, down, or sideways—do not draw the facile assumption that a large move up will lead to a further move up—maybe, or maybe not. The key point is that it is unusual for a market to become volatile and then to immediately go dead again. Volatility shocks tend to persist. Big moves give rise to more big moves. Volatility begets more volatility.

Chapter 3

Module 3–Market Structure & Price Action

This module is the last time we will consider the markets' patterns from a bird's-eye perspective. We begin by reviewing and extending the patterns of trend and trading range. There is, deliberately, some overlap with the previous module's work, but the patterns will be much more meaningful after you have spent some time working through Module 2's exercises.

We then turn our attention to the most complex, from a technical perspective, areas of market behavior: the points at which trends become ranges and ranges become trends. (I have alternately used the words transitions and interfaces to explain these areas; those terms mean the same thing.) In the course videos, we look at some of the complications of these areas, and how various failures and fakeouts can develop. The homework is important because here we drill down into real market data and see both the confusion and clarity as it might develop in actual trading.

This module then looks at some common tools that can help us read trending action better: trendlines and a few indicators that can help to measure trend strength. Combined with a good sense of the underlying structure (this is why we did so much work on swing analysis), a clearer picture of market action can develop.

Next, we turn our attention to a simple, but useful, model of price behavior that I have called the Two Forces Model. This is the idea that price action is shaped by the interaction and conflict between mean reversion, the tendency for big moves in a market to be reversed, and momentum, the tendency for big moves to lead to further big moves. Though this might not seem useful at first glance, it explains both the usual randomness of market action (when the forces are in balance) and the points where we have potential for profitable trading (when they are in imbalance.)

Last, this module concludes with a look at several types of market cycles, and a look at a simple classification system that encompasses every possible type of technical trade.

Section 1: Transitional Pattern Examples

The charts in this section deal with the complicated transitions between trend and range (and back again.) These are some of the most complicated and challenging aspects of technical trading, but it's well worth the time spent to understand them; many of the opportunities, as well as the risks, of trading lie at these areas in which ranges become trends and trends become ranges.

Each chart has a few marked areas and some questions. Answer the questions to the best of your ability, and consider other interpretations of these charts and the market's actions.

Crude Oil Continuous Contract [Nov17]

Assume a trading range starts here. Mark the ongoing expansion of the range until the eventual breakout. How hard would it have been to see this in real time? Would you have ever thought the trend was starting sooner?

175.00
170.00
165.00
160.00
155.00
150.00
145.00
140.00
135.00
130.00

Jul'07 Aug'07 Sep'07 Oct'07 Nov'07 Dec'07 '08 Feb'08 Mar'08

Sugar No. 11 Continuous Contract [Oct17]

26.00
24.00
22.00
20.00
18.00
16.00
14.00
12.00

Assume a range begins here and mark the expansion of support and resistance until the eventual breakout.

May'09 Jun'09 Jul'09 Aug'09 Sep'09 Oct'09 Nov'09 Dec'09 '10 Feb'10

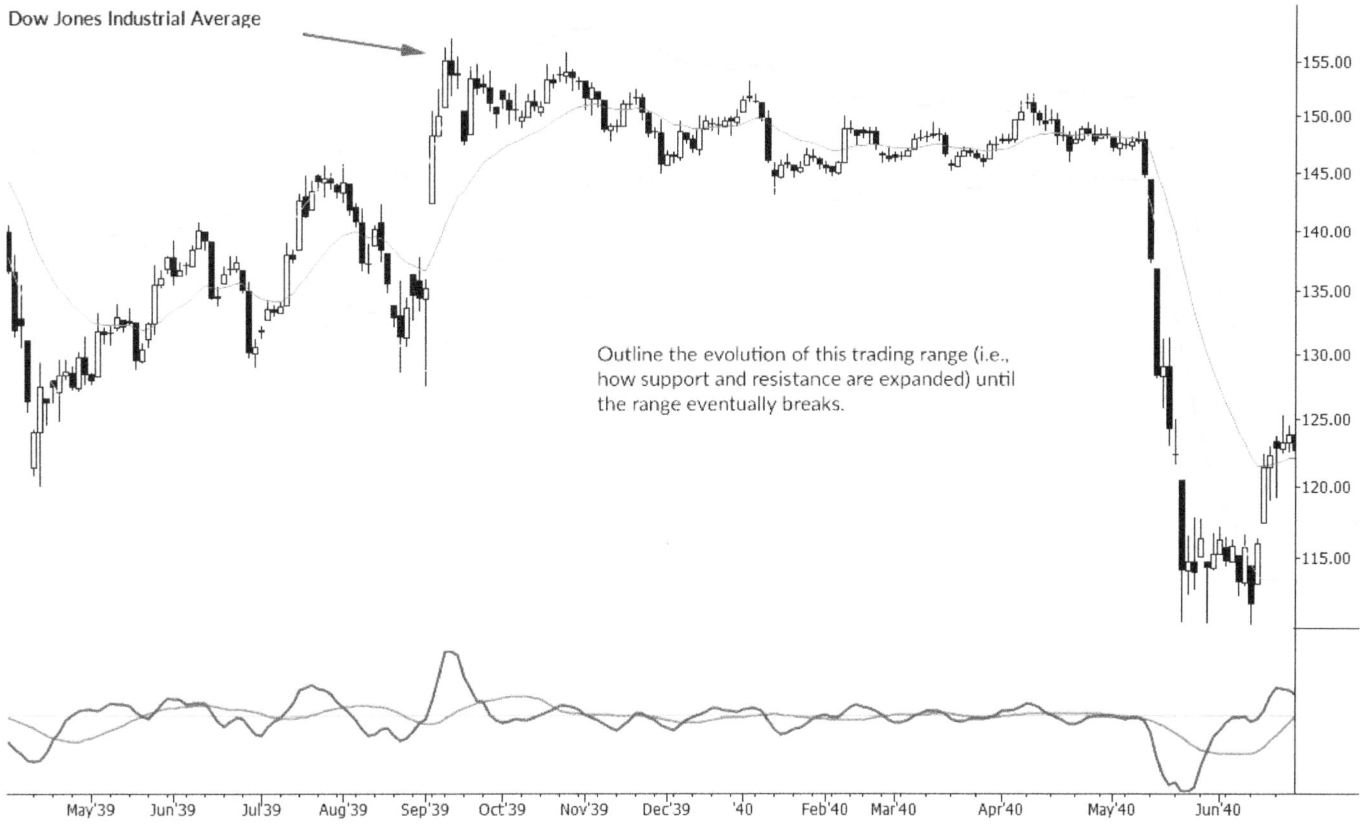
Dow Jones Industrial Average
Outline the evolution of this trading range (i.e., how support and resistance are expanded) until the range eventually breaks.
155.00
150.00
145.00
140.00
135.00
130.00
125.00
120.00
115.00
May'39
Jun'39
Jul'39
Aug'39
Sep'39
Oct'39
Nov'39
Dec'39
'40
Feb'40
Mar'40
Apr'40
May'40
Jun'40

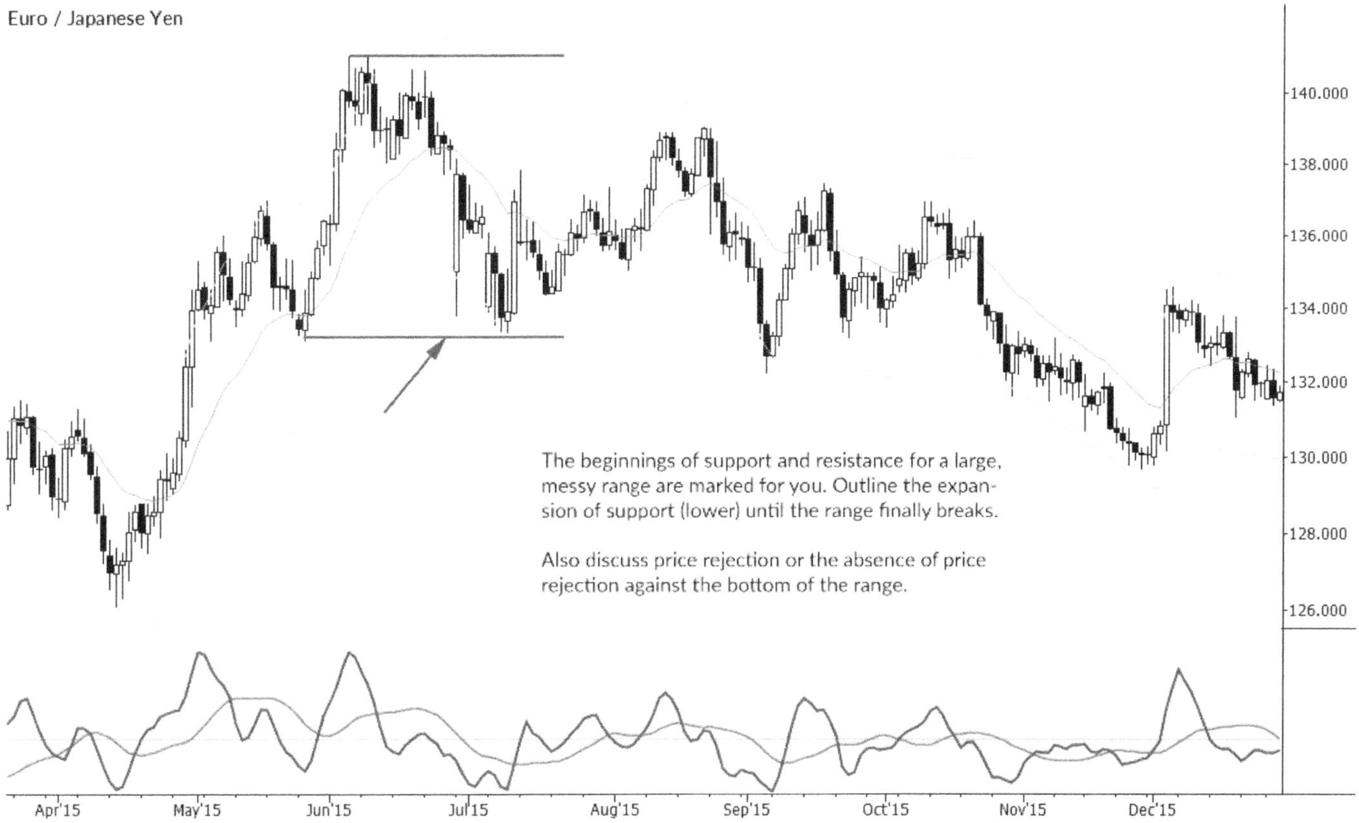
Euro / Japanese Yen
The beginnings of support and resistance for a large, messy range are marked for you. Outline the expansion of support (lower) until the range finally breaks.
Also discuss price rejection or the absence of price rejection against the bottom of the range.
140.000
138.000
136.000
134.000
132.000
130.000
128.000
126.000
Apr'15
May'15
Jun'15
Jul'15
Aug'15
Sep'15
Oct'15
Nov'15
Dec'15

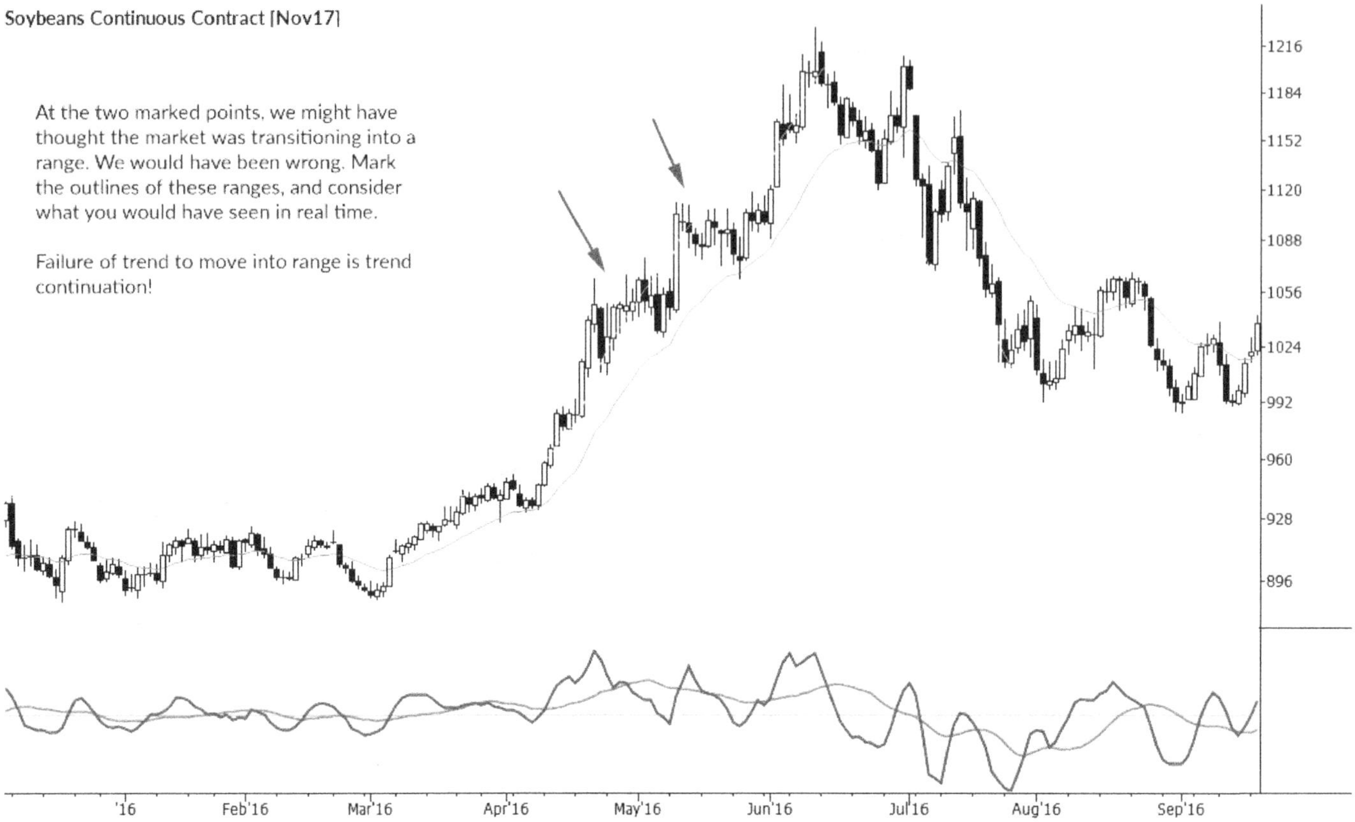
Soybeans Continuous Contract [Nov17]
At the two marked points, we might have thought the market was transitioning into a range. We would have been wrong. Mark the outlines of these ranges, and consider what you would have seen in real time.
Failure of trend to move into range is trend continuation!
1216
1184
1152
1120
1088
1056
1024
992
960
928
896
'16
Feb'16
Mar'16
Apr'16
May'16
Jun'16
Jul'16
Aug'16
Sep'16

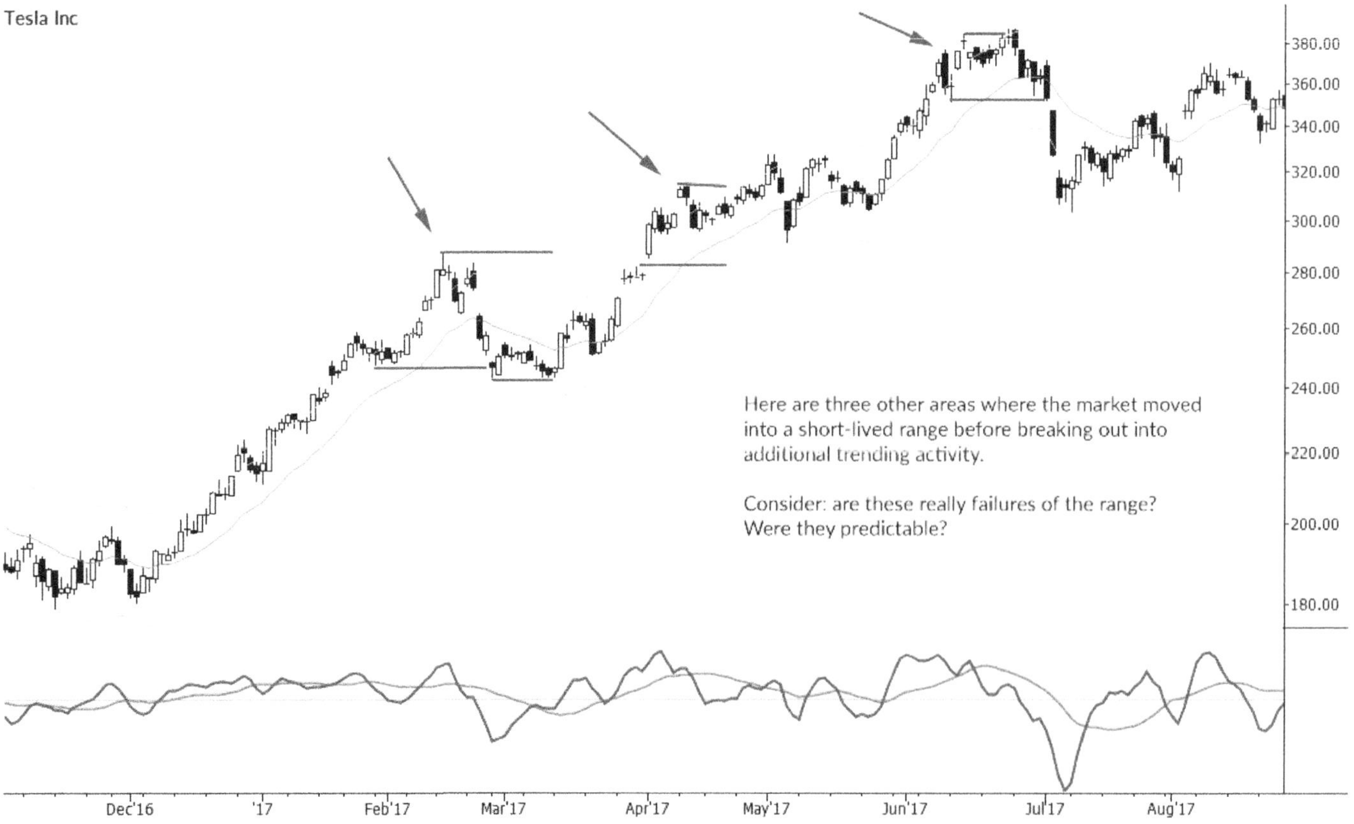
Tesla Inc
Here are three other areas where the market moved into a short-lived range before breaking out into additional trending activity.
Consider: are these really failures of the range? Were they predictable?
380.00
360.00
340.00
320.00
300.00
280.00
260.00
240.00
220.00
200.00
180.00
Dec'16
'17
Feb'17
Mar'17
Apr'17
May'17
Jun'17
Jul'17
Aug'17

Cotton No. 2 Continuous Contract [Dec17]

90.00
85.00
80.00
75.00
70.00
65.00

Mark ranges at the arrows and consider how they break into additional trending action.

Are there any other significant ranges on this chart?

Feb'14 Mar'14 Apr'14 May'14 Jun'14 Jul'14 Aug'14 Sep'14 Oct'14

Nasdaq Composite Index

5,000.00
4,800.00
4,600.00
4,400.00
4,200.00
4,000.00
3,800.00
3,600.00
3,400.00
3,200.00
3,000.00
2,800.00

Use trendlines to define the trend, and note where the uptrend reverses into a downtrend.

Was there a range between, or was this a direct transition from up to downtrend?

Nov'99 Dec'99 '00 Feb'00 Mar'00 Apr'00 May'00 Jun'00 Jul'00

British Pound / US Dollar

This currency goes into a range at the arrow. Mark the evolution of the range, and the eventual break-down.

Note that the actual support of the range should be considered to be the low of the swing before the arrow, but active support appears to be considerably higher. How would you have reconciled this?

1.64000
1.62000
1.60000
1.58000
1.56000
1.54000
1.52000
1.50000
1.48000
1.46000
1.44000
1.42000

Mar'00 Apr'00 May'00 Jun'00 Jul'00 Aug'00 Sep'00 Oct'00 Nov'00

Dow Jones Industrial Average

Trends can reverse directly into opposite trends without going through a range. Consider trendlines as this market evolved. Would you have thought we were in a range at any point? How would you have known this was right or wrong? Are there any ranges to consider to the left of the arrow?

125.00
120.00
115.00
110.00
105.00
100.00
95.00

Nov'41 Dec'41 '42 Feb'42 Mar'42 Apr'42 May'42 Jun'42 Jul'42

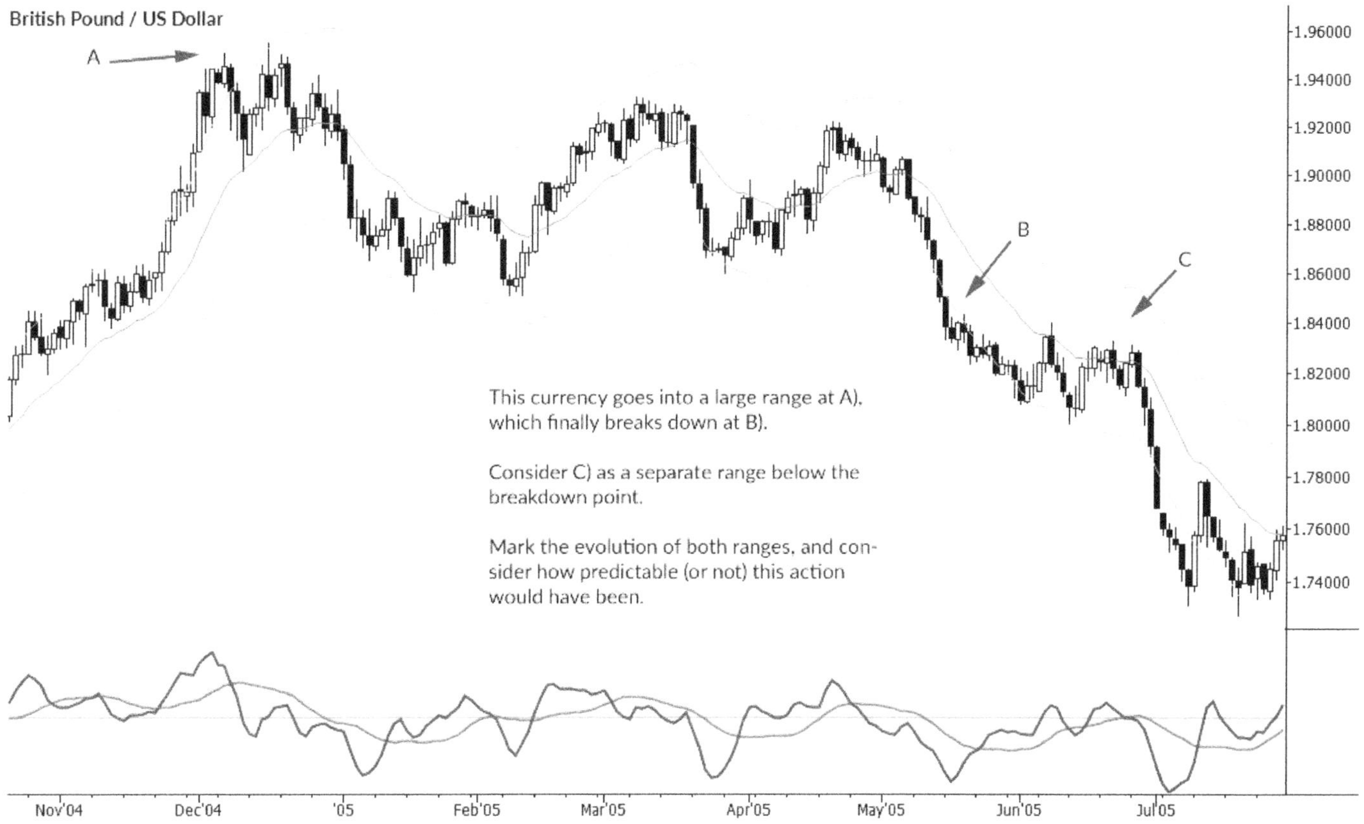
British Pound / US Dollar
A
B
C
This currency goes into a large range at A), which finally breaks down at B).
Consider C) as a separate range below the breakdown point.
Mark the evolution of both ranges, and consider how predictable (or not) this action would have been.
1.96000
1.94000
1.92000
1.90000
1.88000
1.86000
1.84000
1.82000
1.80000
1.78000
1.76000
1.74000
Nov'04
Dec'04
'05
Feb'05
Mar'05
Apr'05
May'05
Jun'05
Jul'05

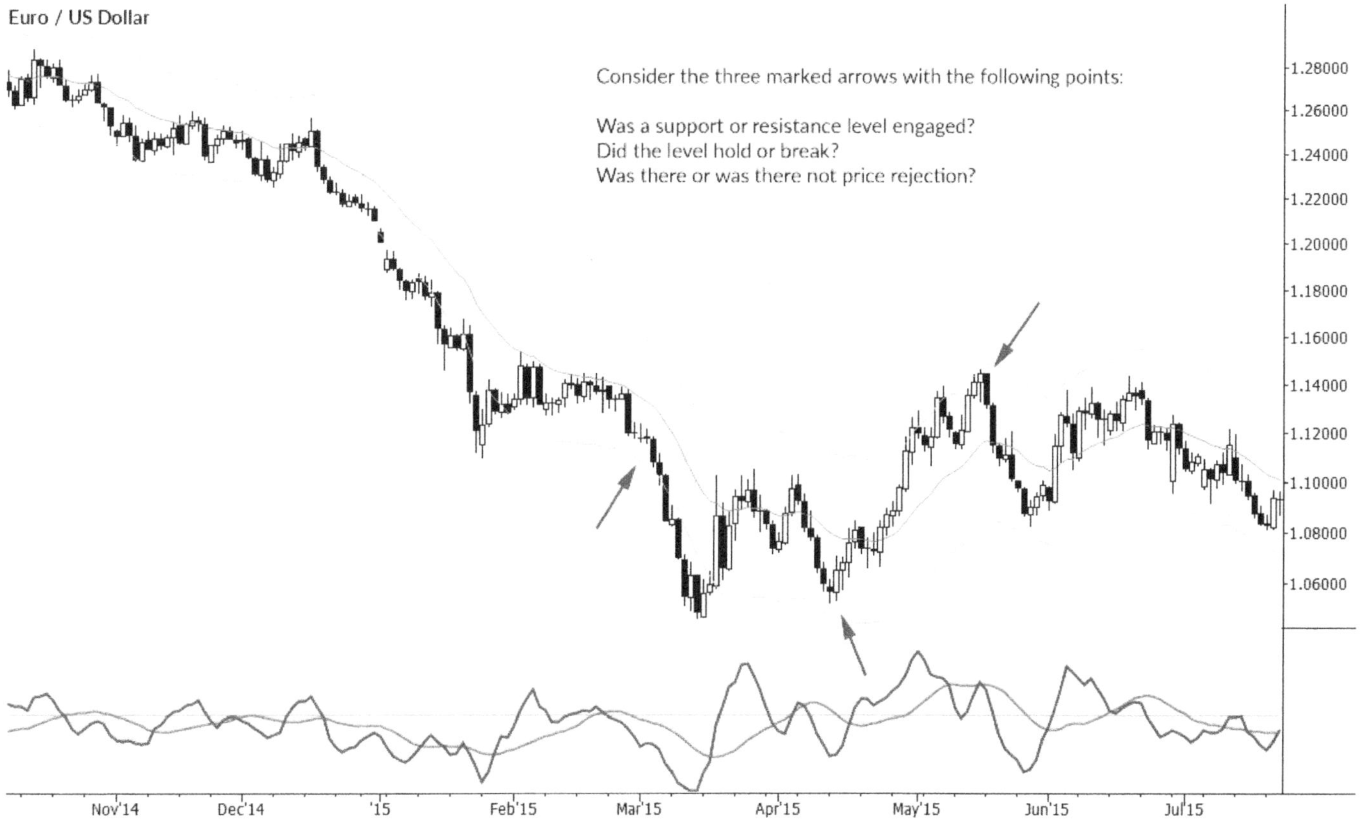
Euro / US Dollar
Consider the three marked arrows with the following points:
Was a support or resistance level engaged?
Did the level hold or break?
Was there or was there not price rejection?
1.28000
1.26000
1.24000
1.22000
1.20000
1.18000
1.16000
1.14000
1.12000
1.10000
1.08000
1.06000
Nov'14
Dec'14
'15
Feb'15
Mar'15
Apr'15
May'15
Jun'15
Jul'15

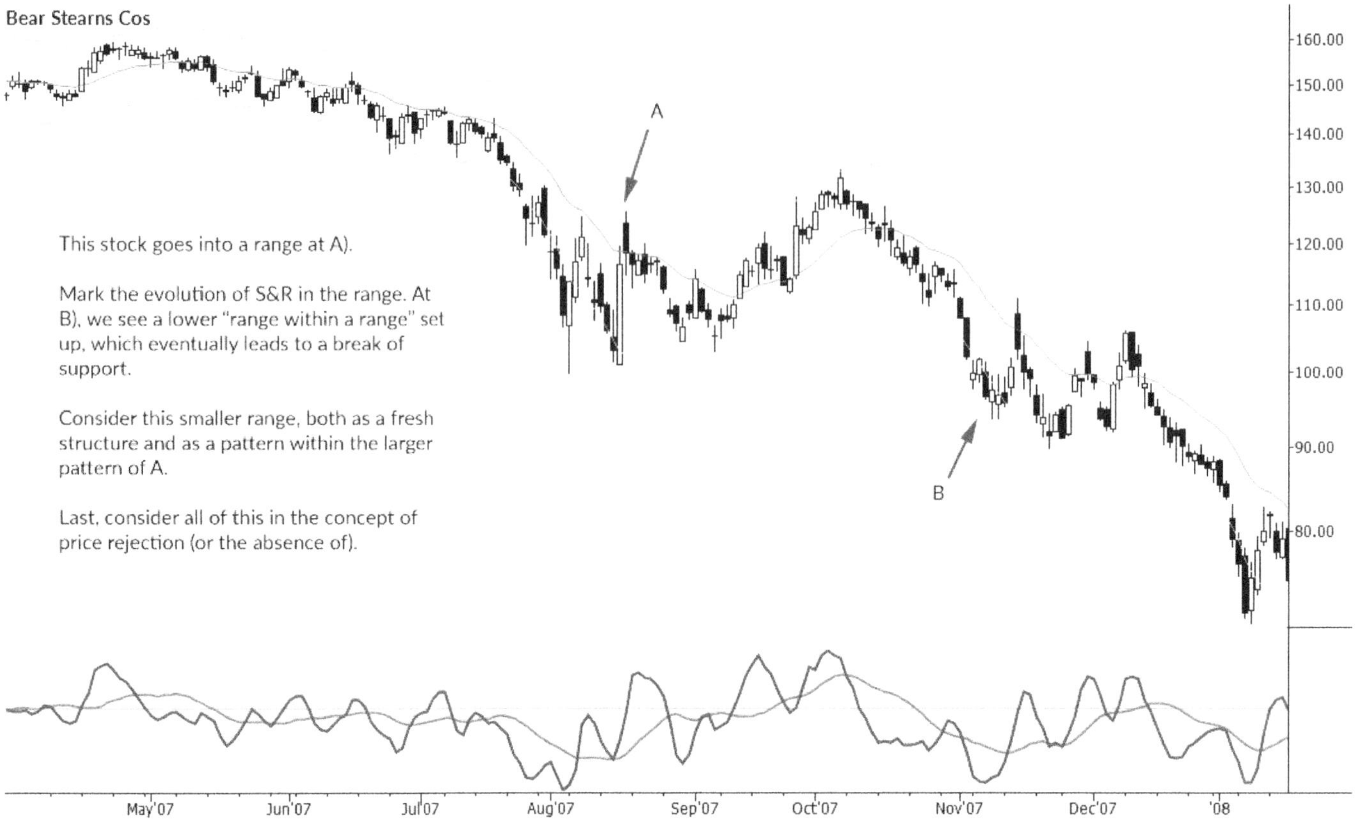

Bear Stearns Cos

This stock goes into a range at A).

Mark the evolution of S&R in the range. At B), we see a lower "range within a range" set up, which eventually leads to a break of support.

Consider this smaller range, both as a fresh structure and as a pattern within the larger pattern of A.

Last, consider all of this in the concept of price rejection (or the absence of).

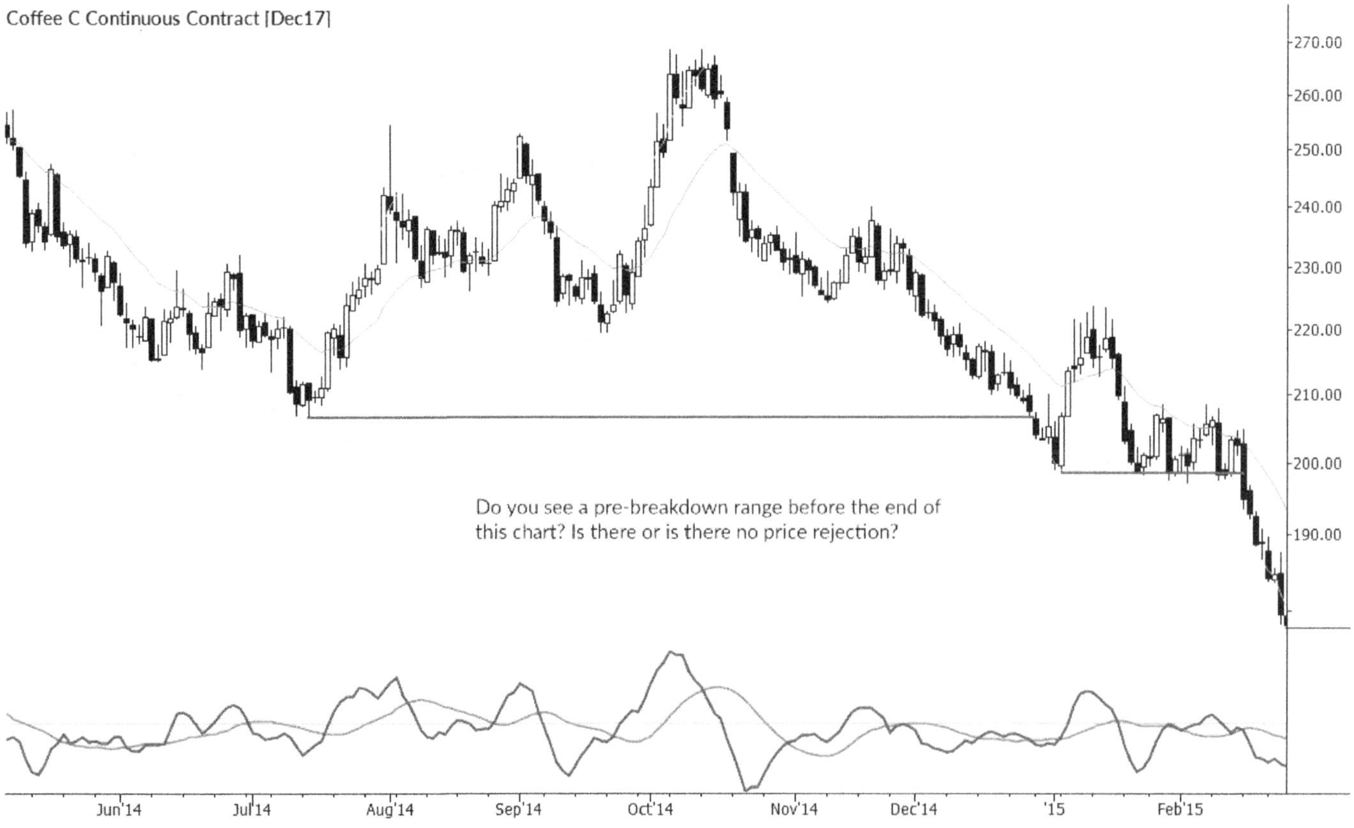

Coffee C Continuous Contract [Dec17]

Do you see a pre-breakdown range before the end of this chart? Is there or is there no price rejection?

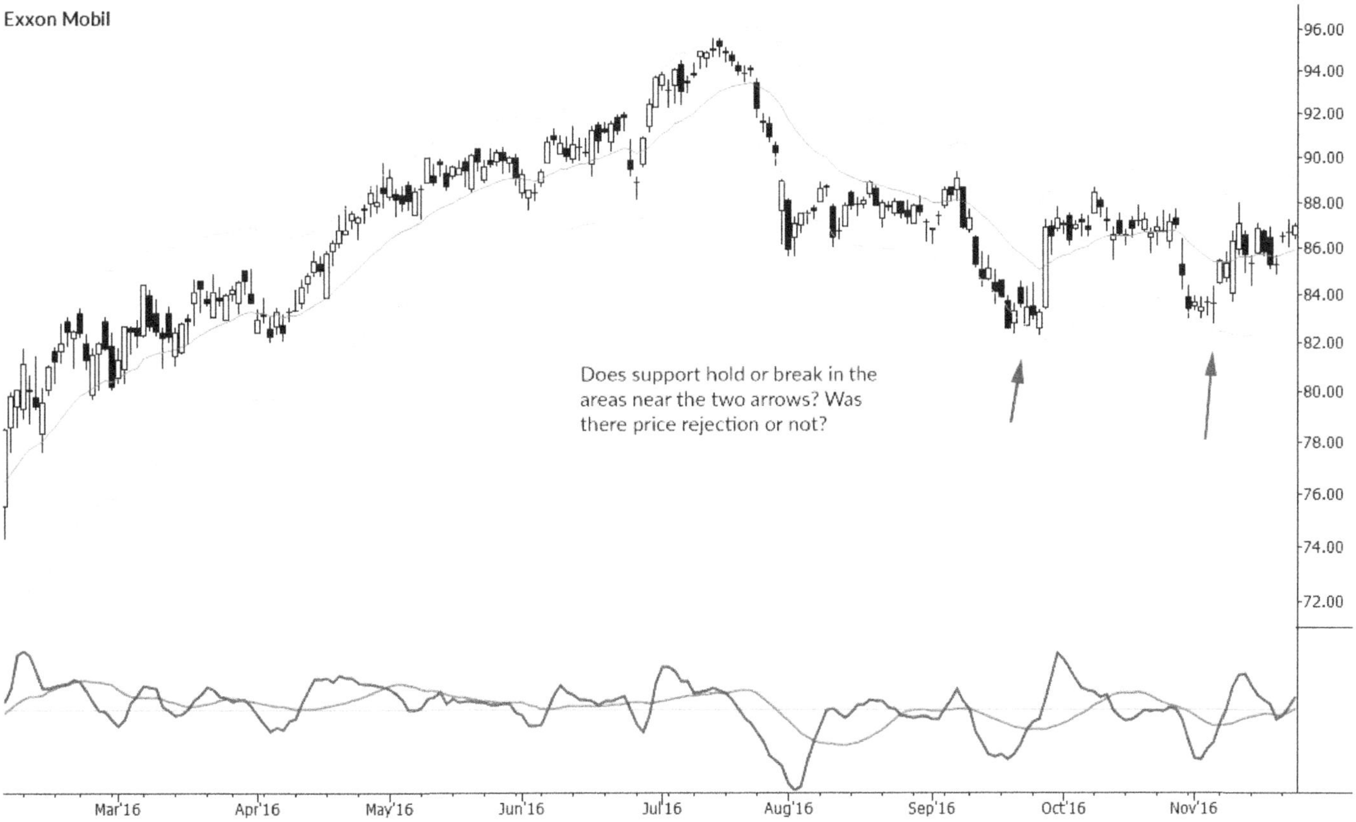
Exxon Mobil
Does support hold or break in the areas near the two arrows? Was there price rejection or not?
96.00
94.00
92.00
90.00
88.00
86.00
84.00
82.00
80.00
78.00
76.00
74.00
72.00
Mar'16
Apr'16
May'16
Jun'16
Jul'16
Aug'16
Sep'16
Oct'16
Nov'16

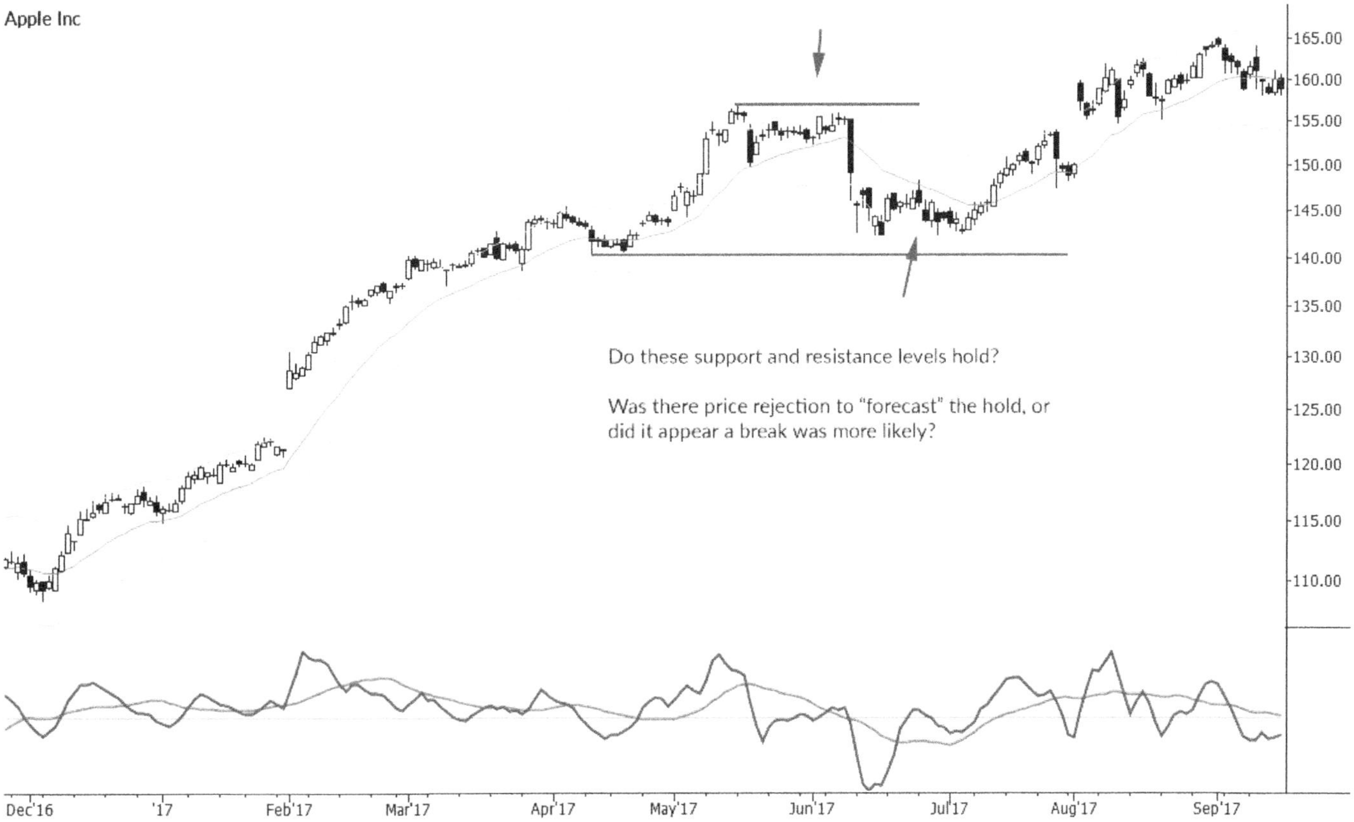
Apple Inc
Do these support and resistance levels hold?
Was there price rejection to "forecast" the hold, or did it appear a break was more likely?
165.00
160.00
155.00
150.00
145.00
140.00
135.00
130.00
125.00
120.00
115.00
110.00
Dec'16
'17
Feb'17
Mar'17
Apr'17
May'17
Jun'17
Jul'17
Aug'17
Sep'17

Section 2: Transitions in Real Market Data

The charts in this section move us one step closer to trading these structures. These charts are daily bars of a specific market. (The choice of market and time period were chosen at random; this is not a carefully chosen-example!) Each chart presents some structures and questions to be answered.

The next chart picks up where the previous chart ended, and slightly greys out the "old" data—in other words, the line between the slightly darker and the light area of the chart was the "hard right edge" on the old chart. This allows you to see what happened as the market moved forward.

It is strongly suggested that you cover up the next chart so you don't see ahead, as even a casual glance will compromise your analysis and thought process. Over the page turns, this will not be a problem, but be careful of seeing the chart at the bottom of the page! Read this section with a piece of heavy paper covering up the next chart.

Do not rush. Some of these charts may require considerable thought and analysis. Some of the questions are obvious and leading, but some of the questions will have no good answer. In all cases, it's a good idea to think of multiple scenarios, and then to consider what market movements would confirm your scenarios, and which would contradict.

To reiterate: this is a chronological sample of actual market data. It is messy. It is complex, and sometimes the simple rules do not fit cleanly. Even then, you will see that they are a good guide to market dynamics and to future market direction.

Established a downtrend and broke below the low of recent support.
What happens next?

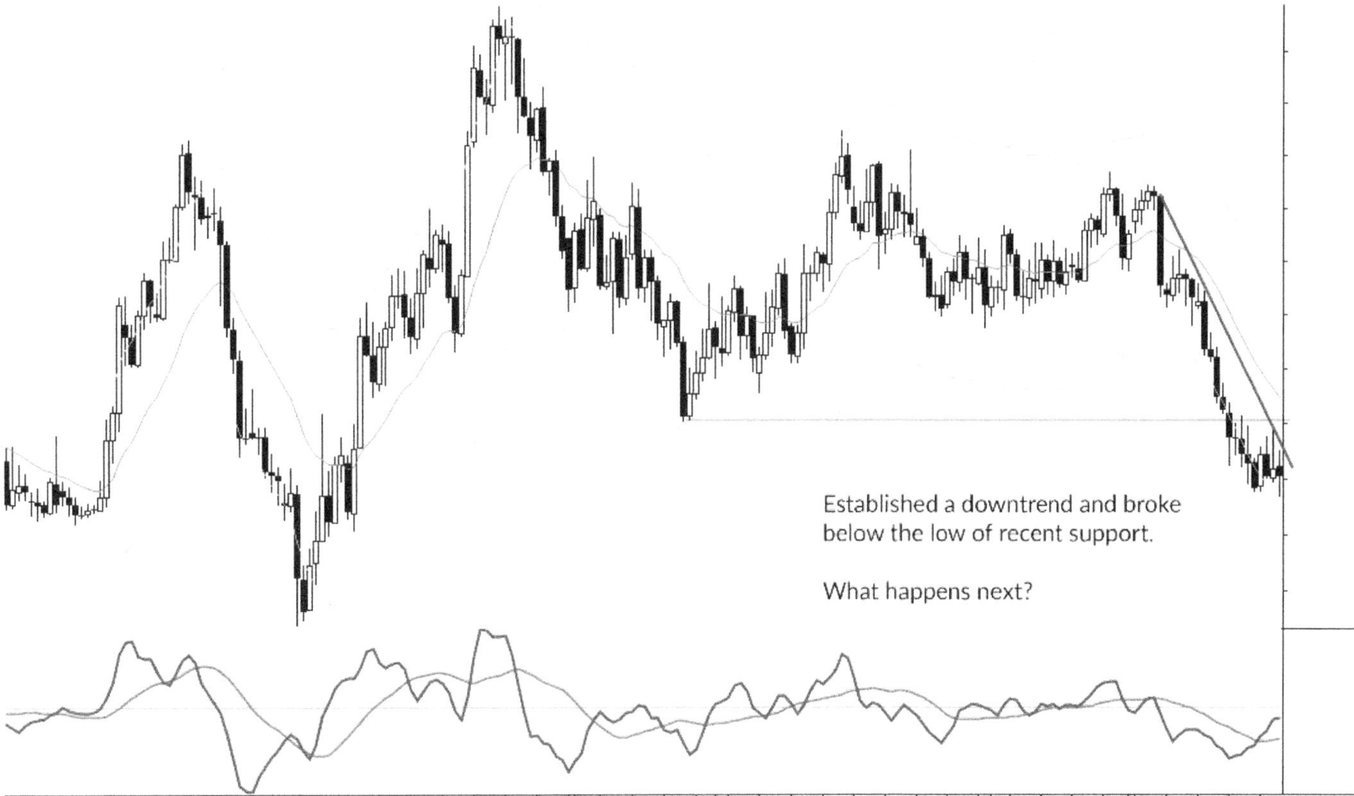

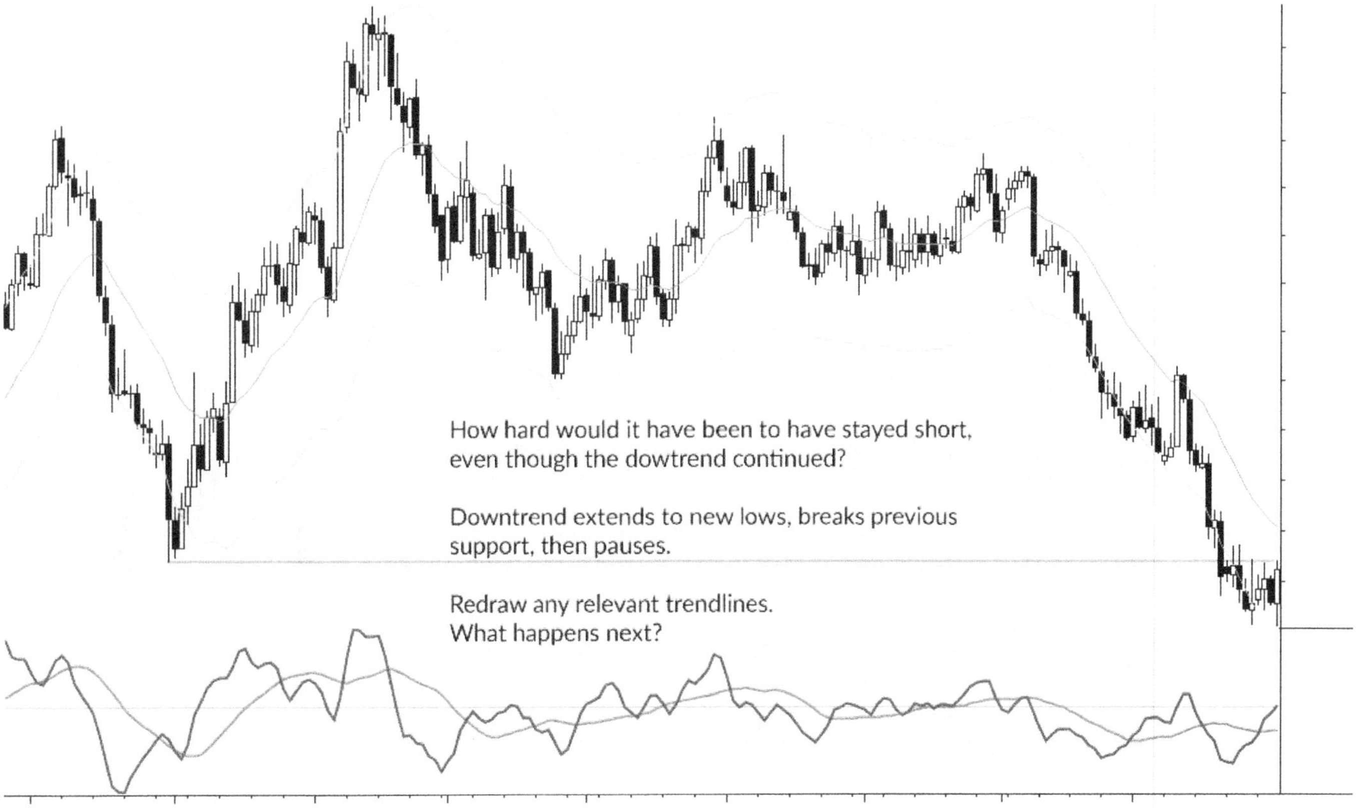

How hard would it have been to have stayed short, even though the dowtrend continued?
Downtrend extends to new lows, breaks previous support, then pauses.
Redraw any relevant trendlines.
What happens next?

Finds support at recent lows.
Does new upside momentum make an uptrend? Update your trendlines.
What next?

Best reading of this is probably as a short-term range, but also consider relevant trendlines.
Is there a trend-ending pattern you know at work here?
What happens next?

The bottom of the range holds, and prices trade back to previous resistance.

Are there still relevant downtrend lines?

Do you think the top of the range holds or breaks?

The top of the range does hold, at least for now.

Do you agree with the reading that we are in a range? Do we see price rejection?

Are there any relevant trendlines?

What do you think comes next?

How about now? Are we still in a range?
Is it possible to define this as a trend?
Do you expect resistance to hold or break?

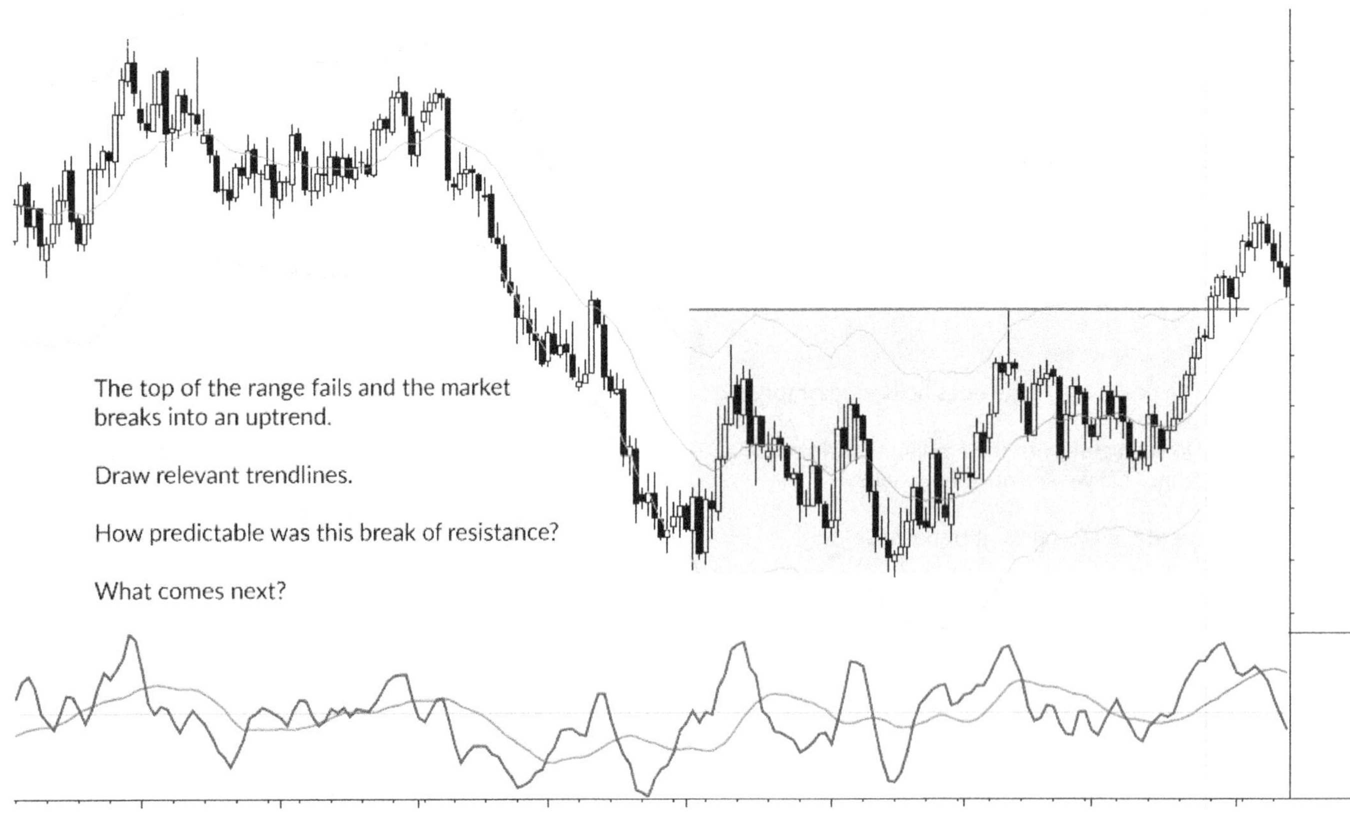
The top of the range fails and the market breaks into an uptrend.
Draw relevant trendlines.
How predictable was this break of resistance?
What comes next?

Uptrend, downtrend or still in the range?
Update trendlines.
Do you think this breakdown will continue lower? Why or why not?

One possible reading is to consider these to be multiple shorter-term trends. Do you agree or disagree with this analysis? Would you see the chart another way?

Do you think the resistance level will hold or break?

What comes next?

We seem to have defined some resistance level.
Is the current rally likely to break that resistance, or do you think it will hold? Why?
Is the market in a trend or range?

What is going on now? What do you think the next steps for this market will be? Why?

Draw any relevant trendlines.
Consider the last bar on this chart in "chart story" format. What do you think the next likely direction is?

Discuss the action just after the shaded area in context of "price rejection."
Is the market in a range or trend?
Draw relevant trendlines.
Do you expect support to hold or to break?

What is going on here? Trend or range? Draw relevant price structures.
What do you think is most likely to happen next? How will you know that scenario is working? What will happen if that scenario is wrong?

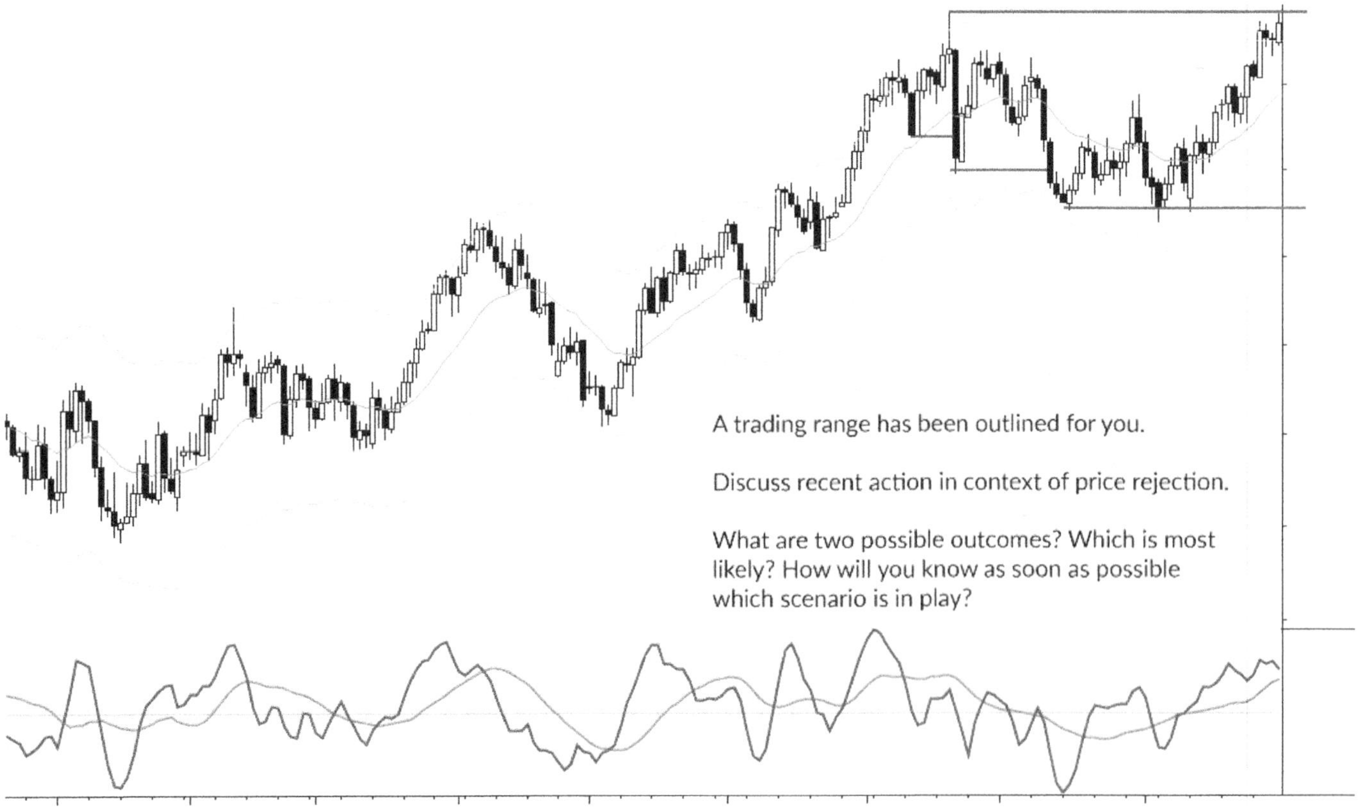

A trading range has been outlined for you.

Discuss recent action in context of price rejection.

What are two possible outcomes? Which is most likely? How will you know as soon as possible which scenario is in play?

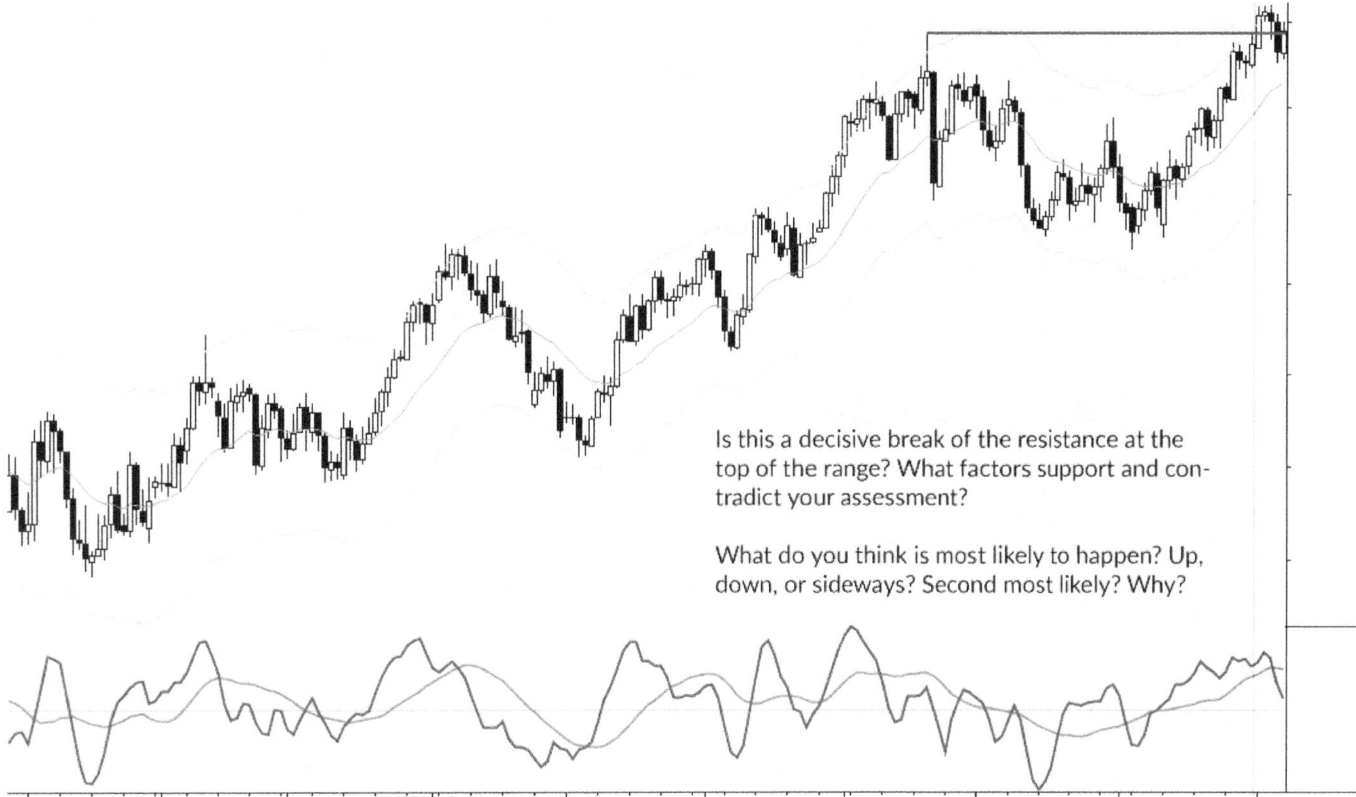

Is this a decisive break of the resistance at the top of the range? What factors support and contradict your assessment?

What do you think is most likely to happen? Up, down, or sideways? Second most likely? Why?

With more data, it is clear the top of the range has broken.

What do you see now? Is the market trending? Any other ranges to consider?

Mark relevant trendlines and/or ranges.

By now, it should be clear the market is trending.

How would you assess trend strength? (Note that there are few actual "swings".)

What is the most likely future direction? What are the dangers? What should you be watching for?

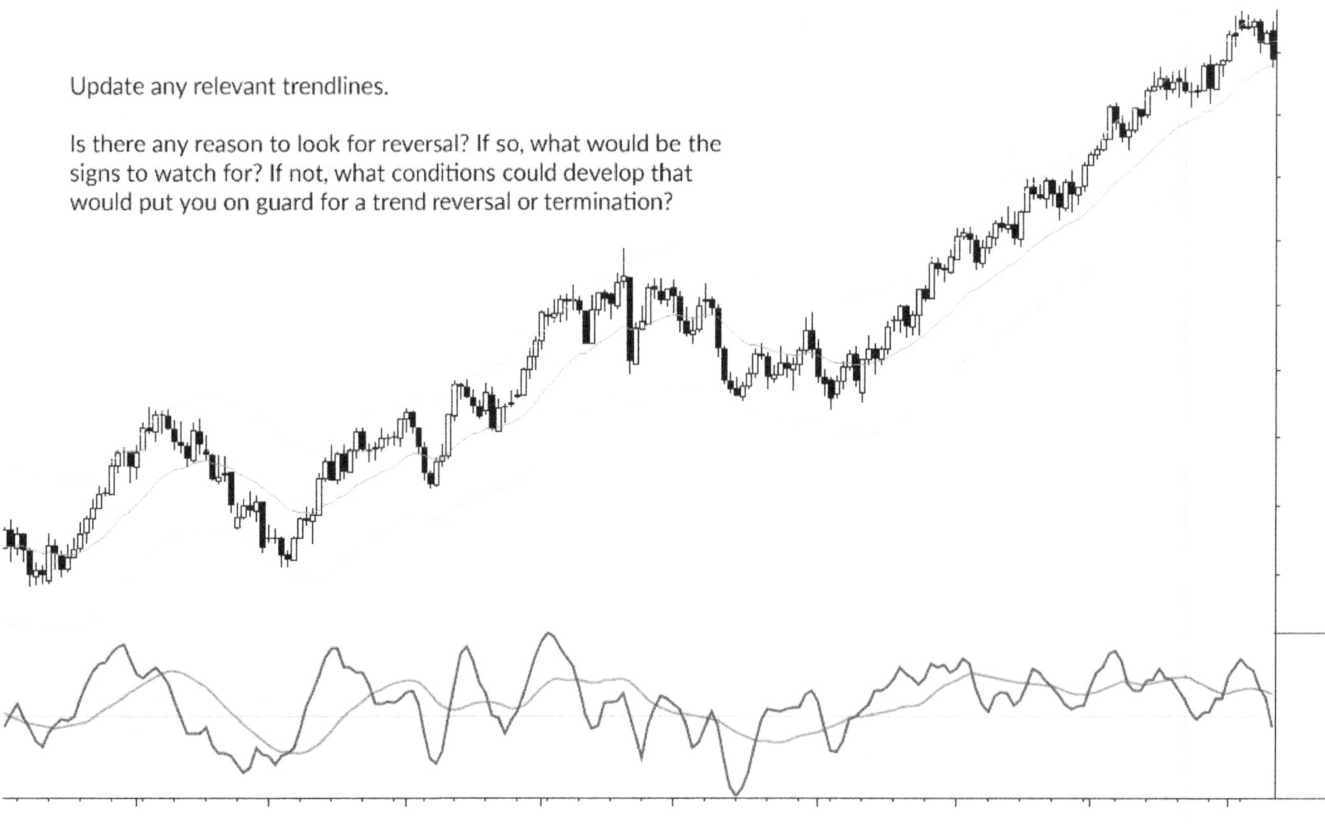
Update any relevant trendlines.

Is there any reason to look for reversal? If so, what would be the signs to watch for? If not, what conditions could develop that would put you on guard for a trend reversal or termination?

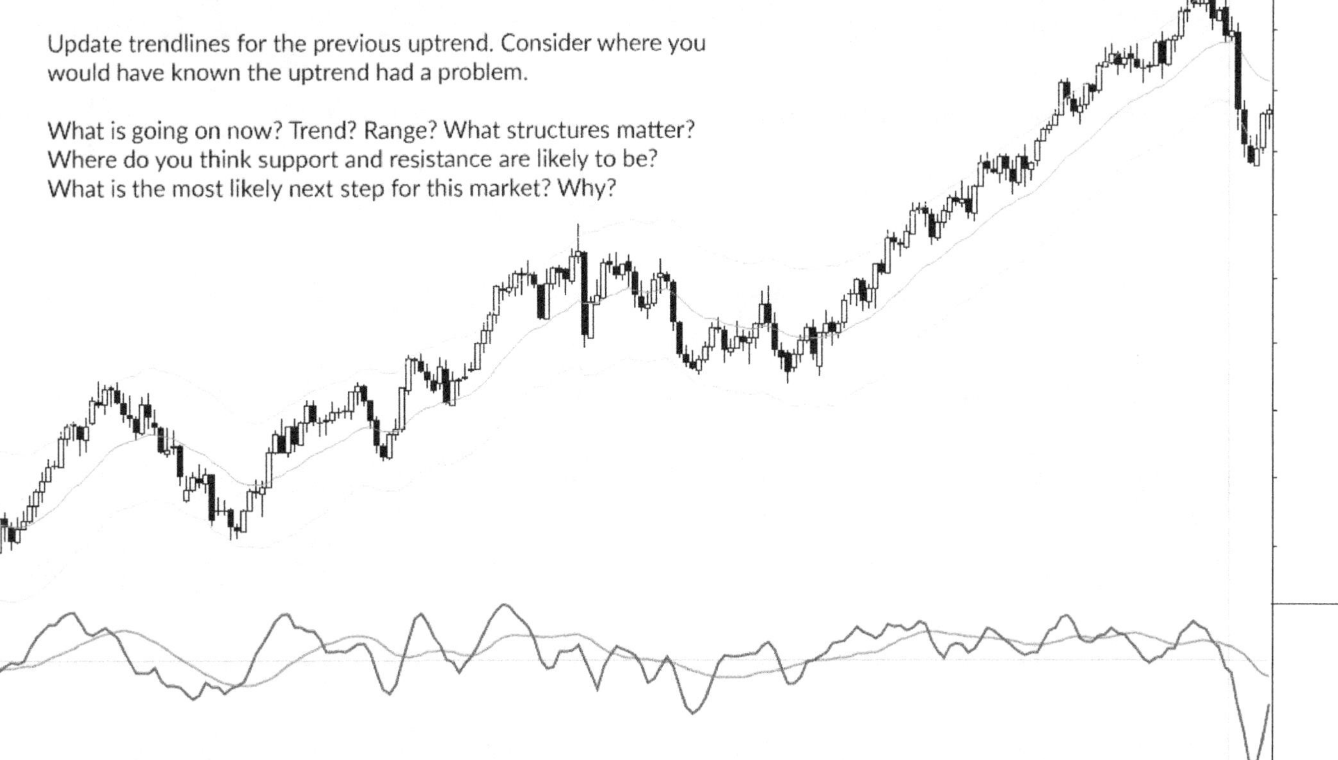
Update trendlines for the previous uptrend. Consider where you would have known the uptrend had a problem.
What is going on now? Trend? Range? What structures matter?
Where do you think support and resistance are likely to be?
What is the most likely next step for this market? Why?

What is going on here? Trend or range?
Draw relevant trendlines.
What do you expect next? Why? What is another possible outcome? What early clues would tell you one scenario or the other is in play?

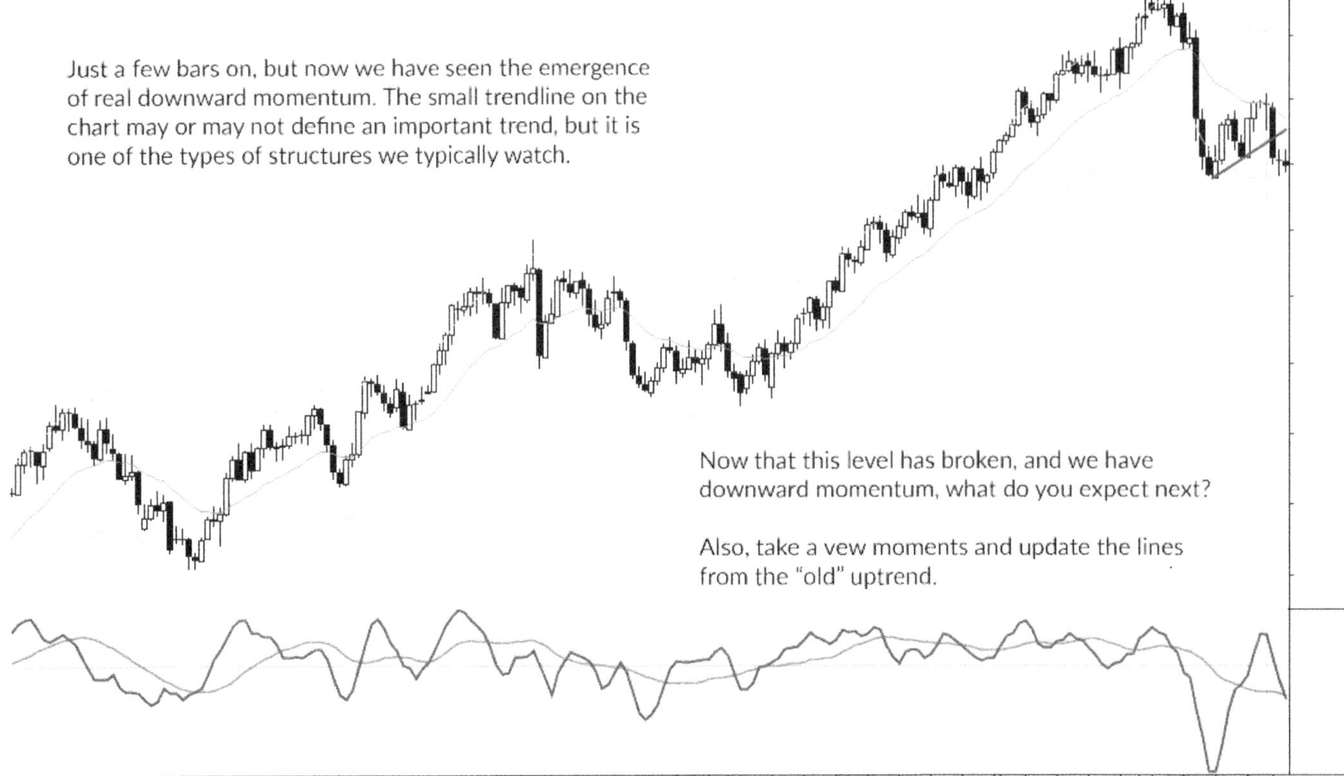
Just a few bars on, but now we have seen the emergence of real downward momentum. The small trendline on the chart may or may not define an important trend, but it is one of the types of structures we typically watch.
Now that this level has broken, and we have downward momentum, what do you expect next?
Also, take a vew moments and update the lines from the "old" uptrend.

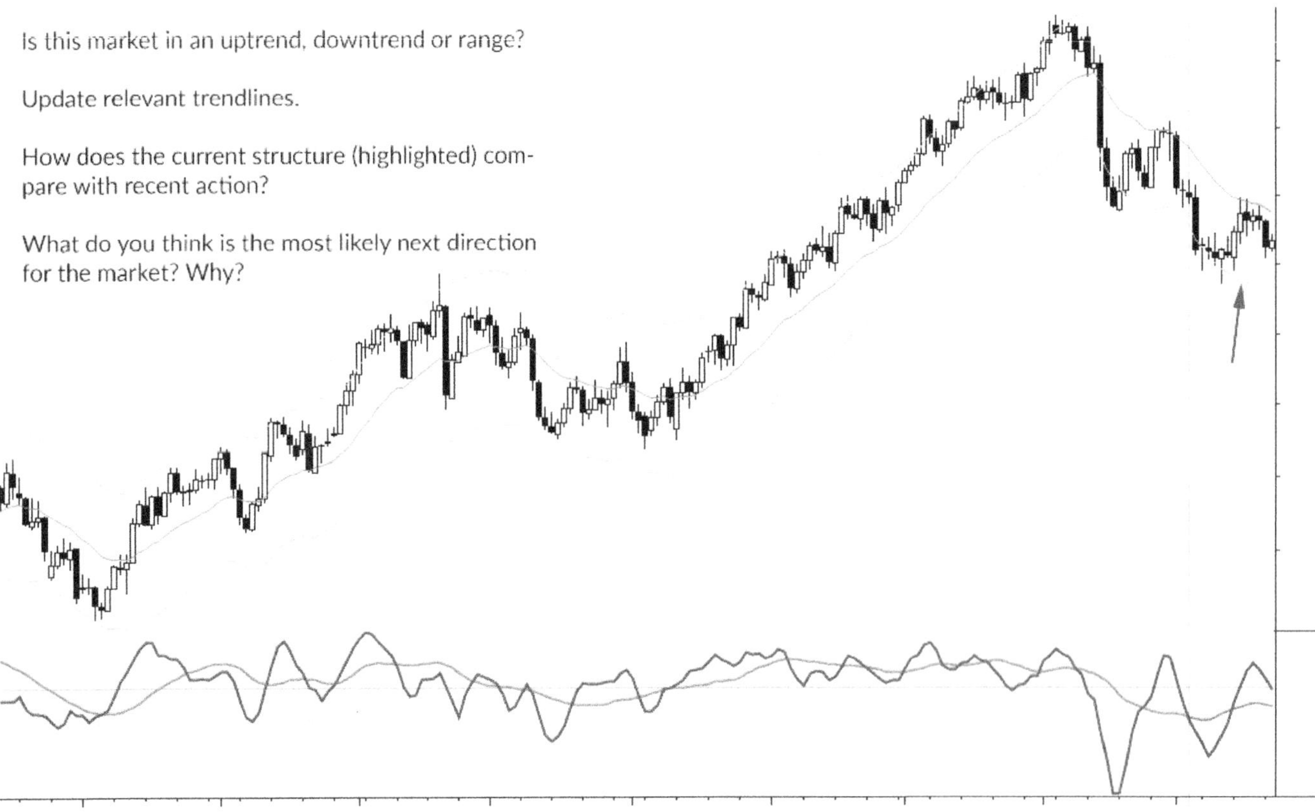
Is this market in an uptrend, downtrend or range?
Update relevant trendlines.
How does the current structure (highlighted) compare with recent action?
What do you think is the most likely next direction for the market? Why?

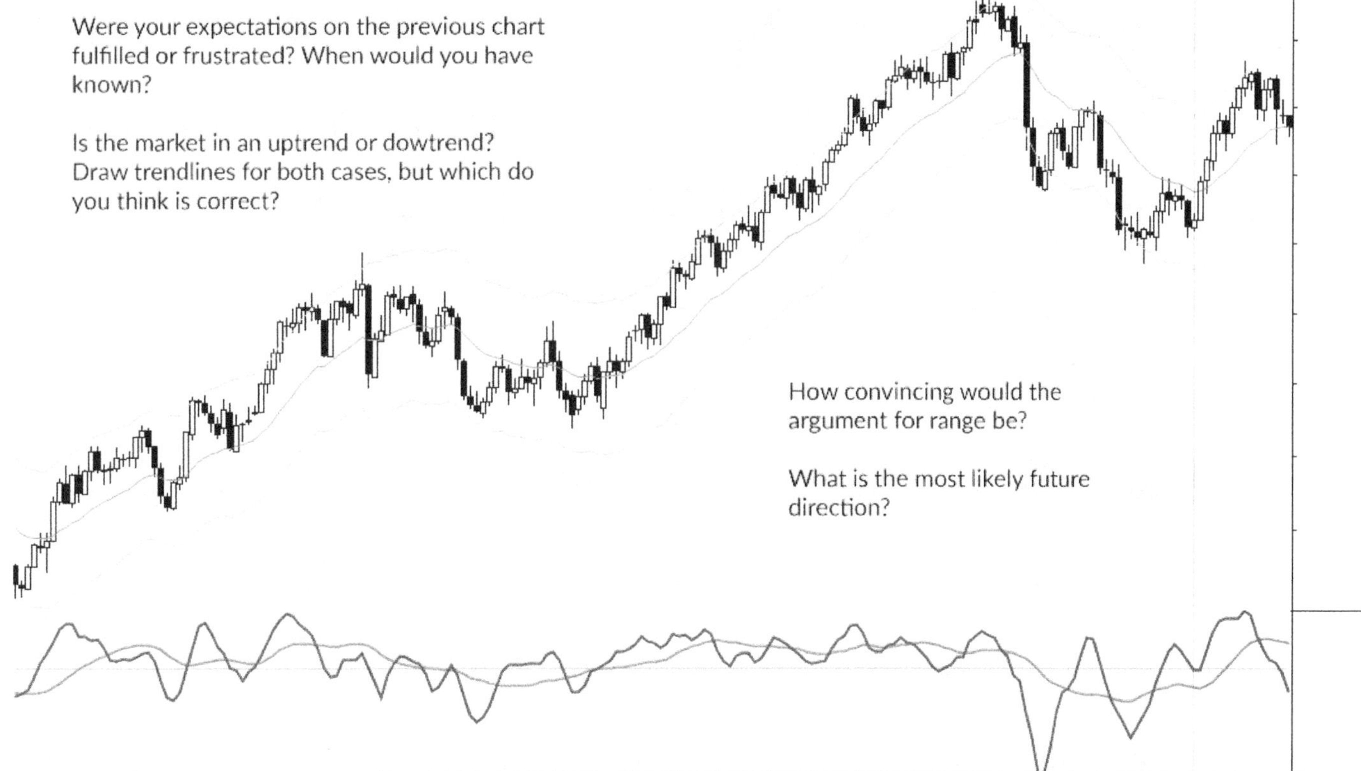
Were your expectations on the previous chart fulfilled or frustrated? When would you have known?

Is the market in an uptrend or dowtrend? Draw trendlines for both cases, but which do you think is correct?

How convincing would the argument for range be?

What is the most likely future direction?

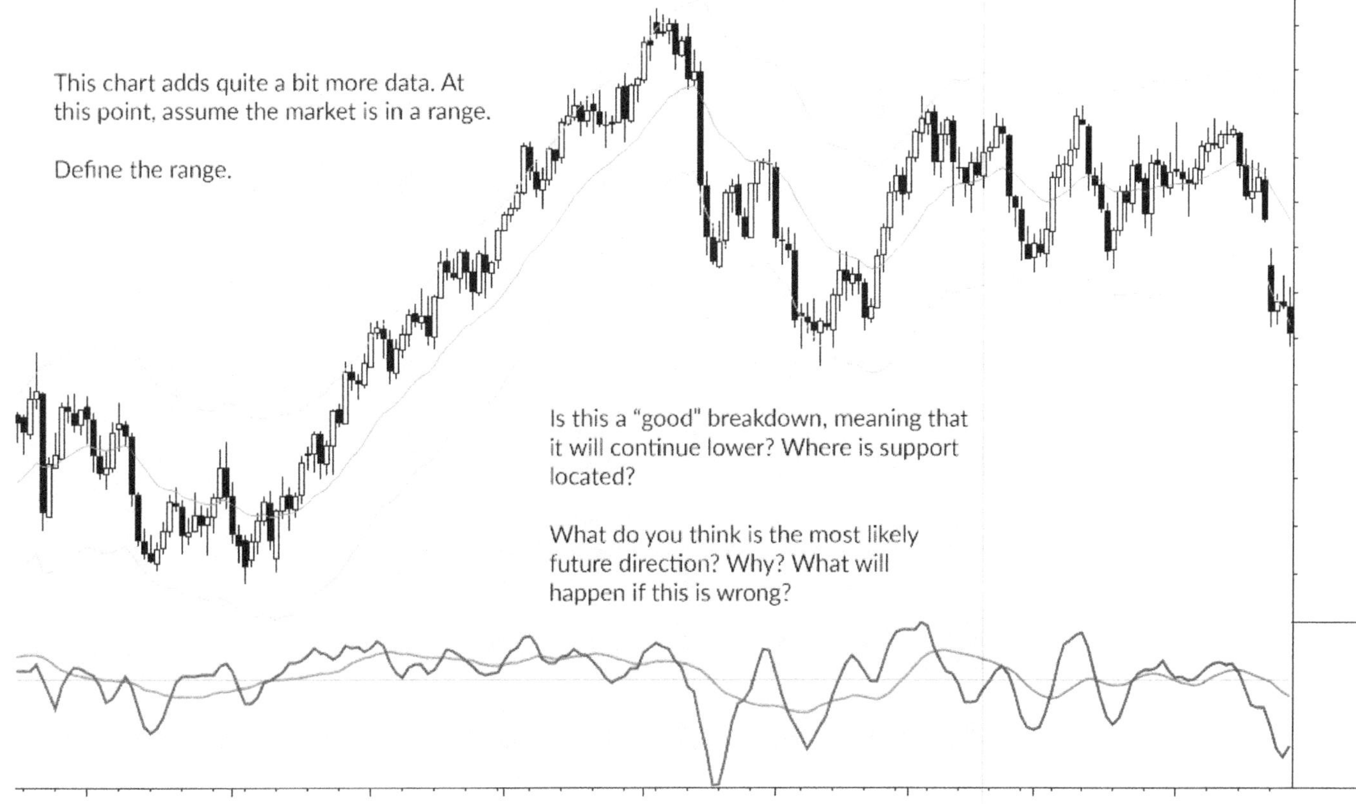
This chart adds quite a bit more data. At this point, assume the market is in a range.

Define the range.

Is this a "good" breakdown, meaning that it will continue lower? Where is support located?

What do you think is the most likely future direction? Why? What will happen if this is wrong?

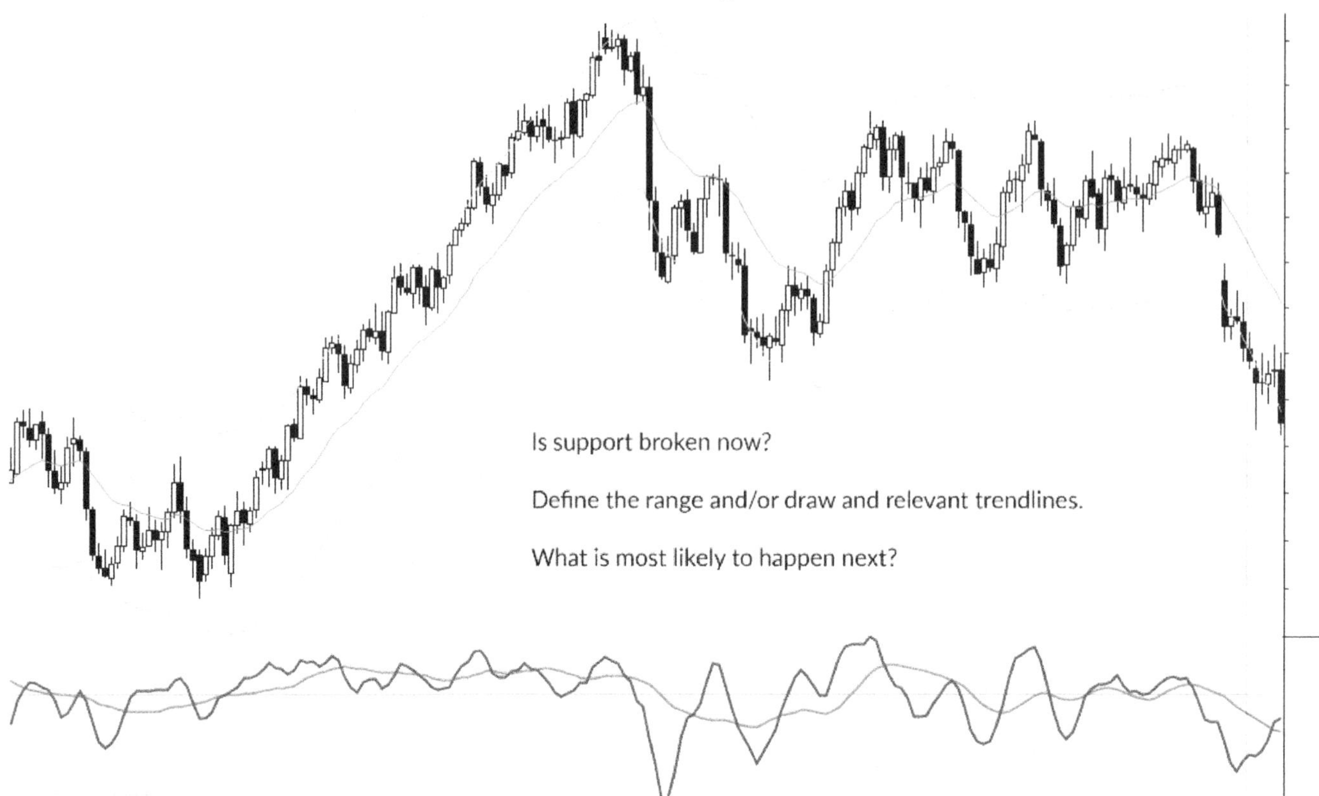

Is support broken now?
Define the range and/or draw and relevant trendlines.
What is most likely to happen next?

Draw relevant market structure (trendlines, ranges, etc.)

What is most likely to happen next? Why? How will you know if this is right or wrong? What should you be looking for?

Section 3: Trendlines

The charts in this section are slightly more compressed and are presented without commentary. Draw trendlines, following the rules from the module (and pp. 84–86 of *The Art and Science of Technical Analysis*). A trendline should:

- Capture the swing low before the high of the trend in an uptrend (and the reverse is true for a downtrend.)
- Be attached as far back into the trend as possible, but capturing the beginning of the trend may not be possible.
- Not cut any prices between the two attachment points. A trendline may cut prices after the attachment point (i.e., the trendline was broken.)

Note the transitions into ranges and then the breaks into trending action, and do whatever analysis you feel appropriate. Many charts will include several trends, and you may find different definitions depending on the timeframes you consider. As long as the trendlines are drawn according to the rule set, they are valid.

These charts were chosen to be a mix of relatively straightforward and more complex patterns.

Carnival Corp

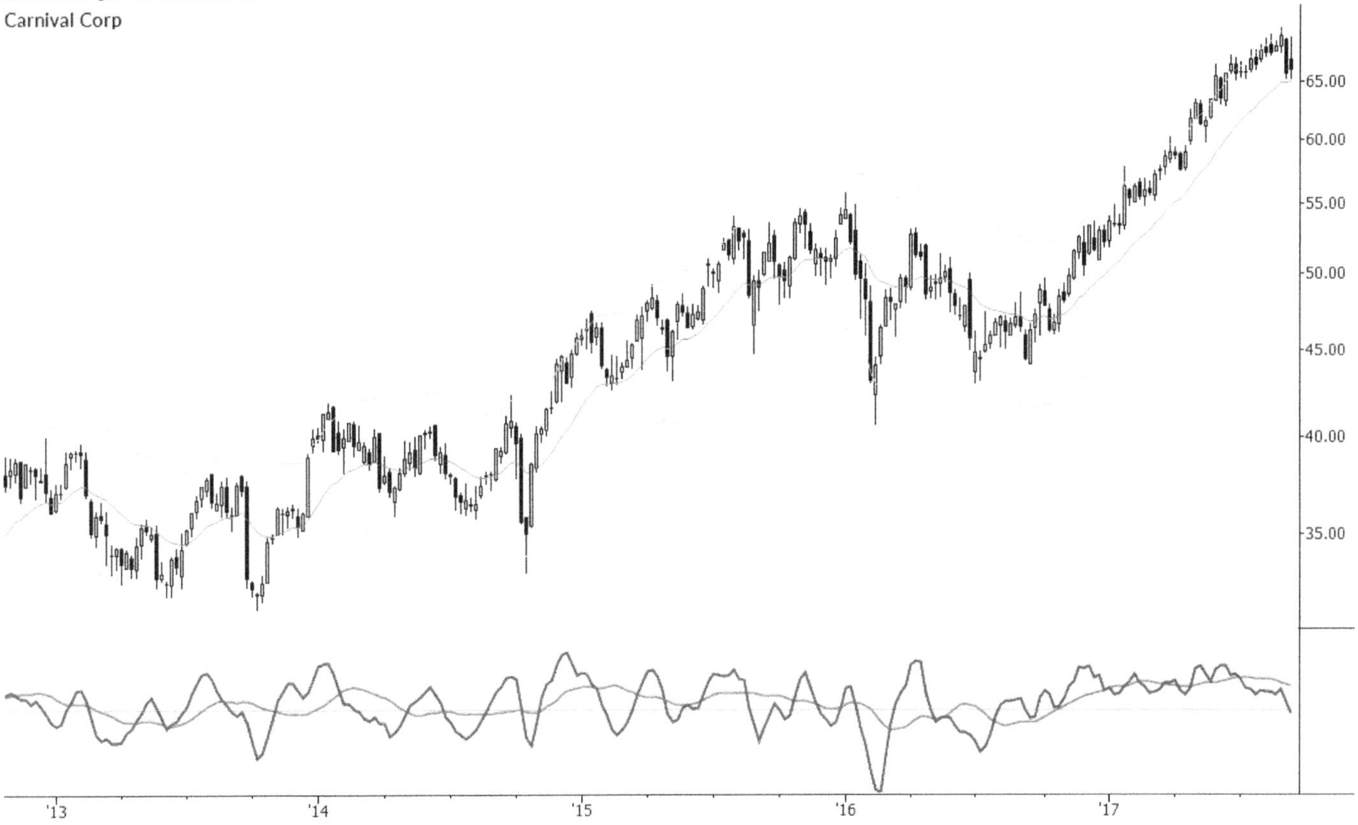

65.00
60.00
55.00
50.00
45.00
40.00
35.00

'13 '14 '15 '16 '17

US Dollar / So African Rand

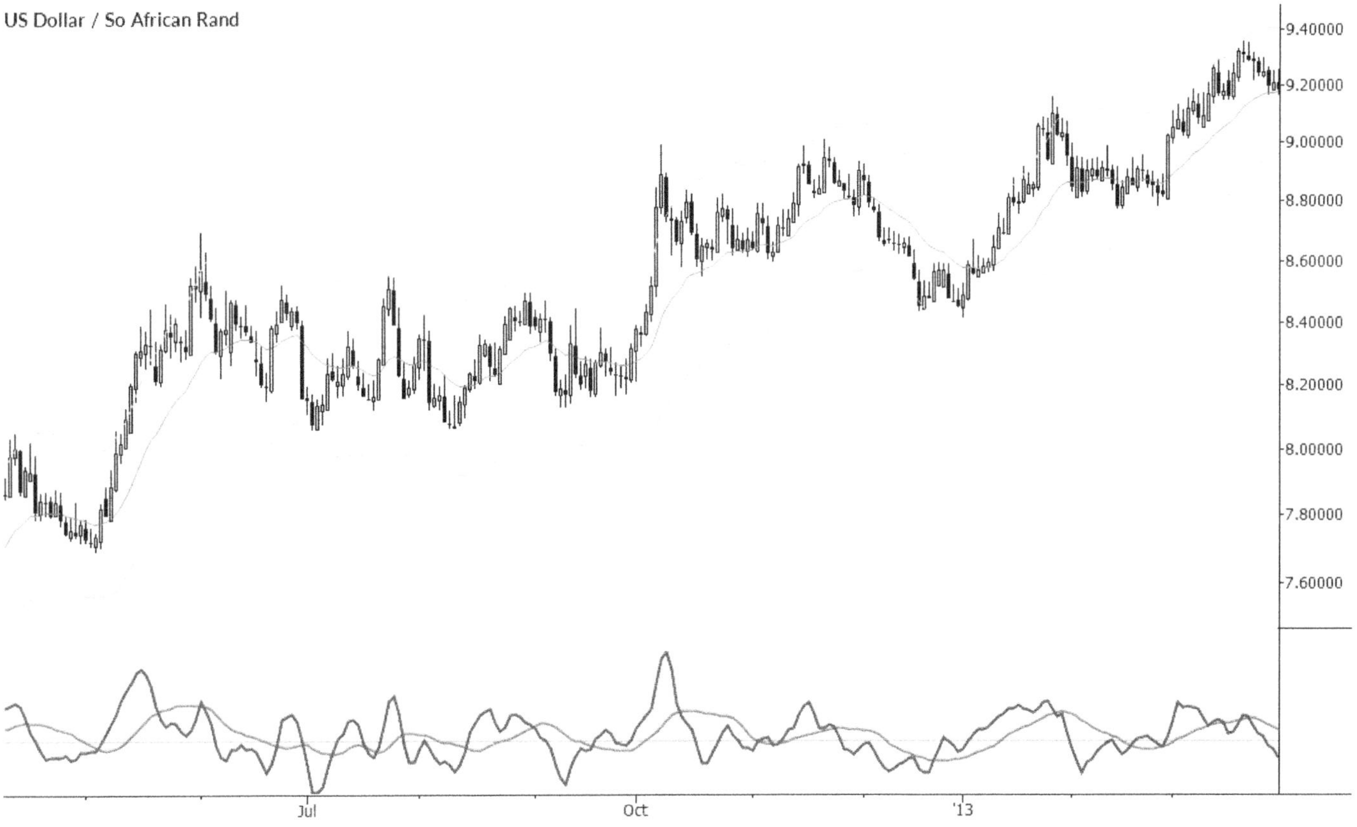

9.40000
9.20000
9.00000
8.80000
8.60000
8.40000
8.20000
8.00000
7.80000
7.60000

Jul Oct '13

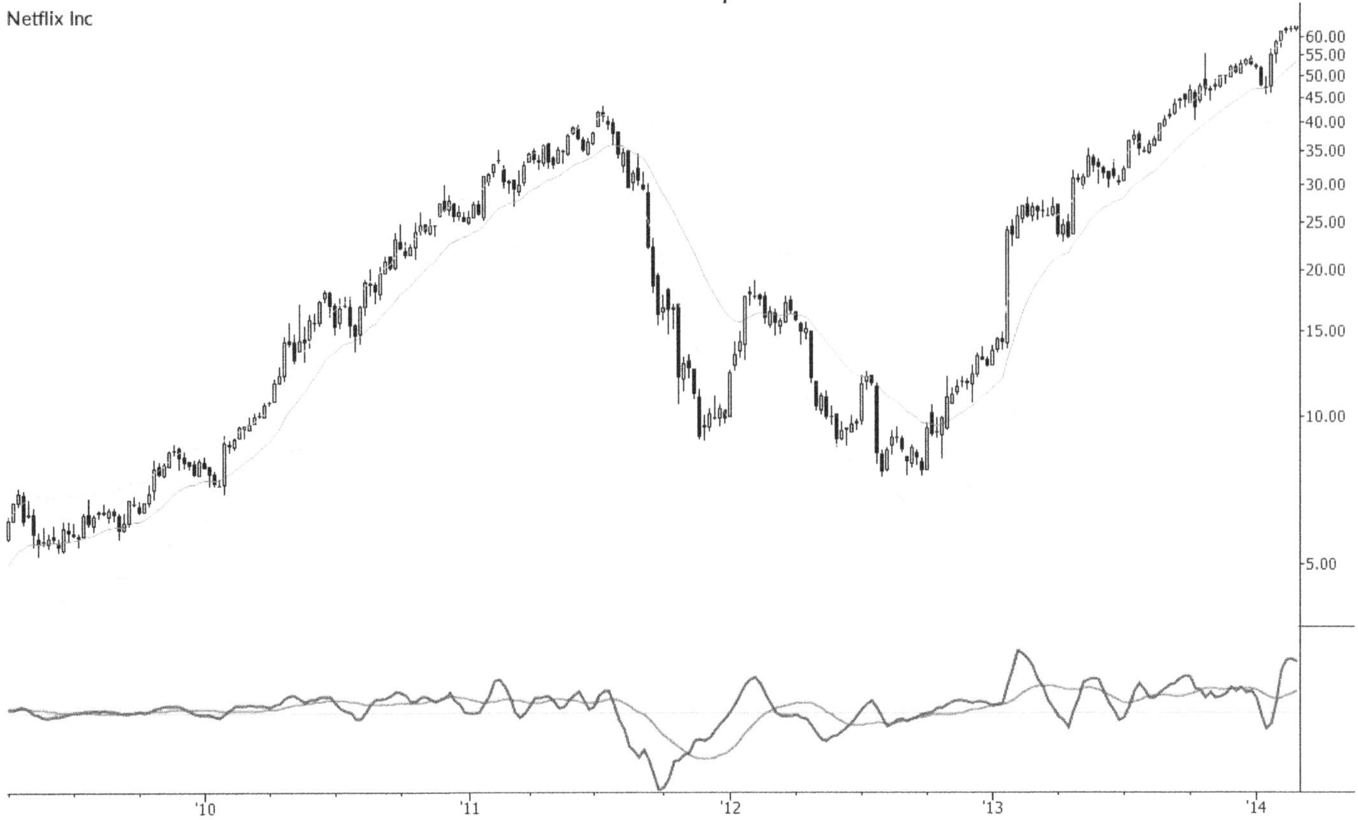

Netflix Inc

60.00
55.00
50.00
45.00
40.00
35.00
30.00
25.00
20.00
15.00
10.00
5.00

'10 '11 '12 '13 '14

Aust Dollar / US Dollar

0.94000
0.92000
0.90000
0.88000
0.86000
0.84000
0.82000
0.80000
0.78000
0.76000

Jul Oct '10 Apr

Euro / US Dollar
1.35000
1.30000
1.25000
1.20000
1.15000
1.10000
Oct
'15
Apr

Wheat Continuous Contract [Dec17]
832
800
768
736
704
672
640
Oct
'15
Apr
Jul

Euro / US Dollar

1.22000
1.20000
1.18000
1.16000
1.14000
1.12000
1.10000
1.08000

Jul Oct '99 Apr

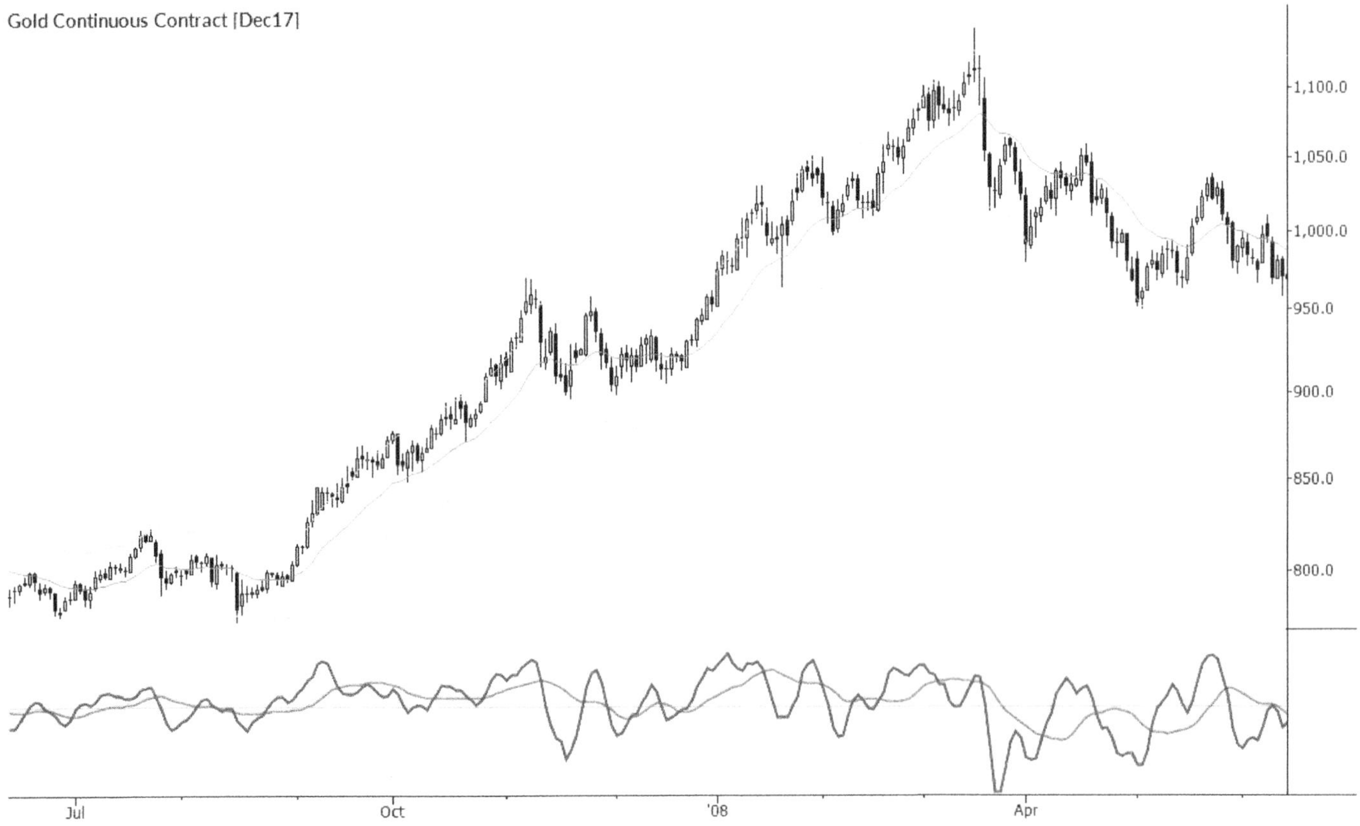

Gold Continuous Contract [Dec17]

1,100.0
1,050.0
1,000.0
950.0
900.0
850.0
800.0

Jul Oct '08 Apr

Euro / US Dollar
1.19800
1.19600
1.19400
1.19200
1.19000
1.18800
1.18600
15:00
20:00
9/14
05:00
10:00
15:00
20:00
9/15
05:00
10:00
15:00
9/17
20:00
9/18

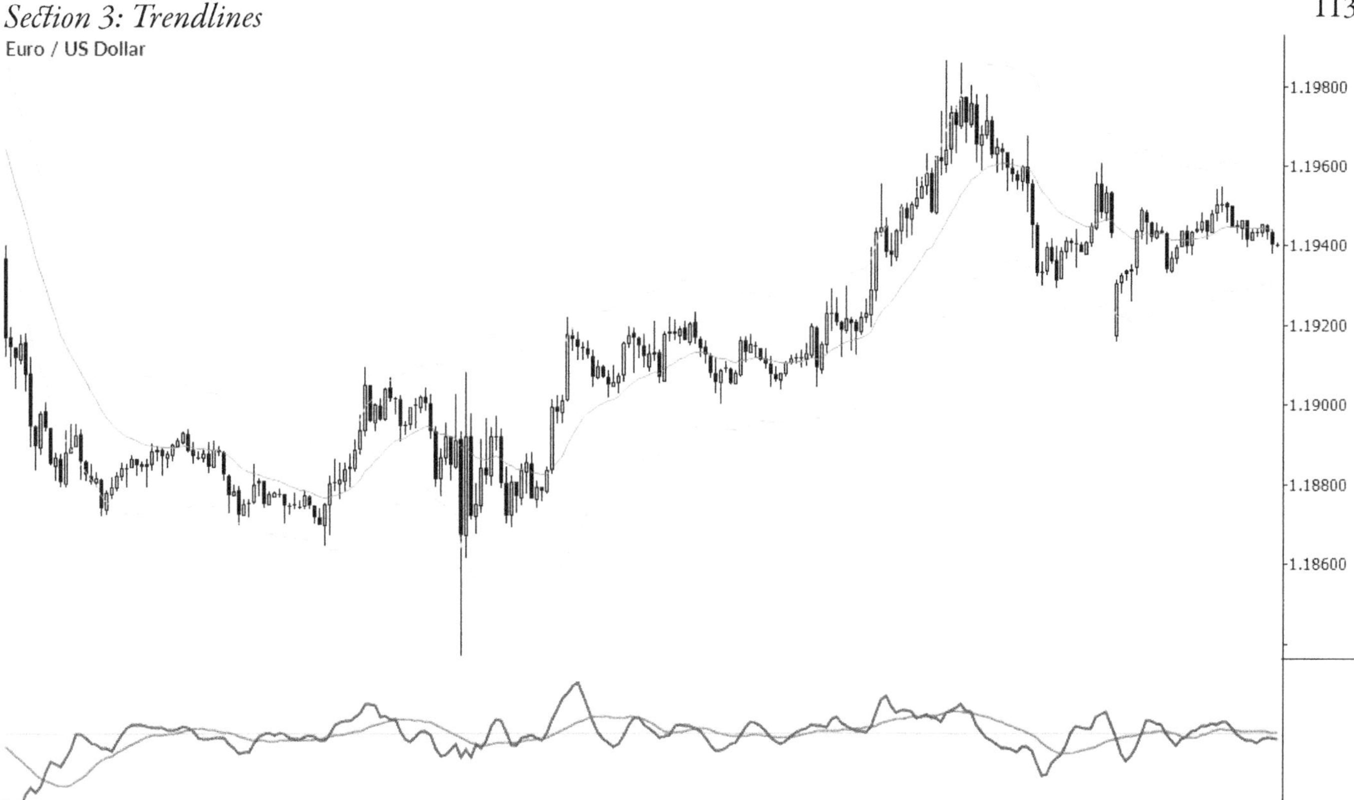

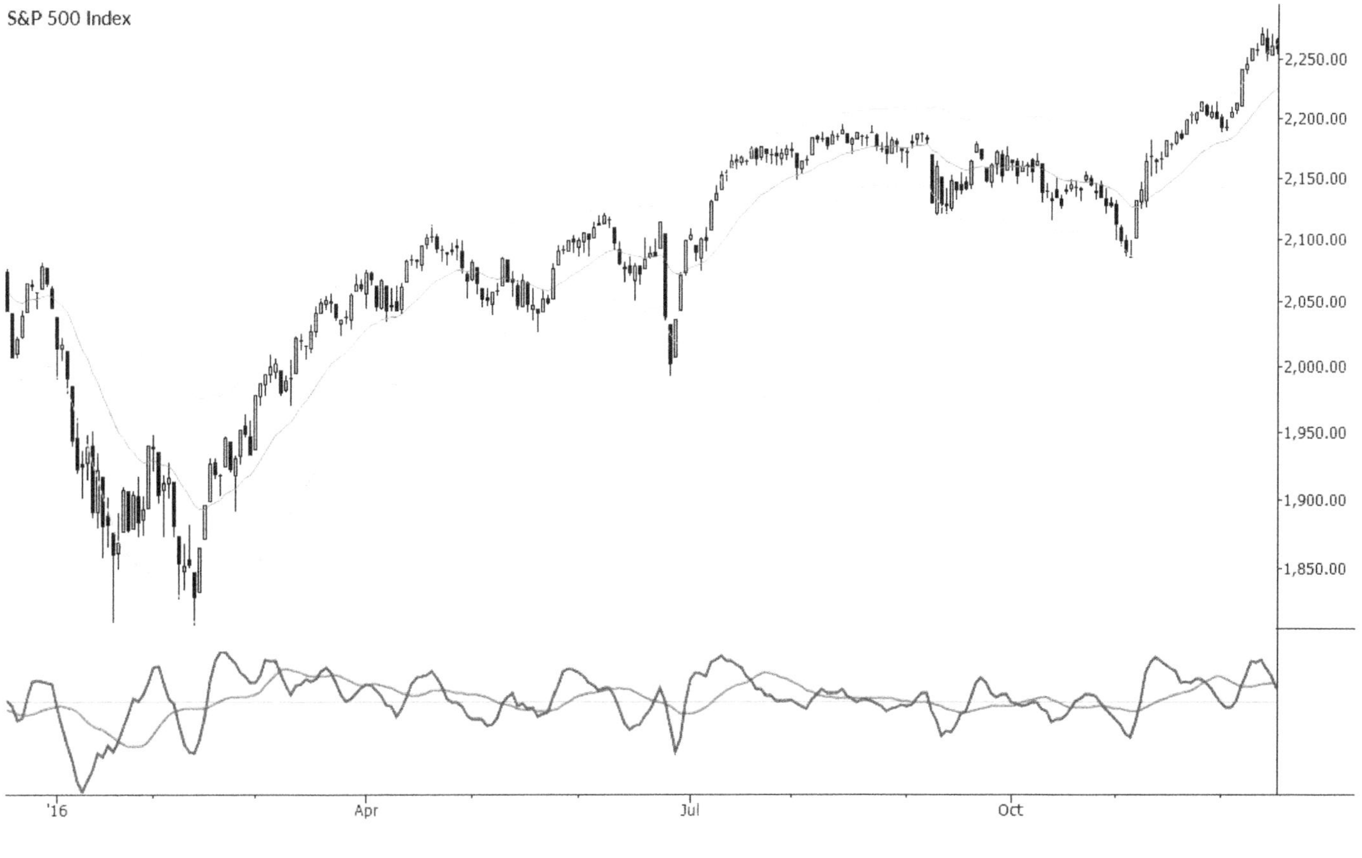

S&P 500 Index
2,250.00
2,200.00
2,150.00
2,100.00
2,050.00
2,000.00
1,950.00
1,900.00
1,850.00
'16
Apr
Jul
Oct

E-mini S&P 500 Continuous Contract [Dec17]

2,504.00
2,502.00
2,500.00
2,498.00
2,496.00
2,494.00
2,492.00
2,490.00
2,488.00

10:00 15:00 20:00 9/14 05:00 10:00 15:00 20:00 9/15 05:00 10:00 9/17 9/18

Crude Oil Continuous Contract [Nov17]

130.00
128.00
126.00
124.00
122.00
120.00
118.00
116.00
114.00
112.00
110.00
108.00
106.00
104.00

'13 Apr Jul Oct

Section 4: Trendline Research Project

A word of warning: done well, this is a big project. It will take some time, but that time will be well rewarded!

The point of the study is to understand what happens as trendlines are drawn in evolving market data. Ideally, you would use a software program that would allow you go one bar at a time (to replicate, as much as possible, the experience of having the chart form in real time.) As the market develops on your screen, decide when and where to draw trendlines. (Review Module 3, Unit 4 from the course for guidelines on drawing trendlines.)

Once the trendlines are drawn, notice what happens when the market touches them. Does the touch of the trendline hold? Does it indicate the end of the trend? What happens if you combine it with bands and/or swing analysis?

Start to think about how you might trade these structures.

You need to keep some type of records. Screencaps of your charts would be one possibility, but it would also be a good idea to somehow score the interaction with the trendlines.

This project is deliberately broad, but should encourage you to spend at least several days investigating action around trendlines. Do not trust what a book tells you—ask the market itself!

If you are not able to generate bar by bar charts, you may work in the middle of a chart but try, as much as possible, to imagine the chart is being revealed one bar at a time. You will not replicate the feeling of hidden information, but you will draw consistent trendlines on correct pivots this way. If you simply start drawing trendlines on charts, you will likely make many mistakes on attachment points and pivots based on what trend information was available at the time.

Remember: draw the trendline, and then see what happens "to the right" of the correctly drawn trendline when the market engages the trendline.

Section 5: Charting by Hand

This is still a valuable exercise. In the first module, we discussed the several ways you can do this exercise. The details are not important; it is far more important that you simply do it.

Do not spend too much time on this exercise. A few minutes every day (but every day!) directed to drawing your charts, or a few minutes each hour if you are an intraday trader, will reward you with deep understanding of price action. This is one tool to stay in the flow and to build your intuitive understanding of market action.

Section 6: Readings

From *The Art and Science of Technical Analysis: Market Structure, Price Action, and Trading Strategies* by Adam Grimes, Wiley, 2012:

85-92 (trendlines)
121-148 (between trends and ranges)
189-212 (indicators and tools for confirmation)
31-48 (market cycles and the four trades)

These readings will lead you deeper into the intricacies of the transitions between trends and ranges, and will give you further examples of correctly and incorrectly drawn trendlines.

On Trends

The Trend Is Your Friend, Except at the End...

Let's talk about endings today. If we can better understand the patterns that often occur when trends end, we are better equipped to manage risk, place stops, and, in general, to trade those trends. Crude oil provides a good example of a dangerous ending in a specific kind of trend.

Recall the "slide along the bands" trend. This is essentially a low-volatility trend, and we can identify it when price goes to one band or channel—it doesn't really matter whether you use Bollinger bands, Keltner channels, or some other similar tool—and stays there while the market "slides" in the direction of the trend. This type of trend doesn't have a lot of the normal pullbacks and retracements that most trends do, and it can be incredibly powerful. Look at this chart of crude oil futures:

It's easy to miss a trend like this because the market may look very dull and boring, but this type of trend can go much further than anyone thinks possible. Identifying this pattern early allowed us to catch the recent downtrend, even though we thought, in early summer, that crude oil might be putting in a long-term bottom. The grinding trend pattern can roll over many obstacles that set up against the trend.

This trend also provides a good example of what happens when everyone is on one side of the trade. In some ways, this pattern quantifies the classic one-sided trade; trading activity and volume dry up as volatility (measured by standard deviation of returns) craters. These trends are a powder keg, and they tend to end in one way: with sharp, volatile counter-trend pops.

Now, call this a "short covering rally" or whatever you will, but the point is we knew, weeks in advance, that this trend was not likely to end politely. We knew that even a minor bounce against the trend was likely to lead to a multi-day pop.

So, how do you use this information? Well, the art of stop placement (and, for discretionary traders, there is maybe more art in this aspect of trading than in any other) depends on understanding expectations. There are times we need to be far from the market—too many traders probably try to use stops that are too tight. However, there are also times that our stops *should* be close; if we know that a minor move against the trend is likely to lead to a nasty move against the trend, why not put our stops close enough that we are among the first out?

This is the lesson: learn to identify these "slide along the bands" trends, which are rare but powerful. Try to get on board, but don't plan to do so via retracements, because those retracements can be painful. If you are in a trend like this, first, congrats, but, second, play defense. Use tight stops, perhaps even tightening them after each bar. This is not a time to endure much pain against the trend—this is a time to lock in profits.

One of the principles of trading is to identify those points when the crowd might be right, to stand with the crowd while they are right, and to try to be among the first out when the crowd turns. It's a nice plan, but usually hard to execute. If you can identify this (rather rare) type of trend and use the correct stops with perfect discipline, you've found trader psychology encoded in the patterns of the market, and this often points the way to winning trades and substantial profits.

Slip and Slide (Along the Bands)

Effective trading patterns are usually simple. The more complicated an idea is, the more likely it is the result of trying to fit random data (i.e., the market) into a preconceived mold. I think many of the patterns and ratios of traditional technical analysis are the result of very misguided Procrustean "analytical techniques"—this is one reason they look so good in the past, but don't have that much utility at the hard right edge of the chart.

First of all, let's take a quick look at a daily chart of crude oil. Notice how crude oil is pressing into the bottom Keltner channel without any real retracements:

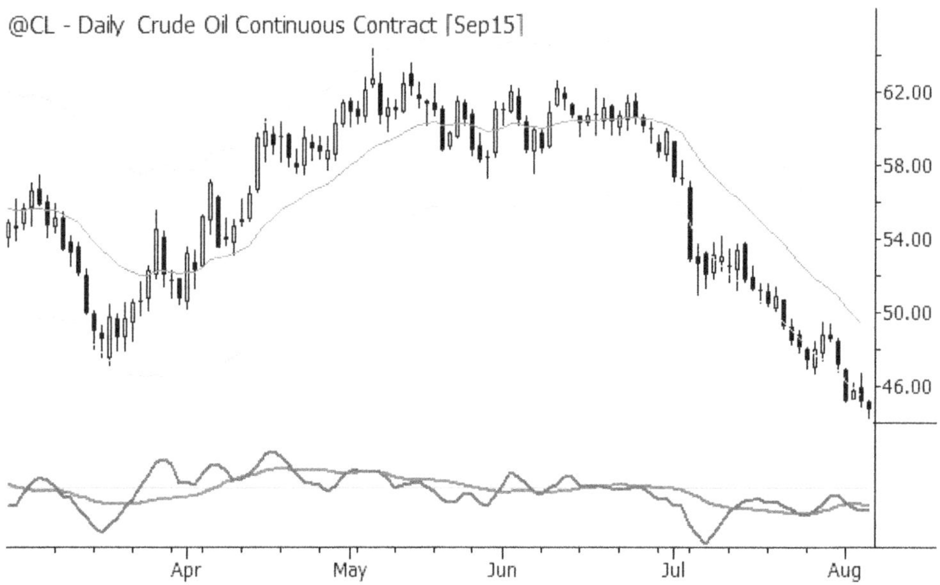

This pattern can be dangerous, and understanding it can save you a lot of grief. I probably need a better name for it, but I've taken to just calling it "slide along the bands", because that's what the market does. In bullet points, here are the main concepts:

- Markets normally move in alternating periods of with-trend movement (up or down), interspersed with pullback against the trend. The normal way markets move is in a zig-zag, which is why trading pullbacks can be such an effective trading strategy.
- Sometimes this pattern gets short-circuited, and the market does not pull back. There are many ways this can happen, but the basic idea is that the dominant group pushes the market in the trend direction at the same time volatility dries up.
- This creates an interesting situation in which the market "drips", "bleeds", or "slides" higher or lower (depending on the trend direction).
- If we use properly calibrated bands, we can see this pattern when the market just presses into one band and sits there while it continues to trend.

This pattern is the proverbial double-edged sword. On one hand, the market can go much further than we might expect. When you are fortunate to be positioned on the right side of such a move, the best thing to do is to focus on trading discipline: maintain a correct stop and tighten that stop every 2-3 bars as the market makes new extremes. Don't look at P&L, and don't over think. Let the market tell you when to get out by hitting your stop.

However, this pattern does bring some unusual risks. When it ends, it often ends in a volatile spike against the trend. We absolutely must respect our stops, and we cannot be upset if we are stopped out in noise. When this pattern ends, the market is probably going to become very emotional. The market can be emotional; you, as a trader, cannot.

So many times, in trading, our entire job description boils down to one simple directive: don't do anything stupid. Don't make mistakes. Understanding this simple pattern can help you avoid many mistakes and navigate this difficult trading environment.

On Developing a Style

Simplify, Simplify, Simplify…

You may know that I studied cooking formally—it was something I'd always wanted to do, and I arrived at a spot in life where I could pursue a culinary degree and apprenticed in the kitchen of one of the top French chefs in America (who was a disciple of Paul Bocuse, but that is a story for another day.) I remember my early days as a trainee chef; I cooked dinner parties for friends often and I had a box that I carried with me that had over forty different herbs and spices. I also had a set of maybe 15 knives that I took with me—a knife for every possible purpose. Today, fifteen years or so later, how has my cooking changed?

First of all, it's better. I would put many of the things I make up against similar dishes made by any restaurant kitchen anywhere, and keep in mind I live in a city with great restaurants. More to the point, I have simplified, simplified, simplified everything to bare essentials. Rather than forty-five different herbs and spices, now it's usually salt and pepper, parsley, garlic and fresh thyme. I almost always have one of two knives in my hand, and I might pick up the paring knife for small jobs. My long study of Japanese cuisine means that when I cook something, I try to express the essence of the thing. For instance, for steak, hot cast iron, salt, pepper and a little butter when it's finished will do the trick. Less can be so much more.

It has been the same with my trading. I've been around the block a few times. I have used multiple indicators with hundreds of lines of code each. I've had complicated systems with rules that fill two pages for bar counts, indicator crossings, and action in related markets. I've traded every possible timeframe from scalping to building baskets and portfolios for monthly/quarterly timeframes and beyond. I've built multifactor econometric models to forecast rates and asset class returns, looked at cross correlations between higher moments of return distributions, and screened for trades across a universe of thousands of assets. Much of this journey was a legitimate part of my learning, but I have realized something over the years—I have truly become a minimalist.

Gone are all the complicated indicators and rules, and, in their place, is a simple system with rules I can explain in five minutes, and two indicators that are non-essential and only used in a supporting role. I do not look at a huge number of supporting (complicating) factors; I try to limit my inputs to only those that I know are significant. The end result is that I can make a trade decision in a matter of minutes or less, and trade and risk management rules are clearly defined. What's more, I find I can trade this system with no emotional involvement, so total, objective control is within grasp. The more I have simplified and removed the unessential, the better my results have become.

You probably don't need many or most of the things you use in your trading. Your results might even be a lot better if you just focused on the things you really do need.

"Hack away at the unessential", as Bruce Lee said. What is unessential in your trading?

What can you simply?

Traders get an edge by thinking in categories

Richard Wyckoff was one of the founding fathers of technical analysis, and one of his useful concepts was to divide the market into an idealized cycle of accumulation, mark-up, distribution, and markdown. Though it can be difficult to apply this model in actual trading, it has many important lessons and can shape the way we think about market action. From a practical perspective, it lays the foundation for a simple categorization of technical trades into four trading categories. There are two trend trades: trend continuation and trend termination, and two support and resistance trades: holding and failing.

Though this may seem like an arbitrary classification system, it is not. Every technical trade imaginable falls into one of these categories. Trades from certain categories are more appropriate at certain points in the market structure, so it is worthwhile to carefully consider your trades in this context.

The first question to consider is: **are all of your trade setups in one category? If** so, this may not be a bad thing—a successful trading methodology must fit the trader's personality—but many traders will find the best results when they have at least two counterbalancing setups. There is an old saying: "If the only tool you have is a hammer, every problem you encounter will look like a nail." There is certainly room for the specialist who does one trade and does it very well, but there's also value in a broader approach.

Some market environments favor certain kinds of plays over others. If you trade within each of these trading categories, then you need to ask yourself: Are you applying the right kind of plays to the right market environments? If you are a specialist who focuses on only one setup or pattern (this is not a criticism if you are successful this way), then you need to realize that only a few specific market environments favor your play and your job is to wait for those environments. You can redefine your job description to include *not* trading most of the time! Wait on the sidelines, and wait for the environments in which you can excel. Clarify your setups. Categorize them into trading categories, and then simplify, simplify, simplify.

Let's look briefly at each of the four broad trading categories:

Trend Continuation

Trend continuation plays are not simply trend plays or with-trend plays. The name implies that we find a market with a trend, whether a nascent trend or an already well-established trend, and then we seek to put on plays in the direction of that trend. Perhaps the most common trend continuation play is to use the pullbacks in a trend to position for further trend legs. It is also possible to structure breakout trades that would be with-trend plays, and there is at least one other category of trend continuation plays—those trades that try to get involved in the very early structure of a new trend, before the trend has emerged with certainty.

There is a problem, though: It is important to have both the risk and the expectation of the trade defined before entry; this is an absolute requirement of any specific trade setup, but it can be difficult with trend continuation trades. The key to defining risk is to define the points at which the trend trade is conclusively wrong, at which the trend is violated. Sometimes it is not possible to define points at which the trend will be violated that are close enough to the entry point to still offer attractive reward/risk characteristics. On the upside, the best examples of these trades break into multileg trends that continue much further than anyone expected, but the most reliable profits are taken consistently at or just beyond the previous highs.

Trend Termination

More than any other category, precise terminology is important here. If we were less careful, we might apply a label like "trend reversal" to most of the trades in this category, but this is a mistake. That label fails to precisely define the trader's expectations. If you think you are trading trend reversal trades, then you expect that a winning trade should roll over into a trend in the opposite direction. This is a true trend reversal, and these spots offer exceptional reward/risk profiles and near-perfect trade location. How many traders would like to sell the high tick or buy the very low at a reversal?

However, true trend reversals are exceedingly rare, and it is much more common to sell somewhere near the high and to then see the market simply stop trending. Be clear on this: This is a win for a trend termination trade—the trend stopped. Anything else is a bonus; it is important to adjust your expectations accordingly.

Trend termination trades are countertrend (counter to the existing trend) trades, and trade management is an important issue. Most really dramatic trading losses, the kind that blow traders out of the water (and that don't involve options) come from traders fading trends and adding to those positions as the trend continues to move against them. If this is one of the situations where the trend turns into a manic, parabolic blow-off, there is a real possibility for a career-ending loss on a single trade. For swing traders, there will sometimes be dramatic gaps against positions held countertrend overnight, so this needs to be considered in the risk management and position sizing scheme. Perhaps more than any other category of trade, iron discipline is required to trade these with any degree of consistency.

Support or Resistance Holding

There is some overlap between these trading categories, and it is possible to apply trades from these categories in more than one spot in the market structure. We might expect that most support/resistance trades will take place in accumulation or distribution areas while the market chops sideways, but a trader trading with-trend trades could initiate those trades by buying support in the trend. Are these trend continuation trades or support holding trades? The answer is both, so traders must build a well-thought-out classification system that reflects their approach to the market. Your trading patterns and rules are the tools through which you structure price action and market structure, and they must make sense to you. Take the time to define them clearly.

Many trading books will show you examples of well-defined trading ranges, where you could buy and risk a very small amount as the market bounces off the magic price at the bottom of the range. These trades do exist, but they are a small subset of support holding trades. Support, even when it holds, usually does not hold cleanly. The dropouts below support actually contribute to the strength of that support, as buyers are shaken out of their positions and are forced to reposition when it becomes obvious that the drop was a fake-out.

For the shorter-term trader trading these patterns, there are some important issues to consider. If you know that support levels are not clean, how will you trade around them? Will you sell your position when the level drops, book many small losses, and reestablish when it holds again? Will you simply position small in the range, plan to buy more if it drops, and accept that you will occasionally take very large losses on your maximum size when the market does drop? Every decision is a tradeoff, and you must understand the consequences of these decisions.

Support or Resistance Breaking or Failing

Support/resistance breaking trades are the classic breakout or breakout from channel trades and, ideally, would be located at the end of accumulation or distribution phases. In fact, these trades define the end of accumulation or distribution, as the support or resistance fails and the market breaks into a trend phase. Another place for support/resistance breaking trades is in trends, but many of these are lower time frame breakout entries into the trading time frame trending pattern. Many traders, especially daytraders, find themselves drawn to these patterns because of the many examples where they work dramatically well. Many trading books show example after example of dramatic breakouts, but there is one small problem with breakout trades—most breakouts fail.

In addition, the actual breakout areas tend to be high-volatility and low-liquidity areas, which can increase the risk in these trades. They occur at very visible chart points, and so they are often very crowded trades. The presence of unusual volume and volatility can create opportunities, but it also creates dangers. Execution skills probably matter more here than in any other category of trade, as slippage and thin markets can significantly erode a trader's edge. These trades can offer outstanding reward/risk profiles, but, especially in short-term trades, it is important to remember that realized losses can sometimes be many multiples of the intended risk, significantly complicating the position sizing problem. This is not a fatal flaw, but it must be considered in your risk management scheme.

Depending on the time frame and intended holding period for the trade, it may be possible to find that there are patterns that precede and set up the best examples of these trades. The best resistance breaking trades will be driven by large-scale buying imbalances, and these imbalances usually show, for instance, as the market holds higher lows into the resistance level before the actual breakout. Breakouts driven by small traders who are simply trying to scalp small profits in the increased volatility are less reliable and are usually not set up by these larger-scale patterns. In the very best examples of these trades, buyers who are trapped out of the market by the suddenness of the breakout will be compelled to buy into the market over coming days or weeks, and this buying pressure will provide favorable tailwinds for the trade. Traders specializing in breakout trades usually spend a lot of time studying the patterns that set up the best trades, and maintain a watch list of potential candidates for trades at any time. Executing unplanned breakout trades in a reactive mode is unlikely to be a formula for long-term success.

On Market Rhythm

Toward a Simple Model of Price Behavior

I am a quantitative discretionary trader: I am a discretionary trader, but everything I do is subject to quantitative and statistical verification. Over the years, I have accumulated a lot of statistical evidence for what works and what does not work in the market, and the results may be surprising. In conversations with other traders, I'm sometimes accused of being overly negative, as it's hard to find real quantitative support for many of the traditional tools of technical analysis (such as Fibonacci ratios, most applications of moving averages, etc.) Many traders find this message challenging, but most people only seek confirmation of their beliefs—a common and dangerous cognitive bias.

I want to share a model of market behavior that I've found very useful. Though this is a theoretical model, it works. It is supported by rigorous statistical research, and, even more importantly, it has proven itself in actual trading for many years. The point of this work is not to disparage anything anyone does; the point is to save your time and money.

The concept is simple. Imagine, for a moment, that there are two forces in the market: *Mean reversion*, the tendency for large moves to be reversed in part or completely, and *Momentum*, the tendency for large moves to lead to further moves in the same direction. When the forces are in balance, and they usually are, markets will move more or less randomly. Price will move up and down in ways that look a lot like a random walk. Future prices and price direction will be unpredictable, and there is no technical reason for having a position. We refer to this as a market in equilibrium, and these are the types of markets we try to actively avoid.

However, there are other points where one force predominates. In trends, momentum-fueled, with-trend thrusts lead to further moves in the same direction, though eventually mean reversion overtakes them and the market rolls over into a pullback. (These concepts are timeframe dependent.) At other times, mean reversion will predominate and large moves can be faded. The question of technical trading now becomes this: "is it possible to identify patterns that show, in advance, when one force is likely to be stronger than the other?" If so, then we have a reason for taking a position, putting risk in the market, and the possibility of harvesting trading profits from markets that are otherwise random and unpredictable. Fortunately, the answer to that question is yes.

That's all there is to the model; it is so simple that it's easy to overlook the importance and usefulness of such a simple framework. These forces shape everything from traditional chart patterns to long-term trends to ultra-short-term HFT behavior. There are many nuances here that may not be appreciated in traditional technical analysis—for instance, the balance of momentum and mean reversion are different in different asset classes and different timeframes. This is why technical tools cannot be simply applied "just as well" to "any market and any timeframe", but, rather, why some adaptation and experience is necessary to translate concepts and tools across different applications. We'll dig into all of this in more depth soon, but, for now, begin to think toward a simpler model of price behavior that is shaped by these two primordial market forces.

Hey, that's different!

It pays to think deeply about markets, how they move, risk, opportunity, and how it all plays out in the grand scheme of probability. We can and should spend a lot of time crafting our trading plans, understanding our risk tolerance, and monitoring our adherence to those plans. But, in the heat of the moment, trading does not have to be complicated. Though there may be tremendous quantitative work supporting a method, often the simplest tools work best. One of my favorite patterns is simply knowing when something has changed in the market.

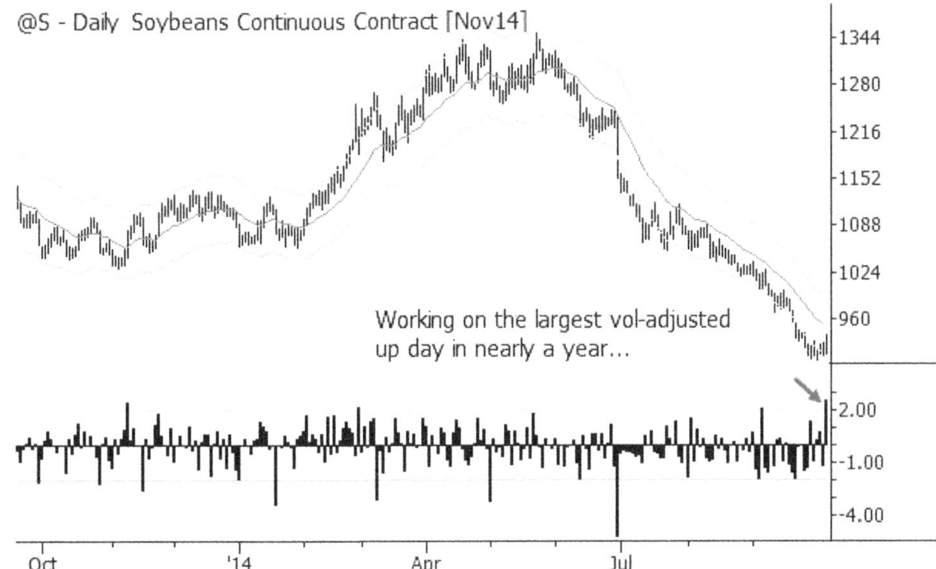

I took the screenshot above in the middle of the day (10/6/14) when I noticed that many of the grains were putting in large standard deviation up days, which is another way to say that they were making large moves relative to their own volatility. Here is also a case where the right tools can be helpful; would you have seen that this was a significant day just by at the chart? Maybe, but the panel below the chart quickly shows the significance of this move. On a volatility-adjusted basis, this was the largest upward move in nearly a year.

Now, this is only the first stage of analysis, but it is an important one. Over the years, when I have worked with, coached, and trained traders, I used to jokingly call this "hey, that's different!" In reality, it is not a joke. Noticing that the dominant market pattern is shifting can be an important piece of information.

The point of this is the concept, rather than the specific example here. Find an obvious break in the existing market pattern, and then pay attention to what happens afterward. So, what can be different? Here are some examples:

- Largest volatility-adjusted move over a certain time period.
- Obvious move that breaks a chart pattern.
- Counter-to-expected breakout, but, again, it must be obvious.
- Sudden, sharp reversal like a single day that reverses the previous week's movement.
- Quiet market goes into an extended period of volatility, or vice versa.

This is just a starting point; you can make a much longer list of things that indicate market dynamics might be shifting. One key point: though this is a simple concept and is simple to use, it must be based on things that really work. If it is based on technical ideas that have no foundation in market reality then you are only analyzing insignificant noise. Understand how markets really move, how they usually move, and then—look for something that breaks the pattern. Look for something that jumps out and say, "hey, that's different!"

Staying in Step: Finding Rhythm of the Market

Rhythm is a fundamental aspect of the human experience: our bodies pulse with the rhythm of blood and breath. We experience the rhythms of day and night, and the longer cycles of the seasons. Rhythm is fundamental to music, whether it's the relentless pounding bass of a rock song, the syncopated stabs of a Jazz guitar, or the nearly baffling asymmetry of Messiaen. Visual rhythm ties together much of architecture, design and visual art. There are natural rhythms in our mood and energy level—rhythm pervades everything we touch or experience, in some way. And, yes, the rhythm of the market is ever present and undeniable.

Philosophically, the understanding of rhythm is a critical division between Eastern and Western thought, with most Western understandings favoring a linear perception of time and experience—history, of individuals, nations, and the world, is seen as a journey along a one-way timeline. In the East, a more cyclical perspective prevails, an understanding that events lead to other events in an ongoing cycle of creation and destruction, and that the rhythmic interplay of forces creates much of the human experience. The Western approach might talk about the march of history, while the Eastern perspective might say, "what is has been before and will be again."

In financial markets, the cyclical approach is usually the right one. This has all happened before, and what has been shall be again, in some form.

The market rhythm

Financial markets move in cycles and there is a rhythm in that movement. Some of this is well-documented: we can measure cycles in prices and returns with tools like Fast Fourier Transforms or Kalman filters, we can measure cycles in volatility with other tools. We also can measure the rhythm between trending and ranging activity with different tools. There are also many more arcane cycles based on time and angles, and there are cycles in instruments that are bounded and in the relative performance of different markets.

Trading cycles is not as easy as we might expect; cycles shift and abort without warning. To stay in step requires frequent adjustment, and the trader often finds himself out of rhythm with the perceived cycle. Traders who discover cycles often think that they are the answer to many trading problems, but actual application is elusive. An understanding of cycles can be useful, but trading them in a pure form can be very difficult. For most traders, understanding the cycles of the market can be a useful "first filter" for knowing when and how to apply specific trading techniques to the market.

The trader's rhythm

Markets have cycles, but so do traders, and there are some lessons here that we can begin to apply right away. First, understand that there is some natural flexibility in all cycles. Do not expect perfect regularity. This applies as much to your trading results and performance as to market action itself—expect that periods of good performance will be followed by lackluster performance. Just know that this is part of the "game": you're never as good as it seems during the good periods and never as bad as you feel when things are hard. Your overall performance (and the right way to think about your performance) lies somewhere in the middle.

Also, realize that your activity in the market will be governed by the market's action and the variation in that action. There will be times when active trading is required, and times when the right thing to do is to do nothing. Sometimes, you may go through long periods of time in which your only job is moving stops and managing open positions, and you may see these open positions stopped out one by one. This is all ok, and all normal.

Staying in step

In my experience, a lot of the bad things that happen to traders happen when we try to apply the wrong tools for current market conditions—the tools may well be great tools, but a great tool at the wrong time is the wrong tool! (Examples: applying a mean reversion system to fade a strong trend, a daytrader forcing trades when markets are dead, etc.) So, the first line of defense is intellectual: know that markets are cyclical and know that your performance will also have some cycles and rhythm.

The next piece of the puzzle comes from good record keeping and analysis of your trading results. Your intuition about your performance may well be valid, but it's a lot better if it's supported by some data. Simply keeping a running total of, say, your last 20 trades' win ratio (assign a 1 if the trade is a win and a 0 if it's a loss (decide what to do with breakeven trades too), and keep a moving average of the last X trades) can give some good insights into performance. Of course, monitoring P&L will get you into roughly the same place, but win ratio is often a good early warning sign.

Last, have good rules that help you decide what to do. The right answer, of course, is the standard and not-immediately-helpful "it depends", but it does depend: it depends on what markets, timeframes, and style of trading you do. At one extreme, a long-term trend follower may well ignore this information, knowing that she is simply going to be out of step with the market for most of the time, and also know that it doesn't matter because she will be profitable over a long enough period. On the other extreme, a daytrader might pull the plug on a day if he has 5 or 6 losses in a row, because he knows that is unusual for his style of trading and probably reflects a market where conditions are not favoring his play. It's hard to know what these rules should be until you've traded a while, but developing these "meta rules" that govern your behavior and trading activity is an important task for the developing and professional trader alike.

Too Much of a Good Thing

When markets trend, they do so in alternating waves of with-trend strength interspersed with countertrend pullbacks. Analysis of these swings can give many insights into the strength and integrity of a trend, and this can be done both quantitatively and qualitatively. Generally speaking, the with-trend legs need to be stronger than the countertrend pullbacks, and the stronger the with trend legs are, the better.

However, *excessive* strength can indicate a climax extreme that can mark the end of a trend, or at least can cap that trend for quite some time. This problem—distinguishing "good" with-trend strength from "overheated" overextensions is one of the core problems of technical analysis. Many solutions have been proposed; all of them work at times and fail at others (one of the recurring problems is that these tools would often take a trader out of a trend too early), but this is another case where simple can be better. Though nothing works all the time, a simple pattern can give important insight into the future direction of prices.

Let's take a look at an example in sugar futures. Many of the Softs (sugar, cotton, orange juice, coffee, cocoa, etc.) can be thin and can have some surprises; inexperienced traders should be cautious, but sugar tends to be a bit more tractable than some of the other Softs. The chart below shows sugar was in a two month uptrend. Don't get too caught up in how you define the trend—the point is simple: Sugar was going up.

This was a reasonably strong trend, possibly threatening to reverse a multi-year downtrend. The next day, Sugar had a sharp spike higher.

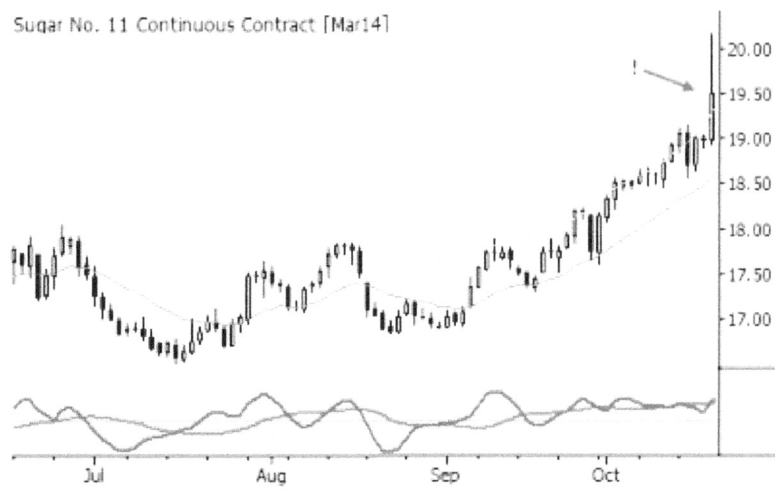

There are several signs of a possible buying climax here. First, the range of this bar is many times the average range of recent bars. (It's not necessary to quantify this, but, in general, a bar that has a range that is three or more times the average range of recent bars should catch your attention.) It also comes to a new trend extreme, and it is obvious that the pattern of the trend has been broken. It's often enough to notice that something has changed, that something is different, and don't assume that violations of the trend only matter if they are against the trend. (In other words, many traders would tend to watch for downward spikes as a warning that an uptrend is weakening. This is not wrong, but upward spikes can also be significant.) Long shadows on candles are often indicative of exhaustion. In this context, it might be ok to think that the large upward shadow ("wick") on the last candle shows where many traders made mistakes.

So, what do we do now? If you're long, you need to play defense. It is appropriate to tighten stops dramatically on long positions, perhaps even working them under the last 1-3 days' lows. If you're looking to short, it might make sense to aggressively pursue short entries following a pattern like this. At the very least, do not enter long positions immediately following a spike like this. Be careful of buying pullbacks or breakouts, and be very reluctant to buy weakness. A buying climax often indicates that the proverbial "last willing buyer" has bought, and the market will often collapse into the vacuum on the other side.

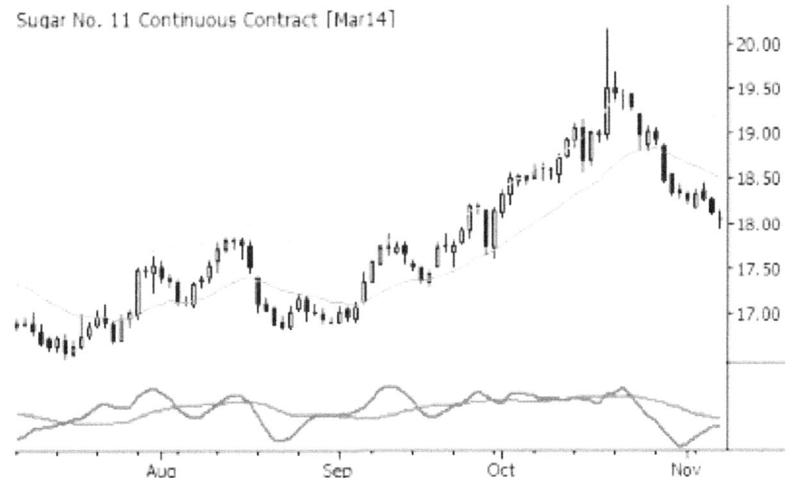

In this case, we can see that the buying climax marked the trend high, at least for several weeks. Generally speaking, if we get a strong enough selloff following a buying climax, the next bounce is often a good, high-probability short setup. It's also possible that the market will pause for a while, absorb the overextension, and then head higher. It's possible that a buying climax could lead to further spikes in the same direction; sugar could have traded to 23.00 on the next day following the "climax" (though the long shadow made that considerably less likely). Anything can happen. Nothing works all the time, and the best we can do is to quantify the probabilities and understand how the balance of buyers and sellers might be shifting in a market at any time, but this pattern, being aware of climax points, can offer great insight for traders in all markets and all timeframes.

Chapter 4

Module 4–The Pullback

This module looks at the pullback: a simple, but powerful, trading pattern that uses the normal fluctuations in trend strength to set up and to manage trades. Though the concept of trading pullbacks is probably familiar to most traders, many traders overlook the power and utility of this pattern.

The second major area of focus is on applying quantitative techniques to market data. On one hand, we are asking a simple question: "does it work?" We quickly find that getting the answer to that not-so-simple question is fraught with complications and difficulties. After a look at calculating expected value, we take a long detour into investigating the patterns in the relationship and geometry of swings, specifically looking at applications of Fibonacci ratios to market data.

This module concludes with a section on journaling and doing manual (bar by bar) backtesting of trading ideas. You will do a research project centering around the pullback concept. The goal of this project is both to understand the edge in the pattern and to familiarize yourself with the process of backtesting a trading idea. This will lay a solid foundation for both discretionary trading and deeper quantitative work.

Section 1: Record Keeping

Your work for this module might appear to be less than for previous modules—certainly, the page count is lower. But that is an illusion! In this module, the emphasis and focus shifts to *you* doing the work, and this begins with record keeping.

Journal

This is the perfect time—today, right now, immediately—to start keeping a journal.

Though you can consider the issues of format and exactly what you want to put into the journal later, this practice will be most effective if it is a routine done consistently. Essentially, you want to make journaling a habit—a very good, constructive habit that will ultimately play a big part in your success.

For the beginning trader, it's sometimes confusing to know what to put your in journal. If you aren't sure what to write, write that. Write about your feelings about journaling, your feelings about building habits. Write about things in your life and world you want to change. Write about your experiences trading. Write about your future trading, and what you think of the work you're doing in this course. Write about kittens. It doesn't matter! Just write a little bit, each day, and let this work evolve as you go along.

P&L Sheet

You also do need a P&L sheet that allows you to record at least the following datapoints for each trade:

- Date In
- Price In
- Price Out
- Initial Stop

You will use this in your research project this week.

Section 2: Pullback Backtest

First of all, it needs to be said that this will not be a proper, rigorous statistical backtest. Rather, it is a process designed to do a few things:

- Train your eye to see the pullback pattern in the market
- Get some idea what edge might (or might not) be in the specific way you see the pattern
- Point you toward some improvements in your perception
- And to get you used to doing some work on historical data

Before you can really do this work, you need access to historical charts and some record keeping system; pencil and paper will work, but electronic formats are much better. You then need to define the pullback pattern. This can be difficult, because there is admittedly (and deliberately) some element of discretion. Do not be discouraged. The way in which you see these patterns will evolve and change, but it is the exposure to market data that will let you evolve. This is truly a case where the only way you learn is by doing.

So, define the pullback pattern. What, specifically, will get you interested in looking for a pullback? How will you define a strong enough or sharp enough move to tell you that a pullback might set up? How will you monitor the shape of the pullback as it develops? Where will you actually get into trades? Where will you place that initial stop?

Take some time to answer those questions, and come up with a rule sheet for pullbacks. (Write it down.) Then, go through some market data bar by bar, recording key stats for each "trade", and see how it works and how it feels; your subjective sense or feeling is valuable. At the first stages, this exercise is as much about you as it is about the market.

Like anything else, this process becomes easier the more you do it. To have a valid test, you need a significant number of trades, but just get started with the exercise this week.

Section 3: Charting by Hand

Continue your work on charting by hand throughout this Module. We have already considered several ways you can do this exercise; choose one that works for you. The details are not important; it is far more important that you do it.

This should also not be a tremendous time suck—this is not a unique form of torture I have devised. A few minutes every day (but every day!) directed to drawing your charts, or a few minutes each hour if you are an intraday trader, will reward you with deep understanding of price action.

Section 4: Readings

From *The Art and Science of Technical Analysis: Market Structure, Price Action, and Trading Strategies* by Adam Grimes, Wiley, 2012:

65-77 (pullback intro)
154-169 (pullback detail)
291-315 (pullback examples)
385 - 388 (journalling)

The readings this week will help us to move from the purely theoretical, high-level perspectives on markets to looking at applied trading patterns. Seeing many examples of the pullback, and considering how to manage trades that set up based on this pattern, will give the trader good ideas for continuing to explore this aspect of market behavior.

On Journaling

Your Best Trading Book Is Your Own

There are a few practices that consistently separate winning traders from the losers. True, there is an incredible diversity of winning strategies, approaches, and personalities. However, we when look at and talk to consistently profitable traders, we start to see a few common threads. There are some things that winners do that losing traders often ignore. Keeping a trading journal, of some kind, is one of those practices.

A reader from by blog asked the following question, which I have paraphrased:

> *What should go into a daily trading journal?*
>
> *should it just narrate the day's activities like "price opened slightly higher than yesterday's close and then it closed lower forming a down trend bar"?*
>
> *should it include my [the trader's] thought process which went through during the day while seeing the price and/or also after seeing the closing price?*
>
> *how to see the last bar in the context of previous bars? Should I look at range of the bars or a doji bar in context of earlier bars?*
>
> *Does it really help to evaluate each bar on daily timeframe (except the sigma spike types bar) if you are swing trading? Or I am just analyzing the noise but if bars seen together will make sense?*
>
> *Of course as you have mentioned in many of your blogs/videos/book the market structure/context plays an important part. But while noting down in my trading journal, I am not sure it is really helping me to improve my decision process.*

So, the answer, I think, is that you need to keep some kind of trading journal, but I don't think you need to keep a *specific* kind of journal. In other words, you probably need to keep a journal, but there's no one, right way. Let me try to simplify this a little bit, and hit some bullet points:

- **The most important thing about your journal is that you do it!** All the planning and best intentions in the world are worth nothing if you don't follow through. Consider this carefully when you plan your journaling—it has to be realistic. If your journal involves filling out three forms and writing a page of text twice a day, you're probably not going to do that. On the other hand, scribbling three lines in your note book at the end of the week ("It was a good week. Made a ton of money. Bought pizza.") probably doesn't really provide a lot of value. If there's a key to successful journaling, it's finding that balance between ease of use and complexity.
- Just to expand on that point, **it's the routine that matters.** Keeping your journal, whether you do it daily, weekly, or monthly (depending on your timeframe) is a matter of discipline. In trading, being disciplined means that you are ***always*** disciplined. This means that you must follow through and do your journal! Get into the routine, and do it without fail. Another note from my own experience: the less you want to do your journal on any period, the more you need to. Never underestimate your mind's ability to avoid tasks that really need to be done.
- I often suggest that traders **keep two journals**: a market research journal and a personal, behavioral, journal. These can be combined, but I've found it useful to understand that I'm shining the

spotlight of my focused attention alternately on the market and on myself. This helps to separate out what is market behavior from errors that I may make as a trader. To me, this is an important part of understanding who you are as a trader.

- Think about the format of the journal. I'm convinced that paper and pencil engage a different part of the brain, and writing things by hand helps us to learn differently. Most of us don't do a lot of writing by hand today, so sitting down with paper, feeling the rhythm of your body as you write, pacing your thoughts to match that rhythm, and focusing your attention on the smooth glide of ink onto paper—knowing that your abstract thoughts are taking form in the outside world—that's powerful magic. However, it's not so easy to go back through five years of trading journals to understand some market tendency if those journals are a Hemingway-esque pile of Moleskine notebooks bound with a string in the corner of a closet. Using a database program or even a searchable word processor document makes for much easier review. My personal answer is to do a lot of stuff on paper, and to separate out "research" from journaling as a separate process. Research is done in Python or Stata or Excel, but I want to hold my journal in my hands. Different strokes for different folks, and there's no right or wrong, here.

These are some points that will get you started on this very important practice

What Do You Believe?

I want to share an important exercise with you. The journey along the path to trading mastery can be difficult because it requires conflicting skills—on one hand, you must rule certain aspects of your behavior with iron discipline and must also begin managing your thoughts and belief systems. On the other hand, learning to trade requires patience and gentleness. You can't force much of what will happen, as some of the changes and adaptations take time—it's a growth process (though we'd like to encourage that growth to be as quick as possible.) This exercise has the potential to give you the power to make sweeping changes in many areas of your life, and maybe to help you a few steps along the path to mastery.

Many authors have pointed out that we don't trade the market, we trade our beliefs about the market, or another way to think of it is that we don't truly interact with the actual market, we face our beliefs, both enabling and limiting, about the market. This is true of many things beyond the market. (For instance, how much miscommunication is happens because people are not really listening to each other? Because they are paying more attention to their own beliefs and preconceptions about what that other person is saying, rather than listening?) Most people careen through life, bouncing from one experience to the other, without really digging into the beliefs and motivations that drive them. Socrates put it in black and white: "the unexamined life is not worth living", yet I wonder if so many of the distractions of day-to-day life are designed to help us avoid that examination—to help us avoid the hard questions.

Today's exercise is about those hard questions. I would like you to block out a full hour's time. Turn off the phone and computer, no texting, no television, maybe put on some background music. Sit down with some blank paper and your favorite beverage of choice, and start to list your beliefs. I would suggest focusing on three areas: your beliefs about the market, your beliefs about the process of trading, and your beliefs about yourself. If you want to go a step further, maybe you can also work on a list of beliefs about the universe and reality itself, but realize that any of these lists is probably enough material to write a substantial book. Do the first part of this exercise with no judgment, simply listing beliefs as fast as you can think of them. List both empowering and limiting (you may choose to think of them as good and bad, but those aren't the best labels) beliefs, and just keep going until no more come.

After you've done this, return to the exercise over the next few days and add things you've missed. You should have several pieces of paper filled with what is probably a jumbled list, and then the second part of the exercise begins: organize and clean those lists. Notice the difference here: the first part of the exercise was stream of consciousness with as little judgment as possible (brainstorming), and now you switch gears to an editor's mindset. There are other ways to think about this division: unstructured / structured, creative / reductive, intuitive / rational, subconscious / conscious, etc.

You will find some of your beliefs overlap, some can be edited, some can be discarded, and some probably were in the wrong list. Clean those lists, and you will end up with a set of beliefs that give you some deep insight into your heart and mind. Incidentally, many of the most effective trading practices work to integrate different types of analysis or different ways of "being", and this little exercise can help you experiment with balancing those sometimes conflicting and contradictory approaches.

The process of trading can be very stressful, and I think many people would find great benefit in working with a mental health professional at different points along the way. This little exercise, however, encourages you to be your own therapist, to do your own work. You can next begin the process of transforming some of those limiting beliefs, or learning how to operate within the belief structure you have. It's difficult to just "change what you believe", but most people are blissfully unaware of the power of their beliefs to influence their actions and their results.

So, once again, I encourage you to find a few quiet moments, shut out the outside world, turn inward, look deeply with, and open yourself to understanding and growth. Why not take those first steps today?

On Quantitative Techniques

Quantitative Analysis: What and Why

I think most traders and investors understand that we live in a world in which markets are becoming ever more competitive. To make money in those markets, you must have an edge, and you must truly understand your edge. But the question remains: where and how do you find an edge and how can be you sure you understand it? I want to share a little bit of my own experience in this regard, and give you some ideas for doing your own work.

At the beginning, I think it's important to understand the questions we are asking. No matter what your trading/investment methodology is, you are assuming that something is more likely to happen than something else, based on whatever tools you are using. Think about that a minute, because some people are confused on this point. Whatever you do to decide when to get in and out of markets, you are doing so because you think one outcome is more likely than another. If we don't have this understanding, then we can easily fall into a mindset that says, "x must happen", "x will happen", or "x has to happen." That way of thinking is dangerous; at best, x is a little bit more likely to happen. So, how do we know that is true?

Quantitative analysis and quantitative tools can seem to be intimidating, but, at their core, they are very simple—all we're doing is looking at a bunch of things that happened in the market, defining some conditions, and seeing if those conditions have been tied to certain outcomes. We then make a (hopefully small) leap and assume, if we've done our work right, that seeing these conditions in the future will make certain outcomes more likely. Here are some concrete examples of statements we can test. Notice that they each include a condition or set of conditions, and an outcome: Stocks with good earnings stability are likely to go up. Stocks making 52-week highs are likely to go up. After a decline in price, if volatility contracts, stocks are more likely to go down. After making new 20-day highs, a commodity is more likely to continue to go higher. (By the way, some of those statements might be true, and some might be false. They are simply examples.)

How do we answer those questions? Well, there are some semi-sophisticated techniques that you may have encountered in a math class a long time ago like linear regression or principal component analysis. These tools do have their place, but we don't need them for much of work. We can do some useful analysis with these steps:

- Get a bunch of market data together. We need to make some decisions about what timeframe (daily, weekly, 1 minute?), what markets, what time span (recent? 5 years? 50 years?) we want to cover. This stage of getting and managing our data is harder than you might think because we have some thorny issues like dividends and splits for stocks and rolls for futures to consider. In addition, nearly all data sources have some errors, so we're going to need to spend (too much of our) time cleaning and wrangling this data.
- Define a set of conditions. These conditions can include price patterns, other technical factors, tools calculated from price inputs (e.g., MACD), fundamental factors, changes in fundamental factors, economic data, macro factors, sentiment data, etc. The only serious caveat here is that these conditions need to be defined precisely because we are going to test them over hundreds or thousands of occurrences.
- Look for every time the condition occurred in every market we are analyzing.
- See what happened following every occurrence of the conditions.
- A useful construct is to frame the question so it's binary: either one thing happens or another.

We can look at magnitude of effects and variability, but, often, this simple binary "counting" approach leads to good insights.

- Compare what happens after the conditions to all other market data. What we're looking for here is some evidence that our condition set has the power to influence markets.

That's really it, and it's not so intimidating: define a condition; test it, and then look at the results. Whether you're working with pencil and paper, a spreadsheet, or working within a programming language, this technique of asking questions and seeing what the data says will help you understand the market better and find opportunities for profitable trading.

How Do You Know If You Have a Trading Edge?

In a recent blog post, I made the statement (borrowed from Jack Schwager), that you must have an edge to be successful in the marketplace, and, if you don't know what your edge is, you don't have one. This, of course, prompted the logical question from a few readers: "how do I know if I have an edge?"

Before I answer, I need to start with a disclaimer: There are a lot of ways to make money in the marketplace. I'll try to be as inclusive as possible in this answer, but just realize that everything here will be somewhat biased from my own perspective as a primarily technical trader who uses hybrid systematic and discretionary techniques. I'll point out some of the places where I'm reasonably sure an edge does not exist, but, undoubtedly, there are things that I'm missing here, too.

Your edge must be realistic. There are many arcane and silly approaches to the market. Sadly, it's not easy to avoid this stuff because it is everywhere. In fact, some certification programs focus on a lot of the this kind of stuff, so we have an army of technicians with letters after their names who talk about, say, the 161.8% Fibonacci extension, or argue over wave counts. Prices in financial markets are driven by buying and selling decisions people make. I've been down the "mysteries of the Universe/probing the Mind of God" rabbit hole myself, earlier in my trading career. If your edge depends on woo-woo and magical thinking, you're probably in trouble before you begin.

Also, being realistic means you must **understand that trading returns are uncertain**; you'll have rich periods and lean periods. Your trading account is not going to be an ATM, and your edge may work for a while and then stop working. It's not uncommon to see a trader make quite a lot of money, and then to enter a period where he cannot make money at all as market conditions change. Even if your edge is solid and stable, it will only be so within the bounds of probability, and those margins can be pretty fuzzy, indeed.

You have to commit to the work and commit to continually evolving as a trader. You must commit to the process.

Your edge must fit your timeframe. Do fundamentals matter? Do short term movements, say on a 5 minute chart matter? How about relationships between prices in different markets? The answer, of course, is yes and no, depending on what kind of trader you are. If you are a short-term trader, focusing on fundamentals probably doesn't make sense. If you're a long term trader, you need to figure out how to filter out the noise. Your edge must respect factors that are relevant to your timeframe.

You probably should be able to verify your edge statistically. This is a good news/bad news situation: you must have some basic knowledge of probability and statistics to tell if you have an edge. There's no way (that I know of) around that, but the good news is that the math is pretty simple. Even someone who is "mathematically challenged" can acquire the skills needed in far less than a year's time, with a little work and focus.

What you're looking for is an understanding of the concepts behind statistical significance, but also some common sense, real-world application. Imagine I shuffle a deck of cards and deal them to you, and you find three red cards in a row. How surprising is that? What if the next ten cards are also red? How surprising is this now? Would you begin to suspect something about the deck? If I assure you the deck is fair and was shuffled (and you know I'm not lying), what are the odds the next card is black? You should be able to do math like that quickly and easily, or at least have some solid intuition about the answers.

As for backtesting, I think there's a place for it, and it's a topic we cover in some depth in this course. There are also limitations, and you need to understand those, as well. The best way to verify your edge is to clearly define your rules, test them, and then out of sample or forward test them before committing real capital and risk. I could list a thousand bad ways to think you have an edge: relying on the authority of a guru, finding a simple pattern and not testing it, etc., but most of those ways would fail at this step. If you can't codify and test your edge, it's very hard to understand it. (Note that this applies to fundamental approaches as well.)

Your edge must fit you. We're all built a bit differently. Some of us have widely varying attitudes toward risk, patience, emotional control, and many other aspects of our personality. I think there are many ways that most traders could trade successfully, but there are also many ways that just will not work. For instance, can you sit through 40% drawdowns that might last 2 years if you knew, with a high degree of certainty, that you'd make money over the long haul? If not, then you shouldn't be a long-term trend follower. Can you devote every second of every day to focusing on the market? If not, you can't daytrade. Are you prepared for a 3-5 year learning curve, and do you have the capital (mental and financial) to sustain your learning through that time period? If not, then you probably can't trade at all.

Good things happen when a trader, who is at the right stage of maturity, finds a system that fits him like a glove. So many of the struggles and problems he has faced will resolve themselves, seemingly effortlessly, but, of course, it's the years of work to get here that make it all happen.

It's hard to have the confidence to execute without having a high degree of certainty that your edge is real—in fact, you *shouldn't* have that confidence! Confidence in the wrong thing is a sure way to financial ruin in the markets. Knowing your trading edge, understanding it, is a critical step in trading successfully.

How Do You Know When You're Wrong?

How can we have a bias and stay out of trouble? One simple rule will solve most of your problems: **if you have a bias on a market, it must be based on something you can *see*.** At the risk of repeating myself, let me say that a few different ways, just to be sure it's clear.

If you have a bias on a market, check yourself for emotional reactions or commitments. Particularly, once you've made a public statement (even a simple tweet or post in a trading room, for developing traders), it is only human to shift your attention to defending that statement. This will get you in trouble. I think many trading problems can be solved with a small adjustment to mindset: *as soon as you are in a trade, begin to shift your focus to finding reasons the trade is wrong.* This is unnatural, to say the least. In everyday life, who argues like that? Who makes a point, and then immediately starts looking for reasons that whatever they just said is wrong? This, however, is a very helpful perspective for the trader because too many traders ignore evidence that they are wrong (even their stops being hit, and it can't get much clearer than that), and hold on to losing trades long past the point they should've exited. Many trading accounts have been destroyed by this practice, and many traders have left the field for some other endeavor simply because they couldn't exit when they were wrong.

A logical extension of that idea is that **a bias is only meaningful if you can clearly state what would disprove or contradict it**. For instance, if I'm short because of a higher timeframe bias on a market, what should not happen? Well, the market should not "go up", but that needs to be better defined—reasonable levels on that higher timeframe should not be broken, but I probably can't use them as stops because then I am trading that higher timeframe.

We also can use price action on the trading timeframe to get clues that our bias is right or wrong. The trading timeframe will trend both up and down within the higher timeframe bias, but we should not see many consolidation patterns resolve easily to the upside, and we should not see too many large standard deviation spikes to the upside. If we do, and if this continues for some time, it's evidence of underlying bullish conviction, which contradicts our bearish bias. The exact points where you "pull the plug", even before your stop is hit, on the bias might be up for debate, but the key is that you have conditions that would contradict your bias.

Compare this to common amateur biases: you hate a stock because you hate the food at a restaurant, you had a bad customer service experience, you think a competitor's product is best, you lost money in a stock so you are out for revenge, someone in a chat room told you it was a great stock, etc. Those types of biases are less meaningful than a disciplined bias that you can understand and monitor as the market unfolds.

There is another potential problem with a bias; it can blind you to trades that set up against your bias. A bias is often nothing more than a higher timeframe structure. If you are a daytrader, maybe you have a bearish bias based on the weekly or daily chart. If you are a position trader, maybe your bias comes from monthly charts, but you do not know your bias is right! It may well be wrong, and, if it is a "good" bias based on structures that have a statistical edge, then, if it fails, it may fail dramatically. Wouldn't it be nice to be able to participate on the right side of that failure, and maybe even make some money? You can't do this if you are emotionally attached to your bias, and if you will not trade against your bias, but a better mindset is something like "I hold a bearish bias, but everything I see is screaming long in my face. Maybe I should get long on my chosen timeframe, manage the trade properly, and see what happens." Easy to write, and easy to do once you've developed the right mindset, but it's usually impossible for the struggling, emotional trader to do this.

Check your biases. See if they are truly based on something you can see, if you can clearly state what would contradict those biases, and if you have the flexibility to trade against them when needed.

What's Wrong with Fibonacci?

I see you don't believe in Fibonacci ratios, but it seems every book and website says they are really important. I read your analysis on your website and it was convincing, but your stance is so different to the CTA program and all the other technical people out there. You've shared stories of your development as a trader and I was wondering Could you maybe talk a little bit more about how you came to the conclusions you have? Maybe seeing the path you walked will help me find more confidence to stand apart from the Fibonacci crowd. Could you tell me what's wrong with Fibonacci and even more how you came to believe this?

This is a tought-provoking question from a student, and one that deserves a good answer. First of all, I'm assuming if you are reading this you understand how Fibonacci is applied to trading. At a bare minimum, you should understand retracement ratios, extension ratios, and time ratios. If you are fuzzy on that, just google it and familiarize yourself with the common practice in today's technical analysis.

As a very short summary, there are two issues here to consider: First, many people believe that the so-called "Golden Ratio" (a number that begins with 1.618) describes many important relationships in the universe and human art. Second, people note that this ratio can be derived from the so-called "Fibonacci sequence" {0, 1, 1, 2, 3, 5, 8, ...} and further assume that the actual numbers have significance themselves—i.e., that the number 13, because it is a Fibonacci number, might have some special qualities that 12 and 14 do not. These ideas are extended to financial markets, usually in measuring length and magnitude of a market's movements in time and price, or in some relation.

I don't know when I first encountered Fibonacci numbers. I was interested and curious about various arcane schools of thought even as a kid, so I'm sure I had some encounters with the idea before I reached high school. My first serious investigation came in college as I was working on a degree in music composition. Part of the process of learning to write music is learning what people have done before you, and there are various schools of thought about how to understand and analyze a composer's work. I was working with a technique called Schenkerian Analysis that basically takes a piece of music and reduces it to a few key elements—a way to see the skeleton of the body or the frame of the building. In reading the works of other analysts, I found that people said the Golden Ratio was very important in the structure of many pieces. I probably looked at 100 examples, and then launched into deep analysis myself.

I'll spare you the gory details, but I spent many months on this project. At first, I was excited because I had unlocked some key to the mysteries of the universe. If I could understand the use of this ratio, then I could improve my own compositions. I could probably use the idea in the computer-generated compositions I was working on, and maybe could develop some alternate tuning systems that would take advantage of different ratios of resonances. What I discovered early on was that the Golden Ratio did not "work". Sometimes important things fell near the ratio, sometimes (quite rarely) exactly on, but often not very close at all. There were also inexplicable things, such as very important features coming at some other ratios, while some very minor detail hit a precise Fibonacci ratio—and "pro-Fibonacci" people would point out how the ratio worked in this case. I scratched my head; maybe there was something I didn't understand, but it seemed like hanging a work of art on a wall and then marveling over some detail of how the floor tiles hit the wall—probably simply due to chance, and almost certainly not significant.

I then encountered the "measurement issue": when I talked to people who were supposed to be experts, they were extremely evasive. I remember a conversation with someone who had written an influential book. When I explained that I could not make the ratio work in a specific Beethoven piano sonata, he told me that was because I needed to measure ratios in space on the page; in other words, inches. This, of course, is nonsense. Our perception of music is ordered in time, not physical space. Physical space on a page is arbitrary; I found examples of the same sonata in different editions that were 4 or 20 pages long, and things were spaced proportionally very differently in those different editions.

I discovered something that I would later encounter in trading: people would use whatever measurement system they needed to make the theory fit the facts. Once I looked at the problem objectively, I saw that "big things" tended to happen later in a piece of music rather than earlier, usually after the middle and somewhere a bit before the end. This, of course, is a dramatic pattern that makes sense in a book, a play, a film, or pretty much any other structure—it's just common sense. But the idea that 61.8% was some magical ratio in music—that just didn't hold water.

When I started digging into relationships between ratios and musical notes, that didn't really "work" either. So, after many months of intensive work, I decided that Fibonacci ratios in music were overhyped and simply didn't represent reality in any meaningful way. Did it make more sense that composers (who, in most cases, were writing music for a living because it was their job) would follow a formula of "big thing happening somewhere after the middle and near the end", adapting it to the flow of whatever piece they were writing, or that someone was staying awake at night trying to hide a secret code of the universe somewhere in between the notes?

Fast forward a few years to where I was learning to trade. I'd had some successes and failures, and realized that I was going to have to study very hard to make this work. I tracked down a bunch of original source material from legends like Schabacker, Gann, and Elliott, as well as a big selection of the modern books written on the subject. In the beginning, I quickly forgot the Fibonacci lessons I learned in music, and was awed by the power of the ratios in financial markets. I read book after book talking about the different ratios and how they described moves, where to put stops, where to put targets, when to predict turns—I saw it worked often. Of course, there were cases where it did not work, but there was also this strong appeal to mysticism in much of the writing: these are "sacred ratios" upon which the "foundation of the universe rests". How could I ignore such portentous information when I was entering a trade on a currency chart?

A few things eventually shook my belief in the concept, best told in bullet points:

- You couldn't be sure which level would work, but *some* level always worked after the fact. I began to realize that levels would be violated in live trades; I had dutifully placed my stop a few ticks beyond, but then another level clearly held at the end of the day. There was no way, and no way in the literature, to predict which level would hold. Once I learned about the idea of confluence, I realized that we were drawing so many levels on charts that it might just be luck that they seemed to work.
- I began to understand randomness. I had a weird formal education. My quantitative training in undergrad was sorely lacking. While I would not recommend this to anyone, it did leave me with a curious hole to fill: I had to re-think the problem of randomness from the ground up, as I did not have a good understanding of things like confidence intervals and significance tests. From practical trading, I saw that there was a lot of noise in data, but I wasn't sure how to tease it out. As I was getting a better education, I came up with a stop-gap; I generated many charts

of random market data according to various techniques and spent a lot of time looking at them. If I had a better formal education I probably would have thought this was a waste of time, but I experienced so many cognitive errors as I did this. It's one thing to know them academically, but when you see how easily your perception is swayed and how easily you find patterns in random data, you start to think deeply. Does it invalidate the idea of patterns in real market data? Of course not, but it certainly challenges the claims of "just look at a chart! You can see it works! How can you question it? Look at these examples..." Armed with that firsthand experience (and, again that word is critical—it was experiential, not academic knowledge) I became very critical of examples and claims.

- I did some background work on the people making claims for the tools. I won't dwell on this because I don't think it's constructive, but suffice it to say that someone could make a good career out of debunking Fibonacci experts, just like Houdini did with mediums in his day. I realized that we have a tendency to put some aura of greatness around past gurus, who, in many cases, were part-time traders who had poor access to data and no analytical tools. Alexander Elder, in his excellent book tells of interviewing the great W.D. Gann's grandson, and that his grandson said there was no fortune and no profits from his trading in the stock market. When I dug into the current gurus on the internet, I discovered that many trades were done at improbable prices ("How do you always get filled on the bid every time?"), and, years later, one of the big gurus from the early 2000's told me that all her trading, scalping NQ futures, was on a simulator and she never had a live trading account. Sadly, I had seen hundreds of people try to replicate her methods, with no success. I could go on and on. I wasn't trying to tear down any idols; rather, I was desperately searching for some evidence that someone was really applying these tools to make money.
- The last straw was adjusted price charts. This might seem odd to newer traders, but when you look at past price charts, those prices may or may not represent prices at which the asset actually traded. Much of the discipline of technical analysis rests on the idea that people have a memory around specific prices. While this may or may not be true, there are different ways that historical charts must be adjusted. With futures, there are at least three common methods (difference, ratio, or unadjusted), and the question of when to roll to new contracts. With stocks, there are issues of dividends, splits, spinoffs, and other corporate actions that may or may not be accounted for on the price charts. You still see this today: ask someone showing a Fibonacci extension on a crude oil chart how their chart is back-adjusted. How many days open interest or volume to roll? How does your chart compare to spot prices? The answer I got from asking many people was either confusion or "it doesn't matter." (I have seen this dismissal over the years from many people who use levels in various capacities. I remember explaining to a stock trader who had traded from more than 20 years why SPY prices were so different today from yesterday—in 20 years of using "levels" he had never accounted for dividends.) Simple logic here: if I tell you I have some powerful pills, but it doesn't matter which pills you take, how much you take—take 1 or 20, or when you take them, is it more likely that it magical medicine or that it does nothing at all?
- The whole thing died, for me, when I realized that it rested on vague appeals to authority. I knew this all along, but once I had been around the block a few times, it was even more obvious. The

> Emperor had no clothes. No one will ever provide you with a quantitative proof of Fibonacci levels working. (I've made this challenge many times, and I will renew it here. Show me something good and I will publish it and admit I'm wrong. Show me something possibly flawed but still substantial, and I'll publish it for discussion. It's possible my thinking on this subject is wrong, and I would love to expand my thinking in another direction. Despite me having said this hundreds of times, I have yet to receive a single shred of actual work done on these ratios.) The last apology for ratios I read was a few weeks ago when someone said that you could just look at charts and see they worked and a lot of his friends, who were medical doctors, said Fibonacci ratios were really important in the body and in art.

So, that's my journey, and that's why I place no emphasis at all on Fibonacci levels. Here's the real key: you do not need them. That's the point. It's not that I'm trying to tear down anything or simply show you that something doesn't work; I'm showing you that this is probably confusing baggage and noise, and does not add any real power to your analysis. Why not focus your attention on things that do work?

On Pullbacks

How to Trade Pullbacks

Some of my readers may have questions as to whether it is possible to trade profitably based on simple patterns, given that so much modern quantitative trading focuses on volatility, spread relationships between two or more markets, and other types of trading that move us away from simple, directional trading. The answer to that is a qualified 'yes': patterns are heuristics, shortcuts, if you will. A trader who can read and analyze patterns can quickly drill down to the essential elements of market structure. Opportunity exists in markets when buying and selling pressure is not balanced, and patterns can help us understand this critical balance very quickly.

Though many of these patterns have a slight edge on their own, I think far better results come with experience and when the trader learns to read the action in the market; we shift from a "take every pullback" to a "find the best pullback" mindset. Traditional technical analysis often focuses on visual symmetry, how the pattern looks on a chart, to find the best trades, and I would suggest that this might not be right. The best patterns are often ugly, but they fall in beautiful spots in the market structure.

How to trade pullbacks

The key to trading pullbacks is that you are trading the fluctuations in a trending market. For this to work, it's obvious that the market must be both trending and fluctuating. It is normal for trending markets to show pullbacks, but some very strong trends do not. Don't try to force trades in this environment—you don't have to be in any move or any trend; wait for the best trades. What might not be so obvious, at first, is that trading a pullback is a prediction that the market will continue to trend. I might suggest that this is slightly different from identifying a trending market.

From a simple perspective, trading pullbacks boil down to:

- Wait for a trending market to make a strong move.
- Look to enter the market when it comes back to some sort of "average" price.

Digging deeper

Both of these elements require a little more information, to be done well. First, you must be able to read market structure and understand trends. It's not enough to say "this market starts at the lower left of the chart and ends at the upper right". That is enough to be able to identify high-level trends, but, remember, you are looking for a market that will likely continue to trend. Being able to juggle elements like length of swing, lower timeframe momentum, exhaustion/strength will help, but, in my experience, these are skills that develop naturally from trading pullbacks.

Identifying a market that has made a strong move can be done with the help of reasonably calibrated bands. There is a wide range of parameters and settings, but I'd suggest that whatever bands you use should contain roughly 80% – 90% of the price action. Consider Bollinger bands: if you set them 0.5 standard deviations, you are probably too close, and 5.0 standard deviations is probably too far. The first case will be hit constantly on trivial movements, while the last will only be hit with the most extreme exhaustion moves. But in the middle there is a wide range of values that can be useful. Play with moving average length and band width, settle on settings you will use, and don't change them. The bands provide structure that will be critical as you develop your intuitive sense of market structure.

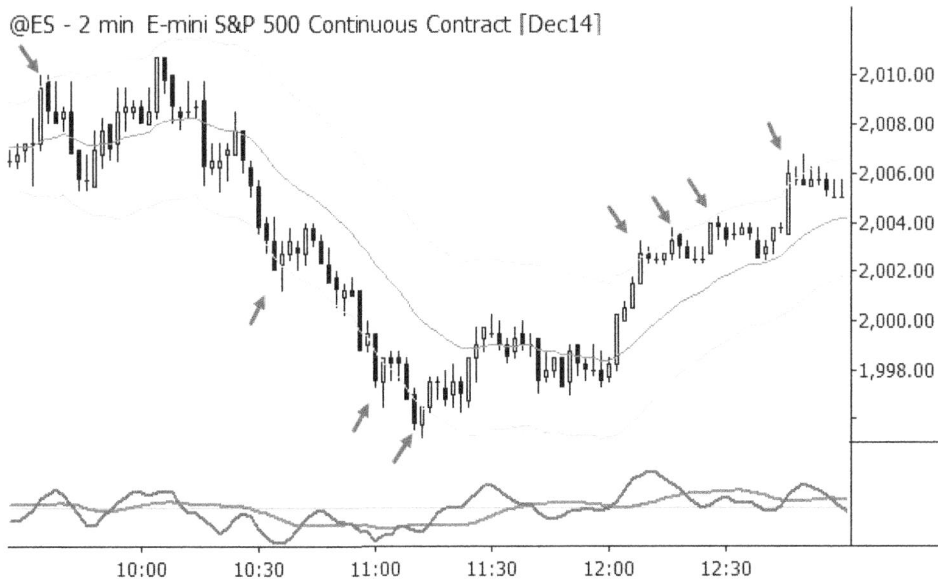

The chart above shows points where 2 minute (we focus a lot of attention on higher timeframes, so let's look at intraday data a bit) bars touch the Keltner channels. Consider this as setting up a trigger condition, and then we look to enter somewhere "around a middle." Now, I've written at great length about how moving averages don't work as support or resistance, so am I telling you to buy and sell at a moving average? No, the average price is not important, but the *concept* of trading near the average is what matters.

If you test this, you will find an edge whether you buy in front of or through the average, and you will also find an edge with many different lengths of moving averages. There is no magic to the average, but perhaps there is magic in a disciplined, consistent approach to trade entry. Look at the following chart, which shows points where we might have executed (long or short) near the average following the setup condition in the first chart.

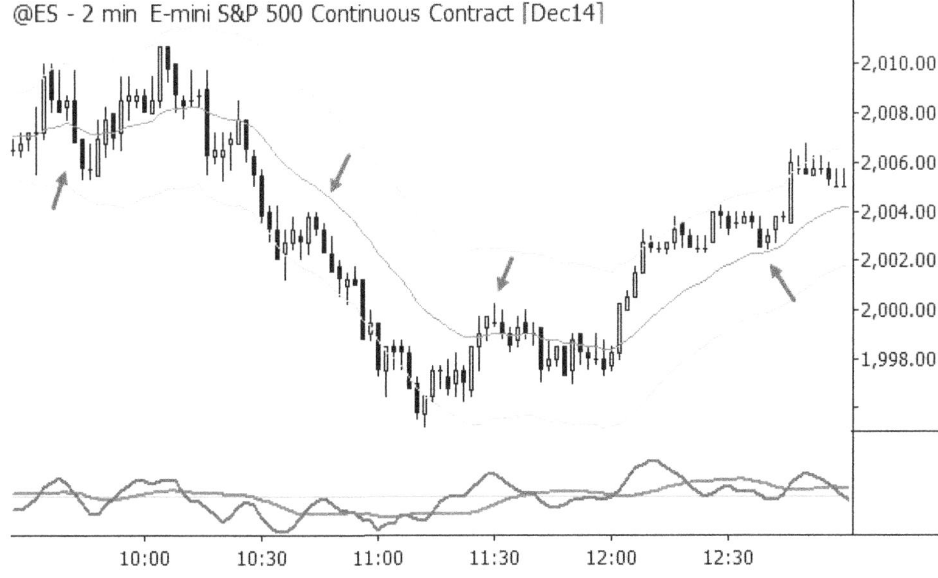

Further refinements for entries

The most important thing to remember that you are looking for a market that you believe will continue to trend, for at least one more trend leg, so it makes sense to avoid patterns that point to end of trends. The most important of these is exhaustion. Avoid buying and selling after potentially climactic moves, which can be identified on the chart as large range with trend bars that often extend far beyond the edge. I believe that identifying true with-trend strength (or weakness, for shorts) and being able to discern it from exhaustion is perhaps *the* key technical skill of with-trend trading. No one talks about it very much, and it can't be done perfectly, but, with some work and hard study, you can learn to dodge the most obvious bullets. (Note that this will also take you into sentiment analysis and understanding crowd behavior.)

The actual entry trigger deserves a little bit of attention too. I've found a useful refinement is to use a lower timeframe breakout as an entry, and this can be as simple as buying a breakout of the previous bar's high. You can also trade around previous lower timeframe pivots (for instance, a failure test), and here is where some of the most powerful multiple timeframe confluences come into play. Other traders will scale into pullbacks, but this requires a level of discipline that can be challenging for newer traders. Because you're entering a market that, by definition, is moving against you, you will be "biggest when wrongest", and this can be a problem if stops are not respected. Now, about those stops...

Stop location

Mark Fisher used to constantly remind traders he worked with and trained that the most important thing is knowing where you're getting out if you're wrong. Know this, on every trade, and respect that point, and you're already far ahead of the game. The problem with pullbacks is that you are often entering a market that is not yet moving in the direction you want, so some degree of error (or play) is required. We can be precise, but there are limits. Without belaboring the point, you will learn where to set stops, and they should go somewhere beyond the previous extreme. As a starting point, 2-3 ATRs beyond the entry is a good, very rough guideline.

Trade management

I've found it helpful to take first profits when my profit is equal to my initial risk on the trade, and then to scale out of the remainder. This doesn't work for those traders who hope to hit homeruns, but it certainly drives toward consistency. There are other ways, but the key is to define your trading style and manage accordingly. I'm a swing trader, usually playing for one clean swing in the market. As such, I need to be proactive about taking risk off the table, but different styles will require different techniques.

Last, it is sometimes possible to use pullbacks in trending markets to build substantial positions. One idea that might be useful is to get in a pullback, take partial profits and hold the rest for a swing, and then get into a second trade if another pullback sets up in the same direction. Manage that new trade in the same way; you are always taking partial profits and moving stops so that you never have on more than a single trade's risk. This is a smart and relatively safe way to "pyramid" into a trend move. Do remember that sometimes "stuff happens" and you may see a very large gap in a market, your stops may get slipped, and you may have a much larger than expected loss. Always respect risk, first and foremost.

Chapter 5

Module 5–The Anti

This Module introduces a new trading pattern: the Anti. Though there are several ways to define this trade, probably the clearest is to see it as the first pullback after a potential trend change, or sometimes within a trading range. At any rate, it is a pullback that must be set up by strong momentum, just like any other pullback; the structural considerations are different, but the actual pattern is simply a pullback.

Next, in the Course videos, we took a deep look at using an event study methodology to consider action around moving averages, and then considered quantitative support for the two forces models. All of this work moves us toward potential opportunities in the market.

We also spent some time on cognitive biases; this is the only psychology-focused chapter in the course before Module 9, which is entirely dedicated to the topic. The work on cognitive biases is especially relevant to this module's investigation of support and resistance and action around those levels.

Once again, this Module seems to be light in page count, the work required of you is considerable. In fact, the studies into action around support and resistance will lay a solid foundation for your understanding of price action and market structure.

Section 1: Anti Backtest

In the previous module, you worked on backtesting the pullback pattern. In this module, we will shift focus to the Anti. The Anti is simply a pullback that occurs after a potential trend change, signaled by strong momentum against the existing trend; contrast this with the classic pullback, which is often a counter-trend movement in an established trend.

Antis are more rare than standard pullbacks (which makes sense, given that they are a subset of pullbacks.) When you quantify this pattern, consider a few points:

- Does the pattern need to be set up by an established trend? If so, do you have guidelines for that trend and for reasons you might consider an Anti trade?
- What degree of countertrend momentum is needed to trigger an Anti? Will you use any indicatord?
- Where will you enter?
- Where will you place initial stops and targets?

Once you have answered these questions, begin a bar-by-bar backtest in the same style you did the pullback test. The objective of this study is twofold: first, to familiarize your eye with the patterns in the market and to get you used to looking for these patterns. Second, to get some sense of the edge that might be in this pattern and in your specific definition of the pattern.

Section 2: Support and Resistance Action Around Levels

Think of this exercise as exploration and training for your visual sense of charts. They question we are investigating is how do markets react around support and resistance? When a market comes down to a potential support level, the following outcomes are possible:

- The support will hold, with immediate price rejection
- The support will hold, without clear price rejection
- The support will fail, with some action around (above or below) the level
- The support will fail with no action, as if it were not even there

Obviously, other variations and combinations of these effects are possible. For instance, we might have a market that significantly penetrates the support, consolidates on the support, and then moves back up with strong momentum—price rejection has occurred, but it happened slowly. Use your judgement to figure out how you will label or define action around these levels.

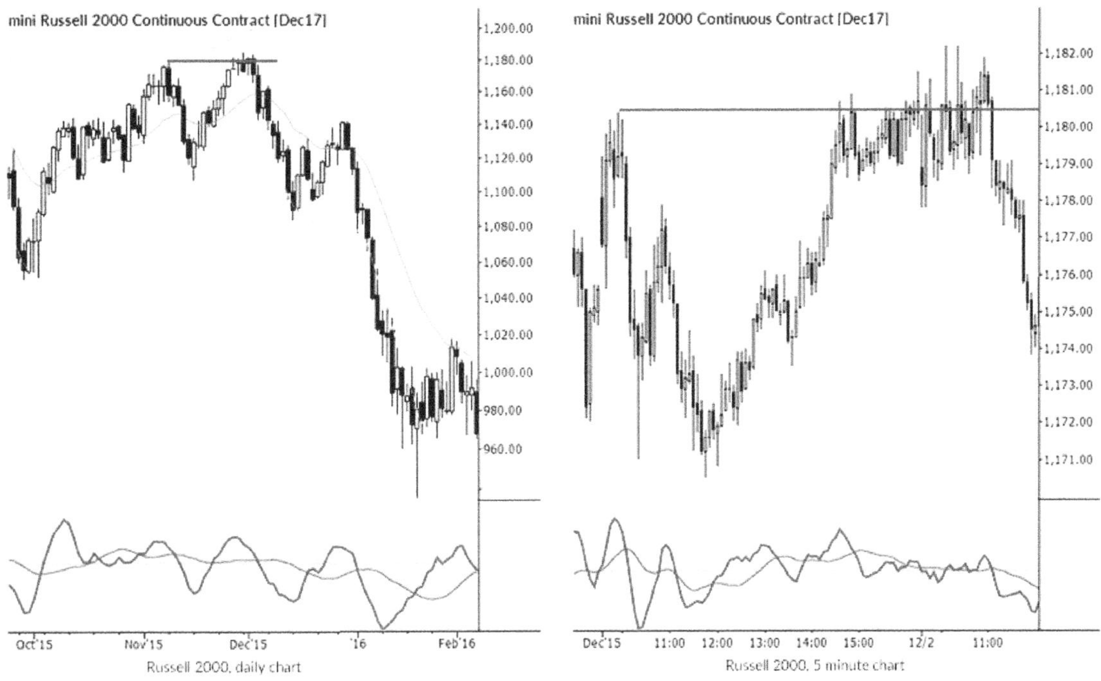

Russell 2000, daily chart

Russell 2000, 5 minute chart

Here is how you should do this exercise: Find examples where market action worked around support and resistance. You may simply find spots in the middle of the chart. (In other words, you do not have to go bar-by-bar for this analysis.) Another interesting idea is to find a market working with support and resistance, and then look at the same area on a lower timeframe, as the chart above shows.

Once you have identified an interesting support or resistance area, look at how the market acted around the area. Did it seem to be one precise price, or was it a large zone? Did the market touch it multiple times, or just once? Did anything happen (think chart stories) around the average? Did the range or volatility of the bars change? Overall, how would you characterize the action?

In the example chart, we see that the market engaged the area several times. It seemed to be a large zone, rather than a single, clear price level. There were significant penetrations beyond the level, and, realistically, we might have thought the level was failing in real time. In the end, the level did hold with price rejection of the level, but after a lot of time was spent and work was done at the level.

This is a deliberately subjective exercise. Make it your own, and take the time to look at many variations of these patterns in the market. If nothing else, you will likely come away from this exercise with a renewed respect for the volatility and random character of market action.

Section 3: Support & Resistance: Looking Deeper

Three exercises to further investigate the patterns of support and resistance

Exercise 1: Action around levels

Find support and resistance levels on charts. This instruction is deliberately broad; you can do this in many ways. One way might be to look for a market to make important pivot highs and lows, and then to see what happens when price re-engages those levels. Another possibility is to find an area in which support or resistance is working, and then zoom in, perhaps on lower timeframes, and look at the action closely.

Keep some kind of notes and records, but this is also a deliberately subjective project. It may be enough to characterize the level as working (holding) or failing (breaking). Many traders find it useful to take screenshots of the charts being investigated. Over time, this will build a library of patterns and variations of patterns around support and resistance.

Exercise 2: Random lines on charts

Of course, the concern with the previous exercise is that we may have been cultivating cognitive bias. Any line drawn on a chart will appear to be significant. It is impossible to stress this enough, so you need to see it yourself to fully appreciate this quirk of human perception.

Take a number (at least 20) charts and somehow draw random lines on those charts. There are many ways to do this, depending how certain you want to be that the lines are random. In many software packages, it is possible to mask the price bars, perhaps setting them to the color of the background of the chart. Another possibility might be to set a chart to a higher timeframe, draw some random lines on that chart, and then "zoom" in to lower timeframe.

Lines may be flat or sloping. Some of your lines, if they are truly random, will not engage prices, but your job is to look carefully every time price comes close to one of these lines. Imagine the line is significant (or that you believe it to be) and then investigate action from the same perspective you did the "real" levels in Exercise 1.

Once you have spent some time with this exercise, you will likely be suspicious of support and resistance in general, and especially of calculated levels. (Think of the so-called "pivot levels" such as S1, S2, R1, R2, ... Is it possible that these levels are no better than your random levels? That is the key question for anyone who would use levels in his work.)

Exercise 3: Statistical Analysis

This exercise is more difficult. Define levels somehow; it might be interesting to use a mixture of some calculated level (ratios, pivot levels, etc.) and levels derived from clearly visible chart points.

Move through the chart bar by bar, seeing what happens as price engages the level.

Make a serious effort to avoid "information leakage" from the future; be very careful of seeing future price data and to focus on information you would have had as the chart unfolded in real time.

Make "mock trades" at each level and record returns for each of several days after. This is a manual approach to the event study methodology. If you have programming skills, you might be able to code a system that could take a discretionary entry on a specific bar and then generate statistics such as those you saw in Module 5 of the course.

Section 4: Charting by Hand

This is still a valuable exercise, and this will be the last module that carries an explicit reminder to do hand charting. You should be thinking about how (and if) you wish to incorporate this practice into your ongoing trading, training, and market analysis. In the first module, we discussed the several ways you can do this exercise. The details are not important; it is far more important that you do it.

This should also not be a tremendous time suck—this is not a unique form of torture I have devised. A few minutes every day (but every day!) directed to drawing your charts, or a few minutes each hour if you are an intraday trader, will reward you with deep understanding of price action.

You may wish to leave this exercise, but come back to it whenenever you feel out of touch with the market, or when you've been away from trading for a period of time. There is something about the practice of writing down prices and/or charting by hand that has deep power to connect us to the flow of the market.

Section 5: Readings

From *The Art and Science of Technical Analysis: Market Structure, Price Action, and Trading Strategies* by Adam Grimes, Wiley, 2012:

170-173 (the anti)
327-336 (anti examples)
353-359 (cognitive biases)
409-424 (a deeper look at the MACD and moving averages)

On Doing Statistical Analysis

Some Important Lessons I've Learned

I thought I'd share a few thoughts today, kind of a "what I've learned in the past 10 years" post. This list was refined and crystallized by the process of writing the book, but this list was also a major reason why I wrote it in the first place. I saw so many people struggling to learn to trade that I wanted to try to put down the lessons and truths I had found in a concrete format. True, there is no one way to trade, and many different approaches can be successful in the market, so long as they are aligned with some fundamental truths. These are some of those fundamental and undeniable truths, as I have come to understand them over the course of my trading career:

Most of the time, markets are very close to efficient (in the academic sense of the word.) This means that most of the time, price movement is random and we have no reason, from a technical perspective, to be involved in those markets.

There are, however, repeatable patterns in prices. This is the good news; it means we can make money using technical tools to trade.

The biases and statistical edges provided by these patterns are very small. This is the bad news; it means that it is exceedingly difficult to make money trading. We must be able to identify those points where markets are something a little "less than random" and where there might be a statistical edge present, and then put on trades in very competitive markets.

Technical trading is nothing more than a statistical game. There are close parallels to gambling and other games of chance; a technical trader simply identifies the patterns where an edge might be present, takes the correct position at the correct time, and manages the risk in the trade. This is a very simplified summary of the trading process, but it is useful to see things from this perspective. This is the essence of trading: find the pattern, put on the trade, manage the risk, and take profits.

It is important to be utterly consistent in every aspect of our trading. Many markets have gotten harder (i.e. more efficient, more of the time) over the past decade and some things that once worked, no longer work. Iron discipline is a key component of successful trading. If you are not disciplined every time, every moment of your interaction with the market, you are not a disciplined trader.

It is possible to trade effectively as a purely systematic trader or as a discretionary trader, but the more discretion is involved the more the trader himself is a key part of the trading process. It can be very difficult to sort out performance issues that are caused by markets, by natural statistical fluctuations, by the trading system not working, or by the trader himself.

There is still a tremendous bias in many circles toward fundamental analysis and against technical analysis. The fundamentalists have a facile argument because it is easy to point to patterns on charts, say they are absurd, and point out that markets are actually driven by supply, demand and fundamental factors—the very elements that fundamental analysis deals with directly. However, many times the element of art involved in fundamental analysis is overlooked. How much does your valuation change if your discount rate is off by a percentage point? How dependent is your model on your assessment of some manager's CapEx decisions in year four? Do you really have a good sense of how the company's competitive position will evolve with the industry over the next decade? Does everyone else? There's a lot more "wiggle room" in fundamentals than most people realize.

One advantage of technical trading is that, done properly, it clearly identifies supply/demand imbalances from their effect on prices. This is a form of look-back analysis, but good technical tools force you to deal with the reality of what is happening right now. There is no equivocation, wishing, or emotional involvement in solid technical trading. The best risk management tools are technical, or are based on patterns in prices themselves.

Most people (and funds) who try to trade will not be successful, and I believe this is because most of them are simply trying to do things that do not work. Taking a good, hard look at your tools, methods, and approach can be scary, but there is no other way to find enduring success in the market.

Bad Stats Lead to Bad Decisions

More and more, we are bombarded with market statistics from every side. Anyone with a spreadsheet can tell you that such and such week has been up 9 times out of the past 7 years; stats are cheap. The problem is that many of those statistics are false or misleading and making market decisions based on those statistics can be hazardous to your financial health.

There have been a lot of statistics floating around about what happens after a weak first day of the month or quarter, claiming that a down first day gives a downward bias to the entire quarter (or month). First of all, let's look at the stats some "experts" are sharing. Using the S&P 500 cash index back to 1961, if the first day of the month is up (which happened 370 months), the entire month was up 64.9% of the time, for an average monthly gain of 1.29%. If that first day of the month was down (which only happened 287 times), the month only closed positive 51.2% of the time, and the average return for all of those months was -0.21%. Here are the results presented in table format:

	All	Day 1 Up	Day 1 Down
# of Months	657	370	287
Monthly Return	0.63%	1.29%	-0.21%
StDev	4.27%	4.09%	4.35%
% of time Up	59.1%	64.9%	51.6%
p =		0.015	0.006

These are strong numbers that seem to show a tremendous edge in the marketplace, but let's dig deeper. We should, first of all, be on guard because the effect is so strong—when we find something that appears to be a statistical homerun, we've probably made a mistake somewhere. Let's find that mistake.

The first step is to ask if the results make sense. I would argue, right out of the gate, that they do not. Why should such a strong effect exist? Perhaps we could make a case for some kind of monthly momentum—maybe managers tend to put money to work at the beginning of the month and that has some persistence through the entire month. Maybe there is another reasonable explanation. It is, at least, possible to make an argument, but we are already suspicious because there is no clear logic driving these results.

However, something interesting happens if we examine day two of the month; we find the same effect. No, not for day 1 and day 2 being a cumulative decline for the month (though we can do that test, too), but simply if day 2 is up, the month tends to be up. Also, day 3... and day 4.... In fact, no matter which day of the month we examine, we find if that day is up, the month tends to be up! If it is down, the entire month tends to be down.

So, now we have a problem. Can we make any possible argument to explain this? How do we feel about the argument of monthly momentum or managers putting money to work on, say, day 17 of the month? Obviously, this is now completely illogical, so we must look elsewhere for an explanation. Maybe we should turn our attention to the way we ran the test. Maybe there is a problem with the methodology.

As an aside, I once knew a trader who had a system that was based on a similar idea. He had done enough research to know that his system "worked", statistically speaking, no matter which day or days of the month (or quarter, or week, or even which hour of the intraday period) used as a trigger. Over the course of about a decade he had traded the system live, and had lost a significant amount of money—high seven figures on this particular system. You might ask why he kept going back to it, but the reason was (bad) statistics. Every way (except the right way) he looked at the system and twisted the inputs, the results were astoundingly strong, yet the system failed to produce in actual trading.

This is not an academic exercise; statistical mistakes are not abstract. For traders, statistics are life and death; statistics are the tool through which we understand how the market moves. Bad statistics lead to bad decisions, and bad decisions cost money.

Before we get to the methodological error, here are the "correct" statistics for the "first day of the month" effect:

	All	Day 1 Up	Day 1 Down
# of Months	657	370	287
Monthly Return	0.63%	0.49%	0.55%
StDev	4.27%	3.96%	4.49%
% of time Up	59.1%	57.8%	58.9%
p =		0.584	0.777

Based on these test results we can say we see no effect—that, whether the first day of the month (or, in fact, any particular day) is up or down has no significant effect on the overall direction of the month. There is no tradable edge here, and, unless our test has missed something ((always a possibility—stay humble!)) there is simply nothing here worth thinking about.

There is a simple solution to mistakes like this, and I'll share it with you later on. For now, spend some time thinking about where the error might be in the method, why it matters, and why it might be hard to catch. Here's a hint: what is a monthly return?

From here on out, I hope to accomplish two things:

- To understand how easily "future information" can contaminate statistical studies, and how even a subtle bias can introduce serious distortions.
- To suggest one simple condition—asking yourself if the statistic could possibly have been *executed* in the market as a trade—can protect us from all errors like this.

The specific error around the first day of the month effect is a common mistake. I've certainly made it myself in tests and analysis enough times to know that it is something always worth checking for, and I've seen it in stats people use for many technical factors like moving average crosses, seasonality, trend indicators, buying/selling at 52 week highs, the January effect, and many others.

Day of the week effect?

Let's re-cast the day of the month effect as the "day of the week effect". Here are (erroneous) stats that show that the return for each day of the week (1 = Monday, 2 = Tuesday, etc.) is a strong influence on the weekly return. For instance, if Wednesday is down, there is a high probability the entire week is down. For comparison, looking first at all weeks (2,856) in the S&P 500 cash index, going back to 1962, the average weekly return was 0.15% with a standard deviation of 2.14%, and 56.1% of all weeks were positive.

Here are statistics for the weekly returns, based on whether any Day of the Week (left column) was up or down for the week. We seem to find a very strong effect, and, again, that's our first warning that something is amiss:

Day of Week	If Day Is Up				If Day Is Down			
	Mean	StDev	% Up	p =	Mean	StDev	% Up	p =
1	0.82%	1.96%	70.1%	0.0000	-0.50%	2.10%	42.5%	0.0000
2	0.79%	1.99%	71.0%	0.0000	-0.56%	2.08%	39.6%	0.0000
3	0.80%	1.90%	70.7%	0.0000	-0.68%	2.15%	37.4%	0.0000
4	0.80%	1.90%	70.6%	0.0000	-0.62%	2.16%	38.8%	0.0000
5	0.85%	1.96%	70.3%	0.0000	-0.76%	2.17%	37.5%	0.0000

Market data is abstract. Think of physical "things" to simplify problems.

To find the mistake, it helps to think of each week as a physical card. On one side of the card, there are five boxes, each of which has a positive or negative number (the daily return). Flip the card over, and you will find a single number that is the return for the week; though not strictly correct, let's just simplify slightly and say the weekly return is all the daily returns added together. You can't add percentage returns (you must compound them), but that's a complication we don't need for this example.

So, put the 2,856 cards in a bag and randomly draw one out. You will find each of the five boxes is more or less just as likely to have a positive or negative number (i.e., each day is just about as likely to be up as down). If you did this a lot, you'd find that the numbers are slightly more likely to be positive than negative—about 52.7% of the days are up—but you would have to look at a lot of cards to see that. At first glance, it just looks like we have a mix of positive and negative days in each small box.

For this exercise, let's focus on box 1, which is the return for the first trading day of the week. Imagine pulling a few cards out, looking at that day, and finding, just like any of the boxes, some are up and some are down. Ok, now put all the cards back in the bag; things are about to get interesting.

Now, dump all the 2,856 cards out on the floor, and separate them into two piles based on one factor: if that day 1 is positive put it in the pile on your left, and if day 1 is negative, put it in the pile on your right. Now, do you see what has happened here? Your selection process has guaranteed that at least one of the days will be positive for the week for every card in the left-hand pile, and there's the mistake.

If you now turn the cards over and average the weekly number for every card in each pile. you'll discover that the pile on your left has a lot more weeks that were positive, and the pile on your right has most weeks in the red. When one out of five days is guaranteed to be positive, the week will overwhelmingly be biased to be positive. While this might not seem that this error would create a large bias in the test, it does. Market data is random enough that even a very light "thumb on the scale" is enough to seriously distort the results.

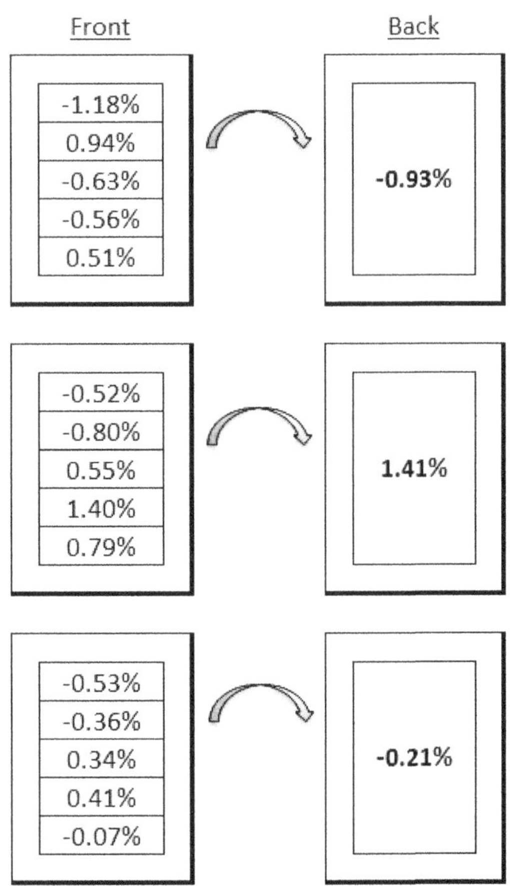

One test can catch many errors

How do we avoid errors like this? Well, the standard I apply to any test is simple: Always ask how could you trade the given effect. In this case, we are looking at weekly returns, which means buying or selling on a Friday and exiting the following Friday (except in shortened weeks); this is the only way we can capture the weekly return as traders. However, we don't know if we should have bought or sold on Friday until we see what the following Monday does! This trade would have been impossible to execute, so the statistic is suspect.

In this case, a better test, and one that would be tradable, would be to define the week in one of two ways: either from the close of the day being examined to the next Friday, or maybe doing a rolling week, always 5 trading days out. In the case of the original test, the month should be defined from the close of the day being examined to the end of the month, and a test like this will find no bias. If you're curious, here is a comparison of the two methods for the first day of the week effect:

	If Day Is Up				If Day Is Down				
	Mean	StDev	% Up	p =	Mean	StDev	% Up	p =	
Friday-Friday	0.82%	1.96%	70.1%	0.0000	-0.50%	2.10%	42.5%	0.0000	← Needs a time machine
Monday-Friday	**0.11%**	**1.80%**	**56.5%**	**0.5853**	**0.27%**	**2.07%**	**57.6%**	**0.0606**	← Could trade

This is a sneaky error, and it's one I've made many times myself. Though the test will work—thinking about whether the tendency was tradable on the timeline—it takes some careful thought as mistakes are not always apparent at first glance. Be ruthless in examining the information you use and be even more vigilant with your own thinking. Bad statistics lead to biases and poor decisions.

On Moving Averages

Death Cross: Omen or Not?

One of the recurring themes in my work is that most of the technical tools most people use do not show an actual edge in the market—in other words, as hard is it may be to say, most things most people do simply do not work. In particular, there are a few technical conditions we hear discussed in the media frequently; I can think of four offhand: any market is "finding support" at its X-day moving average, the ominous-sounding "Hindenburg Omen", and the "Death Cross" and "Golden Cross". What all of these have in common is that they are easy to explain, easy to show visually, and most of them have catchy names. Unfortunately, they are all meaningless—they have, at best, questionable statistical significance.

The Russell 2000 is nearing a potential "Death Cross", as reported yesterday in the media:

> *The Russell 2000, which consists of small-cap stocks, is approaching a key technical level, dubbed the "death cross," that has market-watchers wary. Its 200-day moving average is close to breaking through its 50-day moving average on the upside, which signals a bear market may be on the horizon.*

Laying aside concerns about *anticipating* technical events, or that it is much more accurate to think of the 50-day breaking through the 200 to the downside, we should ask the key question: is the Death Cross really a "key technical level"? Let's ask the market itself and see what the data has to say.

Using the Russell 2000 cash index (6613 trading days, going back to 6/24/1988), we find 19 cases of the Death Cross. A reasonable way to test the Death Cross is to take all the events that have happened, and to see what the market has done following those events. We need to ask some questions and make some decisions like: how far after the event should we look? Should we look at every day or just hit a few spots? What is the correct measure of performance?

For this quick test, let's look at what happens to the market at a few spots following the Death Cross, up to one year out. I will use 5, 20, 60, 90, and 252 trading day windows, which correspond roughly to one week, one month, one quarter, one half year, and a full calendar year. This is not an exhaustive test ((for instance, we could have a distortion due to a weird event 20 days following one of the events, while 19 and 21 days would have shown a very different picture)), but it's good enough for a first look. At least, by looking at a range like this we avoid the error of simplistic analysis that is so common: people will say things like "following the Death Cross, the Russell 2000 was up, on average, x% a month later." When we see a single time period, we should ask what happens over other time windows and why that particular one was the only period examined.

There is another important mistake to dodge here. For instance, this is a completely faulty analysis of a technical event: "Market XYZ was up/down x%, on average, following the event." Something important is missing from that thought process—we should compare the event to the baseline of the market, so we have to say "Market XYZ was up/down x% over/under its baseline return following the event." In other words, we look at what the market normally does, and compare post-event action (condition) to that normal (unconditional) market movement. Only if the market was absolutely flat (i.e., had an average daily return (return, in this case, simply means percent change) of zero) would it be valid to compare the event to zero. The Russell does not have a zero baseline, as the following table shows:

Russell 2000, Cash Index (6/24/88 - 9/18/14)	5 days	20 days	60 days	125 days	252 days
All days (6552)					
Mean	0.20%	0.78%	2.40%	5.04%	10.06%
StDev	*2.84%*	*5.61%*	*9.90%*	*14.02%*	*19.17%*

If we look at returns following every trading day in the history of the Russell 2000, we find it is up, on average, 10.06% a year later. Now, let's compare this with returns following the Death Crosses:

Death Cross

Russell 2000, Cash Index (6/24/88 - 9/18/14)	5 days	20 days	60 days	125 days	252 days
All days (6552)					
Mean	0.20%	0.78%	2.40%	5.04%	10.06%
StDev	*2.84%*	*5.61%*	*9.90%*	*14.02%*	*19.17%*
Event days (19)					
Mean	-1.92%	-0.54%	1.23%	7.15%	11.99%
StDev	*4.08%*	*5.90%*	*10.13%*	*12.47%*	*15.88%*
Diff of Means	**-2.12%**	**-1.32%**	**-1.17%**	**2.10%**	**1.93%**

When you look at that chart, focus your attention on the bottom line, which shows what the Russell 2000 did, relative to its unconditional (baseline) return. For instance, looking at the entire history of the Russell, we find it is up, on average. 0.2% one week later. Following the Death Cross, it is down, on average, -1.92%, meaning that it underperformed its baseline return by 2.12%. So, here is the first interesting point: the Death Cross actually does show a significant sell signal in the Russell 2000 one week later. However, this effect decays; the key question here is how large is the effect, relative to the variation for the period? A year out, we are seeing standard deviations greater than 15.0%, against a very small positive effect of 1.93%. So, what we can say from this test is that we do find a statistically significant, very short-term sell signal in the Russell 2000 in the data examined. This sell signal appears to be strong for a week, and then decays and we see no longer term significance. Interesting.

Where do we go from here? Well, first, I'd flip the test and look at the so-called Golden Cross, which is the inverse of the Death Cross, when the 50 period crosses over the 200 day moving average:

Golden Cross

Russell 2000, Cash Index (6/24/88 - 9/18/14)	5 days	20 days	60 days	125 days	252 days
All days (6552)					
Mean	0.20%	0.78%	2.40%	5.04%	10.06%
StDev	*2.84%*	*5.61%*	*9.90%*	*14.02%*	*19.17%*
Event days (19)					
Mean	-0.10%	-0.05%	0.58%	3.08%	12.21%
StDev	*2.12%*	*7.41%*	*12.79%*	*16.33%*	*15.40%*
Diff of Means	**-0.30%**	**-0.83%**	**-1.82%**	**-1.97%**	**2.15%**

Here, we do not have any significant effects at all; this is not necessarily a condemnation of the test (perhaps there is a reason the effect would not by symmetrical), but it certainly calls for further study. What other questions should we ask? It is entirely possible to find a valid signal just due to chance, so we'd be wise to repeat this test with other assets and other timeframes. We also might dig a bit deeper and look at each of the events, though we should be careful of doing too much work like that because it is easy to "curve fit" and select what we want to see. Still, actually looking into the data can help to build a deeper understanding of how the market looks. A summary test is only that: a very broad, rough, and blunt summary that may miss much significant detail.

Another question that I find very interesting is "why do people focus so much attention on mediocre or, in some cases, absolutely meaningless technical tools?" One reason is probably due to cognitive bias. For instance, one of the largest one-week selloffs following a Death Cross in the Russell was in 2008; anyone who identified it then and remembers the strong selloff is likely to have some emotions associated with that event. Furthermore, the signals certainly can look convincing on a chart:

It would be easy to find a few charts like that, and "show" that these crosses work very well, but this is simply a case of choosing good examples. As I've written before, much of the discipline of traditional technical analysis is visual, not quantitative, so technical analysts are prone to these types of errors, even with the best of intentions. The only defense against these errors is using the tools of statistics to take a proper look at the data and to consider the effects in the cold, hard light of quantitative analysis. In the case of the Death Cross, there does not appear to be any reason to focus on this event, and it appears to have no long-term significance for the market.

Death and Golden Crosses: A Deeper Look

The previous article looked at the (apparently) impending Death Cross in the Russell 2000 index. In that article and the data examined, I found an interesting and statistically significant short-term signal for the Death Cross, but no effect for the Golden Cross. In this post, I will look at the Death and Golden Crosses on much more data. First, the DJIA going back to the 1920's, and then on a large basket of stocks from more recent trading. I'll also discuss a bit more about test procedures, and what I have found to be the most common opportunities to make mistakes that will cost you money.

The sample size for the Russell 2000 test was quite small, with only 19 events to examine. Let's take a look at an index with much larger history, the Dow Jones index going back to the mid 1920's. Here are the statistics for both Crosses on that index:

Death Cross

DJIA, Cash Index (7/8/25 - 9/19/14)

	5 days	20 days	60 days	125 days	252 days
All days (22,345)					
Mean	0.14%	0.57%	1.72%	3.59%	7.59%
StDev	*2.56%*	*5.22%*	*9.24%*	*13.32%*	*20.35%*
Event days (56)					
Mean	0.09%	0.06%	2.09%	3.24%	3.93%
StDev	*3.86%*	*5.28%*	*12.78%*	*16.11%*	*19.31%*
Diff of Means	**-0.05%**	**-0.51%**	**0.37%**	**-0.35%**	**-3.66%**

Golden Cross

DJIA, Cash Index (7/8/25 - 9/19/14)

	5 days	20 days	60 days	125 days	252 days
All days (22,345)					
Mean	0.14%	0.57%	1.72%	3.59%	7.59%
StDev	*2.56%*	*5.22%*	*9.24%*	*13.32%*	*20.35%*
Event days (56)					
Mean	0.05%	-0.01%	0.94%	2.40%	5.97%
StDev	*2.38%*	*5.77%*	*8.56%*	*11.51%*	*16.78%*
Diff of Means	**-0.09%**	**-0.58%**	**-0.78%**	**-1.19%**	**-1.62%**

With more data, this test shows a very different picture from what we saw before. Now, there appears to be no effect at all, though we might note with some curiosity that the excess returns, for both crosses, seem to be pretty consistently negative. (Though we cannot tell from these tables, none of these numbers are statistically significant, meaning that we are quite likely looking at noise.) This test seems to show no effect whatsoever from the Crosses, and we could draw the conclusion that we should probably not pay any attention to them. However, here is our first cautionary note:

Caution: More may not necessarily be better

In examining more data, we have gone back further in time. It is certainly possible that older data does not relate to current conditions. Something (or many things) could have changed. In all analysis, we make the assumption that "the future will look something like the past", but this is an assumption that is worth considering carefully. In this case, it seems reasonable to assume that any effect would be more or less stable, but this may not always be the case.

Crosses on Individual Stocks

Both of these tests have been done on stock indexes. I thought it would also be interesting to look at the test on a basket of individual stocks. Here are the test results (in a different format) for a basket of 100 stocks, using the past 10 years of data. This will be a way to get more events to study, and also to look at a different asset class. (Individual stocks may or may not behave differently than stock indexes.)

"Death" and "Golden" Crosses

Buy Signal: 371 of 125,849 Bars [0.29%]						Sell Signal: 377 of 125,849 Bars [0.3%]					
Day	$\bar{X}_s - \bar{X}_b$	$M_s - M_b$	$p=$	Up	Down	Day	$\bar{X}_s - \bar{X}_b$	$M_s - M_b$	$p=$	Up	Down
1	(0.08%)	(0.08%)	0.41	46.90%	51.48%	1	0.33%	0.11%	0.00	55.44%	43.50%
2	(0.17%)	(0.20%)	0.21	46.90%	52.56%	2	0.30%	0.29%	0.07	55.17%	44.56%
3	(0.19%)	(0.25%)	0.24	46.90%	52.29%	3	0.19%	0.36%	0.32	57.29%	42.18%
4	(0.31%)	(0.19%)	0.10	49.06%	50.67%	4	0.21%	0.45%	0.35	58.89%	40.85%
5	(0.32%)	(0.11%)	0.12	50.94%	48.52%	5	0.39%	0.49%	0.11	58.62%	40.05%
10	(0.28%)	0.10%	0.33	52.02%	47.17%	10	0.16%	0.76%	0.61	60.74%	39.26%
15	(0.72%)	(0.04%)	0.05	52.02%	47.71%	15	(0.28%)	0.62%	0.53	58.09%	41.91%
20	(0.66%)	(0.18%)	0.14	54.99%	44.74%	20	(0.75%)	0.61%	0.14	58.09%	41.64%

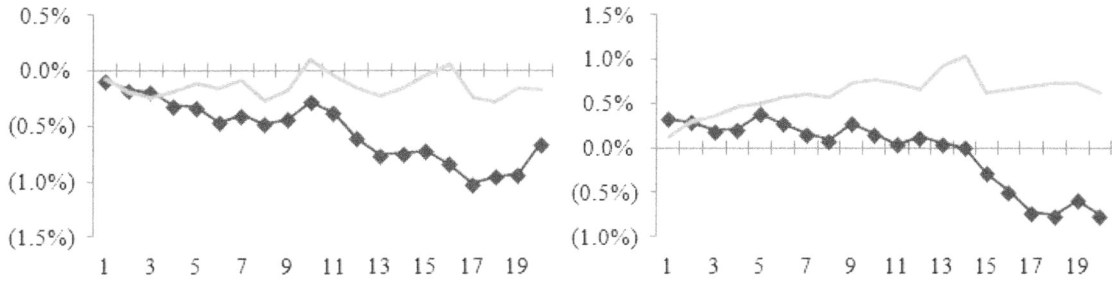

This table is, perhaps, slightly harder to read, but it gives the same type of test results in more depth, focusing on a shorter time period (20 trading days after the event). I would suggest you focus on the second column in each box, which shows the excess return (*X-X* is the signal mean — baseline mean) and the *p*= column, which shows the *p*-value for the test.

In this case, we see echoes of the "weird" negative return that we saw in the DJIA test. (This is, more or less, an artifact. The "juice", i.e., big returns, in stocks appear to happen at the extremes. Tests that select events more likely to be in the "middle" of the data (relative to high/low range), as this average crossing test does, are likely to show a natural element of underperformance.) Most importantly, there is no clear and strong effect here.

Caution: Sample sizes with individual stocks

I just presented a test on over 125,000 daily bars. This would seem to be a lot of data, until you realize that stocks are very highly correlated, and many of these events were driven by the broad market, occurred on or near the same dates. It is easy to do tests on many individual stocks, but avoid being misled by the sample sizes; assume that the tests are not as powerful as we might usually assume, given the apparently (and possibly misleadingly) large sample sizes.

A look at statistical significance

One of the problems with most tests of technical patterns is that statistical significance is rarely reported. When a technical analyst is telling you about a candlestick pattern or some other favorite technical tool, ask a question like "what is the statistical significance for that pattern? Do you have a *p*-value?" You'll be met by blank stares because a) that type of testing has not usually been done in technical analysis and b) traditional technical analysts are not used to thinking like this.

Nearly all data includes some degree of noise or random fluctuation, and market data usually has a lot of noise. What we're trying to do, with any test, is to peer deeply into that data and maybe tease out some real effect. To be able to do that, we must be able to sort out what might be "real" or "significant" from what is random noise. Most traders know if they just go into the market and buy on five days over the past year randomly, there is some chance that they will make money on all five trades. The critical question we need to ask is how sure can we be that these results, no matter how good or bad they look, are something other than randomness? What if we just got lucky?

Traditional tests of significance look at the data, the effect sizes, the amount of variation in the data, sample sizes, etc., and give us one answer to that question. (Note that even this answer only works within the bounds of probability. Stay humble, my friends. We don't truly know anything for certain!) This answer is often expressed as a *p*-value, which is the probability of "seeing a result at least as extreme as the one observed simply due to random chance." (Formally, the last part of this sentence should read "given that the null hypothesis is true", but, for purposes of most market analysis, that null hypothesis is that the effect is due to randomness.)

Without that assessment, any test of a technical effect is bound to be misleading. We don't care that X was up Y% of the time after the event, that stocks rallied Z% following the super-secret signal, or that buying with this system produced any number of wins over the past ten years. Those are examples of how technical results are often presented, but, without an assessment of statistical significance, they aren't terribly meaningful.

Surprise: a hidden gem

Look again at the test table for individual stocks, specifically at the Up and Down columns, that give the % of stocks that were up or down on those days following the event, without regard to the magnitude of those moves. (Note that the baseline was: up, unch, down : 50.6%, 1.02%, 48.38%.) What is going on here? Without going into a lot of supporting detail, this effect is due to mean reversion in stocks, which is a powerful force—almost overwhelming over some timeframes. Individual stocks mean revert strongly. Consider the case of a Death Cross, and the price movement required to generate that event. Nearly always, price will be going down, pulling the short-term average through the longer-term average; furthermore, the day of the event is almost certain to have a lower close than the day before. Simply buying stocks on this condition, a close lower than the day before, will result in a small win in a test, due to the power of mean reversion in stocks. This is also why quantitative trend following systems have trouble with individual stocks.

Perhaps think about your trading experience with individual stocks. What happens when you "chase" entries? How many breakouts fail? How many breakout trades are likely to snap back against you, if you enter on a strong day in the direction of the breakout? What do the statistics from your trading say? Though we might not have found an effect with the soundbite darlings, the Death and Golden Crosses, we have found something important: we've uncovered one of the fundamental principles of price behavior and seen it in action, and that's not a bad day's work.

A Pullback Variation

Patterns Within Patterns

One of the problems swing traders in stocks face is correlation; the sad reality is that stocks mostly move together, and trades in stocks mostly win and lose together. If you buy four names and short four at the same time, there's a pretty good chance that one set four is going to make money and one will lose money. Anything we can do, as technical traders, to loosen the bonds of correlation in our pattern analysis is useful.

Logically, stocks will become less correlated to the market when something company-specific is driving changes in the stock price. In the absence of those company-specific factors, most stocks will drift more or less with the market. There are a handful of patterns, all tied together by urgency (expressed in different ways), that can give an edge to a pattern playing out with less market influence than would otherwise be expected.

One of these is a pattern that I called a "nested pullback"; the pattern occurs when a consolidation or flag is "in force" and is moving toward a target. That move makes a pause of a few bars (on your trading timeframe), and this pause is the nested pullback. It is a way to incorporate multiple timeframe influences without explicitly pulling up a higher timeframe chart; the higher timeframe momentum is "in force", and we are simply looking for a lower timeframe inflection in that momentum. Schematically and conceptually, this is the trade:

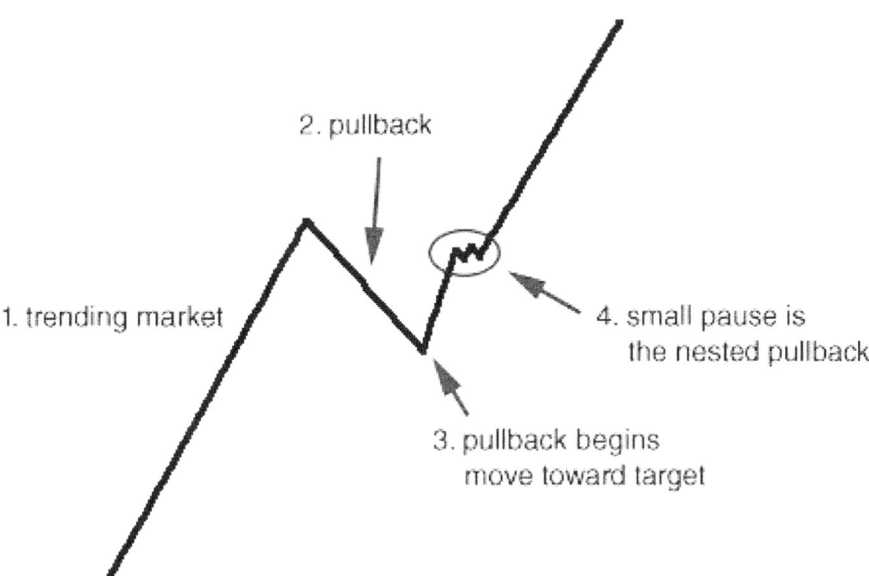

Now, consider this idea in the chart of TWTR:

It's easy to see that the 2nd and 3rd bars from the right of the chart may be a pause in the breakdown that started in the high teens. Though this is a daily chart, the price structure is a complex (two-legged) pullback on the weekly timeframe, so this daily pause is essentially a tiny pullback within the context of that big weekly structure.

What do you do with this information? Well, as always, the answer depends on who you are as a trader and how you make trading decisions. Critically, the action out of this pattern—whether it leads to clean breakdown (confirmation of the trade) or not (possible contradiction) can give insight into the character of the move and to the conviction behind the move.

Many traders will be attracted to the idea of using a little pattern like this to finesse an entry into the weekly trade with tight stops. Conceptually, this is possible, but it's more difficult in practice. One of the biggest mistakes discretionary traders make is using stops that are too tight, and then their stops simply become targets in a noisy market. If you're going to do this, make sure you understand the tradeoffs between tight stops and probabilities.

One last point: this is an example of a pattern that is fairly "easy" for the human trader to handle, but that is very difficult to quantify. You could write code to describe a nested pullback, but that code would take a lot of tweaking and refining before it worked well. (We'd have to define the initial move, what setups are valid, how much momentum would set up the nested pullback, the scope and location of the pullback, and we'd have to strike a balance in all of this between precision and leaving a wide enough range that we catch all the patterns we want—not an easy task!) This is a pattern that puts the human skill of pattern recognition to work in a disciplined framework, and points us toward a type of trading in which discretionary and quantitative tools can work together.

I've written about this pattern before, and even have a section on my blog dedicated to it. Why do I write about the same patterns over and over? Because focusing on a defined subset of patterns can lead to great understanding of complex and complicated markets. Because these patterns work. Because they are important.

Chapter 6

Module 6–The Failure Test

This Module introduces a pattern which I have called the failure test. This is not a pattern I invented; in fact, Wyckoff talked about a similar concept, using the terms of springs and upthrusts. Victor Sperendeo has called this a 2B entry, and other authors have written about this pattern—it is a simple, and enduring aspect of market behavior.

The simplest way to understand this pattern is that the market makes an attempt to break beyond support and resistance, and that attempt fails: it is both a test of the support and resistance level, and a failure to break beyond the level. This is a pattern that is often an aggresive countertrend pattern. Even if a trader does not wish to use such an entry in an outright capacity, it is useful to watch for these failures as they often mark at least short-term ends of trends, and sometimes major turning points.

Next, we think about the concept of papertrading. Many writers have said that papertrading or simulated trading (trading a theoretical account with no real money on the line) is worthless because it does not replicate the emotional aspects of trading. These writers correctly point out that the emotional challenges are where many traders get stuck, but papertrading does have a purpose. Done properly, it is another kind of statistical investigation of the trader's edge. One thing is fairly certain—if a trader cannot make money in a papertrading account, she will not be able to make money in a real money account. Papertrading is an important stage of the trader's development.

This module also includes a look at some basic statistics we can calculate to understand a trader's performance, and how that performance may vary through time. Though this is far from a complete analysis of a trading program, we now have the tools to understand the basic quality of that trading edge.

Last, the Module concludes with a deep look at traditional, classical technical analysis—both its history and examples of chart patterns drawn from the original source material. We consider both the utility and limitations of these patterns, and how understanding the market dynamics behind the patterns can lead to a solid understanding of market behavior.

In the upcoming pages, we also include an in-depth look at nearly a century of market history and data for the US stock market. The trader should now have the tools to analyze price patterns with an eye to supply/demand imbalances, surprises, and probabilities.

Section 1: Failure Test Backtest

Testing patterns should now be second nature, as you've spent considerable time working through pullbacks and the anti pattern. The failure test is a simple and clear cut pattern, but it is not without its problems. It often sets up in a countertrend setting that can lead to stunning, dramatic losses when the pattern fails.

It may require significantly different psychology and trade management skills, compared to the with-trend pullback examples first exampined. In your work on this backtest, consider both the objective aspects of the pattern, and how comfortable you would have been taking the trade. Keep in mind that time in these trades will typicall be shorter, and many trades will hit profits or stops within a few bars. It might also be a good idea to examine both longer-term and intraday charts, whether or not you intend to trade intraday. Price action, particulary around the current high or low of the session, can reveal some interesting aspects of market behavior.

As in previous tests, first define the pattern as precisely as possible. Write a short set of rules, and then turn to the charts and find examples of the patterms. You may now also record your results and consider those results using the basic trading stats from Unit 4 of this Module.

Section 2: First Steps in Papertrading

In this module, you will begin your first explorations of papertrading. Conventional wisdom (correctly) notes that the most significant problems of trading are probably psychological and emotional, and (also correctly notes) that papertrading does nothing to replicate the emotions of actual trading—so many writers and educators, quite wrongly, suggest that papertrading is worthless.

The confusion comes from not understanding what we can and should do with papertrading. Basically, papertrading is a type of forward test of our edge. Backtesting always looks back at historical data, but papertrading does the same type of testing in live market data. The trader papertrading will deal with the unknowable future at every step.

Yes, we need to always remember that a profitable papertrading record is no guarantee of profits with real money. It is very possible to trade well in a simulated account and to lose money when the trader "goes live", but one thing is pretty certain: if you can't make money papertrading, you are unlikely to make money in a real account!

How can we get best value from this exercise? One answer is to take it very seriously. Anything you can do to create some emotional "charge" or accountability around these results will help. This is where working in a community and sharing your results can be valuable. Also, never allow yourself to "recreate history"; there is a temptation to look at a bad decision made a few days ago and say, "what if I had just..." Do not do this—even a simple instance of changing a past decision will completely invalidate your results.

The module discusses how to effectively do papertrading in detail, but a few reminders here:

- You need a system to carefully track your entries and exits. If you've been doing the suggested backtests, then you already have a system that can be used, with little or no adaptation, for your papertrading.
- Clearly define the conditions that will get you in and out of trades. In the next module, we will drill deeper into the creating your trading plan, but have some type of written plan for your papertrading. This plan can always be revised, so don't get stuck on it—just do it!
- Try to do exactly what you will do when you trade real money: do your homework, have a sheet of potential trades, and then note the prices where you would have been filled in your executions. Be pessimistic in your assumptions about slippage or fills.
- Keep doing this consistently for a number of weeks. Initially, this exercise is just to get you in the flow of doing the work. In coming modules, we will spend much more time creating your plan and moving toward actual trading.

Section 3: Classical Charting Research

In this unit, we have seen many examples of classical charting techniques and patterns. This is a good opportunity to investigate the statistical edges behind some of those patterns, but there are some important complications and limitations to be aware of.

First, these patterns are undeniably subjective. Though it may be possible to define some of these patterns algorithmically, the usual application of these patterns comes from being identified by the trader's eye. Before beginning a research project, you should have a clear understanding of the pattern or patterns you wish to investigate: what do they look like and how will you identify what is an example of the pattern and what is not?

Second, trading these patterns involves some nuance. Few classic charting advocates would claim that every occurrence of a head and shoulders pattern will lead to a change of trend. Rather, there are usually other qualifications and complications and triggering price movements that will indicate if a pattern is "in play" or not. These are other issues you should consider before investing time and energy in a research project.

Once you have addressed these issues, write a clear set of rules that explains how you will identify these patterns. Then, move through charts bar by bar and identify the patters as they emerge on the chart. As before, be very careful of any future information contaminating your results; even a glance ahead at the chart will invalidate your test.

Keep theoretical papertrading records of trades around these patterns. You may also consider working this research into some type of event study structure, whether completely by hand or with an automated component for pattern evaluation. The objective of this research project is to gain some insight into the edge behind these patterns, and perhaps to find patterns that might be useful in your own trading plan in the future.

Section 4: Dow Jones Industrial Average: Full History

The charts in this section are weekly charts of the full history of the Dow Jones Industrial Average. They are presented here for your use and analysis.

In most cases, the charts cover roughly a decade from the "zero years" the same year ten years later. In a few cases, you will find charts that snapshot the middle of the decade—for the 1929 crash and the 1987 crash. This was done to allow you to better connect subsequent price action to these distortions in the market.

A few points to considere:

First, *apply the basic tools of trends and ranges* you have learned through the course. Think about both descriptive (ability to define what is happening right now) and predictive (ability to predict what will happen in the near future) power of the tools. Too often, traders make naïve assumptions that do not carry through to actual trading. Doing deep investigation of these historical charts is a good first line of defense—understand what the tools can do, and what they cannot do.

Second, major historical events have been marked on the charts. These fall into two categories: market specific events, such as the 1987 crash, are noted, and also major geo-political events. You should *spend some time considering the market's reaction to geopolitical events.* Though many of these defined culture and thought for decades after the event, market response might not be what you expect. No claim is made that we marked all or even the most relevant historical events, but looking at these events should give you a good starting point.

Third, *spend some time contemplating these charts.* It's easy to glance at a chart in a few seconds, but you hold most of the significant history of the US stock market in your hands. If the events and market movements spark an interest to dig deeper into some of the events marked, this will only deepen your understanding of the market environment and historical context. This is time well spent.

Last, consider the investment returns in the windows below each of the decade-long charts. Though the beginning and ending points are arbitrary, you will begin to gain some respect for the nature of long-term returns in stocks, and for the long-period cycles in these returns.

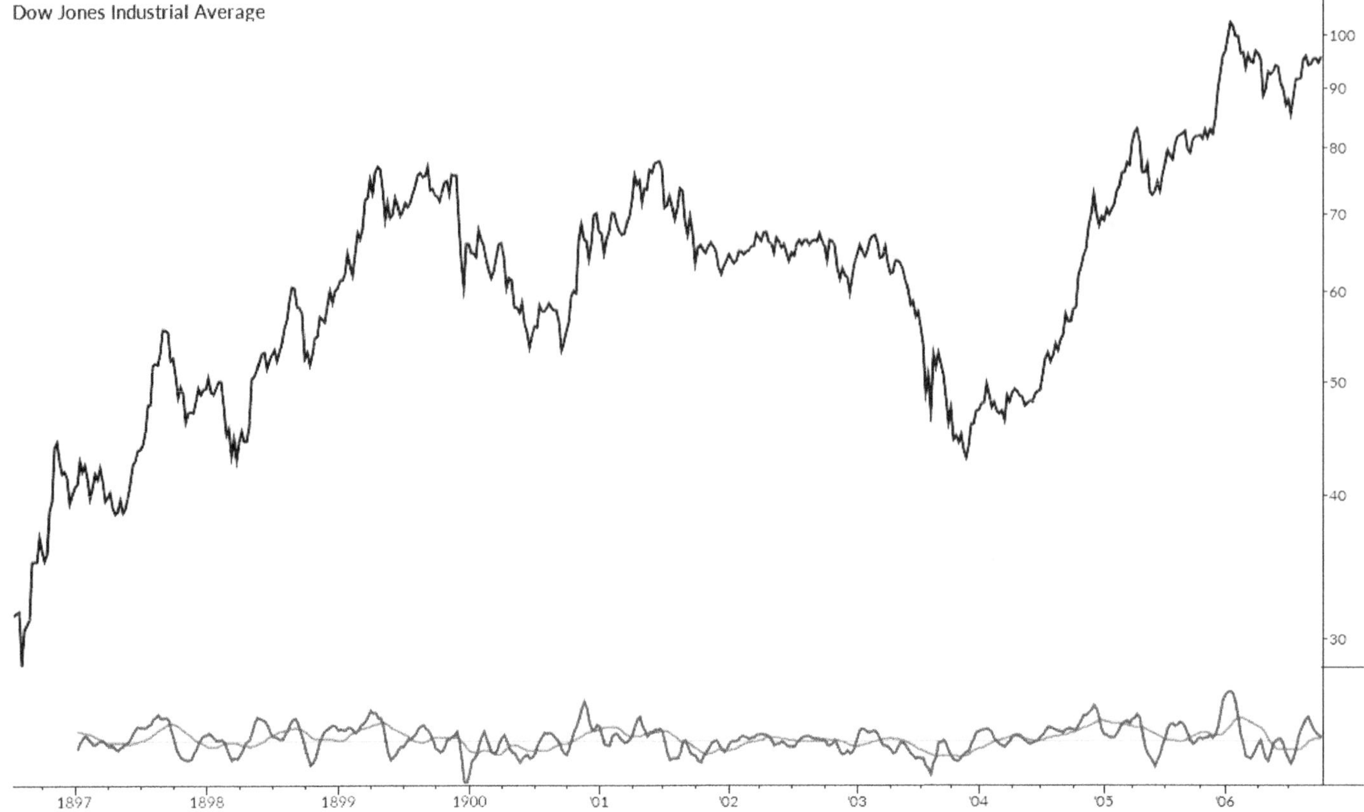

This chart shows the beginning of the DJIA. These early charts are particularly important because this was the environment within which Charles Dow formulated his early Wall Street Journal editorials, and from which most of the principles of classical technical analysis were derived.

Summary stats for 1900-1909

Starting/ending price: 68.13 / 99.05

Total return: 45.4% Average daily return: 1.9bp

Average/highest Hvol(20): 16.3% / 106.2% (3/15/1907)

Highest/lowest price: 103.00 (1/19/1906) / 42.15 (11/9/1903)

Days with new 52 week high/low closes: 163 / 87

Biggest percent gain/loss: 6.7% (3/15/1907) / -8.3% (3/14/1907)

Biggest volatility-adjusted gain/loss: 4.5σ (9/29/1903) / -7.0σ (12/7/1904)

Number of days >2σ/>3σ/>4σ/>5σ: 101 / 21 / 2 / 0

Number of days <-2σ/<-3σ/<-4σ/<-5σ: 126 / 42 / 16 / 3

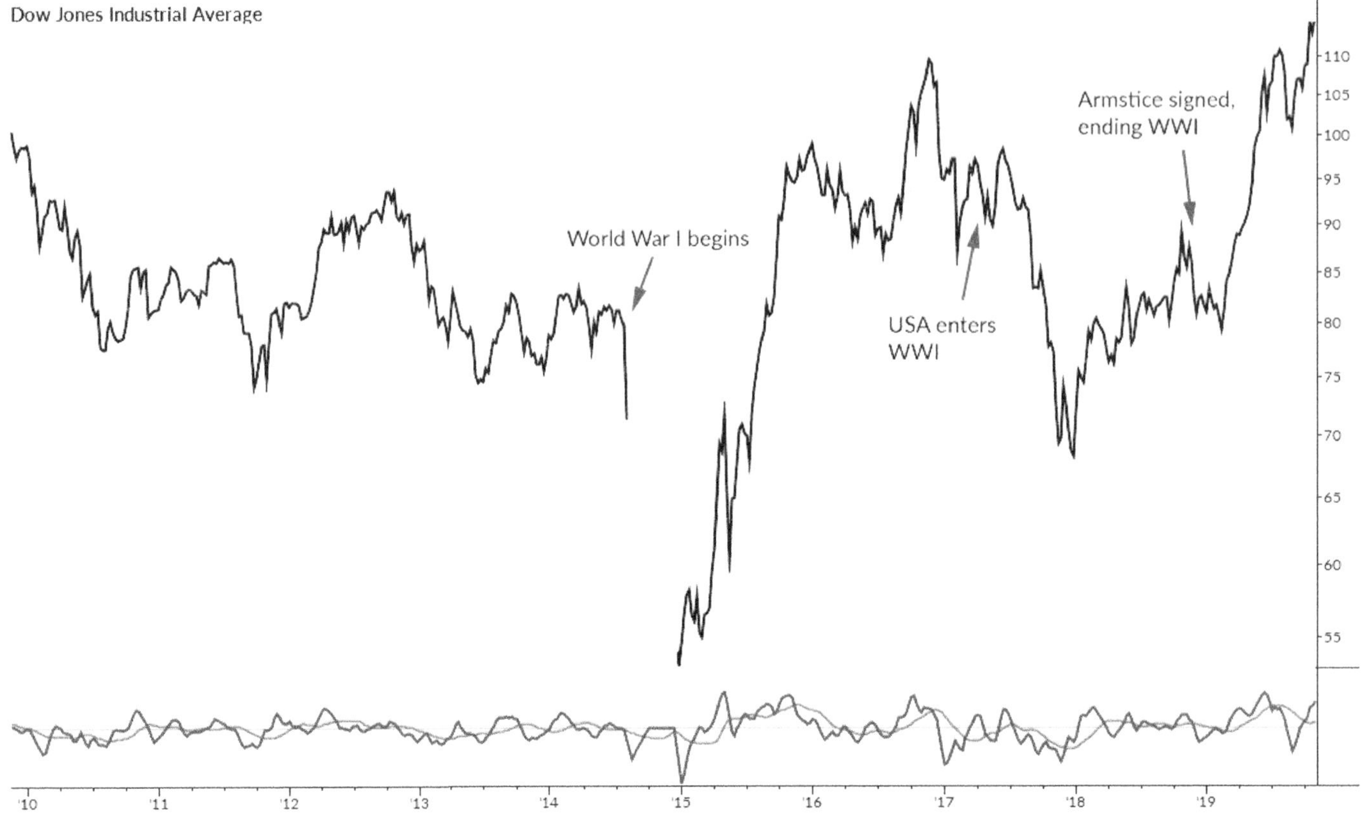

Summary stats for 1910-1919

Starting/ending price: 98.34 / 99.05

Total return: 0.7% Average daily return: 0.5bp

Average/highest Hvol(20): 17.4% / 86.8% (12/22/1916)

Highest/lowest price: 119.62 (11/3/1919) / 53.17 (12/24/1914)

Days with new 52 week high/low closes: 137 / 59

Biggest percent gain/loss: 5.5% (12/22/1916) / -23.5% (12/12/1914)

Biggest volatility-adjusted gain/loss: 5.5σ (8/16/1915) / -13.8σ (12/12/1914)

Number of days >2σ/>3σ/>4σ/>5σ: 92 / 18 / 4 / 1

Number of days <-2σ/<-3σ/<-4σ/<-5σ: 120 / 41 / 19 / 8

Summary stats for 1920-1929

Starting/ending price: 108.76 / 248.48

Total return: 128.5% Average daily return: 3.4bp

Average/highest Hvol(20): 17.6% / 196.0% (10/30/1929)

Highest/lowest price: 381.17 (9/3/1929) / 63.90 (8/24/1921)

Days with new 52 week high/low closes: 324 / 45

Biggest percent gain/loss: 12.3% (10/30/1929) / -12.8% (10/28/1929)

Biggest volatility-adjusted gain/loss: 5.5σ (10/31/1923) / -6.5σ (4/25/1927)

Number of days >2σ/>3σ/>4σ/>5σ: 79 / 15 / 3 / 1

Number of days <-2σ/<-3σ/<-4σ/<-5σ: 121 / 45 / 11 / 6

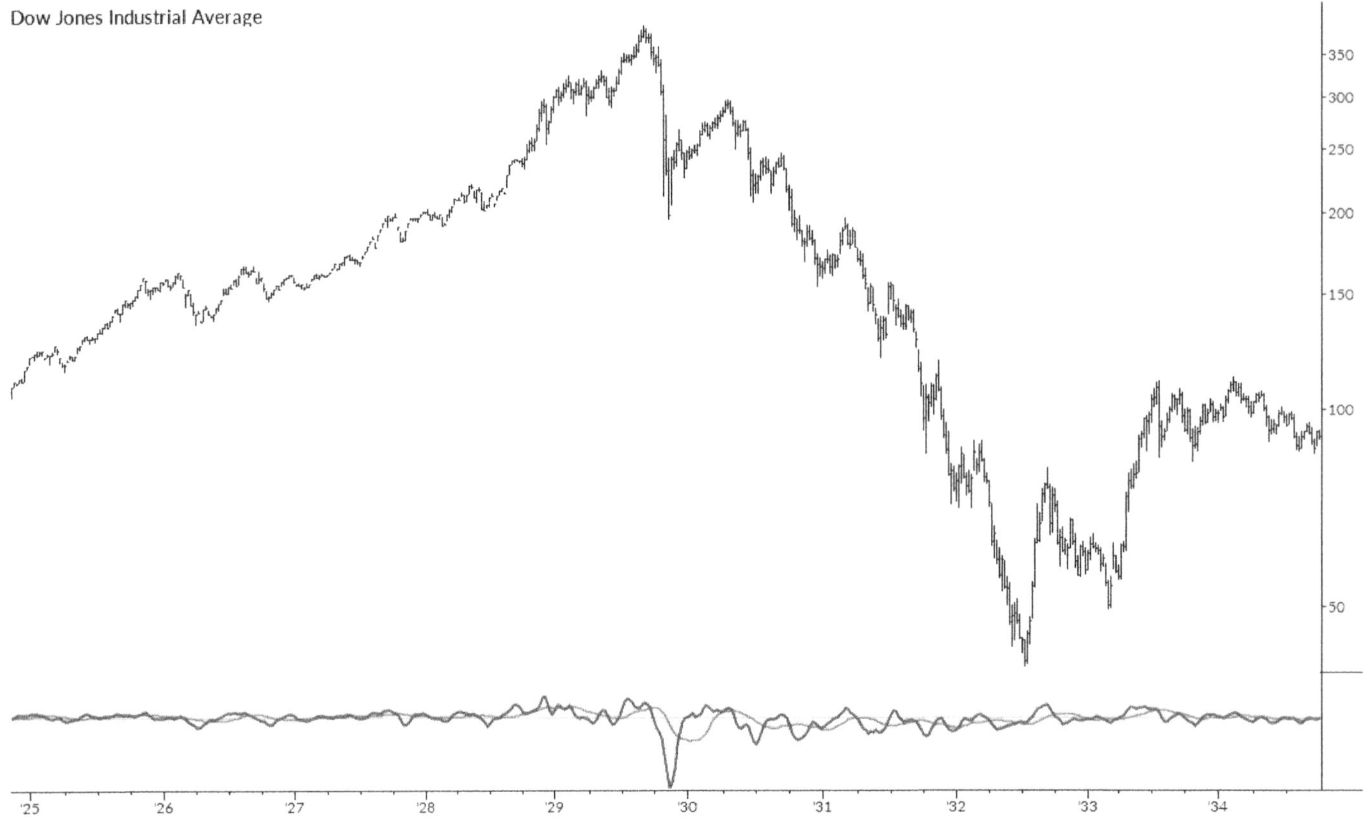

This chart is presented, without commentary, to highlight the magnitude of the 1929 crash and subsequent decline. Consider the price movements as percentage changes to get some respect for the defining psychological impact of this event.

Summary stats for 1930-1939

Starting/ending price: 244.20 / 150.24

Total return: -38.5% Average daily return: 0.0bp

Average/highest Hvol(20): 29.3% / 243.5% (3/15/1933)

Highest/lowest price: 294.07 (4/17/1930) / 41.22 (7/8/1932)

Days with new 52 week high/low closes: 157 / 104

Biggest percent gain/loss: 15.3% (3/15/1933) / -8.4% (8/12/1932)

Biggest volatility-adjusted gain/loss: 6.0σ (3/15/1933) / -5.3σ (7/26/1934)

Number of days >2σ/>3σ/>4σ/>5σ: 88 / 26 / 7 / 2

Number of days <-2σ/<-3σ/<-4σ/<-5σ: 129 / 29 / 5 / 1

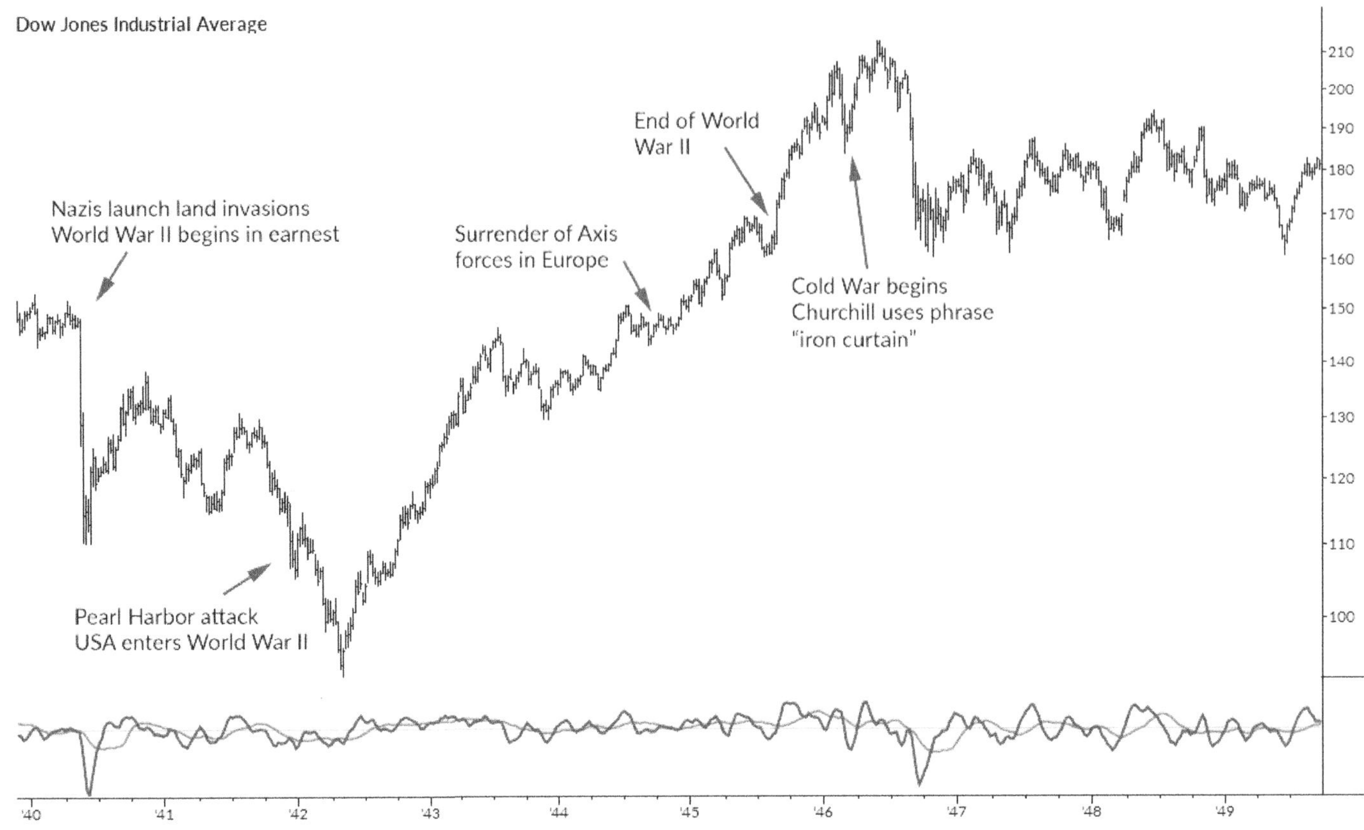

Summary stats for 1940-1949

Starting/ending price: 151.43 / 191.55

Total return: 26.5% Average daily return: 1.1bp

Average/highest Hvol(20): 11.8% / 75.1% (6/12/1940)

Highest/lowest price: 212.50 (5/29/1946) / 92.92 (4/28/1942)

Days with new 52 week high/low closes: 170 / 41

Biggest percent gain/loss: 4.7% (6/12/1940) / -6.8% (5/14/1940)

Biggest volatility-adjusted gain/loss: 6.1σ (7/30/1940) / -7.9σ (5/13/1940)

Number of days >2σ/>3σ/>4σ/>5σ: 91 / 17 / 8 / 2

Number of days <-2σ/<-3σ/<-4σ/<-5σ: 134 / 48 / 26 / 11

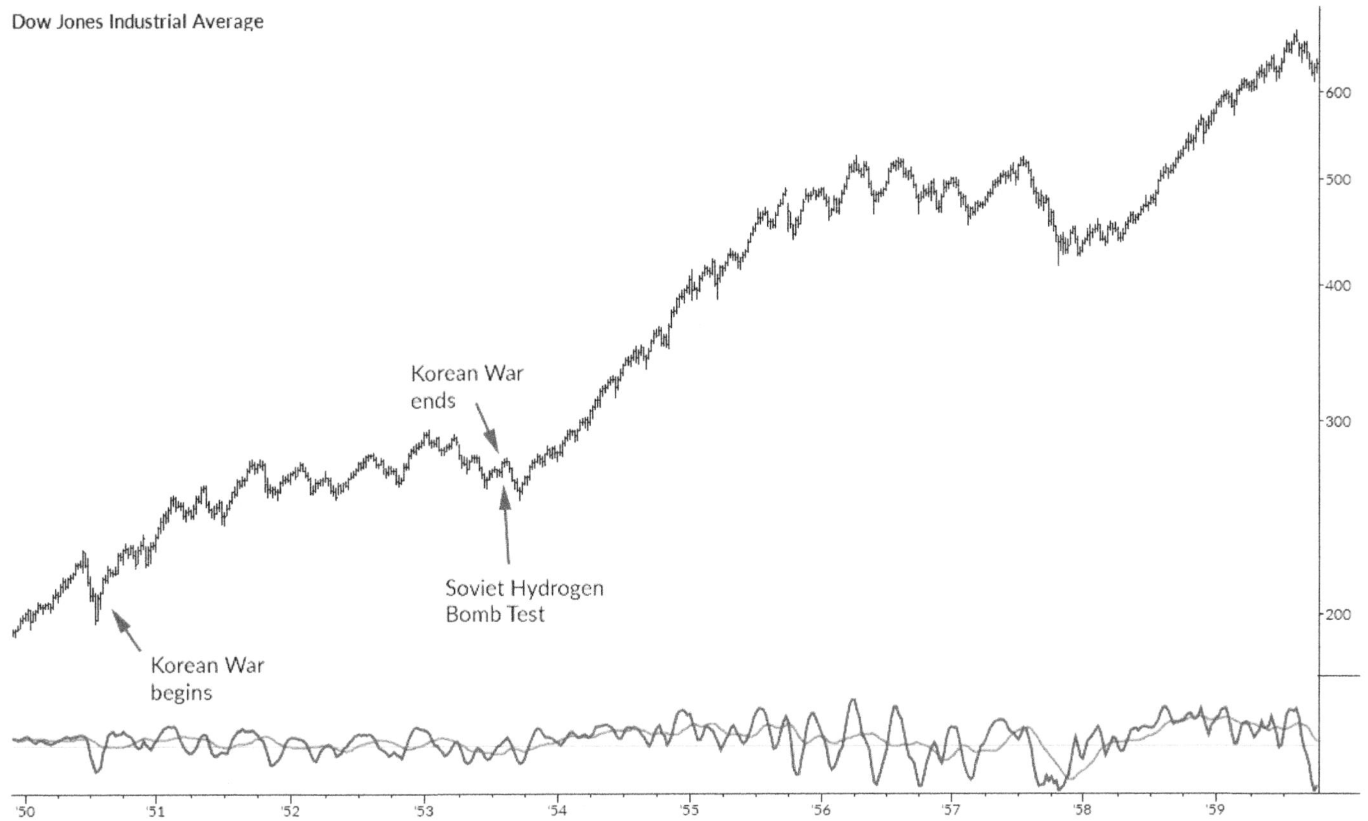

Summary stats for 1950-1959

Starting/ending price: 198.89 / 679.36
Total return: 241.6% Average daily return: 4.9bp
Average/highest Hvol(20): 10.4% / 65.6% (10/23/1957)
Highest/lowest price: 679.36 (12/31/1959) / 196.81 (1/13/1950)
Days with new 52 week high/low closes: 328 / 13
Biggest percent gain/loss: 4.1% (10/23/1957) / -6.5% (9/26/1955)
Biggest volatility-adjusted gain/loss: 4.6σ (11/3/1954) / -18.9σ (9/26/1955)
Number of days >2σ/>3σ/>4σ/>5σ: 68 / 9 / 2 / 0
Number of days <-2σ/<-3σ/<-4σ/<-5σ: 105 / 32 / 8 / 3

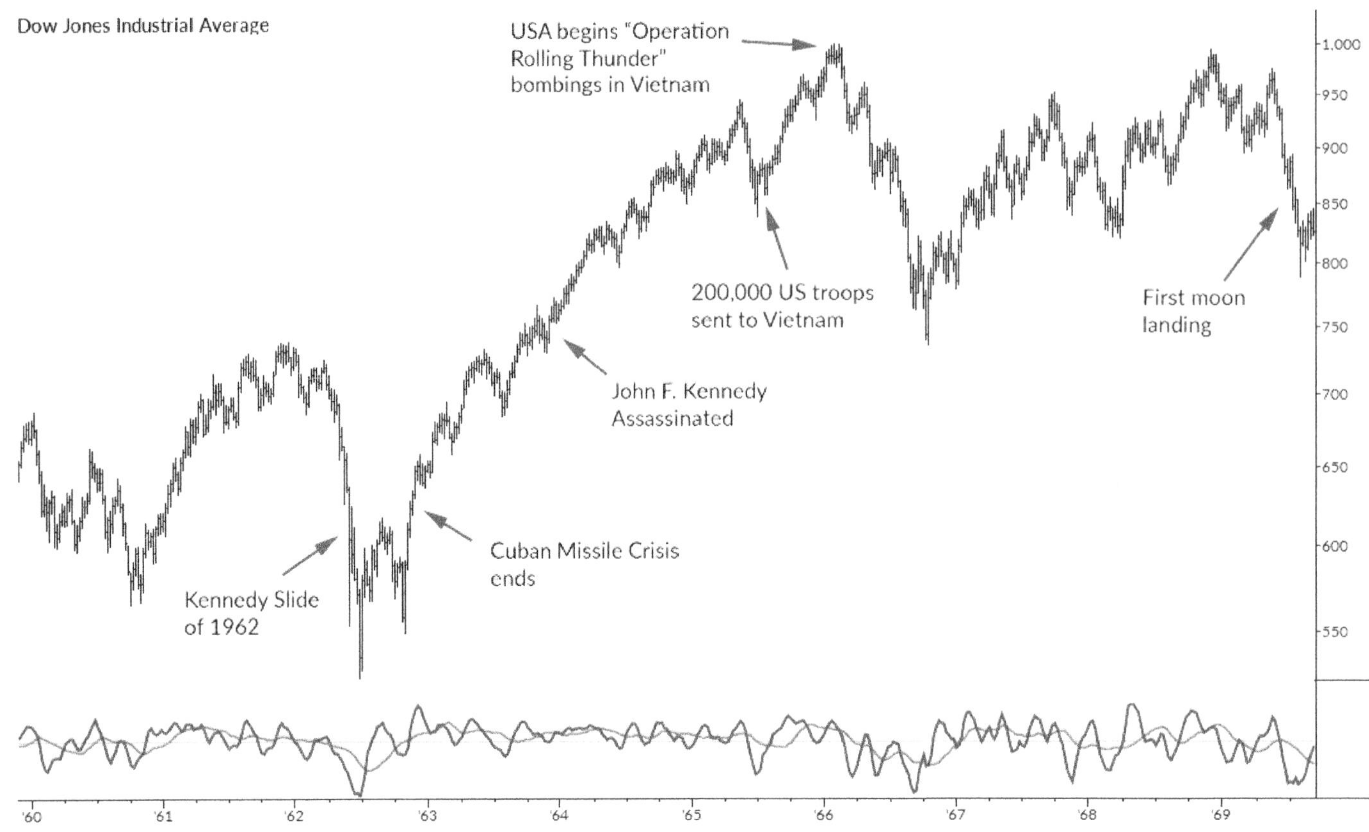

Summary stats for 1960-1969

Starting/ending price: 679.06 / 800.36

Total return: 17.9% Average daily return: 0.9bp

Average/highest Hvol(20): 10.4% / 74.4% (5/29/1962)

Highest/lowest price: 995.15 (2/9/1966) / 535.76 (6/26/1962)

Days with new 52 week high/low closes: 182 / 57

Biggest percent gain/loss: 4.7% (5/29/1962) / -5.7% (5/28/1962)

Biggest volatility-adjusted gain/loss: 5.3σ (11/26/1963) / -6.1σ (5/28/1962)

Number of days >2σ/>3σ/>4σ/>5σ: 85 / 15 / 1 / 1

Number of days <-2σ/<-3σ/<-4σ/<-5σ: 92 / 17 / 5 / 2

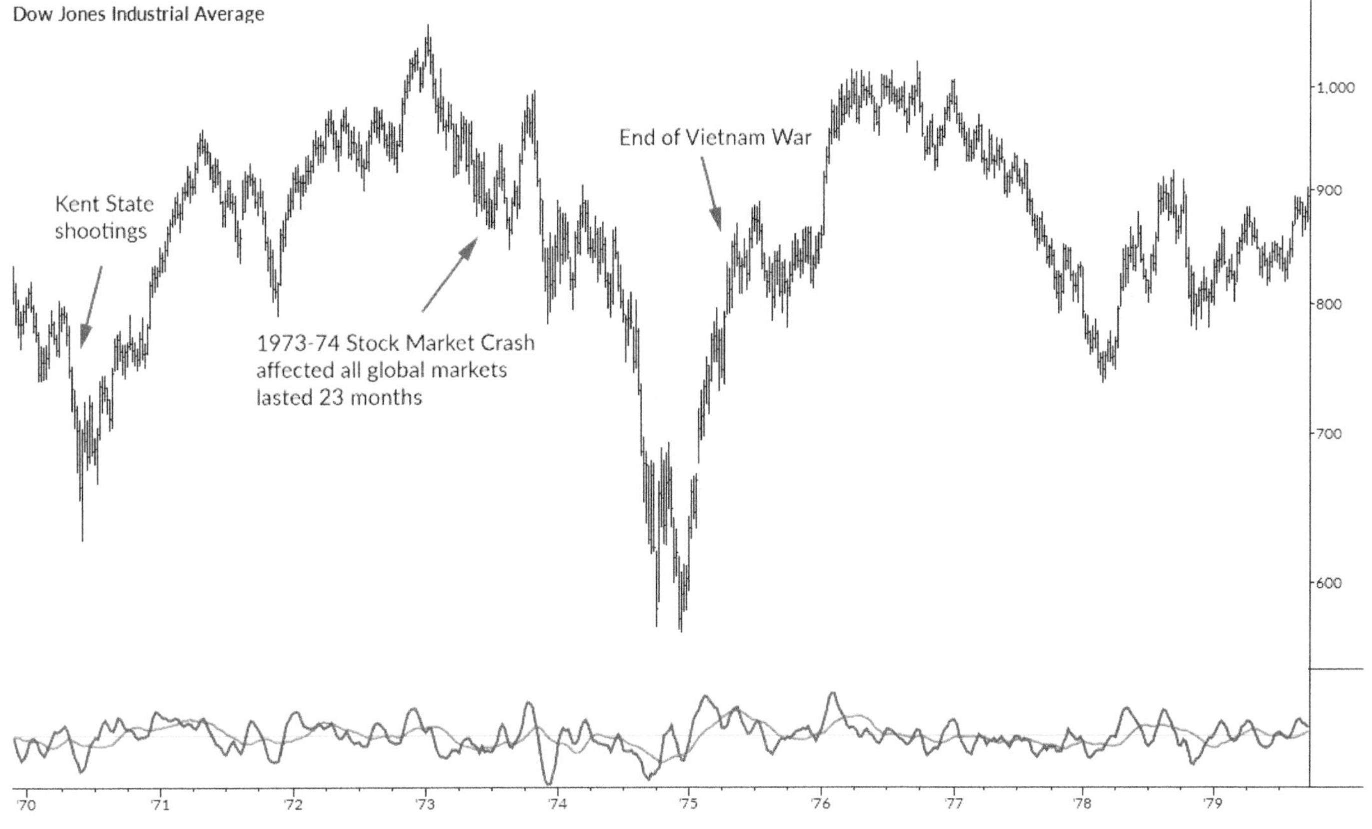

Summary stats for 1970-1979

Starting/ending price: 809.20 / 838.74

Total return: 3.7% Average daily return: .6bp

Average/highest Hvol(20): 14.7% / 80.6% (5/27/1970)

Highest/lowest price: 1051.70 (1/11/1973) / 577.60 (12/6/1974)

Days with new 52 week high/low closes: 94 / 109

Biggest percent gain/loss: 5.1% (5/27/1970) / -3.5% (11/18/1974)

Biggest volatility-adjusted gain/loss: 4.9σ (8/16/1971) / -4.4σ (7/27/1977)

Number of days >2σ/>3σ/>4σ/>5σ: 89 / 13 / 2 / 0

Number of days <-2σ/<-3σ/<-4σ/<-5σ: 67 / 10 / 1 / 0

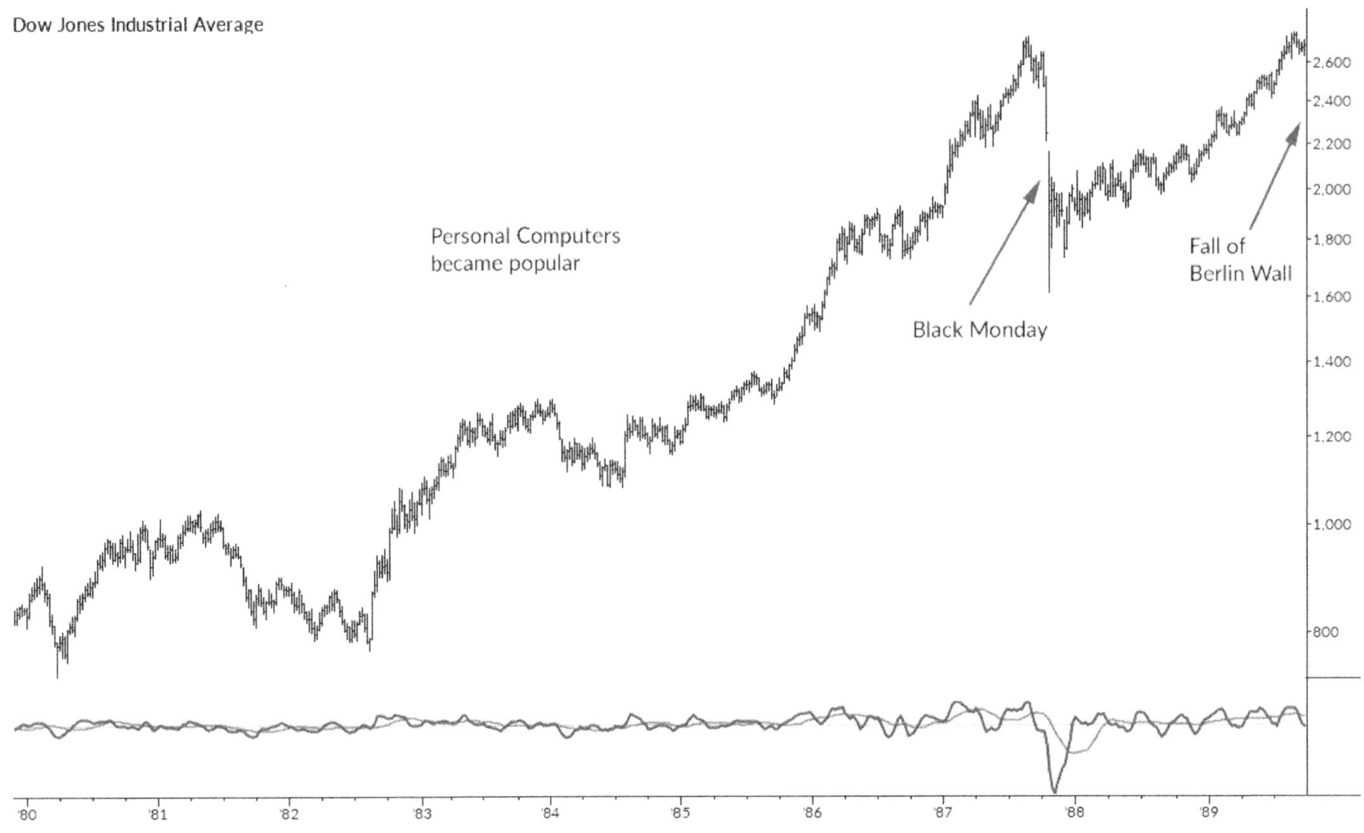

Summary stats for 1980-1989

Starting/ending price: 824.57 / 2753.20

Total return: 233.9% Average daily return: 5.4bp

Average/highest Hvol(20): 18.0% / 161.1% (10/21/1987)

Highest/lowest price: 2791.41 (10/9/1989) / 759.13 (4/21/1980)

Days with new 52 week high/low closes: 232 / 37

Biggest percent gain/loss: 10.1% (10/21/1987) / -22.6% (10/19/1987)

Biggest volatility-adjusted gain/loss: 5.7σ (8/17/1982) / -13.2σ (10/13/1989)

Number of days >2σ/>3σ/>4σ/>5σ: 105 / 24 / 5 / 1

Number of days <-2σ/<-3σ/<-4σ/<-5σ: 80 / 16 / 6 / 3

This chart shows action after the extreme 1987 selloff. The reasons for this selloff are even today not fully understood, but the price acount around this even provides a good template for a market dealing with a large, volatile shock.

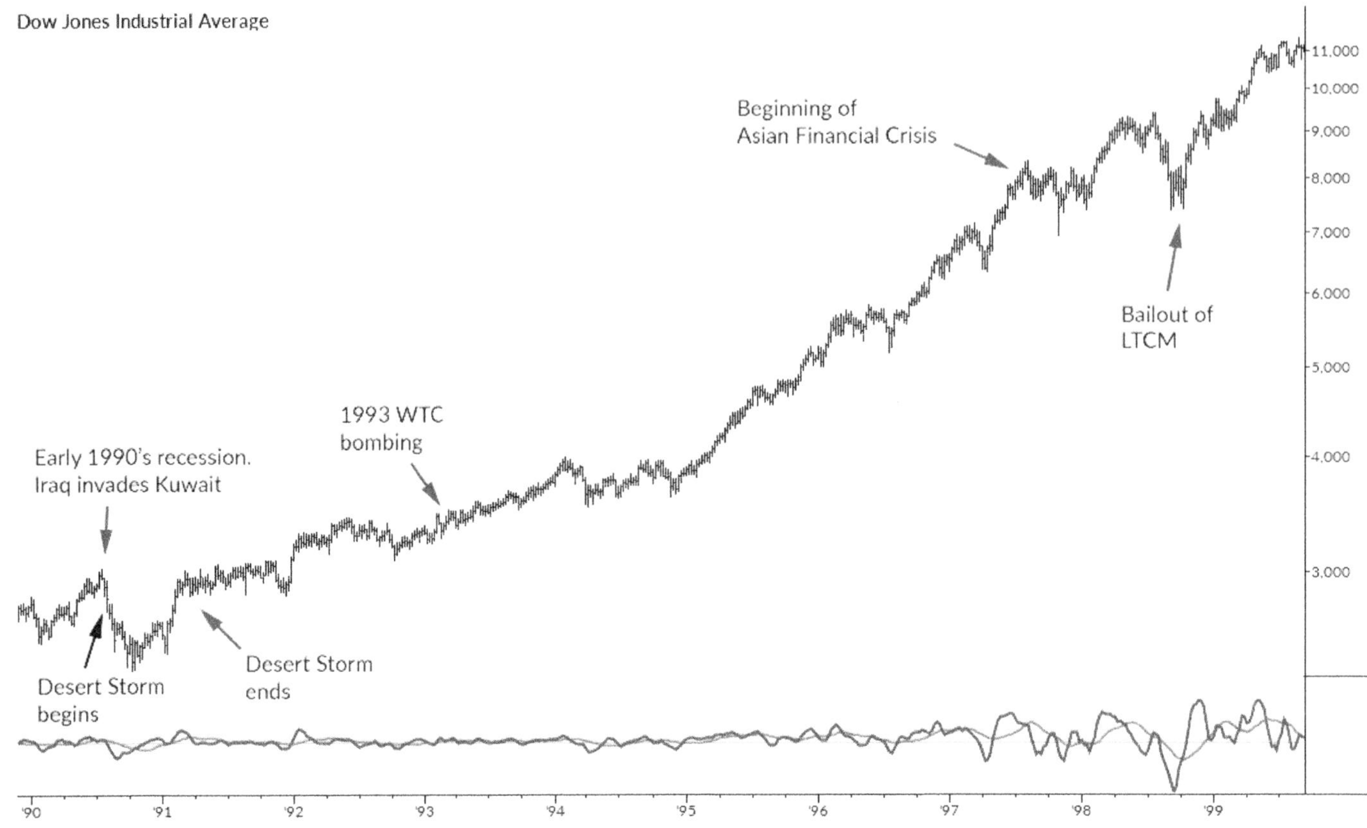

Summary stats for 1990-1999

Starting/ending price: 2810.15 / 11497.12

Total return: 309.1% Average daily return: 6.0bp

Average/highest Hvol(20): 14.1% / 79.1% (9/8/1998)

Highest/lowest price: 11497.12 (12/31/1999) / 2365.10 (10/11/1990)

Days with new 52 week high/low closes: 315 / 5

Biggest percent gain/loss: 5.0% (9/8/1998) / -7.2% (10/27/1997)

Biggest volatility-adjusted gain/loss: 5.5σ (1/17/1991) / -7.2σ (11/15/1991)

Number of days >2σ/>3σ/>4σ/>5σ: 95 / 11 / 3 / 1

Number of days <-2σ/<-3σ/<-4σ/<-5σ: 94 / 23 / 6 / 3

Summary stats for 2000-2009

Starting/ending price: 11357.51 / 10428.05

Total return: -8.2% Average daily return: .5bp

Average/highest Hvol(20): 20.9% / 175.9% (10/13/2008)

Highest/lowest price: 14164.53 (10/9/2007) / 6547.05 (3/9/2009)

Days with new 52 week high/low closes: 128 / 47

Biggest percent gain/loss: 11.1% (10/13/2008) / -7.9% (10/15/2008)

Biggest volatility-adjusted gain/loss: 3.7σ (4/18/2006) / -8.7σ (2/27/2007)

Number of days >2σ/>3σ/>4σ/>5σ: 77 / 7 / 0 / 0

Number of days <-2σ/<-3σ/<-4σ/<-5σ: 88 / 18 / 5 / 2

Summary stats for 2010-September 2017

Starting/ending price: 10583.96 / 22405.09
Total return: 111.7% Average daily return: 4.3bp
Average/highest Hvol(20): 13.9% / 67.3% (11/30/2011)
Highest/lowest price: 22412.59 (9/20/2017) / 9686.48 (7/2/2010)
Days with new 52 week high/low closes: 261 / 3
Biggest percent gain/loss: 4.2% (11/30/2011) / -5.5% (8/8/2011)
Biggest volatility-adjusted gain/loss: 5.5σ (11/7/2016) / -6.8σ (9/9/2016)
Number of days >2σ/>3σ/>4σ/>5σ: 64 / 15 / 3 / 1
Number of days <-2σ/<-3σ/<-4σ/<-5σ: 82 / 26 / 7 / 3

Section 5: US Stock Market Events in Daily Bars

The charts in this section present a handful of major historical events in US stocks. This time, the charts are daily bars, to allow you to zoom in and look at the action around each of these points.

There are many ways to work through these points effectively, but a good idea is to take the best from your work to this point:

- Consider trend and range structures.
- Consider strength of trend measures. In how many of these cases was the market already trending in the direction of the eventual shock?
- What happened after the shock? Which led to persistent strength, and which were quickly recovered?
- This might be another case where doing some "chart story" format work is appropriate, always remember the dangers of overexplaining. Thinking about dynamics and flows as these patterns were formed will give some good insight into market psychology and pattern formation.

This is far from a comprehensive list, but it is interesting to see the common elements of how the market absorbs information and reacts to shocks. Having a good understanding of these patterns will further your intuitive read and understanding of market action.

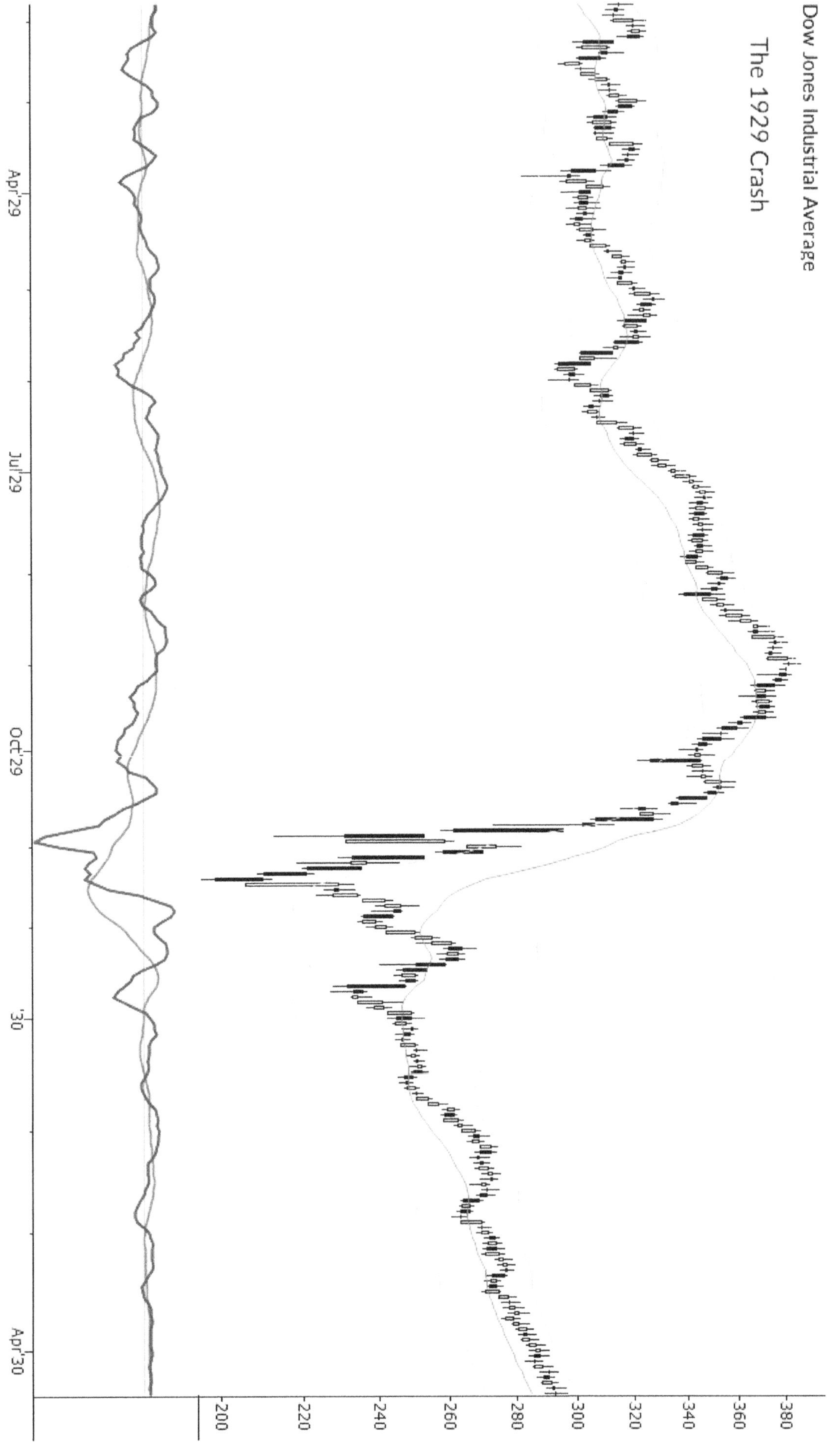
Dow Jones Industrial Average
The 1929 Crash
Apr'29
Jul'29
Oct'29
'30
Apr'30
200
220
240
260
280
300
320
340
360
380

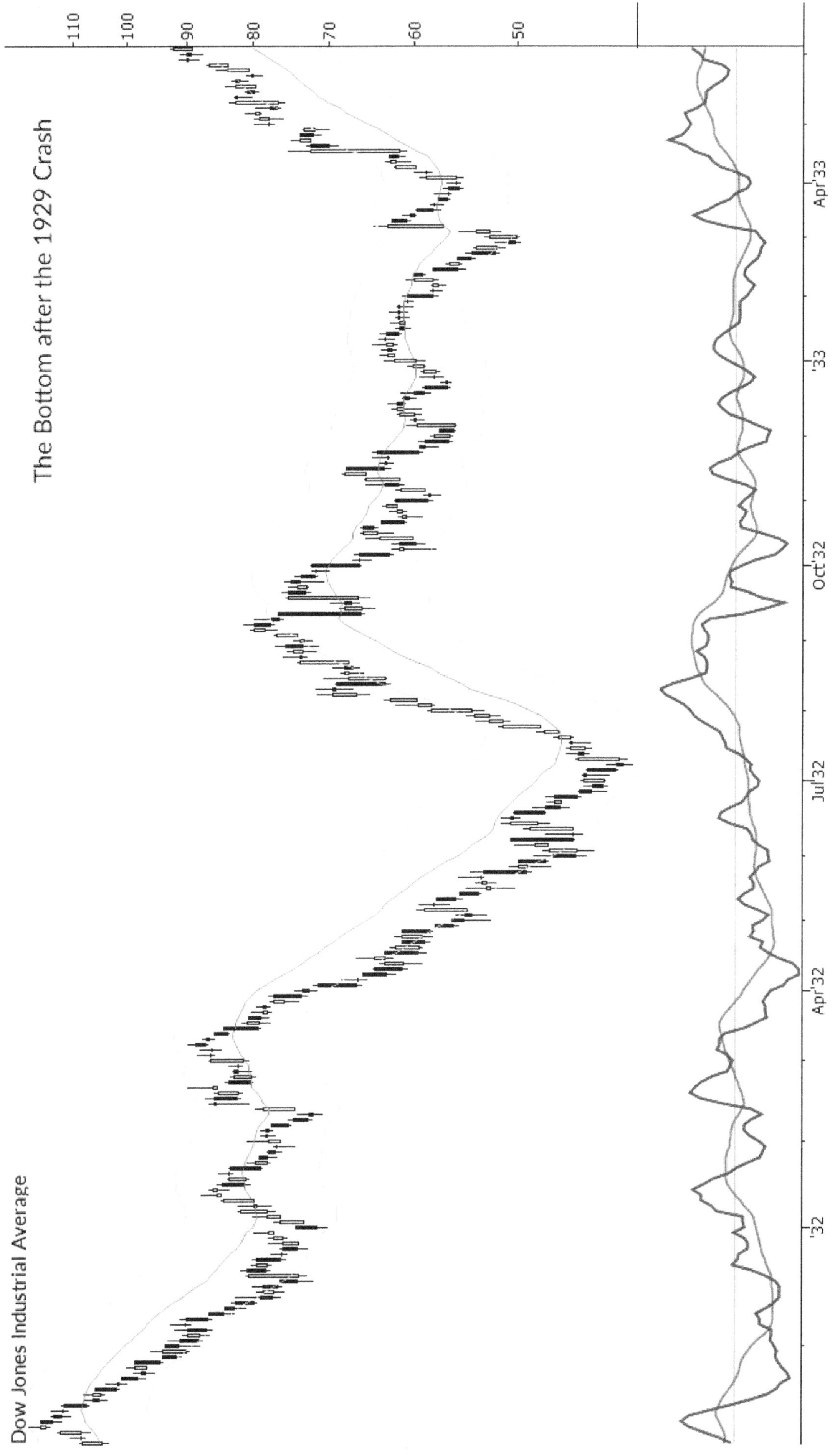
Dow Jones Industrial Average
The Bottom after the 1929 Crash
110
100
90
80
70
60
50
'32
Apr'32
Jul'32
Oct'32
'33
Apr'33

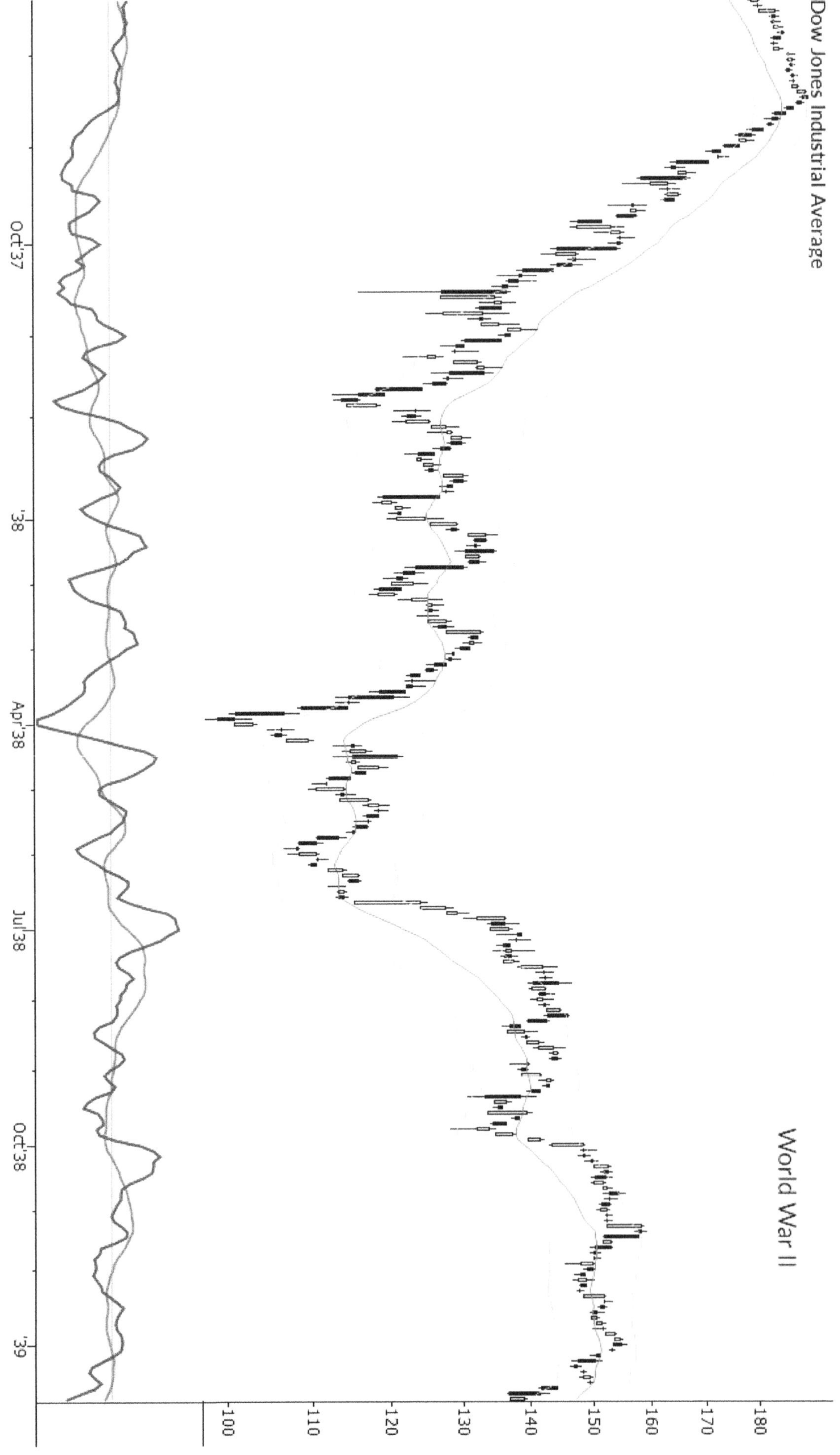
Dow Jones Industrial Average
World War II
Oct'37
'38
Apr'38
Jul'38
Oct'38
'39
100
110
120
130
140
150
160
170
180

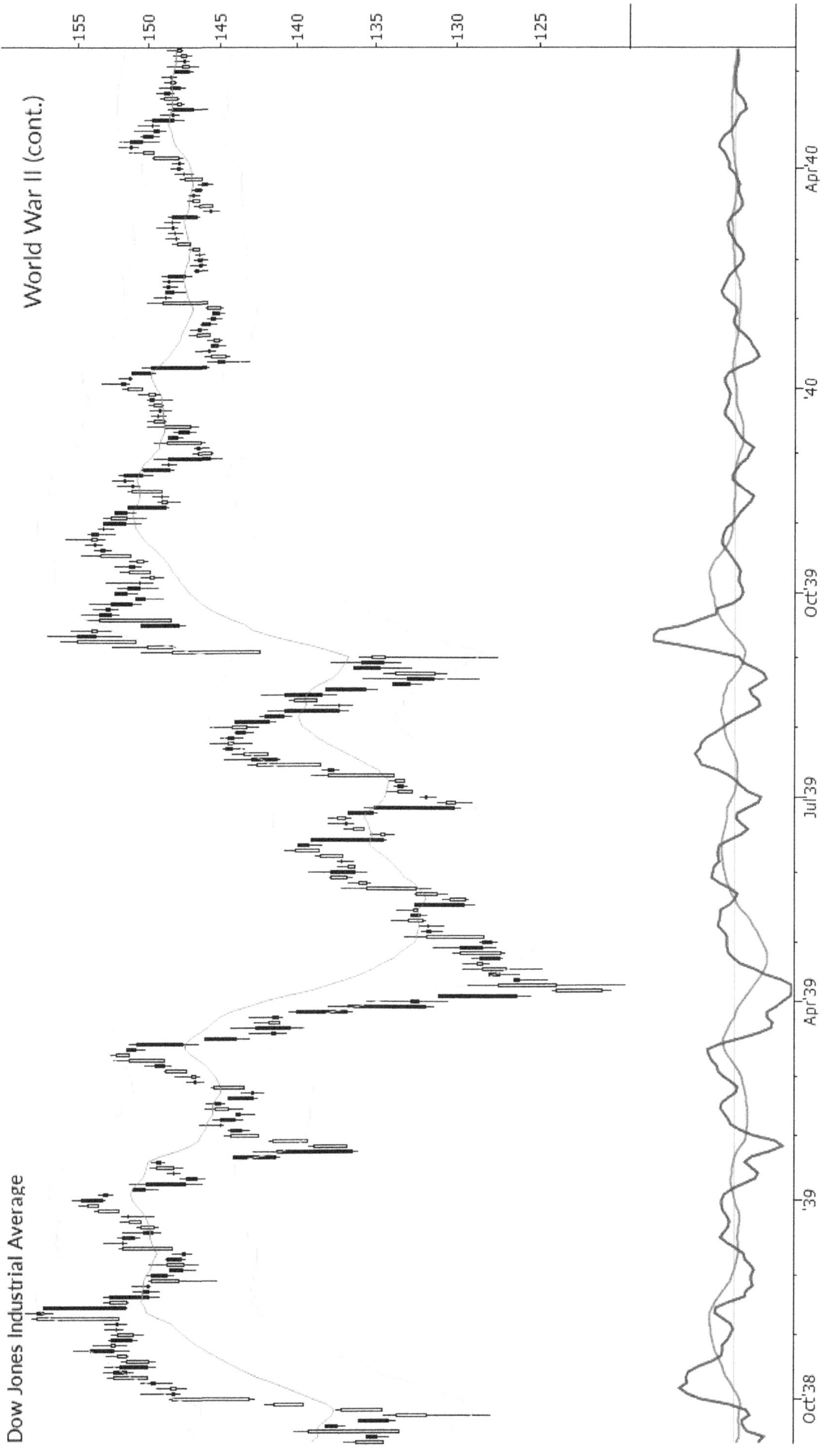
Dow Jones Industrial Average
World War II (cont.)
155
150
145
140
135
130
125
Oct'38
'39
Apr'39
Jul'39
Oct'39
'40
Apr'40

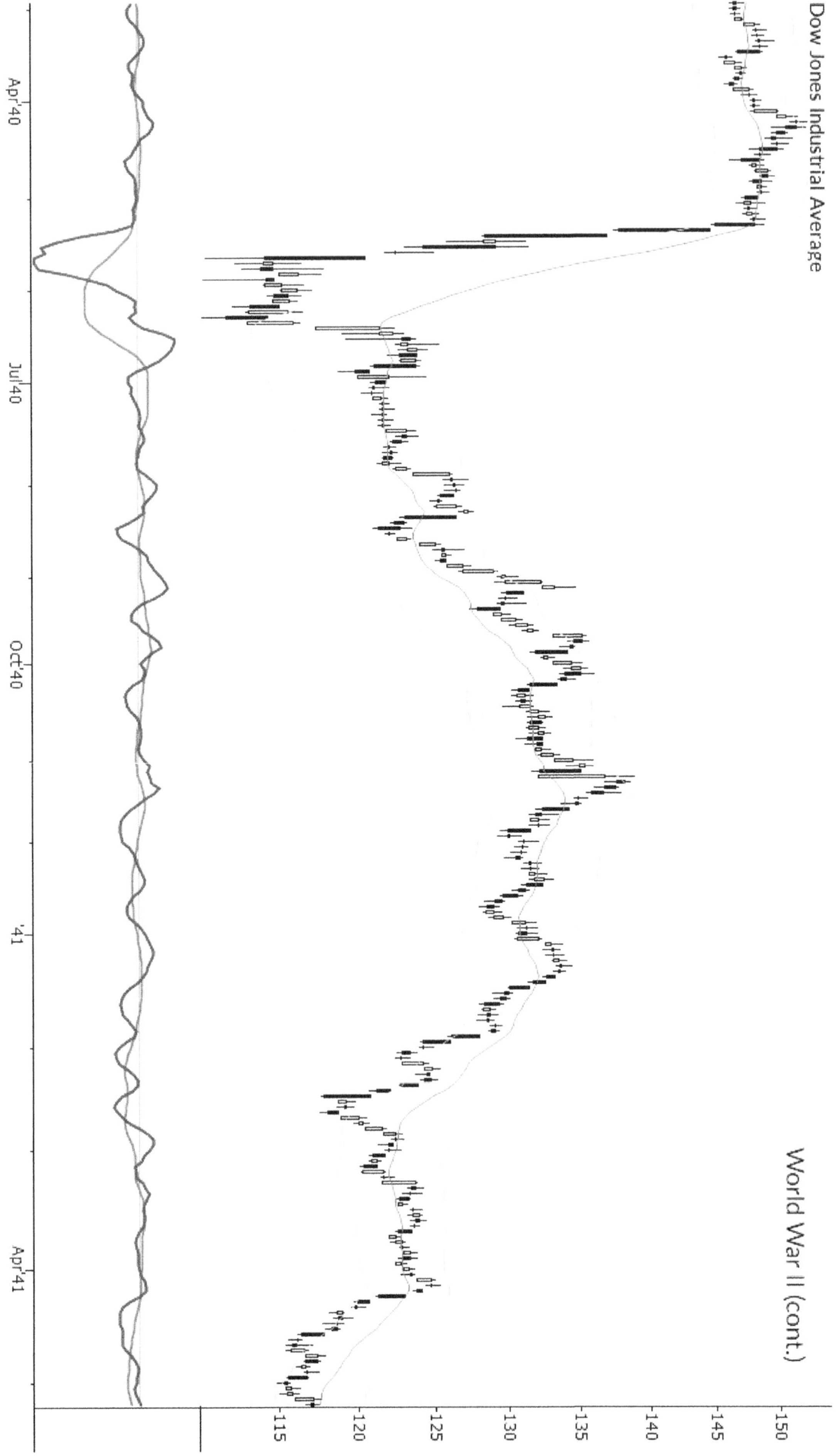
Dow Jones Industrial Average
World War II (cont.)
Apr'40
Jul'40
Oct'40
'41
Apr'41
115
120
125
130
135
140
145
150

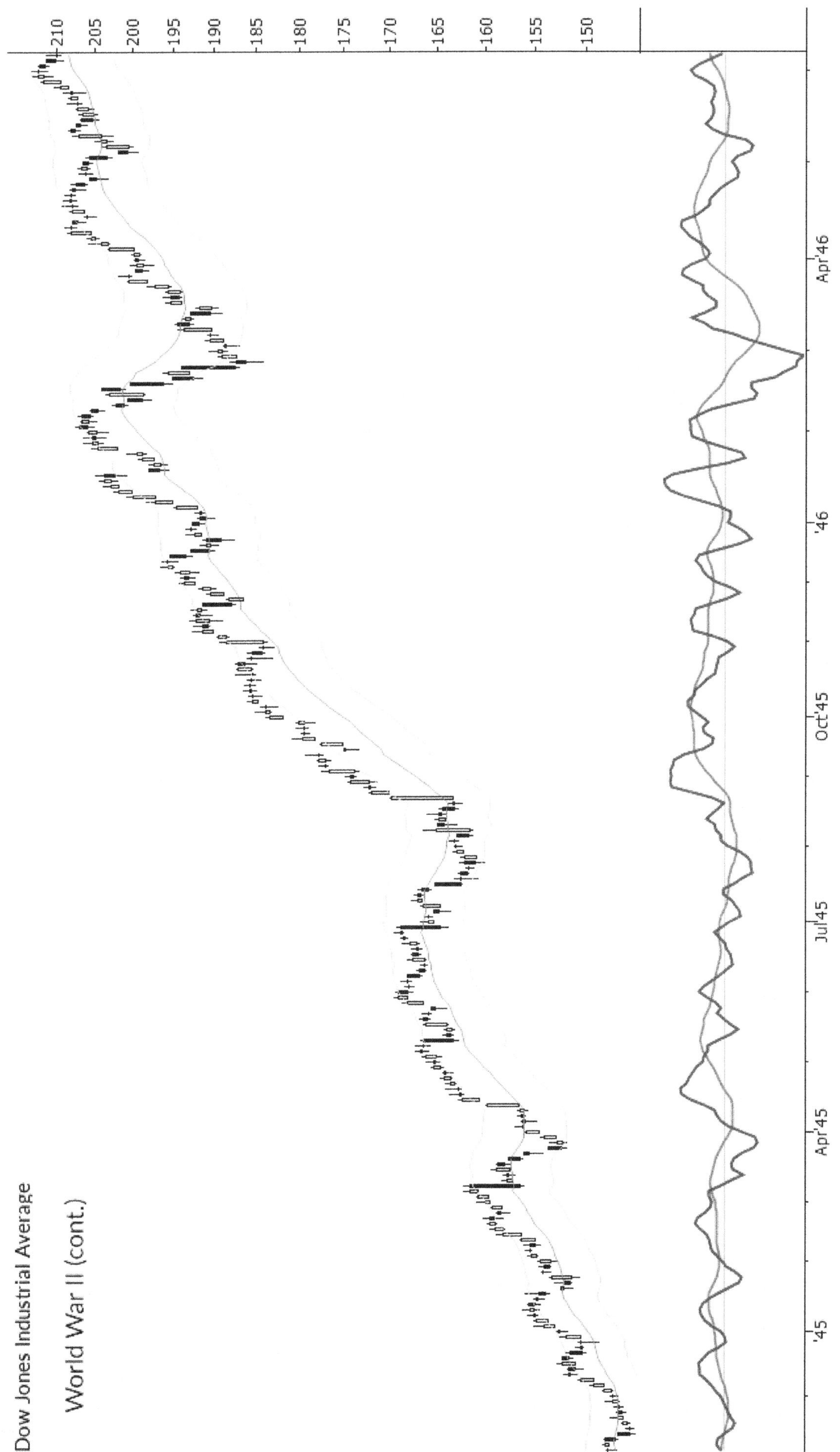
Dow Jones Industrial Average
World War II (cont.)
210
205
200
195
190
185
180
175
170
165
160
155
150
'45
Apr'45
Jul'45
Oct'45
'46
Apr'46

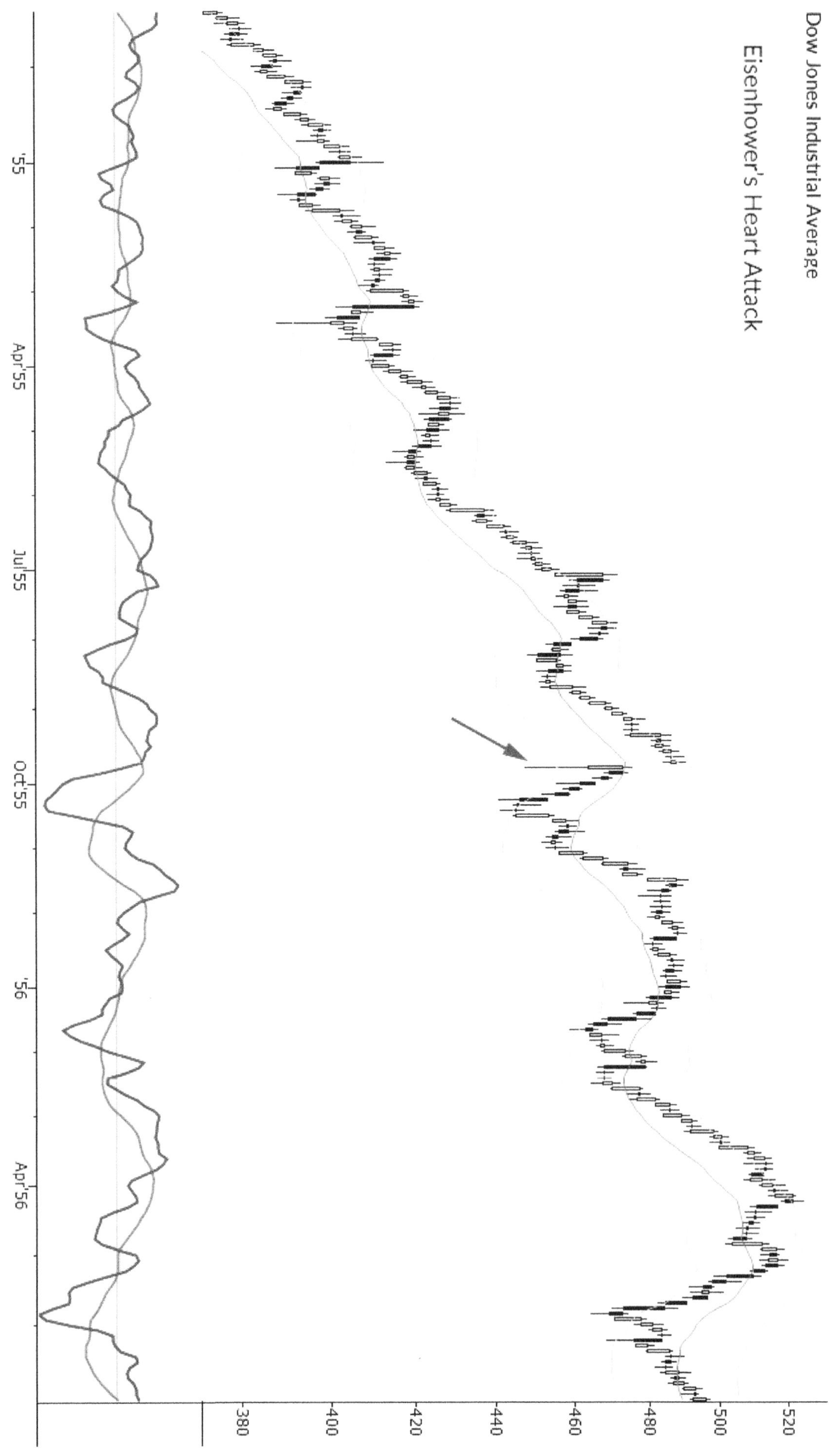
Dow Jones Industrial Average
Eisenhower's Heart Attack
'55
Apr'55
Jul'55
Oct'55
'56
Apr'56
380
400
420
440
460
480
500
520

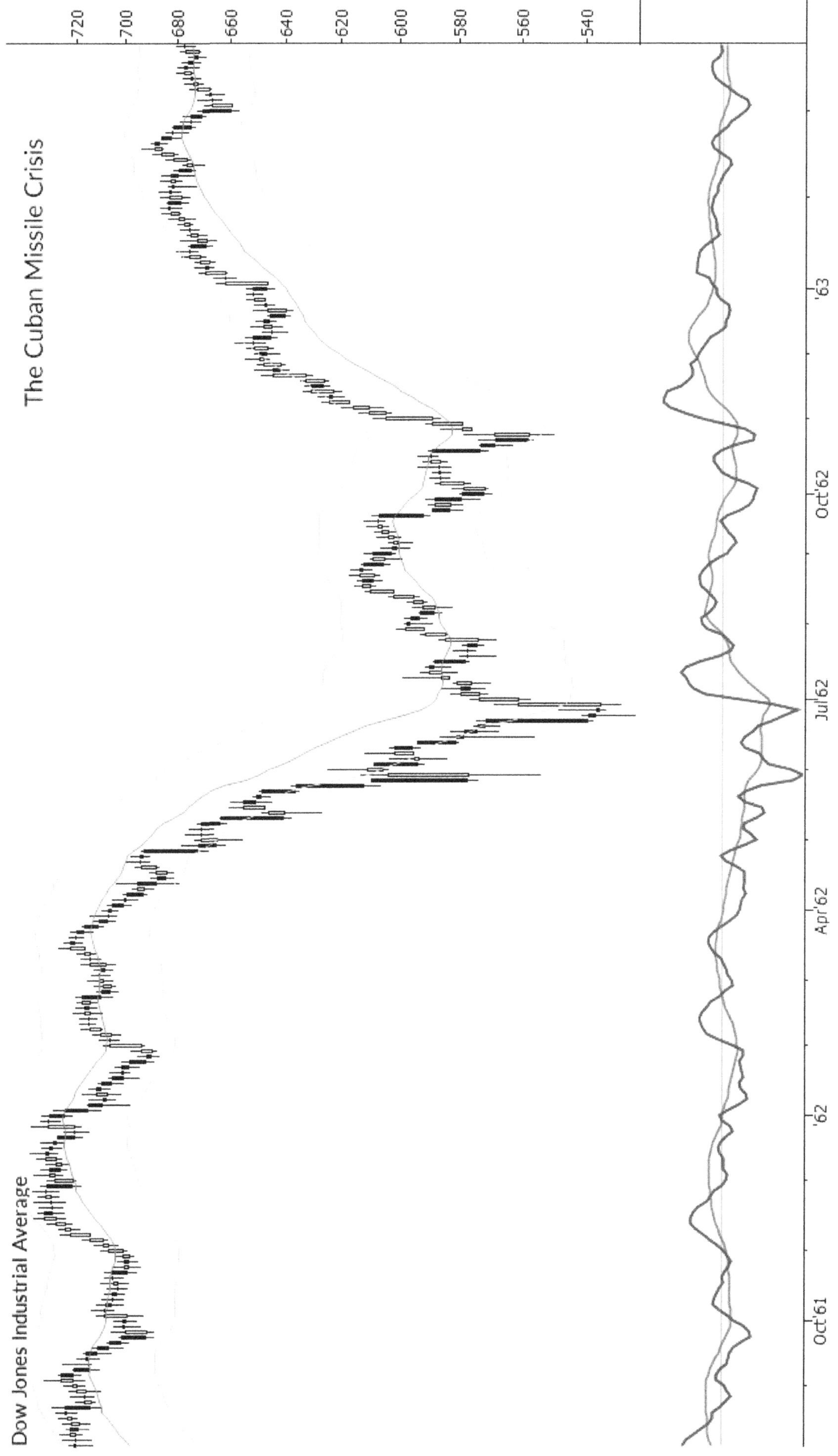
Dow Jones Industrial Average
The Cuban Missile Crisis
720
700
680
660
640
620
600
580
560
540
Oct'61
'62
Apr'62
Jul'62
Oct'62
'63

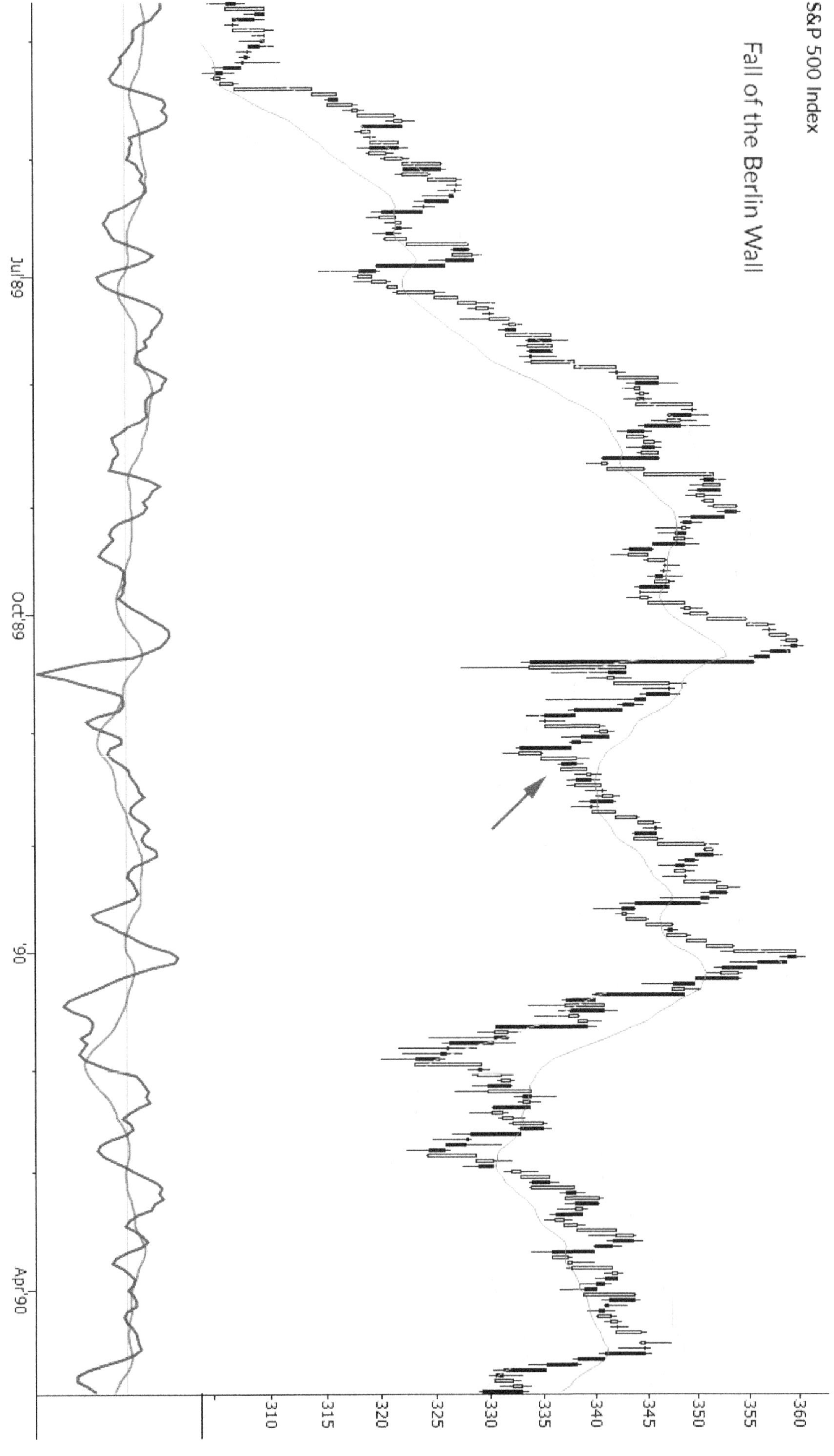
S&P 500 Index
Fall of the Berlin Wall
Jul'89
Oct'89
'90
Apr'90
310
315
320
325
330
335
340
345
350
355
360

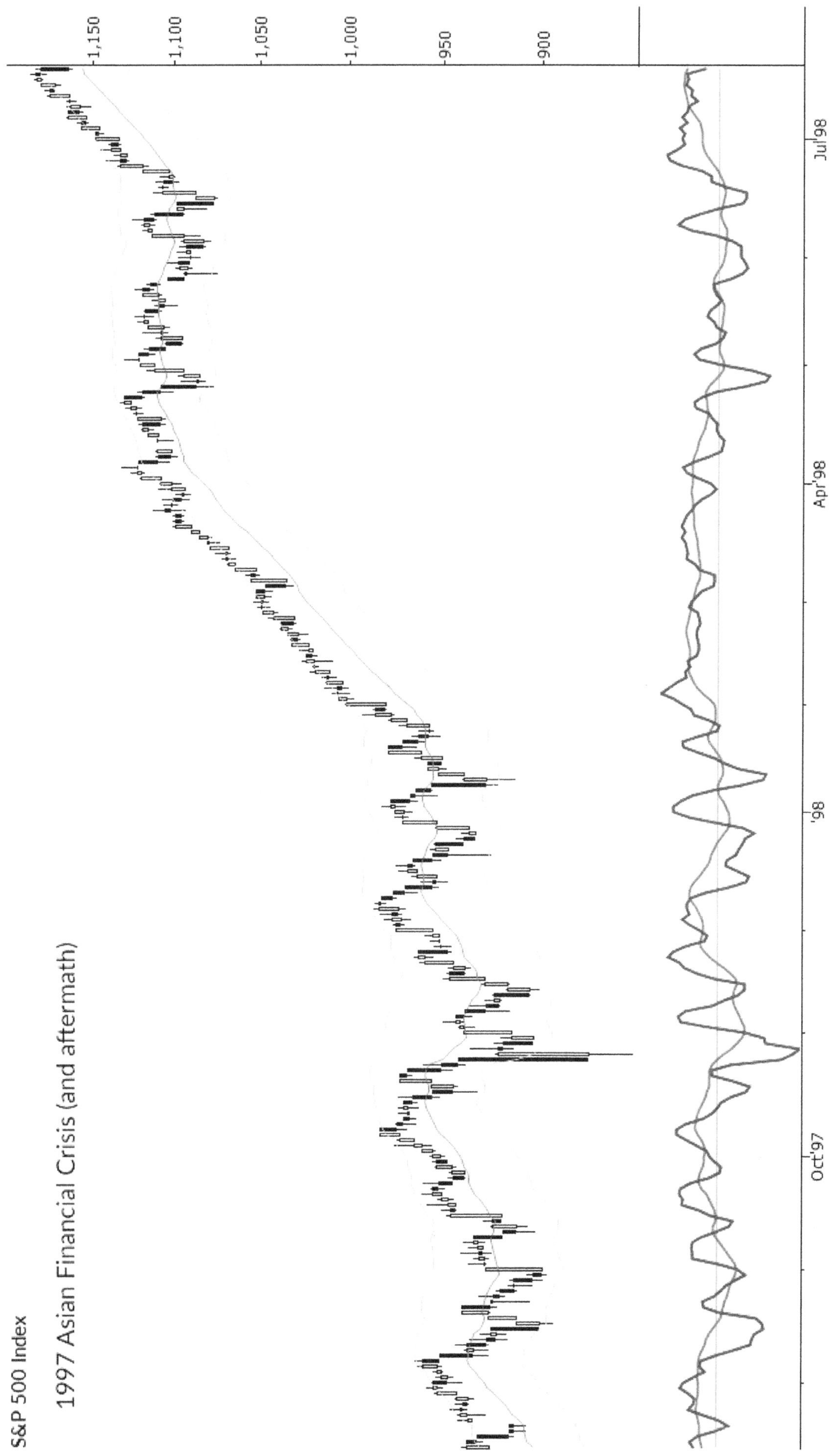
S&P 500 Index
1997 Asian Financial Crisis (and aftermath)
1,150
1,100
1,050
1,000
950
900
Oct'97
'98
Apr'98
Jul'98

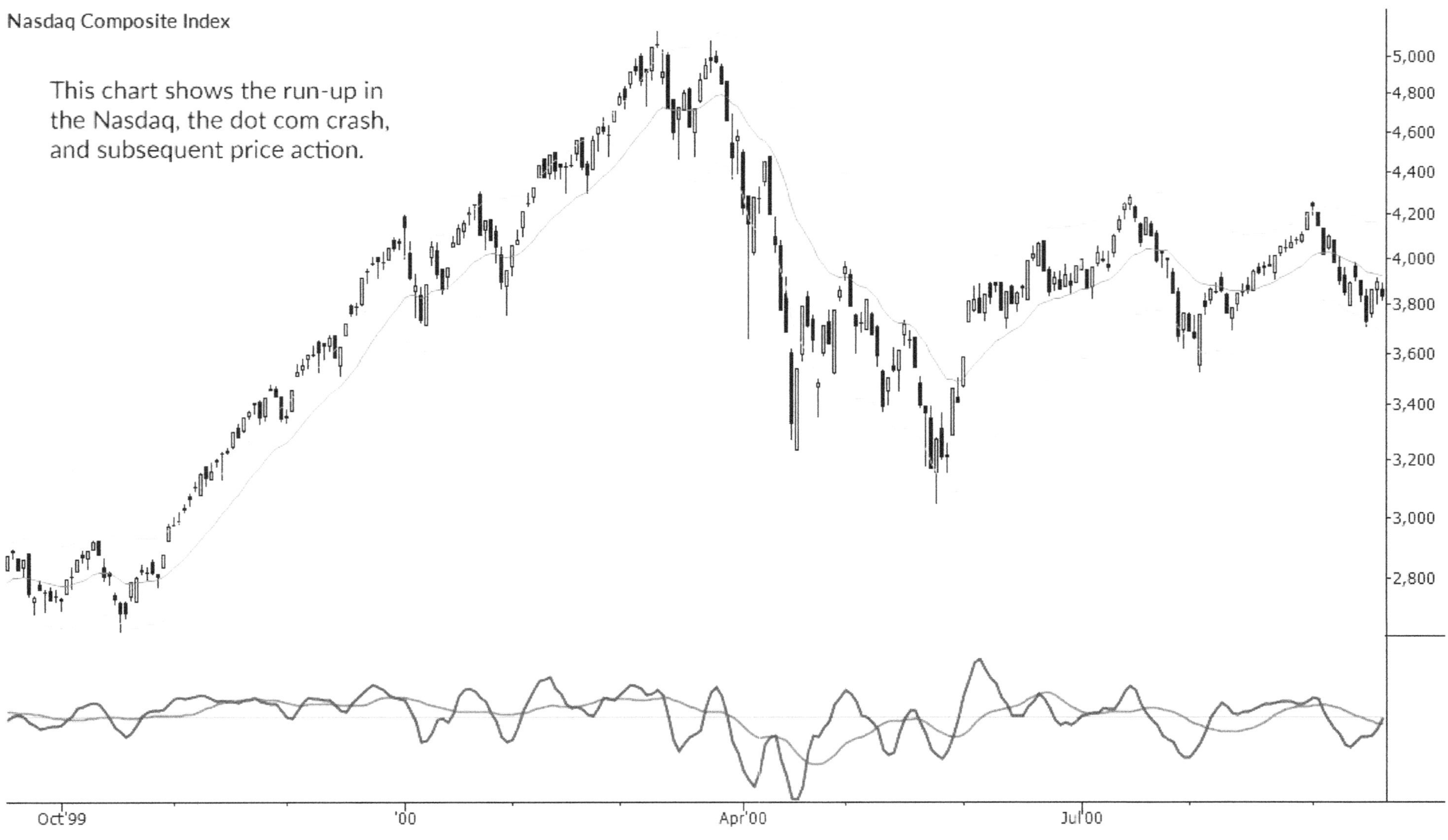

This chart shows the run-up in the Nasdaq, the dot com crash, and subsequent price action.

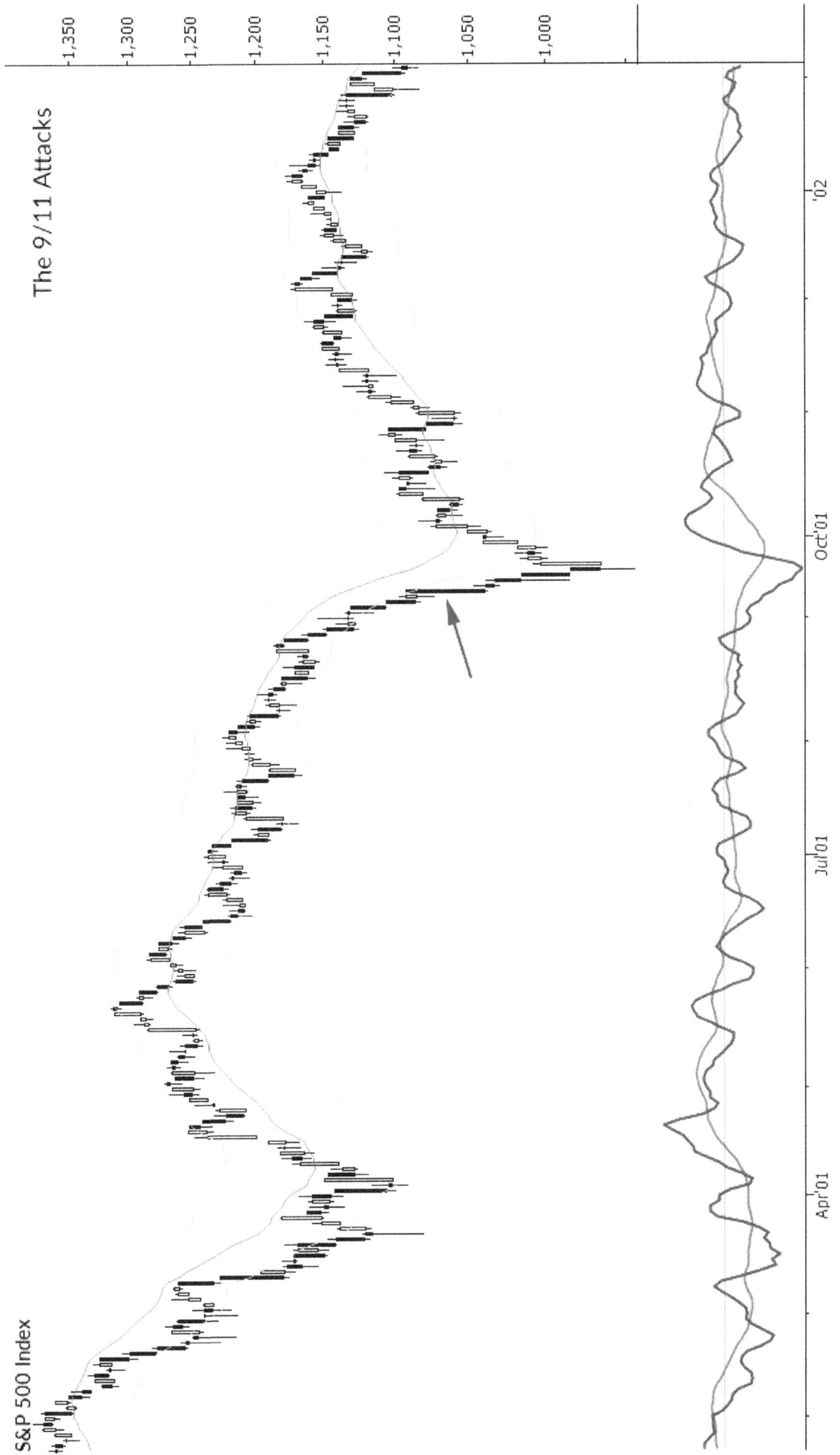
The 9/11 Attacks
S&P 500 Index
1,350
1,300
1,250
1,200
1,150
1,100
1,050
1,000
Apr'01
Jul'01
Oct'01
'02

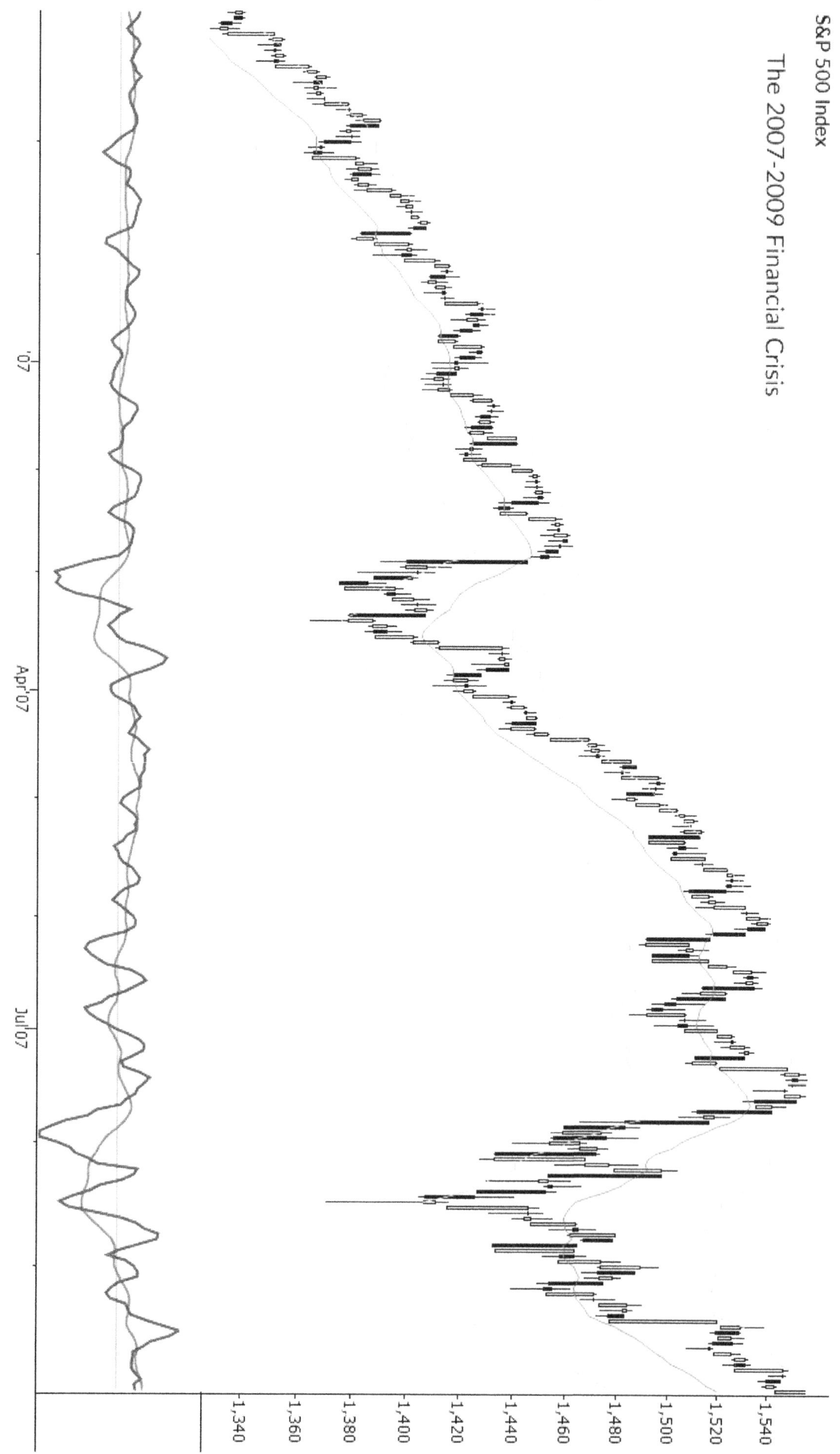
S&P 500 Index
The 2007-2009 Financial Crisis
'07
Apr'07
Jul'07
1,340
1,360
1,380
1,400
1,420
1,440
1,460
1,480
1,500
1,520
1,540

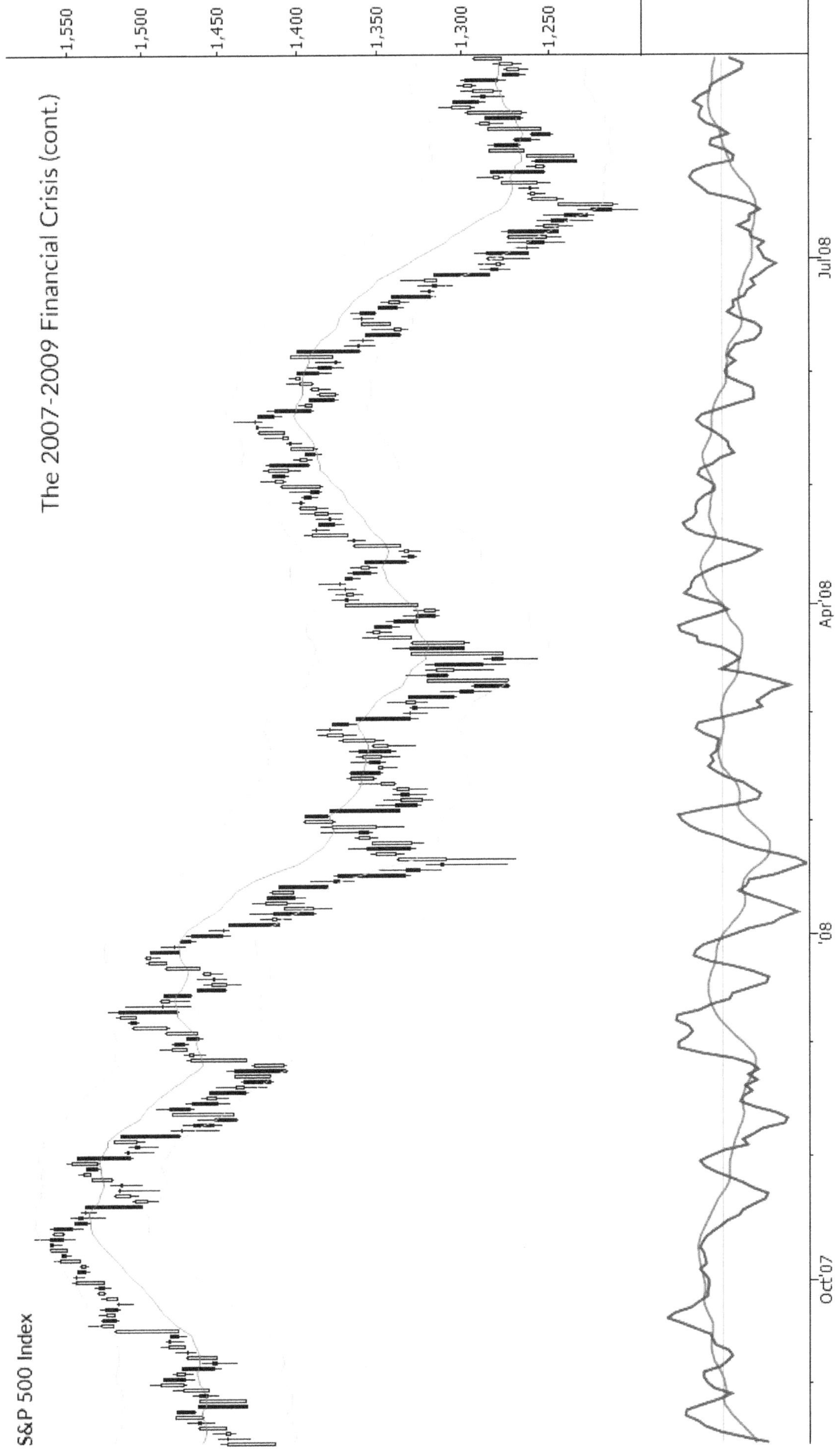
S&P 500 Index
The 2007-2009 Financial Crisis (cont.)
1,550
1,500
1,450
1,400
1,350
1,300
1,250
Oct'07
'08
Apr'08
Jul'08

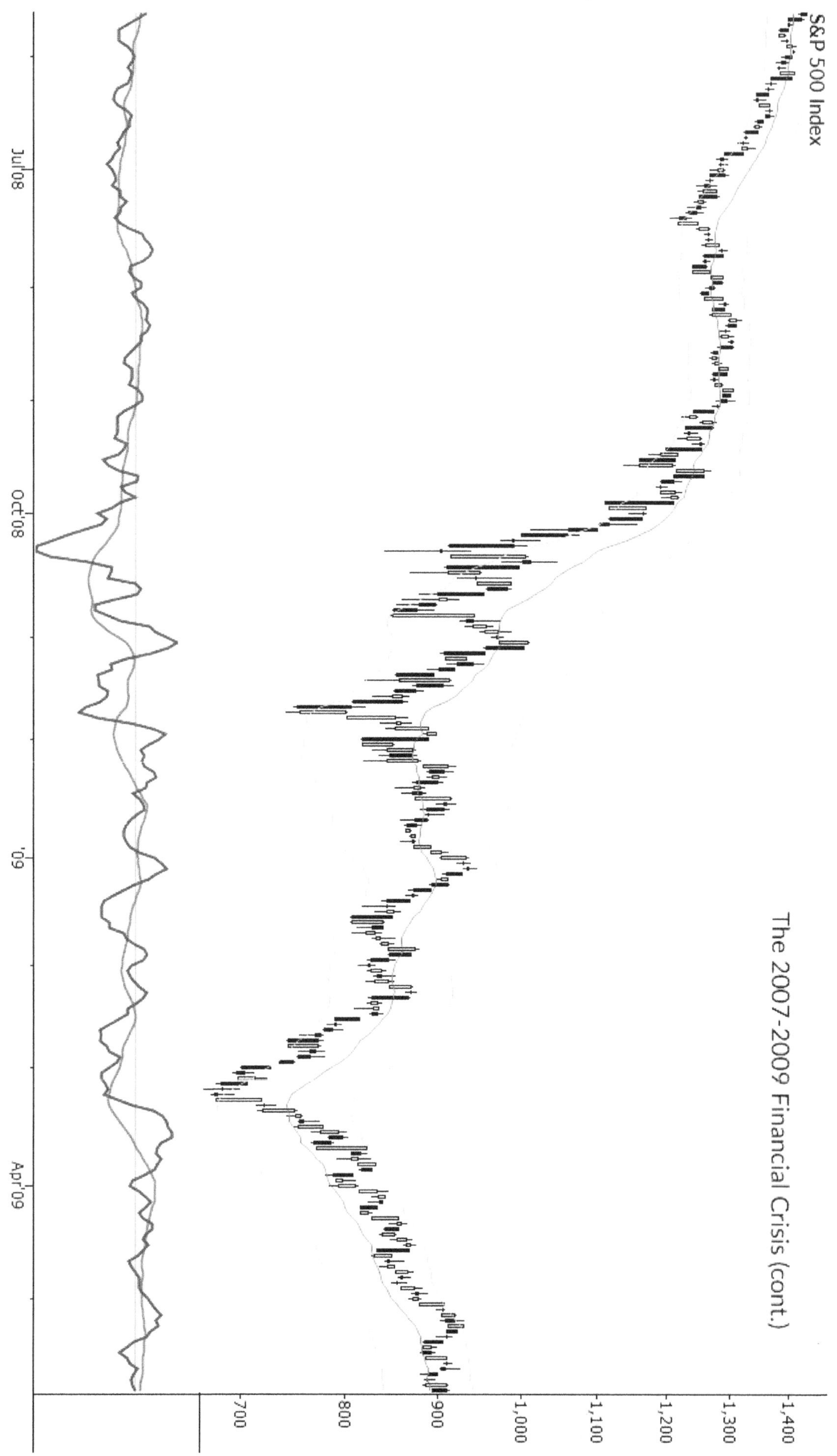
S&P 500 Index
The 2007-2009 Financial Crisis (cont.)
Jul'08
Oct'08
'09
Apr'09
700
800
900
1,000
1,100
1,200
1,300
1,400

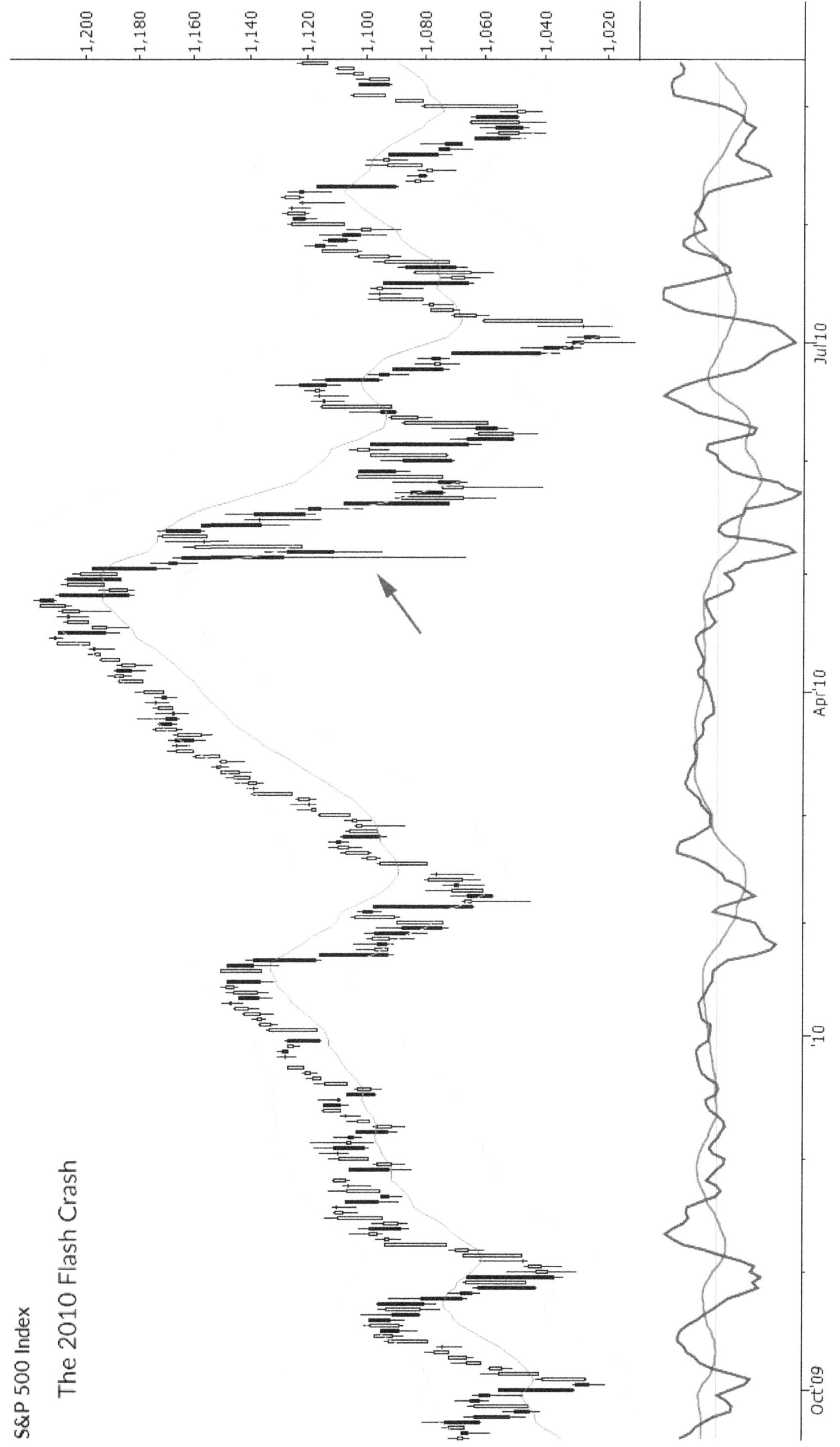
S&P 500 Index
The 2010 Flash Crash
1,200
1,180
1,160
1,140
1,120
1,100
1,080
1,060
1,040
1,020
Oct'09
'10
Apr'10
Jul'10

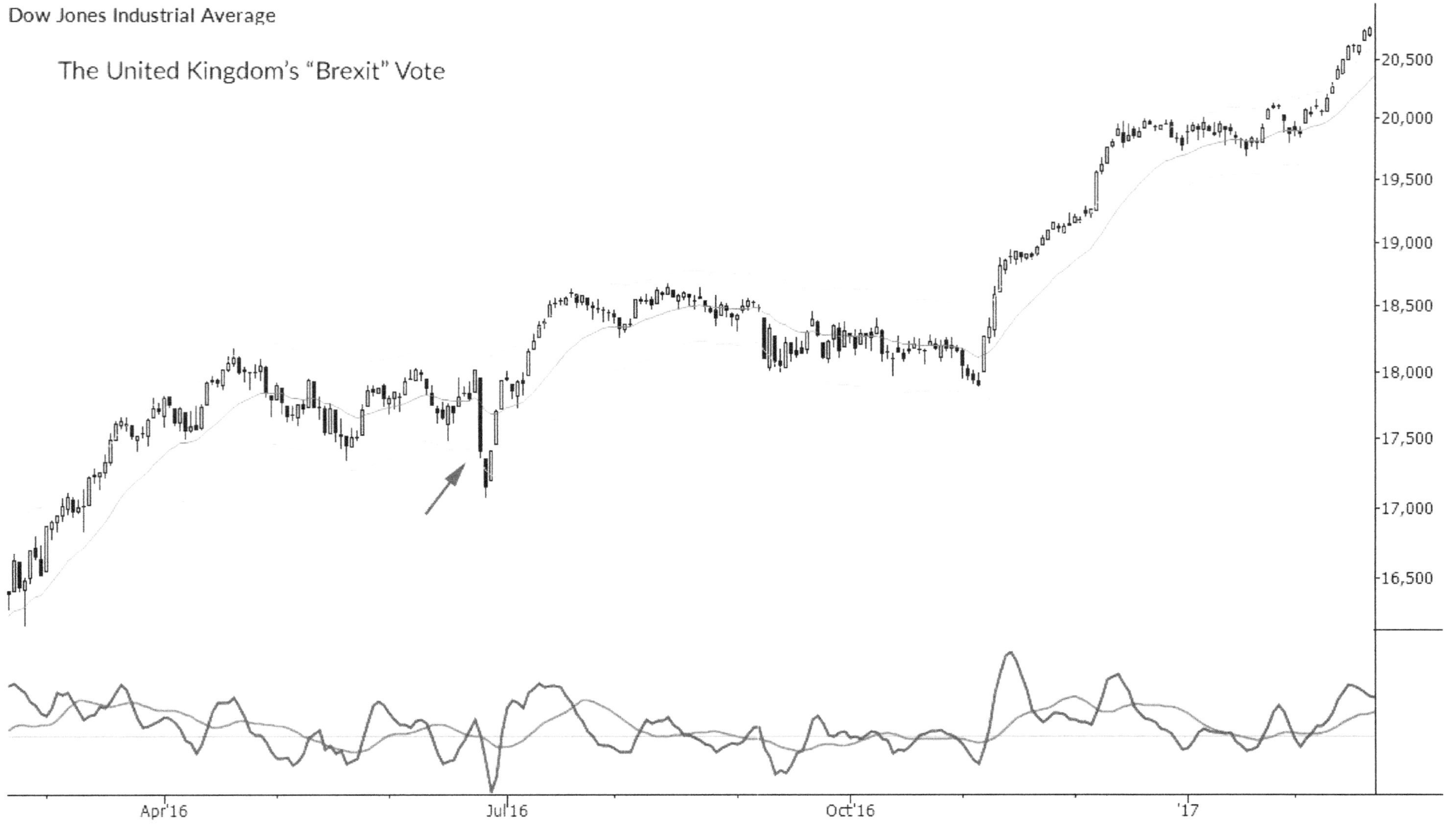
Dow Jones Industrial Average
The United Kingdom's "Brexit" Vote
20,500
20,000
19,500
19,000
18,500
18,000
17,500
17,000
16,500
Apr'16
Jul'16
Oct'16
'17

Section 6: Readings

From *The Art and Science of Technical Analysis: Market Structure, Price Action, and Trading Strategies* by Adam Grimes, Wiley, 2012:

149-153 (failure test)
314-326 (failure test examples)
254-262 (basic trading stats)
389-398 (trading stats)

Challenges to Traditional Technical Analysis

Some Challenges for Technical Analysis

After some success in trading, I started testing ideas quantitatively, and discovered that almost nothing worked "as advertised" in the technical analysis literature.. When I went to experts in the field, I was rebuffed and told that it was wrong to focus too much on statistics, rather "you just have to make it work for you", backed up with vague appeals to the authority. When I dug into that authority, I discovered that most of this work was done in an era when people had little access to data and few techniques to evaluate if something really worked. The field of data analysis was still in development, and access to market data was spotty and limited—certainly not ideal conditions. Furthermore, it was proving difficult to substantiate their findings because the things that I tested generally tested poorly.

What is technical analysis?

The problem might begin with how we define technical analysis. A brief excerpt from Edwards and Magee (1948):

> *...two quite distinctive schools of thought have arisen, two radically different methods of arriving at the answers to the trader's problem of what and when. ...one of these is commonly referred to as the fundamental or statistical, and the other as the technical. (In recent years a third approach, the cyclical, has made rapid progress and, although still beset by a "lunatic fringe", it promises to contribute a great deal to our understanding of economic trends.) The stock market fundamentalist depends on statistics...*

The modern quantitative analyst is likely to be confused by the word "statistics", but, in this case, the term refers to financial statements, aspects of the company's competitive position in the industry. So, what we have here is just a semantic difference, and fundamental analysis today still broadly encompasses the same areas. They go on to say:

> *The term "technical", in its application to the stock market, has come to have a very special meaning, quite different from its ordinary dictionary definition. It refers to the study of the action of the market itself as opposed to the study of the good in which the market deals. Technical Analysis is the science of recording, usually in graphic form, the actual history of trading (price changes, volume of transactions, etc.)... and then deducing from that pictured history the probable future trend.*

And, here, I believe we arrive at the central problem of traditional technical analysis: it is *a visual discipline*: We look at pictures on charts and try to predict the future direction of the market based on those pictures. If we accept that definition at face value (and most practitioners have wholeheartedly embraced that definition), then technical analysis is mostly untestable and highly subjective. People may look at the same picture and draw different conclusions, and who can say who is right and who is wrong? While it might be possible to generate a track record of a specific analyst's calls, it is not possible to test the actual method.

I have defined technical analysis more broadly by saying, "technical traders and analysts make decisions based on information contained in past price changes themselves." That is the key distinction between technical and fundamental: Technical decisions are made based on information contained in the movements of the market (perhaps with additional information beyond price such as volume, whether a trade was on the bid or ask, coincident movements in related markets, etc.), and fundamental analysis incorporates outside factors. With those definitions, we are ready to make some progress.

Charts are useful

Now, don't get me wrong. I'm not saying we should throw charts out. A chart is a visual display of data. The visual display may be useful because it speaks to "more" of our cognitive capacity than a simple list of numbers can. In other words, by seeing pictures and shapes on charts, it is quite possible that we are engaging some inductive reasoning, and some other ways of knowing that may transcend logical analysis. So, don't throw your charts out, yet, and if you laugh at charts because you're tired of hearing people talk about the "double dipping two dog reversal pattern aligning with the harmonic convergence of the third wave's structural retracement ratios", know that your problem is with the way charts are used, not with charts themselves.

There is no free lunch

This is one of the core principles of finance. Though the details may be complex, I believe core truths must always be simple and readily explainable—I use the "smart eight year old" test. (The other principles of modern finance, in my opinion, are also simple: 1) A dollar today is worth more than a dollar tomorrow. 2) People should demand more reward for more risk, and 3) people sometimes make mistakes.) Markets are highly competitive, with a lot of smart people with a lot of money trying to make profits. Arbitrage opportunities (basically, free money) do exist, but they are rare, usually disappear quickly, and can often only be profitable for people with special access or conditions. There's that old joke about an economist who comes upon a $1,000 bill lying on the sidewalk and won't pick it up because it "can't be there", and there's a grain of truth in that joke. We may sometimes find "gifts" in the market, but it is exceedingly rare, and we can't count on it.

There are patterns in prices

Here, I depart from some of the academic research, which suggests that prices are wholly described by random walks. More research, however, supports the idea that there are some patterns and some predictable elements in prices. This should tell you just how thin the statistical edges (if they exist) are. Many traders seem to discount academic research as irrelevant; I think that's a mistake, but if you choose to do so you must at least admit that researchers are highly educated, intelligent, and spend a lot of time carefully looking at data. Some researchers find contradictory evidence. In some cases, this points to problems with methodology, but, more often, it is that different standards of proof are used and the statistical edges only exist in some markets for some time periods. My work suggests that there are some rather simple patterns that work with a degree of reliability, but, again, the edges are small.

We can test patterns objectively, but we must be careful

One of the perennial defenses of technical analysis is "you can't test it. You just have to figure out what works for you", with the emphasis clearly on the *for you*. If you can't make money with the method, then the problem is yours because you just didn't figure out how to use it, or maybe you just need to work on your trading psychology. However, back up a minute. Consider the well-known nugget of statistical wisdom: correlation does not imply causation. Yes, I think most of us know this, but what might not be so clear is that *causation does imply correlation*.

In other words, you can't have a relationship in the data that is both real and important, and also invisible. Now, step back and apply that to technical analysis. If something works, then it should work objectively.

Fibonacci ratios define and limit retracements in financial markets? Ok, then retracements should terminate more often near those ratios. Moving averages provide support and resistance? Ok, then when price touches a moving average, we should see non-random price movement follow. (Note that I don't know what will happen after price touches, but I do know it must somehow be non-random. If what happens to a market after an event is no different from any other time, it was, by definition, a "non-event".) Bollinger bands set +/- 2.0 standard deviations around a moving average contain 95% of price action? Ok, well that's not too hard to test, either.

We must be humble and objective in our testing; any test is a joint test of the test itself and whatever pattern might or might not be in the data. In other words, we must think of a way to test an idea, and maybe we came up with a bad way to test it or missed something important. That's certainly possible, but the idea of asking questions and seeing what the data says is a solid approach.

I don't see much of this data-driven work being done in technical analysis. The examples I gave above range from fairly hard to test to simple. The Bollinger test is extremely simple and anyone can do it with free data in a few hours, yet nearly every book on technical analysis repeats that completely bogus statistic on Bollinger Bands. (Hint: the rule of thumb would only be valid if price deviations from a moving average were normally distributed, and they clearly are not.) The Fibonacci tests are harder; they require many assumptions and we have to create some test structure. If we find no Fibonacci influence, maybe we just didn't structure the question correctly—there will always be another way we can test this idea. However, my thinking is that once we test it enough ways and don't find support, we start to ask how useful it can be. If something is really a strong influence on price movement, can it be that difficult to tease it out of the data?

It is easy to be misled by patterns

I've written on this extensively, as have many other writers, so we don't need to belabor the point here. Just know that we are basically wired to find patterns, and we will find them whether or not they actually exist. (Think of faces in clouds or voices in the seashell.) Furthermore, we tend to attach too much importance to memorable events. It is entirely possible to have a series of trades that are, overall, losing trades, but to remember them as an overall win because of one big or exciting trade. (Be careful how you do your trade review.) You can't "fix" these problems because they are fundamental part of the way we think and process information. What you can do, what you must do, is to counterbalance these foibles with objective, statistical analysis.

You must be literate in basic math and finance

There's no way around this. Though we all like the idea that you just have to learn some pattern and trade it to make money, the world doesn't work like that. (There is no free lunch, remember?) You should understand everything you can about the market, finance in general, the world, human behavior… the list goes on and on. You don't need to do this work to draw trendlines, but you do need a pretty deep understanding of statistics and probability to understand what might happen after a trendline is touched. While you're at it, it would be helpful to have some ability to analyze data. Microsoft Excel is not ideal, but better than nothing (and it has a short learning curve.) Consider Stata, R, Python or learning another "real" programming language. You don't want to be a programmer, but you do need to have the skills to rip through a dataset.

Think objectively

Other writers have made this call, and I will reiterate it. The discipline of technical analysis must move toward understanding the objective tendencies of price movement. Doing so requires correct methodology, careful thought and review, and a willingness to discard what is not useful. This work is already being done by swarms of quantitative analysts, but traditional technical analysis is stuck. Perhaps it is because of the roots of the discipline as a visual exercise, but I also wonder if it is, to some degree, simply laziness and a resistance to change. A friend of mine pointed out that many of the certification programs for technical analysis include a provision that you cannot criticize any work done by any other technical analyst. While that might work toward building a supportive community, that requirement is anathema to scientific progress. Science depends on people asking questions and working to find answers, and part of that process is reviewing the work done by other people, expanding on it, finding problems, and fixing what is wrong. Why is technical analysis any different? Why is peer review so thoroughly shunned by the community?

Intuition is real

Now, I realize I have perhaps just offended some people, so let me offend a different group here. (I'm joking, or at least I hope I am...) Objective, statistical analysis is critical, but there is also a place for intuition. There are other ways of knowing that go beyond rational analysis; intuition is real, valuable, and, I think, it can be trained. I have done extensive work on this subject. I have done some research and statistical work on what might be charitably called the "fringe" of perception, and there appears to be statistical support for intuition, even bordering on some aspects that people might call "ESP" (extra-sensory perception). There are probably aspects of market behavior, and certainly aspects of our individual decisions as traders or managers that we might not be able to quantify, and that is ok. Leave some room for intuition.

However, intuition must be guided by an understanding of how markets really move. For instance, I once sat in a training class for new intraday traders who were told to hold their stocks overnight if they made very large moves the day before. When I asked why, I was told that stocks usually continue the next day after a big move. Now, one of the strongest statistical tendencies in the market is for stocks to mean revert after large one day moves. This is only one example, but does it make any sense to train intuition against a strong statistical bias? There may be situations in which you wish to take a position against the statistical bias, but you still must understand which direction the wind usually blows.

Why does this matter?

This all matters because, very simply, we have a responsibility. If we write books, blogs, or even just share ideas online, don't we have a responsibility to make sure the tools we use are the best they can be? If you are trading your own money, then you have an obligation to yourself and to your family. If you manage client money, then you have a supreme responsibility to the client. The point of all our work and analysis must be to manage risk and find opportunity in the markets, and how can we do that unless we are willing to ask the hard questions of ourselves and of our methodology? Ask those questions, and don't be afraid of the answers.

What's Going On? Thinking Conceptually About Patterns

When I started trading, like many people, I was drawn to traditional technical analysis. I spent hours and hours studying different variations of patterns, often after creating the charts myself on graph paper. I measured ratios, looked at different kinds of averages, relationships of highs and lows within bars within patterns, and basically tried to dig as deeply into the minute details of patterns as possible. After I was fortunate to make some money trading, I started to take an objective look at what I was doing, and realized that the classic 80/20 rule applied, albeit in a different way—over 80% of what I was doing was a waste of time! So much of it didn't matter.

Every tick matters?

I've come to think that there are two ways of thinking about patterns. One is what I might call "detail oriented", and many of the classic charting approaches fall into this category. We might talk about the differences between pennants and flags, and we might also think about where they fall within the bigger picture. Something that looks like a rising wedge could have a very different meaning if it comes after a sharp drop, in the middle of a quiet market, or after a strong advance. (This is what we mean when we talk about context for patterns, and is what many people are looking at when they consider the higher timeframe.) This approach is also carried through in many of the modern books that run into the thousands of pages, looking at the details of every single bar. These approaches are compelling because they offer us answers—authors can create some logic to explain every tiny jiggle of every market in retrospect, but I think there may be a problem with all of this.

The problem is that markets are highly random and full of noise. Yes, there certainly are meaningful things that happen in markets, and sometimes exact, precise things are important. However, I've come to believe that most of what we see is misleading at best, and dangerously seductive at worse. For one thing, not every tick matters. When you've traded long enough to see markets move for stupid reasons or for mistakes, you come to realize that it is not, in fact, all part of some grand scheme. Thinking back to 2007 when I was at the NYMEX, I've seen gold futures make a gigantic intraday jump just because a legendary trader walked into the pit. Why did he do so? Basically, he was bored so he went down to the floor. Other traders, in a quiet afternoon market, saw his arrival as a possible harbinger of doom, and activity in the futures took off. This, by the way, is not an isolated incident—this kind of thing happens all the time, for silly reasons. Also, some things you see are simply mistakes or maybe due to action in related markets. (There's a nasty spike on your XLE charts a few years back that was caused by yours truly making a trading error hedging a large position and clearing the book on both sides. Oops.) If you're trying to divine meaning from every tick, I think you at least must acknowledge that a good percentage of what you see is meaningless, and then you can begin the task of separating out what matters from everything else.

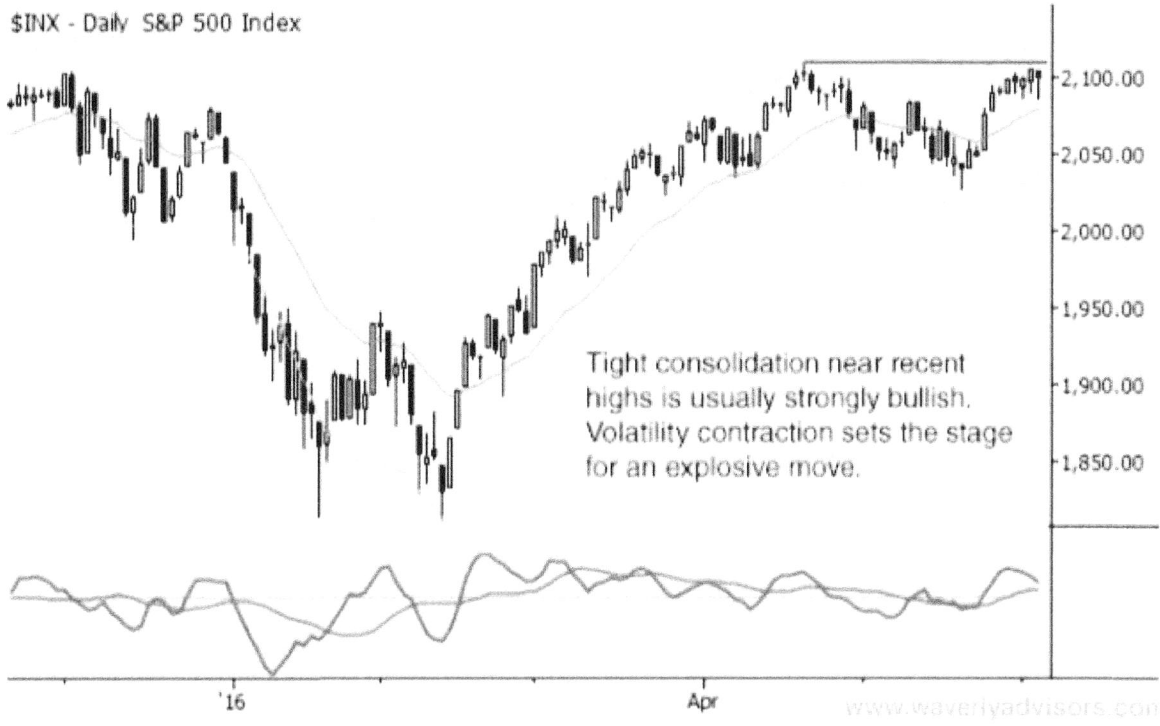
$INX - Daily S&P 500 Index
2,100.00
2,050.00
2,000.00
1,950.00
1,900.00
1,850.00
Tight consolidation near recent highs is usually strongly bullish. Volatility contraction sets the stage for an explosive move.
'16
Apr
www.waverlyadvisors.com

Thinking conceptually

There's another way, and, I think, a better way. Rather than focusing on the details of patterns, we think about what is happening. Consider this situation: a market reverses strongly off the lows, shoots higher, and then goes quiet without backing off much. I would argue that this is a market consolidating to go higher. (Consider the chart of the S&P 500 above.) That is what matters; get the big picture, get the direction right, and everything else is a lot easier. Do we need to spend time analyzing that consolidation? Do we care about the exact shape, how the sides slope, or exactly what retracement ratio it holds? I don't think so.

Focusing on the concept behind the pattern gives us a big picture trading plan. Looking at the chart above, we see clearly that we need to be long. Now, there are some legitimate challenges with this approach. When we get in or out of the market, we must do so at precise prices. How do we reconcile a kind of "fuzzy" big picture approach (strategic view) with the need to have precise execution points (tactics)? It can be done, and that's an important part of developing your specific approach and methodology for the market.

Understanding the Uncertainty of Our Market Predictions

Most of us who write about financial markets look to the future. Yes, there is a place for theory, and any theory lies on a firm foundation of what has happened in the past—history matters. But what probably matters most to us is the future: what is around the next turn, and what lies many years out? Why is it, then, that so many analysts, traders, and technicians say things like "we don't predict the future"? While this might be a comfortable cloak to hide behind, if it were true, there'd be no point to anyone writing anything about the future of financial markets. We *do* predict, but we have to understand what it means to predict, how to understand our predictions, and how to use them in practice.

We don't predict?

Many market technicians are quick to point out that they do not predict the future. I suspect that this saying has emerged for two reasons. First, there are many mumbo jumbo techniques in technical analysis lore that claim to predict exact turning points in financial markets to the exact hour, minute, and second, and to be able to predict highs and lows with extreme precision, usually based on some secret formula. You can't read too much about technical analysis without hearing of these mysterious techniques, and they are usually pinned on some prediction someone made in the past that came true. (Make enough predictions, in a random environment, and some of them will be right; some of them will even be *impressively* right, and legends can be built...) All of this, of course, is nonsense. If we understand what the market is, we will quickly see why such techniques cannot exist.

There's also a certain element of self-defense, and this may be exacerbated in the sometimes highly controversial environment of social media. For instance, a reasonable analysis of market XYZ (assume currently at $50) might be: "we want to buy XYZ if prices advance to $55 within the next 6 weeks. If that happens, we will use a stop (risk point) around $49, and will look for a profit target around $60. If XYZ declines, we have no reason to be long and no trade." Imagine you post an analysis like to any social media network, and XYZ immediately tanks to $40. You'll likely be hit with a flood of gloating messages saying something like "how did your prediction work out? Went down, eh?" Perhaps too many people simply respond to the critics with something like "trading and predicting are not the same thing and we don't predict the future."

There's a grain of truth in all of this, but it also fails to pass the common sense test: if we are saying something about the future, then we are predicting something, or that something is more likely than something else. If we are not saying that, then there's no reason to say anything at all. If we put on a trade, it is because we thinking something is more likely to happen than something else.

The future and uncertainty

We do not predict the future with any degree of certainty. That is impossible. Any financial market is highly competitive, with many people trying to make a profit. There can be many reasons, some logical, some nonsensical, why people buy and sell, so there is a lot of noise (random price jitters) in any market. Nothing, in any market, can be known with certainty, and that is one of the "Holy Grail" revelations of trading. When you start to understand that, you start to understand your job as a trader.

So, if the market is noisy and uncertain, how do we think about the future? Here's one way I teach it: imagine that you are standing in a field that stretches before you to the horizon. You can look behind you, and clearly see the path you took to get here (the path of past prices). However, let's look ahead, to the future. What do we see? Imagine a cone extending out from the point where you currently stand. A few steps in front of your feet, the boundaries of the cone are pretty close. In fact, on the next step you take, the cone is very narrow because you can't go much to your right or left, even if you jump. But, as the cone extends out, it gets wider and wider—the further you go ahead (out in time) the less certain we are where you're going to be.

We can make some better guesses about where you will be. Most people tend to walk mostly forward. What if we were to let you walk a path into the future, fly out with a helicopter, pick you up, and return you to the starting point? What if we did that over and over, recording the path you walked each time? We'd probably find you ended up going more or less straight ahead most times, so a more accurate way to see our cone of uncertainty—a better way—would be that it is darker in the middle, meaning you are more likely to be there than at the edges of the cone. This is the way it is with financial markets.

What can we know?

We can't know the future with certainty. On any trip, we didn't know where you'd end up—even though it's unlikely you'd be really far to one side, it's possible. With financial markets, our "best guess" is that the future will look more or less like the past, meaning that prices will probably end up somewhere around current prices. (This is the assumption behind a lot of options pricing models and other quant models.) But, sometimes, we can tilt the odds in our favor. This is only a small thing, but here's the good news: it is enough. If we can find these "tilts" and know when to place bets aligned with them, we can make a lot of money over time in the market.

If we do not have those tilts (or statistical "edges") then we can't place any bets. These tilts are only small things, but they are enough. Whatever method we use to trade the markets—technical, fundamental, macro, etc.—that's all we are doing. Now, what we do with that information? That's where the art and science of trading truly begin.

The Market is Not a Math Problem

We've been thinking quantitatively about market problems for a while, and now I want to remind you of something: the market is not a math problem. It is easy to get confused, though, because the market often *looks* like a math problem. The market generates a tremendous amount of information, and most of that information comes to us as numbers. It is tempting to blindly apply analytical tools, statistics, and other data processing techniques to market data, and, in fact, we can do that. However, this is a mistake that risks missing the essential nature of the market—the market is a study in human behavior and psychology, first and foremost.

Prices are moved by the buying and selling decisions people make. New information comes into the market, it is processed, and traders make decisions to buy or sell. Even in this day of algorithmic trading, nothing truly essential has changed. (Remember, much algorithmic trading is done by order filling algorithms, which are simply an extension of a human trader's will.) There are recurring patterns in prices because people make, and have made, the same decisions and mistakes in response to risk and opportunity in financial markets for all of recorded history. Behavioral and psychological forces ultimately have the greatest power to set prices.

This does not mean that math is unimportant in markets and trading. Quite the contrary—many developing traders fail because they don't have a good understanding of math. I have seen even experienced traders (some with quantitative backgrounds like engineering degrees) show a poor understanding of randomness in markets. The correct mathematical tools can help us find edges and probabilities in the market, but those tools are best put in context of human behavior.

The markets are noisy, messy places. The mathematical tools that work best in this environment are simple and robust. You do not need fancy, higher math for most trading applications; you need simple, basic math, but you must understand your tools completely. Many times, all that is needed is simple counting, and a way to compare two sets of data. Look into the data deeply, but always think about what is behind the numbers.

On Execution Tactics

Down in the Trenches with Trading Tactics

I've made the argument that the details of patterns do not matter—get the idea and the big picture right, and everything else is much easier. While I firmly believe that this is true, it does leave some important questions unanswered: mostly, exactly where, when, and how do we get into and out of trades? And, if the details of patterns don't really matter, why do we make these choices and how do we know they are the best choices? These are important questions, and we cannot trade without having some answers.

Strategy vs. tactics

Let's make sure we understand the difference between strategy and tactics. (This applies to business and to many other areas other than trading.) Simply put, strategy is what we want to accomplish and tactics covers how we are going to do it: what vs. how. In a military situation, perhaps we have the strategic goal of achieving air superiority over a region. To accomplish this, we need to have our fighters over the contested area without them being shot down, and shoot down anything else that comes into that area—that's the strategy.

Tactically, how will we do that? Well, we need to suppress opposing air defenses, and we have a choice of going after radar sites or SAM sites (what about the portable SAMs?), and have some choices of weapons platforms to get munitions on target, then we need to think about taking out airfields or planes on the ground probably at the same time we get planes out of the sky. Then we need to think about having someone fly CAP over the region and the logistics of refueling and rotating those fighters on and off station, flying those big, expensive AWACs platforms somewhere they can keep an eye on the airspace while we also keep escorts in the area... and this is only a tiny slice of the tactical things that must be considered and accomplished in service of the strategic goal.

In chess, perhaps we want to focus on strategic elements like pawn structure, king safety, or control of space, and we'd do so through tactical moves that might (threaten to) attack two enemy pieces at once, attack a piece through another piece, or force the other guy to make a move he'd rather not make. In business, perhaps we want to increase our social media presence, and we'd do so through tactical elements of email, blogging, tweeting, etc. It's very useful to force ourselves to think about the divide between what we want to accomplish and how we plan to achieve that goal.

Strategy in trading

In trading, tactics refer to how, where, (and maybe why) we execute at the specific prices we choose. Strategy, on the other hand is the big picture perspective. First, get the strategic view right.

I do not think that the minute details of patterns are important, at least conceptually, as traditional technical analysis would have us believe. Rather, an approach that looks at the broad outlines of the market is probably both more useful and more faithful to the realities of the market. Useful strategic tools might include swing analysis, some looks at momentum and volatility, and perhaps even a quick, heuristic glance at a chart. Some legendary traders have famously said things suggesting that a child could do chart analysis, simply answering "is this going up or down or sideways?" I've also advocated an approach where we basically glance or squint at a chart to hide the details, and simply take the first impression. This can be useful for creating a bigger picture, technical, strategic view, but you do need a solid grounding in chart analysis to develop this intuition. This "first glance" is probably not enough, but it's a good start. (And if you've been working through the course this far, you have a *supremely* good start!)

Trading tactics

Don't underestimate the value of that first glance. If you can get the big picture direction right, a lot of the rest falls into place. However, we still have to execute at specific places, and it may be useful to have some "reference levels" or prices to consider. If I've successfully identified a market that is going up, then I need to buy that market. Where I buy it almost doesn't matter: I can buy the high of the previous bar. I can buy the low of the previous bar. I can buy when moving averages cross. I can buy at some silly magical level. I can even calculate my retracements and ratios completely incorrectly and still be ok if I have the big picture right.

Be careful, it's not true that nothing matters: discipline matters. Having rules to govern our behavior matters. Trading patterns that have an edge, and trading them *when* they have an edge matters. In the case of a pullback, there is a range of time and price where we can buy the pattern, but if we buy too early or late, we're not within the pullback at all.

Let's continue with the pullback example, and assume that we have identified a good pullback in a solid trend, and we're looking at it at a time when it makes sense to buy. So how do we actually (tactically) execute? Here are some ideas:

- Buy a breakout of the previous bar's high. If not triggered, roll down to the high of this bar and continue until either the pattern is violated or the entry is triggered.
- Enter at some other breakout level, perhaps based on the patterns of the last 5-10 bars. The same principle will apply.
- In either case, apply a "fudge factor" based on current volatility. If buying a breakout in the S&P futures, perhaps add 2-5 points to the level.
- Another possibility is to require a certain amount of time (on an intraday basis) above the level. In other words, we'd only buy above our breakout level after the market had been above it for X minutes. This will, in most cases, mean that we buy a worse price than expected.
- Just to show the exact opposite concept, buy a failure test of a previous pivot low. This is an example of buying weakness, and can be done on the trading timeframe or on a lower timeframe.

Where to put our stops? Here are some ideas:

- A reasonable distance away from the entry, so that we are quite likely wrong if the market trades to that point. This level could be 3-5 ATRs on the trading timeframe. (This will likely seem wide to many people who are focused on using very tight stops.)
- At the low of X previous bars, with or without the "fudge factor" added. This will likely be a tighter stop.

We could go on, but here is where behavioral factors start to take control: you can do almost any of these things as long as you do them consistently. There's the key—choose your tactical toolkit, but use the same tools in the same way as consistently as possible. This is also where there's room for overlap between systematic and discretionary approaches—perhaps your strategy is dictated by a discretionary synthesis of market factors, but your tactics could be purely systematic. (Example: execute a trend following system only when you have a bullish or bearish bias in a market.) Ideally, both your strategic and tactical pieces should have a statistical edge (and I spend a lot of time in my own work to make sure that this is so), but there could also be room for using a tool that is essentially arbitrary as one piece of the puzzle, especially if it disciplines behavior and creates a tactical framework for effective trade entry and exit within a valid strategic directional bias.

I think there's more to explore here, but, at the very least, start teasing out the difference between strategic and tactical thinking in your own trading and analysis.

On the Failure Test

Chart of the Day: Failure Test in AAPL (11/11/12)

This chart shows a clean failure test in AAPL. The pattern is a brief probe above resistance, followed by an immediate failure and sharp reversal. Many traders would be reluctant to short after a move like this, as it is always possible to point to any number of "levels" that could support prices. However, there is a clear and strong statistical tendency in this pattern (which was the first trading pattern I examined in The Art & Science of Technical Analysis): shorts can be initiated on yesterday's close, or in today's session at the same level or higher, with a stop above yesterday's high. Position sizing with this trade is problematic, as there is always some gap risk in countertrend trades made in strongly trending markets. Regardless, this is a pattern that demands attention.

(It is also worth considering the August (2012) consolidation in the S&P 500 as an example of how this pattern should not play out for shorts. Continued consolidation and pressure against resistance is very constructive for the bulls.)

Failure Test Followthrough in the EUR (5/13/14)

The chart above is a daily chart of the EURUSD. I've written before about some of the challenges with using technical analysis in currencies—it's not that it can't be done, but it does require, in my opinion, a slightly different mindset. Currencies are driven by supply and demand for each currency in the pair, but this supply and demand may itself be secondary to more primary economic pressures (trade balance, interest rates, etc.) Currencies also trade a bit differently than many other markets. This is an important understanding and flies in the face of the claims of traditional technical analysis, that you can apply any tool to any chart and use it with no changes. My work suggests that short-term mean reversion in currencies is muted, as is longer-term momentum, leading to some different characteristics compared to equities or commodities.

Regardless, even in this challenging environment, simple tools and patterns do work. Last week, the EURUSD put in a clean failure test at the top, and followthrough from the pattern has now brought the Euro to the bottom of the range. What now? That's the question. (Note: prudent trade management virtually requires that you will already have covered some of the short if you shorted based on this pattern.) Watch for a possible failure test against the bottom of the range, which could be an entry into the weekly consolidation (leading to more upside) or for downside continuation below the bottom of the range. It's not so much about predicting what will happen (though patterns can sometimes identify spots where the probabilities are tilted in one direction or another) as much as it is about having a gameplan and being able to make intelligent decisions as market action unfolds in the future.

Market Pattern: The Failure Test

There is a theory of market behavior that essentially says that markets exist to create trading activity and volume; whether this is precisely true, or whether it completely explains all market activity, is not important. The concept is valid: markets move to levels where orders are clustered. Markets run stops.

As an interesting aside, this happens on large scales (as in the major stock indexes on 10/4/11), but it also happens on lower timeframes across many markets every day. Back in the days when traders drove much of the activity on the floor, there was often blatant manipulation to trigger stop orders. Imagine that you are a floor trader and you think a broker (a trader who handles orders for traders or firms outside the pit) close to you is holding a large position as the market comes down to the low of the day. You can tell that he's nervous and watching prices closely. You begin to wonder if he has a large position with a stop order under the day's lows. If so, you could get short and cover into the downdraft created by his sell stops, so what do you do? Well, if you're big enough, or crazy enough, you can just sell and sell and maybe push the market to new lows, but that's often suicidal. If the market is thin enough, or close enough to lows, perhaps that's an option, but there is another way.

Markets have bid / offer spreads, and, in nearly all markets, it is illegal to trade outside of that spread (with some exceptions and provisions). What might you do if the market is 40.02 bid, offered at 40.07, and the day's low is 40.00? It's a dirty trick, but perhaps you just call out a trade at 39.98, below the bid, below the day's low—an illegal trade. Now, one of two things happen... either the broker panics and starts selling to whatever bid he can find. In this case, your "accidental" wrong trade will almost certainly be lost in the ensuing confusion and volume, the market will trade much lower as he sells all he can as fast as he can, so no one really cares about your trade anyway. Or, perhaps he does nothing, there's no activity at all and you just say something to the effect of "my bad". The trade never happened, and everyone moves on.

It is harder to do this in today's electronic markets, but there are still many instances where stops are run and orders are spoofed. This is one reason why so many breakouts fail. This is one reason why markets predictably reverse from highs and lows of the day. Markets simply probe beyond levels, trigger stops, and test to see whether there is any further conviction.

One example of this occurred on the 10/4/11 close in most domestic stock indexes. Indexes took out significant lows, but there was no conviction beyond those lows and shorts were in a lot of trouble by the close. This is a predictable pattern; I had warned my short-term trading clients the day before about this scenario, and suggested they not carry heavy short exposure overnight if the bear trap scenario was in play.

A few more examples will show how important context is. Here is a short trade we initiated on the exact day of the high in Gold futures. We had been warning clients for weeks that the uptrend was parabolic (note free bars), and suggested that a retest of the highs was an ideal spot for a bull trap. At the very least, never get caught paying a "breakout" here.

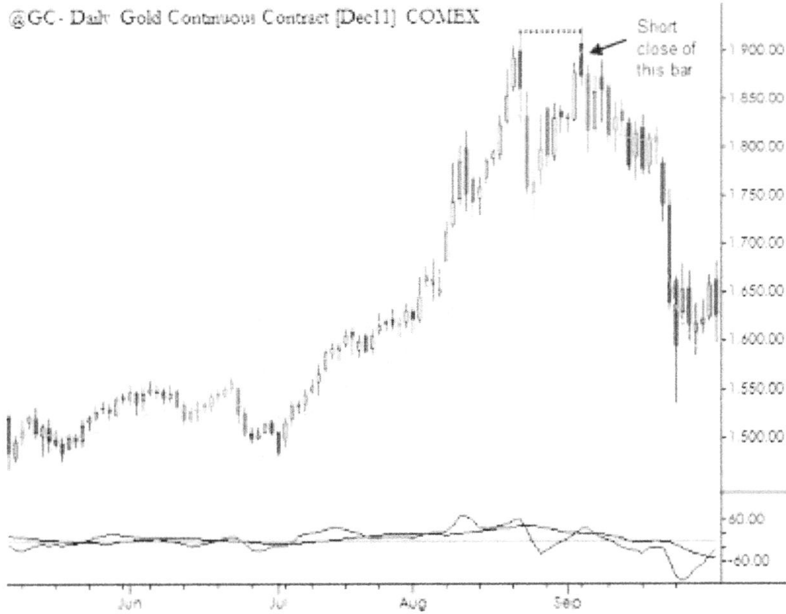

And one more: note here the extended uptrend went parabolic (though only slightly in this case), and then a clean failure test at the highs provided an ideal entry for a short trade. When we entered this trade, we had no idea that the Flash Crash would follow a few weeks later.

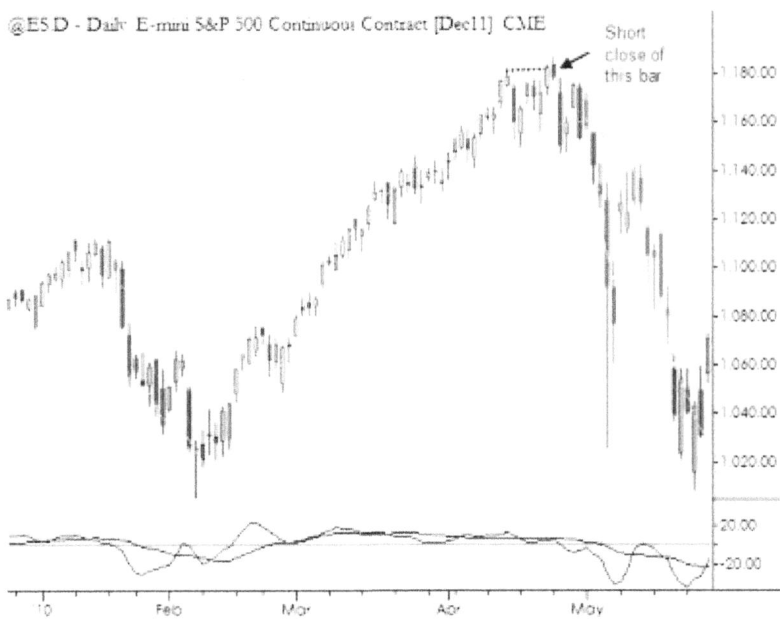

We will look at this pattern in more detail in the future. It is a simple, robust pattern that plays out in all timeframes, and it is also the first of the actual trading patterns I cover in the book. There is, of course, considerable nuance and subtlety to these patterns. (For instance, notice that the second and third examples were set up by overextended trends, while the first set up following only a single, strong downthrust. The first example is not as strong of a trade.) If you are a technical trader, some variation of this pattern belongs in your toolkit, but, as always, make sure you do the work to truly understand the pattern before you commit capital and risk in the market.

Followthrough Matters: Using Subjective Analysis

In our recent work, we've focused heavily on quantitative aspects of trading and market analysis, and just scratched the surface of the thorny subject of intuition. Let's take a detour and look at something slightly different: how we can use some subjective elements in our analysis, and how they might be relevant to the current situation in the broad stock market.

The word "subjective" usually means being influenced by personal opinion or feeling. If we use that definition with market analysis, we might run into trouble; I think the easiest way to understand what we are doing here is to contrast it with firm quantitative work. Understanding the quantifiable tendencies of a market is relatively simple. For instance, one of the clearest cases would be a stock makes a sharp move, and, all other things being equal, we'd then expect some of that sharp move to be reversed in coming days due to the force of mean reversion. If we make a practice of chasing big moves in stocks, we're probably on the wrong side of the market so that much is cut and dried.

If we consider subjective elements, it might be the "what makes this time different" aspect. Sometimes, there are several competing statistical factors, and it's difficult to quantify everything. We could focus on mean reversion on one timeframe, a break and consolidation above a level on another, or a pattern of lower highs on another—which of these is most important? That, to me, is one of the best applications of subjectivity: knowing how to weight different, possibly competing, technical factors at any one time.

One of the problems with subjectivity is that different people may have different interpretations, and experience matters. Anyone, with no experience at all, can have an opinion about any market. But our opinions are likely to have more connection with reality if those opinions are drawn from deep experience seeing many patterns unfold, ideally disciplined and guided by an understanding of the quantitative tendencies that may be present.

One more point: subjectivity is not intuition. The two are related, but not the same, and we don't have to exercise any "special" intuitive insight to incorporate some subjective elements in our understanding of markets. To think about how we can apply subjective elements, let's look at an example from the S&P 500 index.

In this chart, the S&P had been declining a few days, and was approaching a potentially significant inflection. I wrote a post outlining the importance of a potential failure test at the bottom of the range, and how that could be a strongly bullish signal. Today (the trading day that just ended), major indexes closed with very strong gains, appearing to have bounced from that level. Here is the chart, with that level highlighted:

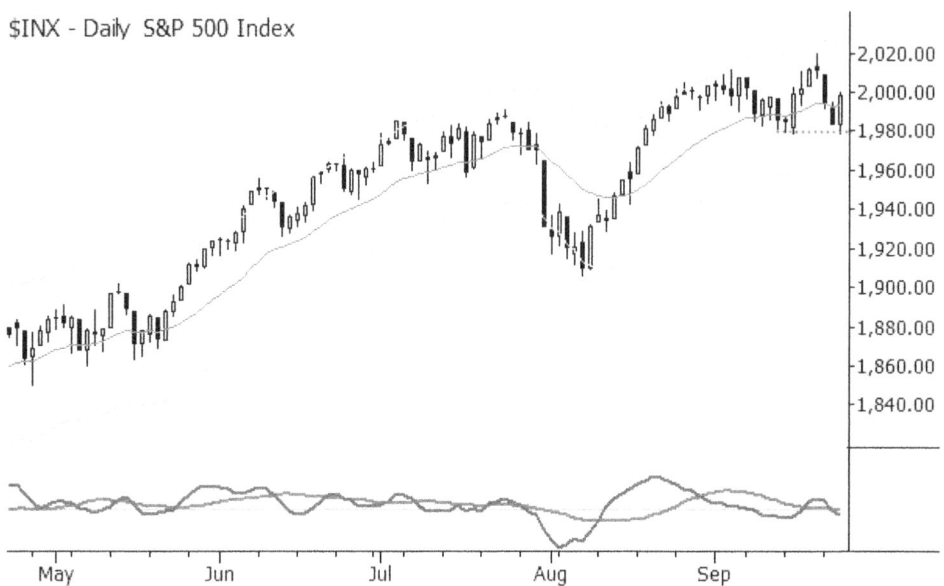

Now, one thing that had been happening at the time of the chart is that many bears had come out of the woods in the past week. People made public calls for a top, and the overall tone of much of the commentary became bearish. There is always a reason—strong dollar, weak metals, slowing growth, fears of a rate hike, blah, blah, blah, but people respond especially strongly to declining prices—it tweaks some deep part of the trader psyche. The rally on that chart was probably primed by a lot of that early bearishness, but there was something about this pattern I did not trust. Markets will move to levels that generate trading volume. In doing so, they will often key in on some of the technical structures and levels we might watch.

For this to have been a best example of a bullish pattern, I would have liked to have seen more bears get hurt. I would have like to have seen more shorts initiate below that previous pivot. A stronger pattern would have been for today to have first traded down dramatically (say 10 handles or more), and then reverse sharply to close on the highs. That's a pattern that I could have some (subjective) conviction about, but this is not what happened. We did not clear the level. We probably did not elect stops. Probably, not enough people were hurt.

Now, we turn to watch the followthrough. If this is a strong buy, we should see very quick followthrough. Markets should trade up to their highs, maybe pause there, and then break higher, and I think this should happen within a week or two. (I think = subjective language.) I can visualize a price path that looks something like this:

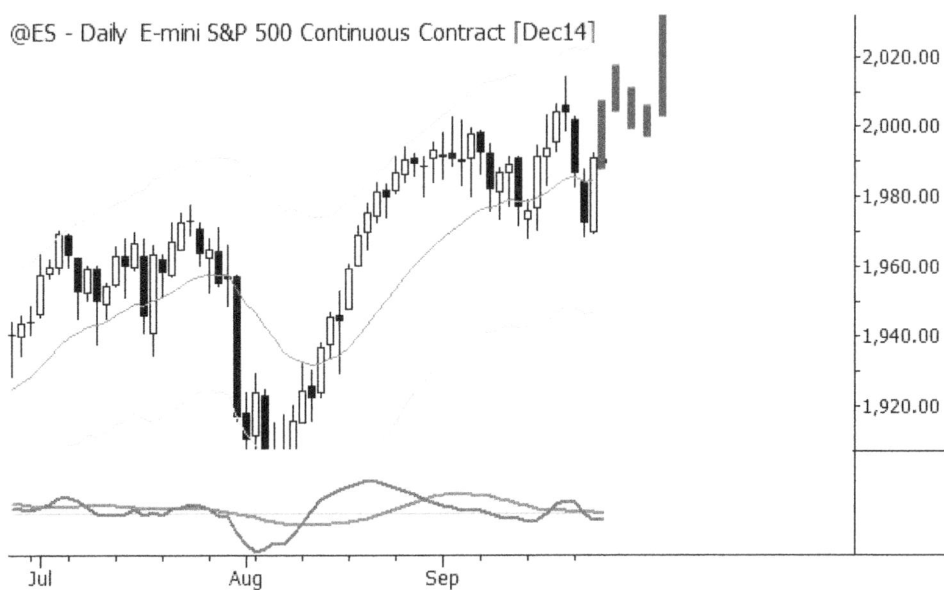

Knowing that, I also know what should not happen. If this is a strong buy, we should not consolidate near current levels. The market should not turn lower (that is obvious), but it also should not "hang out" around here. Going flat and dull near current prices would likely be a consolidation pointing lower. If we do hang out here, much of the commentary we hear will switch back to bullish, so now, what would hurt those complacent bulls? Something like this:

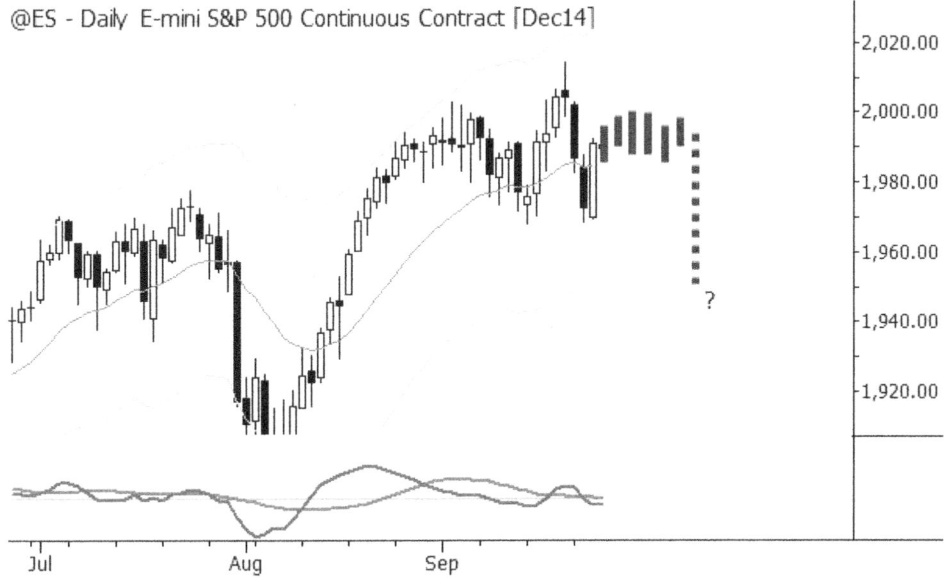

I wrote this just to give you some ideas and insights into how to think about weighing different subjective factors. The quantitative structure is that higher timeframe uptrend is strong and intact, so we must favor the upside. Subjectively, I see factors align that I think could support a flush (and this is why my clients held both long positions in the S&P and short positions in European indexes). One more thing to consider is that, from a subjective standpoint, the landscape can shift quickly. New information (in the form of price movement) can give a very different picture in a single day, so we are always reevaluating. For now, this is what I see in the S&P 500, and I suspect the second scenario, the tricky break lower, is a little bit more likely.

Chapter 7

Module 7–Breakouts

This module rounds out the last of our specific technical patterns with a look at trading breakouts. At this point in the course, the trader is equipped to trade trending markets while they are moving, when the trend might be ending, ranging markets within the ranges, and can now add the ability to trade markets breaking from ranges into new trend legs to the arsenal. This is now a complete tool set and lays the foundation for any type of technical, directional trade possible.

This module also focuses on creating the trading plan, which is one of those critical tasks that separates winning from losing traders. Of course, simply making a plan in no way guarantees success, but the work required to structure and revise a plan will force the trader to think deeply about his performance and any potential issues—this is one of the best tools to help that trader move toward consistent profitability in the markets.

This module also digs into multiple timeframe influences: looking at how patterns and forces from both higher and lower timeframes can influence evolution of patterns on a single timeframe. We also look at different ways a trader can incorporate this information into the trading plan, from explicitly using charts of multiple timeframes to inferring action from other timeframes based on patterns on a single chart.

Last, we will start working on "your own trading book": a research journal with observations and thoughts that will, over time, become a source of your growth and enduring edge in the marketplace.

Section 1: Breakout Backtest

You know what you're doing now, so apply the same techniques to backtesting a variation of the breakout. Create a rule set for the exact types of this pattern you will trade, and then conduct a careful, bar-by-bar manual backtest. As before, track your P&L carefully and consistently to get some idea of the edge that may be in this pattern.

A few things complicate this pattern. One, execution can be challenging, as bid/ask spreads may be wide at breakout points. Two, the volatility around breakout points can be extreme, and this can be hidden within single bars. In other words, your experience trading these patterns, as you watch the bar form, may not be adequately captured on the static price chart on which you will do your backtest. Three, many of these patterns are generated by news or new information flow; consider if this will be (or even could be, given the realistic reaction time) part of your strategy.

There are at least three questions that must be answered before you can begin this test:

- How will you define the levels beyond which you will take breakout trades?
- Will you consider price formations before the breakout in deciding whether or not to take these trades? If so, be careful that you define the formations well, as being too specific can reduce your sample size greatly.
- How will you actually execute? Will you use resting orders, enter when you see the breakout, or execute on the close of the bar? Consider the trade-offs in each possibility, and do your tests on one consistent rule set.

Section 2: Your Trading Plan

A good trading plan is an essential tool for a professional trader. The plan does many things, but we will focus on these points first:

- **The plan is a tool to monitor trader behavior**. You have heard "follow the plan", but that's impossible unless you have a plan!
- **The plan eliminates much psychological struggle and conflict.** When you do have a plan, your only job is to follow the plan.
- The plan is a clear **expression of your trading edge**.
- Changes to your trading plan are **a good record of your evolution as a trader**.

Important considerations

The most important thing to consider about your plan is striking a balance—on one hand, we want it to be complete. Ideally, you could give your plan to someone else who could, with some training, replicate your trading very closely just by following the plan. (There is room for discretionary elements in the plan, and this obviously complicates this.) Since we are going to be evaluating your performance by how well you follow the plan, a vague plan is no help at all.

However, you also want the plan to be usable. If the plan is too detailed, you will simply ignore it. If the plan is too big, then it's impossible to revise and you will find yourself not changing the plan as your trading evolves. This becomes a problem because you then are no longer following the plan, but you know "it's ok to ignore that because I don't really do it anymore but I just didn't change the plan." That line of thinking opens the door to serious breaks of discipline.

This is the balance to strike in all record keeping in a trading operation, and there's no one answer. Here, you must know yourself. Most of us will do well to learn some additional structure and discipline, but this must respect your personality. Someone with an accountant's mind is not likely to keep records and plans in the same way a painter might—and the record and plan must speak deeply to the trader's mind. This is why "one size fits all" plans tend to fail, and one reason we are working together!

So, as you work through this document and the examples I will share, come back to this idea: how much detail, to what level of depth, is appropriate for you? It's hard to answer until you get into this work, but refining and targeting your personality in the plan is one of the early tasks of planning.

Three plans

I think most traders actually need three trading plans, but we are only going to talk about two here, in depth. If you have a desire to work on the first (and you should), we will tackle that next.

Plan #1: Your trading business plan

The first (and the one we will not discuss much) is essentially a business plan for your trading operation as it fits into your life. Some things this plan should cover:

- Your purpose and place in the universe, and how trading serves that. This might seem a bit abstract, but it's important.
- Your trading goals and plans. Timelines can be a problem here, because you don't know how fast you will develop as a trader. But do you want to trade other peoples' money? Be financially independent? Move somewhere different? It's important to keep these goals in mind, and this goes along with the first point. Again, be careful of being too specific too soon with timeline and dollar amounts.
- Your style and approach to trading.
- Markets and timeframes you will trade.
- Your time for work and structure of that work. (I.e., daily or weekly work finding setups, managing trades, journaling, record keeping, etc.)
- Specific structure of trading work and tasks.
- How will you develop and monitor your edge as a trader?
- How will you monitor your development as a trader? How will you know when you move from one stage to another?
- Specifics of your brokerage platforms and financing arrangements
- Disaster recovery plans. Consider an attachment including phone numbers and account numbers.
- Risk management guidelines including trading cutoffs.
- "Strategic alliances" or educational resources you've found to be important

It's not uncommon to see a good Plan 1 include elements of family, spirituality, exercise, health, diet, and many other things. This can be an operating plan for you and your life as a business. Notice that this plan does not include specifics of your trading approach. The "style and approach" section should be kept high level and fairly general. A typical Plan 1 might run from 10-25 pages.

Plan #2: Classes, Risk, and Goals (CRG)

Plan 2 is a document that guides your activity and risk levels. Here's how you create this document:

- Break your trades into "classes" or high-level types of trades. Some traders may have only one class (in which case the class heading can be eliminated, but I'd retain it for later expansion).
- Risk levels. Start with risk per trade, which could be a fixed dollar amount or a percentage of account equity. This is ***not*** number of shares or contracts—this is the dollar amount you will lose on each trade if it is stopped out. Some traders may wish to also allocate risk levels for week and month.

- Goals, including both activity level (how many traders per day/week/month) and profit level (how much money will you net from these trades over those periods?) These are broad goals, and will depend on market action—you can't force trades, so sometimes you will make more or less than these goals. Also, it is difficult to know what to set for a goal until you really understand your system and edge. This is why we refine the trading plan as more data comes in...
- Specific trade setups that fall under each class.

In general, we want to be as specific as possible and avoid suggestions or guidelines. These are rule sheets, not suggestion sheets! But the goals section on this sheet is more flexible than the other sections, and we need to be prepared for normal market variation during trading.

Plan #3: Setup sheets

The CRG sheet should refer to specific setups. There are many ways to format the setup sheets, but I would err on the side of being complete. There is a very good chance that you'll be coming back to some of these sheets years later, and the more complete they are the faster you can understand them. For this reason, many traders write these sheets as if they were teaching a third party to trade the systems.

The basic sections you must cover, in some format are:

- Setup: What conditions tell you that you should be looking for an entry?
- Trigger: What conditions actually get you into the trade. It is possible, in rare cases, that setup and trigger can be combined, but it is far more likely that some setup conditions precede the actual entry and may not trigger entries.
- Stop location: where are you getting out if you are wrong?
- Profit taking: where and how are you getting out if you are right?

These are the basics, but some setup sheets can go into much more depth. Other sections to consider are:

- **General comments** on the concepts behind the setup. If the system is sourced from somewhere other than your own development, mention this here, as well.
- Information for calculating **any indicators or special measures** needed to trade the system.
- **Trade management rules**, such as where to add, other exit rules (time stops), trades in related markets.
- **Size:** Some trades may require different sizes for different setups, and daytraders may prefer a simple X contract or shares size approach. Just remember, if you change how you're trading, you should change this document. (Most sizing issues are better handled at the CRG sheet level.)
- **Comments on discretionary elements:** Writing clear trading rules does not mean you remove all discretion, but explain what you will and will not do clearly. After you make trades, you want to be able to lay your actual trades alongside the Setup Sheet and say "this trade, I followed my rules" or "on this trade, I broke this rule."
- **Specific execution comments:** Some markets and some systems might require special techniques. For instance, will you leg in and out of spreads or not? Market order execution or midpoint?
- **Notes from backtesting:** Notes and experiences from backtesting or previous trading experience with the system might be helpful.

Making your own

So where do you go with this? Chances are, you already have some version of these sheets, but it can be refreshing to start over and build from scratch. Decide what you wish to do, and then work bottom up.

Plan to devote considerable time to this project. A good plan takes at least a few weeks to create. You will first write it, then think and re-think, and have several versions before you have one that is ready to use. Without this written plan, your chances for success are very much smaller.

Create your setup sheet

First, put your setups into clear setup sheet format, following the Setup, Trigger, Stop Location, and Profit Taking format above. Chances are you have a few of these. Most developing traders should probably have two to maybe five of these. (No firm number on that, but 10 is too many!)

Next, work to refine these and get them precisely in line with how you are trading. Every condition you consider—technical, fundamental, news, feelings, etc.—should be in this sheet. This sheet is the complete guide to your personal trading methodology, so take the time to get it right. There is no sense in trading until this is done.

Create your CRG sheet

Next, create a basic CRG sheet, which is, most often, one sheet of paper. You may have no idea what to put in some of those sections, and you may only have one class of trades to start, but start somewhere. Use the Risk, Goals, and Setup headings under each class, and feel free to use "????" as an entry if you do not know what to put there. We will refine this as we go along, but starting here puts you already ahead of most developing traders.

Section 3: Your Research Journal

Start your research journal. This will be a document that you will use, in some way, for the rest of your trading career. No one can tell you how to do this; you have to figure out what works for you and what will work with your lifestyle, but here are a few thoughts:

You will go through cycles in which you use this journal frequently, and then you may go through spells where you do not do much of this type of work. That is normal, but plan for some research-intensive and focused periods in your trading career. Incidentally, one of the best cures for overtrading or forcing trades when the environment does not favor your style (as true for longer-term traders as for daytraders) is to do research. Doing research can be a much better investment of time than making suboptimal trades!

Research is the process whereby you learn from the market itself. Your research journal, which is nothing more than a collection of ideas to investigate, is the document that will guide you through this process. Personally, I find that working in both paper and electronic formats is ideal: the paper format does not allow for revision and gives me a faithful record of what I was seeing and thinking at any time. I keep bound journals, and just jot down observations, ideas, or questions along with dates anytime they hit me.

Then the work begins, and I think of this as a funnel. Now, transferring the idea to some electronic format, where you can keep the ideas that warrant further investigation and discard the rest makes sense. There are many software packages that can do this effectively, and you can even just keep an email draft or a spreadsheet with some notes to get started.

This is a structured tool that will allow you to access your intuition and inner wisdom, even when doing intensive quantitatively-focused work. Though we often think of research as a cold, sterile process, nothing is further from the truth: even if logic dictates every step of the research process, most discoveries depend on some leaps of logic at some point, and even some flashes of "inspiration". Those flashes come from your deep work and exposure to the data, and this journal will keep you in the flow and ready for that inspiration to strike.

Start your journal now, today: get a piece of paper, and write down a few ideas from the course that you would like to investigate further. As with so much of this work, what really matters is that you do it. Start today. Start now.

Section 4: Multiple Timeframe Project

Take this opportunity to investigate what power multiple timeframe analysis might (or might not) add to your trading and to pattern analysis. Here is one suggested way to do this work:

Define precise conditions in which you will allow a timeframe to influence another. These influences may flow from lower or higher timeframe. First, define the timeframe on which you will focus as the *trading timeframe*.

Take a pattern you have found interesting and investigate it on the trading timeframe with either 1) a higher timeframe influence or 2) a lower timeframe influence. Choose one; avoid using both as this introduces too many complicating factors into the analysis at this stage.

As an example: perhaps you will trade pullbacks, and not take trades if the higher timeframe shows one of several trend termination patterns. Another example might be trading pullbacks and looking to enter failure tests on the lower timeframe.

One of the issues with this type of work is that sample sizes will likely be small. With only a few multiple timeframe qualifications, it may be difficult to find a reasonably large number of trades for analysis.

Once you have set up the test structure, work through bars, either in a papertrading or event study format. There is a mechanical issue here, as few software packages will easily allow you to see the higher timeframe bar as it forms; information leakage from the future is almost unavoidable, as you will be looking at completed higher timeframe bars as the trading timeframe unfolds.

It might be interesting to compare your results both to the baseline return of the market you are trading and to the simple pattern on the trading timeframe, unqualified with the multiple timeframe filter. The purpose of this analysis is both to understand the influence (or, potentially, the lack of influence) different timeframes have on each other and to refine your sense of reading charts and multiple timeframe influences.

Section 5: Readings

From *The Art and Science of Technical Analysis: Market Structure, Price Action, and Trading Strategies* by Adam Grimes, Wiley, 2012:

174-188 (breakouts)
337-345 (breakout examples)
213-230 (multiple timeframe analysis)
231-253 (trade management)

On the Trading Plan

How Good Is Your Plan?

We've all heard sayings like "to fail to plan is to plan to fail" and "plan the trade. Trade the plan." These are catchy sayings, but, ask yourself, how good is your plan? Is it good enough? Does it have enough detail? Can it do everything you need it to do? If not, today is the day to fix it.

To my way of thinking, there are two parts of a trading plan. First, you need a proper *business plan* like any other business, and then you need a specific *trading plan*. The difference is that the business plan is an overarching "control document" for you and your trading business, going into details like what time of day you will do your work, disaster recovery plans, how you will find and develop your trading edges, and every other aspect of your business you can think of. The trading plan covers the specifics of how and when you will get into and out of trades. Both are important, and it is worth your time to create both in good detail. It is fairly common to see traders create a trading plan, but few take the time to focus on the business plan. To repeat: traders should have *both* a business plan, and a trading plan. If you don't, you haven't really done your planning.

This became clear as I was working with a few traders I am coaching. Most of them have had some experience and have learned some good lessons from the market, so they have pretty good ideas about what not to do, but they were falling short on the business plan side. Without the big picture plan, you lack guidance and vision. It is as much about you—who you are, what your purpose in life is, how trading fits into your routine and life, and how you will grow—as it is about your trading. A good business plan is a substantial document, perhaps ten to twenty typed pages in length, and it will evolve as your trading business grows and changes. The right way to think about it is that it serves two purposes: First, it controls your behavior, saying clearly what you will and will not do, but you should also think of the second purpose which is to communicate the details of your business to investors. Maybe someday you will grow to the point you solicit investors, but, even if you never want to trade a penny of anyone else's money this level of professionalism is important. You should be as responsible and precise with your own money as you would with anyone else's. You are your own client, and you have a tremendous responsibility to the client and his interests.

Think about the path of trader development. On one end, imagine the completely new trader who just learned how to read a bar chart, and, on the other end, a trader who has traded for years, perhaps is even making some money, but has not yet had the degree of success or the consistency that he wants from his trading. Then taking some time to refine your business plan is time well spent. If you don't have a business plan at all, then today is the day to start crafting one.

Your Many Hats

Calling yourself a "trader" is problematic. Think about other professions: a truck driver drives trucks. A baker bakes things. A teacher teaches. A dentist works on peoples' teeth. In most cases, there is a direct linguistic connection between the job description and what person is supposed to be doing. This is not the case with trading.

It's easy to think that your job as a trader is to trade, to be putting on trades, but this is a mistake. In fact, this understanding leads us to overtrading—you are looking at the markets you follow and nothing is showing an edge, but you are a trader, so you trade—and you simply put on a "boredom" trade. This will not have a good outcome. Rather than thinking your job is to trade, perhaps think about it like this: your job is to put on the trades dictated by your methodology and your system. There's even more good news because if you rethink your job like that, then many pieces of the discipline puzzle automatically fall into place.

What is your job?

I think that's a critical understanding. Your job is not to make money. Your job is not to put on trades. Your job is not to catch any move in the market—it's entirely possible that the market will make a big move that never created an entry signal from your system. That's perfectly ok (depending on what kind of trader you are). *Your job is very simply to follow your system* and to do what the system tells you at the right time. Your job is to be a disciplined trader.

Your two hats

When I mentor developing traders one of the problems I often see is that a trader will do something, make a tweak to the system, do something else, make another tweak, and continue. It can be hard to nail down whether the system actually works because the system is always changing. In the worst cases, the system might change with every trade! Because managing trading psychology is a bit like managing an unruly child, many traders quickly realize that they have an "out"—it is possible to justify any action at any time because one could simply say the system rules now encompass that action. My response to this takes one word: No.

As a very small aside, I think one of the reasons most individual traders fail is poor risk management. I've seen good and bad risk management, but some of the best risk management I ever saw was at the Nymex. When a trader started to have issues, you could tell because he would get a little bit louder and you could almost feel the storm cloud over his desk. This would go on a little bit longer and then the risk manager would magically appear behind him, gently tap his shoulder, and invite him to step away from his desk to have a conversation. Sometimes he'd come back to the screen a changed man, or sometimes you'd see him the next day in a much better frame of mind.

Too many at-home traders (or poorly managed prop traders, which are basically the same thing!) blow out accounts because they don't have a boss. Look at your recent trading history and ask yourself what would happen if you had to sit down with your boss and justify your actions. Would you get a bonus? Would you get fired?

Who's your boss?

So, you must act in several roles, wear several hats, and you have to be clear on the differences between the two. First, you are the trader. You execute the trades and follow the system. When you are the trader, you are in a relatively "dumb" role—you simply follow the system. You don't change the system or supersede the system. You don't ignore the system. If you think something needs to be changed, you can make a note of it for the system developer, but you do not change the system. You, the trader, follow the system.

Now, there's also a time where you change hats and act as the system developer. The system developer is analytical and can tweak the system after an appropriate amount of time. He's not going to give a trader a system because he found it on some website or someone in a chat room told him to buy at some stupid Fibonacci extension. No, he's only going to give the trader something that he has confidence in, and he's always working to make his edge a little bit stronger. He will monitor the performance of the system, and will change what needs to be changed. Once he makes those changes, he gives the new system to the trader… and we already understand the trader's job, don't we?

Switching hats (and more hats?)

The key to making this work is that you wear one hat at a time, and you switch them slowly. If you are an intraday trader, maybe you put on your system developer hat on the weekends, or maybe once a month. You do not—you absolutely do not ever—put on the system developer hat in the middle of the day. That's a serious breach of discipline and will get you fired. You also probably don't stay at your desk until 7 PM and make changes every day. A smart system developer knows you need more data and you should not respond too quickly to emotional results from the previous trading day. The system developer, remember, is an analytical and pretty unemotional dude.

If you are a swing trader, you probably put on your developer hat once a month, maybe less. A long-term investor puts it on maybe a few times a year. Most of the time, your job is simply to execute the trades dictated by your system. Your system may be technical or fundamental or astrological (let's hope not), but you need to be very clear on your different roles: when you trade, and when you may tweak the system.

Accountability

I think there's another piece of this, and this goes back to the risk manager/boss. At some point, the boss will fire you. At some point, if you cannot maintain the discipline of this kind of structure, you can't be a trader, so you also need to put on the "boss hat" sometimes and take a serious look at what you're doing.

An effective boss is tough, but nurturing, and does what needs to be done to help the trader and system developer grow. Still, *at the end of the day, it's all about doing the right thing and if you don't have that discipline, you cannot be a trader.* This system, thinking of yourself in discrete roles and wearing separate hats, can get you closer to being that disciplined trader you must be, and closer to your ultimate success.

What Matters More Than Your Process?

Process has become something of a buzzword, but it's a useful word. Process covers *everything* we do, and is a reminder to do those things *consistently*. If I have patterns or indicators or even a system, I might doubt it. I know they work about half the time, so maybe I should just skip this trade? It's easy to think like that, but if I have a defined process, then I have a pretty simple job: I follow my process.

You need a trading plan, and we've covered that. A process goes beyond the plan, and covers every aspect of everything you do in relation to the markets. How do you do your homework? How do manage conflicts? How do you allow your actual trading plan to evolve? How do you evaluate your performance? How do you take care of yourself? How do you manage your process? A process covers all of this, and somewhere in your process should be the instruction to "follow the trading plan".

Handling conflicts

It's pretty common to see trades set up against the conventional wisdom. I might have looked silly shorting Gold and Silver in 2011, buying stocks in October 2014, shorting the EUR in 2014, or shorting crude in 2015. Each of those trades would have been hard to defend on CNBC at the time, and it would have been easy to say, had they failed, "I should have seen _____."

I think the best way to handle these conflicts is to think about narrative, news, and the conventional wisdom as a potential input to your process and plan. Is there some way you can measure the influence they would have on your trades, so we can know if it makes sense to pay attention to these things or not? If you can't do that, then think about what you're doing—you have a methodology for trading, and then you add this extra "thing", this extra influence, at the end of the process. This extra thing hasn't been measured, and you don't understand it, so how can it help? It's just another degree of freedom.

Personally, my life quest seems to be to simplify and remove degrees of freedom; this is where I have found much of my edge. I've seen enough market action and have accepted that I can only see the future through a very cloudy glass of uncertainty and probability; the best guide I have is only a slight statistical tilt. All I can do, and all I need to do is to follow my process. What's more import than my process? Nothing. How do we handle conflicts? Work the process.

Working your process

So, the short answer is that I can safely ignore narrative and news and what everyone else thinks and simply follow my process. As an aside, this means that I will be brilliantly contrarian at times, but I don't actively seek to be a contrarian. I'll also be a brilliant trend follower at times, jumping on before everyone else sees the move and squeezing most of the juice out of the move. I know not to get too caught up on how "brilliant" I look, though, because I'll look equally dumb at other times: I'll get ticked out of trades, buying the exact high or selling the exact low. I'll be in trades that immediately explode against my trade direction. I'll hold trades for a very long time, only to get stopped out right before the trade rockets in my favor. That's all part of the game—unpleasant, but unavoidable.

Process is the hub that holds the wheel together. In a very real way, process is all that matters. Process is all there is.

Five Questions to Ask Before Each Trade

Successful trading and investing is largely about asking the right questions. Many of the most serious mistakes we make come from blindly accepting our ideas and perceptions at face value. I would like to offer you a short checklist of questions that will challenge you to think more deeply and to work out your process more thoroughly.

1. **Do I understand this idea?** Every investment or trading decision rests on an idea. On one extreme, perhaps the signal to buy or sell something is generated by an algorithm (a set of rules); even in this case, the algorithm is built on an idea that something should happen in the market after a set of conditions are fulfilled. On the other hand, maybe you are trading off a hunch or a gut feel. Ideas can come from many places: are you following someone on social media? Is your idea based on fundamental, macro, or technical ideas? I think the key questions to ask are do you really, fully, understand the idea and were it comes from? Also, is your idea reproducible? Is this an idea you can execute, in some form, over and over? Good investment and trading programs are built around consistency, and, for this to happen, the idea must be something you can repeat.

2. **Do I understand how the market should move if I am right?** This is important, and not as simple as it seems. You think something is going up so you buy, but when should the market move? How long is it ok if the market is flat? What if it goes down a little bit, or a lot? What would be strongest confirmation of your idea? What might mean the idea has become consensus and is now vulnerable to reversal—when is good, too good?

Another variation of this question is asking if your position will properly capture the market move. In some cases, this is simple: you think the Nasdaq futures should go up beyond the high of the day in the next 30 minutes, so you buy Nasdaq futures—simple. But what if you think volatility is going to increase in stocks and you're trading the VIX futures, or a leveraged ETP, or options on one of the above? Do you truly understand how those products will respond to market movements? What if you think Delta Airlines should do better than its competitors? Is buying DAL the right play there?

3. **Do I understand my risk?** No, not do you know where your stop is; I mean do you really, truly understand your risk? What is the worst that can happen, and what is the probability of that worst case outcome? Once we've accepted that worst-case risk, we should then begin to think about less serious risks. Do not just assume that your risk is your stop; think deeper.

4. **What might I be missing?** This is hard one, because the question you're asking is what do you *not* know. The problem, of course, is that we don't know what we do not know! Many people find it challenging to think along these lines, but this is one way that we grow as traders and investors. Always ask what you don't know. Always be learning.

5. **What mistakes might I be making?** More and more, the investment literature focuses on cognitive mistakes. There are important lessons here, but, to me, one of the most important is that things are "wrong" with the way we perceive patterns, risk, and probability. These errors are a fundamental part of human perception and cognition, and you aren't going to *change* them—you cannot *fix* most cognitive biases, so how do you work with them? How do you minimize their ability to harm you? Asking these questions can help you protect yourself from some serious and dangerous errors.

These questions will not solve every problem you have, but they can point you in the right direction and help you work toward solutions to some of your most serious challenges.

Five Steps to a Successful Investment Process

It's easy to make money in the market. Anyone can place a winning trade; no expertise, experience, knowledge, or edge is possible. It's not so easy to make money in the long run, or to make any kind of consistent money in the market. Knowing that you have something you can replicate, month after month, year after year, and bring in some type of consistent profits? That's a lot harder, and to do that, we need a process.

A process defines what you will do, how you will do it, when you will do it, how you will evaluate it, and how you will modify it. A comprehensive trading plan includes all of these things, and, so, the plan can be considered a guide to your process. Once you have that good plan, discipline is "simply" a matter of following that plan.

No matter where you are in your trading journey, working on some aspect of your process can lead to significant rewards. Beginning traders often fly by the seat of their pants with little plan and no process, but even experienced traders can smooth some rough edges and find things to refine in their process. It's an ongoing journey. Let me share a few thoughts, and encourage you to work on your own trading or investment process:

Five questions

1. **Do you have an edge?** If you don't have an edge in the market, nothing else you do really matters. Maybe you can lose money more slowly with good money management, maybe you can avoid blowing out in one disastrous trade with discipline, but you can't make money if you don't have an edge. So, before you go deeper, make sure you understand your edge. Your process serves the edge, but if you don't have an edge, your process should be squarely aimed at developing that edge.

2. **What and how will you trade?** What markets will you trade? What size will you trade? What timeframe will you trade? How, exactly (and I emphasize exactly) will you find your trades? Lay out the precise details of your trading rules—how you get into and out of trades—in detail.

3. **When will you do the work?** What will your schedule be on a daily or weekly basis? Work includes both finding trades and evaluating your results. Also, what does that workflow look like? Do you start looking at charts, reading news, looking at a watchlist of markets?

4. **How will you evaluate the process and your performance?** It's easy to err on both sides: look too short-term, and you analyze noise. Take a too-long-term perspective, and you might not be correcting errors often enough.

5. **How and when will you change the process?** Changing trading plans, looking at some indicator you don't use, or doing a trade on a different timeframe—these are all potential warning signs that can point to a bad break in discipline. Once you have a plan, your job is to follow the plan, but the plan is a living thing. The plan can and should change; it should evolve and grow as you change, but it must do so in a disciplined way. Plan for change.

Get to work!

One last thought: *create a realistic plan*. There is no point in creating an 80 page document that has a list of rules you will not follow. If something is in your plan, it should be meaningful, important, and real. On the other hand, your plan needs to have enough detail—a rough outline is probably not useful for most traders—especially for developing traders. Strike a balance between detail and ease of use, and degree of detail.

Take a few moments today, sit down with a pen and paper, and spend a few moments writing freely on the questions I have asked above. Then, pull out your trading plan, and look at your plan with fresh eyes. What can you do better? What are you not doing that your plan says you will do? What needs to change? (Wait, you don't have a plan?! Well, I think you know what to do about that...) Process makes us better. Process leads us to consistency. Process matters.

Is Your Trading Boring? It Should Be.

I remember my first trades: the months of fevered study and preparation, the excitement of filling out those first brokerage forms, getting the first statements in the mail, and then the overwhelming rush of picking up the phone to put on those first trades. Though I had no easy access to live price data, I'm sure I would have been glued to the screen watching every tick if I did—counting the seconds until the fountain of money started flowing into my account. I also remember the agony of the botched trades, or, the horrible pain of loss when I had to get out—and, it should be said, sometimes well past my stop.

As I've written before, those first trades were not happy trades; success was elusive. In fact, nothing I did seemed to work, but the emotional roller coaster was, shall we say, extreme. Though I have never particularly liked gambling (because I can so clearly feel the odds are not ever in my favor), I could understand how someone could become addicted to the rush, and how even rare, fleeing, partial success could be powerful reinforcement.

Anyway, I struggled for a very long time, and I can point to something that marked a real turning point. I remember putting on a trade, and just not caring about the outcome. Win? Lose? Both? On a very deep level, *I simply did not care.* I had turned a corner, and I didn't even realize it at the time.

I had stumbled onto what I think is one of the keys to proper trading psychology. You must be unattached to the outcome of any trade, and, especially for developing traders, this can be scary. Too many people are attracted to trading because of the perceived excitement. (Q; Why do you want to trade? A: I want to work in a fast-paced, exciting environment where every day is a new challenge.... BZZZZ! Thank you for playing. Next...)

Proper, professional trading is anything but exciting—it is routine, and, hopefully, predictable. As a friend of mine said, being a trader is a lot like being a bricklayer. You put a brick down, you put mortar down, you smooth it, and you put another brick down... repeat. All day. Every day: today, the next day, the day after—always the same thing. Eventually, you build a big wall, but the act of putting the bricks down is just routine.

On some level, professional trading is boring, and it should be. What we need is structure, routine, and a methodology that points toward repetitive elements of market behavior. What we don't need is excitement. Be a bricklayer.

We all know Ed Seykota's now-famous quote: "Win or lose, everybody gets what they want out of the market." Too many traders come to the market seeking excitement. If you do, you will find excitement. You can have whatever you want, but just know that exciting trading and making money do not often overlap in the marketplace.

You can have whatever you want. What do you really want?

On Multiple Timeframes

Hidden In Plain Sight: Trading Multiple Timeframe Influences

Multiple timeframe analysis is almost a buzzword in technical analysis. I have been involved in markets actively for more than two decades, and have been an active participant in dialogue about markets for most of that time. It is interesting to see different techniques take the spotlight as groups of traders hold out hope that some new technique offers solutions to consistent profits: neural nets, quantitative analysis, scalping, and multiple timeframe analysis are some examples that immediately come to mind. These tools tend to move through the public awareness almost like a fad, eventually fading from notoriety when they fail to deliver on over-hyped promises.

Of course, no technique offers a simple solution to all the problems of trading. We know this: There is no magic formula; there is only the disciplined management of risk, in alignment with the (very small) underlying statistical edges in the market. However, though none of these techniques could possibly be the Holy Grail, they often do hold some important lessons. One of the key lessons from multiple timeframe analysis is understanding how trends develop, and, eventually, end on multiple timeframes, and we can use this awareness to give us an edge in some specific trades.

Multiple timeframe analysis does not always have something to say about a market or a trade. This is true, for one reason, because market action is mostly random, and most markets do not offer any tactical edge at most times—trading opportunities are fleeting. When these opportunities, imbalances of buying and selling pressure, do appear, even then there are not always multiple timeframe influences. Multiple timeframe analysis is a tool we use and apply in some situations.

Fighting the trend?

One of those situations arises when we are contemplating a trade that is against the trend on the higher timeframe. For instance, look at the chart of crude oil futures below, and imagine you are holding a long trade based on the uptrend on the daily timeframe (green arrow).

While this trade might make sense, the weekly timeframe—quite literally, the bigger picture—shows that this market has been in a downtrend for some time, and very well could still be in a downtrend. It is certainly possible that this daily uptrend we have identified could be a pullback setting up another selloff on the weekly timeframe.

What do we do with this information? There are many choices, and the right answer will depend on who you are, how you trade, and how you think about risk. Here are some possibilities:

- Skip the trade on the daily timeframe because we don't want to trade counter to the longer trend. This is ok, but there is a possibility that the weekly chart has bottomed. If we always skip trades like this, we will never be able to catch turns on the higher timeframe.
- Take the long trade, but tighten stops faster and take profits quicker. We know if the daily trade fails it could fail into a pretty dramatic selloff driven by the higher timeframe pattern.
- Ignore the higher timeframe considerations and just focus on what we see on a single timeframe. If we've done our work properly in creating our trading system, we have an edge and can just focus on that edge.

Those are some possible answers, with good arguments for each. They are all valid, but the key is that you must have all of this decided before you start trading—it has to be part of your trading plan.

Triggering entries

We can also use multiple timeframe influences to trigger trade entries. Look at the chart of gold futures below. I've highlighted a fairly unimpressive failure test (short entry) on the daily chart. However, what does the weekly timeframe show?

In this case, the weekly chart showed some kind of pullback in a market that is putting pressure on what appears to be a multi-year support level. That's a situation where we might want to be short into that pressure, and the unimpressive daily failure test may take on more significance. How do we categorize this trade? Is it countertrend? Failure tests are countertrend trades, and the daily was in an uptrend at the time, but it is also with-trend on the higher timeframe. You can label this however you wish, but be clear on the influences and what you are trying to accomplish with the trade.

This is a rich subject, and one that is often glossed over. The typical advice we hear is to not take trades against the higher timeframe trend, but I think there are some serious problems with that advice. A better plan is to learn to read market structure, to try to understand these conflicting flows, and to have a clear trading plan for handling these conflicts. Whether you ignore them, use them to trigger entries, or use them in a risk management context, you do have to have a clear plan for these patterns.

On Trade Management

Reader Question: Cutting Losses Quickly or Properly?

A few questions/comments. Define "cut losses quickly"? If you are trading pullbacks and you set a stop loss that would signify the pattern has failed, would that not be "cutting losses quickly"? I can see how a trader might take such a comment and introduce a level of dabbling in one's trading that would produce mental turmoil. For example, a pullback starts sputtering and the trader closes the position only to see the trade go in his direction. The opposite is true as well. Is not setting your stops and targets based on your risk management principles and letting the trade play out a more consistent approach?

Absolutely. I think you've hit on one of the critical elements of trading: we must give trades "enough room". What is "enough room"? It will vary with the market, but it's at least clear that it has to somehow incorporate the volatility of the market being traded—more volatile markets will require more room (larger stops) than less volatile markets. You can certainly quantify that in many different ways, and I might suggest that this is a case where ATR or other "range-aware" measures of volatility are probably better than, say, historical volatility. Why? Because historical volatility is calculated from the standard deviation of closes, and you are going to execute your stops if they are violated intrabar (probably), meaning that you will be responding to market information based on highs and lows of each bar. Since historical volatility doesn't see highs and lows, it might be a slight logical disconnect to use it in this context.

So, it's clear we can't put our stops extremely close to the market, in what would essentially be the noise of the market. As a general rule of thumb, stops placed less than 1 ATR are probably too close, with a few exceptions. Beyond that, you can adjust and tweak for elements of your style and the pattern you are trading.

Very close stops actually carry very large risk. This is one way that a lot of the marketing done to beginning traders is really disingenuous: it's so common to see people talk about "low risk trades". There's no such thing as a low risk trade, if you are sizing everything appropriately. If you have a very tight stop you will have a very large position size, and that, ironically, can represent very large risk, especially on a gap. Even if you're a one lot trader, a tight stop has a high probability of being hit, and the actual risk is the size of the loss times the probability of it happening.

Putting all these considerations aside, even if you do have a low risk trade, you also have a low reward trade, so what are you doing? Why waste your time with a small exposure that takes a disproportionate amount of mental and emotional capital for the potential financial return? If you truly understand probability, you will see that tight stops are very rarely a good thing. As I said there, "good risk management means using the *proper* stop, not necessarily a very tight stop."

Cutting losses quickly means cutting losses appropriately. For some traders, this may mean minutes; for others, it could mean weeks. I do think one of the key trading skills is allowing markets to fluctuate appropriately—giving trades enough room. There has to be a point at which you can step back and let the market move. People who can't do that find themselves getting into trades, getting nervous, and then immediately doing something silly like exiting and getting right back in.

It's really about doing the right thing, but there are two parts to that: first, you have to know what the right thing is. This means you must understand how markets move, what works and what doesn't, and how probabilities and statistics rule your trading results. Second, you have to do the right thing. You must be able to monitor and control your behavior, and execute your plan with perfect discipline.

Exits: Know When to Hold 'Em, Know When to Fold 'Em

We all focus a lot of attention, perhaps too much attention, on where to buy and sell a market, on where to enter trades. Let's spend some time looking at the other side: where are you getting out?

Some categories are useful here. First, we have exiting at a loss, or at a profit. (This is not necessarily the same as saying exiting on a stop or at a profit, because a (trailing) stop can often be a profit-taking technique.) Both of these can then be divided into two more categories: Exiting at the initial loss or a reduced loss, and profit taking against a stop or at a limit. Let's spend a few moments thinking about each of these.

Initial stops

The most important thing about initial stops is that you have one. Though so many trading axioms and sayings do not apply universally, one that does is "know where you're getting out before you get in." For every trade, you should have a clearly defined maximum loss, and you should work hard to make sure that loss is never exceeded. (There may be some styles of trading where this is not true, but if you know that you already know the lesson!)

In practice, bad things will happen. You will have the (hopefully rare) experience of a nasty gap beyond your stop, and sometimes will see losses that are whole number multiples of your initial trade risk. (I remember one lovely -4.5x loss in YHOO years ago. Though these events are rare, they are also a good reminder of we do not, for instance, risk 10% of our accounts on a trade. A 45% loss on a single trade would be a disaster, but 4.5x a reasonable risk (1% – 2%) is merely annoying.)

Initial stop placement is an art in itself, but, in general, I think too much of the material on the internet probably uses stops that are too tight. I've never seen anyone trade successfully with stops that are a few ticks wide. For me, initial stops usually end up somewhere around 2-4 ATRs from the entry. These stops are wide enough that many traders find them uncomfortable, but simply reducing position size to manage the nominal loss is an obvious solution. Taking losses is perhaps the most important thing you will do as a trader, so do it well and do it properly.

Partial Profits: Tightened Stops

We have defined that initial "never to be exceeded" (ideally) stop at trade entry, but many traders find it effective to move that stop rather quickly. Another possibility to consider is the time stop, in which we take steps to limit the position risk if the trade does not move in some defined time. There are many possibilities here, ranging from tightening the stop, to reducing the position, to exiting completely.

I have made a good case for not reducing the position at a loss because it effectively "deleverages" your P&L in the "loss space." Personally, I've found that simply taking whole, but smaller than initial, losses is more effective, but your experience may be different. A key point here is that all of this—entry, exit, position size, moving stops, taking targets, re entries, adding to positions, partial exits, etc.—all of this must work together. You change one piece, and the whole system will change. This is why some techniques may be effective in some settings but not in others.

To simplify, think of reduced stops as being moved when the trade does not immediately go far enough in your favor, and consider the use of time stops.

Partial Profits: Profit Targets

Profit targets are usually limit orders, as opposed to stops (which, not surprisingly, are usually stop orders.) In general, I find that it makes sense to have profit taking limit orders working in 24-hour markets, though we may not wish to work stops in the same after hours environments. People sometimes make mistakes or do silly things in afterhours, and I'm always happy to provide liquidity at the right prices.

There is a school of thought that says that all trades should simply be exited at profit targets, while there is a conflicting school that says we must let our winners run. How to reconcile these two approaches? I think the answer lies in trading style. For trend traders, we must let our profits run. As countertrend traders, we must take quick profits, usually at pre-defined areas. I have not found chart patterns or points to be any more effective than simply setting a target 1X my initial risk on the "other side" of the entry. Many people like to use pivots or trend-lines, but I've executed tens of thousands of trades (one of the advantages of spending years as short-term trader) and have simply not found these to be that effective. (For intraday traders, highs and lows of the day do deserve respect.) Consider the tradeoffs in simplifying your approach.

Trailing stops

Trailing stops can be managed in many ways, and I have found these to be very effective in many types of trading. We can trail at some volatility-adjusted measure, and there are even times we trail a very tight stop, effectively hoping to be taken out of the trade. This is a good problem to have: sometimes you may trail a stop at yesterday's low, and be shocked as the trade grinds in your favor week after week—there's nothing to be done in these cases but be forced to stay in the trade and make more money, but guard against hubris: many of the times this has happened to me I have been properly positioned into a climax move. When these moves end, they often end dramatically, so simply ring the register and step away from the market.

Putting it all together

This is certainly not an exhaustive list of all the possible ways to exit trades, but it will get you started in the right direction. I find that combining these techniques, using a pre-defined target for part of the trade, trailing the stop on the rest, and moving quickly to reduce initial risk on my rather wide initial stops, this works very well for swing trading the markets I follow.

Consistency certainly matters, but consistently doing something that does not work will, not surprisingly, lead to consistently losing money. Make sure you have a well-designed system with an edge, and that the system is one you can follow in actual trading. Make sure you trade with appropriate size and risk, and that you monitor your performance accordingly. With these guidelines, you can be a few steps closer to developing your own system and approach to trading.

Reader Question: What Does "Good Risk Management" Mean?

[This is the very first question I answered on my blog!]

I often see and hear people talking about good risk management being a good part of trading. What does this mean exactly? Limiting the size of your losses? Something else? Thank you.

I have summarized the process of technical/tactical trading basically as: 1) find patterns that suggest a statistical edge might be present, 2) take the appropriate position in the market, and 3) manage the risk in the trade. All of those steps are important, but I think most developing traders (and many firms, by the way) often stumble on risk management.

There also seems to be a misconception in much of the retail trading literature that suggests that effective risk management simply means making sure your losses are small. This is a mistake because many very small losses add up quickly. Though the actual size of each loss might be very small, the end result of consistently taking small, but nearly certain, losses is a constant drain on the trading account. It might be hard for a trader to see this, because most developing traders are fairly blind to costs of trading such as commissions, fees, and paying the spread in the instrument you're trading.

I think the root of effective risk management is to *make sure that no one loss can take you out of business*. This means, of course, taking the appropriately sized positions (and too small is as bad as too large because then you are not being correctly compensated for the risks you are taking), but it also means being aware of things that could have an impact on the volatility of that position. Most of us size positions based on anticipated volatility, and if something happens that causes future volatility to be dramatically higher than expected, the position carries more risk than we expected. Oftentimes, these things can be predicted: earnings reports, upcoming economic reports, scheduled macro events, earnings reports in an important competitor—these types of events are often priced into the implied volatility of the options market, so prudent risk management usually includes at least a cursory look at implied pricing. However, there are nasty surprises out there that cannot be foreseen: classic "acts of God", takeovers, surprise announcements, weather-related events, etc. Some of these can cause tail events that lead to losses many times larger than what was initially planned on a position. These risks, in most cases, cannot be hedged effectively, but are essentially a cost of doing business. Trade long enough, and you'll have some of these nasty surprises.

Another part of risk management is position management. First of all, this means getting out of your position at your initial loss point—though some developing traders struggle with this, there are really no excuses here. It is very simple: have a stop point when you get in a trade and exit when the price gets there. Book your loss; the market just told you your position is wrong and there is no point in fighting that. Position management goes far beyond that, though. Do you have a plan for taking profits at specific points? What about for booking partial losses? Will you add back to a position? It is important to understand the consequences of each of these decisions, and to have a clearly defined trading plan that tells you what to do in every situation.

Adding to Positions: A Simple Rule

I want to share a simple rule that has worked well for me over the years. I'll explain the how and why, and then wrap up with some thoughts about when this rule might not be appropriate.

So, imagine you are in a position, and then, for whatever reason, you know it's right. In fact, it's so right that it's time to add to the position, and so you do. Now, think about what happens if the trade turns out to not be right, or to not develop as you expected—what do you do? Here's the rule: *if you add to an existing position and it does not work out as expected, you must get out of more than you added.* Simple rule, but effective.

To put numbers to the idea, say you are long 5,000 shares of a stock. As the trade moves in your favor, you get a signal to add to the trade (and that "signal" could cover many possibilities.) So, you add 2,000 shares. Somewhere down the road, the trade does not work out, and probably is under the price at which you added. Now, you know the right thing to do is to reduce the position size, and you must do so, but how much do you sell? Answer: more than 2,000, and probably more like 4,000 than 2,100. You now hold less than the original position size, and you've booked a loss on part of the position, but you've also reduced your risk on a trade that was not developing as you thought it might.

One of the classic trading mistakes is to have on a winning trade, add inappropriately, and have that trade become a losing trade. For some traders, being aggressive and pressing when they have a good trade can add to the bottom line, but there is a tradeoff: when you become more aggressive you do so by taking more risk. The psychological swing—going from aggressive to wrong—can be one of the most challenging experiences for a trader, and many mistakes happen in this heightened emotional space. The rule of exiting more than you added is a simple rule, but it protects you from yourself.

Now, no rule fits all styles of trading all the time. There could be styles of trading for which this is inappropriate, (for instance, when we add planning to scale in as the trade moves against the entry.) However, for "simple", directional technical trading, this rule might be helpful in many cases. So much of the task of trading is just about avoiding errors and mistakes, and correct rules lead to good trading.

On Research

How to Find Trading Ideas

There are patterns in market prices—of this, there is no doubt. Some small set of these patterns even can help us with our trading and investing. Some are worthless. And some aren't even there at all—they are literally figments of our imagination-laden cognitive biases! What do we do about this, and how do we learn to understand and to read the market's patterns well? We have focused a lot of attention on how to separate the gold from the dross, how to test for statistical significance, and how to protect yourself from cognitive errors. But before that, there must be an idea. Where do we get ideas about how the market moves and what might be worth testing?

Finding ideas from the market itself

When we get into the later stages of testing, system development, and then actual trading, there is clearly a right way and a wrong way. There are ways to do things that will probably make you money, and ways that will probably cost you money. But, in the early stages, there is no right or wrong. There's no way you can make mistakes in the very early stages of idea generation. In fact, you must approach this work with a childlike sense of wonder and play.

So where do the ideas come from? While it's remotely possible that someone with no experience could have an idea that turns out to be a good idea, that's not the way it usually works—it's far more likely that your ideas, the ideas that eventually turn out to be profitable, will come from your experience and exposure to the market. The best way to get ideas is to be in the flow of the market.

With that in mind, here are a few things you can do to speed your idea generation along:

- **Be exposed to a lot of market data. Pay attention.** This seems like a silly thing, but it isn't. Attention is a precious resource, and you consciously decide where and how to allocate it. Focus your attention on the market. Pay attention to what happens after other things happen. Eventually you will start to draw some connections.
- **Look at a lot of charts.** People talk about "screen time", which means that you have to spend a certain amount of time in front of the screen looking at charts. Look at charts on different timeframes. Look at charts of different markets. Look at relationships between charts. Look at charts on timeframes you don't normally trade. Just look at patterns on charts.
- **Take some notes.** How you want to do this is up to you, but keep in mind this is not testing. This is opening the doors of your perception very wide, and letting everything in. So, jot down pattern ideas. Make pages where you sketch outlines of chart patterns you want to trade. Make text notes about relationships of highs and lows and closes that look potentially interesting. Keep another page of ideas and other questions to explore. Even just doodle mindlessly while looking at charts—these doodles might be a communication from a deeper part of your mind.
- **Read a lot and listen to a lot of people talk about markets.** The vast majority of what you hear and read will be garbage, but so will most of what you see. What we're looking for are the few seeds of good ideas that can grow into something more. Higher quality inputs will lead to higher quality results. So books with titles like Dude, Crush the Freakin' Market! or a $0.99 ebook on using moving averages probably won't add a lot to your thinking. Better books might, and so might academic research. You might even find some ideas in interviews and news articles.

What next?

Next, some hard work comes, but don't worry about that at first. At first, you need to immerse yourself in the flow of data and allow that powerful pattern recognition machine in your head to draw connections. Later, we'll do the work of sorting out the false connections from the good ones, and the illusion from the real—this is the work of statistics and system development, but all of this work starts with ideas.

Quality Matters

I've written a lot about the need for simplicity in trading. I've suggested you could probably throw out the vast majority of the tools you use and the things you look at, and your results would likely improve. There is a problem with this plan, though—as we simplify more and more, the individual components, the ingredients in our trading recipe, if you will, become much more important. Let me explain a bit more what I mean.

Think about food for a moment; I love eight course tasting menus, plates with three sauces and multiple garnishes, wine pairings, and dessert progressions. These things make me happy, but they don't feed my soul. The foods I literally dream about are things like the tomato sauce I can only make about two weeks out of the year, ideally with tomatoes picked in the early morning still covered in dew, peeled, cooked with a little sea salt, butter, and half an onion that is thrown out before the sauce is eaten. My thoughts often go back, decades past, to a meal of scrambled egg, butter, a grated black truffle and a crust piece of rye levain bread. Or, the single best thing I have ever eaten: a dashi broth made from kelp and shaved dried fish, infused with matsutake mushrooms (which taste a bit of pine forests) and a hint of yuzu rind, prepared by a master Japanese chef. What do all of these things have in common? Flawless ingredients prepared simply and perfectly, but first of all: perfect, flawless ingredients.

It is the same in trading, or in virtually every other endeavor I can think of. You can hide a lot behind complexity. If you're doing something wrong or there is some serious fault, it may be so deeply buried in the noise from competing influences that you don't see it at first. Your performance isn't good, but you cannot pinpoint the problem. You can be using something that doesn't add anything, but it gets lost in the mix. If you are going to simplify, it is important that you simplify to things that actually work.

If your trading is going well and you are pleased with your results, then take everything I say with a grain of salt. If you make changes or adjustments, make small tweaks or incremental adjustments rather than sweeping changes. (Many traders find something that works for them, and abandon it in the search for a shinier piece of gold. This is usually a mistake as well.) However, if you are struggling, I'd encourage you to ask yourself some hard questions. What tools are you using? How well do they actually work? Do they provide a real, verifiable edge in the market? (Most of the tools commonly used in technical analysis do not.) How do you know they work? How can you simplify your process and only use the best tools that provide you the best edge in the market? We'll keep digging, and hopefully find some answers to questions like these in some future blog posts. For now, dare to ask the right questions, and don't be afraid of the answers.

Chapter 8

Module 8–Pattern Failures

In some sense, this module is a "bringing it all together" perspective on the patterns we have studied throughout the course. We focus special attention on how these patterns fail. Some traders will choose to specialize in entries around pattern failures, and other traders will use this information to more effectively manage risk. All traders can gain good insights into pattern development and evolution through this study of pattern failures.

The course material and readings also include some thoughts on position sizing. This is an important question: how much to trade? Trade too much, and even a good system can blow up and take all your money. Trade too little and everything you do is meaningless—it's important to understand the tradeoffs and consequences for your particular approach to trading, and this section includes an exercise you can return to as your trading develops.

Last, this section concludes with a few thoughts on risk and how to effectively manage the risks of trading and investing. It's no exaggeration to say that trade is mostly about risk management, but we must define our terms for that statement to be meaningful and useful.

It is also worth noting that this module continues to move you in the direction of personal responsibility. The actual number of pages in this module's supplementary materials is less, but this is because more of the work is your own work. You are ultimately responsible for your own success or failure in the markets. The tools here can help you grow and develop, but the hard work is yours... and so are the rewards.

Section 1: Trading Plan: Revising and Refining

Your trading plan is a living document. Over the years, you will revise it as your trading style grows and progresses.

In this module, take some time to revisit your plan. If you did not do the work in the last module, stop and do it. This section is here to re-emphasize the supreme importance of having a solid trading plan—without it, you're just guessing!

What, exactly, you need to do in this module will vary for each trader. At a bare minimum, make sure you have the documents discussed in the previous module, and have them completed in a format you would feel comfortable sharing or presenting to investors. You will likely reconsider or want to change many aspects of these documents as you grow and progress in your trading.

You should also begin to work toward a backtest-able and backtested trading plan: now that you have all the pieces and can formulate your trading thoughts in a good format, create the plan that explains exactly how you wish to trade. Subject this plan to some backtesting, some papertrading, and only then are you ready to move into live trading.

Though creating a plan is a terribly unexciting topic, it truly is one of the most important steps in a trader's development.

Section 2: Your Own Research Project

You should, by this point, have some ideas about things you might want to research and examine in the market. Ideas do not have to be complicated, nor do they have to be unique. You may be interested in revisiting one of the pattern research projects you have done earlier in the course, and changing the way you structure that pattern as your trading plan has developed.

You should be very interested in examining your trading plan from a backtesting/research perspective. You will certainly find ideas in conversations with other traders you wish to test. You may get ideas from books, and all of this will probably filter down to your research journal, which will become a burgeoning source of ideas for further exploration.

Begin the work of doing this research. The bar-by-bar testing you have worked with certainly has its place, and I suggest it even for the more quantitative-able traders I work with. You may also wish to begin exploring some ideas using other backtesting frameworks, building simple Excel spreadsheets, or coding in language such as R or Python.

So, use this as a departure point, and begin doing your own work. You now have a good sense of what to do, what skills you may need to develop, and what you need to learn. If you continue to trade and to work on becoming a trader, much of that work will be in testing and examining trading ideas.

Begin your own research and keep good records of the results.

Section 3: Position Sizing Project

Intellectual understanding of the math behind position sizing, drawdown, and the volatility of an equity curve is one thing, but deeper investigation will bring further insights. One way to dig deeper is to create a simple, model trading system and to run many iterations of the system with different position sizing rules. Doing this effectively will require use of some programming structure or a spreadsheet.

Here is one possible procedure:

Define the "trading system" with three conditions (each of which can be a variable): the probability of a win or loss, the size of a win, and the size of a loss. For instance, you might have a 50% chance of a win. If the trade is a win, assume you make 1.1. If it is a loss, assume you lose 1.0.

Create a series of 100 trades drawn from this distribution. If you are using a spreadsheet, each one of these trades will be a row.

Assume a starting capital of $100,000. Decide the amount risked on each trade. (To begin, assume you will risk $1,000 per trade, but this should be a variable you can change in subsequent tests.) If the trade is a win, multiply your size of a win variable times the amount risked and add the resulting amount to the previous account balance. (If the trade is a loss, make sure the amount is subtracted.)

Repeat for each trade so you will have a running account balance beginning at $100,00 and changing for each of 100 trades in the series. Calculate basic stats for the equity curve and graph it.

Add one more refinement: if the equity curve goes to or below zero, terminate trading for the run and leave the account balance at that value. In your analysis, you will want to flag this as a run that went bankrupt.

Your random number generator should create a different equity curve each time the system is run. Generate multiple curves and consider how variable the results are.

Repeat this work with different amounts risked for each trade. Build a system that will allow you to risk a percentage of the previous account balance rather than a simple, fixed dollar mount. Last, repeat this work with different values for your base system. How does a stronger or weaker edge affect the variability of your results?

With a system that has a positive edge, you will generally see that there's truth to the "risk more/make more" approach, but also consider the variability and risk of ruin, both of which increase as trading size increases.

Section 4: Belief Inventory

Our beliefs define much of who we are, and drive our behavior, sometimes in ways we do not fully understand. The market environment is extremely challenging; most of the obstacles that stand in a trader's way are, to some extent, self-imposed. Much of the work on trading is work on ourselves.

This project asks you to spend some time considering your beliefs. This exercise appears to come out of nowhere: we have not spent much time focusing on the psychological and mental issues of trading. Rather, we've focused on the intellectual aspects of learning patterns, the math behind successful trading, and exploring how to put a trading approach together. This exercise is a bridge to carry you forward to the work on yourself.

The exercise is simple: spend a few minutes a day, for several days, in quiet reflection and write down some insights into what you think your core beliefs are. Of course, these can be explored and broken down on many levels, but it's enough to get the high-level perspective. Do not pay attention to whether beliefs or "good" or "bad" (empowering or limiting might be better labels), and do not think too much about where the beliefs came from.

Suggested topics to think about might be:

- Yourself
- Health
- Career
- Universe
- Family
- Relationships
- Money
- Success

Belief language typically begins with phrases such as "I am...", "People are...", "Life is...", etc. Many of these belifs are things that probably have not considered carefully; you simply accept and believe them to be true. You might be surprised what you find when you starting digging into these, and this exercise will reveal some important things about you and how you understand the world in which you live.

You may be inspired to think about other topics, but if you can end this exercise with a handful of most important beliefs about these, or similar, topics, consider the exercise a success. We will go deeper in the next module.

Section 5: Readings

From *The Art and Science of Technical Analysis: Market Structure, Price Action, and Trading Strategies* by Adam Grimes, Wiley, 2012:

263-290 (risk)

On Risk

Where Are Your Risks?

Traders talk and think about risk all the time, and for good reason: this is a risky business! A lot of things can go wrong, and some of those things can be very dangerous. Understanding your risks is the first step in managing them.

Risk can be counterintuitive; in so many walks of life, our goal is to reduce or to eliminate risk—reduce the risk of fire, take steps to reduce the chances of a car crash, and the list goes on. In trading, we want risk; we need the right kinds of risk because risk and opportunity are locked together—you cannot have one without the other. (Again: there's no free lunch.) However, they key is to take on the right kinds of risks, and to understand what those risks really are.

Think about risks, in four big categories:

Low consequence / high probability of happening: These are the common risks, and managing them is routine. Because we see them so often, we can handle them easily, and even if we make a mistake the consequences are (usually) not that serious. These are common, forgiving mistakes. An example of this type of risk might be a simple, normal, losing trade. It's worth spending a few moments to make sure that you are categorizing risks appropriately; if you put something in the low consequence category that is not low consequence, bad things can happen!

Low consequence / low probability of happening: These risks can be disruptive, but they usually aren't terribly dangerous. (Imagine a longer-term trader losing his datafeed or internet connection for a moment. (And also think, for a moment, about how these risks are relative. For a short-term trader, this might be a very high consequence event!)) The main dangers here are usually psychological, as the annoyance or break in the routine can lead to further mistakes, but these risks are usually not serious.

High consequence / high probability of happening: The true risk of an event (its expected value) is the product of the magnitude of the risk and the probability of that risk happening. By that math, these risks seem to be the most serious, but I would argue that they don't really matter for most traders. They are so serious and represent such an immediate risk to the trader—anyone who takes on these risks is quickly and efficiently eliminated from the game. You might look at these risks (e.g., violating your risk level per trade and then doubling up on the trade) as "just stupid". You can't take these kinds of risks and be a trader for very long.

High consequence / low probability: Here is where the true dangers, for most traders, lie. We, all humans, have poor intuition about these kinds of events. Maybe we choose to obsess about them, which reduces our ability to trade, or maybe we ignore them, and are blissfully blind to the upcoming day of reckoning. Options traders deal with these risks: anyone who has been in the business a while has heard stories of options traders who made money every week for 20 years, and who then lost their entire net worth in one catastrophic trade. If you're naked short premium, ask yourself what would happen if all those deltas went to 1.0—because some day, they will.

These risks exist for other traders too: if you swing trade stocks, there will be a day that your entire portfolio gaps far beyond stop levels due to an "act of God". If you short-term trade, there will be another Flash Crash that might take you to your margin limit if you are fading the move. This category, to paraphrase a well-known children's book, is where the wild things are. This category demands the best of your intention and discipline.

Six Keys to Effective Risk Management

1. It is not just that risk is hard to understand—**some risks may be *impossible* to understand.** Your risk management plan must leave room for the unknown and the unknowable. This is why advice from great traders always includes a reminder to "stay humble" or to avoid hubris. There's a lot you don't know in the market, but there's also a lot you cannot possibly know. And, in markets, what you don't know certainly *can* hurt you.

2. **Think about the extremes.** Understand the most extreme events that have happened in your market, then look backward and out: look at related markets and go back in history. What is most extreme thing that has ever happened, in the entire recorded history of markets, in markets that might be like yours? Once you understand this, realize that more extreme events lie in the future. Ask the questions: What would happen if you had a position on? How bad could it be? Then, assume that your answers vastly understate the risks.

3. **Think about the "middles"**. What are the common risks you will face in this market? What happens a few times a year that could be unsettling? How can you prepare for and protect yourself against these events? Many traders only focus on the extreme risks, but a lot of trading accounts die sad deaths from a thousand cuts. Mundane risks add up, and mundane risks can take you out of the game permanently.

4. **Your trading strategy is a risk.** One of the biggest risks most developing traders face is that they are doing something that simply doesn't work. How well do you know your strategy and its characteristics, and how sure are you of those numbers? The unexamined life may not be worth living—Socrates was probably right—but the unexamined trading system is certainly not worth trading!

5. **You are the biggest risk.** Yes, that's right, *you*. All of your talk of discipline, preparation, planning, all of the hours of screentime, all of the chats with trader friends—all of that isn't worth much if you don't follow through and do the right thing. If you aren't disciplined, every moment of every trading day, you are not a disciplined trader. The market environment is harder than you can imagine, and it will challenge you, at times, more than you imagined possible. Spend a lot of time thinking about the most critical part of your trading system: you, yourself.

6. **Plan for risks outside the market.** Everyone, from the institutional scale to the individual trader, will have outside influences challenge their market activities. Institutionally, regulatory changes and developments in market structure can dramatically change the playing field. Your investors will make mistakes—becoming fearful and exuberant at exactly the wrong times. If you're an individual investor, you will face outside financial stresses, personal issues, health issues, etc. All of these things will have an effect on your trading that is hard to capture in the numbers, but prudent planning will allow you to navigate these challenges.

What's Luck Got to Do With It?

Let's cut straight to the punchline: the answer is, "it turns out, quite a lot." Here's a look at probability and luck, and the part they play in our investing results.

People selling investment tools or advice are, in some sense, selling an illusion of certainty. We can use whatever words we like—consistency, security, risk management—but what it comes down to is that humans have a very natural desire (and need) for safety and security. We want to know what the right actions are, and that those actions will lead to the desired results. We think we are prepared, and that we can handle some variability and surprises the market throws our way.

Think about it like this: let's say we want to cook a steak. We might know that sometimes the piece of meat will be tougher, more flavorful, or have a little better fat marbling—so we know that the steak we cook tonight will not be identical to the one we cooked last week. But what if we cut the meat, get the grill to just the right temperature, season the meat perfectly, start to sear it, and then our house gets hit by a small asteroid that wipes out our entire town? That's a degree of variability we, generally, are not expecting. Though the example becomes a little silly (and the steak overcooked), surprises like this happen in financial markets far more often than we'd like to admit.

Randomness is a problem for traders and investors. It's a problem objectively because it makes our results highly variable (even if we're doing exactly the right thing), and it's a problem subjectively because we have very poor intuition about randomness. Looking at any market, most of the time, most of what you see is random fluctuation—meaningless noise. We don't deal well with meaningless noise; our brains are fantastic pattern recognition machines; they find patterns with ease, even when no patterns exist. Many pages have been written about cognitive biases in investing, but one of the most serious is that we don't understand randomness intuitively very well. Consider these questions:

- How many people do you need to get together in a room to have a 50% chance that two of them share a birthday?
- If you flip a perfectly fair coin a million times, is there a good chance or a bad chance you will have 500,000 heads at the end of that run?
- If I flip that coin only 30 times, what is the chance I have 5 heads in a row, given that it's a fair coin? You don't have to give me a number, just tell me is there a "pretty good chance" or "almost no chance".
- How likely is it for someone to win a lottery twice?

You probably get the point that, unless you've studied probability and statistics, your first answers to those questions are probably dramatically wrong.

Because we don't naturally understand randomness and variation, few traders are prepared for the natural degree of randomness in their results., and, yes, let's use that dirty word: some traders get lucky and some get very unlucky. It's easy to show models where traders have radically different results trading the same system with no errors (on different time periods). Even with no mistakes, no emotions, no analytical prowess, no tweaking of the system, results diverge, dramatically, due to luck.

So, that's great, right? Some people get lucky in the market and some don't. If that's all I have to say, maybe we should just go to Vegas and put it all on black for the first roll, but hold on, there's a better way.

Managing your luck

Now for the good news: you are not powerless against luck. People say many different things about luck, like "luck is what happens when opportunity meets preparation." Well, there's certainly some truth to that (and value, from a motivational perspective), but that is not exactly how we are using the word here. Luck, in this case, means random variation that you cannot control. Luck can be good or bad, but it is, by definition, unpredictable and uncontrollable. Even if we can't control it, there are some things we can do to better understand and to manage the impact it has on our trading results:

You absolutely must have an edge. In the short run, you can get lucky and make money doing something that has no edge, but expected value will catch up with you. Don't gloss over this point, because it might just be the single most important thing we can say about trading—you have to have an edge.

You must be consistent. You must trade with discipline. Nearly everyone who writes anything about trading says these things, but the why is important: you must be consistent because the market is so random. You cannot change your approach based on short-term results because those short-term results are confounded by the level of noise in the market. In other words, you can lose doing the right thing and make money doing the wrong thing. Too many traders make adjustments based on evaluating a handful of trades, and this is likely a serious (fatal) error. Markets are random; you don't have to be.

Luck matters. There's no denying that, but so does skill and so does edge. In fact, the more skillful you are as a trader, paradoxically, the more luck matters. You can be successful without luck, but the wildly successful traders (who are outliers) always have some significant component of luck. If the overall level of investment skill in the market is rising (far from a certain conclusion, in my opinion), then performance will converge and luck will play a bigger part for the top performers.

If you understand the part luck plays in your results, you will realize that emotional reactions to your results are largely inappropriate. Too many traders ride the emotional roller coaster from euphoria to depression based on their short-term results, and this really doesn't make sense because you're letting luck (random fluctuation) jerk your emotions around.

Some people take this message, that luck, good or bad, is important and unavoidable, as bad news. It isn't bad news at all. You are still responsible for developing your trading method and your skill as an investor. Without those things, you won't make it. It's very unlikely that you can do everything right over a long period of time and not perform adequately well. However, many people focus on outlier-type stories as their motivation for getting into the market: people who took a few thousand dollars to hundreds of millions, people who make incredible returns in a short period of time, etc. If you understand the part luck plays then you will understand that this cannot be a goal or motivation for getting into the markets, because those outlier returns were people who got lucky. Maybe you will too (by definition, you probably won't), but your focus must be on building a disciplined, core trading methodology rather than trying to get lucky.

If this topic interests you, let me recommend a fantastic book. In *The Success Equation: Untangling Skill and Luck in Business, Sports, and Investing,* Michael Mauboussin takes a deep look at measuring the contribution of skill and luck to success, and draws some fascinating parallels from sports. This is one of the most important books I've read in a long time, and I'd highly recommend it to anyone who manages money or trades in the markets.

On Trading Styles

Discretionary and Consistent? How?

I've been asked a few variations of the same interesting question recently. Here are a few examples:

> *The one thing I keep struggling with is finding an edge I can use in a disciplined and consistent way. How do you define an edge? To me an edge can't be discretionary; an edge can only be defined by a set of rules. Otherwise it can't be applied in a disciplined and consistent way, am I right?*

Or, as another reader asked in the comments to one of my blog posts:

> *As an avid reader of your posts and your book it strikes me how often you mention the importance of discipline and consistency. Does this mean that your trading is more rule based than discretionary? Or are some parts... more rule based and other parts... more discretionary?*
>
> *In my opinion, consistency is only possible if you have rules, but on the other hand it is also important to be adaptive and flexible and this might sometimes challenge consistency.*

So, the question really comes down to something like "how can we be discretionary and consistent at the same time?" Let's think, first, about what "discretionary" means.

I think many people would categorize trading approaches across a spectrum from discretionary to systematic. A purely systematic trader has a set of rules and simply always applies those rules; a computer could do it, probably better than a human. On the other extreme, imagine a purely discretionary trader who simply buys or sells whatever he wants based on his opinion or mood at the time with no consistency (1 share or 1,000 shares; holding 1 minute or 10 years; etc.) The problem in this (flawed) classification system comes from a misunderstanding of what it means to be a discretionary trader.

To my way of thinking, discretionary trading simply means that we allow some degree of human intuition into the trading process. This does not mean that trading becomes unstructured and undisciplined. On the contrary, the application of discretion can be highly structured. Here are some ways this might be done:

- First, specify where discretion is allowed. In choosing entries only? Sizing? Trade management? Stop location? Getting out early? Doubling up? All of the above? Depending on your trading methodology, some of these choices may make more sense than others.
- Have a rule that specifies what you will do if intuition and other rules are strongly in conflict. This requires some thought because it may be different at different points in the process. For instance, if your intuition is to skip an entry specified by your system, perhaps that would not be allowed, but if you are inclined to exit a trade early, that might be ok.

Note the words used here: "specify", "have a rule", etc. This means that you have rules, in advance, that say what you will and will not do in the market.

That last point is the key to consistency. We do not have to remove all human input from the trading process. In fact, we can't. For instance, a purely systematic trader follows a set of rules, but where did those rules come from? In most cases, from some type of statistical or scientifically-informed (hopefully) research process, but, even here, things are not absolute. Research involves decisions, and those decisions are made, at least on some level, by humans. Why some markets and not others? Why certain parameters? Why was this particular approach to the data explored in the first place? Why did we choose to look at certain data sets and exclude others?

Even more important, someone (or something) is probably monitoring our systematic guy. If market conditions change in some way we don't understand, his rigid set of rules may no longer work, and, at some point, he will get be pulled out of the game. Following that event, there's a good chance that humans (again, using some intuition and discretion) may look at his rule set, refine it in the context of recent data, and might send him in to play again. Even in this most rigid systematic approach, human discretion and intuition dance in the margins. The key is that discretion can be structured and disciplined, just as any other input to the trading process.

I will agree that exact adherence to bullet point rules is easier than incorporating discretion into your trading. It takes a lot of experience to use discretionary inputs in a way that is not unduly influenced by emotion. (Note: removing all emotion from trading should not be a goal.) Being consistent and being disciplined simply means we follow a set of rules with consistency, and those rules certainly can include an element of discretion.

On Reversals

The Problem with Reversals

One of the curious elements of human psychology is the tendency to fade moves or to try to pick turning points in trends. When I started trading, this was how I started out: looking for patterns that showed a trend was ending and trying to take a counter-trend position. Over the years, I've seen many traders focus on fading moves—a few do so successfully, but most struggle. We must be aware of this bias, know that it colors our thinking, and work very hard to see market action with objectivity and clarity.

Calling tops and bottoms is seductive. If you have a public platform, all you have to do is get it right once; it's amazing to see people consistently calling for reversals, being wrong time after time, and yet to see other people still following that advice. One reason this works is that we look so smart and feel so right when we do call those tops and bottoms that it's easy to forget the accumulated losses from the failed trades would be very large indeed.

It's also difficult because this is a very inconsistent game. For instance, many stock traders at prop firms specialize in fading large moves. They will wait for a news item to hit and for a stock to make a huge move relative to its normal trading history. (Think about a $50 stock that normally has an ATR of $1 making a $5 move in less than a minute. Those are the kinds of moves we are talking about.) These traders will take a position against that move and are prepared to add to it if the stock keeps moving against them. Down, buy more. Down, buy more. Down more, keep buying. These traders will often have long strings of winning weeks (or even years), but then may give back years of profits in a single trade, and may even be taken out of the game completely. I've seen it happen more than once.

There are psychological reasons behind many traders' focus on fading, but I think this is really driven by a deep, fundamental misunderstanding of how markets work. Ask yourself: when a market makes a large move, a very large move out of all proportion to its recent history, what is more likely to happen? Is that move more likely to lead to another move in the same direction, or is it more likely to reverse? Though our inclination is to think the market has gone "too far" (and, perhaps, to be sorry we missed the move so we look for a reversal), it's far more likely for a market to make another large move in the same direction after it has made a large move. (Mandelbrot makes this point in *The Misbehavior of Markets* and explains why it is so.) If we do not understand that, then we are doomed to be forever biased to reversal.

Are you automatically inclined to look for reversals? Do you see trending charts, and immediately try to find where you can jump on board against the move? If so, you have a bias. It may even be a bias that can be harnessed constructively. I am not advocating blind adherence to "trend following" as a methodology, and there are tools that can be used to find trend termination trades. There's room for many different styles of trading, but we need to understand how we think, how we see, and work to manage our biases with ruthless efficiency. Fail to do so, and we will fail as traders.

Don't Be This Guy

Take a look at this picture which I took a few years ago, on a Friday afternoon, on a New York / New Jersey ferry. After a long and stressful work week (it was 2008), the gentleman in the photo was more than a little inebriated (i.e., could barely stand up), probably the victim of an early happy hour. Now, you should also know that these ferries are fast, and the winds on the river are strong—the wind is often strong enough to blow glasses off your face. This poor soul had urgent business that was unable to wait for the trip across the river, so he walked to the front of the ferry, unzipped, and relieved himself over the bow—directly into what was probably a 35 knot headwind.

Though this happened a while ago, the lesson and the aftermath made a lasting impression (probably more so on the people who did not see it coming and did not step out of the spray). Though few of us might commit the Technicolor version of this error, financial commentators do it all the time, in other ways.

I have spent some time doing a lot of reading—everything from social media, "big" media, gurus and pundits, and paid research. It is always interesting to see the commonalities across the group (a less kind assessment might be "groupthink"), but one error crops up repeatedly: attempts to catch or call a trend turn with no justification. This error can be hazardous to your financial health, so let me share a few thoughts.

Why we are always looking for the turn

I think there are good reasons why traders are always looking for the end of the trend. Many of us who do this are competitive and contrary in the extreme. I joke with people that I could have a conversation like this: Me: "Look at the pretty blue sky." You: "Yes, that really is a pretty color of blue." Me (now concerned because I agree with someone else): "Well... is it really blue? Isn't it more blue green? And we know it's essentially an optical illusion anyway..."

This tendency is natural and pretty common among traders. On one hand, it's a very good thing—you will do your own work, be naturally distrustful of outside opinions and cynical about information, and will work to think critically about everything. But it's also a weakness because it makes us naturally inclined to see any market movement and think that the crowd is wrong. The crowd is not always wrong; often, they are right and they are right for a very long time.

I think this is a simple reason why so many of us are always looking for the turn—many traders are simply wired to be contrary and to think in a contrary way. We are different, and we want to stand apart from the crowd. For many of us, this is a part of our personality and we must learn to manage it, and to understand that it is the lens that can distort everything we see.

Trading lessons and psychology

Beyond this element of personality, there are also some trading and market related reasons why we are always looking for a turn. There's a misguided idea that we have to catch the turn to make money. Decades of trend following returns (for example., the Turtles) have proven that you don't have to catch the turn; it's enough to take a chunk out of the middle. There's also a natural inclination to be angry and distrustful of a move we missed—if we see a long, extended, multi-month trend in which we are not participating, it's natural to be scornful of those who did participate and to look for reasons the trend might be ending.

Many classical chart patterns are taught and used out of context. Any trend will always show multiple "head and shoulders" patterns, and inexperienced chartists will not hesitate to point these out. The problem with poorly defined chart patterns (out of context) is that you can see anything you wish to see in a chart—it's always possible to justify being long, short, or flat a market, so it's always possible to find evidence to support whatever you want to do, at least in the absence of clearly defined trading rules and objectives.

Another problem is that many traders use tools that are supposed to somehow measure extremes. Overbought/oversold indicators, sentiment indicators, ratios, bands—the problem is that these all measure the same thing, in a different way. If I get an oversold signal from sentiment, RSI, and some Fibonacci extension, I do not have three signals; I only have one because the tools are so tightly correlated. This is important to understand—if we don't understand this (the correlation of inputs into a trading decision), then we will have false confidence in our calls, and performance will suffer. Better to know you don't know, than to think you know more than you do.

Commentators and asymmetrical payoffs

If a trader places a trade, she makes money if the trade is profitable and loses money if it is not. This is simple, logical, and just. However, for a commentator (blog writer, research provider, tv personality, guru, etc.), the payoffs are very different—the public remembers the times we are right, and very quickly forgets the times we are wrong. The fact there even are permabears (people who have been bearish stocks for decades) who are called to be on TV and in the paper when the market goes down is proof of this fact. It's possible to run a newsletter or blog business for years making outrageous claims that never come true such as "end of the financial world", "the coming crash", "how to protect your assets from the coming seizures", "where to bury your gold", etc.

The crazier and more outlandish the forecast, the better: if someone says the S&P is going down 500 points tomorrow and he's wrong, no one will long remember because it was a dumb call. If, however the S&P should, for some reason, go down 500 points, that person is, instantly and forever, the expert who "called the crash". In fact, if that forecast doesn't come true but there's some mild decline in the next few months, creative PR can still tie the forecast in.

Why does this matter? You can read blogs and listen to commentators, but read with skepticism. Realize that the person writing has a reason for calling ends of trends and turns. Your trading account, however, has a different standard: if you lose more on your losing trades than you make on the sum of your winners, that's going to be a problem, in the long run.

Finding ends of trends

One way I have found to avoid the situation where I'm going against the trend is to require some clear signal from the market that the trend might have ended. There are specific patterns that can help: (exhaustion, climax, three pushes, failure tests, price rejection), and then seeing the change of character (new momentum in the other direction) to set up a pullback in the possibly-new trend is key.

In the absence of that sequence: 1) something to break the trend and 2) new counter-trend momentum and change of character, the best bet is to not try to fade the trend and to wait for clear signals. And that guy back at the top of this post? Yeah, don't be that guy.

Chapter 9

Module 9–Practical Trading Psychology

Psychology is not an afterthought. In the first version of the Course, each Module had a component focused on psychology, so the topic was taught throughout the course. One of the most significant changes in the 2017 revision was the most of the psychology-focused units were moved into the last Module.

There are two reasons for this change: progress in the psychological tasks of trading are more individual and each trader will progress at her own pace. One of the most consistent pieces of feedback was that students would find themselves working many units in the past on psychology while they continued to forge ahead with the market pattern work.

Second, the ending of this Course really is the beginning. Putting the psychology and inner work here highlights the importance of this material, and should help the developing trader and experienced trader alike to better integrate this material into their continued learning.

The readings, carefully selected from my blog posts over the years, are more extensive for this Module and should be read carefully as they include some hints and directions that are not covered elsewhere.

Section 1: Introspection

Introspection is not easy. We spend much of our lives lying to ourselves; some of this is even constructive, but with can easily either over or underemphasize weaknesses or strengths. Looking at other people, we easily identify people who think too much of their abilities, or can probably also think of someone who we think should have far more confidence. Having an accurate and balanced assessment of our strengths, weaknesses, and potential is not normal, but that is your goal in doing this work!

First, we can define the scope of the project a little more clearly. We want to understand our:

- Skills and abilities, natural, developed, and as-yet undeveloped
- Core beliefs and principles
- Motivations
- Needs
- Fears
- Strengths and weaknesses
- Directions for growth
- Anything else that catches your attention as you work through the project

There is no right or wrong way to do this, but here are some ideas that work for other people. Feel free to adapt and expand them for your own practice and exploration.

Sit down with a blank piece of paper and write stream of consciousness lists of your strength and weaknesses. Spend time doing this, and come back to it every day for a week. At the end of the week, edit and categorize the list. Reflect on the list, and let it grow over another week or two. Make sure that you bring your focused attention back to this list several times each day, even if for only a few minutes.

Alternatively, make five lists (personal attributes, values, emotional characteristics, habits, needs and desires) and work in filling out those lists.

Though this is introspection, you may find value in talking to people who know you well and getting feedback from others. It can be very helpful to work with people from different settings (friends, coworkers, family members), but use their perspectives to spark your own work and self-reflection.

This exercise is an important part of knowing yourself. Once you have a clearer picture of your motivations, strengths, and weaknesses, you will be better equipped to figure out how to shape yourself into the person you want to be.

Be honest—not brutal, not cruel—be fair and honest with yourself. The goal of this exercise is to see clearly and accurately.

Section 2: Understanding Beliefs

Do not begin this project until you have completed both the Belief Inventory in the previous module, and the introspection in this module. Once those two projects are done (and they will take considerable time to do well), we can turn our attention to understanding our beliefs and motivations better, and to transforming some of the limiting beliefs into beliefs that are useful and empowering.

To do this exercise, take your work from both the introspection and belief inventory, and focus on the beliefs. Separate them into categories based on two criteria. First, is the limiting-empowering spectrum. For instance, a trader might hold the belief that "money is dirty", and it's easy to see how that belief could limit all of his operations in the market. An empowering example of the same belief might be "I live in a universe of abundance."

The second category is "how strongly you believe this." Rank your beliefs on a scale from "deeply held, almost certain to be true" to "very uncertain, and essentially a guess." You should also mark beliefs that you believe (deliberate word choice, there) are very important and not very important to you. Come up with a system that makes sense to you.

You will need to trust your intuition on this project, and may well need to revisit it several times. It has only taken me a few paragraphs to explain a profoundly important exercise. If you do this well, you will have a much better understanding of who you are, why you are, and perhaps even have some insights for how you might grow into the person you want to be.

Section 3: Transforming Beliefs

Now we begin the fun stuff! Here is where you transform the beliefs that have held you back, that have separated you from your potential. Before you start, consider that this is work that might benefit from an outside perspective. A coach can be particularly effective as you do this work, but so can a friend, a therapist, or a counsellor. Sometimes it's much easier to see someone else's limitations and problems than it is to understand our own. The work you have done to this point has laid a strong and solid foundation for transforming your beliefs. You can make great progress on your own (perhaps adapting your journal or self-talk for the project), but don't be afraid to avail yourself of some outside help. Even a few sessions with someone who is used to doing this work can be life-changing.

You have arrived at your beliefs as the total of all your learning, thinking, and life experiences. Many of these beliefs have been reinforced time and time again, and these beliefs form an important part of the fabric of your reality. However, some of these beliefs are not true. Some of them are unimportant, but some of them are harmful. If you want to change yourself—if you want to change the results you get from the Universe—one of the best ways to do so is to change your beliefs.

I should say up front that the common approaches of positive affirmations (e.g., writing down a new belief and saying it repeatedly, perhaps with strong emotion, every day, maybe while looking in the mirror, etc.) are not usually very effective. We hold our beliefs, for the most part, because they are anchored in our perception of reality. If we simply try to change a belief by force, our minds will rebel. (Take a silly example of trying to transform the belief "I cannot walk through walls" with positive affirmation. That belief is going to be strongly reinforced, no matter how you frame your affirmation!)

There is no one, right way to do this work. (Indeed, for some people the positive affirmation approach may be very effective.) A framework that I have found useful is this:

Identify where you want to be or what you want to do, and then think about why you are not there.

Identify beliefs that have gotten in your way. These are limiting beliefs.

Think about these limiting beliefs. Where do they come from? Why do you believe these things? What anchors, things you see or experience, reinforce this belief and lead you to think it is true? What emotions and life experiences are associated with this belief?

Think about what this belief is doing. Every piece of your mental framework serves some purpose. If it's not a useful purpose, it's at least intended to be useful—many things that become problems could be constructive in another context. Think about why you believe this, and what it is doing for you. What are you getting from this belief?

Spend a little bit of time thinking about what you might be missing? Is it possible you are missing information or misinterpreting experiences that you have always taken to support this belief? You know there are people in the world who don't believe the same things you do. Can you imagine what it would be like to see through someone's eyes who did not have this belief? How would that person interpret the data you think supports the belief?

Working with intention—with responsibility, care, and love for yourself—you will likely see some paths to transform your beliefs. Simply working through this approach will cause you to see the belief from another perspective, to be able to question its foundations. You can choose, in many cases, to replace the belief with something that is more constructive and more empowering. Perhaps here there is a place for some positive-affirmation-type reminders that can help you see the world through new eyes.

This is only the very surface of this work. If it interests you, you can easily find additional sources and materials that will carry you deeper. Change your beliefs, and you change your world. Change your beliefs, and you change yourself.

Section 4: Readings

From *The Art and Science of Technical Analysis: Market Structure, Price Action, and Trading Strategies* by Adam Grimes, Wiley, 2012:

346-374 (trader's mind)

On Psychology

Are Beliefs All That Matter? Thoughts on Trading Psychology

Here's an interesting question on a controversial topic—trading psychology. A reader sent me a note asking:

> *Hi. I hope you can help me with a question. I am a developing trader and am having a friendly argument with some trading friends. One person says that trading psychology is all there is. She says that we don't trade the markets we trade our beliefs about the markets and all we need to do is act with our beliefs and we will make money. Another person says psychology is just an excuse to sell courses and books and that anyone who has a system can follow it. Can you give us a final answer on this?*

I know this is a good question because there's no way I can answer it without making someone, somewhere very angry. People have passionate feelings on this topic, and, no, I don't think I can give you a final answer. What I *can* do is to share some thoughts based on my experiences—my personal experience as a trader, working with other traders, and conversations with other traders, both developing and professional. Also, it should be said up-front that I'm not a trained mental health professional and anything I say here is just the observation of a layman in the field.

My personal belief is that trading psychology is often overemphasized at the expense of actually having an edge in the market. I bet I know the books your friend who says "we just trade our beliefs about the market" is reading, and those books also suggest that it's very easy to find a system that works—all you have to do is have a trend following and a range system and just know when to switch back and forth between the two. In my experience, there are some serious and deep problems with this line of thought.

First the statement "you only trade your beliefs about the market" is a non-falsifiable statement. I could give a list of reasons why I think this statement is not true, but then someone who believes it could say "well, that's your belief..." This is a statement that has almost religious overtones. Because it holds out such promise, it inspires strong emotion and almost fanatical defense from people who believe it is true. Also consider the statement: "it's all psychology. Trading psychology is all there is." Plenty of books and people say this, but since there is nothing anyone could do to disprove the statement, no evidence that would make believers stop believing, a reasonable, logical, course of action is to consider the statement is meaningless. (If you're not familiar with this idea: a statement must be potentially falsifiable, work it into your thinking. It will change the way you see the universe.)

Methodologically, there's another perspective: it's a tautology to say that successful traders trade their beliefs about the market. Of course they do, and those beliefs are well-aligned with the way markets work; that's why these traders are successful. It's quite another thing to tell a developing trader you just have to believe something, and then trade in alignment with your beliefs because there are plenty of market beliefs that are wrong. Successful traders have beliefs that explain how the market really moves. I think we should teach beginning traders how to understand how the market works rather than focusing too much, early on, on psychology.

Now, there's another side to this coin: there are plenty of examples of traders who know what to do and can't do it. There are traders who have a solid system and just can't execute. There are investors who do good research, have a good plan, and then panic when the market goes down 5% and sell everything. It's not enough to just know what to do; some of the most serious challenges of trading relate to actually doing what we know is right.

There are significant overlaps between human peak performance in other endeavors (athletics, chess, music, etc.) and trading. I personally spent some time working with a therapist when I saw that I needed better skills and strategies to deal with the pressures of trading. Knowing what to do isn't enough; it's the doing that matters. And, to actually *do*, we need the psychological strength and resilience to deal with the stresses of the markets—psychology is indeed important.

I apologize for the long-winded answer to your question, but there is no definitive answer: the answer is different for traders and investors in different stages of the journey. I do think—and I know that this is a controversial stance—many, if not most, psychological questions can be addressed through trading methodology. If we don't have an edge then no psychological work will stop the bleeding from our accounts. Maybe we'll lose money and feel better about it, maybe we will be happier, but we will still lose money. We must have an edge.

It seems counterintuitive to say this: but many problems that are assumed to be trading psychology problems can be fixed by correct trading, with an edge, in alignment with the realities of the market.

Six Keys to Managing Trading Psychology

We live in a "quick fix" world in which everyone is looking for "hacks" to solve and shortcut problems. The internet is filled with "you're doing it wrong" posts that purport to show you how to do everything from tying your shoes to drinking orange juice correctly. For traders struggling with psychological weaknesses—and, to be clear, this is all of us! *All* traders are vulnerable to making mistakes driven by psychological issues—there are no shortcuts to solving psychological issues. It's hard work, but if you don't do it you're going to lose a lot of money in the market. It is work that must be done. Here are six of the most important tools I've found to help you manage your psychological issues in the marketplace.

1. **Make sure you have an edge.** This seems elementary, but so many traders begin to trade without knowing they have an edge. Yes, there are many ways to find an edge in the markets, but an edge is a precise and delicate thing. If you don't know what your edge is, you don't have one. In my experience, I've seen many struggles that appear to be psychological—both my own and others'—and, in most of those cases, the issues were not psychological. They were methodological: the traders had no edge in that time and that environment.

There are psychological issues in trading, and even experienced traders sometimes hit roadblocks. It would be wrong to say that there are no legitimate psychological issues in trading, but I suspect that most of the psychological issues people face are the result of doing something in the market that does not work—not having an edge. If you're trading without an edge you *should* have psychological issues because you are going to lose money!

2. **Have a trading plan.** We hear and read the same, boring things from people who write about how to trade, right? Have a plan. Plan the trade; trade the plan. Fail to plan; plan to fail. Well, this "boring" thing is the difference between success and failure.

People want shortcuts. It would be nice if I could tell you some magical hand position and way to look at a special plant on the corner of your desk that would make all of your trading issues go away, wouldn't it? The world doesn't work like that; there really are no shortcuts. If you create a good trading plan, then your job, as a trader, is to simply follow that plan. When you are evaluating your actions, the only question you really need to ask is "did I follow the plan?" ("Does the plan work?" is another question that should be asked and answered separately. I refer you to point #1 above.)

3. **Have a written gameplan for each day or trade.** The trading plan in #2 is more of a business plan/control document, but I've also found it helpful to have notes for each trade I execute. If you're a swing trader, then you can write down your initial stop loss, target, and perhaps some trade management guidelines for each trade you enter. These don't have to be extensive or formal; maybe you even write them on scrap paper, but the act of writing them down gets the ideas out of your head and into the real world. If you're a daytrader, this is impractical, but you still need to have guidelines for each trading day. Where will you execute? What kinds of trades will you look for? Is this a day to be aggressive or lay back? If these questions aren't relevant to your style, find the questions that are.

4. **Keep a journal.** I've written about this before in great depth, so I won't beat that horse again. Keeping a journal, of some kind, is perhaps the single most important thing in your development as a trader. Everything, from execution issues, to developing methodology, to dealing with psychological issues, can be addressed, over time, through the journaling process. This is something you probably aren't doing, and, frankly, you probably aren't going to be successful unless you start doing it. Enough said?

5. **Know yourself.** Easier said than done, but it's worth spending time understanding who you are in relation

to risk, money, hard work, uncertainty, and a number of other things you will face as a trader. While you're at it, also consider what skills you need to develop: a better understanding of probability? Deeper knowledge of financial markets? Any specific analytical techniques?

There are many ways to work toward the goal of knowing yourself, and it's probably the process that matters more than anything. Some people will talk to a therapist, some will go on long walkabouts, some will journal and reflect, and some may work on the answers in the quiet moments each day. There's no wrong way to do this, but the market is going to make you face the best and worst in yourself, so you might want to get a jump on that.

6. **Work on pattern interrupts.** If you were looking for a simple, shortcut technique, this might be it. A pattern interrupt, to put it very simply, means you notice when you're about to do something dumb or make an emotional mistake, and you break that pattern. Again, there are many ways to do this: go for a walk, make a phone call, go to the gym, stop trading for a few days, snap a rubber band on your wrist—but the key is *awareness*. You have to build awareness of your own mental and emotional state, first, and then somehow disrupt the negative cycle.

For instance, assume you get angry after losses and make emotional trades to try to get even. These trades are impulsive and ill-considered and, over time, you lose more money on them, so you want to stop doing that. First, you must have a plan, and then maintain the awareness of your own mental state to be able to say "I'm emotional right now. I might make a revenge trade." Now, simply not making that revenge trade might be beyond your capability, but you can make yourself get up and go outside, can't you? The pattern interrupt is a way to get some leverage against your behavior, even when you might be very emotional.

Trading Edge vs. trading edge

I did an interview with Abraham Thomas, one of the co-founders of Quandl. I love doing interviews because a thoughtful interviewer makes me ask questions and think about things in a new way. Part of our discussion centered around the idea of having and maintaining a trading edge, and I realized that I may not have shared the full picture of a trading edge with my readers.

My work is heavily quantitative, possibly to a fault at times. If I cannot nail down an edge in a tool or a pattern, I will not use it in my trading. This is a conscious decision, because, if I have to choose an error (and, make no mistake, you *do* have to make this choice) I'd rather eliminate potentially useful tools rather than allowing useless junk to creep into my analytical process. When I've talked about trading edges before, I focused strongly on the mathematics: the easy way to explain this is that you, over a large set of trades, are going to have two piles of money—money you made and money you lost. At the end of that large set of trades, the pile of money you made should be larger than the pile of money you lost. In other words, you need to make more than you lose.

We can slice this many different ways, and dig into the tradeoff between win ratio and average win/loss size (the classic expectancy discussion), and we can expand it to be a benchmark for analyzing raw patterns, indicators, or setups. This is important work, and anyone trading should understand how to do it. But, it's not the full picture. There are other parts of your trading Edge that might transcend the mathematics.

Trading is a high-performance endeavor with parallels to professional athletics, chess, music, or any other pursuit where humans try to do something as well as possible. Many of these pursuits are competitive; to stand out from the crowd, we must be better than the crowd. (This is so obviously true in trading.) In any high-performance pursuit, the performer himself is critically important—*you* are perhaps the most important part of your edge.

What does this mean, practically? Well, here are a few thoughts that came up in the interview:

Do you take care of your working environment? Not that everything has to be perfectly ordered, but do you have a space and a time in which you feel comfortable and settled doing your work? At times, this might mean doing analysis in a noisy coffee shop. (I wrote a large part of my book in various Irish pubs, fueled by Guinness...) Understand how and where you work best, and make sure your environment reflects this.

Do you take care of your body? Do you walk regularly, or perhaps go to the gym? Move! Is your diet a reflection of who you are and who you want to be? All things in moderation, but it's hard to imagine performing at an elite level if all you are eating is junk food.

Do you have vibrant connections to friends, family, and professional colleagues? Are the relationships in your life additive and supportive? Are you finding a balance between solitude and social life? For different personalities, this balance will look very different, but both aspects are important.

Are you finding some time away from the markets? I'm very much in favor of obsession, and I think there's great value in single-minded focus, but, at some point, it becomes detrimental. You must have a reason for existing outside of the markets, and you need a reminder that there is so much else to existence. Hobbies are good!

So much of this is about balance, and it is a subtle call to think about your own mental health. At times, therapy can help a trader out of some rough spots or over some humps, but there is also therapeutic value in a sunset.

What is your purpose? You can define this however you wish—for some, it is intertwined with questions of religion and deeper meaning, but basically this, perhaps the most important question, asks us to think about who, what, and why we are. Throughout history, the people who have accomplished great things—even if those things appear somewhat unremarkable (like surviving a period of profound hardship)—most of those people had some guiding star, some bigger sense of purpose. I have come to believe that one of the keys to a happy life is having this sense of purpose. What is yours?

Yes, the math is important. Having a trading edge is essential, and if you don't have that then you can have everything else right, and you will still lose money. Maybe you will feel better about it, but you're going to lose without that mathematical edge. However, applying that edge requires that you have an Edge—a constructive framework to guide all of your activities. We touch on aspects of this when we look at trading and performance psychology, but, I found myself wondering in this interview, if I was missing and not communicating the big picture to you, my readers.

So, what's your Edge, and what are you doing to take care of yourself?

The Illusion of Control

I've written and said many times before that simplicity is a good thing—if you have a methodology that is overly complex, there's a pretty chance it won't work. However, so many traders feel drawn to complexity—it feels right and good. Why is that? Why would we not prefer the simpler path. One reason might be a psychological quirk called the "illusion of control".

There are a lot of ways to be successful in the markets—you can use a fundamental approach, you can allocate to a long-term portfolio, you can use a trend following system with the right asset classes, you can use a technical approach, you can combine all of these ideas... and the list goes on. But, however we find success, we have to acknowledge that the markets are a difficult and conflicted environment. It's hard to make money and it's hard to maintain the discipline required to do so. Markets are capable of an almost infinite range of events, though they spend a lot of their time doing almost nothing, which can lull us into a dangerous sense of complacency.

Because markets are so complex, it is tempting to meet them head on with a very complex approach. Many traders think the more indicators, tools, and things to tweak, the better—and then they tweak things differently for different stocks and different timeframes. I knew a trader who loved moving averages (though he had never made money trading) and had an approach that was based on using a different combination of moving averages for each stock he tried to trade!

The Illusion of Control

More moving parts often means more ways we can lie to ourselves. There is a well-known psychological effect called the "illusion of control" that works like this: imagine I put you in front of a computer screen, tell you it's going to flash random numbers, and then, after you watch it a while, I ask you how well you were able to affect the numbers higher or lower. You would probably look at me like I was a little crazy, and reply that of course you had no effect on the numbers.

But then I give you a button. I can even tell you the button does nothing, but you're allowed to push it while you watch the numbers (which will still be random.) After doing this for a while, I ask you how strongly you were able to affect the numbers, and you would almost certainly tell me that you had some success. Even though we know it's an illusion, having the ability to do *something* (change something, push something, move something) makes us feel that we have some control over a random situation. This effect has been replicated in psychological research time and time again.

Now, think about your trading platform and ask yourself if a similar thing could be happening. Could you tweak indicator settings and colors, or screen setup and feel that you are somehow doing something that must be effective? We, all humans, have such poor intuition about random events that it's difficult for us to trust our gut. (This is why statistics and performance evaluation are so important to traders.) Even if you were trading with no edge at all, could you legitimately feel that some tweak to an entry technique or a stop setting made a real difference? Remember that, if this illusion is in effect, you will be utterly convinced of your ability to control something that is completely random and beyond your control. That kind of determination can be fatal in the marketplace.

It might not be all bad, except in the markets...

Some of the researchers have suggested that there's a good reason we have this illusion of control. First of all, in most areas of human endeavor, it probably isn't all that harmful; if you're doing something pretty random then whether you keep doing it or stop probably makes little difference to your long-term survival. In fact, the illusion of control might help you to continue at tasks long enough to develop skill. Imagine the developing archer whose early results are random, but, if he's convinced he's developing skill, he might keep shooting just long enough that he actually develops real, solid skills.

In the market, and with trading, I think it's a little bit different and more dangerous. One of the things I have become convinced about over the course of my career is that many people are doing things that make no sense and have no edge. They often think they have an edge, but they don't. But why can that conviction—that they actually do have an edge and that success is just around the corner—be so very strong?

It's likely that many of these people have fallen prey to this illusion. Many traders bash their heads against screens and desks (sometimes, not so metaphorically) for years with no success because they are doing something that does not work. They feel, often very strongly, that they have an edge and that's it working, but the numbers don't add up at the end of the day. They change things, and each small tweak brings a new sense of hope and control, but, again, the bottom line doesn't improve. This happens because the trader does not have a solid understanding of what matters and what doesn't in trading.

What we can do about it

The answer is deceptively simple: we have to analyze our results with hard statistics and then understand what those numbers say. Proper performance metrics, either of live trading or of systems under development, are key, but the work has to be done correctly. Even system development offers many opportunities to tweak this and that and create the illusion of an edge—and that will likely fail the first time the system meets live markets. If we are working with proper methodology and statistics, it's harder to lie to ourselves, and much easier to combat this illusion. Statistics are only a tool, but they are a powerful tool.

This illusion of control is, on one hand, just another one of those cognitive quirks and biases, but it's an important one. If we overestimate our ability to control our results, we can become overly confident, make mistakes, and quickly fall to ruin. If we have proper respect for our ability within the bounds of probability, we will respect the market. We will avoid hubris and stay humble.

Understanding this illusion also points the way to psychological balance and control because we will know that we are not as good as we think we are in the good times, and we're also not as bad as we feel in the rough spots. It's all part of the normal flux of probabilities in trading, and we are all traders in the hands of an all-too-often angry market.

On Process

The Practice of Conscious Gratitude

I want to share a practice that has made a real difference for me—as a trader, and for me as a human being. It's a simple thing, but it matters—the practice of conscious gratitude.

Every word in that phrase is important: "practice of conscious gratitude." It is not enough to sometimes think of things that we're happy about, to think things could be a lot worse, or to say a little prayer of thanks when we have some narrow escape from a problem. No, I think this only works—only has the power to transform us—if we commit to doing this every day, as part of a conscious practice. It does not have to be an elaborate thing, and it doesn't have to take even five minutes, but it does need to become a part of your daily practice, as much as brushing your teeth or checking your email.

Here's how I do it: go buy a small notebook, and I'd spend some money to make it a nice one. I'm a big fan of the Moleskine notebooks, but what matters is that you take the time, effort, and make a small expense to say to yourself, "this is special. This is important." So, go get that notebook (and maybe get a nice pen while you're at it!)

Next, take a few minutes every day, and craft some small practice or ritual that is meaningful for you. For me, I sit at my desk, close the computer desktops, and take out the notebook. I take a few deep breaths and invite myself to be fully present in the moment. I make an effort to silence all distractions and thoughts of what I must do that day, and take a few minutes just to *be* and just to experience. To some of you, that sounds very esoteric and obtuse, but it doesn't have to be—there's value in just focusing your mind and being fully present, if even for a single instant each day.

After a few breaths, probably not a full minute's time, I then think of three things for which I am grateful. They can be mundane or profound, and can cover any aspect of life. Do not overthink this and do not become frustrated—three things should come easily. (I wrote once that I was thankful for warm socks. This morning I might have mentioned a particularly juicy orange. You get the idea.) You can repeat things from day to day, but try to think of new things each day. Just don't worry that you've already written something you will write today. Then, open the notebook to a blank page, write today's date, and write three sentences each beginning with "I am grateful for..." Take a few more breaths, and allow yourself, no matter what is going on in your world and in your life, to truly feel grateful for these three things, even if just for a moment.

Then, close your book and go about your day. Your mind might turn to the book and your ritual throughout the day, or you might forget it until the next day. That's fine—what matters is that you do this and you do it regularly. Limit yourself to three things each day. Of course, you may live your whole day in a state of conscious gratitude some days, and that would be great—but don't write 15 things in your notebook some day! Pick three, and then do three more tomorrow. The next day, do three more. Do the practice, and allow it to become part of what and who you are.

This is one of those simple practices that really does have the potential to make us better than we are—this simple little daily practice can change you. Perhaps it's simply seeing that you can take control and can create a good, constructive habit for yourself. Perhaps there is something more to it. So, I invite you to try this for one month and see what it does for you. Every day for a month, carve out a few minutes, focus your mind, and give conscious gratitude to the universe. The results might surprise you.

Five Steps to Being Fully Present

What you *think* you see is not what you see. What you *think* is happening is not what *is* happening. Everything we experience is filtered through our inner dialog and experience. We can think of simple examples: three people watching a person on a subway train with a dog will likely have three very different experiences—maybe one thinks fondly of an old pet, another has a phobia, and another remembers a movie she saw last night. What is clear is that pretty much no one is "just seeing a dog"—the dog brings up memories, associations, and past experiences.

Too many writers treat the "normal" human experience as something that is bad or something we need to change, but we've survived long enough as a species that it can't really be all that bad! In many ways, it is actually very good because it increases the connections we have between datapoints in our brain. This way of experiencing the world makes us smart, but it also keeps us closed off from another level of experience. There's a way to achieve a radically different perspective, and to bring different strengths of your analytical tools to every situation.

This different way of being and experiencing might be called "being in the moment." (Be careful with the word "mindfulness"—it's often applied to this type of work, but it really means something else. It's a specific set of meditation techniques, not a way to sit at your desk and answer emails.) For traders in financial markets, being in the moment can be a powerful perspective: you can see with clarity. You are free from emotional baggage and past mistakes. You are free to be your most powerful and successful self.

Achieving this state takes two things: first, you have to want to do it. You must have a clear intent to be more in the moment. Second, it requires attention and a gentle patience to bring your attention back to the work when it wanders. In some ways, this is a framework for extending meditation to your everyday life, and here are some ways to do it.

- **Work with intent.** Too often, we are robots. I find that I focus much better if I declare an intent—for the day, for a specific task, or for an entire venture. Simply working with intent will focus the power of your will, and you'll get things done that might seem impossible.
- **Use a list.** Use two lists! One of the best pieces of time management advice is to start each day by writing a list of the three to five things you must do that day. When something goes on that list, you get it done, no matter what. Putting something on the list declares a clear intent for the day. (Nice when things are coherent, isn't it?) You also might have a longer-term list of projects and things you are working on that will require days, weeks, or months to accomplish, but start with the daily list. If you do nothing else, do this.
- **Create ritual and structure.** There is great power in the little rituals of everyday life. Do it when you sit at your desk. Do it when you leave the house and when you return. Do it when you eat—there's power in conscious eating—take a few moments to extend gratitude for the fish, animal, or plant that is no longer what it was so that you can eat. This might sound touchy-feely, but it's also an invitation to really understand where we fall in the dance that is life.
- **Be careful of "I am ____" language.** I am afraid. I am nervous. I am angry. No... you are *not*. You are *feeling* afraid, nervous, or angry, but *you are not these emotions*. Particularly for traders, the flood of emotions can be overwhelming. Simply being aware of the self-talk and natural tendency to think "I am ____", and then to gently contradict that—this is one way to achieve powerful clarity and perspective.

- Spend a few moments **paying attention to your breathing.** Do this right now. Read this paragraph, then close your eyes and bring all of your attention to your breathing… in… and out… for the next three breaths you take. That's it—very simple and it will only take maybe half a minute to do that. Don't alter your breathing pattern and don't try to think anything; just focus on your breathing. Do this a few times a day, and you'll begin to interrupt the "normality" of our everyday experience.

We could go on and on with these ideas, but these will get you started. The key concept is that we want to shake things up just enough that we can achieve a new perspective. Simple things work. Simple things are powerful.

You Are What You Read: Try an Information Diet

A developing trader said something to me a few years ago that has stuck in my mind: he said that he has to be careful what websites he reads because negativity can be dangerous; when you live in a constant state of fear, it colors everything you see. Be careful: you are what you eat (and read and think about!)

I think it goes even deeper. Negativity and fear change our perception deeply. When we absorb certain kinds of information, or information placed in emotional contexts, we create blind spots for ourselves. We are not *able* to see and think rationally if we allow too much emotion, and too much emotional contamination from others, into our thought process. Emotional context changes how we think and how we can think.

I'd challenge you to take a moment and think about the information you consume on a daily basis. First, major media is not perfectly unbiased. Anyone who works in media wants to engage an audience. We (I'm including myself here because, among other things, I'm a blogger) all know that emotion generates clicks, shares, and reads and negative emotion resonates much more strongly than positive. So, news stories naturally come wrapped in an emotional wrapper with a provocative and emotional headline, and our brains naturally accept the emotion with the facts. And what about blogs and newsletters and sources that are intended to be biased? Some of the most popular sites on the internet feature an incredible dose of emotion—fear and hate will provoke and engage an audience and build a core audience very well.

So, take a few moments today and do an information inventory. Ask yourself what sites and sources you regularly read and how much emotion is baked into them. (I'm not going to call out any specific sites or authors, but I think you will be able to read between the lines.) For traders, there are a few specific things to watch for:

- Do you frequent discussion forums that are filled with frustrated, failed traders and investors? Some of these forums also include a healthy dose of constructive work by traders who are either committed to figuring out the game or helping others, but be sure you can separate out the wheat from the chaff. I've been involved in these forums since they were mailing lists, and I can say the degree of anger that comes from failed traders is astounding. They are certain the system is rigged, and just throw abuse at anyone and everyone in the forum like a monkey throwing poop at the zoo. You can hang out in these forums, but watch out for the flying poop.
- Speaking of flying poop, there's been a lot of focus lately on fake news, especially politically-driven news on Facebook and other social media feeds. It takes less than a minute to do some basic fact checking, so please do this before you share and get upset about something you read.
- Do you read newsletter writers who constantly predict the end of the financial world, World War 3, or who focus on conspiracy theories? If so, you're probably hurting yourself. There are writers who have built multi-million-dollar industries playing on the emotions of the public. These newsletter writers have been constantly predicting THE END for decades, and they've been wrong. They will continue to be wrong, but the harm they have done to their readers is almost beyond measure. If you read anyone like this, consider carefully what your world would be like without this influence.
- Do you frequent blogs that repost or aggregate content like this? Is there a constant flood of posts predicting crashes, talking about why the system is rigged, or drawing great significance from hidden datapoints? Is everything blamed on HFTs? Again, this stuff generates clicks and shares, but it does not help you as a trader and investor.

Once you've taken a serious look at the information you consume, then you're in a position to figure out what do to about it. I suggest trying an information diet: First, cut out virtually everything you read. If you are a news junkie, this may feel uncomfortable. You may feel blind or cut off, but give it a chance. Avoid clicking or reading for a week, and see how your emotional state changes.

Then you can start adding things back, a little at a time, and monitoring your emotional state while you do so. If you find yourself sucked into hours of clicking and sharing emotional and negative articles, first of all congratulate the blog owner on building an engaging blog, but then step away and rethink. You can absorb information, but you need to be careful about the emotion that goes with it.

On Dealing with Loss

Managing your Fear of Loss

People talk about "learning how to lose" and "losing gracefully". Truth be told, that's a concept I've always had trouble understanding. Though I know there is some wisdom in the idea of losing gracefully, I am very competitive in most things and a terrible loser. I hate to lose.

But trading is different. In trading, I am a great loser, and, in fact, I have actively cultivated the skill of learning to lose. Early on, I struggled with the same emotions any new trader faces; when I put on a trade my palms would sweat, my heart would race, and I would find myself taking a bathroom break every five minutes. It soon became obvious that being emotional to that degree was overwhelming whatever rational analysis I was capable of making, and that I simply was not going to be successful until I learned to manage those emotions to some degree.

The breakthrough, for me, came when I understood something very important about risk and loss. (And this is important. It might even be the single most important thing I know about trading psychology.) There *are* risks in trading you should be concerned about. Yes, but the risk of losing on your next trade is not one of them. In fact, that risk, of any one trade being a loss, is not actually a risk at all!

Think about the things that probably should concern you as a trader: if you are trading too large (overleveraged), then you should be terrified. In fact, you should be so scared you can't do anything else until you reduce your position size and are trading with an appropriate degree of risk. (Fear can be good.) Maybe you should be afraid about tail risk, or about the impact of some unforeseeable geopolitical risk. Perhaps you should be concerned about breaking discipline and doing something dumb. You should definitely be concerned that maybe you're trading without an edge and your approach doesn't actually have the potential to pull profits out of the market, and a lot of your work should be aimed at proving this fear unfounded.

In all of this, I'd argue that that last trade you just put on, whether it is in Apple, Facebook, the euro, gold, or the crush spread—whether that trade wins, loses, or breaks even is not something you should even be thinking about. In fact, the best mental state is simply to not care about the outcome of any one trade.

Why is this? Well, your trading results are the sum of your wins and losses, and you absolutely *are* going to have losses. Trying to avoid those losses is very dangerous; you must accept them and welcome them. The grocery store owner with a thriving business (i.e., his business is working—just like a trader with an edge) does not agonize over buying inventory, or that some percentage of his lettuce will spoil before it can be sold. This is simply a cost of doing business, and he could have no profits without lettuce—some of the lettuce he sells, and some of it spoils. As a trader, *your losses are your cost of doing business and you cannot have profits without those losses*. You must learn to think over the next 20 trades, not the next single trade. You must avoid attaching too much importance to any outcome.

When I realized this, trading changed for me. I knew it was different the day I put on a position, asked myself what I thought would happen, and found the answer "I really don't care." That's the key: you have to be able to not care. (This does not mean you are irresponsible. You still must do the hard work of trading, be perfectly disciplined, and manage all of the other risks of trading. About those things, you must care deeply.) I think this is also something that goes beyond intellectual understanding. I can point you toward the realization. You can read the words I write here and understand them, but you have to accept the lesson into a deeper part of your self, and that takes some time. If you truly understand loss, you can accept that loss, make it a part of who you are, and use it for your success.

A Little Mental Trick...

I want to share a quick thought with you—a little trick in thinking that made a big difference in my trading a few years ago. One of the problems with traders is that we can be stubborn. This happens to everyone, and no one is ever immune to it. It takes a lot of confidence to pull the trigger, and sometimes much analysis and hard work has gone into justifying the trade. What do we do when contradictory information emerges? Well, sometimes the shock of seeing that the trade is wrong can cause traders to freeze, with disastrous consequences, or sometimes a trader is just unable to process the conflicting information.

I developed a little trick that might seem trivial, but it is very important. Simply put, *anytime to you put a trade on, assume that the trade is going to be a loser*. No matter how much analysis, how many supporting factors, or how perfect the pattern is, assume that the trade will lose money. This creates a profound shift in your focus because, rather possibly discounting contradictory evidence (which can sometimes be as simple as "I just bought and now it's going down..."), you will be open to and will readily accept that contradicting information.

Of course you will, because you *assumed* the trade was wrong to begin with. When you find confirmation that the trade is right, it is almost a pleasant surprise. Shift your thinking into this mode, and you will be much less likely to overstay your welcome in suboptimal setups that are not working out—you'll be far more likely to do the right thing, which is usually to pull the plug on the trade and look for a better opportunity.

Wins Live in the Land of Loss

I'm sitting here at my desk looking out the window. On my desk is a (perfectly normal and fair) coin that I had been flipping a while. Question: can you tell me how many heads I flipped?

Now, think about that question a few moments. If you had to guess, what would you guess? Maybe I've been sitting here watching Netflix for a couple of hours flipping a coin. Maybe I flipped it while I was on the phone for just a few minutes. Maybe I just flipped it once or twice. You probably could figure out some reasonable estimate of how long a (mostly sane) person would sit flipping a coin, add into it an estimate of how many times you could flip each minute, and come up with some kind of answer. You can probably guess that there's some practical upper limit to how many times I flipped it, and the probability distribution of how long I've been flipping probably has a lot of weight near the origin and not much out in the tail. If this was an interview question for a consulting firm, you could come up with an answer!

Now, here's another question: how sure are you of that answer? How confident can you be that you're within 10% of the right number of coin flips? This is the question that really matters. Ok... hold on to that thought.

Let me give you one more piece of information. If I tell you I flipped 67 tails, does that change your answer to how many heads I flipped? It should—now you know if 5, or 65, or 65,000 is a better guess. How confident are you about your guess now? Much more confident, yes?

Here's the point of this post, and it's not a math lesson: heads and tails go together. You can't have one without the other. The same process that generates the tails generates the heads. You might even say that heads and tails "live together" or that "tails live in the land of heads".

This is such a simple observation that it's easy to miss, but I want you to think of this in two ways. First, this lesson generalizes to life. I think you can often tell how successful someone is by asking how many times they have failed. Most big, successful businesses (and individuals) have a string of dramatic failures behind them. In some sense, we learn from those failures, move forward, and eventually get "lucky".

But there's another way to think about this—life and business are really about the odds. Chance and luck do play a part, but you must put yourself in those situations where chance and luck can work in your favor. The more times you're at bat, the better the chance you're going to hear that crack and everyone can just stand and watch the ball sail over the fence. One of the most inspiring quotes I've ever heard—and maybe it's as much for its gritty realism as anything else, comes from Mark Cuban:

> *It doesn't matter how many times you fail. It doesn't matter how many times you almost get it right. No one is going to know or care about your failures, and neither should you... All that matters in business is that you get it right once. Then everyone can tell you how lucky you are.*

If you're a trader, think about your losses in this context. How do you feel about those losses? Do you feel shame? Fear that your next trade might be a loser? Do you do things designed to minimize the size and chance of your losses? (Be aware that those two things work against each other—fearful traders often generate very small, but very certain losses. This is one way to die as a trader.)

Or do you *welcome* your losing trades?

Do you know that all of your winning trades live in the land of loss? Do you realize, wholeheartedly, that your losses and wins are two sides of that same coin? Do you know your losses are essential to your success? The more winning traders you have in the course of your career, the more losing trades you will have—winning lives in the land of losing, just like the heads and tails on that coin I flipped.

When we understand this—and if we are sure that we are trading with an edge—then trading becomes easy. Fear of loss simply melts away. To me, this is a simple, but profound truth. It also just happens that this simple thing is one of the keys of approaching trading with a professional mindset, and becoming fully comfortable with probability, risk, and the nature of a trading edge—all essential to your eventual success as a trader or investor.

Four Steps to Mastering Your Fear of Trading

Every trader faces fear, sooner or later. In a perfect world, we'd be fearful at exactly the right times and use that fear to manage our risk, but we all know it doesn't work like this—markets naturally seem to provoke the "wrong" emotions at the wrong turns, and following those emotions blindly can get us in a lot of trouble. For some traders, fear can be nearly debilitating, and this is as true for purely systematic/quantitative traders as it is for discretionary daytraders. Here, I'll share a few ideas that have helped me, and many traders I know and have worked with, to manage the emotions of trading.

Acknowledge the fear and allow yourself to experience it. There's a natural tendency to avoid our fear; we aren't that much different from the child who knows monsters lurk in the darkness under the bed, but pulls the covers over his head to avoid looking. While this is a very effective strategy for children dealing with monsters at bedtime, it is not so effective in most other walks of life. The first step is to allow yourself to experience your fear, and one of the ways to do that is simply to say, "I am feeling fear right now." Whatever works for you, just invite that emotion of fear to be fully present in your experience—this also has the effect of grounding you in the "now" and bringing you into a mindful awareness of the present moment. It just so happens that this present moment is tinged with fear, but that is perfectly fine. However you do it, first, allow yourself to fully experience the fear.

Ask if the fear is there for a reason. Fear often serves a good purpose. The Darwin Awards (would I date myself too much if I said I remembered the early days of this Usenet phenomenon, when the cost of connecting was a long-distance phone call for my Apple II modem?) are full of humans who probably should have had more fear at critical points in their existence. Though we usually are not going to *reason* fear away—it is counterproductive to try to rationalize most emotions away—there's a good chance that your fear is telling you something. Are you afraid to put on 25 long positions and no shorts in stocks, risking 2% on each trade? Are you afraid to put on 5 large currency pairs in the same direction against the USD? Do you have some issues with all that naked short option premium you just sold? Good. Listen to your fear; it's telling you not to be stupid. On a deeper level, do you have a nagging fear because you might be trading without an edge, are undercapitalized, or are simply doing something that doesn't work? Your fear might be doing something useful, and it's worth thinking about that before we try to casually dismiss that fear.

Inflate the fear to ridiculous extremes. This might seem counterproductive, but asking "what's the worst that can happen?" can be a useful step. In some cases the worst that can happen is unacceptable, and you might need to take some steps to manage that scenario. In many more cases, we see that the fear is unjustified, and that the possible consequences are much smaller than the fear we are feeling. Allowing your fear to expand to extremes, without being afraid of experiencing it, can often make a cartoon mockery of that fear, and it will naturally release. You might even find yourself laughing at the fearful state you were in just a few moments before; fear has a very difficult time surviving where there's laughter. If nothing else, this step will help you to understand your fear on a deeper level.

Work on releasing the fear. There are many ways to do this. In several podcasts I talked about the Sedona Method, which is a simple, targeted method to release unhealthy emotions. It's so simple that you might overlook it, but it can be powerfully effective. Give it a chance, or maybe simply take a few deep breaths and allow the fear to dissipate. There's no right or wrong here—managing emotions is a personal journey and we all find what works well for each of us.

Those few, simple points can reshape your experience of fear in trading. Let me remind you that we are not going to eliminate emotions in trading, nor would that be a productive outcome. As humans, every decision we make includes some mix of rational analysis and emotion. Many traders find fear is an essential emotion in trading, but there are different kinds of fear: if you are "white knuckling it" through trades, or experiencing a high "pucker factor" every time you look at a chart, then you won't be able to trade effectively—the emotions of trading will drown everything else out. Everything in its place, in its time, and in the correct proportion. These simple ideas will help you get there.

The Power of Vulnerability

> *"I'm looking for a portfolio that will make about 20% a year but I don't want any down years."*

> *"Can you give me a hedging strategy with options that will protect me from all downside without limiting my upside and at zero cost?"*

> *"I'm working on my trading plan and I plan to just eliminate my losing trades."*

Believe it or not, I didn't make those quotes up—they are exact quotes from questions or conversations I've had with either professional managers or developing traders. They are all tied together by one thing: fear of loss.

We spend much of our lives taking reasonable precautions. We look both ways before crossing the street. We smell fish before we cook it. We buy insurance, hopefully after carefully considering the cost and risks. In trading, we find ways to limit or to define our loss and we avoid taking stupid risks. It is good that we do these things, and good that we are aware of the risks.

Healthy respect for risk is one thing, but when it becomes fear, problems arise. Fear leads to tension and conflict; we don't see information correctly and clearly, and we will make mistakes. Cognitive biases and emotional reactions seize control of our behavior, and, in the worst cases, traders are completely unable to act and end up quitting in desperation. Attempts to counteract this, by focusing on risk control and aspects of the trading plan, can often work against us as they simply highlight the probability of losses. Too many traders get stuck in this spiral.

What's the solution? One powerful solution is to accept vulnerability. If we know, with certainty, that losses will happen—and they will; losses are a part of every trading methodology—then we are not afraid of those losses and certainly are not surprised when they happen. For "scarier" things, like tail risk, we must first accept and emotionally open ourselves to the reality of those risks before we can turn rational analysis to understanding the tradeoffs between magnitude and probability of these risks.

Life, existence itself, is fragile. There are no guarantees in anything—by opening ourselves to this reality, we can understand our trading and interaction with financial markets as part of that web, and can better understand our place in the universe.

Something else happens here too: risk and opportunity truly do go together. To answer all of those questions at the top of this post, we could eliminate the risk or cost. Just get out of the market completely! But we cannot have any upside if we eliminate all the risk. There's always going to be a cost or a chance of a cost or the chance of a loss with any valid approach. If we fully accept this, it will shape our understanding of markets and may even point out some hidden opportunities we might've missed if we were only focused on the possible loss.

On Discipline

A Letter to Myself: Pattern Interrupts

A reader's question:

> *Hi. I know that most of what you talk about isn't really about daytrading, but I am a daytrader and I have a question. Overall, I'm not making money. I've found that my problem is that I have a few big losing days each month. I set a daily loss limit and am supposed to stop when I reach the limit but I find myself getting angry and trading bigger the closer I get to it. Yesterday I lost almost three times my limit. How do I stop myself from hurting my trading account? Thank you, I know I'm not the only person who does this to myself.*

Well, no—you are not the only person who does this. In fact, it's very common for traders on all timeframes to do some kind of "revenge trading". Getting this aspect of trading under control is crucial; if you don't do it, you aren't going to succeed in this business. Whatever profits you make will leave faster than you make them. Sadly, it's not so easy as just saying "follow your rules" and leaving it at that. It's vitally important to avoid emotional, revenge trading, and to avoid "going on tilt".

People have different psychological makeups and respond to this kind of stress differently. Some people do well being down and behind and fighting to get back—there are even successful traders who do their best work like this, and some of them do manage to constructively harness an impressive degree of emotion. For others, cultivating a detached perspective is important because any strong emotional content sends them over the edge. You must work hard to understand yourself, your triggers, and how to deal with them. This is a critical part of the "know yourself" aspect of trading.

For me, there were two parts to the solution: 1) realizing how stupid this is and 2) creating pattern interrupts. Both of those were important; the first is intellectual, but that cannot adequately and fully address the problem. Understanding, reason, analysis—these are all great, but we are dealing with an emotional and behavioral problem and reason has limited power. I spent a lot of time in reflection after some of the times I went on tilt and became an irrational trader. I finally realized that this was not how I wanted to live my life and I couldn't trade well if I continued to be stupid. (The image of a video game character getting stuck in a loop and running into a brick wall was powerful imagery for me—seeing him keep hitting it, then getting bloody, then making a bloody splat on the wall, but his legs won't stop—they are out of his control and keep picking him up and running him into the wall again and again and again, even after he starts bleeding, even after his head falls off, even after he turns into a big, gross, bloody pulp... you get the idea. This was the equivalent of what I was doing to myself as a trader about once a month... and it didn't feel good!)

Bad things happen to us often because we make them or let them happen; we go through chains of behavior that lead to predictably bad results. After the fact, we are driven to ask, "why would you do that to yourself? Wasn't it obvious?" Well, it is obvious when we look at it rationally, but in the heat of the battle we are not rational. Our brains are flooded with flight or fight chemicals, and we are not able to make good decisions. What you need is some really simple tool to break that usual pattern of behavior and change it. This is where pattern interrupts come in.

I had a friend who stopped a serious smoking habit with the classic "snap the rubber band on the wrist" method—cliché, but it is a pattern interrupt and it works. Consider situations outside of trading: Do you typically have a fight with your spouse? Can you identify what leads up to it? Then do something different: when ____ happens, go for a walk, get a glass of water, randomly say "I love you"... do something different. How about minor road rage? Instead of getting angry at the "idiot" who someone got in front of you, what would happen if you made yourself take a deep breath and smile? Do you think you might forget to get angry?

As a daytrader, my answer was to write myself a letter. The letter was to be read when I had reached a specific loss limit, either in numbers of consecutive losses or in actual dollars lost. Today, I realize that some small fraction of those days I might have been down just due to bad luck (anyone can have 4 losing traders in a row), but I also know that, far more often, I was in that spot because I was doing something stupid. I attach the letter below so you can adapt it to your own situation. Here are the points I found useful:

Write simply. Write to yourself as if you were a small child. Use simple sentences and words. Be tough on yourself. Maybe not Gunny Sgt. Hartman Full Metal Jacket tough, but be tough. You're reading this to yourself because you are doing something pretty dumb and destructive and let's just say things as they are. Don't sugar coat it. Include specific behavioral alternatives. Tell yourself what to do. In my case, it was get up and go for a walk. Above all, stop trading. Include some positive reinforcement. Remind yourself that you don't actually suck at trading, even though you might suck today.

So, here is my "open letter to myself: today, a loser, but tomorrow, probably not:"

> *If you are reading this, it is because you are within ______ of your loss limit today. Let's slow down and consider how we got here.*
>
> *There are three ways this usually happens. If you got here because you lost track of your risk on a trade or a number of trades, you are just an idiot and I can't help you. It is also possible that you just aren't seeing the market clearly today, for whatever reason. Think hard about that. If either of those things are true, maybe you should pack it in and just go home. Tomorrow is a new day.*
>
> *However, it is more likely that today's market is not the kind of market that plays to your strengths. You have a specific skill set, and within this realm you are probably as good as anyone out there. You understand the ebb and flow of a trending market, and how to press trades in those markets to maximum advantage. You usually don't get shaken out by noise—you can hold trades in this kind of market better than almost anyone else... and, more often than not, you catch the turn at the end so you know when to get out. You do need to remember that maybe 1 in 5 trading days really rewards this style of trading. Chances are, today is not one of those days or you wouldn't be reading this right now.*
>
> *What do you do now? Well, first of all take a deep breath and go for a short walk. Now. You are not going to make a brilliant trade in the next 15 seconds. You do not have to be here. In fact, your brain chemistry is compromised so you aren't quite in your right mind—you cannot make good decisions right now. There is a really good chance the next trade you make will be your last one for the day, and then you can sit there and think about what an idiot you are for the rest of the day. Not pleasant or productive, so go for that walk right now.*
>
> *When you come back to the screen, the right course of action is to chip away at this loss. Think carefully about your next trading decision. You are going to be tempted to put on a lot of risk to try to make a big dent in your loss, but you know that almost never works. On a day you're really in sync with the market, you can recover this loss in a single trade in a few minutes, but this clearly is not that day or you wouldn't be reading this right now. Make a few ticks on small size and then use that cushion to take larger risk. Make $10 at first... $5 is even ok. Green is good. Hit singles, not home runs.*

The Discipline Rule

You have to be disciplined to trade successfully; we all know that, and it's one of the few pieces of trading advice that might apply universally. No matter what your trading style, market, timeframe, risk profile—whatever you do, you have to do it consistently and with discipline. It's easy to overlook something we hear this often, but the reason this advice is so often repeated is that it really is that important. However, there is one little detail that makes all the difference—if you are going to be disciplined, you must be disciplined all the time.

So, you make your trading rules, and you refine those rules. You monitor how they work in real time, and you make adjustments as necessary. Your job is now "simply" to follow those trading rules—do what the rules say always. Again, I'd be willing to bet that every one of you reading this knows what I just said is important, but can you truly say that you are disciplined every moment, in every interaction with the market?

Sometimes you will hear traders say they are "usually disciplined" or they "almost always" follow their trading rules. Wrong. You are either disciplined or you are not—it's a yes or no thing. If you are disciplined 999 times out of 1,000, but you break discipline that one time, you are not a disciplined trader. There is no halfway, usually, mostly, or almost always—either you are or you aren't.

This way of thinking is a good reminder because it forces us to be mindful of the damage we can so easily do to ourselves. All it takes is one slip—one trade held too far past the stop, one crazy addition to a losing trade, or one impulsive entry—to undo weeks of disciplined work. Not only can the financial impact be extreme (it's not that hard to lose a month's profits in five minutes), but the emotional and behavioral impact can be devastating. Once you've opened the door and done something silly, you are much more vulnerable to future mistakes. And, if you make money doing something stupid... well... that's almost the worst possible thing that can happen to any trader because you will do it again, and eventually the bill will come due.

You must be disciplined, and you must be disciplined every day, every minute, every moment, and every interaction with the market. If you are not always disciplined, you do not have the right to call yourself a disciplined trader. Another simple rule, but one that can make all the difference in the world.

Five Steps to Trading Discipline (And Why You Should Care)

You have to be a disciplined trader. This is one of the nuggets of trading wisdom we hear constantly, and for good reason—it's true. Without discipline, we will make many mistakes in the highly competitive market environment. But it's not as simple as saying to yourself "be disciplined" and watching all your trading problems melt away. Discipline, for many traders, is a battle to be fought over many years and a goal that is only achieved with some maturity as a trader. Here are five things you can start doing, today and right now, that will move you a little further along the path to being a disciplined market participant.

1. **Understand, intellectually, the reasons why discipline is important.** Many of the battles you will fight with discipline are emotional and behavioral, so you cannot simply reason them away, but you are unlikely to be successful unless you understand why it matters so much.

2. **Have a plan.** This is another perennial nugget of trading wisdom that holds great truth. By this point in the course, you should have spent a lot of time constructing a full and detailed trading plan. Discipline, then, is "simply" following that plan. Without the plan, it's pretty hard to evaluate discipline.

3. **Evaluate your performance regularly.** In this context, I don't mean whether you made money or not; I mean one simple thing: did you follow your plan? That's the only question that matters. If you aren't disciplined every moment in the market, you aren't disciplined. Every second, every day, every tick, every trade, every exit, every interaction with the market—you must be disciplined. If you aren't a disciplined trader all the time, then don't say you are a disciplined trader. Evaluate your ability to stick the plan regularly, and be aware of the times you've fallen short. (Hint: keep a journal. Write this stuff down!)

4. **Become aware of your "tells" and behavioral triggers**. We all have things that set us off. Maybe it happens when someone cuts us off at an exit driving. Maybe it's the way someone looks at us or uses a certain tone of voice, or a passive aggressive tone in email—for traders, there are certain things in the market that can cause our discipline to waver. What are those things, for you? It's different for everyone, so you must understand yourself and what makes you tick. Are there things outside of the market that are likely to make you more vulnerable to having a break of discipline? Even more important, how can you tell when you're about to have a lapse? Learn to see yourself as an outsider, perhaps to take the role of a manager, therapist, doctor, or friend to the "you" that is the trader, and learn to tell that person when he is in danger.

5. **Learn to break the cycle**. We often do the same stupid things in response to the same behavioral cues—this is, in some ways, the very definition of self-destructive behavior. You don't have to be at the mercy of your emotions and reactions; you can take control. There are many tools and techniques you can use to protect yourself. (And they aren't complicated; they can be as simple as: go for a walk. Get away from the market, etc.) You can't, however, use them if you don't know you need to, which is why step #4 is so important. If you don't know yourself, it's very hard to manage yourself.

Nothing here is a quick fix, but these are ideas and tools that have served me well in the market. Look at your own trading and investing; work through these steps and think about what you could do better and how you can work toward the goal of being a perfectly disciplined trader.

Steps to Mental Strength

Mental strength or toughness basically means that you are able to do what you need to do, no matter how hard it is. The emotional stresses of trading, and particularly of learning to trade, are extreme. Mental strength doesn't mean that we are immune to those emotions; it means that we are able to do the right thing no matter how uncomfortable we are.

One of the answers to developing mental strength you are not going to like: **part of the answer is time**. The more time you spend trading, the more times you have the experience of putting on risk in the markets—most people experience the emotional charge getting weaker over time, so that's often part of the answer. But how can we make sure that process happens in the best way, and how can we keep it from going wrong? Here are some ideas for developing mental strength and toughness in trading:

Refine your expectations. This is a theme I've beaten to death, but one of the biggest reasons traders struggle is that they have unrealistic expectations. You are learning to do something difficult, and it will likely take you several years to learn to do it. Once you've learned to do it, it will probably take you a decade to reach true expertise. Past that, we're always learning. Also, results have a wide range of outcomes because of how probability works. Having realistic expectations can help you weather the emotional stresses of the learning curve.

Embrace uncertainty. You don't have a choice on this one. Your P&L will go through good times and bad times. Some of that will be due to performance issues, but some of it is just going to be random fluctuation. Work to understand the practical implications of probability and statistics. That's not as easy as understanding some equations or knowing what a probability distribution looks like. Get comfortable, deep down in your bones, with uncertainty and the range of possible outcomes. You might argue that if we truly understand these topics we will never be comfortable, and I suppose there's some truth in that. In that case, get comfortable being uncomfortable.

Understand your emotional makeup. There's not a whole lot I can do about this one in a paragraph, but the process of learning about you and your relationship to risk is a big part of the learning curve. What sets you off? What are your emotional triggers? What can cause your attention to flag? You've heard the injunction "know thyself"; if you don't know yourself, the market is a very expensive teacher.

Make sure you have an edge. Again, you'd think this one is obvious, but it's not. Too many traders struggle for too long simply doing something that does not work. There is maybe not enough emphasis on finding a true edge in much of the traditional literature. Too many traders thank that "basically, anything works", but I'd suggest to you maybe the opposite is true. Maybe it's very, very hard to find an edge. Maybe it's even harder to apply that edge, and maybe it's even more difficult to maintain it over a long period of time. If you don't have an edge (or get one), none of this other stuff is going to work.

Love the markets, the process, and yourself. Yes, I realize this one is a little softer than the others, but I think it's critical. If you don't love this, you won't be very good at it. If markets are not your passion, go find your passion wherever it is. But you also have to be able to detach your sense of self-worth from your results (because those results will be highly variable), and you must have motivation that goes beyond the markets.

The One Thing—The Only Thing—That Matters

One of the problems with successful trading is that everything matters. In the scope of: when to get in, when to get out, how much to buy or sell, how often to adjust your position, etc., every decision matters. There's no one thing that is most important. You can't become a successful trader by focusing on entries or on position sizing—you have to have it all. (What's the most important part of a submarine? You can have a power plant, a screw, a pressure hall, or a hatch. Pick one. Obviously, this is not going to end well.) However, there really is only one thing that matters in the market, and it's what you do: your actions are all that matters.

Orthopraxy is a term you may not have encountered before, but it's easy to take apart: "ortho" meaning "correct", and "praxy" meaning "practice"—doing the right thing. Though it's a mouthful, the market rewards us for being orthopractical traders—for *doing the right thing at the right time.*

You can have all the belief, confidence, knowledge (all of this might be orthodoxy: "right belief") in the world, but if you don't do the right thing, none of it matters. If you're paralyzed by fear, you lose. If you are excited and take positions too large when it feels right, you lose. If you ignore your exits and hold on, hoping for the best, you lose. If you are lazy and aren't at the table when it matters, you lose. On the other hand, if you're fearful, excited, bored, tired or whatever and you still do the right thing, then you have a chance.

This is why so many of the good and correct "trading sayings" focus on discipline and why so many successful traders say, over and over, with almost boring regularity, that you must have discipline to succeed in the markets. I invite you to take a few moments and review your trading history—both short term (recent weeks) and longer-term (maybe the whole span of your career) perspective. Realize that the market does not care about your system or analysis. The market does not care how hard you work. The market does not care how passionately you believe in your own success. All that matters is you do the right thing at the right time.

This is very basic, but it's also a profound truth. If you're falling short on your executions, think about why, and think about what you're going to do about it.

Doing the Right Thing: Bias, Opinion, and Action Points

One of the great things about writing a daily research piece is that it serves as a good record of my thought process and perspective on markets on each and every trading day. (Hint: developing traders might try the same thing. When I was figuring all this out, I wrote a daily "newsletter" years ago even though I had no clients. The discipline of doing the work every day, staying in the workflow, and expressing my ideas in a concrete format were an important part of my development process.) In the piece I write for my firm, Waverly Advisors, we publish a broad perspective on a wide range of markets, but also "actualize" those perspectives into executable "trade ideas." Today, I want to spend a few moments thinking about the difference between bias, opinion, and executing concrete trade ideas.

Three layers deep and more ways to lose

To put this into context, I tend to think of each market activity as having at least three components:

- my opinion about what might happen in the market
- my longer-term perspective
- shorter-term "action points."

Let's start with the first one of those: having an opinion can be hazardous to your financial health. Right away, here's where I think a professional, technically-driven approach separates itself from the pack; so much of what is written or said about financial markets is opinion and speculation. Even experienced, wise people will talk a lot about what might or might not happen, and possible fallout, and then make emotional decisions. Many smart people get into markets thinking they are going to "figure it out." If you have an engineering background, then you think you're going to apply one set of tools. If you have an MBA, then you think another set of tools will work. The problem is that none of this really works very well.

Markets are beautifully, wonderfully, and maddeningly counter-intuitive. If you think you're going to figure out the news and be positioned correctly, good luck. In actuality, it just becomes more ways to lose. For instance, let's say you have a thesis that you want to buy oil stocks because you think the US Dollar is going to be weak and so crude oil prices will rise. How could this go wrong? Well, perhaps you're wrong on your USD forecast so you do not pass go. However, you could be right on the USD, but then oil doesn't move how you think it will. Or maybe the USD forecast is right, crude oil moves as anticipated, but the stocks don't move in response to oil because something is holding down the stock market.

This is an admittedly simple example, but a lot of "macro thesis" ideas fall into the "more ways to lose" camp. In this example, the actionable part is that you think the USD will be weak. Trade that. Get short the Dollar instead of making all these connections to other markets. Trading is not an intellectual exercise and it's not a chance to show how smart you are by creating business school case studies.

In my experience, you can't help but have some opinion and bias on what you think might happen. You'll have to find the right answer for yourself, but, in my experience, the right thing to do is to ignore that opinion. It's often emotional, perhaps driven by political considerations, and swayed by the zeitgeist, social and mainstream media, and by my own unstoppable contrarian slant. I know, or rather have learned, that my opinion is a very unreliable guide, and so I ignore it.

Longer-term bias

The other two parts, my long-term bias and action points, are more important. The challenge comes when action points align against your long-term bias. There are many traders who will tell you not to trade against your bias or the longer-term trend, but I'd suggest that might be wrong. Your longer-term bias will sometimes simply be wrong. Your action points may align against your bias (which, let's say, is driven by the longer-term trend), and those action points may show where the longer-term trend is breaking down. Consider this: you have a market that is a strong downtrend on the weekly/monthly timeframe and then you start getting daily buy signals. Do you ignore those? Maybe you should, but these can often be outstanding trades since those long trades might show where the trend is ending.

To assume we never trade against the longer-term bias is to give too much importance to longer-term trends. Trend indicators are unreliable. We've looked at some of those in this course, and you've seen they don't have a statistical edge. In fact, some of the common trend indicators put you, very reliably, on the wrong side of the market.

Too many people complicate things too much with multiple timeframe analysis. If you are going to have a bias, you've got to figure out how to manage it and how to keep it from hurting you. I'll make it simple: any bias you hold should be based on something you can see in the market. (This removes "opinion" from consideration.) It also should be falsifiable, meaning that you should be able to explain what would invalidate your bias. If those two things are not true—it's not based on something you can see and you can't say what would make the bias wrong—then you don't have a bias; you have an opinion. The great thing about this business is you get to choose—you can lose your opinion or you can lose your money.

Action points

Action points are easy—when you get a signal to do something, you do it. This is the discipline of trading, and it's also how you build consistency. This point really could have been a lot shorter and could have simply been: when you get a signal from your system, do what it says to do. Period. All of these other things might be part of your system, but they need to be incorporated in a way that makes sense.

On Skill Development

Why You Think You're Getting Worse

Do you ever work really hard and feel like you got nothing out of it? Or, even more to the point, ever work a long time on developing a skill, and have the feeling that you're getting worse instead of better? Chances are, no matter what you're into, you've experienced this: in sports, in academics, in music, in chess, and, certainly, in markets and trading. This feeling can be frustrating, and is one of the reasons why many learners quit before achieving mastery, but there's a good reason for it.

Developing skills

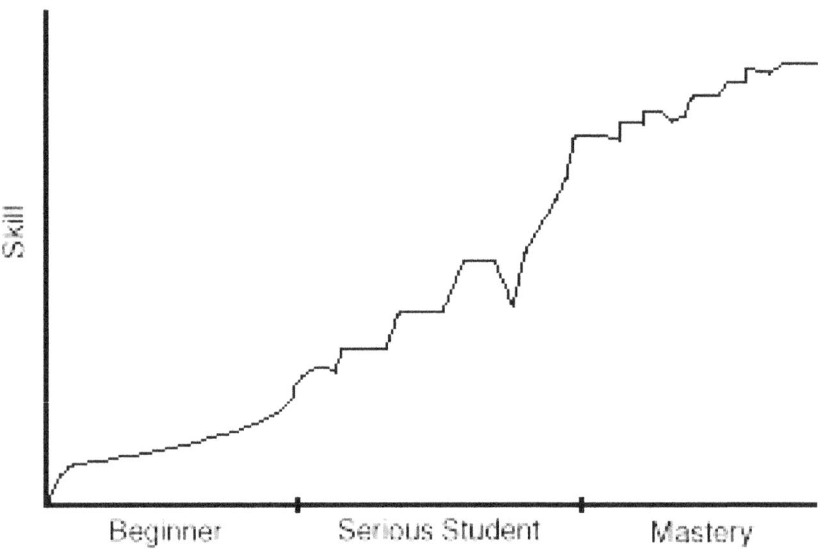

Skill development over time

Take a look at the chart above, which shows a learner's skill in a task (vertical axis) as a function of time spent learning (horizontal axis). I've divided her learning into three broad categories of beginner, serious student, and mastery. A few points to think about:

- From the very beginning, a new learner picks up a lot of new skills quickly. This is the "honeymoon" period. It's real and it's important motivation—you can go from knowing nothing to having some legitimate skills in just a few days or weeks in pretty much any field. However, the beginner's learning soon slows down to a more gradual growth.
- At the intermediate stage, progress is usually a series of long plateaus followed by sudden jumps. We very rarely increase skills in any field in a predictable line or curve, and sometimes we might even experience dramatic setbacks. For the intermediate learner, time spent working is important, but we might not see the payoff for a very long time.

- For someone approaching mastery, progress comes in probably more predictable, but smaller jumps. As we climb higher, it's harder to go ever higher in the rarefied air. Learning and progress slow down, but we have a significant body of skill and knowledge behind us.

This applies to actual skill: how good you are at catching the ball and getting to where you need to be on the field, how good you are at understanding patterns and potential on the board, how good you are at playing the right notes at the right time. Though the chart above is just one possible path, the concepts probably apply to a wide range of fields. But wait, there's more...

Knowing what good is

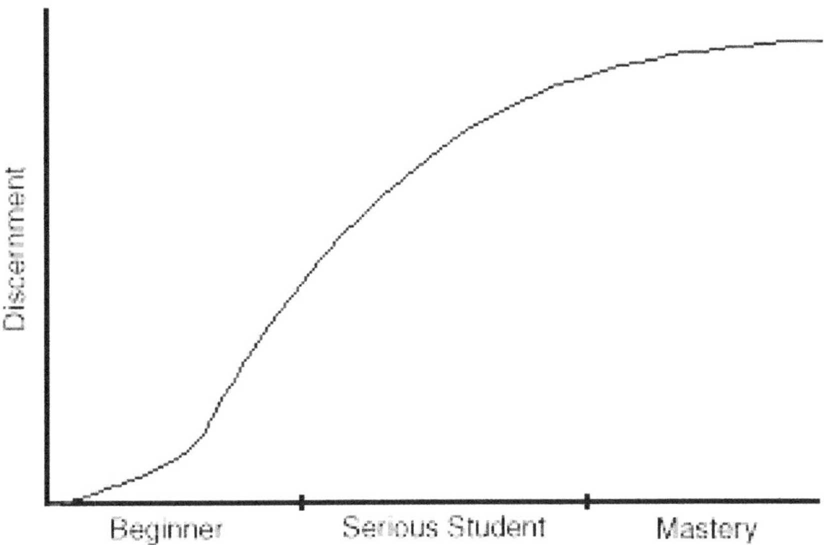

Knowledge and perception of skill, over time

This chart shows something entirely different: your understanding and perception of skill in a field. For instance, the beginning musician is likely to be dazzled by anyone who can play a lot of notes fast. He doesn't understand subtlety or style, and probably can't even tell the difference between something played well or not so well. As our learner digs deeper, he starts to get some wisdom. He starts to understand what good (in his field) really is, and begins to understand the difference between really good and great.

- The beginner probably doesn't know much and doesn't know he doesn't know much. When I see someone swing a golf club, I just see someone swing a golf club. I don't understand angles, grip, body position, addressing the ball, how to connect all parts of the body to a swing—but if I spent many hours learning to swing a golf club, I'd start to see it. The beginner's understanding probably grows slowly at first, but this soon speeds up.
- The intermediate student likely develops this knowledge at a faster and faster rate. Spurred by her own learning, working with a teacher or mentor, and watching/listening to peak performers in her field, she starts to get a very good idea of what is possible.
- For the master, we continue to refine this discernment, but it grows slower and slower as we near the peak. A master's understanding in a field can look superhuman to the layperson.

So, this is our understanding of skill, which is something different from skill itself. What happens if we consider both of these curves together on the same chart?

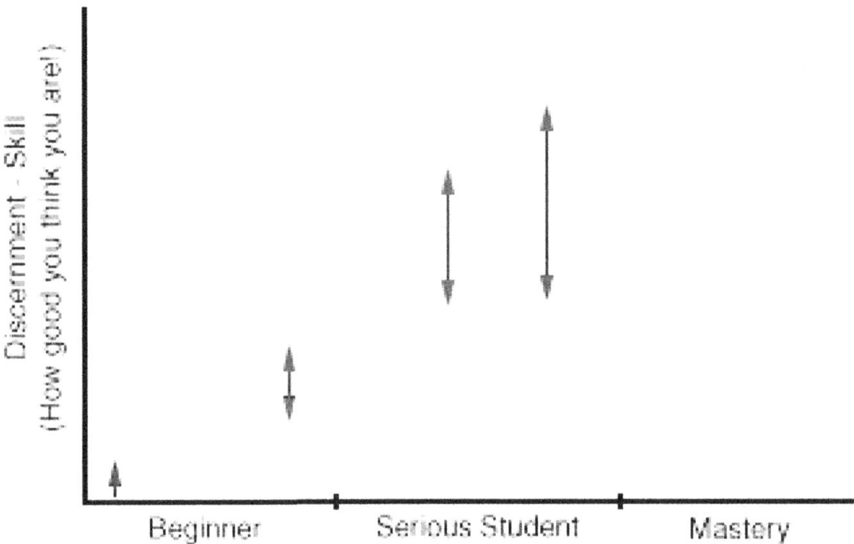

Perception of own skill

- Here's where things get interesting. In the chart above, I've put both of our lines, but I've also highlighted the difference between them. This is important: your understanding of your own skill (self-skill) depends on your general perception of skill in the field! For the beginner, who we just said knows very little, his own early skill seems very impressive indeed. Very often the "honeymoon" period in which he gains some new skills happens before he really understands very much. Realistically, he doesn't have great skills, but he also doesn't know enough to know this!
- In the intermediate stages, which is where the foundation of mastery lies, things get a lot messier and a lot more complicated. Skill development often plateaus while discernment does not. If this is hard to understand, imagine that you are practicing, but are stuck in a long plateau stage in which your skills don't really grow. (Remember, this is normal for most fields.) However, what if you're continuing to develop more discernment and refining your perception during this period? You will very likely have the sense that you are actually getting worse, because your impression of self-skill is based on this difference. (Heaven forbid we have an actual minor setback in skill in this emotionally-charged environment—this can feel like the end of the world!)
- For the master, things start to get more realistic as perception and skills come into alignment, but this is many years down the road in most fields, if not decades.

What to do with this?

This is an idea I've been trying to articulate for a long time. You may disagree with the specifics of the charts above, but I do think the concept is sound: we often increase our understanding and perception of skill in a task faster than our own skill can develop. I can't put it more simply than this: this feels bad. Really bad. This is one reason why many people quit.

Forewarned is forearmed. If you know that this will likely happen, that you will hit plateaus and they'll feel worse than they are, that you may feel stuck at a level for months (or even years), you'll be prepared for it. You'll understand that it is a normal part of skill development, and, most important, you will not quit. The path to mastery is difficult at best, but our perception of our own skill can shape the emotional context and lead to our eventual success or failure.

Patience... patience

An interesting debate emerged in the comments to one of my blog posts. In the post, I had suggested that discipline was the most important thing; a reader countered that patience was more important. Now, I could (and did) argue that patience is a subset of discipline, but the discussion could quickly devolve into an argument over the exact meaning of words—all of this could so easily miss the point: patience is absolutely essential for success in trading. And learning to have patience... well... it sucks!

The patience to wait for an entry

People who haven't traded often have trouble understanding the psychological stresses of trading. I can remember my early days: I'd have a plan and I would know exactly what I would/could/should do and which markets I would trade. I would review this plan, write it down on paper so it was "real", and then resolve to follow it exactly. Then, when the hoped for entry didn't develop, I found myself almost magically in another trade in an unrelated market. I wish I could tell you this only happened once, but it was a part of my struggle several times, and then again when I switched markets and asset classes.

From a logical perspective, this is baffling. It's beyond stupid. But nearly all traders do it, and some never get over it. The simple patience to wait for the right entry to develop is truly an essential skill in trading, and, if you can't manage to do this, I don't think you can be a trader.

We can come up with whatever powerful and correct imagery we wish: for instance, a hawk sitting motionless on a pole, watching the grass below for the telltale whisper of lunch. That hawk will sit for hours if need be, and then pounce at exactly the right moment. Far more often than not, things work out well for the hawk and badly for the "lunch animal". Ideas like this should be compelling to a developing trader, but we can rehearse and pound the ideas into our heads, only to do something stupid in an I MUST TRADE NOW moment the next day. What to do about it? Hold on, we'll get to that, but let's look at a few other ways patience is important.

The patience to be sure you have an edge

This one seems obvious: It shouldn't be too hard for me to convince you that the markets are a difficult place and that you don't stand a chance without an edge. It's also not terribly hard for someone to learn how to develop and verify an edge. Knowing this, it would seem to be logical that any trader should carefully do the work to be sure he has a reason to risk money in the market, right? Of course, this doesn't always happen.

Again, the solutions I'm going to offer will help here, but it's also worth spending a few moments on the intellectual side of this. Whether you are trading or investing, you don't have any reason to risk money or time until you are sure you have an edge. If you got a system idea from a chatroom, are trading some indicator or candle pattern, or just think you can figure out what companies make really cool products, you don't have an edge. I would argue you can't be reasonably certain you have an edge until you have some good data (ideally back and forward tested) that shows an edge, so consider this carefully before you risk money. Solutions in a few lines, but let's look at one more kind of patience we need.

The patience to become a trader

Now, I know this borders on New Agey-touchy feely stuff, but there's truth here: if you want to do this well, you don't trade, you must *become* a trader. I think this is true whether you develop computer trading systems, actively trade technical patterns, or invest in longer-term stocks based on fundamental criteria—no matter how you are involved in the market, you aren't likely to be successful until you have become a trader. This journey can be long and frustrating; it takes time and conviction. You'll probably want to give up along the way. You'll kill a few dragons and maybe rescue a damsel in distress here and there. You will, absolutely, go in some very dark places and fight some battles you're not sure you can win. It's a long, hard journey, but just know that this is really the only way to succeed.

Many disciplines have clear apprenticeship paths, so the developing cook/shoemaker/architect is assured of putting in the time needed. While learning, growing, and developing skills, an apprenticeship program forces patience. Yes, you can find someone selling you programs for trading that claim to do this, but the true apprenticeship path probably lasts 3-5 years. Does your two-month course do the same thing? Of course not. You must be patient with yourself and give yourself time to grow into being and becoming a trader—there's no other way. (Despite the already brewing arguments from the quants who think it might be different if we're coding. Even here, there's a long path to being able to actually and effectively implement these ideas in the market.)

What to do about it

I can remember, as a very young boy, my grandmother telling me to never pray for patience because that was a lesson usually taught in miserable ways! Know this: if you have decided to be a trader, you've already committed to accepting the brutal lessons of developing patience, and the market god is a ruthless teacher! Though the market will certainly teach you these lessons if you stay in the game long enough, let me share a few thoughts that might help:

- **None of this makes rational sense.** Accept that from the beginning, and don't expect that you can rationalize your way around these issues. Here, we are confronting behavioral and emotional factors that are, to a large degree, outside the umbrella of rational control. Fixing behavioral problems requires a different tool set, and you be careful of emotions (e.g., anger, frustration, despair) that can make the process harder. Be kind and... um... patient with yourself as you work through these issues.
- **It is a discipline problem.** At the same time you are being kind to yourself, inject a healthy component of "tough love." If you can't solve these issues, you're probably going to eventually lose every dollar you risk in the market. This stuff matters, and you have to hold yourself to the highest standards. Demand perfect compliance to your rules.
- **Rules and accountability help.** If you don't know what you're supposed to do, then it's pretty hard to do it. Even with those rules, most of us will discover that it's still harder than we might expect. Setting up some kind of accountability—to a mentor, to a family member, to a community, or even to yourself—is a good idea. Get some rules and then get some accountability.
- **It just takes time.** Back to my grandmother's point—developing patience sucks because there's a lot of this that just takes time. The new trader is too hungry for action, and hands will often seem to make trades without conscious control. The new trader is a swirling mass of emotions and energy; we can try to channel those, but a pressure cooker needs a vent—otherwise we have a bomb.
- **Limit the damage while you learn.** If there's one truth I've learned about learning to trade, it's this: you're going to make mistakes. As a new trader, you're going to make a lot of them, and you may make them for years. Make yourself earn the right to trade bigger. Monitor your growth and performance, and be smart about it. Don't plan on supporting yourself from your trading income, perhaps for a very long time. All of this is designed to give yourself the time and space you need to grow and develop as a trader.

Just a few thoughts here that may help someone to take a few more steps along their path. Be prepared for how hard this is and how long it can take, and limit the damage while you learn—simple stuff, but powerful solutions.

The end is where we start from.

-T.S. Eliot

Part the Second

Chapter 10

Academic Theories of Market Behavior

It can scarcely be denied that the supreme goal of all theory is to make the irreducible basic elements as simple and as few as possible without having to surrender the adequate representation of a single datum of experience.

-Albert Einstein

The line between theory and practice is perhaps more clearly drawn in finance than in nearly any other field. On one side, an army of traders goes to battle every day in an attempt to pull profits out of the markets. The vast majority of these traders will fail in their attempts, a few will be successful, and only a handful will sustain that success over many years. These traders come to the market with a wide range of strategies at all levels of sophistication, but they are all looking for an answer to the same question: how do we make money in the markets? On the other side are the academics, who apply rigorous quantitative techniques to the same markets; many of them come to the conclusion that markets are essentially random and unpredictable. If they are right, then it is impossible to make consistent money trading and all of the traders' efforts are in vain.

The Efficient Markets Hypothesis

The *efficient markets hypothesis* (EMH) is one of the cornerstones of modern finance. One of the core tenets of the EMH is that all available information about an asset is encoded in the price of that asset. Prices are determined by the actions of traders who make rational decisions based on the arrival of new information and an analysis of the relevant probabilities and marginal utilities associated with various scenarios. The arrival of new information is essentially random and unpredictable, so price movements in response to that information are also unpredictable. Traders, however, tend to dismiss the theory out of hand, perhaps because they do not see a real-world application, or perhaps they are uncomfortable with the implications of the theory. If what the EMH tells us about markets is true, then trading in any form is an exercise in futility—it is not possible for traders to make consistent, risk-adjusted profits.

Classically, the EMH exists in three forms: strong, semi-strong, and weak. *Strong-form EMH* states that all information, even secret inside information, is reflected in the price. If this were true, it would be impossible to make money by trading, even with secret inside information. Not surprisingly, very strong evidence exists to contradict strong form EMH, both in theory and in practice, and it exists more as a theoretical construct than anything else. The situation is considerably more complex in the case of the semi-strong and weak forms, as there is good evidence to support and to contradict both of these. *Semi-strong-form EMH* states that all *publicly* available information is immediately and accurately reflected in the asset price. In practical terms this would mean that the instant an earnings report is released for a company or a crop report for an agricultural product, prices jump to the correct level justified by the report and stay there (with some allowance for random influences due to noise traders). Again, since the arrival of new information is unpredictable, so are price movements in response to that information.

For traders who base their buying and selling decisions on technical analysis, even *weak-form EMH*, which is largely accepted as correct in the academic community, poses some serious questions to consider. Weak-form EMH states that all information that was publicly available in the past is reflected in past and current prices, and therefore it should not be possible to make any predictions about future prices using information encoded in past prices. They key concept here, once again, is that since information flow is essentially random with respect to both timing and content, the impact of that information on market prices will be random and unpredictable. If this were true, there are no price patterns with any predictive value, and technical analysis (or fundamental analysis, for that matter) is a waste of time. This is a difficult perspective for many traders to even consider, but, at the very least, the academic research offers some important points to ponder.

The Random Walk Hypothesis

Another, closely related theory is the *random walk hypothesis* (RWH), which states that that price changes in assets can be described by random walks. (See Chapter 2 for discussions of random walks and ways that random walks can be used to model price changes.) The obvious question is how well this theory fits the changes in asset prices, and the answer is that no one is really sure. Academic studies have found both support for and violations of the RWH, with the general consensus that random walks seem to describe what happens on longer time frames (daily to monthly) fairly well. On shorter time frames, particularly intraday, violations of the RWH appear to be common, but there are a number of factors that could prevent traders from making easy profits based on these violations. (Liquidity, transaction costs, and bid-ask bounce top the list.)

In addition, violations of random walk do not appear to be stable over time. There are many examples in the literature (see Lo and MacKinlay 1999) of inefficiencies and violations of the RWH disappearing after they are published, and it is certainly possible to find that a subset of an asset's history conforms to random walk while another time period does not. It is worthwhile to consider that, even if a trader is able to find tradable patterns, they may not endure forever. Without going into the research and mathematical arguments in depth, it is probably enough for the average trader to realize that random walk describes market prices much more often than most traders wish it did. Most of the time, most asset prices wander in a path that can be described as more or less random, and it is impossible to find a trading edge in that environment.

What Does Not Constitute Disproof

The EMH is the cornerstone of much modern academic thinking about finance and markets. A large body of sophisticated literature and research has grown around the theory; much of it is fairly inaccessible to nonmathematicians, but the punch line is clear: if markets are truly efficient, then "such markets do not allow investors to earn above-average returns without accepting above-average risks" (Malkiel 2003).

Practitioners and traders generally have one of two broad approaches to the EMH. Many choose to ignore it altogether as something too abstract and too academic (in a pejorative sense) to be relevant or useful in actual trading. Others will offer a variety of points in an attempt to refute or disprove parts of either of the theories. Sadly, many of the attempts at disproof in the practical trading literature fall well short of significance because they fail to understand a few critical points.

One key mistake that many people make is to assume that the EMH and RWH are basically the same thing. This is not correct. Random walks are neither a necessary nor a sufficient condition for market efficiency (see Lucas 1978). In other words, it is possible for markets to be informationally efficient and to have prices move in ways that are not described by random walks. On the other hand, even if we could definitively prove that prices do follow random walks, we would not have enough information to declare that markets are fully efficient. It is important to separate the two in our analysis and thinking, but, for most technical traders, a focus on finding nonrandom price behavior is natural and reasonable. If sufficiently reliable and stable patterns can be found that also offer economically significant opportunities for profit, traders could justifiably ignore much of the theoretical debate and simply focus on application.

It is also important to realize that the EMH is a set of theories and ideas, and is not constructed in a way that allows simple contradiction or disproof. There are many variations of the EMH, and, in some sense, challenges to the EMH are met with "moving goalposts" as they are sometimes absorbed into the body of the theory and the theory is redefined. As Andrew Lo and A. Craig MacKinlay (1999) say:

> *The Efficient Markets Hypothesis, by itself, is not a well-defined and empirically refutable hypothesis. To make it operational, one must specify additional structure, e.g., investors' preferences, information structure, business conditions, etc. But then a test of the Efficient Markets Hypothesis becomes a test of several auxiliary hypotheses as well, and a rejection of such a joint hypothesis tells us little about which aspect of the joint hypothesis is inconsistent with the data.*

Any test of the theory is a joint test of the theory itself and of one particular specification of the theory—strong refutation of that particular specification would not necessarily invalidate the entire theory. In a very real sense, the EMH is not one thing or one set of beliefs; it is a way to think about financial markets and the problems facing market participants.

Non-normal Distributions

The normal distribution is commonly used in many statistical and mathematical applications because it describes a wide range of phenomena in the natural world. The so-called bell curve is used in many disciplines to model complex systems, and it serves a useful role in the fields of statistics and probability. Despite its utility in other applications, many writers (Taleb 2008 and Mandelbrot and Hudson 2006, among others) note that the normal distribution fails badly when applied to financial markets. In Figure 10.1, which shows the distribution of returns for the Dow Jones Industrial Average (DJIA) from 2000 to 2010, the solid line shows the shape the distribution would have if price changes conformed to the normal bell curve. Note that there are many more events clustered in the center of the distribution, and also many more far out in the tails; the extra weight is taken from the "shoulders" of the curve. For practical purposes, what this means is that markets are both more boring (more events clustered around the average) and far wilder (more events in the tail) than predicted by a normal bell curve.

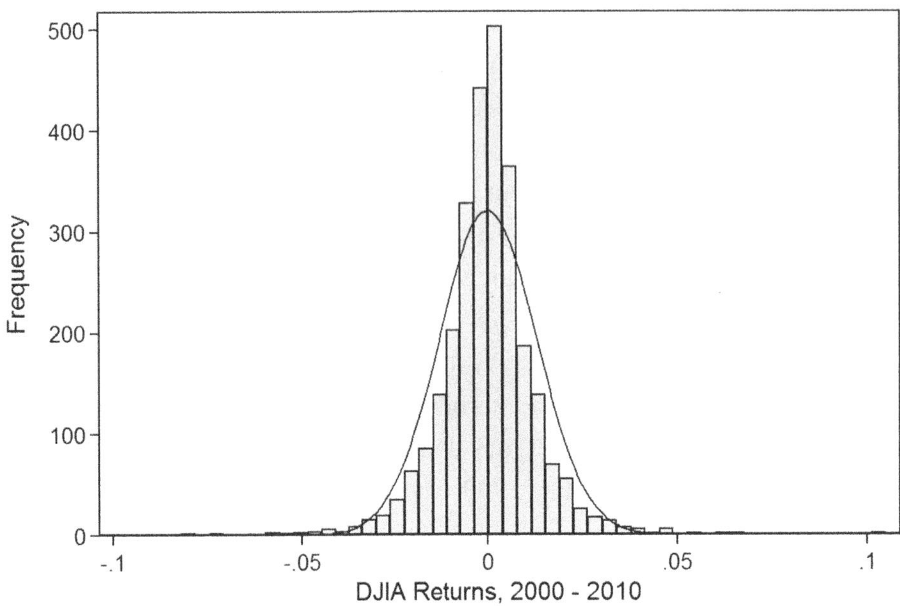

Figure 10.1 Distribution of Returns for the DJIA with a Normal Distribution Overlay

The most striking element of the diagram is the extra events in the tails. In fact, there are price changes on eight days in this sample of 2,772 trading days that should occur less than one day out of a million in our sample *if*—and this is the key point—the normal distribution is the correct one to use. (The full history of the DJIA includes a whopping 22 standard deviation outlier on the day of the 1987 crash. The probability of a 22 standard deviation event in a normal distribution is so remote that it is completely incomprehensible. If we had been generating a million normally distributed price bars every second since the Big Bang, it would still be exceedingly unlikely to find a single 22 standard deviation event in that entire set.) A distribution with many more events in the tails of the distribution is said to be leptokurtic, but it is more common to hear people speak of "fat tails." The 2007–2008 financial crisis brought the dangers of these fat tails squarely into the public focus, as many stocks, indexes, and derivatives made one-in-a-million moves day after day. The choice is simple: either we are seeing events nearly every week that should not happen once in a million years or the mathematical models we are using to describe those events are wrong.

Many traders and authors offer this evidence of nonnormality as proof against the EMH or the RWH. That a normal curve fails to adequately describe financial market data is true and well established—it would be difficult to find anyone willing to take the other side of that argument. (As an interesting aside, many risk management systems and option valuation models still use this assumption of normality as one of their core assumptions.) However, the presence of fat tails or any other kind of nonnormal distribution is no evidence at all against either the EMH or the RWH.

Baseline Drift

When we look at long price histories of some assets, we observe a baseline drift. For instance, if you were to randomly buy a large basket of stocks and hold them over a significant time, you would likely make money: over any extended holding period, stocks tend to go up. It would be easy to assume that this kind of slight bias might be evidence of nonrandom price action, but it is not. Mathematically, we could express the probability of a step up or down in our original random walk equation like this:

$$Prob_{up} = Prob_{down} = 0.50$$

But there is no reason that the probabilities in that equation have to be equal. Making a simple change—allowing the probability of a step up to be slightly larger than the probability of a step down—would generate a random walk with a positive drift component.

The presence of a baseline drift in stock prices is well established, and it is the reason behind the prevalence of index funds, which seek to capture this drift for their investors. One of the goalposts for traders seeking to outperform markets is that they must beat this baseline return without incurring extra risk (volatility) compared to the baseline. It is trivial to create a system that captures the baseline return with baseline volatility (buy and hold), and also simple to increase both the baseline capture and the risk through leverage. It is also not that difficult to create an active trading system that will outperform the baseline, albeit with increased volatility and risk. In this case, investors receive no benefit over what would be achieved through a simple leveraged portfolio, and in many cases are worse off because they are assuming risks that may not be well-defined or completely understood. The challenge is to achieve superior *risk-adjusted returns*, which is not a simple task. Far from disproving either the EMH or the RWH, this baseline drift is embraced by both. This is the "above-average" that Malkiel was referring to when he said that efficient markets "do not allow investors to earn above-average returns without accepting above-average risks."

Examples of Outperformance

Critics of the EMH often point to examples of funds or traders who have outperformed the market as evidence against the theory. The academic world, of course, is also aware that a group of traders consistently outperforming the market would be a serious challenge to the theory, so these cases of claimed outperformance have been carefully examined in the literature. The EMH does not say that no one can make money trading, as is commonly assumed. First of all, survivorship bias and the prevalence of counterintuitive runs in random data will result in a handful of traders showing exceptional performance purely due to chance. For instance, imagine a room with 10,000 people who will all flip a fair coin. If the coin comes up heads, the flipper is declared a winner and can stay in the room; tails, the flipper leaves the game. After the first flip there will be about 5,000 flippers left in the room since roughly 50 percent will win this game of chance. If we continue to 10 flips, there will be, give or take, 10 remaining flippers of the original 10,000, all of whom have displayed remarkable coin flipping acumen.

Assume, for a minute, that you are presented with the coin flipping record of one of these remaining star flippers without being told the selection process that produced them. The probability of someone being able to flip 10 heads in a row is less than one in a thousand, so we could reasonably assume that someone able to do this had a remarkable skill. However, when we do consider the selection process, that these 10 expert flippers are the remnants of the 10,000 who began the game, we may regard the one-in-a-thousand odds a little differently. Taken out of context, these flippers look like experts, but they are obviously the result of random chance when the process is considered.

We could structure a simple test to see if these flippers have actual skill. All we would need to do is to monitor their performance going forward; if they do not have any skill above random chance (which should be our initial assumption), then roughly half of them should leave the game on the next flip, and so on. If we see this group has remarkable performance, say 75 percent of them flip heads on every flip from the time we identified the group, then we might begin to consider that they have a real edge in this game. If they continue to exit the game at a rate of about 50 percent per flip, then we realize that their past flipping records, however impressive, are simply the result of a random process.

There are, of course, examples of traders and funds that outperform the market, but the academic argument is that they may well be the result of a selection process not unlike the coin flipping game. In fact, mutual funds sometimes cultivate this process by launching a number of products with various strategies in diverse asset classes, selecting the winners after a period of time and then marketing those products to the public. Going forward, however, these funds do not, as a group, show outperformance. Market history is littered with stories of winners with extended periods of outperformance and seemingly inexplicable track records that eventually revert to the mean. (Value Line, as well as Bill Miller and the Legg Mason Value Trust are two well-known examples of track records that have faltered a bit in recent years.)

There are several possible explanations here. One that should not be dismissed out of hand is that perhaps EMH advocates are correct in their claims. Perhaps consistent risk-adjusted outperformance is not possible in the long run. For traders trying to make profits in the market, this would be disheartening, to say the least, but there are other possibilities to consider. Market efficiency may be an evolving process, and it may be possible to identify profit opportunities that are eroded over a period of time. (Whether a trader can successfully identify new inefficiencies in the future is another question entirely.) It is also possible that there are traders with impressive track records who simply have no economic motivation to offer those records for analysis. At any rate, we must realize that a simple example of fund or trader outperformance (even on a risk-adjusted basis) does not present a credible challenge to the EMH.

Inefficiencies Due to Market Microstructure or Transaction Costs

Traders doing initial research into price patterns will observe that there appear to be glaring inefficiencies in illiquid instruments such as inactive futures contracts, less frequently traded currency rates, and microcap stocks. A word of caution is needed here, because price records in these instruments may not present realistically exploitable opportunities. Price changes in illiquid instruments can often be nothing more than bid-ask bounce, where prices trade back and forth between wide bid-ask spreads. Exploiting these opportunities would require being able to reliably buy on the bid and sell on the offer—a most unrealistic assumption.

Another issue, especially when comparing relationships between two markets, is that quoted prices almost always consist of the last actual trade. Imagine two markets that are very closely related, one of which trades actively but the other rarely trades. Examining the price records of these markets, a trader would find long periods when prices seemed to diverge, but this is only because current trades in the active instrument are being compared to a single stale print in the inactive one. If the trader attempts to actually execute on this apparent divergence, he would probably find that there is no divergence at all because the bid-ask spread of the illiquid instrument tracks the liquid instrument very closely. The bid-ask spread represents true value, as any trade will execute there first, certainly not against a stale price from many minutes or hours ago. This is not just a hypothetical example—the same issue occurs every day in options, in back months of futures, and in stocks that trade multiple share classes or that are listed in different international markets.

It is also important to consider whether inefficiencies are economically significant. Volume in some illiquid instruments may be very light, for instance, with only a few hundred shares a day trading in very thin stocks. Even if actual inefficiencies were found after accounting for market structure issues, it might not be possible to exploit them on any economically meaningful scale.

There have also been cases throughout market history of one group of participants gaining a structural or transaction costs–based advantage over the rest of the marketplace for a period of time. The New York Stock Exchange specialist system, floor traders in most open-outcry markets, and the SOES bandits of the dot-com boom are obvious examples. These traders' profits are the result of structural imbalances in the market, and are not evidence against efficient markets. In addition, markets have tended to evolve and erase these inefficiencies over time.

Credible Challenges to the Theory

Before proceeding, it is important to clarify one point. There are many people on both sides of the argument for and against the EMH; it is a very polarizing subject, and some people in academia and in some areas of the finance industry have built careers out of defending the theory. Our goal in this section is not to disprove the EMH, but to understand what types of information could potentially present a serious problem for believers in the EMH. If markets are, in fact, less than efficient, it is possible that some of these legitimate challenges could point the way to potential profits.

Assumptions Are Flawed

In classic EMH, the assumption is that market participants receive new information, process it, and immediately act in a rational manner. Their immediate, but well-considered, actions cause prices to instantly adjust to the correct level justified by the new piece of information. Models are important because they can help us understand reality, but it also important to consider the limitations of those models. A model must, by definition, simplify elements of reality. No one thinks that a model is a perfect representation of reality, but no one is quite sure how far models can diverge from reality and still be useful. Model building, even in the case of simple models, is a blend of both art and science. (Think of the old joke about a group of scientists stranded on a desert island with a case of canned food and no way to open it. After the physicist, the chemist, and the biologist tried unsuccessfully to open the cans, they asked the economist for help. He replied, "This one is easy. You see, first we must assume a can opener exists. ...")

Some of the assumptions of the EMH fall well short of reality. First of all, there is great debate about whether people act rationally. There is a growing body of evidence that is confirming what traders have probably known since the beginning of time—people make emotional decisions, sometimes they make mistakes, and they do not always act in their own best interests. Furthermore, information is not received and processed by all market participants simultaneously, and sometimes errors are made in analysis. In the case of breaking news, traders make immediate and emotional decisions that can have a dramatic impact on prices. Particularly intraday, when news breaks in a stock, the stocks of companies with similar ticker symbols (e.g., AAP and AAPL, PCBC and PCBK) will sometimes have large moves as well. It does not matter that the two companies are completely unrelated or are in completely different industries. This is a clear example of traders reading the news and simply making a mistake by executing in the wrong symbol. If markets were truly informationally efficient, if investors always made rational decisions, this should not happen.

Overreactions and Underreactions to News

When new information comes into a market, most EMH models assume that the information is processed and the stock immediately moves to the correct level justified by the news. This process would look something like the example in Figure 10.2.

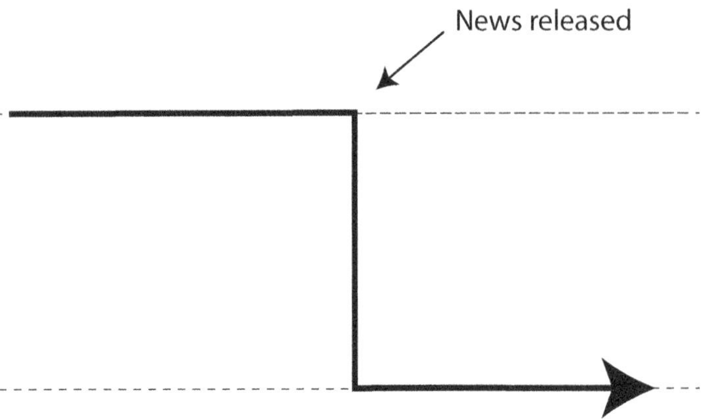

Figure 10.2 Idealized EMH-Style Reaction to News

It rarely works like this. Prices are much more likely to overreact or underreact to news, or even to move initially in the wrong direction entirely. These are sometimes periods of great uncertainty, and the situation is often exacerbated by wide spreads and low liquidity. Markets work, but the process of price discovery is sometimes messy, noisy, and even dangerous. Market makers and liquidity-providing traders step back, spreads widen, and large orders have a disproportionately large impact on price. In reality, it is exceedingly unusual for a market to move cleanly and instantly to the new price level; the process is much more likely to look something like Figure 10.3.

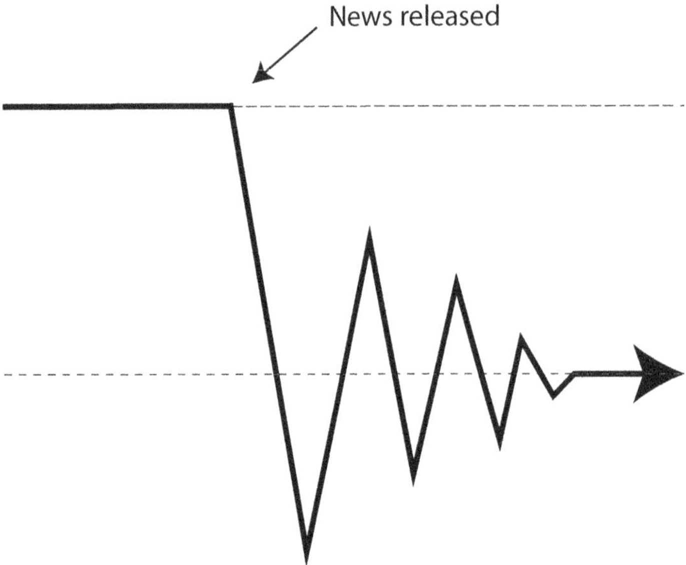

Figure 10.3 A More Realistic Reaction to News

In addition, not all market participants receive all news items at the same time, and some certainly do their homework on a different schedule. Imagine that news breaks in the middle of a trading day that a prominent pharmaceutical company has been denied a much-anticipated Food and Drug Administration (FDA) approval for a new drug. The news is inarguably bad, though there could be some debate and disagreement about the exact extent of the impact on the company's profits, margins, and competitive place in the industry. Within seconds of the press release, a small army of algorithmic news-reading robots has processed the news with linguistic artificial intelligence, made buy or sell decisions, and placed orders that are immediately executed in the market. From start to finish, the process takes seconds; many of these machines have executed their orders before the first human even sees the headlines.

Next comes a group of human day traders who pay for access to fast news feeds. They execute within seconds to minutes, and many of them will be in and out of the market several times within the first few seconds. These are people, and they are fallible, so mistakes can and do happen. Some of them may initially execute on the wrong side (buying instead of selling) and may flip their positions several times as they attempt to position for the move. Some of them will establish positions they plan to hold for hours to weeks, but, on balance, these traders tend to be very focused on short-term price movements and are looking to take fairly small profits out very quickly.

A few minutes to many hours later, the news propagates to the major media sources, where it is run as breaking news. Members of the public finally hear the news item, and some of them act on what they believe is fresh news. Their orders will be executed in a flurry around the major media release, but some of the orders may not be executed until quite some time later. Of course, what many of these traders don't realize is that they are not getting breaking news at all—the battle is over and much of the process of price discovery has already happened by the time they hear the news. (The fact that there are some people who repeat this process many times argues against the assumption that people make rational decisions in their own self-interest.)

In this environment, it would certainly be possible for a $40 stock to experience a $10 price swing within the first hour, but there is still a very large pool of money that has yet to vote. Large funds and pools of institutional money (hedge funds, pension funds, etc.) may hold a significant percentage of the company's stock, but they are not able to make decisions within seconds because there are many decision makers involved in the process. Furthermore, many of these funds have policies that prohibit them from reacting immediately to news. Even if they wanted to execute, as a group they may own most of the outstanding shares of the company and positions like this cannot be unwound in seconds—they must be cut up into smaller pieces and sold over a period of days to weeks in a manner that will not have an extremely adverse impact on prices.

Researchers are quick to point out (quite correctly) that, while markets may not move immediately and cleanly to new price levels, overreactions are about as common as underreactions. This, they claim, prevents traders from making easy, reliable profits off reactions to news events. Even if markets do fluctuate, overreact, and underreact to new information, if these fluctuations are random and unpredictable, market efficiency is maintained. (Note that here is a case where the RWH could be violated and the EMH still hold.) Based on my experience, I would say that they are correct in pointing out that there are no easy profits to be made in this environment. Of course, it is also possible that there are opportunities to profit from these initial mispricings of news events, but that the academic tests have failed to capture some of the factors that traders consider in their decisions.

This is reality. It is messy, dirty, and ugly, and it is very different from the idealized world presented in some forms of the EMH. Some of these traders are making emotional reactions, and many of them are actually making trading decisions based off the price movements themselves rather than a rational analysis of the news. In the idealized world, if $40 were the correct price for the stock based on its future earning potential (and it would be, because market prices always accurately reflect all available information in this idealized world) and the news item now justified a drop to $30, this adjustment to $30 would happen instantly with no intervening prices. But this is simply not the way the world works. There would be tremendous volatility around the announcement, and the impact of large funds adjusting their positions (some of whom will be selling and some will be buying because they will find the stock trading at a discount to the fundamental value justified by their models) will be felt for days or weeks afterward.

Inside Information

Strong form EMH says that all information, even secret inside information, is priced, so it is not possible to make a profit trading off that information. Obviously, in the case of the aforementioned drug stock, a group of people knew the drug approval would be denied before the news was released to the public. Those people had a chance to initiate short positions at $40 and could have taken profits as the news hit the wires. For strong form EMH to be valid there would have to be some mystical adjustment mechanism that moves price to the correct level the instant the FDA committee votes to deny the drug approval, before the information hits the newswires, even before the company knows the news, and even before the news leaves the room. (We should be suspicious of market explanations and models that require a deus ex machina. Buying and selling move prices—only those and nothing else.) It is also worth considering that regulatory agencies, at least in the United States, spend an enormous amount of time, energy, and resources prosecuting traders who trade on inside information. Why would this be so if there were no money to be made on that information? Obviously, there are some serious logical problems here, so strong form EMH has few adherents today, even in academia.

Long-Term Mispricings: Booms, Bubbles, and Busts

Some forms of the EMH could allow for short-term mispricings due to market microstructure issues, but there is also evidence that markets may stay mispriced for extended periods of time. In an efficient market, such mispricings would represent a profit opportunity for rational investors, and the pool of educated, rational arbitrage money should be able to quickly overcome any irrationality. This does not seem to be the case. Market history has many examples of markets that reached irrational bubble valuations and then deflated with astonishing speed. The financial crisis of 2007, crude oil at $150 in 2008, Nasdaq stocks in the dot-com bubble, the collapse of Long-Term Capital Management in 1998, the Asian financial crisis of 1997, and the Hunt Brothers' impact on the silver market in 1980 are recent examples, but the South Sea Bubble of 1720 and the Dutch Tulip Mania of 1634 suggest that this has been going on for a long time. Figure 10.4 shows a chart that could be the chart of a high-flying tech stock from the dot-com bubble of 2000, but it actually is the price history of shares of the South Sea Company from January 1719 to mid-1721. In fact, we even have evidence from ancient Babylon that there were commodity bubbles in antiquity—it seems likely that, far from being an aberration, bubbles and busts are natural features of markets. There is nothing new under the sun. In these bubbles, valuations typically expand to hundreds or thousands of percentages of fair, justifiable valuations over a period of months or years. When the bubble pops, as it always does, there is the inevitable bust as the market quickly recalibrates. It is difficult to reconcile this behavior with the idea that investors always make rational decisions. At the very least, it seems like something else is going on here.

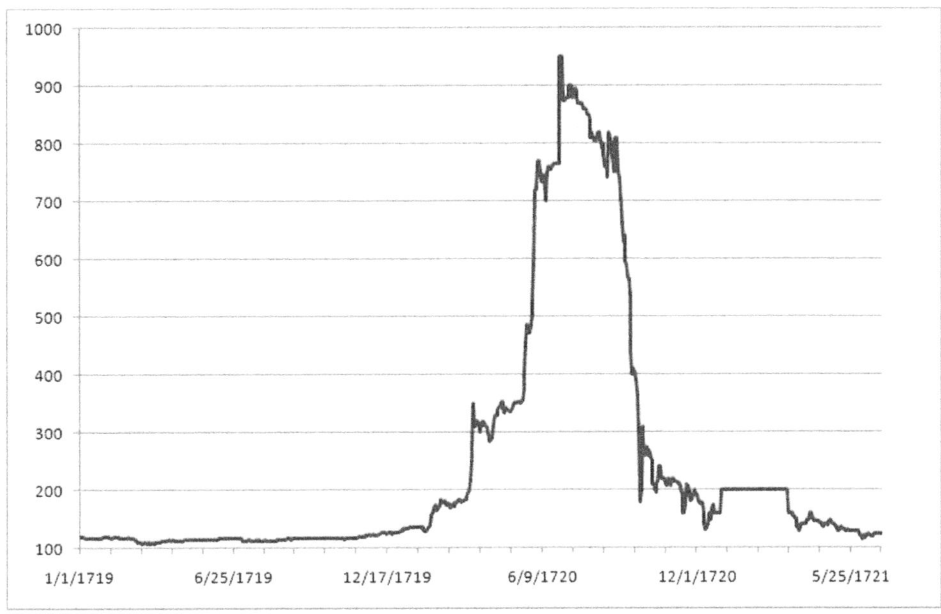

Figure 10.4 Stock Price of the South Sea Company

Cost of Information

Semistrong form EMH states that no one can earn above-average profits based on analysis of any publicly available information. Therefore, there is no value in doing any fundamental analysis or, indeed, any analysis at all, because all information is already reflected in the price. Again, we run into a logical absurdity in the limit. If the theoretical construct were true, then no one would do any analysis, so how would the information be reflected in price? In fact, there would be no motivation for anyone to ever do any analysis of any information, and, eventually, no reason to ever trade. Markets would collapse and cease to exist (Grossman and Stiglitz 1980). However, in the real world, market-related information is quite expensive. Institutions, traders, and analysts pay a lot for information, and they pay even more to get it quickly. Why would they do that, and continue to do so decade after decade, if this information were worthless?

Autocorrelation in Returns

In a random walk, the probability of the next step being up is usually very close to 50 percent (plus or minus any drift component), and that probability does not change based on anything that has happened in the past. In other words, if the probability of a step up is 50 percent, after three steps up the probability of the fourth being up is still 50 percent, exactly as it would be for flips of a fair coin. Under the assumptions of random walks, price has no memory and each step is completely independent of previous steps. Autocorrelation is the statistical term that basically deals with trends in data. If a series of price changes displays high autocorrelation, a step up is more likely to follow a previous step up. Though this is a simplification that is not always true, prices tend to trend in an autocorrelated price series.

Many academic studies have found no autocorrelation in returns, but the evidence is mixed, with other studies finding strong autocorrelations. The question seems to depend heavily on the sample being examined, as different time frames or time periods of the same market may exhibit radically different qualities. It is worth mentioning that this is consistent with what I have come to expect as an experienced trader in a wide range of markets and time frames. One of the major themes of this book is that all market action exists in one of two broad states: range expansion or mean reversion, or, to use terms that might be more familiar, trends and trading ranges. In a trending environment, over any given time period, the next price change is more likely to be upward if the preceding price change was also upward, or downward if the preceding change was downward. In a trading range environment, negative autocorrelation is more likely—the following price change is more likely to reverse the previous price change. If these two environments are aggregated, the end result is that the autocorrelations essentially counterbalance each other, and the overall sample shows near-zero autocorrelation.

I would suggest that one of the potential problems with the academic studies regarding autocorrelation is that they begin with the assumption that prices move randomly, so perhaps not enough effort has been made to find patterns that could differentiate, a priori, between these discrete regimes. Note that some writers supporting technical analysis have made the suggestion that trending and trading range environments should be analyzed separately. This is a mental exercise on par with dividing a set of random numbers into those greater and less than zero, and then being surprised that the former set has a higher mean than the latter! For the analysis to be useful, it must be possible to define a set of conditions that will have some predictive value for autocorrelations over a finite time horizon. This is actually one of the core tasks of competent discretionary trading—to identify the most likely emerging volatility environment. One of the major focuses of this book is to identify conditions and factors that will help a discretionary trader make just such a distinction.

Volatility Clustering

Real market prices show at least one very serious departure from random walk conditions. A random walk has no memory of what has happened in the past, and future steps are completely independent of past steps. However, we observe something very different in the actual data—large price changes are much more likely to be followed by more large changes, and small changes are more likely to follow small changes. For practical purposes, what is probably happening is that markets respond to new information with large price movements, and these high-volatility environments tend to last for a while after the initial shock. This is referred to in the literature as the persistence of volatility shocks and gives rise to the phenomenon of volatility clustering. Figure 10.5 shows the absolute value of the standard deviations of daily changes for several years of daily returns in the S&P 500 Cash index. Note that the circled areas, which highlight clusters of high-volatility days, are not dispersed through the data set randomly—they tend to cluster in specific spots and time periods.

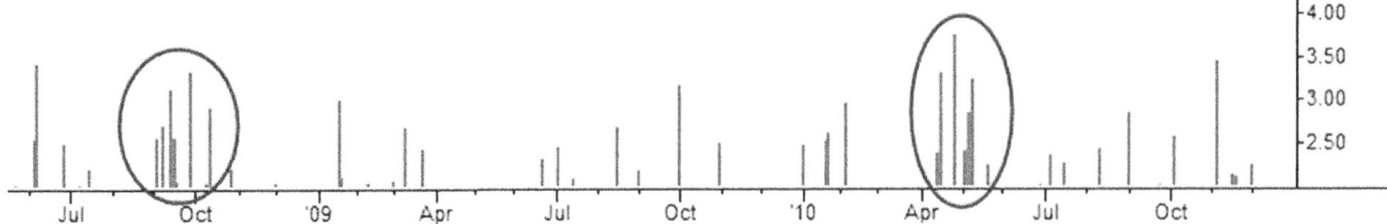

Figure 10.5 Absolute Values of Standard Deviation of Returns, S&P 500 Index, Mid-2008 through 2010 (Values < 2.0 Filtered from This Chart)

What we see here is autocorrelation of volatility. Price changes themselves may still be random and unpredictable, but we can make some predictions about the magnitude (absolute value) of the next price change based on recent changes. Though this type of price action is a severe violation of random walk models (which, by definition, have no memory of previous steps), do not assume that it is an opportunity for easy profits. We have seen practical implications of an autocorrelated volatility environment elsewhere in this book—for instance, in the tendency for large directional moves to follow other large price movement—but it is worth mentioning here that there are academic models that capture this element of market behavior quite well.

Autoregressive conditional heteroskedasticity (ARCH), generalized ARCH (GARCH), and exponential GARCH (EGARCH) are time series models that allow us to deal with the issue of varying levels of volatility across different time periods. A simple random walk model has no memory of the past, but ARCH-family models are aware of recent volatility conditions. Though not strictly correct, a good way to think of these models is that they model price paths that are a combination of a random walk with another component added in. This other component is a series of error components (also called residuals) that are themselves randomly generated, but with a process that sets the volatility of the residuals based on recent history. The assumption is that information comes to the market in a random fashion with unpredictable timing, and that these information shocks decay with time. The effect is not unlike throwing a large stone in a pond and watching the waves slowly decay in size. If this topic interests you, Campell, Lo, and MacKinlay (1996) and Tsay (2005) are standard references.

Behavioral Perspectives

Strictly speaking, it is not possible to disprove either the EMH or the RWH, but sufficient empirical evidence has accumulated to challenge some of the core beliefs. Strong form EMH, in particular, exists today more as a vestigial intellectual curiosity than as a serious theory. In addition, the price adjustments under other forms of the EMH cannot occur through some magical, unexplained mechanism; they must be the result of buying and selling decisions made by traders. There will necessarily be temporary and intermediate mispricings as prices move from the preevent to the postevent levels, and there may be some degree of emotion (irrationality) along the way. New theories have evolved in an effort to better explain the conditions we observe in the real world, and many of those focus on investors' behavior.

Markets Are Mostly, but Not Always, Efficient

Many of the potential issues with and challenges to the EMH essentially go away if we allow for some form of intermittent efficiency. Perhaps markets are informationally efficient most of the time, interspersed with periods where prices diverge from fundamental values. This model sacrifices one of the key advantages of the EMH—consistency ("Markets are efficient and market prices are the correct prices. Always.")—but the trade-off could be a model that more closely fits the real world. Temporary mispricings such as bubbles and crashes could be embraced by a theory that allows intermittent efficiency, but work would need to be done to understand the mechanism by which markets enter and leave the state of efficiency. It seems likely that some understanding of the participants' emotional reactions and behavioral issues would be necessary to understand that mechanism, and that the actions of rational traders would ultimately be the driving force behind a return to efficiency and equilibrium. It is also worth considering that, if these models are correct, there could be profits for traders who can identify and act on inefficiencies. These traders could well be the process through which markets become efficient, and they could be compensated for their efforts and risk through superior risk-adjusted profits.

Reflexivity

Reflexivity is a term coined by George Soros to describe the process where asset prices have an impact on fundamentals and fair valuations. Most theories suggest that prices are a reflection of actual value, but Soros (1994) suggests that the causative link runs both ways. In his own words:

> *The generally accepted theory is that financial markets tend towards equilibrium, and on the whole, discount the future correctly. I operate using a different theory, according to which financial markets cannot possibly discount the future correctly because they do not merely discount the future; they help to shape it [emphasis mine]. In certain circumstances, financial markets can affect the so-called fundamentals which they are supposed to reflect. When that happens, markets enter into a state of dynamic disequilibrium and behave quite differently from what would be considered normal by the theory of efficient markets. Such boom/bust sequences do not arise very often, but when they do, they can be very disruptive, exactly because they affect the fundamentals of the economy.*

Essentially, Soros's argument is that the traditional causative model in which asset prices correctly reflect fundamentals is flawed because it assumes a one-way link between fundamentals and prices. There are times when markets become so irrational and so mispriced that market participants' biases and impressions actually change the fundamentals that are supposed to be driving valuations.

The academic world has taken little note of this theory, but it does seem to describe many elements that we observe in boom-and-bust cycles. Perhaps the clearest example of this concept would be to imagine a wildly changing currency rate. Exchange rates are supposed to reflect fundamentals, but it is not terribly difficult to imagine an unbalanced situation where the rates actually become so extreme that they have an effect on the fundamentals of each country's economy. Similarly, how hard is it to imagine an extreme price for a commodity affecting fundamentals of production, transportation, or marketing for that commodity? Do farmers not make planting decisions based on grain prices? This certainly is not the normal mode in which markets operate, but these types of extremes occur several times each decade. Even if we do not wish to wholeheartedly embrace the theory of reflexivity, it is worthwhile to spend some time considering the concept that prices may influence fundamentals, that the observer may affect the outcome of the experiment. Perhaps far more complex relationships exist in financial markets than classic economic models suggest.

Market Efficiency Is an Evolving Process

Victor Niederhoffer (1998) offers the intriguing idea that markets may be viewed as ecosystems, with each participant playing some role in the food chain. In nature, there is an ongoing arms race between predators and prey: ecosystems rest on a large base of prey animals, which evolve new forms of deception and camouflage over time. In response, predators also become more efficient over time. Both predators and prey depend on each other in a complex network of relationships, and neither side can truly win the arms race. If predators win the battle, then they eventually die because there are no more prey animals. If prey animals evolve to the point where none of them are eaten, predators first die from starvation, but prey animals quickly follow as they overpopulate and consume all available food. The process of evolution is not an option. Ecosystems are locked into these processes, but they must, by definition, end in stalemate.

What happens if we replace the ecosystem with the market, prey animals with small individual traders, and predators with market makers and HFT algos? There is also an arms race here, and many parallels exist between the deceptive practices animals evolve in nature and the behavior of market participants. Technology evolves, the marketplace itself evolves, but there has always been a hierarchy in which some traders are predators and some are prey.

Under these assumptions, market efficiency is not a static state, but an evolving process itself. There are many examples from market history of large groups of traders making outsized profits. These profits persist for a period of time, but then something changes in the marketplace and they are unable to adapt. Two glaring examples are floor traders on commodity exchanges and stock daytraders in the latter part of the 1990s. Floor traders had access to order flow and the ability to execute orders for their own accounts much faster than the public could. A floor trader could literally trade 20 times in the amount of time it took a member of the public to place an order and get confirmation of the fill. In addition, floor traders' transaction costs were extremely low, enabling them to profit from very small moves in the market. Eventually, the major commodity exchanges moved away from the floor structure to an electronic market, and the vast majority of these traders were unable to make profits under the new paradigm.

In the case of some stock traders, there were specific inefficiencies that also allowed them access to order flow in the form of visible, large orders in the early electronic trading systems. This group also had the ability to execute at much higher speeds and for much lower costs than the general public, and, as a group, these traders were wildly profitable for several years. Over time, markets evolved. New execution technology for large orders made it impossible for this group of day traders to consistently identify large orders and to trade in front of those orders. At the same time, the general public began to access the market electronically through low-cost direct-access brokers, also eroding the day traders' informational and cost advantages. Last, a new predator evolved in this ecosystem as high-speed electronic trading systems were developed to target the order flow generated by this group of day traders. The predators had become prey.

In both of these examples, there was a group of traders who were able to pull consistent, outsized profits out of the market for a number of years (or decades). Their advantage was based on access to information, execution speed, and lower transaction costs—taken together these things are the very definition of a market inefficiency. In the end, markets changed and evolved, and these traders, as a group, were no longer able to profit.

New Directions: The Adaptive Markets Hypothesis

One of the most exciting ideas from academic research in the past decade is the adaptive markets hypothesis (AMH), from Andrew Lo (2005) at MIT. As he says,

> *[T]his new frame-work is based on some well-known principles of evolutionary biology—competition, mutation, reproduction, and natural selection—and I argue that the impact of these forces on financial institutions and market participants determines the efficiency of markets and the waxing and waning of investment products, businesses, industries and, ultimately, institutional and individual fortunes. In this paradigm, the EMH may be viewed as the "frictionless" ideal that would exist if there were no capital market imperfections such as transactions costs, taxes, institutional rigidities, and limits to the cognitive and reasoning abilities of market participants. However, in the presence of such real-world imperfections, the laws of natural selection, or, more appropriately, "survival of the richest," determine the evolution of markets and institutions. . . . Although the AMH is still primarily a qualitative and descriptive framework, it yields some surprisingly concrete insights.*

The EMH and the AMH begin with the same assumption: that individuals always intend to act in their own self-interest, after careful consideration of the probabilities, payoffs, and marginal utilities attached to all possible scenarios. However, where EMH postulates consistently rational actions, AMH acknowledges that traders and investors make mistakes and learn from those mistakes. Over a period of time, specific groups of market participants grow and evolve, while other groups are unable to adapt and eventually perish. The market environment also evolves as these groups wax and wane in influence, and this process of evolution drives market dynamics. Under the EMH, market prices reflect all available information, but the AMH points out that prices reflect all available information and the specific ecology of the market environment at that time.

The efficient markets hypothesis poses some serious questions that traders must consider. Even if the theory is not entirely correct, traders need to acknowledge that markets are usually informationally efficient. New directions in academic thinking about markets, including concepts of evolving efficiency, reflexivity, and Lo's adaptive markets hypothesis, suggest that the academic world is beginning to acknowledge that there may be legitimate opportunities for traders to profit. Markets usually trade with a high degree of randomness, and price action usually approximates some form of a random walk quite well. I suggest that the trader's job is to find those very few times when markets are something less than random, when there is an imbalance of buying and selling pressure, and when there is some degree of inefficiency. This is the first task of trading and is the point of all of our quantitative thinking about markets.

Summary

Much modern academic research suggests that markets are efficient, meaning that new information is immediately reflected in asset prices and that price movements are almost completely random. If this were true, then it would not be possible to make consistent risk-adjusted returns in excess of the baseline drift in any market. However, many studies and much empirical evidence exists that challenge the EMH, and new directions in academic thinking leave open the possibility that some skilled traders may be able to profit in some markets. Trading is not easy, for markets are very close to being efficient and price movements have a large random component. However, with skilled analysis and perfect discipline, traders can limit their involvement to those rare points where an imbalance in the market presents a profitable trading opportunity. The final two chapters of this book look at some tools for that analysis and lay out some specific market patterns that offer verifiable edges to short-term traders.

Chapter 11

Tools for Quantitative Analysis of Market Data

If someone separated the art of counting and measuring and weighing from all the other arts, what was left of each of the others would be, so to speak, insignificant.

-Plato

Many years ago I was struggling with trying to adapt to a new market and a new time frame. I had opened a brokerage account with a friend of mine who was a former floor trader on the Chicago Board of Trade (CBOT), and we spent many hours on the phone discussing philosophy, life, and markets. Doug once said to me, "You know what your problem is? The way you're trying to trade ... markets don't move like that." I said yes, I could see how that could be a problem, and then I asked the critical question: "How do markets move?" After a few seconds' reflection, he replied, "I guess I don't know, but not like that"—and that was that. I returned to this question often over the next decade—in many ways it shaped my entire thought process and approach to trading. Everything became part of the quest to answer the all-important question: how do markets really move?

Many old-school traders have a deep-seated distrust of quantitative techniques, probably feeling that numbers and analysis can never replace hard-won intuition. There is certainly some truth to that, but one of the major themes of this book is how traders can use a rigorous statistical framework to support the growth of real market intuition. Quantitative techniques allow us to peer deeply into the data and to see relationships and factors that might otherwise escape our notice. These are powerful techniques that can give us profound insight into the inner workings of markets. However, in the wrong hands or with the wrong application, they may do more harm than good. Statistical techniques can give misleading answers, and sometimes can create apparent relationships where none exist. I will try to point out some of the limitations and pitfalls of these tools as we go along, but do not accept anything at face value.

Some Market Math

It may be difficult to get excited about a chapter about market math, but these are the tools of the trade. If you want to compete, you must have the right skills and the right tools; for traders, these core skills involve a deep understanding of probabilities and market structure. Though some traders do develop this sense through the school of hard knocks, a much more direct path is through quantifying and understanding the relevant probabilities. It is impossible to do this without the right tools.

Many trading books have attempted an encyclopedic presentation of mathematical techniques, but I see little value in this. It is not a good use of your time to read a paragraph on harmonic averages in this section, never to see the term again. In fact, this may do more harm than good, as most mathematical techniques will give misleading answers if they are incorrectly applied. I have attempted a fairly in-depth examination of a few simple techniques that most traders will find to be immediately useful. If you are interested, please explore these further through some of the resources in the bibliography. For some readers, much of what follows may be review, but even these readers may see some of these concepts in a slightly different light.

The Need to Standardize

It's pop-quiz time. Here are two numbers, both of which are changes in the prices of two assets. Which is bigger: 675 or 0.01603? As you probably guessed, it's a trick question, and the best answer is: "What do you mean by bigger?" There are tens of thousands of assets trading around the world, at price levels ranging from fractions of pennies to many millions of dollars, so it is not possible to compare changes across different assets if we consider only the nominal amount of the change. Changes must at least be standardized for price levels; one common solution is to use %ages to adjust for the starting price difference between each asset.

When we do research on price patterns, the first task is usually to convert the raw prices into a return series, which may be a simple %age return calculated according to this formula:

$$\text{Percent return} = \frac{price_{today}}{price_{yesterday}} - 1$$

In academic research, it is more common to use logarithmic returns, which are also equivalent to continuously compounded returns.

$$\text{Logarithmic return} = \log\left(\frac{price_{today}}{price_{yesterday}}\right)$$

For our purposes, we can treat the two more or less interchangeably. In most of our work, the returns we deal with are very small; %age and log returns are very close for small values, but become significantly different as the sizes of the returns increase. For instance, a 1 % simple return = 0.995 % log return, but a 10 % simple return = 40.5 % continuously compounded return. Academic work tends to favor log returns because they have some mathematical qualities that make them a bit easier to work with in many contexts, but, for the sake of clarity and familiarity, I favor simple %ages in this book. It is also worth mentioning that %ages are not additive. In other words, a $10 loss followed by a $10 gain is a net zero change, but a 10 % loss followed by a 10 % gain is still a net loss. (However, logarithmic returns are additive, which is one reason why researchers prefer to use them over simple %age returns.)

Standardizing for Volatility

Using %ages is obviously preferable to using raw changes, but even % returns (from this point forward, simply "returns") may not tell the whole story. Some assets tend to move more, on average, than others. For instance, it is possible to have two currency rates, one of which moves an average of 0.5 % a day, while the other moves 2.0 % on an average day. Imagine they both move 1.5 % in the same trading session. For the first currency, this is a very large move, three times its average daily change. For the second, this is actually a small move, slightly under the average. This method of *average returns* is not a commonly used method of measuring volatility because there are better tools, but this is a simple concept that shows the basic ideas behind many of the other measures. Note that if you are going to use average % returns as a volatility measure, you must calculate the average of the absolute values of returns so that positive and negative values do not cancel each other out.

Average True Range

One of the most common ways traders measure volatility is in terms of the *average range* or *Average True Range* (ATR) of a trading session, bar, or candle on a chart. Range is a simple calculation: subtract the low of the bar (or candle) from the high to find the total range of prices covered in the trading session. The *true range* is the same as range if the previous bar's close is within the range of the current bar. However, suppose there is a gap between the previous close and the high or low of the current bar; if the previous close is higher than the current bar's high or lower than the current bar's low, that gap is added to the range calculation—true range is simply the range plus any gap from the previous close. The logic behind this is that even though the space shows as a gap on a chart, an investor holding over that period would have been exposed to the price change; the market did actually trade through those prices. Either of these values may be averaged to get average range or ATR for the asset. The choice of average length is, to some extent, a personal choice and depends on the goals of the analysis, but for most purposes, values between 20 and 90 are probably most useful.

To standardize for volatility, we could express each day's change as a %age of the ATR. For instance, if a stock has a 1.0 % change and normally trades with an ATR of 2.0 %, we can say that the day's change was a 0.5 ATR% move. We could create a series of ATR% measures for each day and average them (more properly, average their absolute values) to create an average ATR% measure. However, there is a logical inconsistency because we are comparing close-to-close changes to a measure based primarily on the range of the session, which is derived from the high and the low. In some sense, this may be comparing apples to oranges.

Historical Volatility

Historical volatility (which may also be called either *statistical* or *realized volatility*) is a good alternative for most assets, and has the added advantage that it is a measure that may be useful for options traders. Historical volatility (Hvol) is an important calculation. For daily returns:

$$Hvol = \text{StandardDeviation}\left[\ln\left(\frac{p_t}{p_{t-1}}\right)\right] * annualizationfactor,$$

$$annualizationfactor = \sqrt{252}$$

where p = price, t = this time period, $t - 1$ = previous time period, and the standard deviation is calculated over a specific window of time. Annualization factor is the square root of the ratio of the time period being measured to a year. The equation above was specifically for daily data and there are 252 trading days in a year, so the correct annualization factor is the square root of 252. For weekly and month data, the annualization factors are the square roots of 52 and 12, respectively.

For instance, using a 20-period standard deviation will give a 20-bar Hvol. Conceptually, historical volatility is an annualized one standard deviation move for the asset based on the current volatility. If an asset is trading with a 25 % historical volatility, we could expect to see prices within +/−25 % of today's price one year from now, if returns follow a zero-mean normal distribution (which they do not.)

Standard Deviation Spike Tool

The standardized measure I use most commonly in my day-to-day work is measuring each day's return as a standard deviation of the past 20 days' returns. I call this a *standard deviation spike*, and use it both visually on charts and in quantitative screens. Here is the four-step procedure for creating this measure:

1. Calculate returns for the price series.
2. Calculate the 20-day standard deviation of the returns.
3. Spike = Today's return ÷ Yesterday's BaseVariation.

Keep in mind that this tool does have the term *standard deviation* in its name, but, because it compares today's move to a very small window, extremely large standard deviation moves are not uncommon. If you have a background in statistics, you will find that your intuitions about standard deviations do not apply here, and the purpose of the tool is not to use standard deviations in any traditional concept. Even large, stable stocks will have a few five or six standard deviation moves by this measure in a single year, which would be essentially impossible if these were true standard deviations. The value is in being able to standardize price changes for easy comparison across different assets.

The way I use this tool is mainly to quantify surprise moves. Anything over about 2.5 or 3.0 would stand out visually as a large move on a price chart. After spending many years experimenting with many other volatility-adjusted measures and algorithms, this is the one that I have settled on in my day-to-day work. Note also that implied volatility usually tends to track 20-day historical volatility fairly well in most options markets. Therefore, a move that surprises this indicator will also usually surprise the options market unless there has been a ramp-up of implied volatility before an anticipated event. Options traders may find some utility in this tool as part of their daily analytical process as well.

Some Useful Statistical Measures

The market works in the language of probability and chance; though we deal with single outcomes, they are really meaningful only across large sample sizes. An entire branch of mathematics has been developed to deal with many of these problems, and the language of statistics contains powerful tools to summarize data and to understand hidden relationships. Here are a few that you will find useful.

Probability Distributions

Information on virtually any subject can be collected and quantified in a numerical format, but one of the major challenges is how to present that information in a meaningful and easy-to-comprehend format. There is always an unavoidable trade-off: any summarization will lose details that may be important, but it becomes easier to gain a sense of the data set as a whole. The challenge is to strike a balance between preserving an appropriate level of detail while creating a useful summary. Imagine, for instance, collecting the ages of every person in a large city. If we simply printed the list out and loaded it onto a tractor trailer, it would be difficult to say anything much more meaningful than "That's a lot of numbers you have there." It is the job of descriptive statistics to say things about groups of numbers that give us some more insight. To do this successfully, we must organize and strip the data set down to its important elements.

One very useful tool is the histogram chart. To create a histogram, we take the raw data and sort it into categories (bins) that are evenly spaced throughout the data set. The more bins we use, the finer the resolution, but the choice of how many bins to use usually depends on what we are trying to illustrate. Figure 11.1 shows histograms for the daily % changes of LULU, a volatile momentum stock, and SPY, the S&P 500 index. As traders, one of the key things we are interested in is the number of events near the edges of the distribution, in the tails, because they represent both exceptional opportunities and risks. The histogram charts show that that the distribution for LULU has a much wider spread, with many more days showing large upward and downward price changes than SPY. To a trader, this suggests that LULU might be much more volatile, a much crazier stock to trade.

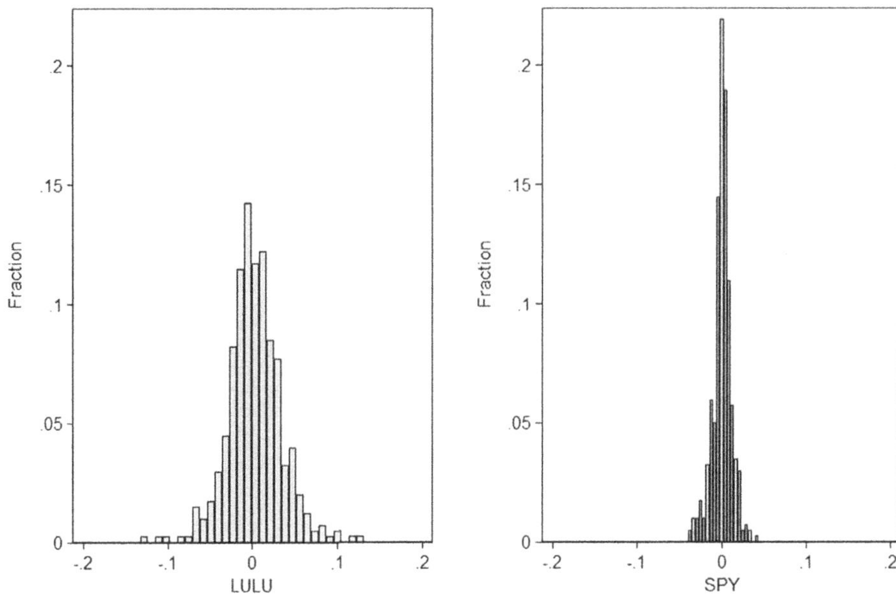

Figure 11.1 Return Distributions for LULU and SPY, June 1, 2009, to December 31, 2010

The Normal Distribution

Most people are familiar, at least in passing, with a special distribution called the *normal distribution* or, less formally, the *bell curve*. This distribution is used in many applications for a few good reasons. First, it really does describe an astonishingly wide range of phenomena in the natural world, from physics to astronomy to sociology. If we collect data on people's heights, speeds of water currents, or income distributions in neighborhoods, there is a very good chance that the normal distribution will describe that data well. Second, it has some qualities that make it very easy to use in simulations and models. This is a double-edged sword because it is so easy to use that we are tempted to use it in places where it might not apply so well. Last, it is used in the field of statistics because of something called the *central limit* theorem, which is slightly outside the scope of this book. (If you're wondering, the central limit theorem says that the means of random samples from populations with any distribution will tend to follow the normal distribution, providing the population has a finite mean and variance. Most of the assumptions of inferential statistics rest on this concept. If you are interested in digging deeper, see Snedecor and Cochran's *Statistical Methods* [1989].)

Figure 11.2 shows several different normal distribution curves, all with a mean of zero but with different standard deviations. The standard deviation, which we will investigate in more detail shortly, simply describes the spread of the distribution. In the LULU/SPY example, LULU had a much larger standard deviation than SPY, so the histogram was spread further across the x-axis. Two final points on the normal distribution before moving on: Do not focus too much on what the graph of the normal curve looks like, because many other distributions have essentially the same shape; do not assume that anything that looks like a bell curve is normally distributed. Last, and this is very important, normal distributions do an exceptionally poor job of describing financial data. If we were to rely on assumptions of normality in trading and market-related situations, we would dramatically underestimate the risks involved. This, in fact, has been a contributing factor in several recent financial crises over the past two decades, as models and risk management frameworks relying on normal distributions failed.

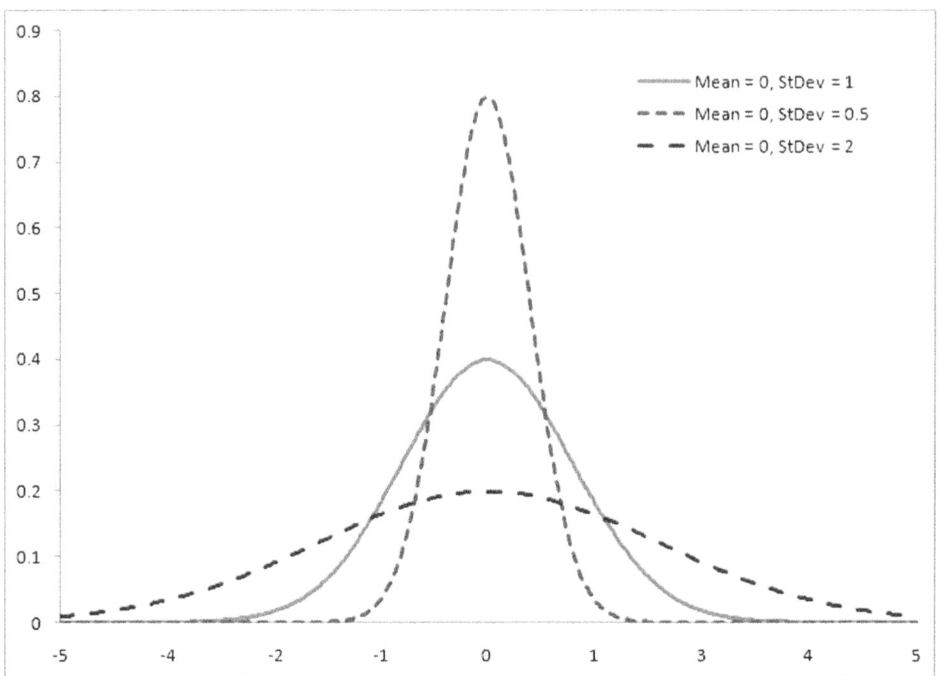

Figure 11.2 Three Normal Distributions with Different Standard Deviations

Measures of Central Tendency

Looking at a graph can give us some ideas about the characteristics of the data set, but looking at a graph is not actual analysis. A few simple calculations can summarize and describe the data set in useful ways. First, we can look at measures of *central tendency*, which describe how the data clusters around a specific value or values. Each of the distributions in Figure 11.2 has identical central tendency; this is why they are all centered vertically around the same point on the graph. One of the most commonly used measures of central tendency is the *mean*, which is simply the sum of all the values divided by the number of values. The mean is sometimes simply called the average, but this is an imprecise term as there are actually several different kinds of averages that are used to summarize the data in different ways.

For instance, imagine that we have five people in a room, ages 18, 22, 25, 33, and 38. The mean age of this group of people is 27.2 years. Ask yourself: How good a representation is this mean? Does it describe those data well? In this case, it seems to do a pretty good job. There are about as many people on either side of the mean, and the mean is roughly in the middle of the data set. Even though there is no one person who is exactly 27.2 years old, if you have to guess the age of a person in the group, 27.2 years would actually be a pretty good guess. In this example, the mean describes the data set well.

Another important measure of central tendency is the median, which is found by ranking the values from smallest to largest and taking the middle value in the set. If there is an even number of data points, then there is no middle value, and in this case the median is calculated as the mean of the two middle data points. (This is usually not important except in small data sets, but it is important to understand this small refinement.) In our example, the median age is 25, which at first glance also seems to explain the data well. If you had to guess the age of any random person in the group, both 25 and 27.2 would be reasonable guesses.

Why do we have two different measures of central tendency? One reason is that they handle outliers, which are extreme values in the tails of distributions, differently. Imagine that a 3,000-year-old mummy is brought into the room (it sometimes helps to consider absurd situations when trying to build intuition about these things). If we include the mummy in the group, the mean age jumps to 522.7 years. However, the median (now between 25 and 33) only increases four years to 29. Means tend to be very responsive to large values in the tails, while medians are little affected. The mean is now a poor description of the data set—no one alive is close to 522.7 years old! The mummy is far older and everyone else is far younger, so the mean is now a bad guess for anyone's age. The median of 29 is more likely to get us closer to someone's age if we are guessing, but, as in all things, there is a trade-off: The median is completely blind to the outlier. If we add a single value and see the mean jump nearly 500 years, we certainly know that a large value has been added to the data set, but we do not get this information from the median. Depending on what you are trying to accomplish, one measure might be better than the other.

If the mummy's age in our example were actually 3,000,000 years, the median age would still be 29 years, and the mean age would now be a little over 500,000 years. The number 500,000 in this case does not really say anything meaningful about the data at all. It is nearly irrelevant to the five original people, and vastly understates the age of the (extraterrestrial?) mummy. In market data, we often deal with data sets that feature a handful of extreme events, so we will often need to look at both median and mean values in our examples. Again, this is not idle theory; these are important concepts with real-world application and meaning.

Measures of Dispersion

Measures of dispersion are used to describe how far the data points are spread from the central values. A commonly used measure is the *standard deviation*, which is calculated by first finding the mean for the data set, and then squaring the differences between each individual point and the mean. Taking the mean of those squared differences gives the variance of the set, which is not useful for most market applications because it is in units of price squared. One more operation, taking the square root of the variance, yields the standard deviation. If we were to simply add the differences without squaring them, some would be negative and some positive, which would have a canceling effect. Squaring them makes them all positive and also greatly magnifies the effect of outliers. It is important to understand this because, again, this may or may not be a good thing. Also, remember that the standard deviation depends on the mean in its calculation. If the data set is one for which the mean is not meaningful (or is undefined), then the standard deviation is also not meaningful.

Market data and trading data often have large outliers, so this magnification effect may not be desirable. Another useful measure of dispersion is the interquartile range (IQR), which is calculated by first ranking the data set from largest to smallest, and then identifying the 25th and 75th %iles. Subtracting the 25th from the 75th (the first and third quartiles) gives the range within which half the values in the data set fall—another name for the IQR is the *middle 50*, the range of the middle 50 % of the values. Where standard deviation is extremely sensitive to outliers, the IQR is almost completely blind to them. Using the two together can give more insight into the characteristics of complex distributions generated from analysis of trading problems. Table 11.1 compares measures of central tendency and dispersions for the three age-related scenarios. Notice especially how the mean and the standard deviation both react to the addition of the large outliers in examples 2 and 3, while the median and the IQR are virtually unchanged.

Table 11.1 Comparison of Summary Statistics for the Age Problem

	Example 1	Example 2	Example 3
Person 1	18	18	18
Person 2	22	22	22
Person 3	25	25	25
Person 4	33	33	33
Person 5	38	38	38
The Mummy	Not present	3,000	3,000,000
Mean	27.2	522.7	500,022.7
Median	25.0	29.0	29.0
Standard Deviation	7.3	1,107.9	1,118,023.9
IQR	3.0	6.3	6.3

Inferential Statistics

Though a complete review of inferential statistics is beyond the scope of this brief introduction, it is worthwhile to review some basic concepts and to think about how they apply to market problems. Broadly, inferential statistics is the discipline of drawing conclusions about a population based on a sample from that population, or, more immediately relevant to markets, drawing conclusions about data sets that are subject to some kind of random process. As a simple example, imagine we wanted to know the average weight of all the apples in an orchard. Given enough time, we might well collect every single apple, weigh each of them, and find the average. This approach is impractical in most situations because we cannot, or do not care to, collect every member of the *population* (the statistical term to refer to every member of the set). More commonly, we will draw a small *sample*, calculate statistics for the sample, and make some well-educated guesses about the population based on the qualities of the sample.

This is not as simple as it might seem at first. In the case of the orchard example, what if there were several varieties of trees planted in the orchard that gave different sizes of apples? Where and how we pick up the sample apples will make a big difference, so this must be carefully considered. How many sample apples are needed to get a good idea about the population statistics? What does the distribution of the population look like? What is the average of that population? How sure can we be of our guesses based on our sample? An entire school of statistics has evolved to answer questions like this, and a solid background in these methods is very helpful for the market researcher.

For instance, assume in the apple problem that the weight of an average apple in the orchard is 4.5 ounces and that the weights of apples in the orchard follow a normal bell curve distribution with a standard deviation of 3 ounces. (Note that this is information that you would not know at the beginning of the experiment; otherwise, there would be no reason to do any measurements at all.) Assume we pick up two apples from the orchard, average their weights, and record the value; then we pick up one more, average the weights of all three, and so on, until we have collected 20 apples. (For the following discussion, the weights really were generated randomly, and we were pretty unlucky—the very first apple we picked up was a small one and weighed only 1.07 ounces. Furthermore, the apple discussion is only an illustration. These numbers were actually generated with a random number generator so some negative numbers are included in the sample. Obviously, negative weight apples are not possible in the real world, but were necessary for the latter part of this example using Cauchy distributions.) If we graph the running average of the weights for these first 20 apples, we get a line that looks like Figure 11.3.

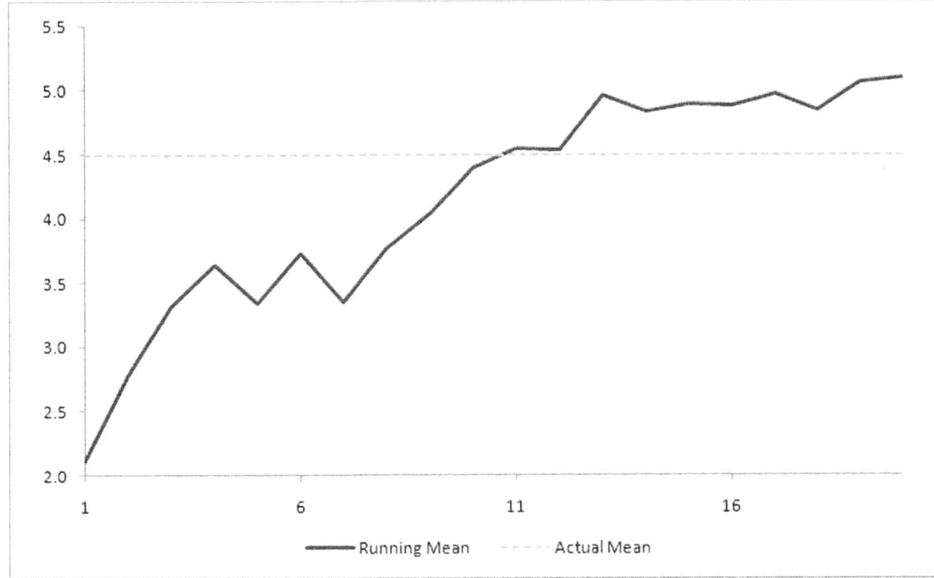

Figure 11.3 Running Mean of the First 20 Apples Picked Up

What guesses might we make about all the apples in the orchard based on this sample so far? Well, we might reasonably be a little confused because we would expect the line to be settling in on an average value, but, in this case, it actually seems to be trending higher, not converging. Though we would not know it at the time, this effect is due to the impact of the unlucky first apple; similar issues sometimes arise in real-world applications. Perhaps a sample of 20 apples is not enough to really understand the population; Figure 11.4 shows what happens if we continue, eventually picking up 100 apples.

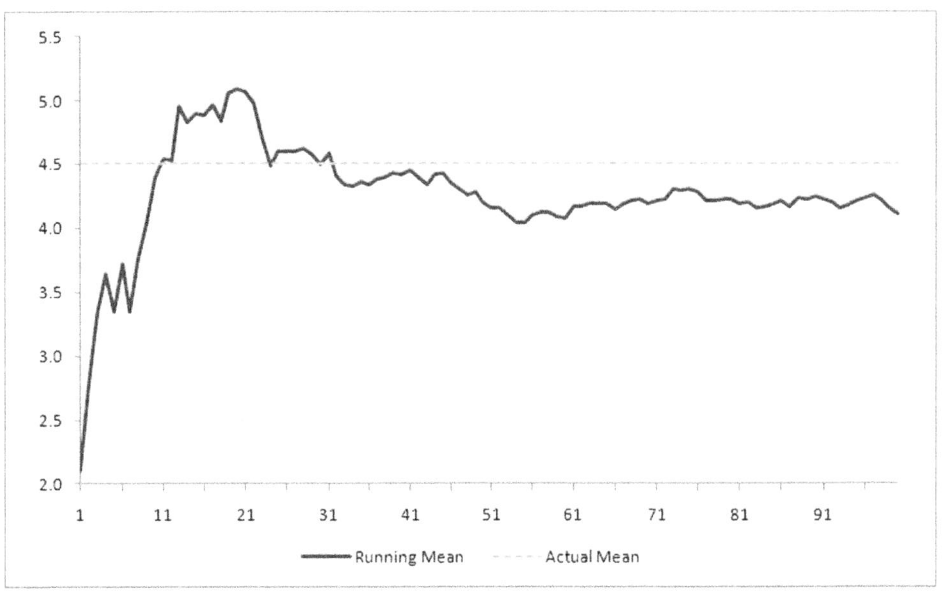

Figure 11.4 Running Mean of the First 100 Apples Picked Up

At this point, the line seems to be settling in on a value, and maybe we are starting to be a little more confident about the average apple. Based on the graph, we still might guess that the value is actually closer to 4 than to 4.5, but this is just a result of the random sample process—the sample is not yet large enough to assure that the sample mean converges on the actual mean. We have picked up some small apples that have skewed the overall sample, which can also happen in the real world. (Actually, remember that "apples" is only a convenient label and that these values do include some negative numbers, which would not be possible with real apples.) If we pick up many more, the sample average eventually does converge on the population average of 4.5 very closely. Figure 11.5 shows what the running total might look like after a sample of 2,500 apples.

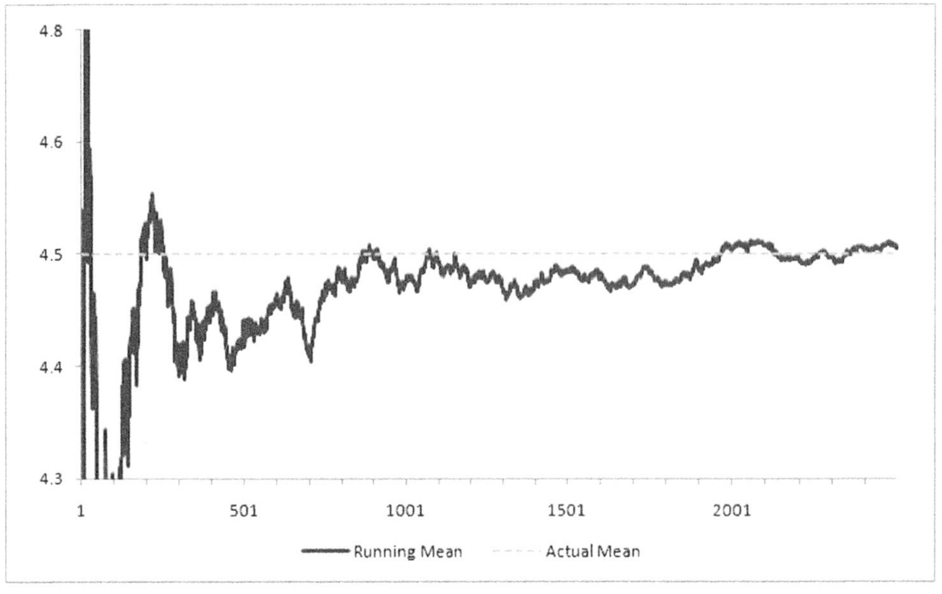

Figure 11.5 Running Mean After 2,500 Apples Have Been Picked Up (Y-Axis Truncated to Show Only Values Near 4.5)

With apples, the problem seems trivial, but in application to market data there are some thorny issues to consider. One critical question that needs to be considered first is so simple it is often overlooked: what is the population and what is the sample? When we have a long data history on an asset (consider the Dow Jones Industrial Average, which began its history in 1896, or some commodities for which we have spotty price data going back to the 1400s), we might assume that that full history represents the population, but I think this is a mistake. It is probably more correct to assume that the population is the set of *all possible returns*, both observed and as yet unobserved, for that specific market. The population is everything that has happened, everything that will happen, and also everything that *could* happen—a daunting concept. All market history—in fact, all market history that will ever be in the future—is only a sample of that much larger population. The question, for risk managers and traders alike, is: what does that unobservable population look like?

In the simple apple problem, we assumed the weights of apples would follow the normal bell curve distribution, but the real world is not always so polite. There are other possible distributions, and some of them contain nasty surprises. For instance, there are families of distributions that have such strange characteristics that the distribution actually has no mean value. Though this might seem counterintuitive and you might ask the question "How can there be no average?" consider the admittedly silly case earlier that included the 3,000,000-year-old mummy. How useful was the mean in describing that data set? Extend that concept to consider what would happen if there were a large number of ages that could be *infinitely* large or small in the set? The mean would move constantly in response to these very large and small values, and would be an essentially useless concept.

The Cauchy family of distributions is a set of probability distributions that have such extreme outliers that the mean for the distribution is undefined, and the variance is infinite. If this is the way the financial world works, if these types of distributions really describe the population of all possible price changes, then, as one of my colleagues who is a risk manager so eloquently put it, "we're all screwed in the long run." If the apples were actually Cauchy-distributed (obviously not a possibility in the physical world of apples, but play along for a minute), then the running mean of a sample of 100 apples might look like Figure 11.6.

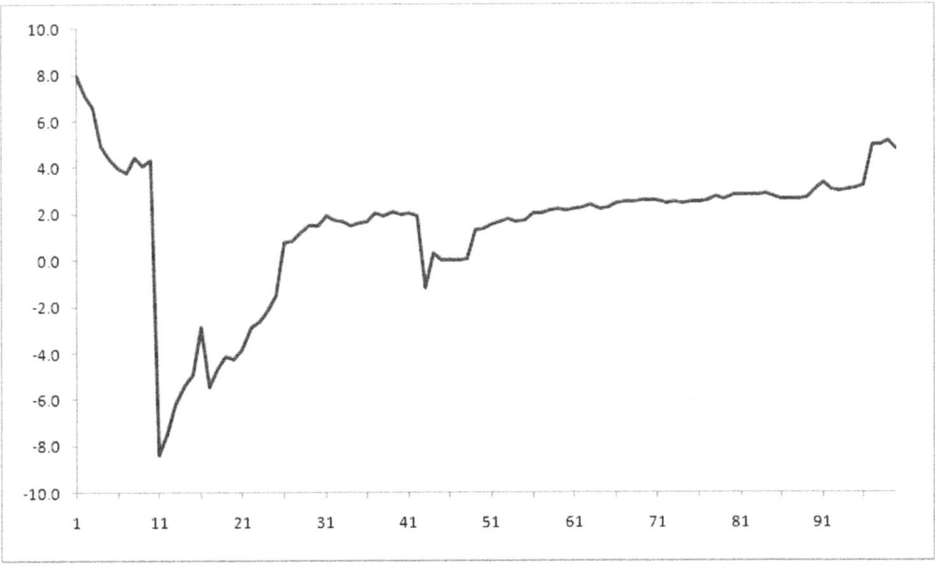

Figure 11.6 Running Mean for 100 Cauchy-Distributed Random Numbers

It is difficult to make a good guess about the average based on this graph, but more data usually results in a better estimate. Usually, the more data we collect, the more certain we are of the outcome, and the more likely our values will converge on the theoretical targets. Alas, in this case, more data actually adds to the confusion. Based on Figure 11.6, it would have been reasonable to assume that something strange was going on, but, if we had to guess, somewhere in the middle of graph, maybe around 2.0, might have been a reasonable guess for the mean. Let's see what happens if we decide to collect 10,000 Cauchy-distributed numbers in an effort to increase our confidence in the estimate (see Figure 11.7).

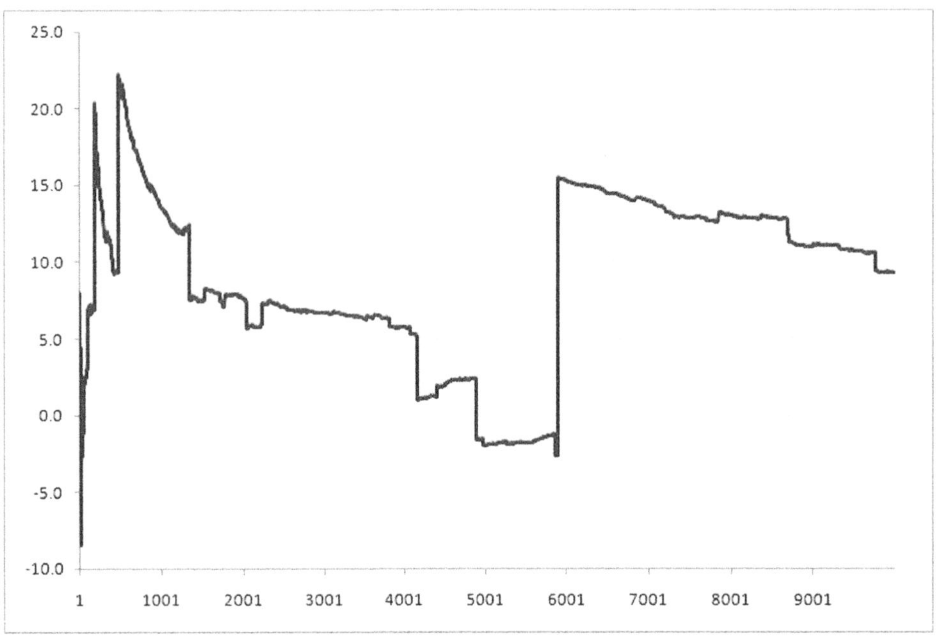

Figure 11.7 Running Mean for 10,000 Random Numbers Drawn from a Cauchy Distribution

Ouch—maybe we should have stopped at 100. As the sample gets larger, we pick up more very large events from the tails of the distribution, and it starts to become obvious that we have no idea what the actual, underlying average might be. (Remember, there actually is no mean for this distribution.) Here, at a sample size of 10,000, it looks like the average will simply never settle down—it is always in danger of being influenced by another very large outlier at any point in the future. As a final word on this subject, Cauchy distributions have undefined means, but the median is defined. In this case, the median of the distribution was 4.5—Figure 11.8 shows what would have happened had we tried to find the median instead of the mean. Now maybe the reason we look at both means and medians in market data is a little clearer.

Three Statistical Tools

The previous discussion may have been a bit abstract, but it is important to think deeply about fundamental concepts. Here is some good news: some of the best tools for market analysis are the most simple. It is tempting to use complex techniques, but it is easy to get lost in statistical intricacies and to lose sight of what is really important. In addition, many complex statistical tools bring their own set of potential complications and issues to the table. A good example is data mining, which is perfectly capable of finding nonexistent patterns in random data. It is fair to say that nearly all of your market analysis can probably be done with basic arithmetic and with concepts no more complicated than measures of central tendency and dispersion. This section introduces three simple tools that should be part of every trader's tool kit: bin analysis, linear regression, and Monte Carlo modeling.

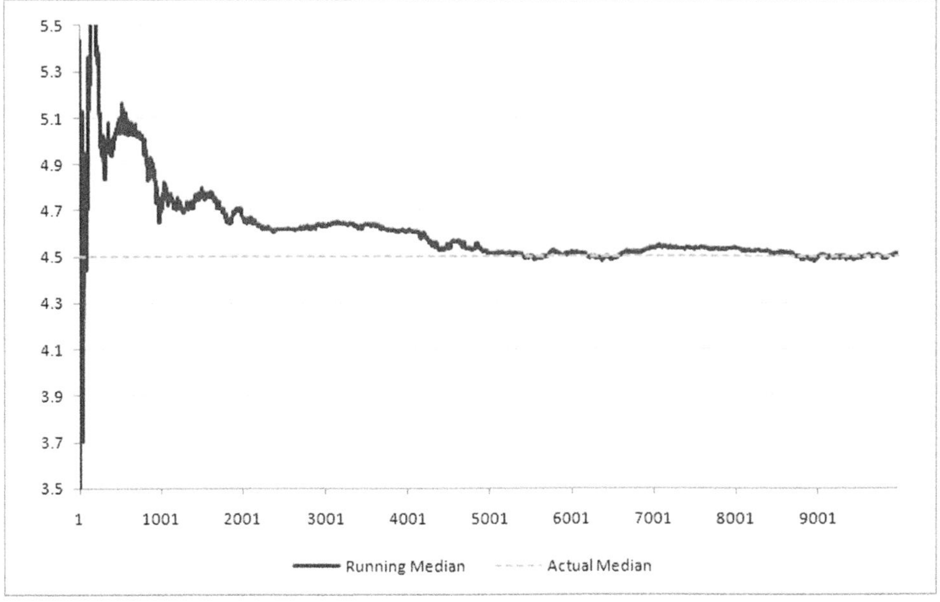

Figure 11.8 Running Median for 10,000 Cauchy-Distributed Random Numbers

Statistical Bin Analysis

Statistical bin analysis is by far the simplest and most useful of the three techniques in this section. If we can clearly define a condition we are interested in testing, we can divide the data set into groups that contain the condition, called the signal group, and those that do not, called the control group. We can then calculate simple statistics for these groups and compare them. One very simple test would be to see if the signal group has a higher mean and median return compared to the control group, but we could also consider other attributes of the two groups. For instance, some traders believe that there are reliable tendencies for some days of the week to be stronger or weaker than others in the stock market. Table 11.2 shows one way to investigate that idea by dividing the returns for the Dow Jones Industrial Average in 2010 by weekdays. The table shows both the mean return for each weekday as well as the %age of days that close higher than the previous day.

Table 11.2 Day-of-Week Stats for the DJIA, 2010

Weekday	% Close Up	Mean Return
Monday	59.57%	0.22%
Tuesday	53.85%	(0.05%)
Wednesday	61.54%	0.18%
Thursday	54.90%	(0.00%)
Friday	54.00%	(0.14%)
All	56.75%	0.04%

Each weekday's statistics are significant only in comparison to the larger group. The mean daily return was very small, but 56.75 % of all days closed higher than the previous day. Practically, if we were to randomly sample a group of days from this year, we would probably find that about 56.75 % of them closed higher than the previous day, and the mean return for the days in our sample would be very close to zero. Of course, we might get unlucky in the sample and find that it has very large or small values, but, if we took a large enough sample or many small samples, the values would probably (very probably) converge on these numbers. The table shows that Wednesday and Monday both have a higher %age of days that closed up than did the baseline. In addition, the mean return for both of these days is quite a bit higher than the baseline 0.04 %. Based on this sample, it appears that Monday and Wednesday are strong days for the stock market, and Friday appears to be prone to sell-offs.

Are we done? Can the book just end here with the message that you should buy on Friday, sell on Monday, and then buy on Tuesday's close and sell on Wednesday's close? Well, one thing to remember is that, no matter how accurate our math is, it describes only the data set we examine. In this case, we are looking at only one year of market data, which could possibly not be enough; perhaps some things change year to year and we need to look at more data. Before executing any idea in the market, it is important to see if it has been stable over time and to think about whether there is a reason it should persist in the future. Table 11.3 examines the same day-of-week tendencies for the year 2009.

Table 11.3 Day-of-Week Stats for the DJIA, 2009

Weekday	% Close Up	Mean Return
Monday	56.25%	0.02%
Tuesday	48.08%	(0.03%)
Wednesday	53.85%	0.16%
Thursday	58.82%	0.19%
Friday	53.06%	(0.00%)
All	53.97%	0.07%

Well, if we expected to find a simple trading system, it looks like we may be disappointed. In the 2009 data set, Mondays still seem to have a higher probability of closing up, but Mondays actually have a lower than *average* return. Wednesdays still have a mean return more than twice the average for all days, but, in this sample, Wednesdays are actually *more likely to close* down than the average day is. Based on 2010, Friday was identified as a potentially soft day for the market, but in the 2009 data, it is absolutely in line with the average for all days. We could continue the analysis by considering other measures and using more advanced statistical tests, but this example suffices to illustrate the concept. Sometimes just dividing the data and comparing summary statistics are enough to answer many questions, or at least to flag ideas that are worthy of further analysis.

Significance Testing

This discussion is not complete without some brief consideration of *significance testing*, but this is a complex topic that even creates dissension among many mathematicians and statisticians. The basic concept in significance testing is that the random variation in data sets must be considered when the results of any test are evaluated, because interesting results sometimes appear by random chance. As a simplified example, imagine that we have large bags of numbers, and we are only allowed to pull numbers out one at a time to examine them. We cannot simply open the bags and look inside; we have to pull samples of numbers out of the bags, examine the samples, and make educated guesses about what the populations inside the bag might look like. Now imagine that you have two samples of numbers and the question you are interested in is: "Did these samples come from the same bag (population)?" If you examine one sample and find that it consists of all 2s, 3s, and 4s, and you compare that with another sample that includes numbers from 20 to 40, it is probably reasonable to conclude that they came from different bags.

This is a pretty clear-cut example, but it is not always this simple. What if you have a sample that has the same number of 2s, 3s, and 4s, so that the average of this group is 3, and you are comparing it to another group that has a few more 4s, so the average of that group is 3.2? How likely is it that you simply got unlucky and pulled some extra 4s out of the same bag as the first sample, or is it more likely that the group with extra 4s actually did come from a separate bag? The answer depends on many factors, but one of the most important in this case would be the sample size, or how many numbers we drew. The larger the sample, the more certain we can be that small variations like this probably represent real differences in the population.

Significance testing provides a formalized way to ask and answer questions like this. Most statistical tests approach questions in a specific, scientific way that can be a little cumbersome if you haven't seen it before. In nearly all significance testing, the initial assumption is that the two samples being compared did in fact come from the same population, that there is no real difference between the two groups. This assumption is called the null hypothesis. We assume that the two groups are the same, and then look for evidence that contradicts that assumption. Most significance tests consider measures of central tendency, dispersion, and the sample sizes for both groups, but the key is that the burden of proof lies in the data that would contradict the assumption. If we are not able to find sufficient evidence to contradict the initial assumption, the null hypothesis is accepted as true, and we assume that there is no difference between the two groups. Of course, it is possible that they actually are different and our experiment simply failed to find sufficient evidence. For this reason, we are careful to say something like "We were unable to find sufficient evidence to contradict the null hypothesis," rather than "We have proven that there is no difference between the two groups." This is a subtle but extremely important distinction.

Most significance tests report a *p*-value, which is the probability that a result at least as extreme as the observed result would have occurred if the null hypothesis were true. This might be slightly confusing, but it is done this way for a reason; it is very important to think about the test precisely. A low *p*-value would say that, for instance, there would be less than a 0.1 % chance of seeing a result at least this extreme if the samples came from the same population, if the null hypothesis were true. It could happen, but it is unlikely, so, in this case, we say we reject the null hypothesis, and assume that the samples came from different populations. On the other hand, if the *p*-value says there is a 50 % chance that the observed results could have appeared if the null hypothesis were true, that is not very convincing evidence against it. In this case, we would say that we have not found significant evidence to reject the null hypothesis, so we cannot say with any confidence that the samples came from different populations. In actual practice, the researcher has to pick a cutoff level for the *p*-value (5 % and 1 % are common thresholds, but this is only due to convention.) There are trade-offs to both high and low *p*-values, so the chosen significance level should be carefully considered in the context of the data and the experiment design.

These examples have focused on the case of determining whether two samples came from different populations, but it is also possible to examine other hypotheses. For instance, we could use a significance test to determine whether the mean of a group is higher than zero. Consider one sample that has a mean return of 2 % and a standard deviation of 0.5 %, compared to another that has a mean return of 2 % and a standard deviation of 5 %. The first sample has a mean that is 4 standard deviations above zero, which is very likely to be significant, while the second has so much more variation that the mean is well within one standard deviation of zero. This, and other questions, can be formally examined through significance tests. Return to the case of Mondays in 2010 (Table 11.2), which have a mean return of 0.22 % versus a mean of 0.04 % for all days. This might appear to be a large difference, but the standard deviation of returns for all days is over 1 %. With this information, Monday's outperformance is seen to be less than one-fifth of a standard deviation—certainly well within the noise level and not statistically significant.

Significance testing is not a substitute for common sense and can be misleading if the experiment design is not carefully considered. (Technical note: The *t-test* is a commonly used significance test, but be aware that market data usually violates the *t-test*'s assumptions of normality and independence. Nonparametric alternatives may provide more reliable results.) One other issue to consider is that we may find edges that are statistically significant (i.e., they pass significance tests), but they may not be *economically significant* because the effects are too small to capture reliably. In the case of Mondays in 2010, the outperformance was only 0.18 %, which is equal to $0.18 on a $100 stock. Is this a large enough edge to exploit? The answer will depend on the individual trader's execution ability and cost structure, but this is a question that must be considered.

Linear Regression

Linear regression is a tool that can help us understand the magnitude, direction, and strength of relationships between markets. This is not a statistics textbook; many of the details and subtleties of linear regression are outside the scope of this book. Any mathematical tool has limitations, potential pitfalls, and blind spots, and most make assumptions about the data being used as inputs. If these assumptions are violated, the procedure can give misleading or false results, or, in some cases, some assumptions may be violated with impunity and the results may not be much affected. If you are interested in doing analytical work to augment your own trading, then it is probably worthwhile to spend some time educating yourself on the finer points of using this tool. Miles and Shevlin (2000) provide a good introduction that is both accessible and thorough—a rare combination in the literature.

Linear Equations and Error Factors

Before we can dig into the technique of using linear equations and error factors, we need to review some math. You may remember that the equation for a straight line on a graph is:

$$y = mx + b$$

This equation gives a value for y, to be plotted on the vertical axis, as a function of x, the number on the horizontal axis; x is multiplied by m, which is the slope of the line; higher values of m produce a more steeply sloping line. If $m = 0$, the line will be flat on the x-axis, because every value of x multiplied by 0 is 0. If m is negative, the line will slope downward. Figure 11.9 shows three different lines with different slopes. The variable b in the equation moves the whole line up and down on the y-axis. Formally, it defines the point at which the line will intersect the y-axis where $x = 0$, because the value of the line at that point will be only b. (Any number multiplied by x

when $x = 0$ is 0.) We can safely ignore b for this discussion, and Figure 11.9 sets $b = 0$ for each of the lines. Your intuition needs to be clear on one point: the slope of the line is steeper with higher values for m; it slopes upward for positive values and downward for negative values.

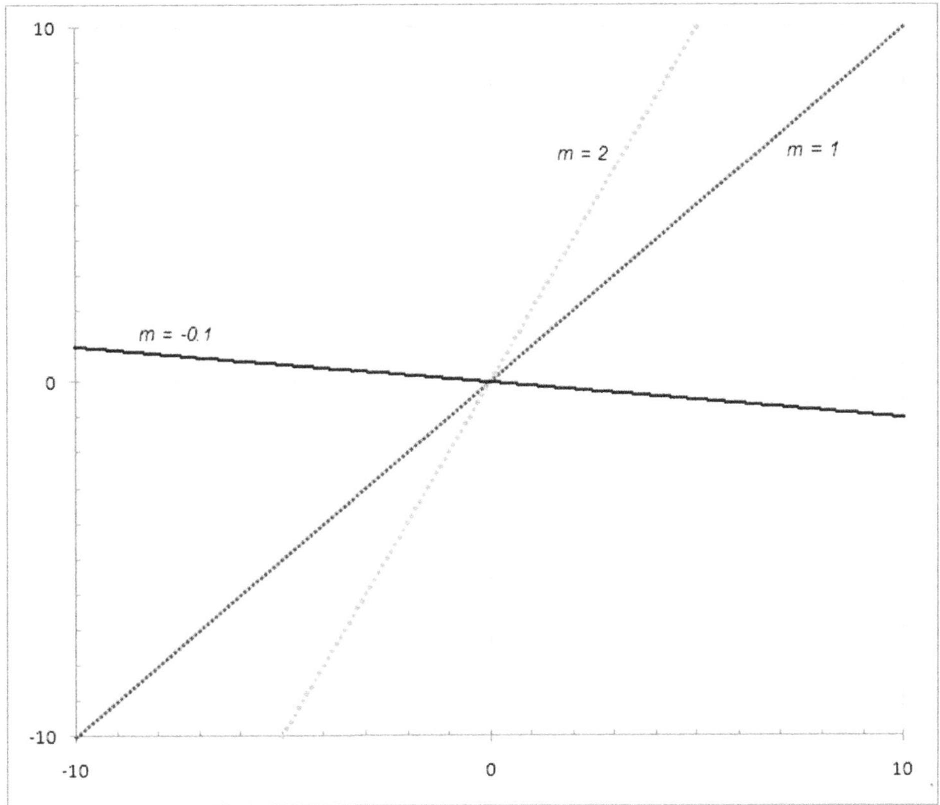

Figure 11.9 Three Lines with Different Slopes

One more piece of information can make this simple, idealized equation much more useful. In the real world, relationships do not fall along perfect, simple lines. The real world is messy—noise and measurement error obfuscate the real underlying relationships, sometimes even hiding them completely. Look at the equation for a line one more time, but with one added variable:

$$y = mx + b + \varepsilon$$
$$\varepsilon \sim \text{i.i.d. } N(0, \sigma)$$

The new variable is the Greek letter epsilon, which is commonly used to describe error measurements in time series and other processes. The second line of the equation (which can be ignored if the notation is unfamiliar) says that ε is a random variable whose values are drawn from (formally, are "independent and identically distributed [i.i.d.] according to") the normal distribution with a mean of zero and a standard deviation of sigma. If we graph this, it will produce a line with jitter, as the points will be randomly distributed above and below the actual line because a different, random ε is added to each data point. The magnitude of the jitter, or how far above and below the line the points are scattered, will be determined by the value of the standard deviation chosen for σ. Bigger values will result in more spread, as the distribution for the error component has more extreme values (see

Figure 11.2 for a reminder.) Every time we draw this line it will be different, because ε is a random variable that takes on different values; this is a big step if you are used to thinking of equations only in a deterministic way. With the addition of this one term, the simple equation for a line now becomes a random process; this one step is actually a big leap forward because we are now dealing with uncertainty and stochastic (random) processes.

Figure 11.10 shows two sets of points calculated from this equation. The slope for both sets is the same, $m = 1$, but the standard deviation of the error term is different. The solid dots were plotted with a standard deviation of 0.5, and they all lie very close to the true, underlying line; the empty circles were plotted with a standard deviation of 4.0, and they scatter much farther from the line. More variability hides the underlying line, which is the same in both cases—this type of variability is common in real market data, and can complicate any analysis.

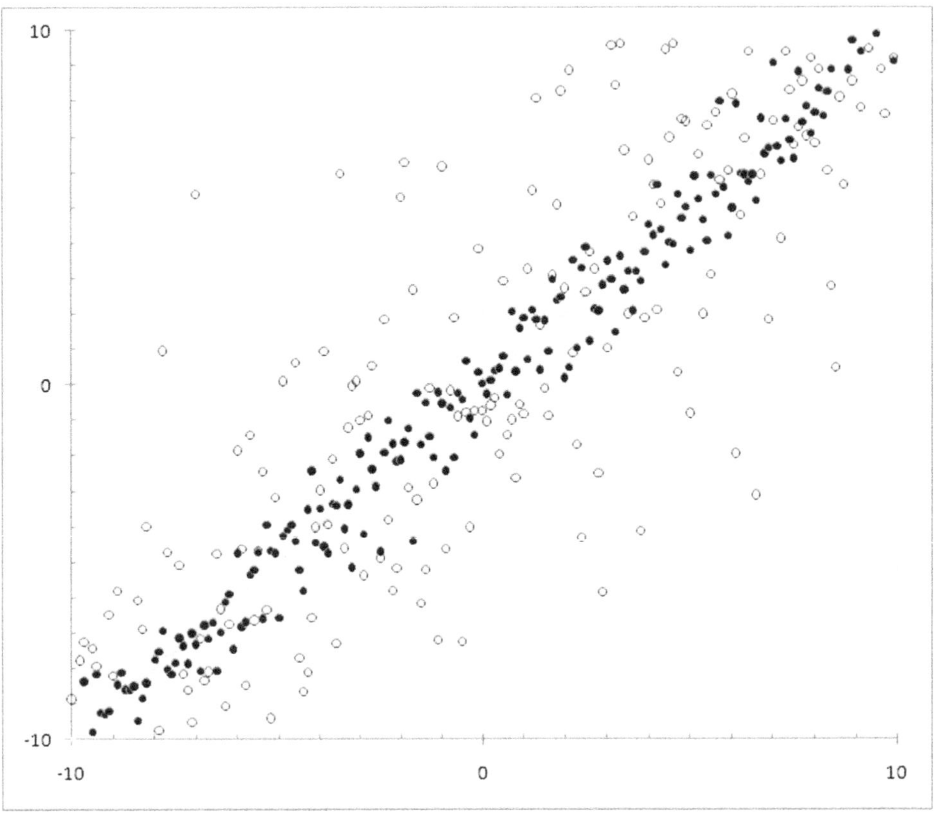

Figure 11.10 Two Lines with Different Standard Deviations for the Error Terms

Regression

With this background, we now have the knowledge needed to understand regression. Here is an example of a question that might be explored through regression: Barrick Gold Corporation (NYSE: ABX) is a company that explores for, mines, produces, and sells gold. A trader might be interested in knowing if, and how much, the price of physical gold influences the price of this stock. Upon further reflection, the trader might also be interested in knowing what, if any, influence the U.S. Dollar Index and the overall stock market (using the S&P 500 index again as a proxy for the entire market) have on ABX. We collect weekly prices from January 2, 2009, to December 31, 2010, and, just like in the earlier example, create a return series for each asset. It is always a good idea to start any analysis by examining summary statistics for each series. (See Table 11.4.)

Table 11.4 Summary Statistics for Weekly Returns, 2009–2010

Ticker	N=	Mean	StDev	Min	Max
ABX	104	0.4%	5.8%	(20.0%)	16.0%
SPX	104	0.3%	3.0%	(7.3%)	10.2%
Gold	104	0.4%	2.3%	(5.4%)	6.2%
USD	104	0.0%	1.3%	(4.2%)	3.1%

At a glance, we can see that ABX, the S&P 500 (SPX), and Gold all have nearly the same mean return. ABX is considerably more volatile, having at least one instance where it lost 20 % of its value in a single week. Any data series with this much variation, measured by a comparison of the standard deviation to the mean return, has a lot of noise. It is important to notice this, because this noise may hinder the usefulness of any analysis.

A good next step would be to create scatterplots of each of these inputs against ABX, or perhaps a matrix of all possible scatterplots as in Figure 11.11. The question to ask is which, if any, of these relationships looks like it might be hiding a straight line inside it; which lines suggest a linear relationship? There are several potentially interesting relationships in this table: the Gold/ABX box actually appears to be a very clean fit to a straight line, but the ABX/SPX box also suggests some slight hint of an upward-sloping line. Though it is difficult to say with certainty, the USD boxes seem to suggest slightly downward-sloping lines, while the SPX/Gold box appears to be a cloud with no clear relationship. Based on this initial analysis, it seems likely that we will find the strongest relationships between ABX and Gold and between ABX and the S&P. We also should check the ABX and U.S. Dollar relationship, though there does not seem to be as clear an influence there.

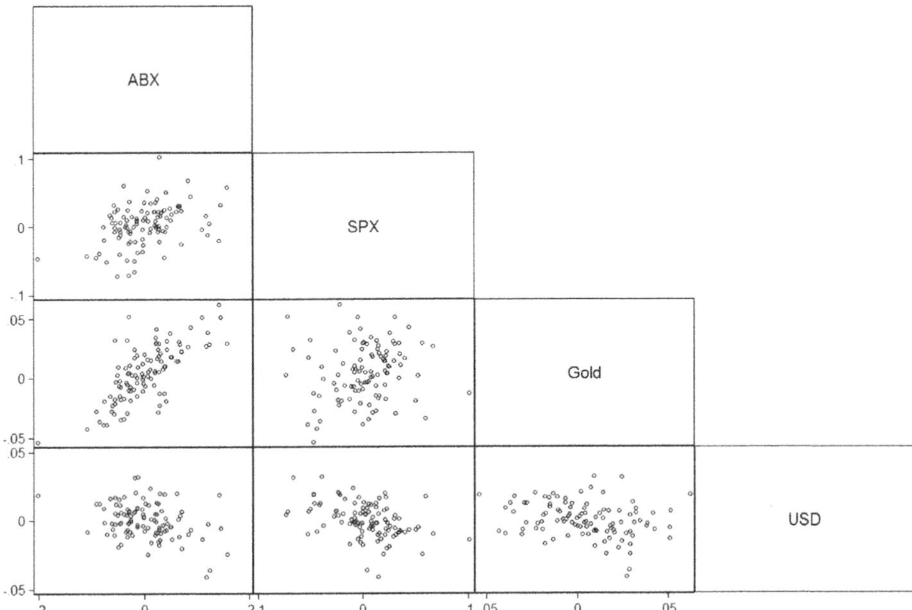

Figure 11.11 Scatterplot Matrix (Weekly Returns, 2009–2010)

Regression actually works by taking a scatterplot and drawing a best-fit line through it. You do not need to worry about the details of the mathematical process; no one does this by hand, because it could take weeks to months to do a single large regression that a computer could do in a fraction of a second. Conceptually, think of it like this: a line is drawn on the graph through the middle of the cloud of points, and then the distance from each point to the line is measured. (Remember the ε's that we generated in Figure 11.11? This is the reverse of that process: we draw a line through preexisting points and then measure the ε's (often called the errors).) These measurements are squared, by essentially the same logic that leads us to square the errors in the standard deviation formula, and then the sum of all the squared errors is calculated. Another line is drawn on the chart, and the measuring and squaring processes are repeated. (This is not precisely correct. Some types of regression are done by a trial-and-error process, but the particular type described here has a closed-form solution that does not require an iterative process.) The line that minimizes the sum of the squared errors is kept as the best fit, which is why this method is also called a *least-squares* model. Figure 11.12 shows this best-fit line on a scatterplot of ABX versus Gold.

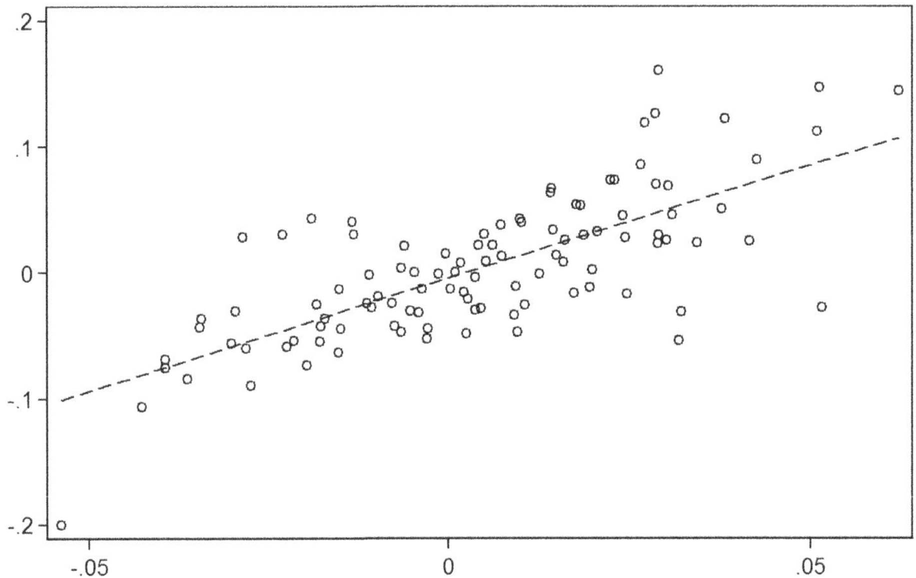

Figure 11.12 Best-Fit Line on Scatterplot of ABX (Y-Axis) and Gold

We now look at a simplified regression output, focusing on the three most important elements. The first is the slope of the regression line (*m*), which explains the strength and direction of the influence. If this number is greater than zero, then the dependent variable increases with increasing values of the independent variable. If it is negative, the reverse is true. Second, the regression also reports a *p*-value for this slope, which is important. We should approach any analysis *expecting* to find no relationship; in the case of a best-fit line, a line that shows no relationship would be flat because the dependent variable on the *y*-axis would neither increase nor decrease as we move along the values of the independent variable on the x-axis. Though we have a slope for the regression line, there is usually also a lot of random variation around it, and the apparent slope could simply be due to random chance. The p-value quantifies that chance, essentially saying what the probability of seeing this slope would be if there were actually no relationship between the two variables.

The third important measure is R^2 (or *R-squared*), which is a measure of how much of the variation in the dependent variable is explained by the independent variable. Another way to think about R^2 is that it measures how well the line fits the scatterplot of points, or how well the regression analysis fits the data. In financial data, it is common to see R^2 values well below 0.20 (20 %), but even a model that explains only a small part of the variation could elucidate an important relationship. A simple linear regression assumes that the independent variable is the only factor, other than random noise, that influences the values of the independent variable—this is an unrealistic assumption. Financial markets vary in response to a multitude of influences, some of which we can never quantify or even understand. R^2 gives us a good idea of how much of the change we have been able to explain with our regression model. Table 11.5 shows the actual regression output for regressing the S&P 500, Gold, and the U.S. Dollar on the returns for ABX.

Table 11.5 Regression Results for ABX (Weekly Returns, 2009–2010)

	Slope	R^2	*p*-Value
SPX	0.75	0.15	0.00
Gold	1.79	0.53	0.00
USD	(1.53)	0.11	0.00

In this case, our intuition based on the graphs was correct. The regression model for Gold shows an R^2 value of 0.53, meaning the 53 % of ABX's weekly variation can be explained by changes in the price of gold. This is an exceptionally high value for a simple financial model like this, and suggests a very strong relationship. The slope of this line is positive, meaning that the line slopes upward to the right—higher gold prices should accompany higher prices for ABX stock, which is what we would expect intuitively. We see a similar positive relationship to the S&P 500, though it has a much weaker influence on the stock price, as evidenced by the significantly lower R^2 and slope. The U.S. dollar has a weaker influence still (R^2 of 0.11), but it is also important to note that the slope is negative—higher values for the U.S. Dollar Index actually lead to lower ABX prices. Note that p-values for all of these slopes are less than zero (they are not actually 0.00 as in the table; the values are just truncated to 0.00 in this output), meaning that these slopes are statistically significant.

One last thing to keep in mind is that this tool shows *relationships* between data series; it will tell you when, if, and how two markets move together. It cannot explain or quantify the causative link, if there is one at all—this is a much more complicated question. If you know how to use linear regression, you will never have to trust anyone's opinion or ideas about market relationships. You can go directly to the data, and ask it yourself.

Monte Carlo Simulation

So far, we have looked at a handful of fairly simple examples and a few that are more complex. In the real world, we encounter many problems in finance and trading that are surprisingly complex. If there are many possible scenarios, and multiple choices can be made at many steps, it is very easy to end up with a situation that has tens of thousands of possible branches. In addition, seemingly small decisions at one step can have very large consequences later on; sometimes effects seem to be out of proportion to the causes. Last, the market is extremely random and mostly unpredictable, even in the best circumstances, so it very difficult to create deterministic equations that capture every possibility. Fortunately, the rapid rise in computing power has given us a good alternative—when faced with an exceptionally complex problem, sometimes the simplest solution is to build a simulation that tries to capture most of the important factors in the real world, run it, and just see what happens.

One of the most commonly used simulation techniques is Monte Carlo modeling or simulation, a term coined by the physicists at Los Alamos in the 1940s in honor of the famous casino. Though there are many variations of Monte Carlo techniques, the basic pattern is:

- Define a number of choices or inputs that will create different decision branches in the model.
- Define a probability distribution for each branch.
- Run many trials with different sets of random numbers for the inputs.
- Collect and analyze the results.

This is can be slightly confusing without an example, and the simple cases of a trader attempting to trade on a random walk binomial tree in earlier chapters provide a good framework for a very simple Monte Carlo example. Each node of the tree can be modeled as a random coin flip (formally, ~i.i.d. [–1, 1]). The simplest example would be the first, in which the trader was taking a loss at –1 and a profit at +1 on the first step in the tree. We could run many trials through this tree using a computer program to simulate the steps at the first node, and could collect the trader's P&L at the end of each run (in this case, only a single step). After accumulating hundreds of thousands of ending P&Ls from individual runs, we could add them up and probably find that they sum to something very, very close to zero. The computer simulation is used here to reproduce and to prove what should happen probabilistically. This is an extremely simple example, but it is possible to create much more complex rule sets and run them through the same modeling process.

We touched earlier on the possibility of using stop loss rules on a random walk tree, and saw that these problems quickly become intractable because there are so many possible branches. It is not practical to evaluate all of the possibilities in a moderately complex scenario by hand, but it is possible to create a Monte Carlo model that can handle even the most complex rule set. For instance, after thinking through the various trailing stop and target scenarios, maybe it would make sense for the trader to not have a profit target. He could simply trail a stop some distance below his peak P&L, leaving himself open to literally unlimited upside if he catches a lucky run in the tree. I have already pointed out that random data has more runs than most people would expect, and it seems like a single good run could make up for a lot of smaller losses, as long as the trader controls the size of those losses. Many traders also wonder if bigger stop sizes would help since it would allow for more room without getting hit in the noise (though, I would point out, the tree is random so it's all noise!). It makes sense to try to apply these ideas to the random walk market because in real-world trading they do sometimes make sense, but nothing will help us in the random walk world. Consider the following rule set as an example:

- The trader is trading on a binomial tree with a fixed step size of +/–1 and probability of 0.5 at each node in the tree.
- An initial stop-loss level is established at –25.
- This stop will be trailed 50 points under the high-water mark of the trader's P&L. In other words, if the first step in the tree is +1, the stop adjusts to –24. The stop never moves down, only up.
- These rules will be applied on 100,000 runs through the tree, recording the high, low, and ending P&L for each individual run.

For 100,000 runs through the tree, the trader ended up with an average P&L of 0.02. Have we found a trading edge? Is this a positive expectation? Be careful—remember that it is actually very unlikely that the average of the P&Ls would be *exactly* zero in an experiment like this. Some variation above and below zero is to be expected; the level of variation in the results must also be considered. Though not a formal significance test, we can apply the same concept and assume that the mean return is equal to zero. We have an observed return of 0.02, which is not equal to zero, but the standard deviation of the ending P&Ls is 15.2. Normally, as a rough rule of thumb, we would probably start to think a result might be statistically significant if the mean is two or more standard deviations from zero. In this case, considering the size of the standard deviation, the mean return is well within the noise level and does not provide any evidence that this trailing stop technique would provide a trading edge.

Monte Carlo techniques offer a good alternative to deterministic techniques, and may be especially attractive when problems have many moving pieces or are very path-dependent. Consider this an advanced tool to be used when you need it, but a good understanding of Monte Carlo methods is very useful for traders working in all markets and all time frames.

A Warning against Sloppy Statistics

Applying quantitative tools to market data is not simple. There are many ways to go wrong; some are obvious, but some are not obvious at all. The first point is so simple it is often overlooked—think carefully before doing anything. Define the problem, and be precise in the questions you are asking. Many mistakes are made because people just launch into number crunching without really thinking through the process, and sometimes having more advanced tools at your disposal may make you more vulnerable to this error. There is no substitute for thinking carefully. The second thing is to make sure you understand the tools you are using. Modern statistical software packages offer a veritable smorgasbord of statistical techniques, but avoid the temptation to try six new techniques that you don't really understand. This is asking for trouble. Here are some other mistakes that are commonly made in market analysis. Guard against them in your own work, and be on the lookout for them in the work of others.

Not Considering Limitations of the Tools

Whatever tools or analytical methodology we use, they have one thing in common: none of them are perfect—they all have limitations. Most tools will do the jobs they are designed for very well most of the time, but can give biased and misleading results in other situations. Market data tend to have many extreme values and a high degree of randomness, so these special situations actually are not that rare. If you are really interested in using some of these tools in your own trading and analysis, you owe it to yourself to understand everything you can about them.

Most statistical tools begin with a set of assumptions about the data you will be feeding them; the results from those tools are considerably less reliable if these assumptions are violated. For instance, linear regression assumes that there is an actual relationship between the variables, that this relationship can be described by a straight line (is linear), and that the error terms are distributed i.i.d. $N(0, \sigma)$. It is certainly possible that the relationship between two variables might be better explained by a curve than a straight line, or that a single extreme value (outlier) could have a large effect on the slope of the line. If any of these are true, the results of the regression will be biased at best, and seriously misleading at worst.

It is also important to realize that any result truly applies to only the specific sample examined. For instance, if we find a pattern that holds in 50 stocks over a five-year period, we might assume that it will also work in other stocks and, hopefully, outside of the five-year period. Many technical analysts assume that the same patterns work in all asset classes—that something that could be traded in equities, futures, forex, and fixed income—but this may or may not be true. In the interest of being precise, rather than saying, "This experiment proves ... ," better language would be something like "We find, in the sample examined, evidence that ..."; this is a subtle distinction, but phrases like this have great power to shape our thinking.

Some of the questions we deal with as traders are actually epistemological. Epistemology is the branch of philosophy that deals with questions surrounding knowledge about knowledge: What do we really know? How do we really know that we know it? How do we acquire new knowledge? These are profound questions that are usually ignored by traders who are simply looking for patterns to trade, only looking for the next big win. Spend some time thinking about questions like this, and meditating on the limitations of our market knowledge. We never know as much as we think we do, and we are never as good as we think we are. When we forget that, the market will remind us. Approach this kind of work with a sense of humility, realizing that however much we learn and however much we know, much more remains undiscovered.

Not Considering Actual Sample Size

In general, most statistical tools give us better answers with larger sample sizes. If we define a set of conditions that are extremely specific, we might find only one or two events that satisfy all of those conditions. (This, for instance, is the problem with studies that try to relate current market conditions to specific years in the past: sample size = 1.) Another thing to consider is that many markets are tightly correlated. If the stock market is up, most stocks will tend to move up on that day as well. If the U.S. dollar is strong, then most major currencies trading against the dollar will probably be weak. Most statistical tools assume that events are independent of each other, and, for instance, if we're examining opening gaps in stocks and find that 60 % of the stocks we are looking at gapped down on the same day, how independent are those events? (Answer: not independent.) When we examine patterns in hundreds of stocks, we should expect many of the events to be highly correlated, so our sample sizes could be hundreds of times smaller than expected. These are important issues to consider.

Not Accounting for Variability

Though this has been said several times, it is important enough that it bears repeating: It is never enough to notice that two things are different; it is also important to notice how much variation each set contains. A difference of 2 % between two means might be significant if the standard deviation of each were half a %, but is probably completely meaningless if the standard deviation of each is 5 %. If two sets of data appear to be different but they both have a very large random component, there is a good chance that what we see is simply a result of that random chance. Always include some consideration of the variability in your analyses, perhaps formalized into a significance test.

Assuming That Correlation Equals Causation

Students of statistics are familiar with the story of the Dutch town where early statisticians observed a strong correlation between storks nesting on the roofs of houses and the presence of newborn babies in those houses. It should be obvious (to anyone who does not believe that babies come from storks) that the birds did not cause the babies, but this kind of flimsy logic finds its way into much of our thinking about markets. Mathematical tools and data analysis are no substitute for common sense and deep thought. Do not assume that just because two things seem to be related or seem to move together that one actually causes the other. There may very well be a real relationship, or there may not be. The relationship could be complex and two-way, or there may be an unaccounted-for and unseen third variable. In the case of the storks, heat was the missing link—homes that had newborns were much more likely to have fires in their hearths, and the birds were drawn to the warmth in the bitter cold of winter.

Especially in financial markets, do not assume that, because two things seem to happen together, they are related in some simple way. These relationships are complex, causation usually flows both ways, and we can rarely account for all the possible influences. Unaccounted-for third variables are the norm, not the exception, in market analysis. Always think deeply about the links that could exist between markets, and do not take any analysis at face value.

Too Many Cuts Through the Same Data

Most people who do any backtesting or system development are familiar with the dangers of overoptimization. Imagine you came up with an idea for a trading system that said you would buy when a set of conditions is fulfilled and sell based on another set of criteria. You test that system on historical data and find that it doesn't really make money. Next, you try different values for the buy and sell conditions, experimenting until some set produces good results. If you try enough combinations, you are almost certain to find some that work well, but these results are completely useless going forward because they are only the result of random chance.

Overoptimization is the bane of the system developer's existence, but discretionary traders and market analysts can fall into the same trap. The more times the same set of data is evaluated with more qualifying conditions, the more likely it is that any results may be influenced by this subtle overoptimization. For instance, imagine we are interested in knowing what happens when the market closes down four days in a row. We collect the data, do an analysis, and get an answer. Then we continue to think, and ask if it matters which side of a 50-day moving average it is on. We get an answer, but then think to also check 100- and 200-day moving averages as well. Then we wonder if it makes any difference if the fourth day is in the second half of the week, and so on. With each cut, we are removing observations, reducing sample size, and basically selecting the ones that fit our theory best. Maybe we started with 4,000 events, then narrowed it down to 2,500, then 800, and ended with 200 that really support our point. These evaluations are made with the best possible intentions of clarifying the observed relationship, but the end result is that we may have fit the question to the data very well and the answer is much less powerful than it seems.

How do we defend against this? Well, first of all, every analysis should start with careful thought about what might be happening and what influences we might reasonably expect to see. Do not just test a thousand patterns in the hope of finding something, and then do more tests on the promising patterns—this is an example of the worst possible statistical practice. It is far better to start with an idea or a theory, think it through, structure a question and a test, and then test it. It is reasonable to add maybe one or two qualifying conditions, but stop there. In addition, holding some of the data set for out-of-sample testing is a powerful tool. For instance, if you have five years of data, do the analysis on four of them and hold a year back. Keep the out-of-sample set absolutely pristine. Do not touch it, look at it, or otherwise consider it in any of your analysis—for all practical purposes, it doesn't even exist.

Once you are comfortable with your results, run the same analysis on the out-of-sample set. If the results are similar to what you observed in the sample, you may have an idea that is robust and could hold up going forward. If not, either the observed quality was not stable across time (in which case it would not have been profitable to trade on it) or you overoptimized the question. Either way, it is cheaper to find problems with the out-of-sample test than by actually losing money in the market. Remember, the out-of-sample set is good for one shot only—once it is touched or examined in any way, it is no longer truly out-of-sample and should now be considered part of the test set for any future runs. Be very confident in your results before you go to the out-of-sample set, because you get only one chance with it.

Multiple Markets on One Chart

Some traders love to plot multiple markets on the same charts, looking at turning points in one to confirm or explain the other. Perhaps a stock is graphed against an index, interest rates against commodities, or any other combination imaginable. It is easy to find examples of this practice in the major media, on blogs, and even in professionally published research in an effort to add an appearance of quantitative support to a theory. This type of analysis nearly always looks convincing, and is also usually worthless. Any two financial markets put on the same graph are likely to have two or three turning points on the graph, and it is almost always possible to find convincing examples where one seems to lead the other. Some traders will do this with the justification that it is "just to get an idea," but this is sloppy thinking—what if it gives you the wrong idea? We have far better techniques for understanding the relationships between markets, so there is no need to resort to techniques like this. Consider Figure 11.13, which shows the stock of Harley-Davidson, Inc. (NYSE: HOG) plotted against the Financial Sector Index (NYSE: XLF). The two seem to track each other nearly perfectly, with only minor deviations that are quickly corrected. Furthermore, there are a few very visible turning points on the chart, and both stocks seem to put in tops and bottoms simultaneously, seemingly confirming the tightness of the relationship.

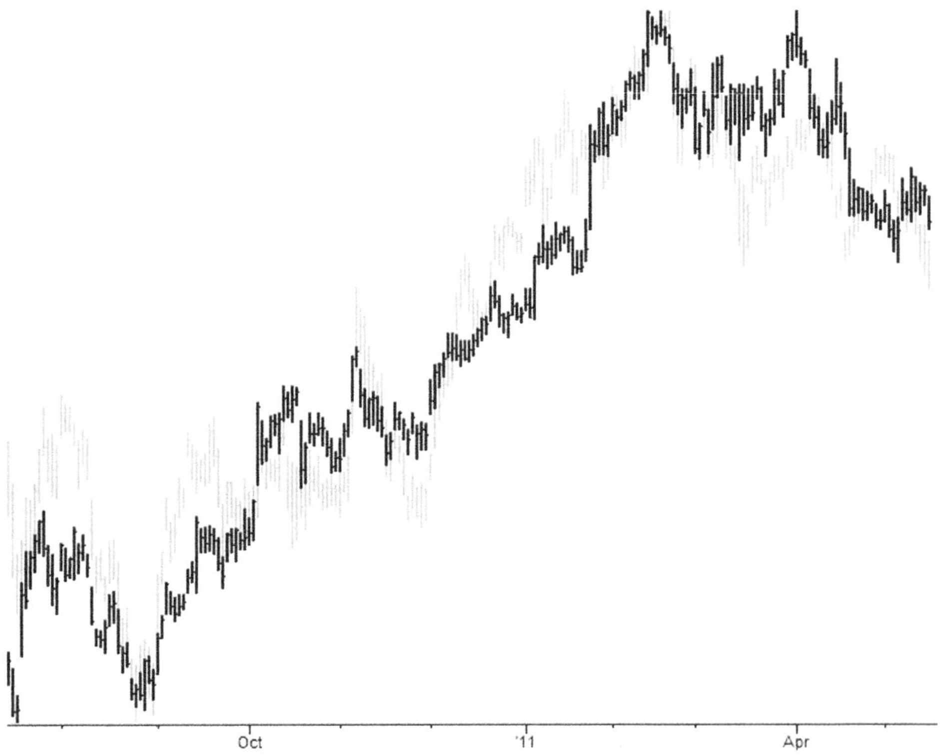

Figure 11.13 Harley-Davidson (Black) versus XLF (Gray)

For comparison, now look at Figure 11.14, which shows Bank of America (NYSE: BAC) again plotted against the XLF over the same time period. A trader who was casually inspecting charts to try to understand correlations would be forgiven for assuming that HOG is more correlated to the XLF than is BAC, but the trader would be completely mistaken. In reality, the BAC/XLF correlation is 0.88 over the period of the chart whereas HOG/XLF is only 0.67. There is a logical link that explains why BAC should be more tightly correlated—the stock price of BAC is actually a major component of the XLF's calculation, so the two are linked mathematically. The visual relationship is completely misleading in this case, and in many others as well.

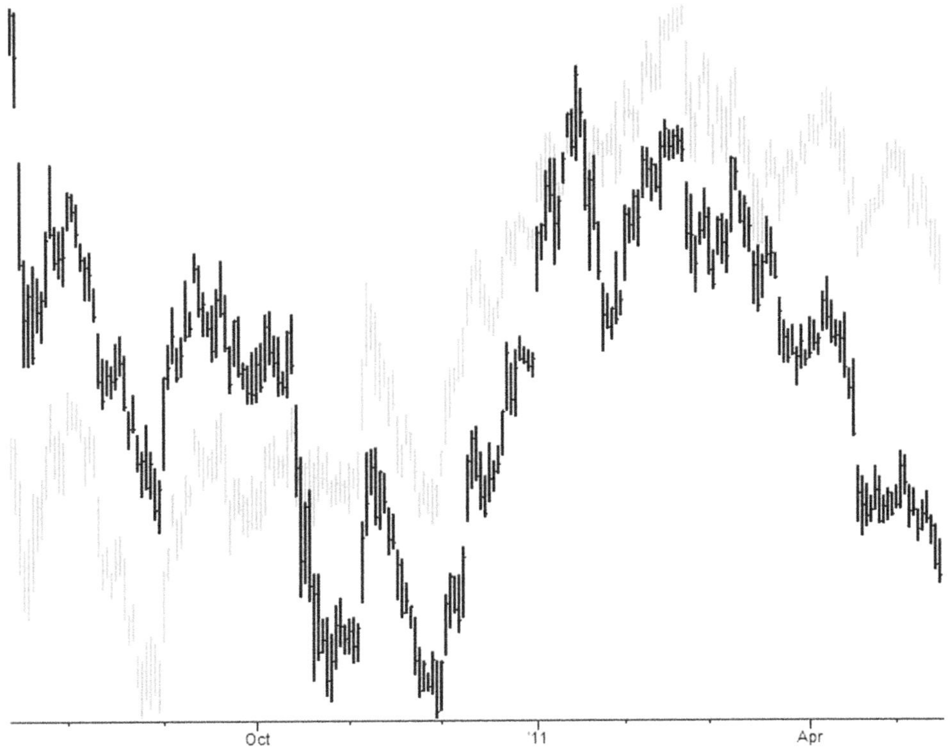

Figure 11.14 Bank of America (Black) versus XLF (Gray)

Percentages for Small Sample Sizes

Last, be suspicious of any analysis that uses %ages for a very small sample size. For instance, in a sample size of three, it would be silly to say that "67 % show positive signs," but the same principle applies to slightly larger samples as well. It is difficult to set an exact break point, but, in general, results from sample sizes smaller than 20 should probably be presented in "X out of Y" format rather than as a %age. In addition, it is a good practice to look at small sample sizes in a case study format. With a small number of results to examine, we usually have the luxury of digging a little deeper, considering other influences and the context of each example, and, in general, trying to understand the story behind the data a little better.

It is also probably obvious that we must be careful about conclusions drawn from such very small samples. At the very least, they may have been extremely unusual situations, and it may not be possible to extrapolate any useful information for the future from them. This is an important reminder in your own work, but be especially suspicious of very small sample sizes presented by someone else. Maybe they did not examine enough raw data or maybe it was just a quick back-of-the-envelope study, in which case it may have something useful to say, but more work is needed. In the worst case, it is possible that the small sample size is the result of a selection process involving too many cuts through data, leaving only the examples that fit the desired results. Drawing conclusions from tests like this can be dangerous.

Summary

Quantitative analysis of market data is a rigorous discipline with one goal in mind—to seek to better understand the market's movements. Many traders feel that tools and techniques such as the ones presented here are too abstract or too complex to be useful, especially to the individual trader. However, without them, the trader is blind, and it is impossible to separate valid trading edges from random noise. The next chapter shows some concrete applications of these tools in finding verifiable edges in the marketplace.

Chapter 12
Universe & Methodology

People almost invariably arrive at their beliefs not on the basis of proof but on the basis of what they find attractive.

–Blaise Pascal

This part presents several examples of quantitative techniques applied to real market data. There are at least two goals here: First, by actually working through several analyses, I show some of the issues that can arise when studying market problems. It is important to carefully think through the questions and goals of the study, as even the simplest questions often have many complicating factors. If the study is poorly designed or overlooks important points, the answers obtained will be misleading or incorrect.

The second point of the studies is to provide quantitative support and background that supports my style of trading. Most traders are using tools and techniques that have not been submitted to rigorous analysis, so they do not understand the statistical edges (or the lack thereof) behind their trading methodologies. If traders were encouraged to do their own work like this, there would be far fewer traders losing money trading support and resistance at moving averages or basing trades off of meaningless Fibonacci ratios. To this end, we have examined two commonly used technical tools:

1. *Fibonacci ratios* are commonly used by many traders to define entry levels and risk points for pullbacks, and targets for trend trades. However, we are unable to find any evidence to support the claim that Fibonacci ratios have any significance in the market. This casts serious doubt on any trading systems or methodologies that rely on these magical ratios.

2. Traders believe many things about *moving averages*; two of the most common beliefs are that they provide support and resistance, and that they are useful trend indicators. An investigation into moving averages will show that they do not, at least in our very large sample covering a decade of market data, function as significant support or resistance levels. Furthermore, many systems define the trend by moving average crossovers or slopes of moving averages, and we will also examine these tools. Last, we look at a simple, but powerful, way to use moving averages that may reduce portfolio volatility for longer-term investors.

Though the first part of this work focuses on contradicting some common errors in thinking, it is far more important to know what does actually work. To this end, the chapter concludes with a high-level look at the two main modes of market behavior, and provides statistical evidence of nonrandom price movement under specific conditions:

- *Mean reversion* is the tendency for large moves to reverse themselves, and for the market to move back toward a middle value.
- *Range expansion* is the tendency for markets to continue in the same direction after a large move.

As these two modes are polar opposites in many respects, we will look at different ways to quantify them, at conditions that may show that subsequent price action is more likely to display one mode than the other, and will demonstrate that there is a verifiable statistical edge to support these tendencies. Though we may trade discretionary methodologies, they must be firmly rooted on a solid foundation of statistically significant market behavior.

Any analysis of market tendencies gives an answer that is specific to the data set that was examined. Furthermore, the results may say as much about the techniques used as about the data itself, so it is important that tests be properly structured and specified. Hopefully, results generalize to other markets and time periods, and they are more likely to do so if the tests and the test universe are well constructed. However, we must always remain humble; we will never have absolute truth. For instance, it is possible that aberrations in the data set examined may cause some results that will never be replicated in the future. It is also possible that something worked well in the past, but markets evolve and the pattern may not work in the future. Even with the most care and the best of intentions, it is also possible that a mistake was made at some stage of the analysis. Properly constructed tests can, at best, guide us to a better understanding of market action, but much always remains unknown.

The Test Universe

When doing any analysis of markets, one of the most important issues to consider is the universe on which the tests are run, in terms of composition (specific choice of stocks, etc.); time frame (intraday, daily, weekly, etc.); and time period covered. Most traders tend to believe that "everything trades the same," meaning that if we find patterns that work on stocks those patterns should work on futures and forex as well. How do they know this, and it is true? (That, by the way, should be a question you find yourself asking constantly—How do they know that?) We must structure tests in a way that lets us see if the tendencies hold for different markets, different timeframes, and whether they have been stable over time. Proper selection of the test universe is the first step in this process.

From a quantitative perspective, one of the main questions about markets is whether asset returns are *stationary*. This is a slight oversimplification, but, mathematically, a stationary process is a stochastic (random) process whose probability distribution does not change over time. In market data, if returns were stationary, we would not see a shift in such things as measures of central tendency or dispersion when the same market is examined over different time periods. There is a significant debate in academia over whether returns are stationary, but, from a trader's perspective, they do not seem to be. For instance, consider the stock of a company that in its early days was a minor player but later rose to be the industry leader, or a commodity that might at one time have been primarily produced and consumed domestically, but for which a large global marketplace developed as domestic supplies were depleted. As these large, structural changes occur we know that the assets will, in fact, trade very differently. (Note that there are also processes that are cyclostationary, meaning that they appear to be stationary except for having a fairly predictable cyclic or *seasonal* component. If something is predictable, it can be backed out of the data, and the cyclostationary data can be transformed to a stationary set. Examples of real market data that have a strong seasonal component might be retail sales and volatility of natural gas prices.)

Non-stationarity of asset returns is a challenge to the enduring validity of any technical methodology; any trading edge should be examined over a long enough time period to assess its stability. Our results will vary greatly depending on the time period examined and whether it was a rip-roaring bull market, a flat period with no volatility, or a bear market. Traders doing analysis must consider this factor. Too many tests are presented to the public that were run on the last year or two years of data. These tests may be valuable if the future looks like these recent years, but that is a tenuous assumption on which to build a trading program.

Assets and asset classes are also correlated to varying degrees. In times of financial stress, it is not uncommon to see everything trading in the same direction, and to see, for instance, coffee, cocoa, crude oil, stocks, and even gold futures being crushed on the same day. One of the assumptions of many standard statistical methods is that events are independent, but if we examine a set of 1,000 stocks, we may find that more than 800 of them have large moves in the same direction on the same day. Of course, this violates any reasonable definition of independence, so we need to be aware that large tests on many different assets may be considerably less powerful (in terms of the information they give us) than a comparable test in another field. In addition to challenging assumptions of independence, tight correlations can effectively reduce the same size for many tests. For instance the equities sample for these tests includes over 1,380,000 trading days, but, because of correlations, these are *not* 1,380,000 independent events.

For the tests in this book, I have attempted to address some of these issues in three ways: by using a diverse sample of assets and asset classes, by focusing on a reasonably large historical period that includes several volatility regimes, and through a methodology that adjusts for the baseline drift inherent in each data set. In terms of asset class selection, I have taken a basket of 600 individual equities, randomly sampled from three large market capitalization tranches, 16 different futures markets, and 6 major world currencies trading against the U.S. dollar. All tests were also run on a set of stochastic (random) price models for calibration: a random walk i.i.d. ~ normal (the notiation "i.i.d. ~" means "independent and identically distributed according to the ... distribution"), a random walk i.i.d. ~ actual returns from the Dow Jones Industrial Average of 1980 to 2010, and a GARCH model.

All tests in this chapter are run on the time period from 1/1/2001 to 12/31/2010. This period was chosen partially out of convenience, and partially because of the assumption that the most recent data are likely to be more relevant going forward. (There could be less value in examining results from, say, 1940 to 1950.) In addition, this period includes, for equities, a period of protracted low volatility in the first part of the decade, the dramatic and volatile bear market associated with the 2007 to 2008 financial crisis, and the sharp recovery bull market of 2009 to 2010. One could, quite correctly, make the argument that this period does not include a large-scale secular bull market, which is likely to be the focus of many equities traders, but it is possible to replicate these tests on other time periods to check for consistency. It is also worth considering that these 10 years include some dramatic transitions for nearly all of these assets, many of which underwent a change from open-outcry to electronic markets. For others, such as U.S. equities, the electronic marketplaces matured and evolved as they underwent significant regulatory and structural changes.

Equities

For the equities universe, the entire set of domestic equities (N = 7,895) was ranked by market capitalization as of 1/1/2011, and break points were set at the 500th, 1,500th, and 2,500th members to approximate the divisions into large-cap, mid-cap, and small-cap universes. Note that though there are nearly 8,000 tickers listed, only a few thousand of them trade actively; many of the very small market capitalization stocks are extremely illiquid, sometimes going days or weeks without so much as a single trade. Exchange-traded fund (ETF) products and stocks with very short trading histories, and then 200 stocks from each market cap group were randomly chosen as the sample for that market cap. Table 12.1 presents industry statistics by each group.

Table 12.1 Industry Statistics for Equities Sample

	Large-Cap	Mid-Cap	Small-Cap
Basic Materials	7	15	15
Capital Goods	13	18	7
Consumer Cyclical	6	8	8
Consumer Noncyclical	15	9	7
Energy	15	19	8
Financial	33	31	44
Health Care	21	9	14
Services	50	41	46
Technology	17	21	28
Transportation	5	6	7
Utilities	17	23	16
Totals	199*	200	200

*One company was designated as a conglomerate and is missing from this tabulation.

In general, smaller market capitalization stocks tend to trade less actively and are less in the public focus. As a consequence, smaller-cap stocks are also usually less liquid and often trade more erratically than their large-cap cousins. In the sample used for this research, we see clear evidence of this as measures of dispersion are considerably larger for the mid- and small-cap tranches. One other common characteristic of smaller stocks is that they tend to outperform their large-cap cousins with higher average returns, which is a well-known anomaly in academia called the size effect. The explanation commonly offered for this is that smaller companies carry more risk than larger companies, so investors demand a higher return to hold these stocks. Though not a comprehensive study of the size effect, it is interesting to note that we see no evidence of the effect in our samples. Table 12.2 presents simple summary statistics for the equities test universe. Note that many of these are very small numbers, so they are presented here in basis points rather than percentages. (For most people, a number like 2 is much more intuitive than 0.0002.)

This sample, no doubt, suffers from *survivorship bias*. Many of the companies in the large-cap sample grew into that market cap; the companies did well and their stocks appreciated in value. Similarly, many of the small caps may have been mid caps at one time, but the companies faltered and the stocks declined. This is a likely explanation for why we do not see the classic size effect in this sample: because the market cap slices were taken at the end of the trading period. Had we taken a sample by market cap in early 2009 and then followed the returns going forward, we almost certainly would have seen dramatic outperformance in small caps over large caps.

Table 12.2 Summary Statistics for Equities Universe, Daily Returns

	All Stocks	Large-Cap	Mid-Cap	Small-Cap
Total Trading Days	1,381,685	484,002	454,649	443,034
Mean	5.6 bp	5.2 bp	5.9 bp	5.8 bp
Median	2.3 bp	2.5 bp	3.4 bp	0.8 bp
Standard Deviation	248.7 bp	230.8 bp	246.2 bp	270.9 bp
Interquartile Range (IQR)	227.2 bp	215.3 bp	223.5 bp	244.0 bp
Coefficient of Variation	44.4	44.8	41.4	47.1
Up%	50.07%	50.21%	50.43%	49.56%
Unchanged%	1.42%	1.15%	1.46%	1.66%
Down%	48.51%	48.64%	48.11%	48.78%

For our tests in this book, this is not a fatal flaw, but it is something that needs to be considered carefully for many other kinds of tests. If we were really interested in different trading characteristics by market caps, one way to compensate for survivorship bias would be to create a dynamic universe. For instance, it could be resampled, say, every six months and the membership based on current market cap rankings at each resampling point. On 1/1/2006 you could segregate the stock universe into market caps based on 1/1/2006 rankings, take your samples, and do your analyses over the next six months. You would then need a list of market caps as they stood on 7/1/2006, take your sample, and repeat. This is a laborious process, but it may be the only way to correct for this bias in some kinds of studies. Be clear that these market cap tranches were done on a look-back basis for the purpose of the studies in this book; the goal of these tests was to understand the behavior of equities as a whole rather than focusing too much attention on market cap division, so this was not a significant limitation for these tests.

Another factor to consider is that the test universe was created from stocks trading as of 12/31/2010, so companies like Enron, Bear Stearns, and Lehmann Brothers are not included, nor are stocks that did exceptionally well and were taken over, sometimes at significant premiums to their market values. This introduces an element of survivorship bias that could distort or alter our results. Particularly for traders developing rule-based trading systems, the impact of these events can be very significant, even to the point of making unprofitable systems appear to be very good in backtests. For rough tests of price tendencies like the ones on this chapter, this factor may be less significant, but the potential impact of survivorship bias cannot be quickly and casually dismissed

There are several ways in which this research could be extended. For one thing a number of companies in the sample are American depositary receipts (ADRs), which are foreign companies that also list on U.S. exchanges. For most of these companies, U.S. trading hours are not the primary trading session and there may be significant differences between the way these companies trade and domestically domiciled companies. It also may make sense for interested traders to drill down a bit deeper into segregating stocks by sectors, because biotech companies, for instance, trade very differently from utilities or technology companies. There may be some important quantitative differences that these tests have not captured, because they did not segregate the equity groups by these or other factors.

Last, many traders access markets through a variety of indexes and ETF products. We should not assume that the behavior of a large number of stocks in aggregate will mirror the behavior of an index; traders who choose to focus on index products should probably conduct similar research on the indexes themselves. However, research done exclusively on indexes is subject to several deficiencies: limited data history, changing index composition, and potential microstructure issues such as nonsynchronous trading are a few of the most common. Even traders who choose to focus on these products will find their work significantly enhanced by a deeper understanding of the behavior of the individual components that make up the index.

Futures

Selecting a universe of domestic futures was more complicated. For instance, one of the most active futures markets is the S&P 500 futures, a futures contract based on the S&P 500 index, which is a basket of stocks, many of which are already included in our equities sample. We need to be aware of issues of potential overlap, but this market could not be eliminated from our sample because this market is the primary focus for many futures traders. A selection of 16 markets was chosen to represent financial futures (S&P 500, 30-year Treasury Bond futures); metals (Gold, Silver, and Copper); petroleum products (WTI Crude Oil, Natural Gas); softs (Coffee, Sugar, Cotton, and Frozen Concentrated Orange Juice); grains (Soybeans and Wheat); and meat products (Live Cattle and Lean Hogs). Conspicuously absent are currency futures due to overlap with cash forex, and derived products (petroleum distillates and soybean products).

Another potential issue with futures is the roll: futures contracts are listed for delivery in various months and years, sometimes many years in the future. However, nearly all trading activity is restricted to the current contract (called the front month) or to a very small set of specific delivery months. Futures traders typically move their focus from contract to contract as one nears expiration and delivery. The problem is that, for a number of reasons, the prices of the contracts are different so it is not possible to simply chain together front month contracts to create a historical price series—doing so creates an apparent price movement, a distortion, usually called the roll. The solution is to create a continuous returns series (not a price series) that adjusts for the effect of the roll, and then to build a price series from that continuous return series. Table 12.3 presents basic statistics for the futures group used in this research.

Table 12.3 Summary Statistics for Futures Universe, Daily Returns

Sample Size	40,104
Mean	2.7 bp
Median	3.5 bp
Standard Deviation	144.0 bp
IQR	141.6 bp
Coefficient of Variation	52.6
Up%	50.59%
Unchanged%	1.72%
Down%	47.70%

Currencies

Currency rates are always expressions of the relative value of one currency against another. Though there are many currency pairs traded today, a great number of them are illiquid, having large spreads and little trading activity for most of the day. In an effort to simplify, to avoid a "double counting" effect, and to represent the currencies that are most accessible, these tests avoid cross-rates and focus only on the following currencies against the U.S. dollar: Australian dollar, Canadian dollar, Swiss franc, Eurocurrency, British pound, and Japanese yen. Table 12.4 presents summary statistics for this test universe.

Table 12.4 Summary Statistics for Forex Universe, Daily Returns

Sample Size	15,570
Mean	1.7 bp
Median	2.1 bp
Standard Deviation	69.1 bp
IQR	76.8 bp
Coefficient of Variation	40.2
Up%	51.00%
Unchanged%	0.87%
Down%	48.13%

It is worth mentioning here that, from a purely quantitative perspective, the currency markets often approximate random walks much more closely than our other samples do. It may be reasonable to assume that these, the largest of the world markets in notional terms, are the most closely watched and tightly arbitraged of all markets. The currencies are dominated by large, well-capitalized players who, in many cases, have legal access to information before it is available to the public. Also, much of the buying and selling in currencies is driven by other factors perhaps only peripherally related to the currency itself. This is true in other markets as well, but speculative buying and selling represent a smaller slice of the market activity in currencies than in most other asset classes.

Random Walk Universe

These tests were also run on a number of different random walk models. These tests, of course, show no trading edge (none is possible in random markets), so the results are not presented here. Why expend the time and energy to run tests on random markets? I continue to believe that traders who do not have intuition about random price movement will find it difficult to fully understand price action, and I also believe that many developing traders should spend far more time examining charts and running tests on random walk data. If you have built a good testing framework, it is easy enough to feed it randomly generated data along with actual market data for comparison; this will beging to build a type of intuition that cannot be developed in any other way.

Probably the most important ideas are the basic concepts behind random walks and the binomial tree. If you have a good grasp of these concepts, you can conduct many interesting experiments using Microsoft Excel. While it is not ideal for quantitative work, it is adequate for many applications, and has the advantage of being ubiquitous and fairly easy to use. One problem that will be encountered early on is that the random number generator in Excel (=rand() function) has some fairly serious limitations. All random numbers generated by computer code should actually be called pseudo-random because the code that generates them will eventually start repeating the same sequence; Excel's native number generators repeat after just a few million numbers. Users generating reasonably long price histories, especially with open, high, low, and close, will run into this limitation more quickly than might be expected. If you are going to use Excel, it is worth your time to find a better random number generator than those provided with the program. The tests in this book use the MT19937 variant of the Mersenne twister algorithm developed by Matsumoto and Nashimura in 1997. This is a high-quality pseudo-random number generator that produces uniformly distributed numbers that pass most statistical tests for randomness, and it has a very long period (before the values repeat). The numbers generated by this algorithm do not repeat until the $2^{19,937}$ value (that's a 1 followed by about 5,800 zeros—a big number), which would get you through a lifetime of testing nearly any financial concept imaginable.

If you have not done any serious work with randomly generated data, a good place to start is to generate random charts and look at them as though they were price charts. Though this is highly subjective, most traders are very surprised to see many of the patterns they look for in the market also appearing in random data. To get you started, here are step-by-step instructions for building a simple random walk with returns that are distributed according to the standard normal distribution (mean: 0%; standard deviation: 1%) in Excel.

1. Type the value 1000 in cell B1, the starting value for your random walk.
2. In cell A2, type: =NORMINV(RAND(),0,0.01)
3. In cell B2, type: =B1*(1+A2)
4. Select cells A2 and B2 (drag select with mouse) and copy them down the column one of two ways. Either grab the little black bump in the lower right corner of the selection box and drag it down or type Ctrl-C, hold down Shift, and press Page Down until you have gone as far down as you want to copy, and then type Ctrl-V.
5. Column B now contains your random walk price series. You may graph it by selecting the entire column (left click on the B above the column), going to the Insert menu, and selecting a line graph type.

If you create a random walk about 1,000 steps long (determined by how far you copy the rows down in step 4), you can produce some charts that would be the equivalent of several years of daily price changes. Once you have built this graph, each time you press the F9 key the sheet will recalculate and produce a completely new series. Spend some time looking at these and imagining that they are real market prices. Do you see trends? Trading ranges? Many of the chart formations you have come to trust? If you are honest about it, you will see remarkable similarities between these charts (which you know are randomly created) and price charts of real stocks. Even though you see patterns here, remember it would not be possible to trade them profitably because the resolution of those patterns is completely random. This is only a starting point, but seeing patterns appear in randomly generated data will make you reconsider the validity of a simplistic approach to chart patterns.

Pythia

The tests in the following section utilize simple counting and comparison methods along with simulation. The majority of the quantitative tests presented in this part were done using Pythia™, which is an event-study testing methodology. All of the ideas behind this testing protocol are very simple; the power comes from its ability to objectively evaluate a large number of patterns and to summarize the results in a readily comprehensible format.

The basic Pythia procedure is:

- For each market tested, calculate baseline stats, including measures of central tendency, dispersion, and the probability of closing up, down, or unchanged in any trading period. These statistics represent the market conditions a naive buy-and-hold investor would have realized, so this is also the hurdle rate that any valid signal must overcome.
- If multiple markets are used in a testing set (as in a set of stocks, futures, etc.), create a weighted average of the summary statistics; this is the equivalent of creating an index from the test universe.
- This baseline summary is calculated for every day in the test universe, averaged across the entire universe. The single-day return and associated dispersion can then be compounded and extrapolated to further days for comparison with actual tests.
- Define a precise condition that will result in a trading signal. There can be no subjectivity in this signal condition, but it may be complex An example of a very simple signal condition would be "buy if this bar's close is lower than the previous bar's low." All of the tests in this book are symmetrical, meaning that the conditions for entering a market short are merely the buy conditions inverted. This is not a requirement, but it usually makes sense to test symmetrical ideas.
- Go through each of the markets in the test universe one bar at a time, examining each bar for the entry conditions. When a valid entry condition is found, use the close of that bar as the entry price, assuming the trade is entered without slippage on that bar.
- Calculate a return for the next bar and label it bar 1. Continue for as many bars desired after the signal. (The tests in this book use 20 bars following the signal.) At this point, you will have a list of returns by bars following the signal: bar 1, bar 2, and so on. Save this set and continue working through the rest of the test universe.
- Once all bars have been examined, align all bar 1, bar 2, and so on returns. You will now have a matrix ordered by bars following the signal on one axis and by date of entry on the other.
- The results of the first column's summary statistics (first bar after entry) are compared to the benchmark for each specific market and for the set of markets as a whole. Most of the tests in this book do not present test statistics for each individual market (stock, currency, etc.), but only summary results for the entire set of related markets. We are interested in differences between measures of central tendency, in dispersion, and in significance tests for each day following the signal, in aggregate.

Many traders attempt to test technical signals or trading ideas in the context of trading systems. Many software packages can take simple inputs and run backtests on historical data to see what gains or losses would have resulted. It needs to be emphasized early on that this is not an acceptable testing methodology. Any test like this is a joint test of the entry criteria well as the exit. Some studies attempt to overcome this by setting time limits for the exits, as in "the results of taking this signal and exiting five days later," but this is an arbitrary constraint. These P&L style or trading system style tests also give no insight into the character of the return distributions for each day following the event, nor do they allow for easy comparison to the baseline drift. Last, these tests do not allow for significance testing, which is a crucial step in any real statistical analysis. Beware of any published tests showing theoretical P&Ls for trading tools or for systems masquerading as quantitative tests.

Event-study methodologies are well established in the academic literature, so, in some sense, Pythia is not revolutionary. What is unique is the disciplined application of this methodology to a large number of patterns over a carefully constructed test universe. Statistically speaking, there are, at best, slight edges in the marketplace. This tool can reveal those edges and their directionality, magnitude, and stability across asset classes and time frames. Without this kind of information, technical traders are forced to rely on untested market lore and ideas that may or may not have value. Eventually, some traders will accumulate enough information to understand some of these edges intuitively, but few new traders survive the learning curve, nor do they trade with the discipline necessary to build that intuition.

Chapter 13

Fibonacci Retracements

Scientific truth by conesnsus has had a uniformly bad history.

-David Douglass

The Fibonacci sequence is a sequence of numbers obtained by starting with the numbers 0 and 1, summing them, and then continuing the process, always creating the next number in the series by summing the last two: {0, 1, 1, 2, 3, 5, 8, 13, 21, 34, 55, 89, 144, 233, ...} The first mention of this sequence in Western literature is attributed to Leonardo of Pisa (called Fibonacci, a contraction of filius Bonacci, "son of Bonacci"), an Italian mathematician who used the sequence as an example in his 1202 book, Liber Abaci. In the midtwentieth century, Ralph N. Elliott came to believe that this sequence of numbers was the foundation for something he called Nature's Law, and pointed to applications of this Law in such diverse phenomena as the construction of the human body (one head, two arms, three divisions in each arm and leg, five senses); the musical keyboard (eight notes to an octave, eight white keys, and five black keys—a miscounting because if eight white keys span an octave, six black keys are the equivalent—and 89 keys to a "complete keyboard"; confusion reigns on that count as well), the construction of the Great Pyramids of Egypt (which he claimed were the fulfillment of Biblical prophecy); and the number of signers of the Declaration of Independence. He also points out that there are "approximately" 89 primary chemical elements. (Actually, there are 94 naturally occurring elements.) Elliott naturally reasons that if this number series is so significant in nature, it certainly should have application to the fluctuations of financial markets. As convoluted as Elliott's writings were on the subject, the situation has not improved over time.

The basic claim of Fibonacci traders is that the magnitude and timing of swings in the market are described by ratios derived from the Fibonacci sequence. If a number in the sequence is divided by the number that follows it, the result is a number very close to 61.8 %, which is a constant called Φ (phi), also known as the Golden Ratio. This is a number that truly does describe many relationships and ratios in art, in architecture, and in nature—on this count, the Fibonacci followers are correct. If a number is divided by the second number following it in the sequence, we get »38.2 %, and »23.6 % for the third number following. (The further out in the sequence these divisions are done, the more closely the quotients converge on these values. For instance, 89 divided by 144 is much closer to 0.618 than is 3 divided by 5.) In addition to using these ratios from the Fibonacci series, Fibonacci traders inexplicably focus attention on the 50 % ratio, which is not a Fibonacci number at all.

Some Fibonacci traders also use the actual numbers from the sequence in ways that are, simply, illogical. There is nothing special about numbers that are in the sequence (which some traders call Fibonacci numbers), because the magic ratio will be generated from any series that is summed this way. (Try creating a Fibonacci-style sequence with the procedure $X_t = X_{t-1} + X_{t-2}$ using different seed numbers. For instance, the ratio will appear further out in the sequence {2, 5, 7, 12, ...} or even {3; 9,785; 9,788; ...}. Any seed numbers will generate the famed ratios, so there is absolutely no reason to attach any significance to the standard Fibonacci numbers.) For instance, some traders will trade only time frames that are Fibonacci numbers; that is, they will trade 5- or 13-minute bars because those numbers are in the sequence, but not 6- or 12-minute bars. They may also use them as inputs for indicators, perhaps using 55 or 144 bars for their moving averages. There is no justification for this practice, but it is very common in the literature and practice of Fibonacci traders

Structuring the Data

All serious fields of study have a consistent lexicon. This allows teachers, students, and practitioners to communicate easily and clearly; energy can be spent discussing concepts rather than making sure everyone is on the same page. (Imagine the confusion that would reign in an operating room if a surgeon had to say, "No, the other squiggly pink thing!" (I'm sure that happens sometimes, but that's another story.)) This is a real problem in technical analysis because every author invents his own terms, and often reuses terms from earlier authors in completely different contexts. In addition, there have been cases in the past where authors tried to hide muddled thinking behind a proliferation of new and confusing technical terms. In referring to market structure, I have used the same terms consistently throughout this book. The line marked AB in Figure 13.1 is called the preceding trend leg or the setup leg, because it is the move that sets up the next trend leg. The swing marked BC is called the retracement or the pullback, and CD is called the extension or, simply, the next trend leg. Note that the next trend leg can become a setup leg for another push in the same direction. (CD would be relabeled AB when the next pullback begins.)

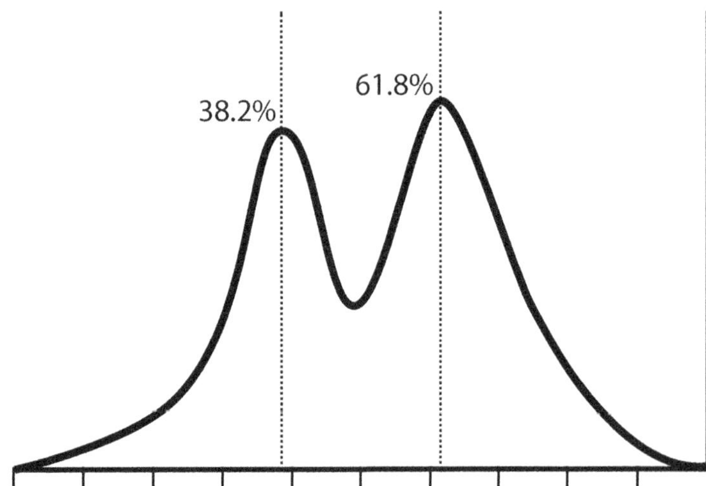

Figure 13.1 Schematic of Basic Market Structure

Fibonacci ratios are most commonly used to predict the following:

- The most probable stopping points for retracements in trends. The idea is that pullbacks are more likely to stop around Fibonacci ratios of the preceding trend leg. For example, if the previous upswing was 10 points, Fibonacci traders would expect the pullback to terminate around 3.82 points from the high. If that level fails to hold, they would then watch 5.00 and 6.18 for potential turning points. It is widely understood that these are not precise levels, but general guidelines.

- The magnitude of the extension (CD in Figure 13.1). There are several common variations of this plan, but a good working example is expecting the next trend leg to extend 161% (the length of the previous swing + 61.8% of that length) of the previous trend leg in the same direction. Again, these are guidelines, not exact levels.
- The timing of turning points. Traders will often count the number of bars (weeks, days, or minutes) in a swing, and anticipate future turning points at Fibonacci ratios of that count.

Figure 13.2 shows a simple example of Fibonacci retracements applied to several swings in the stock of Apple Inc. (Nasdaq: AAPL) from mid-2006. Yes, this is a carefully chosen example, but notice that the retracements are contained by the 38.2%, 50%, and 61.8% retracement levels nearly perfectly.

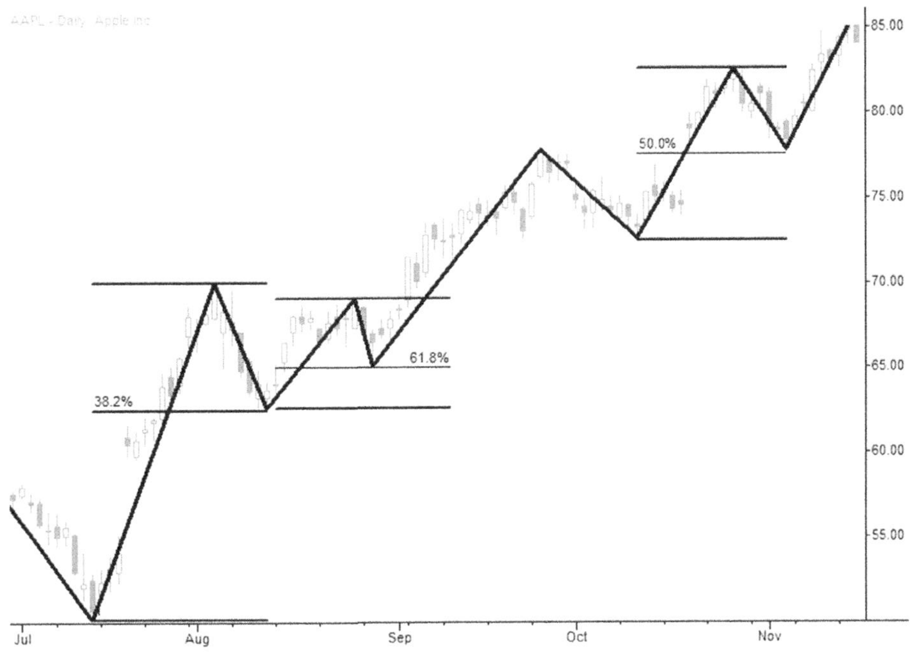

Figure 13.2 Fibonacci Retracements in AAPL (2006)

Another concept that Fibonacci traders use is confluence. Ratio relationships do not have to be limited to the previous swing; we can combine several smaller swings into one larger structure, and we can also look at swings far back in the structure and at higher time frames—each of these possibilities offers additional anchor points for ratios that can be considered on the trading time frame. If important Fibonacci ratios from different swings or time frames line up at approximately the same price level, we say there is a confluence at that level. Traditionally, Fibonacci traders have believed that these confluences are more powerful than simple ratios and that they have a higher probability of changing the direction of prices. Figure 13.3, which shows an example of a Fibonacci confluence on the same chart of AAPL, may help to clarify (or to further confuse) the issue. Relevant points on the chart have been labeled, and four different sets of retracement lines are overlaid on the chart. Remember, the object is to explain how the stopping point at G could have been anticipated based on a confluence, or a lining up, of multiple Fibonacci levels.

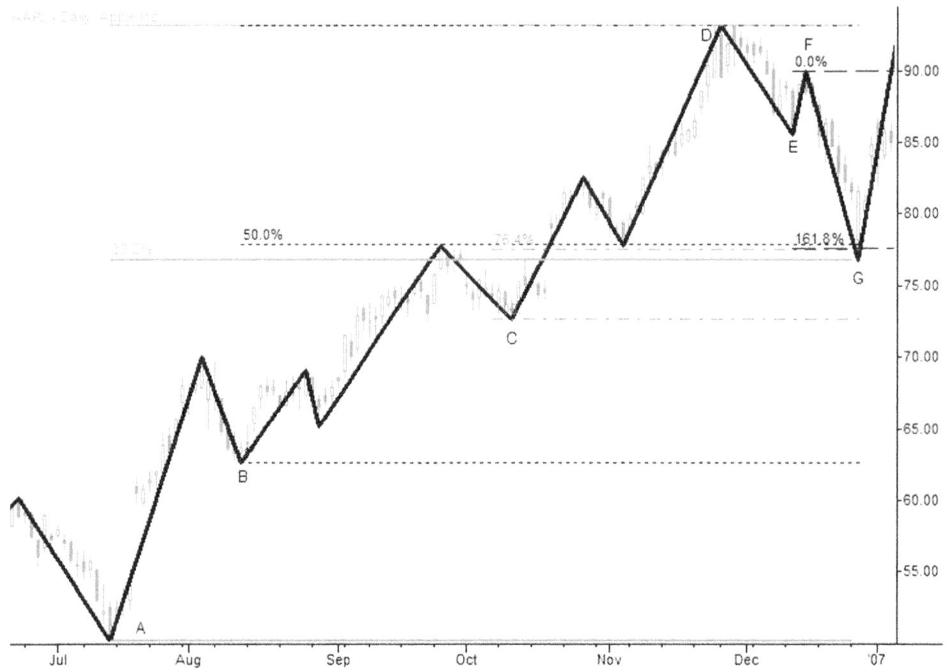

Figure 13.3 Fibonacci Confluence in AAPL

In this example, note the following:

- DG is a very close to 38.2% retracement of AD (thick gray line on chart).
- DG is between the 50% and 61.8 % retracement levels of BD (dotted line).
- DG is close to a 76.4% retracement of CD (long-short dashed line). (Yes, Fibonacci traders also use this ratio, because 76.4 = 100% – 23.6%.)
- FG is a little more than a 161.8% extension of DE (black dashed line). Fibonacci traders use extensions based on the ratios as well as retracements. Since extensions are supposed to predict likely profit targets, they also can be used to project anticipated turning points.

These examples do look very convincing, but keep two points in mind. First, as you add lines to the chart, there is a very good good chance that some of those lines will appear to be significant. Add enough lines, and it is virtually certain. Second, it is always possible to find impressive illustrations to support any point. No matter how convincing the examples look, it is not always possible to trade the underlying concepts. The question is not whether we can find good examples, but whether these levels actually represent something significant over a large set of swings. Over a substantial number of swings, are Fibonacci ratios more informative than any other randomly selected ratio would be? To answer that question, we turn to the market data itself.

Testing Fibonacci Levels

From the beginning, we need to be clear that it is not possible to devise a test of Fibonacci levels that will satisfy all practitioners and believers in the concepts. My goal here is simple: to incorporate in my trading process only tools that have objective and strong support from the data. If these levels are truly important, if there really is a mystical connection between the "sacred geometry" that laid the foundations of the universe and swings in markets, it should not be hard to structure a test that reveals this relationship.

The approach here is guided by two overriding principles: simplicity and objectivity. Avoid highly structured and potentially overspecified tests, and instead focus on whether you can gently tease out any Fibonacci relationships from the raw data. Second, all results and analysis will be conducted according to absolutely objective rules. There will be no inspection of charts, no human input, and no subjectivity at all; an algorithm will go through the data and pull out events according to well-defined rules.

It is also important to define the question and goals of the study precisely. In this case, the question is: "Are retracements in markets more likely to stop at Fibonacci levels than any other place?" If so, we should be able to collect a large number of retracements, analyze them as ratios of previous swings, and expect to see more of them terminate at the common Fibonacci levels of 38.2%, 61.8%, and, perhaps, 50%. The testing methodology is simple: we will treat every swing in the market as an extension (CD in Figure 13.1) and will record two measures: the retracement preceding the extension and the extension itself, both a %age of the setup leg. Again, referring to Figure 13.1, these measures would both be recorded at point D:

In an upswing (if D > C)

- Retracement: (BC)/(BA)
- Extension: (DC)/(BA)

In a downswing (if D < C)

- Retracement: (CB)/(AB)
- Extension: (CD)/(AB)

Figure 13.4 shows two swings in a theoretical market. In the one marked example #1, the setup leg was 15 points (25 – 10), and the retracement was 5 (25 – 20). We would record this is a retracement of 33%, meaning the length of the retracement was one-third of the length of the setup leg. The extension was 15 points (35 – 20), for a 100% extension, exactly equal to the setup leg. These data points cannot be recorded until the swing marked 35 terminates, so, for every swing in the market, we are collecting both the measure of extension and of the retracement that preceded it. Note that when the market turns down from the point marked 35, a downswing will be recorded. Assume that this downswing (not shown in the diagram) terminates at 25. For that swing, we would record an extension of 200% because it is twice as long as the setup leg, which is now the 25 – 20 leg, and a retracement of 300%, because the 20 – 35 leg, which is now the retracement, was three times as long as the setup leg. Look at example #2 to make sure you understand the calculations. At the terminal point of 25, we would record an extension of 66% following the retracement of 66%. The key to understanding this is that all measurements refer to the setup leg as the denominator for the ratio, and this setup leg is the preceding swing in the same direction as the extension.

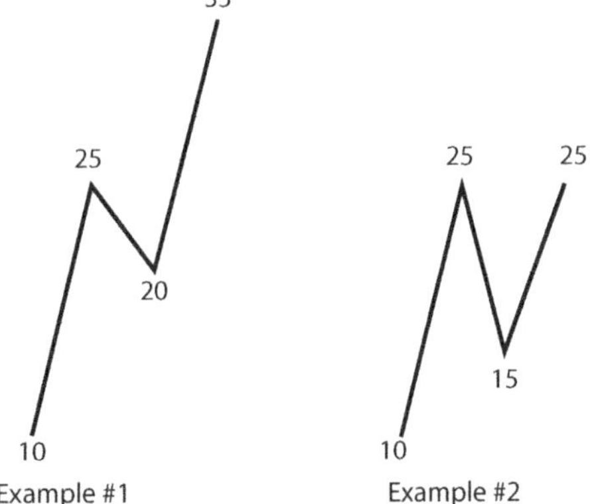

Figure 13.4 Extensions and Retracements

With this measurement system in place, all we have to do is to draw swing points for every swing in the market and collect these measurements, which is no trivial task. Figure 13.5 shows swings drawn in the market according to a rule set that looks at simple elements of price structure and volatility to determine when a market swing has changed direction. The rule set is the very epitome of simplicity—it defines swings as first level pivot highs and lows, qualified by a movement of a certain ATR away from those pivots.

Though the precise rule set is my own, it is not that important; many charting packages offer similar tools to draw swings on charts, and it is fairly easy to devise your own. Remember, this test is specifically a test of swing ratios as defined by my model, and these results may or may not generalize to other definitions. In other words, it is possible that another set of rules to define swings in markets could find that different ratios are more or less significant. Figure 13.5 shows the swing extension and retracement measurements for the swings on the AAPL daily chart. Remember, the key to these measurements is that each swing is measured twice: as retracement, as a %age of the setup leg; and as an extension, also measured as a percentage of the same setup leg. Make sure you understand these measurements before reading further.

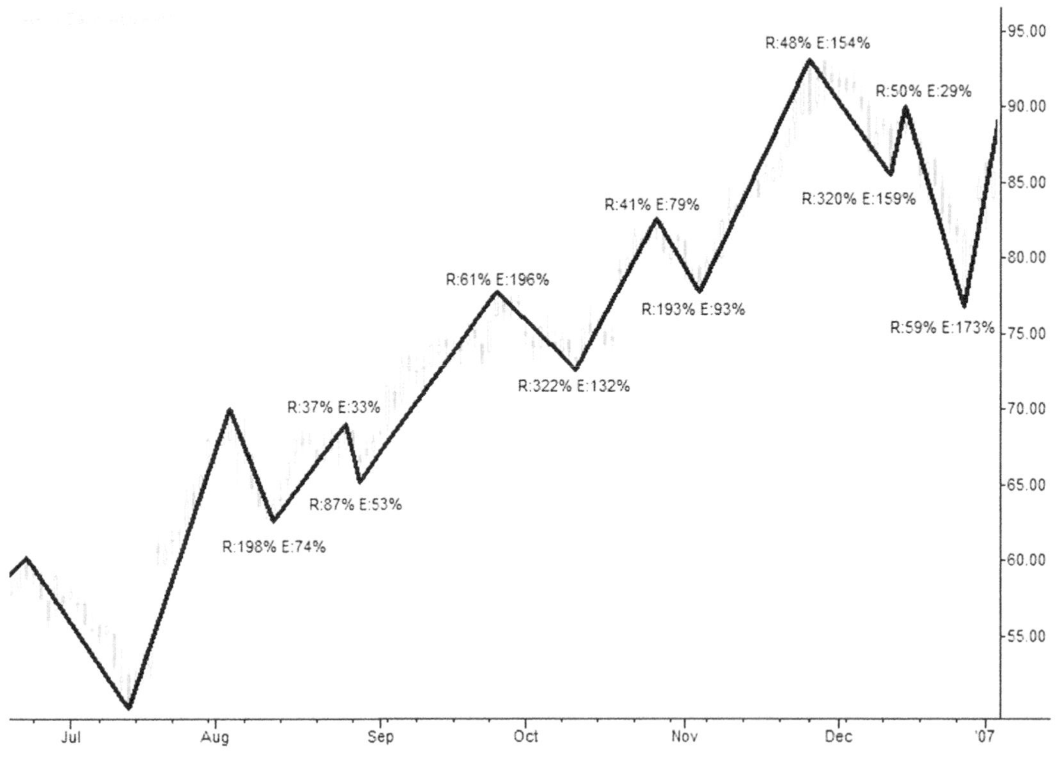

Figure 13.5 Swing Ratios for Swings on AAPL Daily Chart

Assume that Fibonacci ratios really do describe retracement ratios in market data. How could we structure a simple test, imposing as few external measurements and structures on the data as possible, that would reveal this tendency? One approach might be to go through the data set, collect every retracement measured as a ratio of the preceding setup leg, and simply draw a histogram of those ratios. Though this is complicated by the sheer number of events involved, at its root this is nothing more than simple counting. If Fibonacci levels are truly significant in market structure, we might expect to see more retracements stop around those levels, creating a distribution like that in Figure 13.6. At the very least, it is reasonable to expect some sort of peak or distortion around the

Fibonacci levels, even if it is not as clear as this idealized example. Furthermore, this could be a case in which a comparison of real market data to random walk data is useful. If there is some mystical force shaping prices, we should see a difference between the actual market data and random walk data. This is what we are looking for in a nutshell: if Fibonacci levels are truly significant, then we should see that they describe retracements and extensions—these levels cannot be important and also be invisible in the data.

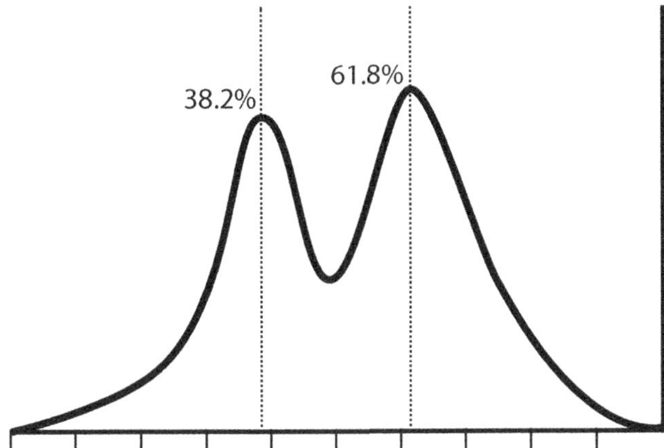

Figure 13.6 A Retracement Length Distribution That Would Reveal Significant Fibonacci Level Influence

The Raw Data

As an initial test, the swing definition rule set was run through the entire test universe from 2000 to 2010, recording retracement and extensions for each swing. As a check for liquidity, swings in which any equities traded less than an average volume of 50,000 shares a day were removed from the results; this affected 20,212 equities swings, or 11.7% of the results. (The swings removed were not substantially different from those that were kept, having a mean swing length of 124% with a standard deviation of 104%. The choice to remove them was made because price action in very illiquid markets is subject to a number of potential microstructural distortions, and few traders will be placing technically motivated trades in this kind of environment, anyway.) As another liquidity check, any swings that had a single trading session in which the high was equal to the low of the session, probably indicating no trading activity, was also removed. Table 13.5 shows the resulting raw retracement statistics broken down for each asset class in the test universe.

Table 13.5 Raw Retracement Stats for Swings

	N=	Mean	StDev	Median	IQR	Min	Max
Equities	152,863	122.1%	87.9%	98.4%	85.6%	1.2%	1,890.2%
Futures	4,832	124.9%	99.5%	98.8%	88.2%	4.9%	1,359.9%
Forex	1,639	122.6%	87.5%	96.6%	84.6%	16.6%	636.2%
Random	2,420	123.3%	89.1%	99.9%	83.5%	10.9%	1,092.5%
Total	161,754	122.2%	88.3%	98.5%	85.6%	1.2%	1,890.2%

Several things are apparent from the data. First, there is a lot of variability, evidenced by the high standard deviations relative to the means. In addition, the results are probably skewed by large right tails, as the means are greater than the medians and the maximum is very large relative to the mean for all asset classes. We see no evidence that the means or medians are different for any asset classes, suggesting that all asset classes trade with approximately the same ratio relationships between swings. Furthermore, based on the limited data in this table, the relationships in actual market data do not appear to be significantly different from those generated by the random walk processes. Last, we do note that both the forex and random walk classes show higher minimum and lower maximum swings than the other classes, but this could simply be a result of sample size. The total number of forex swings is about 1.1 % of the total number of equity swings, so it is possible that, if we were able to collect substantially more forex data, we would eventually see more of these very large and very small swings.

Focusing on Trends

The goal of this study is to examine retracement percentages in trends, which is where Fibonacci ratios are most commonly assumed to hold. Most traders would not consider retracements that retraced more than 100% of the setup leg to be retracements at all, as they may be properly viewed as extensions of a trend in the other direction, or as a failed pullback. A pullback in an uptrend that violates the pivot low of the setup leg is actually more likely to be a losing trade for most trend traders. At this point, there are two ways to continue this study. One option is to add a definition of trend and a trend filter, and take measurements only in the direction of that trend. For instance, if the overall market structure were judged to be in an uptrend, we would measure uptrend extensions and contra-uptrend retracements while ignoring downtrend extensions. This approach brings with it many complications and areas of potential disagreement—how will the trend be defined? How do we deal with ambiguous situations in which the trend may have changed but is unclear? Do we allow for nontrending, trading range states, and, if so, how do we measure swings in those areas? It is certainly possible to structure a test that deals with these questions, but each step takes us further away from the raw data.

A much simpler option is to eliminate all retracements that are greater than 100% of the setup leg and their subsequent extensions. Note that this is also a simple definition of a trend: a retracement less than 100% will hold a higher low in an uptrend or a lower high in a downtrend, which is a key structure in most market structure–oriented (as opposed to indicator-derived) definitions of a trend. Table 13.6 shows summary stats for all swings in the test universe that are less than or equal to 100% of the setup leg.

Table 13.6 Retracements Less Than or Equal to 100% of the Setup Leg

	N=	Mean	StDev	Median	IQR	Min	Max
Equities	78,455	65.4%	20.7%	66.4%	33.4%	1.2%	100.0%
Futures	2,459	64.4%	21.0%	64.9%	35.4%	4.9%	100.0%
Forex	858	66.1%	20.5%	67.5%	34.9%	16.6%	100.0%
Random	1,215	64.5%	21.8%	65.4%	35.8%	10.9%	100.0%
Total	82,987	65.3%	20.7%	66.3%	33.6%	1.2%	100.0%

This specification removes about 50% of the swings. As expected, it removes many large outliers; the mean moves much closer to the median and the measures of dispersion drop dramatically. In addition, we now see something very curious: both the mean and median are close to one of the most important Fibonacci ratios, 61.8 %, but are conclusively larger. Figure 13.7 shows a histogram of the retracement %ages; a visual representation can help us to understand what the results of this test. This histogram does not show any clear peak or distortion around either the 38.2 % or the 61.8 % Fibonacci ratio. The 38.2 % level seems to be a nonevent; there is no peak around the 61.8 level—80 % seems to be about as important as 50 %, and both are about as important as 61.8 or any other randomly chosen number in that general range. This is not what we should see if these Fibonacci levels are truly important.

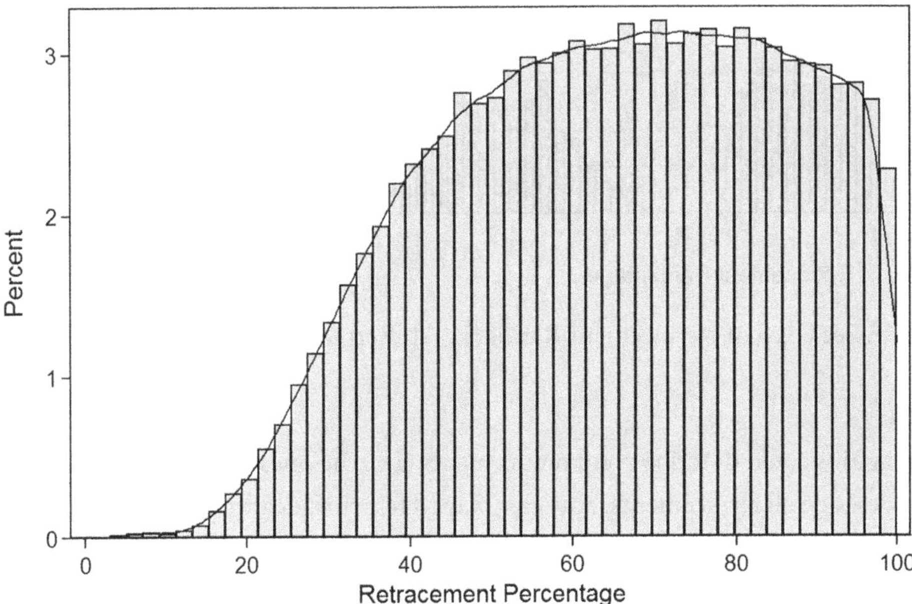

Figure 13.7 Histogram of Retracement Ratios for All Retracements Less Than 100%

It may also help to break this down by asset class, remembering, as Table 13.6 showed, that the sample sizes are small for both the forex and the random walk samples. Figure 13.8 shows the same data as Figure 13.7, but this time broken down into asset classes. The forex distribution immediately catches our attention, as the bimodal (having two peaks) distribution is reminiscent of the idealized Figure 13.6. However, this, and the shape of the random histogram, could be a result of the much smaller sample sizes, and at any rate the bump is around 48 %, not the 31.8% suggested by the Fibonacci ratios. The second peak in the forex histogram is centered around the 80 % area, again not a significant Fibonacci-derived ratio. From this breakout, there is, again, no evidence to support the claims that Fibonacci ratios are important.

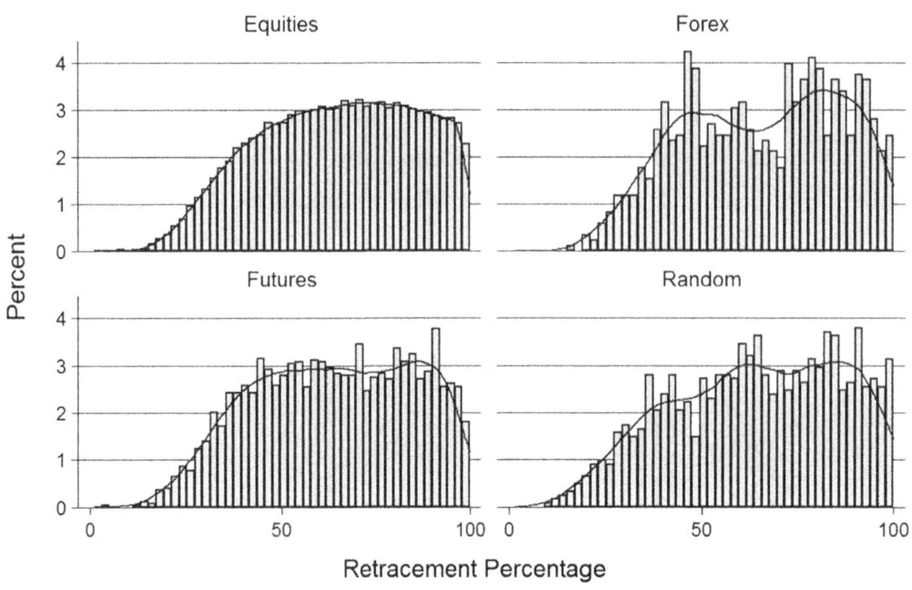

Figure 13.8 Histograms by Asset Class of Retracement Ratios for All Retracements Less Than 100%

Only the Best Trades

It is possible that Fibonacci ratios could describe good retracements (i.e., the ones that would be most profitable to trade) better than they describe all retracements. Any easy way to test this idea would be to identify good retracements using a set of post hoc criteria, being aware that we are creating a construct that could not be traded in real time. If we could find evidence that these Fibonacci ratios are more significant in these best-case examples, then it is not beyond the realm of possibility that a trader could develop the skill to identify them in real time. Remember, the key concept is that the trader would be positioning in the retracement leg for the extension. So, the trader would be buying into the downward retracement, looking to profit from the upswing of the extension, and vice versa in a downtrend. This test filters out qualified retracements using the following criteria:

- Length of the extension is greater than 25% of the setup leg. This condition assures that there was adequate profit potential in buying the pullback, and is actually quite conservative, as only perfect entries would give profits with such a small extension. (Note that the mean extension was much larger at 120%.)
- For long trades, the retracement held a higher low relative to the A point of the setup leg. This is equivalent to saying that the retracement is less than or equal to 100% of the setup leg.
- The extension must make a new high relative to the B point of the setup leg. An extension that fails to do so is a failure in a trend and cannot be considered an example of the best possible trade.

Table 13.7 gives summary statistics for qualified retracements.

Table 13.7 Summary Stats for Qualified Retracements

	N=	Mean	StDev	Median	IQR	Min	Max
Equities	49,062	63.3%	20.6%	63.6%	33.4%	1.2%	99.9%
Futures	1,566	61.9%	20.9%	62.1%	34.9%	4.9%	99.7%
Forex	544	64.9%	20.9%	66.1%	35.4%	16.6%	99.7%
Random	786	62.6%	21.4%	62.9%	35.8%	10.9%	100.0%
Total	51,958	63.3%	20.6%	63.6%	33.5%	1.2%	100.0%

This further specification removes approximately another 40 % of the swings. It is interesting to note that the measures of central tendency and dispersion are practically unchanged between the two sets. Figure 13.9 shows the distribution for all qualified swings, and Figure 13.10 breaks the distribution down into asset classes. Once again, it is clear from these distributions that there is no evidence of an unusual number of retracements terminating at or near important Fibonacci levels.

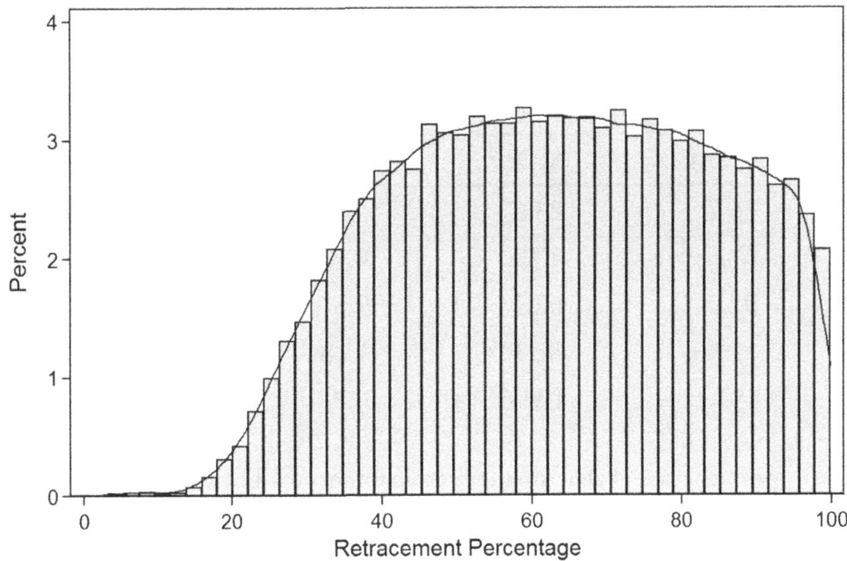

Figure 13.9 Histogram of Retracement Ratios for Qualified Extensions

Retracement Depth and Extension Length

It is also said that smaller retracements lead to larger extensions, or, more commonly, that shallower pullbacks lead to better, more powerful trend moves. One way to test this would be to categorize extensions by the depth of the preceding retracement. If this statement were true, the average extension should be larger for smaller pullbacks. Table 13.8 is a simple investigation of this idea. (Note that the swing definition methodology included a volatility filter that required the market to move a certain distance from previous swings to confirm a change in swing direction. This filter removes most very shallow retracements, which is why the sample size for this group is much smaller than the other groups. This is an artifact of the measurement methodology and not a reflection of market structure.)

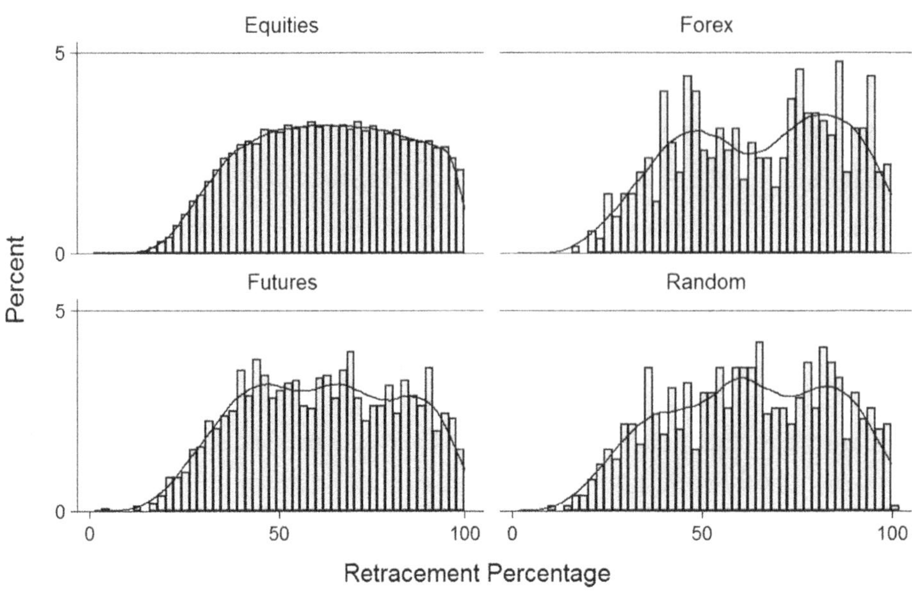

Figure 13.10 Histogram of Retracement Ratios for Qualified Extensions, by Asset Class

Table 13.8 Extensions Categorized by Retracement Depth (r)

Retracement	N=	Mean	StDev	Min	Max
r ≤ 25%	1,752	36.7	23.6	1.2	189.2
25% < r ≤ 50%	19,995	63.5	40.9	6.7	753.1
50% < r ≤ 75%	30,835	92.0	62.2	9.8	1,203.7
75%< r ≤ 100%	30,405	119.6	82.1	11.8	1,560.4
r > 100%	78,767	157.1	105.6	6.7	2,215.7

This simple test does not seem to support the belief that smaller retracements lead to strong extensions, but we could be missing something. It is possible that there are many very shallow retracements that lead to very powerful moves; this test would be blind to those retracements because they are filtered from the sample by the measurement methodology. The main purpose of these tests was to investigate Fibonacci retracements; very shallow retracements fall well short of the main Fibonacci levels, so they can be removed with no ill effects, but perhaps we want to see them for this specific test. It is possible to remove the volatility filter criterion to see if it is somehow distorting the data. Table 13.9 shows summary stats for all retracements less than 100 % of the setup leg, with the volatility filter removed. Compared to Table 13.6, we see that the number of total swings has increased nearly threefold, which is not surprising because many of these very small swings were essentially folded into larger swings by the volatility filter. Also, as expected, the measures of dispersion are considerably larger, as we now have many smaller swings. It is, however, very interesting that the mean and median of the swing proportions were not much affected by this dramatic change in sample size and measurement methodology. The actual size of the individual swings is considerably smaller with the filter removed, but the proportions and relationships are roughly maintained. This suggests that the volatility filter was not introducing a significant structural distortion.

Table 13.9 Summary Stats for Retracements Less Than or Equal to 100 % of the Setup Leg, No Volatility Filter

	N=	Mean	StDev	Median	IQR	Min	Max
Equities	120,405	63.9%	21.4%	64.6%	34.4%	1.4%	100.0%
Futures	3,718	62.9%	21.8%	63.3%	36.6%	2.2%	100.0%
Forex	1,515	64.2%	21.3%	64.0%	35.6%	16.8%	100.0%
Random	2,110	62.6%	22.2%	64.3%	35.6%	10.7%	100.0%
Total	127,748	63.8%	21.4%	64.6%	34.5%	1.4%	100.0%

Last, Table 13.10 reproduces the test in Table 13.8, this time with no volatility filter. Again, the number of swings increases dramatically, especially for the smaller swing sizes. However, the relationship is the same—we see no evidence that shallower retracements lead to strong extensions. In fact, the opposite is true, at least in this data set and time period examined: larger retracements actually set up larger proportional extensions, in clear contradiction of the standard teachings of technical analysis. Keep in mind that these are proportional measurements; a very small setup could lead to an extension that is proportionally much larger, while being nominally smaller, relative to an extension off a larger setup leg.

Table 13.10 Extensions Categorized by Retracement Depth, No Volatility Filter

Retracement	N=	Mean	StDev	Min	Max
r ≤ 25%	247,517	130.8	108.9	4.5	4,554.6
25% < r ≤ 50%	214,842	140.8	112.0	4.5	4,554.6
50% < r ≤ 75%	168,338	154.3	118.0	4.5	4,554.6
75%< r ≤ 100%	125,277	166.9	124.5	6.6	4,554.6
r > 100%	123,832	188.6	107.2	5.4	2,773.7

Conclusions

In this sample and these tests, we see no evidence that Fibonacci numbers are structurally important in the market. Furthermore, the received wisdom that shallower retracements lead to larger extensions is also strongly contradicted by the data. What we do see from the retracement histograms is a large plateau of retracement terminations, extending from roughly 40 % to 75 % of the setup leg. Though some of these tests on qualified extensions assumed foresight that is not possible in actual trading, the proportional relationships were not much affected by filtering out only these best trades—reinforcing the idea that we should look for retracements to terminate at about 50 % of the setup leg, with a very large margin of error.

There is a useful message here for discretionary traders: it is likely a serious mistake to use Fibonacci ratios as entry points, stops, or targets. This will be challenging to many traders, as it calls them to question many of their dearly held beliefs, but so much of the literature and thinking of Fibonacci traders is based on superstition and esoterica. It is also possible that these tests have missed some essential elements or structure (though they were repeated over a wide range of swing definition parameters), and that they do not offer conclusive disproof of Fibonacci ratios. Indeed, it is the nature of scientific inquiry that disproof is not possible, but it is difficult to see any utility in these ratios when they fail such simple high-level tests. There are far better tools for understanding the market's movements.

Chapter 14

Moving Averages

Statistics are used much like a drunk uses a lamppost; for support, not illumination.

-Vin Scully

Traders use moving averages for many purposes; we have seen a few ideas for specific applications earlier in this book, but it is worthwhile to now take a deep look at price action around moving averages. It is always surprising to me how many of the same concepts are repeated by traders, in the literature, and in the media without ever being tested: moving averages are support and resistance, moving averages define the trend, moving average crosses predict future price movements, and so forth. In devising quantitative tests of moving averages, we immediately run a problem: many traders use them in ways that are not amenable to testing. They may be part of a more complex methodology incorporation many discretionary factors, but there may also be some sloppy thinking involved in many cases. For instance, traders will argue that moving averages sometimes work as support and resistance, or that a moving average crossover is sometimes a good definition of trend. It is always possible to find an example of something working, and traders often tend to focus undue attention on a few outstanding examples. However, the real question is whether it is repeatable and reliable over a large sample size, and whether the tool adds predictive value to the trading process.

If you flip a coin whenever you have a trading decision you will find that the coin sometimes does seem to help you. It is also likely that, at the end of many trades, you would be able to remember a few dramatic examples where the coin made you a lot of money; perhaps it got you out of a losing trade early on, or kept you in a winner for the big trend. In fact, you might conclude that the coin doesn't work all the time, but nothing in trading works all the time. Perhaps you realize that it does help in certain cases so you are going to keep it and just use it sometimes. In fact, you might say, as many traders do of their indicators, that you "have to know when to look at it." Obviously, I am making a bit of a joke here, but the point is important. You have to be sure that the tools you are using are better than a coin flip, that they are better than random chance.

Moving Averages as Support or Resistance

A moving average is an average of a window of prices that is moved forward and recalculated for every bar. For instance, a standard 50-period moving average averages the last 50 closing prices, including the current bar's close. Since today's close, or the close of whatever time period is being used, cannot be known in advance, the current price is used until the closing price of the bar is established. This brings up an important point about moving averages: a standard moving average, calculated for the current bar, will change with every tick as the bar unfolds. For longer-term moving averages, today's price might be one of several hundred prices, so it would take a very large change today to significantly move the average. For shorter-term averages—some traders use averages as short as three to five bars for some purposes—the last price may have a dramatic impact. This effect creates a serious problem when examining moving averages on historical price charts, because the moving average you see on the chart did not exist in real time.

Moving Moving Averages?

Some writers (for instance, Kirkpatrick 2006) claim that moving averages function as support and resistance levels. This claim may be based, at least in part, on a casual inspection of historical charts, but it is important to remember that some of the most dramatic examples of moving average tests never actually occurred. Points where price appeared to have touched and moved away from an average may not have existed in real time because the moving averages actually move while the bar is being formed. Figure 14.1 shows an example of a near-perfect, to-the-tick test of a 20-period moving average on a daily chart of the S&P 500 index (NYSE: SPY). Based on this chart, we could assume that price traded down to the average, touched it, and was immediately pushed away as the market exploded to close at the highs of the day. This chart suggests that a trader who buys at the moving averages could have practically bought the very low of the day, as that is where the moving average intersects the price bar. Furthermore, this was at a structurally significant point in the market; catching this trade off the moving average would have given the trader a shot at catching a 13% advance over next few months.

Figure 14.1 Near-Perfect Example of a Moving Average Appearing to Act as Support

However, it was not possible to execute this trade at the average. Figure 14.2 shows the daily bar as it unfolded, at five separate points during the trading day, with the actual value of the moving average highlighted to the right of each small price chart. On the open, the moving average was well below the low of the day, and, later, as the market traded down to put in the low for the session (which was 108.94), the average was still well below the low of the day. As price rallied in the afternoon, the average also moved up, but it was still below the low of the day. It is important to remember that every time the current price changed, it pulled the moving average with it; try to see these five charts as snapshots in time. Finally, as the market exploded to close near the day's high, the average was pulled up into the low of the day, but this low had already been set many hours before. A trader executing on this signal would have had to buy the close of the day, not the moving average test at the low. This is not an example of a moving average acting as support—this is an illusion. The trade simply never happened. Any backtesting or system development based on price touching a moving average, including some of the tests in this chapter, suffers from this effect.

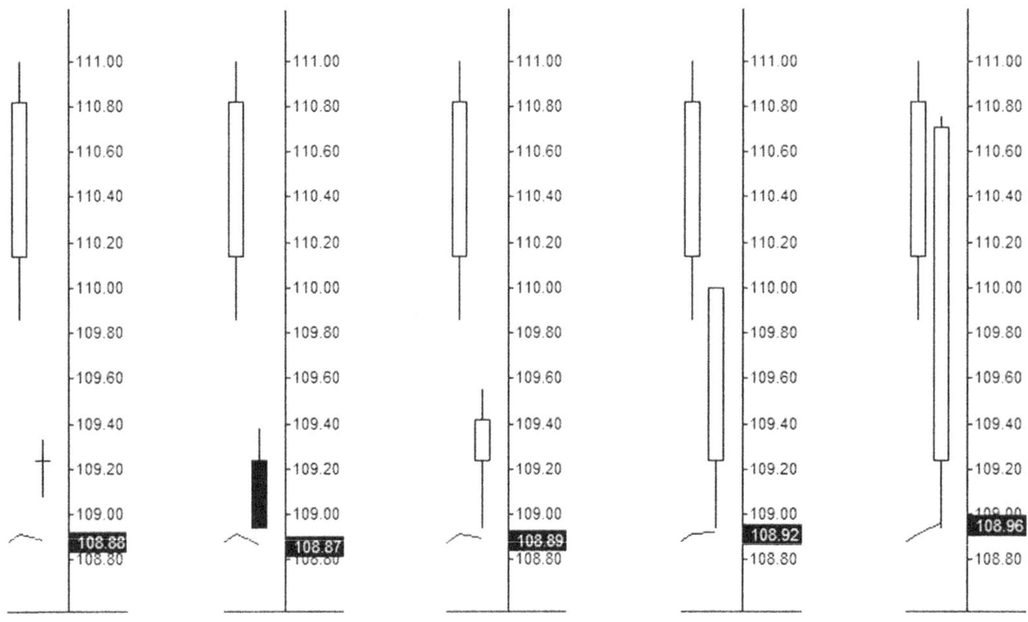

Figure 14.2 The Moving Average Is Pulled Up to Touch the Low of the Day as Price Rallies into the Close

Moving Average Variations

To deal with this issue, some traders offset the moving average a number of bars. For instance, you may use yesterday's moving average value, calculated on the close of that day, as today's average, or even the average of 5 to 10 bars ago. This has the benefit of being defined before the current bar begins, and, depending on the specific application of the moving average, may or may not have an impact on its ultimate utility. In addition, there are several variations of moving averages, including averages that weigh recent prices more than past prices, and averages that do not drop data points but rather decay them exponentially. Chapter 8 examines the behavior of simple moving averages (SMAs) and exponential moving averages (EMAs) in considerable detail from a perspective that might be useful to a discretionary trader. In this section, we focus on the hard facts of price behavior around simple moving averages.

The Tests

For the tests that follow, I make no attempt to test complete trading systems or complex methods. Instead, I am simply looking to see whether there is discernible, nonrandom price movement around moving averages. Does it make sense to make buying or selling decisions based on the relationship of price to a moving average? Do moving averages provide support? Are some moving averages more useful (special?) than others? Can moving averages define the trend of a market? Consider these to be fundamental tests of the building blocks and basic principles. There could well be modifying factors, not addressed in these simple tests, that do show an edge when combined with moving averages, or there could be ways to trade them profitably that are outside the scope of these tests. For now, let's start at the beginning and consider what happens when price touches a simple moving average.

Moving Average Touch and Hold on Close

There are only two possible outcomes as price engages a moving average: either the moving average level can hold on the close—meaning that, if price traded down to the moving average, the bar closes above the level—or it can fail as the bar closes under the average. Let's consider the first case, in which price touches the moving average but the moving average holds on close. Figure 14.3 shows visual examples of valid tests of a 20-period EMA. We will use the Pythia framework for testing purposes, which takes a criteria set, generates a buy or sell signal if a bar fulfills the condition, and then generates a composite return for each day after the signal. Note that I am not suggesting this or any signal could be traded based on such simple criteria; this is just a robust way to do a pure test of tendencies around a potential trading signal. Also, it is very possible that I have the buy and sell signals flipped—in other words, what I think is a buy may actually be a sell. This is not a problem within this testing framework, as we would simply see that buy signals had an edge for negative excess returns and sell signals showed positive excess returns.

Criteria for Moving Average Touch and Hold Test

```
AVG = Average(close, N)            //Set average length here.
IF all of the following are true:
Low of previous bar > AVG on previous bar.
Low of current bar ≤ AVG           //Moving average touched on this bar.
Close of current bar ≥ AVG         //Market is unable to close below moving average.
THEN buy this bar on close.
Conditions are symmetrical for sell signal.
```

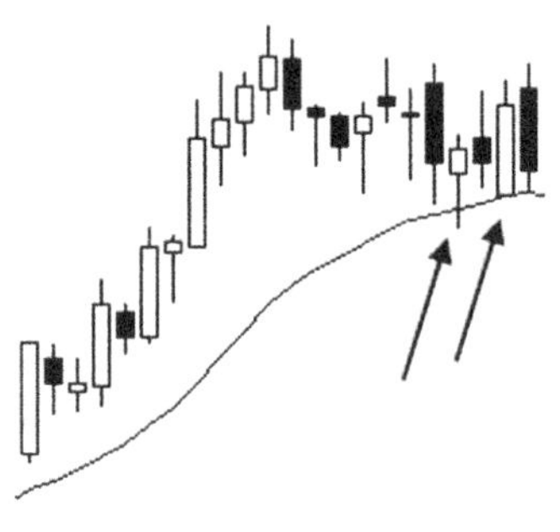

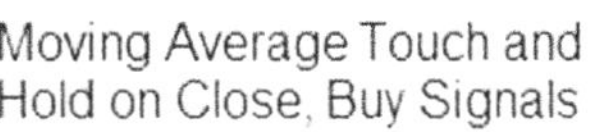

Moving Average Touch and
Hold on Close, Sell Signals

Figure 14.3 Examples of Valid Moving Average Touch and Hold on Close

Many traders watch the 50-day moving average, with the justification that it provides support or resistance because "hedge funds watch it" or that many other traders like to buy around the 50-day moving average. Of course, there's an important assumption here—do people really watch and use this level? If this were true, it should be possible to find nonrandom price tendencies around this average. Table 14.1 shows summary statistics for successful tests and holds of a 50-period simple moving average. Take a minute to familiarize yourself with the table format, because you will be seeing it many times throughout the rest of this chapter.

- The rows in the table are for days following the signal event. Days one to five are presented, and the table then switches to a weekly format. This allows assessment of short-term tendencies while still maintaining a longer-term perspective.
- Excess mean returns (labeled $\mu_{sig} - \mu_b$), may be the most useful summary statistic for these tests. To generate this number, the mean return for the baseline of the sample universe (e.g., the drift component of stock returns) is subtracted from the mean of all signal events.
- Diff median is the excess median, or the baseline median return subtracted from the signal median return.
- Because these may be very small numbers, they are displayed in basis points (one basis point equals one-hundredth of a percent: 0.0001 = 0.01% = 1 bp) rather than percentages.
- Asterisks indicate statistical significance at the 0.05 and 0.01 levels.
- The percentage of days that close higher than the entry price is also indicated in the %Up column, but this number needs to be compared for the raw %Up in the baseline.

In an ideal trading signal, working as we supposed it would, the buys would show a positive excess return, indicating that they went up more, on average, than the baseline, and the sell signals would show a consistently negative excess return. This may not be intuitive at first glance, so consider it carefully: buys should show positive excess returns while sells show negative excess returns. There is a lot of information in this table, and it is only a summary of the more complete information presented in Appendix B.

Based on the information in this table, it does appear that there is statistically significant activity around the 50-period simple moving average, but, as you might have expected, there is more to the story. First of all, notice that there is inconsistency between asset classes: Futures and forex show slight positive tendencies for the buy setup, while equities show a consistently negative return for buying bounces off the 50-period SMA. (This is not technically a problem with the test, but it does suggest that we mis-specified the criteria. What we thought was a buy has turned out to be a statistically significant sell, at least in equities.) The magnitude of the excess returns in both futures and forex are insignificant for the buy test, while forex actually does show a slight edge (means and medians both consistently negative) for the sell setup. Equities are more complicated; remember, the idea is that funds and large traders are supposed to be watching this average, so the received wisdom is that their buying pressure at the average provides support. We find that this claim is not supported by this test. In this sample, if you were to buy every successful test of the 50-period moving average, you would have shown a loss for many days following the signal, as indicated by the negative and statistically significant mean return. There is no clear edge for the sell setup in equities, as mean and median returns diverge significantly.

Though this is a complex and unclear relationship, one thing is clear: it is not what we should have seen if what traders say about the 50-period moving average were true. Certainly, if we had refined the test with multiple conditions (perhaps considering specific price patterns, distances from the moving average, or overall market conditions), we could have arrived at a test that showed a positive edge—it is always possible to massage statistical data to give a desired answer, but the point here is to see if there is an actual, quantifiable edge to this moving average. The answer is not as clear as might have been hoped, but simple, clear answers are unusual in market data.

There seems to be some unusual activity going on in at least two of the "boxes" of this test—the buy signal for equities and the sell signal for forex. It might be instructive to take a look at another, similar moving average to see if there is, in fact, something special about the 50-period moving average. It stands to reason that, if institutions are watching the 50-period average, they are not watching the 45-period. (If this logic does not hold, it becomes kind of silly in the limit; eventually every possible moving average is a potentially significant level, and literally every possible price is intersected by some moving average.) Figure 14.4 shows a 45-period SMA compared to a 50 period SMA; they are very similar, but the 45-period average tracks price more closely since it responds to recent data more quickly. If there is unusual institutional support at the 50-period moving average, it is reasonable to assume that we should be able to see a difference between that average and the 45-period. Table 14.2 shows the results of a test on the 45-period moving average.

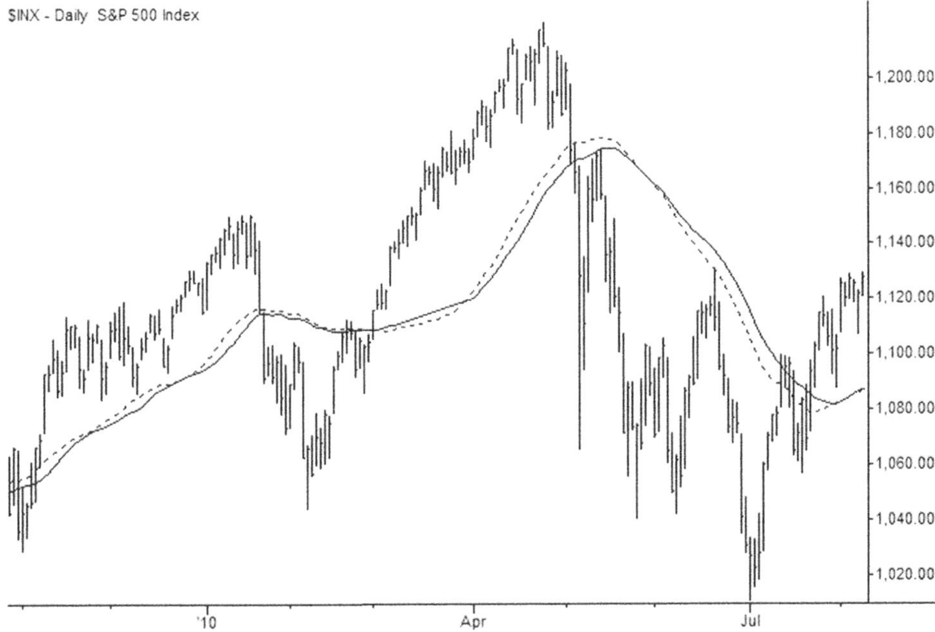

Figure 14.4 Comparison of 50-Period (Solid Line) and 45-Period (Dotted Line) Moving Averages

Table 14.1 Touch and Hold Test, 50-Period SMA

	Equities—Buy			Futures—Buy			Forex—Buy		
Days	$\mu_{sig} - \mu_b$	Diff. Med.	%Up	$\mu_{sig} - \mu_b$	Diff. Med.	%Up	$\mu_{sig} - \mu_b$	Diff. Med.	%Up
1	(5.1)**	(2.3)	49.6%	0.2	(3.5)	48.4%	0.7	1.0	54.0%
2	(6.3)**	2.3	50.9%	6.7	(3.4)	50.9%	0.7	3.8	53.6%
3	(8.8)**	(0.4)	50.7%	6.3	(9.8)	50.1%	3.3	(12.1)	48.3%
4	(10.5)**	5.7	51.6%	9.4	(20.0)	48.2%	9.1	6.8	52.5%
5	(4.9)	12.8	52.3%	15.2	(14.3)	50.6%	12.4	(1.1)	51.7%
10	(24.9)**	15.8	52.8%	18.5	(26.0)	50.6%	3.5	6.1	57.9%
15	(41.0)**	25.0	53.3%	23.7	(45.0)	50.9%	(6.3)	0.5	54.0%
20	(62.9)**	16.5	53.2%	41.0	(41.4)	52.4%	(7.0)	(12.0)	55.6%
	Equities—Sell			Futures—Sell			Forex—Sell		
Days	$\mu_{sig} - \mu_b$	Diff. Med.	%Up	$\mu_{sig} - \mu_b$	Diff. Med.	%Up	$\mu_{sig} - \mu_b$	Diff. Med.	%Up
1	3.7	3.3	50.9%	(4.9)	(10.2)	46.0%	(8.5)	(5.3)	47.0%
2	4.7	6.5	51.6%	2.0	(9.8)	48.8%	(16.6)*	(13.1)	43.9%
3	(2.5)	7.0	51.7%	0.8	(11.1)	49.1%	(15.6)	(18.2)	46.1%
4	(3.1)	6.8	51.8%	3.6	(5.6)	51.4%	(16.5)	(29.6)	46.1%
5	(9.1)*	10.2	52.1%	4.1	(8.2)	51.1%	(15.9)	(22.3)	47.0%
10	(13.1)*	26.3	53.7%	18.1	(6.6)	52.6%	(29.5)*	(44.1)	46.1%
15	(22.4)**	48.2	55.1%	2.8	(21.9)	52.3%	(36.0)*	(50.0)	47.0%
20	(27.0)**	63.3	55.8%	(10.5)	(85.3)	48.9%	(30.5)	(56.7)	48.7%

Results for means and medians are in basis points, excess returns over the baseline for that asset class. %Up gives the number of days that closed higher than the entry price on the day following the signal entry. For comparison, the% of one day Up closes in the Equity sample is 50.07%; in the Futures sample, 50.59%, and in Forex 51.0%.

* indicates difference of means are significant at the 0.05 level, and ** indicates they are significant at the 0.01 level.

This table shows that there is little difference between the 45- and 50-period moving averages, which strongly contradicts the claims that the 50-period is somehow special. We might not expect to find dramatic, easily exploitable results in a blunt test like this, but, if the 50-period moving average is significant, it should at least be distinguishable from the other lengths of moving averages. Remember, we are not looking for an actual trading signal here; we are looking for at least some hint of a statistical anomaly around this moving average. You will find results that are similar to the previous tables regardless of the average length examined. Reproducing all of those tables is not a constructive use of time or space, but there is another way to structure an interesting test. Figure 14.5 shows an unusual moving average: the period of this average random walks between 30 and 70. On every bar, the length of the moving average is either increased by 1, decreased by 1, or stays the same, based on the outcome of a pseudo-random number generator. The average is literally different every time the chart is recalculated. Table 14.3 shows the results of the moving average test on this random moving average. The results show that the 45- and 50-period moving averages for equities are, literally, indistinguishable from any other random level.

Table 14.2 Touch and Hold Test, 45-Period SMA

	Equities—Buy			Futures—Buy			Forex—Buy		
Days	$\mu_{sig} - \mu_b$	Diff. Med.	%Up	$\mu_{sig} - \mu_b$	Diff. Med.	%Up	$\mu_{sig} - \mu_b$	Diff. Med.	%Up
1	(4.1)*	(2.3)	49.4%	(3.0)	(3.5)	49.9%	(0.8)	(3.1)	48.7%
2	(7.3)**	0.9	50.7%	(6.2)	(7.0)	49.3%	(4.1)	(5.2)	48.4%
3	(7.2)**	0.3	50.9%	2.7	(3.4)	51.1%	4.7	2.4	51.3%
4	(9.3)**	5.7	51.5%	6.2	(10.9)	50.2%	1.5	(3.6)	51.3%
5	(3.8)	12.3	52.4%	(2.7)	(13.1)	50.6%	8.0	(2.1)	51.6%
10	(23.5)**	13.0	52.8%	2.6	(14.1)	52.4%	0.7	(4.4)	52.3%
15	(45.7)**	18.2	53.1%	7.1	(40.3)	51.4%	(6.9)	(8.0)	53.8%
20	(64.8)**	15.1	53.2%	17.0	(44.5)	52.7%	(6.9)	(25.5)	52.7%
	Equities—Sell			Futures—Sell			Forex—Sell		
Days	$\mu_{sig} - \mu_b$	Diff. Med.	%Up	$\mu_{sig} - \mu_b$	Diff. Med.	%Up	$\mu_{sig} - \mu_b$	Diff. Med.	%Up
1	2.6	1.9	50.6%	(2.3)	(6.7)	48.6%	(12.9)**	(13.0)	42.5%
2	5.2	5.8	51.4%	(0.2)	(2.5)	51.6%	(16.7)*	(12.1)	44.6%
3	(1.5)	5.2	51.4%	10.2	16.0	54.7%	(23.5)**	(24.4)	42.5%
4	(4.0)	6.3	51.5%	12.7	6.4	53.3%	(25.4)**	(18.3)	47.2%
5	(13.8)**	4.4	51.4%	1.9	(4.6)	51.7%	(31.0)**	(20.4)	46.8%
10	(21.2)**	25.7	53.4%	5.1	(23.2)	51.0%	(39.2)**	(39.0)	46.4%
15	(25.4)**	49.2	54.9%	(1.9)	(26.7)	52.9%	(32.1)	(48.5)	48.5%
20	(29.6)**	66.1	55.7%	3.4	(18.1)	53.6%	(40.5)*	(50.9)	48.1%

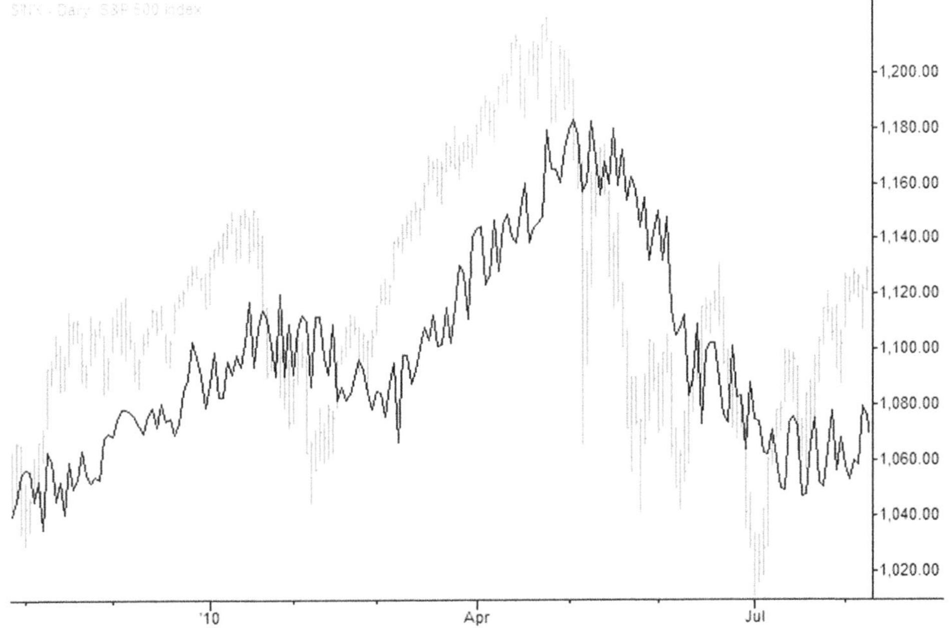

Figure 14.5 S&P 500 Chart with Random Walk Period Moving Average

Table 14.3 Touch and Hold Test, Random Period SMA

	Equities—Buy			Futures—Buy			Forex—Buy		
Days	$\mu_{sig} - \mu_b$	Diff. Med.	%Up	$\mu_{sig} - \mu_b$	Diff. Med.	%Up	$\mu_{sig} - \mu_b$	Diff. Med.	%Up
1	(7.2)**	(2.3)	49.1%	1.3	0.9	51.6%	(0.3)	(2.1)	49.1%
2	(5.7)**	1.2	50.7%	(4.7)	(8.5)	48.7%	(2.6)	(7.0)	48.3%
3	(4.1)	5.4	51.5%	(7.1)	(10.5)	49.5%	(4.5)	(5.5)	50.1%
4	(6.6)*	5.6	51.6%	(5.9)	(17.3)	49.3%	(4.1)	0.8	52.6%
5	(2.5)	14.1	52.4%	(6.1)	(15.2)	50.1%	(7.5)	(10.5)	49.7%
10	(25.0)**	11.9	52.6%	(8.0)	(20.1)	51.8%	(10.0)	(12.9)	51.9%
15	(39.2)**	24.5	53.7%	(20.1)	(39.5)	51.4%	(7.7)	(16.6)	53.3%
20	(61.4)**	20.1	53.6%	(16.7)	(62.8)	50.7%	(13.4)	(23.3)	52.6%
	Equities—Sell			Futures—Sell			Forex—Sell		
Days	$\mu_{sig} - \mu_b$	Diff. Med.	%Up	$\mu_{sig} - \mu_b$	Diff. Med.	%Up	$\mu_{sig} - \mu_b$	Diff. Med.	%Up
1	2.7	3.1	50.9%	1.6	(2.1)	50.2%	(1.6)	0.3	51.2%
2	2.7	3.7	51.1%	(1.3)	(4.4)	50.4%	(0.9)	5.4	54.6%
3	(3.7)	5.9	51.5%	2.7	(5.8)	51.0%	3.5	9.3	56.5%
4	(4.2)	7.1	51.6%	5.4	(9.2)	50.9%	6.3	12.1	55.1%
5	(9.6)*	9.4	52.0%	4.8	(0.4)	53.3%	(1.8)	(3.7)	52.9%
10	(18.7)**	27.8	53.3%	(0.5)	(19.4)	52.1%	3.4	9.1	57.5%
15	(17.5)*	51.9	54.9%	0.5	(35.1)	52.1%	(0.5)	(2.8)	55.7%
20	(18.9)*	70.1	55.8%	(1.9)	(57.2)	51.0%	(4.4)	2.9	56.8%

Before moving on to another type of test, I know many readers are probably saying, "What about the 200-day moving average?" The 200-day moving average has been important in the investment literature for decades, at least since Joseph Granville wrote about it in the 1940s. To many casual chart readers and traders, the 200-day is the ultimate line in the sand. Supposedly, many funds are able to own only stocks that are above their 200-day moving averages, and the major media are quick to print stories every time a stock market index crosses this level. Surely, such a well-watched and respected level must be statistically significant. Table 14.4 presents results for the touch and hold test for the vaunted 200-day moving average. Compare this table to the previous ones. The numbers, in this case, truly do speak for themselves.

Table 14.4 Touch and Hold Test, 200-Day SMA

	Equities—Buy			Futures—Buy			Forex—Buy		
Days	$\mu_{sig} - \mu_b$	Diff. Med.	%Up	$\mu_{sig} - \mu_b$	Diff. Med.	%Up	$\mu_{sig} - \mu_b$	Diff. Med.	%Up
1	(13.3)**	(4.5)	48.1%	(5.7)	0.0	50.8%	(3.1)	2.9	55.7%
2	(10.6)**	(3.3)	50.0%	0.8	(4.8)	50.8%	(0.0)	14.5	59.4%
3	(13.2)**	2.2	51.0%	(12.3)	(22.4)	47.1%	9.5	18.4	60.4%
4	(16.6)**	6.1	51.4%	(6.3)	(14.0)	49.5%	4.3	12.1	58.5%
5	(11.0)*	10.5	51.9%	(12.1)	(8.2)	51.1%	(0.6)	(1.5)	54.7%
10	(57.5)**	(6.2)	51.1%	9.2	(23.2)	51.1%	12.9	1.5	52.8%
15	(78.6)**	11.9	52.6%	31.2	(13.1)	53.8%	11.6	(23.3)	53.8%
20	(97.4)**	9.6	53.1%	23.5	(20.1)	56.9%	5.5	(15.2)	53.8%
	Equities—Sell			Futures—Sell			Forex—Sell		
Days	$\mu_{sig} - \mu_b$	Diff. Med.	%Up	$\mu_{sig} - \mu_b$	Diff. Med.	%Up	$\mu_{sig} - \mu_b$	Diff. Med.	%Up
1	(3.6)	(2.3)	49.5%	(4.0)	(13.4)	41.2%	0.1	(6.8)	44.4%
2	(8.5)*	0.6	50.5%	(11.3)	(8.8)	49.1%	3.2	(3.1)	50.9%
3	(15.0)**	4.6	51.4%	(15.6)	(10.5)	49.8%	(1.0)	(4.8)	50.9%
4	(6.3)	9.3	52.3%	(10.9)	(34.2)	46.8%	9.5	8.4	54.6%
5	(11.3)	8.7	52.4%	(11.0)	(12.9)	50.6%	11.3	(1.8)	52.8%
10	(28.0)**	30.2	54.0%	(9.0)	(22.7)	50.9%	13.9	25.3	59.3%
15	(49.4)**	43.1	54.7%	(26.4)	(52.8)	49.8%	5.1	12.7	57.4%
20	(62.4)**	48.7	54.5%	(14.0)	(50.0)	53.2%	(1.3)	(14.8)	52.8%

Price Crossing a Moving Average

Though the Touch and Hold test is a logical way to examine price action around moving averages, it might be a good idea to consider some other possibilities. For instance, what happens after price breaks through a moving average? If moving averages are, in fact, important support or resistance levels, if large traders are making trading decisions based on the relationship of price to the average, we should see some reaction after the moving average fails to contain prices. It would be reasonable to assume that traders will exit or adjust positions on the break of the average, and this buying or selling pressure should cause distortions in the returns. We call this test the Moving Average Penetration test.

Criteria for Moving Average Penetration Test

Use the following criteria to define the buy signal:
AVG = Average(close, N) //Set average length here.
IF all of the following are true:
Low of previous bar > AVG on previous bar.
Close of this bar < AVG //Market closes below moving average.
THEN buy this bar on close.
Conditions are symmetrical for sell signal.

This set of conditions would have the trader always fading, or going against, price movements through a moving average: if price breaks below a moving average after being above it, this rule set will generate a buy signal. It is entirely possible that this is backwards, and perhaps these should be traded as breakouts by going with the direction of the price movement. Again, it does not matter; if the criteria are flipped for buy and sell signals, we will simply see negative excess returns for buys and positive for sells. Figure 14.6 shows examples of both buy and sell signals for this test.

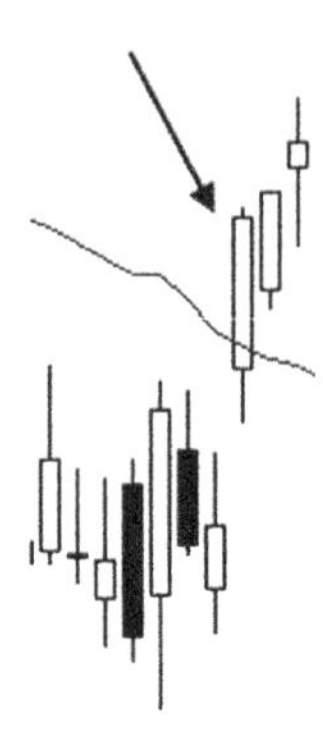

Moving Average Fade
Break, Sell Signals

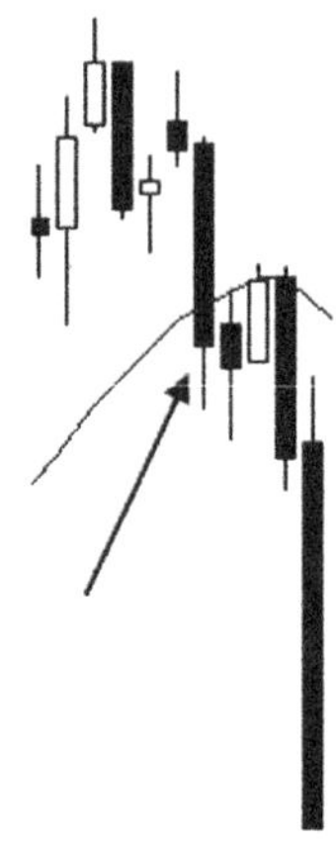

Moving Average Fade
Break, Buy Signal

Figure 14.6 Moving Average Penetration (Fade Break) Signals

Table 14.5 and Table 14.6 show the results of this Moving Average Penetration test, using 50- and 200-day moving averages.

Table 14.5 Penetration (Fade Break), 50-Period SMA

	Equities—Buy			Futures—Buy			Forex—Buy		
Days	$\mu_{sig} - \mu_b$	Diff. Med.	%Up	$\mu_{sig} - \mu_b$	Diff. Med.	%Up	$\mu_{sig} - \mu_b$	Diff. Med.	%Up
1	2.8	2.7	50.7%	3.3	6.3	54.0%	(4.7)	(6.0)	46.4%
2	1.5	4.3	51.2%	(5.6)	(7.0)	48.6%	(10.3)	(16.5)	42.0%
3	1.7	4.8	51.4%	(10.8)	(20.3)	47.7%	(4.8)	(11.7)	47.8%
4	(2.0)	2.7	51.4%	(3.8)	(24.5)	47.8%	0.2	(9.4)	49.6%
5	(1.9)	9.1	51.8%	(1.7)	(23.3)	48.7%	(6.0)	(17.2)	48.2%
10	(15.2)**	17.9	52.9%	(6.4)	(39.7)	49.0%	(2.9)	(12.4)	51.8%
15	(32.7)**	26.1	53.5%	(8.5)	(41.0)	51.4%	(3.2)	(8.0)	54.5%
20	(35.6)**	38.1	54.0%	(4.1)	(63.9)	50.4%	18.6	12.6	57.6%
	Equities—Sell			Futures—Sell			Forex—Sell		
Days	$\mu_{sig} - \mu_b$	Diff. Med.	%Up	$\mu_{sig} - \mu_b$	Diff. Med.	%Up	$\mu_{sig} - \mu_b$	Diff. Med.	%Up
1	(12.6)**	(5.2)	48.6%	0.4	(3.5)	48.9%	0.2	(3.4)	46.9%
2	(14.6)**	(1.2)	50.3%	9.5	0.1	52.5%	(7.4)	(8.1)	46.9%
3	(16.8)**	1.4	50.9%	14.1	11.7	54.7%	(6.7)	(3.7)	51.4%
4	(19.8)**	2.9	51.2%	12.8	12.3	56.4%	(1.9)	3.5	53.1%
5	(22.6)**	6.2	51.7%	12.8	8.8	54.0%	(5.6)	0.4	51.4%
10	(32.7)**	20.5	53.2%	9.4	4.7	55.6%	8.3	20.2	57.6%
15	(43.4)**	33.3	54.2%	9.1	0.2	55.0%	20.2	12.8	55.9%
20	(40.2)**	51.4	54.8%	20.6	9.6	56.8%	17.8	13.1	58.0%

These results appear to be interesting, at least for the equities sample. The sell signals (which, remember, are based on shorting the first bar that closes above a moving average) show a consistent negative edge, and this edge is statistically significant. The buy signals also show an interesting pattern, but it is not as clear or as strong. The buys (again, this is buying the first bar that closes below a moving average) show an initial small positive edge that appears to decay into a negative edge between 5 to 10 days from the signal. This decay of a positive signal into a statistically significant sell signal may be a bit surprising; to better understand the dynamics involved we should ask if it could be due to the effect of a large outlier. Though the data is not reproduced in these tables, this effect does not seem to be attributable to a single outlier; when the equities universe is split into large-cap, mid-cap, and small-cap samples, the same signal decay is apparent in all market capitalization slices. If this were due to an aberration in a single stock, the decay would most likely be limited to a single market cap. It is also interesting to note that, while we have interesting patterns in equities, the futures and forex groups do not show any predictable pattern. This is the strongest clue we have had so far in these tests that perhaps not all assets trade the same from a quantitative perspective. If we continue to see evidence that assets behave differently, this would seem to present a significant challenge to the claims that all technical tools can be applied to any market or time frame with no adaptation.

Table 14.6 Penetration (Fade Break), 200-Period SMA

	Equities—Buy			Futures—Buy			Forex—Buy		
Days	$\mu_{sig} - \mu_b$	Diff. Med.	%Up	$\mu_{sig} - \mu_b$	Diff. Med.	%Up	$\mu_{sig} - \mu_b$	Diff. Med.	%Up
1	9.4 **	7.7	51.7%	5.7	6.2	53.3%	(2.1)	(4.7)	47.9%
2	9.4 *	13.2	52.6%	(0.4)	7.1	52.4%	10.2	2.5	54.5%
3	5.1	10.3	52.1%	(3.2)	(10.5)	49.8%	9.5	(3.5)	52.1%
4	(3.8)	7.5	51.7%	(4.9)	(7.6)	50.5%	8.3	(5.8)	50.4%
5	1.4	14.8	52.6%	(7.9)	(22.5)	49.2%	14.5	2.8	54.5%
10	(25.1)**	16.2	52.4%	2.4	(24.2)	50.5%	27.1	35.7	55.4%
15	(44.8)**	29.7	53.5%	29.3	(13.3)	55.8%	52.4 *	40.7	61.2%
20	(57.2)**	35.2	54.0%	(0.8)	(57.8)	50.2%	37.5	20.2	61.2%
	Equities—Sell			Futures—Sell			Forex—Sell		
Days	$\mu_{sig} - \mu_b$	Diff. Med.	%Up	$\mu_{sig} - \mu_b$	Diff. Med.	%Up	$\mu_{sig} - \mu_b$	Diff. Med.	%Up
1	(16.2)**	(9.6)	47.6%	(3.6)	(3.5)	48.2%	(4.7)	(2.8)	48.1%
2	(28.1)**	(9.2)	48.8%	(3.2)	(12.5)	47.9%	(2.3)	4.2	54.6%
3	(31.6)**	(11.9)	49.0%	1.3	(11.9)	49.6%	(6.7)	5.9	55.6%
4	(31.9)**	(11.2)	49.5%	1.1	5.7	54.6%	(1.7)	1.3	55.6%
5	(35.5)**	(11.3)	49.9%	15.2	(5.9)	52.4%	7.1	14.4	58.3%
10	(55.5)**	3.8	52.0%	10.9	(11.6)	52.1%	19.0	24.2	58.3%
15	(83.9)**	8.4	52.6%	11.0	(36.1)	52.1%	20.1	19.8	57.4%
20	(91.7)**	23.5	53.5%	(12.7)	(31.4)	52.6%	9.0	11.0	54.6%

Results from other tests, though not reproduced here, look very similar regardless of period (from 10 to 200) or type (exponential or simple) of moving average used in the test—the curious distortion in equity returns persists. Also, running the test on the random walk period moving average, not surprisingly, generates similar results. This might be a good place to pause and to think about what is going here. Based on these tests, we see absolutely no evidence validating moving averages as important levels. In the data and the results, we cannot distinguish between the different periods of moving averages: 20, 45, 50, 65, 150, 185, 200, 233, and any others basically all look the same. However, there is an unusual pattern in the Moving Average Penetration tests that warrants deeper investigation. Regardless of what moving average is used, there appears to be a statistically significant edge, at least in equities, for buying closes below and shorting closes above the moving average. Here is a radical thought: what happens if we repeat this test without the moving average?

Yes, a test of moving averages without the average. Before you decide I have gone completely insane, consider the criteria for this Moving Average Penetration test. For a buy, price has to close below the average, and the previous bar's low had to be above the average. In almost all cases, this means that the entry bar's close is below yesterday's low. Sure, it is possible that, in a few rare cases, the moving average could actually have risen enough that it is above yesterday's low, but this is unlikely. It is far more likely that a close below the moving average is also a close below yesterday's low. Figure 14.7 and Figure 14.8 show graphical examples of fading a close outside the previous day's range, and Table 14.7 presents summary statistics for this test.

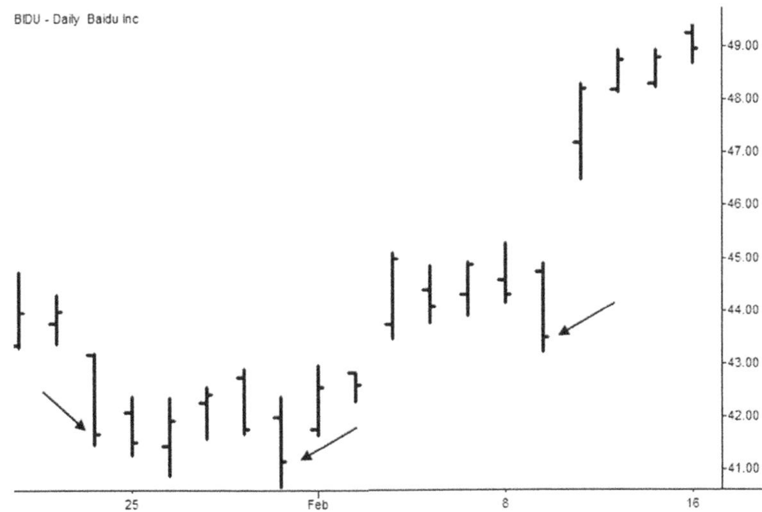

Figure 14.7 Fading (Buying) Closes Below the Previous Day's Low

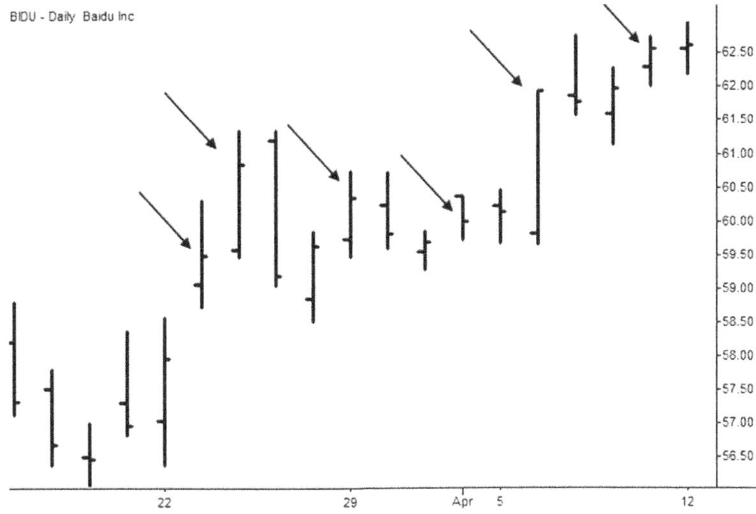

Figure 14.8 Fading (Shorting) Closes Above the Previous Day's High

Now we are getting somewhere, and this is important, so make sure you understand this next point: First of all, these results look remarkably similar to the moving average breaks, at least for the first five days: Equities show a fairly large and statistically significant negative return after the sell condition. Equities also show a much smaller, but still significant, positive return following the buy condition. Though this is not conclusive evidence, it strongly suggests that the observed statistical edge around the moving average is simply a function of stocks' tendency to reverse after a close outside of the previous day's range. This is an expression of mean reversion, which is one of the verifiable, fundamental aspects of price movement.

Table 14.7 Fade Close Outside Previous Day's Range

	Equities—Buy			Futures—Buy			Forex—Buy		
Days	$\mu_{sig} - \mu_b$	Diff. Med.	%Up	$\mu_{sig} - \mu_b$	Diff. Med.	%Up	$\mu_{sig} - \mu_b$	Diff. Med.	%Up
1	9.1 **	7.1	51.9%	1.6	4.0	52.6%	1.8	4.3	54.2%
2	12.1 **	13.8	52.8%	1.9	(2.2)	51.2%	2.1	3.8	54.2%
3	12.7 **	16.8	53.0%	1.0	(4.9)	51.0%	2.1	0.4	52.4%
4	14.6 **	21.5	53.3%	0.4	(8.2)	50.9%	(0.4)	0.9	53.1%
5	20.7 **	29.0	54.0%	0.7	(9.5)	50.9%	(2.7)	(4.4)	51.5%
10	17.9 **	50.8	55.2%	0.1	(22.3)	51.3%	(5.3)	(5.2)	53.3%
15	16.2 **	69.0	55.9%	1.0	(29.7)	52.1%	(5.6)	(2.9)	54.4%
20	12.4 **	79.5	56.2%	(3.6)	(43.6)	52.0%	(11.8)*	(10.5)	54.4%
	Equities—Sell			Futures—Sell			Forex—Sell		
Days	$\mu_{sig} - \mu_b$	Diff. Med.	%Up	$\mu_{sig} - \mu_b$	Diff. Med.	%Up	$\mu_{sig} - \mu_b$	Diff. Med.	%Up
1	(8.9)**	(4.5)	48.7%	(3.3)*	(5.6)	47.9%	(2.8)*	(4.2)	47.5%
2	(14.6)**	(4.5)	49.6%	(2.9)	(4.1)	50.5%	(2.1)	(4.2)	49.6%
3	(15.3)**	(2.8)	50.3%	(0.9)	(1.3)	52.0%	(1.9)	1.0	53.1%
4	(19.4)**	(2.8)	50.6%	(1.3)	(1.7)	52.4%	0.0	3.1	53.8%
5	(23.5)**	(2.0)	50.9%	(2.1)	(3.1)	52.4%	(0.0)	4.3	54.3%
10	(35.1)**	9.1	52.4%	(4.4)	(17.3)	52.0%	0.9	6.9	55.1%
15	(43.8)**	23.0	53.6%	(1.9)	(31.4)	52.0%	1.2	2.3	55.7%
20	(48.0)**	38.7	54.5%	3.8	(38.6)	52.8%	3.1	(1.3)	56.0%

It is also worth considering that what you see in Table 14.7 is significant on another level as well—these results strongly suggest that equities do not follow a random walk. Random walk markets would not show this anomaly. (Though the results are not presented here, in general, deviations of less than 2 basis points were seen from the baseline when this test was reproduced on random walk markets.) This is an extremely simple test with one criterion that produces a result that raises a serious challenge to one of the accepted academic hypotheses. We can say, based on this sample of 600 stocks over the past 10 years, that we find sufficient evidence to reject the random walk hypothesis for equities.

We're not done yet, however. The situation for futures and forex is a bit more complicated. On one hand, there is a measurable difference in the proportion of positive closes on the first day after the signal. The Futures baseline closes up 50.6% of the time, compared to 52.6% and 47.9% for the buy and sell signals, respectively, and the forex baseline closes up 51.0 percent, compared to 54.2% and 47.5% for buy and sell signals. These differences are statistically significant, and could potentially give an edge in some situations. However, we have to note that the magnitude of the signal, in terms of deviation from the baseline, is very, very small. This is certainly too small to be economically significant on its own, but perhaps could be a head start when combined with some other factors. This is something we are going to see again and again in quantitative tests: futures and forex consistently tend to more closely approximate random walks than equities.

You might also ask why they will not rewrite the academic books if we have just disproved the random walk theory. Good question, and there are several answers: One, the size of the effect, even in the equities sample, is fairly small at 29 basis points for buy signals and 24 bp for sells five days after the signal. Would you really run a trading system designed to hold a $100 asset for a week to capture $0.25? The answer to that may well be yes; there are some traders who could capture an edge this small, but in our case, it does not matter since we do not intend to trade these ideas systematically. They are useful only as a hint or a guidepost to suggest where trading opportunities might lie, and to reveal some otherwise hidden elements of market structure. You could also challenge these results on the basis that they might not be representative of the whole market. I would disagree because a large sample of stocks from all market caps and industries is represented, along with most major futures and currencies, but it is a valid criticism to consider. Last, this is not a standard and accepted test for random walk, even though the results strongly suggest a nonrandom process is at work in this sample.

Moving Average Crossovers

Moving average crossovers occur when a short-term moving average, which tracks price more closely, crosses over or under a longer-term moving average. These events are commonly regarded as good trading signals or as indicators of trend because they are supposed to identify inflection points where markets have changed direction. In their purest form, these systems are traded on an always-in (the market) basis, meaning that the system goes long on a buy signal and immediately reverses to a short position on a sell signal, without any intervening flat period. The idea is that always being in the market, whether long or short, will allow the trader to be positioned to take advantage of a large trend when it emerges. Figure 14.9 shows an example of an excellent trade that would have been captured, in its entirety, by a moving average crossover system. This brings up an important point about moving average crossovers: they will always capture the majority of a large trend. To be sure, there is some lag depending on the length of the moving averages chosen, so they will never sell the exact high or buy the exact low of a move, but, in backtests, they will always take a big chunk out of a large trend move.

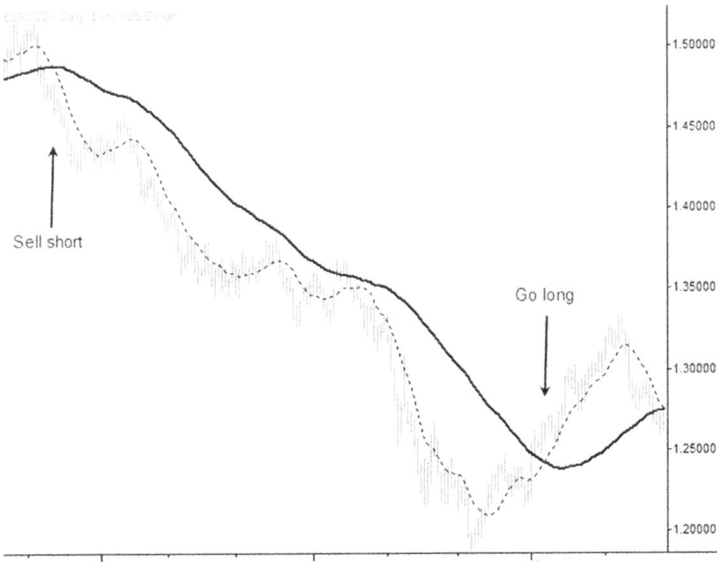

Figure 14.9 Trading a 10-/50-Day Moving Average Crossover System in a Trending Environment

However, this is only part of the story. Moving average crossover systems always work well in trending environments, but, just as surely, they will get destroyed in ranging markets. If there is no clear trend, the market will chop back and forth, forcing the moving average system to buy at the highs and sell at the lows. These whipsaws usually end up giving back all of the profit made in the trending environment, and sometimes even more. Contrary to what some authors and books suggest, it is not economically feasible to trade basic moving average systems on a stand-alone basis, because whipsaws and trading frictions make them breakeven at best. Figure 14.10 shows an example of a moving average applied in a range-bound market, where it finds itself repeatedly buying at the high and selling at the lows. Significant losses would have accrued in this period.

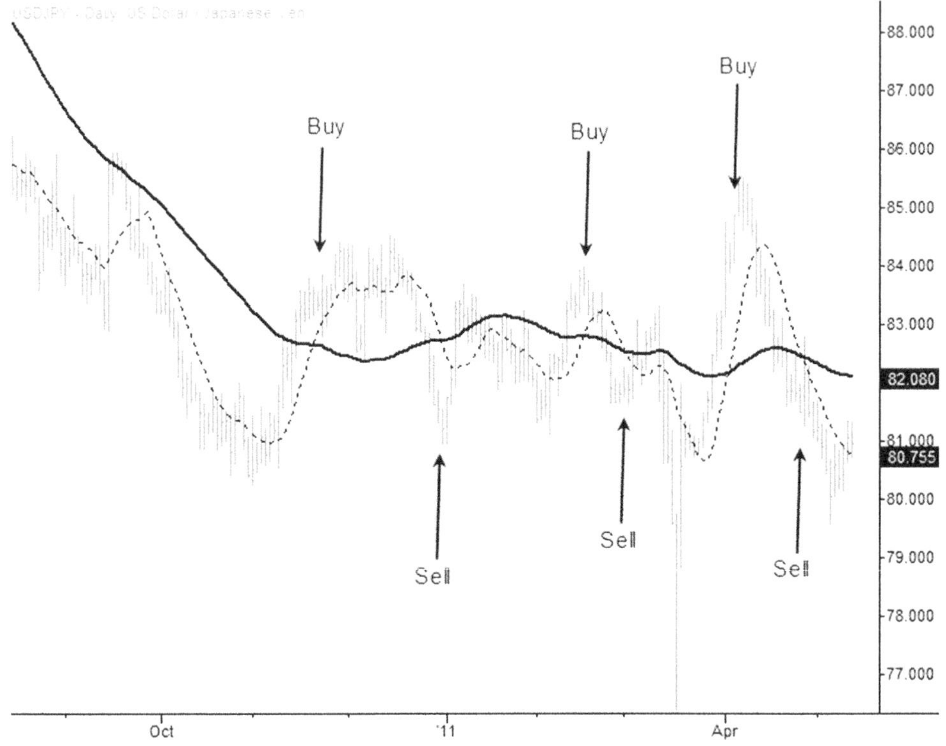

Figure 14.10 Trading a 10-/50-Day Moving Average Crossover System in a Range-Bound Environment

Academic Research

There is a significant body of academic research investigating the profitability of trading rules based on moving average crossovers. Brock, Lakonishok, and LeBaron's landmark paper, "Simple Technical Trading Rules and the Stochastic Properties of Stock Returns" (1992) is noteworthy because it was one of the first papers to show evidence that technical trading rules could produce statistically significant profits when applied to stock market averages. They used a set of rules based on moving average crossovers and channel breakouts on the Dow Jones Industrial Average from its first record day in 1897 to the last trading day of 1986. The results, as they say in the paper, are striking: they find statistically significant profits on both the long and short side for every moving average combination they examined.

For traders familiar with moving average studies in modern trading applications, the choices of moving averages that Brock et al. chose may be surprising: for the short average 1-, 2-, or 5-period, and 50-, 150-, or 200-period for the longer. A 1-period moving average is not actually a moving average at all—it is simply the price of the asset, so many of their moving average crossovers were actually tests of price crossing a moving average. Most authors and system developers tend to use averages much closer in length, like 10/50, 50/200. The original 1992 paper is fairly accessible to the lay reader and should be required reading for every trader who would trade based on technical signals. However, it might also be instructive to investigate their results in terms that traders will more readily understand.

The most profitable signals in their study were not the stop and reverse versions, but rules that entered on a moving average cross and exited 10 days later. In addition, some of their tests added a band around the moving averages and did not take signals within that band, in an attempt to reduce noise and whipsaw signals. For the sake of simplicity, let's look at their 1-/50-period moving average crossovers with no filter channel. Figure 14.11 shows the equity curve calculated for every day from 1920 to 1986, assuming the trader invested $100,000 on each trading signal, or sold short an equivalent dollar amount for the short signals.

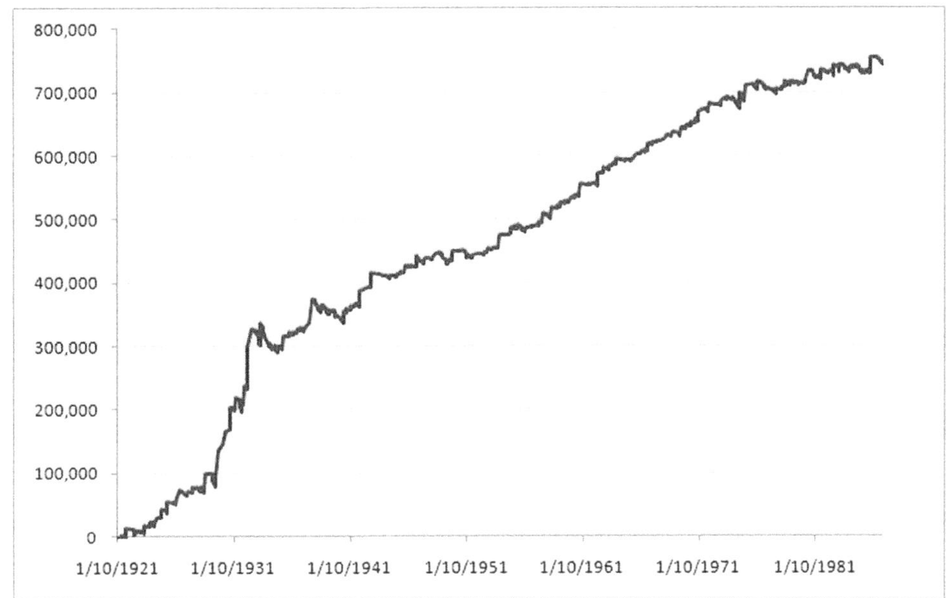

Figure 14.11 Daily Equity Curve for 1/50 Moving Average Crossover on DJIA, 1920–1986 ($100,000 Invested on Each Signal)

These results do appear to be remarkable at first glance: a steadily ascending equity curve that weathered the 1929 crash, both World Wars, and several recessions with no significant drawdowns. In addition, this system was stable for most of a century, while the economy, the sociopolitical landscape, and the markets themselves underwent a number of dramatic transformations. This stability is exactly what systematic traders are looking for. Table 14.8 shows a few summary stats for this system, assuming no transaction costs or financing expenses.

Table 14.8 Summary Stats for 1/50 Moving Average Crossover on DJIA, 1920–1986 (Total Net Profit Assumes $100,000 Invested on Each Signal)

N=	911
Total Net Profit	$743,794
% Profitable	28.0%
Mean Trade	84 bp
Mean Winning Trade	589 bp
Mean Losing Trade	–112 bp

These numbers are not bad, though traders not used to seeing long-term trend-following systems might wish for a higher win percentage. It is not uncommon for these types of systems to have win rates well under 40 percent, and, as long as the winners are substantially larger than the losers, such a system can be net profitable. In this case, we have to wonder if the average trade size is large enough to be profitable after accounting for trading frictions. It is important to remember that this is a backtest on the cash Dow Jones Industrial Average (DJIA), which is the average of a basket of 30 stocks. Today, investors can access this market through a variety of derivative products, but, for most of the history of this backtest, it would have been necessary to have purchased each of the stocks in the average individually and to have rebalanced the basket as needed to match changes in the average. In addition, financing costs, the impact of dividends, and tax factors also need to be considered with a system like this. Considering financing costs alone, if an investor were able to earn 4% risk-free for 66 years (the actual rate would vary, but this is probably in the ballpark. See Dimson, Marsh, and Staunton 2002), the initial $100,000 investment would have grown to over $1.3 million over the same time period. Also, the actual price of the DJIA itself increased 2,403% over this period—a simple buy-and-hold strategy would have returned over $2.3 million, albeit with impressive volatility and drawdowns along the way.

Stronger condemnation, though, comes from an out-of-sample test. Since the published results end in 1986, this is an ideal situation to walk forward from 1/1/1987 to 12/31/2010, which effectively shows the results investors might have achieved had they started trading this strategy after the end of the test period. (This is not a true out-of-sample test, as it is likely that Brock et al. examined some of the later history in their tests, even if the results were not published.) Figure 14.12 and Table 14.9 show the results for this time period, which are disappointing to say the least. It is also worth noting that a simple buy-and-hold strategy would have returned over $550,000 over the same time period.

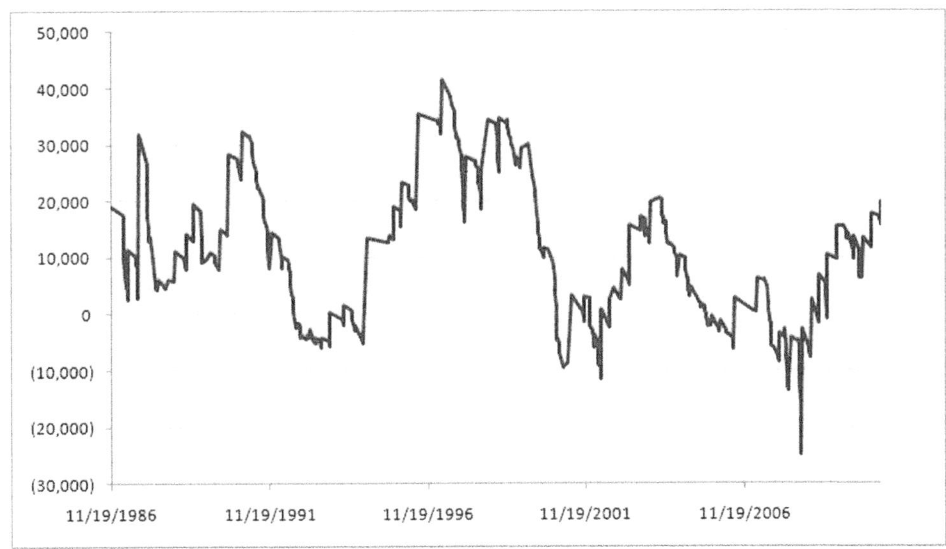

Figure 14.12 Daily Equity Curve for 1/50 Moving Average Crossover on DJIA, 1987–2010, Quasi Out of Sample ($100,000 Invested on Each Signal)

Table 14.9 Summary Stats for 1/50 Moving Average Crossover on DJIA, 1987–2010, Quasi Out of Sample (Total Net Profit Assumes $100,000 Invested on Each Signal)

N=	449
Total Net Profit	$19,830
% Profitable	20.9%
Mean Trade (Basis Points)	7 bp
Mean Winning Trade	477 bp
Mean Losing Trade	–117 bp

What is happening here? The first question we should ask is: is it possible that this is simply normal variation for this system? Just by looking at the equity curves, this seems unlikely because we are not able to identify any other 15-year period when the curve is flat and volatile, but this is not an actual test. Comparing the in- and out-of-sample returns, the Kolmogorov-Smirnov test, which is a nonparametric test for whether or not two samples were likely to have come from the same distribution, gives a p-value of 0.007. Based on this result, we can say that we find sufficient evidence to reject the idea that the out-of-sample test is drawn from a similar distribution as the in-sample test; this suggests that something has changed. It might be unwise to trade this system in the future after such a significant shift in the return distribution. This is not to say that anything was wrong with the research or the system design; market history is littered with specific trading ideas and systems that eventually stopped working. This is especially common after working ideas have been published, either in academic research or in literature written for practitioners.

Optimization

Though this is not a book on quantitative system design, a brief discussion of the value and perils of optimization is in order. (System optimization is also sometimes wrongly referred to as "curve fitting".) In a nutshell, optimization is simply taking trading systems and changing inputs until you find a set of conditions that would have performed well on historical data. In the case of the moving average crossover system just discussed, using a 65-period short moving average and a 170-period long moving average would have made the system profitable over the 1986 to 2010 window, producing a profit of $169,209 in over just 35 trades, with an impressive 40% win ratio. These numbers were found through an exhaustive search of many possible combinations of moving averages, but had we also searched for the inverse of this system (allowing shorting when the slow moving average crossed over the long and vice versa), we could have found combinations that made well over a million dollars during the same time period. The danger of overoptimization is that the best historical values will rarely be the best values in a walk-forward test or in actual trading. In the worst case, it is possible to create an optimized system that looks incredible on historical data, but will be completely worthless in actual trading.

Overoptimization can be accidental or deliberate. In the case of system vendors selling trading systems to the public, optimized systems can produce very impressive track records. Some systems are built by system designers who lack the education and experience to avoid this trap; they may truly believe they are producing something of value and are surprised when the actual trading results do not match their backtests. More often, overoptimized systems are created in a nefarious attempt to extract money from the public. Designers can build and optimize a trading system in a single weekend that shows dramatic results on a handful of markets. If they can sell a few copies of the system for $2,000 to $3,000, that's not a bad return for a few days' work.

In these examples, the method and effect of optimization is obvious, but it can also be more subtle and much harder to detect. It is even possible to overoptimize a simple market study yourself, without realizing you are doing so. The term overoptimization implies that there might be an appropriate degree of optimization—which is correct. Some optimization is necessary and is actually a vital component of the learning process. For instance, if you wanted to do a research project on gap openings what would be the appropriate gap size to study? You might first start with 400 percent, but would quickly discover that there may not be a single market gap that size in your entire test universe. If you next look at 0.25% gaps, you will discover that these are so common as to be meaningless; eventually you might settle on gap openings between 5 and 20%. Each step does bring some dangers because you are potentially overspecifying the question, but this is also how you learn about the market's movements. Here are some guidelines that will help you to guard against overoptimization:

- Understand the process. If this is your own work, think critically about every step in the process. If you are only seeing the product of someone else's work, you cannot trust the results unless you also understand their process. Knowing and trusting the person who created the results is a good first step, but remember, anyone can make mistakes. In general, do not pay money for systems designed by unknown third parties.
- Good systems and good research questions usually have few conditions. A set of conditions like "Buy when RSI is below X and price is above Y" is preferable to "Buy when RSI is below X, MACD is above Y, the A- and B-period moving averages are above the C-period and rising, while the C-period is declining, and only execute entries on a Monday, Thursday, or Friday, avoiding the last three days of the month." Though the first criteria set could well be the result of overoptimization, the second is almost certain to be.

- Guard against small sample sizes. It is not possible to draw good conclusions from most tests with a small number of events, and someone presenting you a study based on six occurrences has probably pared that down from a much larger starting universe. Large sample sizes can also be misleading, but very small ones are a huge red flag.
- Be suspicious of incredible results. In trading, if something looks too good to be true, it almost certainly is not true. There are no systems that crush the market over a long period of time. There are no systems that return, unlevered, 100% a year on capital. There are no systems with an extremely high win rate and extremely high reward/risk ratio. These things simply do not exist, because the markets are too competitive and efficient, but historical results like this can be created through optimization.

This is a deep subject and we have only scratched the surface. For the automated system designer, this is an important area of study, and ideas like systems that reoptimize themselves on a walk-forward basis, optimizing for outcomes other than maximum net profit or considering the results of optimization tests as multidimensional surfaces, are an important part of that study. Most discretionary traders will only use quantitative studies as a departure point for developing trading ideas, so it probably is sufficient to have an idea about the most serious dangers and risks of optimization. When in doubt, disregard the results of any study that you feel may be the result of overoptimization or overspecification. Better to simply know you do not know than to be misled by spurious information.

Testing Moving Average Crosses

Frankly, it is well established that moving average crosses cannot be traded as stand-alone systems, so there is little point in presenting study after study that confirm this. There is, however, another application that is very common. There are many books and trading methodologies that suggest that some kind of moving average–derived trend indicator can be a useful tool. The idea usually presented is that, in an uptrend, the upswings will be larger than the downswings, so traders should use a tool to identify the uptrend and then trade only with that trend. Because these ideas are so common in the trading literature, it is worth our time to investigate them here.

First, think about what you would need to see from a trend indicator to make it useful. Though there could be different answers to this question, I suggest that they all are probably some variation of this: long trades should work better when the indicator shows an uptrend, and the downtrend condition should produce a more favorable environment for short trades. A simple way to test this would be to identify the trend indicator and then categorize all days according to whether the indicator labels them uptrend, downtrend, or neutral. (Note that if you are testing this mathematically, you need to assign the current bar's return to the previous condition. For instance, imagine a situation where a large up day turns the trend indicator to an uptrend. If you include that day in the uptrend designation, you will assume that you were holding a long position from the previous day's close, which is possible only if you knew what was going to happen the next day in advance. This is a small, but critical, adjustment.) Once we have categorized the days according to trend condition, we can measure the mean return and volatility for each group. If the trend indicator provides useful information, we should be able to see some difference between the two groups. Ideally, the uptrend days would have a higher mean return and perhaps a higher probability of closing up than in the downtrend days.

Consider a very simple trend indicator: the slope of a moving average. Immediately, we face the ubiquitous moving average question: "What length of moving average?" By changing the length of the moving average, we can usually make a trend flip to either up or down on almost any bar, so there is an arbitrary element to this definition. The 50-period average is commonly used in this capacity, so we will limit our testing to this one choice. Another issue to consider is that, though a trader can easily identify the slope of a moving average visually, doing so in a structured, quantitative manner is a little bit more difficult. In this case, we draw a linear regression line through the last five data points, equally weighted, of the average itself, and use the slope of that linear regression line as the trend indicator.

Table 14.10 shows the results of a test of a 50-period moving average slope trend indicator; it shows excess returns (in this case, excess return is the raw return for the signal group minus the raw return for all bars) for the up and down trend conditions relative to all days in this test. (Note that "All" excludes days categorized as neutral when the slope of the average was flat.) In addition, we have calculated two measures of volatility: the standard deviation of raw (not excess) returns, and the mean of the 20-day historical volatility readings for each set. Last, the percentage of days that close up is calculated for each category.

Table 14.10 Trend Indicator: Slope of 50-Period Moving Average, Categorical Returns

	Equities	Futures	Forex	Random	Total
Down					
N=	580,302	18,818	6,581	22,205	627,906
Mean Excess Return (bp)	177.2	(94.1)	15.5	(85.2)	157.7
StDev Raw Returns (bp)	302.8	152.4	75.6	119.9	293.2
Mean HisVol	39.9	20.4	10.5	18.1	38.2
% Close Up	50.2%	50.1%	50.5%	51.0%	50.2%
Up					
N=	793,221	21,827	9,223	26,283	850,554
Mean Excess Return (bp)	(129.6)	81.1	(11.1)	72.0	(116.4)
StDev Raw Returns (bp)	218.9	150.2	65.2	114.1	213.8
Mean HisVol	30.2	20.5	9.8	17.2	29.3
% Close Up	50.0%	51.1%	51.5%	51.7%	50.1%
All					
N=	1,373,523	40,645	15,804	48,488	1,478,460
Mean Raw Return	2.3	1.8	1.5	1.2	2.3
StDev Raw Returns	257.7	151.2	69.7	116.8	250.6
Mean HisVol	34.3	20.5	10.1	17.6	33.1
% Close Up	50.1%	50.6%	51.1%	51.4%	50.2%

The results are not impressive for this trend indicator. Considering the random column first to better understand the baseline, we do see a negative excess return for the downtrend and a positive return for the uptrend condition, with a slightly higher chance of close up (51.7% of days close up in uptrend condition versus 51.4% for all days. (This is not statistically significant.) Volatility is slightly higher for the downtrend, but roughly in line across all groups. Turning to equities, we find something surprising: the downtrend shows a very large, over 3 percent, positive excess return, while the uptrend shows well over a 1% negative excess return; this is precisely the opposite of what we should see if the uptrend indicator is valid. In fact, for equities, this suggests we might be better off taking long trades in the downtrend condition because we would be aligned with a favorable statistical tailwind. Futures show a situation that is more like what we would expect, with a fairly large negative excess return for downtrend, and a large positive excess return for uptrend. Forex, paradoxically enough, looks more like equities, but the actual excess returns are very small, and are not statistically significant.

How can this be? If you try this experiment yourself, put a 50-period moving average on a chart, and just eyeball it, you will see that the slope of the moving average identifies great trend trades. It will catch every extended trend trade and will keep you in the trade for the whole move—actually, for the whole move and then some, and there's the rub. The problem is the lag, the same problem that any derived indicator faces. Whether based on moving averages, trend lines, linear regression lines, or extrapolations of existing data, they can respond to changes in the direction of momentum of prices only after those changes have happened. A moving average slope indicator will also get whipsawed frequently when the market is flat and the average is rapidly flipping up and down. It is possible to introduce a band around the moving average to filter some of this noise, but this will be at the expense of making valid signals come even later.

Figure 14.13 illustrates the problem with a 50-period moving average applied to a daily chart of the U.S. Dollar Index. It would have been slightly profitable to trade this simple trend indicator on this particular chart, but notice how much of the move is given up before the indicator flips. The chart begins with the market in an uptrend (moving average sloping up), and nearly one-third of the entire chart has to be retraced before the moving average flips down. Once the market bottoms in November, a substantial rally ensues before the trend indicator flips up. This lag, coupled with the fact that markets tend to make sharp reversals from both bottoms and tops, greatly reduces the utility of this tool as a trend indicator.

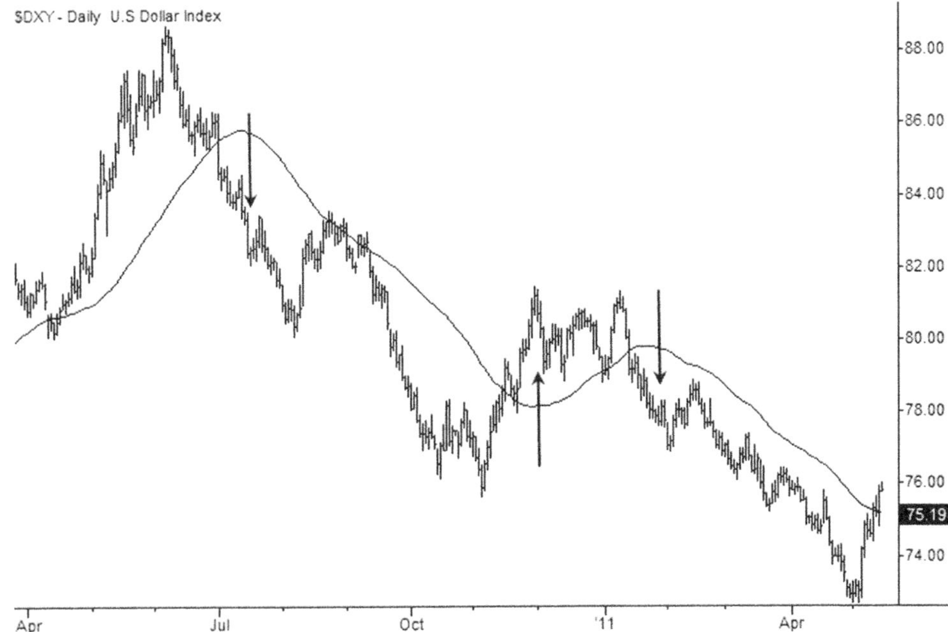

Figure 14.13 Slope of 50-Period Moving Average as a Trend Indicator
Notice how much of each trend move is given up by this tool.

Another common idea is to use the position of two or more moving averages to confirm a trend change. For example, three moving averages of different lengths could be applied to a chart, and the market could be assumed to be in an uptrend when the averages are in the correct order, meaning that the shortest average would be above the medium-length average and both of those would be above the longer-term moving average, with the reverse conditions being used for a downtrend. This type of plan allows for significant stretches of time when the trend is undefined; for instance, when the medium-length average is above the longer-term average, but the shortest average is in between the two. This, like all moving average crosses, is attractive visually because the eye is always drawn to big winners, to the clear trends that this tool catches. However, like all moving average crosses, the whipsaws erode all profits in most markets, leaving the tool with no quantifiable edge. In addition, more moving averages usually introduce more lag, with no measurable improvement compared to a simple moving average crossover.

One of the most popular moving average trend indicators today is based on simple 10-, 20-, and 50-period moving averages. Traders using this tool are told to take long trades only when it indicates an uptrend and to short only when it indicates a downtrend. It is reasonable to ask how the market behaves in both of those conditions. Table 14.11 shows that traders using this tool in Equities (and it is primarily used by stock traders) will consistently find themselves on the wrong side of the market, fighting the underlying statistical tendency. Simply put, stocks are more likely to go down when this tool flags an uptrend, and up when it flags a downtrend—traders using it as prescribed are doing exactly the wrong thing. For the other asset classes, the message is mixed. There is possibly an edge in futures, particularly on the short side, and forex looks more random than the actual randomly generated test set. At least in this sample of markets, this test suggests that traders relying on this trend tool or on tools derived from it are likely to have a difficult time overcoming these headwinds.

Table 14.11 Triple Moving Average Trend Indicator, Categorical Returns

	Equities	Futures	Forex	Random	Total
Down					
N=	365,690	12,372	4,204	14,621	396,887
Excess Ret	166.9	(203.0)	43.6	(74.9)	144.5
StDev Raw Returns	319.2	158.8	78.0	119.9	308.6
Mean HisVol	40.8	20.7	10.7	18.5	39.0
% Close Up	50.2%	49.8%	50.5%	50.9%	50.2%
Up					
N=	537,896	14,652	6,137	17,515	576,200
Excess Ret	(157.9)	80.7	43.9	98.6	(141.5)
StDev Raw Returns	217.6	152.3	66.4	114.6	212.7
Mean HisVol	30.2	20.2	9.6	17.2	29.4
% Close Up	49.9%	51.5%	51.7%	52.0%	50.0%
All					
N=	903,586	27,024	10,341	32,136	973,087
Raw Returns	2.0	1.3	1.9	1.4	2.0
StDev Raw Returns	263.5	155.3	71.3	117.0	256.2
Mean HisVol	34.5	20.4	10.1	17.8	33.3
% Close Up	50.0%	50.7%	51.2%	51.5%	50.1%

Equity Volatility in Relation to Moving Averages

So far, these tests of moving averages have not shown good results, but there is one use of moving averages that long-term investors might want to consider. Table 14.12 shows mean returns, standard deviation of returns, and coefficients of variation for two simple systems applied to the daily Dow Jones Industrial Average from 1/1/1960 to 12/31/2010. The first system is simply buy and hold, which returns an impressive 1,504% over this time period, with a daily mean return of 2.2 basis points and a standard deviation of 101.5 basis points. The second system is long-only, and is in the market as long as the market is above the 200-day moving average. On the day the Dow Jones Industrial Average crosses its 200-day average, the system moves fully to cash on the close of that day and does not reenter the market until the close of the first day that closes back above the moving average. The moving average system returns are still a very satisfactory 1,408% by being in the market approximately two-thirds of the time that buy and hold was invested. Furthermore, this system achieves its returns with a higher mean return and a lower daily standard deviation. (For this test, no interest was paid on cash balance, and no financing costs or trading frictions were assumed.) Buy and hold has a coefficient of variation of 46, compared to 24.3 for this simple moving average system—this is a clear example of superior risk-adjusted performance from a simple technical system. How many money managers realize that they could beat the market by applying simple technical criteria like this? How many dollars of investors' money could have been saved in the form of management fees in the often futile effort to achieve the goal of superior returns with lower risk?

Table 14.12 Buy and Hold Compared to Long-Only above 200-Day Moving Average, DJIA, 1960–2010

	Buy and Hold	Long above 200-Day MA
Total ROI	1,504%	1,408%
Mean Return	2.2	3.3
Standard Deviation	101.5	79.8
Coefficient of Variation	46.0	24.3
Days Invested	12,842	8,450

Conclusions

This section has looked at many variations of tests on moving averages. On one hand, the answers were not crystal clear because there were some interesting and statistically significant tendencies in some of the tests. However, the same tendencies are present regardless of the specific period of average tested, even if the length of the average changes randomly from bar to bar, and often even without the moving average being present. This evidence strongly contradicts the claim that any one moving average is significant or special. Traders depend on moving averages because they are lines on their charts and they sometimes seem to support prices, but this is a trick of the eye. If you are depending on moving averages, considering the 50-, 10-, or 100-day moving average to be support or resistance, you are trading a concept that has no statistical validity.

This section also taught us some potentially useful things about market movements. For example, we saw that equities, futures, and forex markets sometimes show significant differences in the way they trade. It probably does not make sense to approach them all the same way and to trade them with the same systems and methods. We also saw evidence that some of the tendencies that seem to be around moving averages may actually be deeper, more universal elements of price action. For instance, the tendency for some asset prices to bounce after trading down to a moving average may simply be the tendency for prices to bounce after trading down. We also took a brief look at trend indicators derived from moving averages, and saw that they suffered from enough lag and mean reversion that they may often put the trader on the wrong side of the market.

Last, we saw that there is some truth to the claim that declining markets are more volatile than rising markets. A simple 200-period moving average system has produced superior risk-adjusted returns over the past 50 years. The power of this system is not in the 200-day moving average, for the system also works with nearly any other period of moving average; it simply captures the tendency of declining markets to become more volatile. The message here is simple: Know your tools. Understand the statistical tendencies around them, and how they work in the market. There is no substitute for careful thought and analysis.

Chapter 15

The Opening Range Phenomenon

Every new beginning comes from some other beginning's end.

-Seneca

Many traders, probably following in the footsteps of Toby Crabel's 1990 book, *Day Trading with Short Term Price Patterns and Opening Range Breakout*, attach great significance to the opening range of each day's trading session. While there is good reason for doing so—profitable systems have been constructed based on moves from the open, many traders note that the opening print is very near to the high or low of the day much more often than it seems we should expect.

At first glance, the distribution of the opening print appears to be striking, and here traders and authors make a mistake: from this apparently unusual distribution, many writers have drawn the conclusion that markets do not move randomly. This conclusion is based on a misunderstanding of random walk motion; the purpose of this chapter is not to "disprove" any trading methodology or system that works around the opening range. Rather, it is to investigate a specific aspect of random walk movement, and to show that markets moving randomly have some surprising characteristics. If we do not understand this, we are led to draw false conclusions about markets, and, possibly, about our trading edge. The following is a good example of the flawed reasoning surrounding the opening range:

> *If you subscribe to the random walk theory ... then the opening range would not be any more important than any other price level during the trading day. Let's say that you divide the trading day into roughly 64 five-minute intervals. Random walk theory would state that the opening, five-minute range would be the high 1/64 of the time or the low 1/64 of the time. So it would be either of those extremes 1/32 of the time. However, in volatile markets that five-minute opening range is actually the high or low of the day about 15 to 18% of the time. So, instead of about 3% of the time as random walk theory would predict, the first five minutes of the trading day turns out to be the high or the low 15 to 18% of the time. Again, this is statistically significant. (Fisher 2002)*

For traders, who are paid on price rather than time, the *location* of the open within the day's range is arguably more important than the timing of the high or low. It could be more valuable to know that the opening print was likely to be within a certain percentage of the session's high or low than to know that the high or low would be put in within the first X minutes of the day's session. This is a slightly different question—rather than investigating time intervals of intraday data, we can gain much of the same intuition by studying the relationship of the opening price of a session to that session's range. For the purposes of this section, we will use a measure I call the Opening as percentage of Range (*O%Rng*), which is calculated as:

$$O\%Rng = [(Price_{Open} - Price_{Low}) \;/\; (Price_{High} - Price_{Low})] \times 100$$

where $Price_{Open}$ is the price at the opening tick of the session and $Price_{High}$ and $Price_{Low}$ are the highest and lowest prices reached during that session.

An *O%Rng* of 100 would mean that the opening print was at the highest extreme of the day; an *O%Rng* of 0 would be at the bottom, while an *O%Rng* of 50 would indicate that the opening was exactly in the middle of the session's range. Figure 15.1 shows bars for four daily trading sessions with the associated *O%Rng* measures for each bar. (Remember, the tick to the left of each bar shows the position of the opening price for that session.) Assuming, for the sake of argument, that the opening print should be in the middle of the bar, we will refer to any tendency for the open to cluster near the high or the low as opening skew.

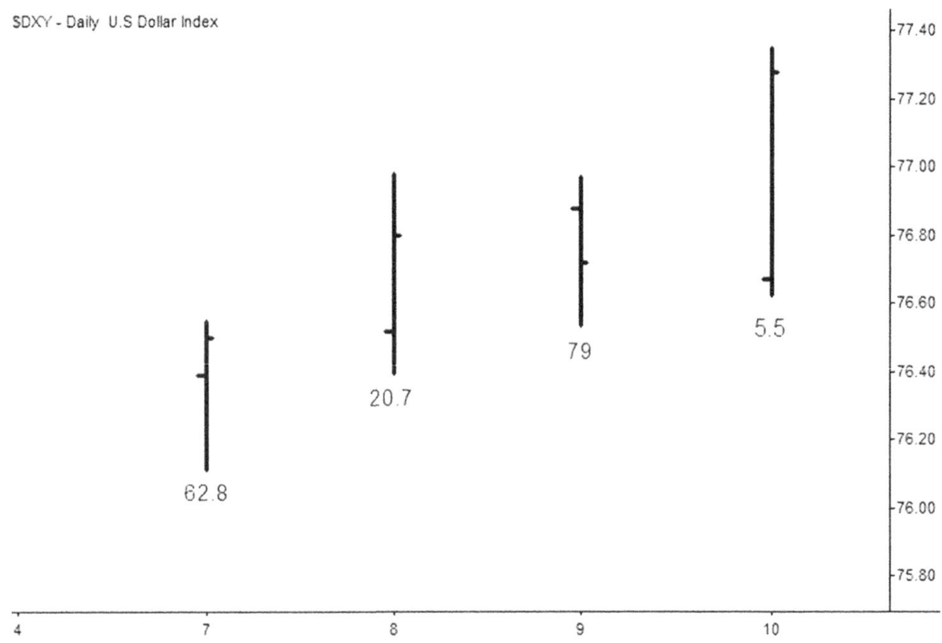

Figure 15.1 Bars with O%Rng Values, or the Opening Print Expressed as a percentage of the Day's Range

To paraphrase, most traders and writers who focus on the opening range make points roughly like this. They would say that, if markets move by random walks:

- Any trade (tick) randomly selected from any time during the trading day should fall anywhere within the range of the day with equal probability.
- The opening is just like any other tick, so it should fall anywhere within the day's range with equal probability.
- In actual markets, we observe that the open is near the high or low of the session much more often than it is in the middle. This is evidence that markets do not follow a random walk. Since this is a nonrandom element of price behavior, the position of the open within the day's range may offer profitable trading opportunities and evidence of market inefficiency.

Each of those points is logical and intuitive, but each is, unfortunately, also wrong. This is a case where faulty intuition about the nature of random walks can lead to bad decisions about the nature of the market.

What Does the Data Say?

To understand the issues involved here, let's start with the actual market data and work backward into a random walk scenario. We start by examining the opening range anomaly, the opening skew. Table 15.1 shows the percentage of the bars for which the *O%Rng* statistic is within the top or bottom 5% of the day's range. Based on the arguments in the previous section, we see that the top and bottom 5% of the day's range comprise a total of 10% of the day's range, so we might expect the opening tick to fall within that area 10% of the time.

Table 15.1 Percentage of Bars with O%Rng Within 5% of the Bar's High or Low, Actual Market Data

Sample	5 ≥ O%Rng ≥ 95	Sample Size
Active Markets, Daily Bars	14.7%	46,433
Active Markets, 60-Minute Bars	18.1%	139,616
Active Markets, 39-Minute Bars	18.9%	231,288
AAPL, Random Intraday	16.3%	4,413

Let's think about these results carefully. The Active Markets sample is a selection of actively traded stocks, futures, and currencies from the years 2007 to 2010. (This is a different selection than the large test universe used for the rest of this chapter, because that universe includes some periods of inactivity in some assets—here, we are focusing only on active assets.) Illiquid assets show much larger opening skews than liquid markets; the full test universe reported a 20.2% skew compared the 14.7% in the active sample. Again, if we expect to see this opening skew at 10%, every value in this table appears to be remarkable—the open really does occur near the high or low of the session with some consistency. Opening skew is real.

Many traders postulate that some element of market dynamics might be driving this, perhaps order flow around the open. This would seem to be a plausible explanation for the daily bars, and perhaps even for 60-minute bars. It is possible that large traders or funds are making trading decisions based on each 60-minute interval? This seems unlikely, but it is *possible*. However, the last two lines of the table descend into absurdity. If we accept that order flow is driving the daily and 60-minute intervals, how can we believe that is also true of 39-minute intervals? (If you checked to see if 39 was a Fibonacci number, go directly to jail. Do not pass Go. Do not collect $200.) Perhaps it would be possible to construct some arcane explanation for the 39-minute interval, but the last line shows Apple, Inc.'s (NASDAQ: AAPL) 2007 to 2010 trading history, cut into random intraday bars that are each 2 to 60 minutes long; each bar is a different, random length. We still see significant open skew above the 10% we would expect, even in this absurd example.

Traders who write about opening range systems have long noted that you can define the opening range according to any time period and still see the same patterns—5-minute, 15-minute, 60-minute—it doesn't matter. There are also systems that look at weekly or monthly opening ranges, and strange variations (e.g., Tuesday-to-Tuesday weeks, or months tied to expiration cycles in options or futures) are even used in some applications. Here is an important clue: if we see something that "always works" no matter what we change or tweak, our first assumption should be that there is some error in our thinking. The other alternative, that the tendency is so strong and the pattern so powerful, easily descends into magical thinking and becomes a self-sustaining proof. (A parallel outside of markets might be a panacea medicine—a powerful medicine that can cure any ill in any range of unrelated conditions, but can do no harm, regardless of how much is taken. This type of medicine does not exist, and any medicine not capable of doing harm most likely does nothing at all.)

If you can randomly define the parameters and get the same result, isn't that suggestive of some random process at work? This should be our first warning that perhaps our intuition is faulty, and there is something else going on here. Figure 15.2 shows a random walk path with the with the maximum, minimum, and open marked. The next tests will replicate this procedure thousands of time to help build intuition about the location of the open under a random walk.

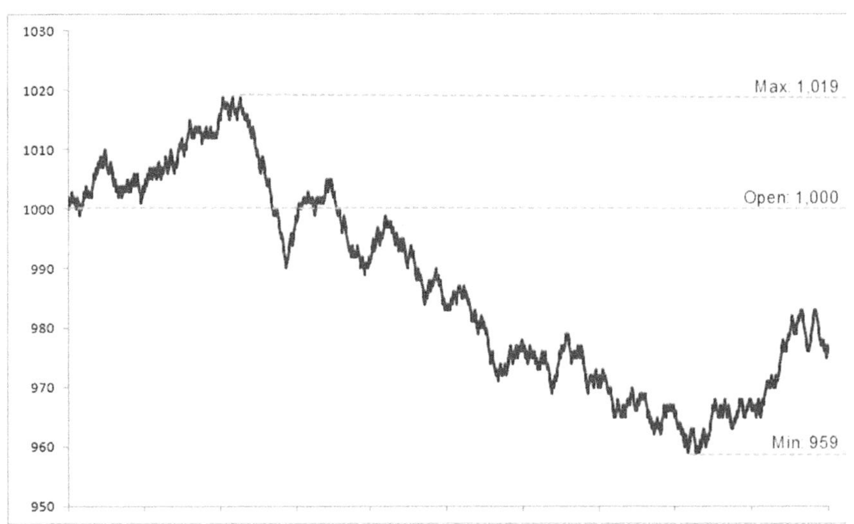

Figure 15.2 A Single Path Through a Random Walk Tree, with the Max, Min, and Open Marked

Random Walk Models

Let's first deal with a more elementary question. Most people would assume that, if we randomly select a tick from any point in a random walk model, it should fall anywhere in the range covered by the random walk with equal probability. We can test this easily through the following procedure: run multiple paths through a binomial tree, recording the range (Max – Min) for each path, and the value of a single randomly selected tick. Figure 15.3 shows the distribution for the location of this randomly selected tick for 500,000 trials. The results are conclusive: *a single, randomly selected tick will not fall anywhere within the session's range with equal probability in a random walk*, but instead will cluster much more often around the middle of the range.

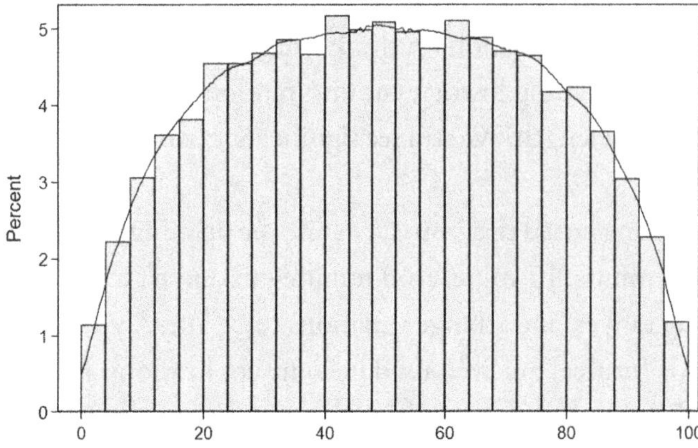

Figure 15.3 Distribution of Randomly Selected Ticks Within the Session's Range for a Random Walk Model

Upon further reflection, it becomes apparent that we would expect a random walk to spend more time around the middle of its range than at either extreme, so perhaps this is not surprising. This is also true in real markets. There are tools that show the distribution of volume inside each individual bar (see Figure 15.4). MarketProfile is the best known of these, and it shows that most sessions have clusters of volume and activity at one or more prices; it is extremely unusual to see activity evenly distributed over the range of an actual trading session in a real market. If activity clusters in certain places, a randomly selected tick is more likely to fall in those clusters than anywhere else.

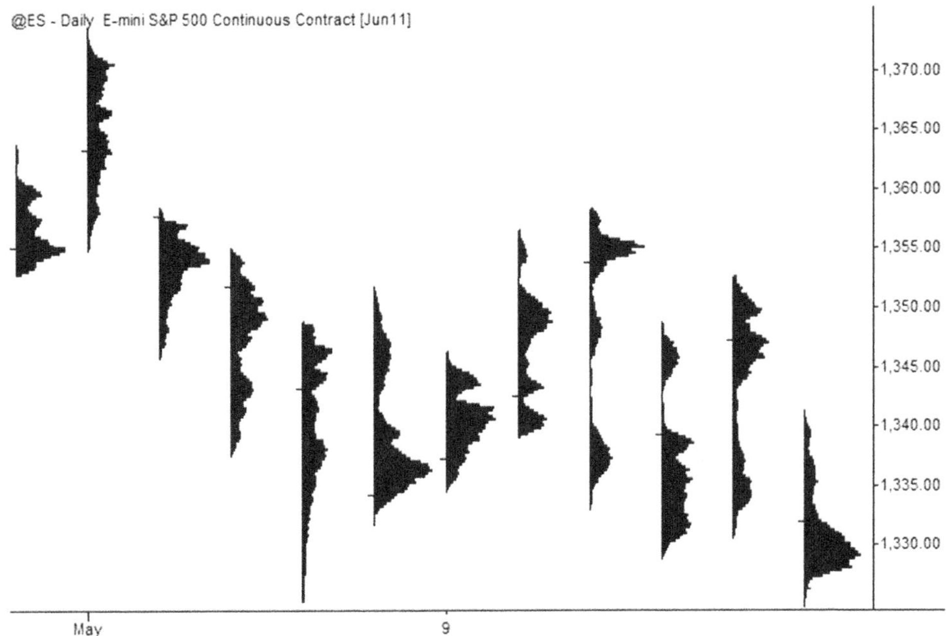

Figure 15.4 Distribution of Volume Within Daily Bars
Note that volume and trading activity are not *evenly distributed throughout the range.*

Position of the Open

At this point, you may be saying, "Wait a minute. You have just shown that a random tick is more likely to be in the middle of the range than at the extremes, so doesn't this strengthen the case for the open being special?" The problem here is the assumption that the open is just like any other tick.

To build some intuition about this, imagine that you are standing at the beginning of a binomial tree that will soon begin its random walk forward. (Perhaps you are standing at the precipice of a ski slope or something equally dramatic.) You can squint and visualize the most probable future path of the random walk as a fuzzy cone of probability that starts from your current position. If you move, the center of the cone, indicating the most probable terminal point of the random walk, moves with you. This is true because, in the absence of any drift component, the expected value of a zero-mean random walk process is the initial point; in other words, the best guess for the ending point is the starting value. So, at the beginning of the run before the first step, the probability cone extends downward, centered on your starting location. It is equally likely that you will end up to the left or the right, but you most likely will end somewhere around the middle of that cone.

Now, take the very first step of the random walk. Assume it is to the right, and notice that the cone of probability has shrunk a little bit because you are one step closer to the end of the tree, but much more importantly, it has also shifted to the right with you. Think carefully about this: You are now more likely to continue on the right side of the initial point than to cross back to the left, because more of the weight of the probability cone is on the right. Should your second step happen to be to the right again, now the cone has shifted even more. True, these shifts are infinitesimal, but over a large number of trials they do add up, just as a slightly weighted coin can win a gambler a fortune. The point is that the first step of the random walk defines the most probable future range, so the starting point is not like any other tick; it is actually very special.

This is not idle theory; learning to think about market movements like this can build deep intuition about price movement and the most likely outcome of many scenarios. Let's consider this one other way, by carefully enumerating all of the possible paths through a small binomial tree. Figure 15.4 shows a four-step tree with each step labeled, so that we can record the path to any endpoint. For instance, the highest endpoint could only be reached via A-1-a-i, but the second highest could be reached in two ways: A-1-a-ii or A-1-b-ii.

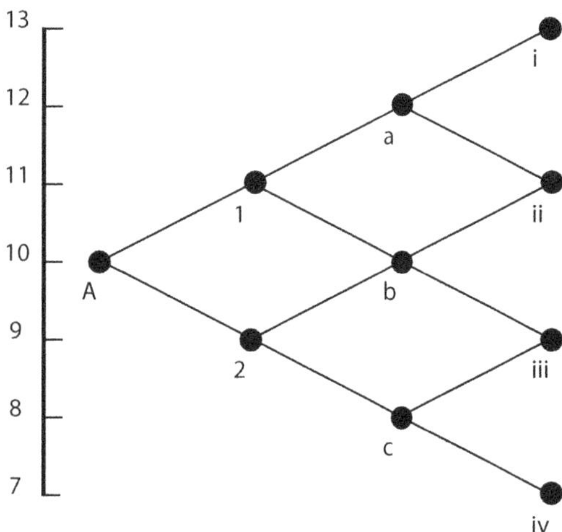

Figure 15.4 A Simple Four-Step Binomial Tree

For each path through the tree, we can record the starting price (always 10 in this case), the minimum, and the maximum, and can also calculate the O%Rng statistic for the run. Table 15.2 shows all of the possible paths for this trivial example; the important point is that there are more paths that put the open near the extreme than in the middle of the range. If you find yourself with some time on your hands, reproduce this exercise with more nodes on the tree, recording the minimum and maximum for each path and checking the O%Rng stats at the end of the whole set. There are 2n possible paths for an n-step tree, so this can become time-consuming very quickly. If you are having trouble intuitively grasping why the open should cluster near the high or low in a random walk, repeating this exercise with, say, an eight-step tree and thinking about each of the possible resulting paths might be helpful.

Table 15.2 O%Rng Stats for All Possible Paths Through Figure 15.28

Path	Max	Min	O%Rng
A-1-a-i	13	10	0
A-1-a-ii	12	10	0
A-1-b-ii	11	10	0
A-1-b-iii	11	9	50
A-2-b-ii	11	9	50
A-2-b-iii	10	9	100
A-2-c-iii	10	8	100
A-2-c-iv	10	7	100

Simulation Results

Figure 15.5 shows the distribution of the *O%Rng* statistic for actual market data, in this case, the Active Markets, Daily Bars sample (N = 46,433) from Table 15.23. This graph is interesting because it does show the marked tendency of the open to occur near the high or low of the session, and it is easy to see why traders, noticing this pattern, might think that some nonrandom force was creating this result. Though the earlier examples may explain why the open should be near the high or low more often than in the middle of the range, the extent of the observed effect may seem to be too large to explain by a slight statistical skew.

Table 15.3 reproduces the market data from Table 15.23, and adds the results of two random walk simulations: a random walk with uniform steps up or down with equal probability, and an AR(2) model. The real market data shows that the open is in the top or bottom 5% of the range between roughly 15 and 19% of the time. Many traders assume that, since the top and bottom 5% of the day's range total to 10% of the day's range, the open should be there 10% of the time under a random walk. Table 15.25 shows that this is not true—these traders have faulty intuition about random walks.

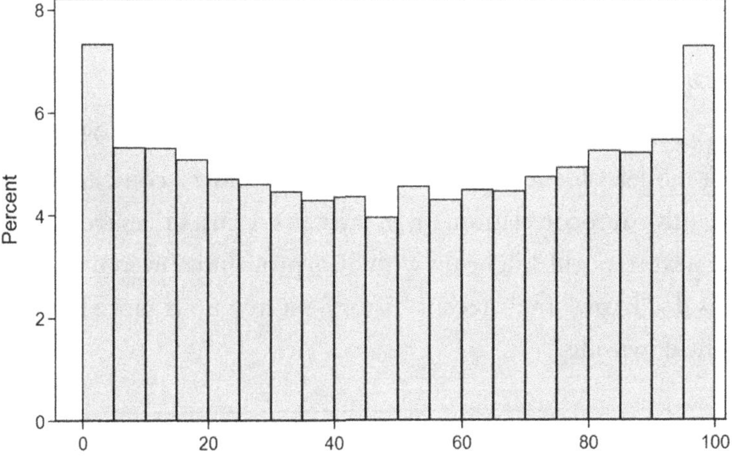

Figure 15.5 Real Market Data: Distribution of O%Rng for Active Markets, Daily Bars

Table 15.3 Distribution of the O%Rng Statistic for Market Data, Random Walk Simulation, and an AR(2) Model

Sample	5 ≥ O%Rng ≥ 95	Sample Size
Active Markets, Daily Bars	14.7%	46,433
Active Markets, 60-Minute Bars	18.1%	139,616
Active Markets, 39-Minute Bars	18.9%	231,288
AAPL, Random Intraday	15.7%	4,413
Random Walk Model	15.6%	500,000
Second-Order AR Model	18.1%	~100,000

The results closely approximate market data. In the random walk model, the open is in the top or bottom 5% of the session's range 15.6% of the time, more often than in the observed daily data of active markets. This is conclusive proof that the opening skew at least could be the result of a purely random process. Figure 15.6 shows the return distribution for the *O%Rng* statistic for the random walk model, which is virtually indistinguishable from Figure 15.5, the actual distribution from observed market data.

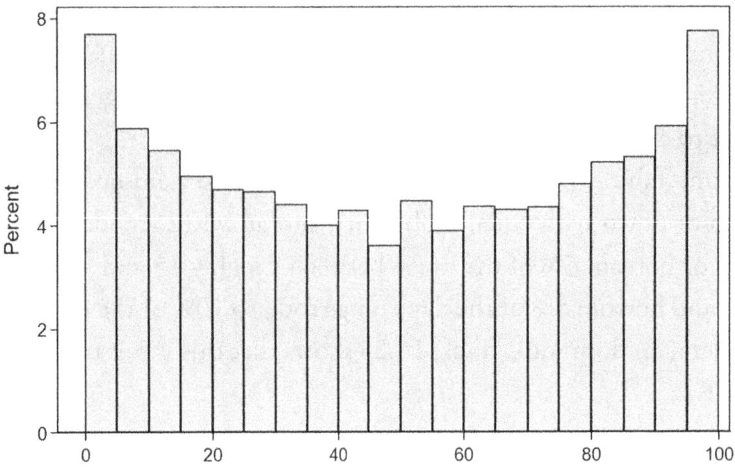

Figure 15.6 Simulated Data: Distribution of O%Rng for a Random Walk Model

If we consider illiquid markets or intraday data, we will often find opening skews closer to 19%, which is not fully explained by the simple random walk model. One reason that actual prices show a consistently larger opening skew could be that real prices show positive autocorrelation, or, in layman's terms, prices trend. A pure random walk has no memory of past steps; the next step will still be up with 50% probability even if the past six steps have also been up. Autoregressive models do "know" their recent history—a step up is more likely to be followed by another step up and vice versa to the downside.

The AR(2) model in this test generated its returns from this equation:

$$r_t = \alpha + \beta r_{t-1} + \gamma_{rt-2} + \varepsilon_t,\ \varepsilon \sim \text{i.i.d. } N(0, \sigma)$$

meaning that the return at time t is the sum of a constant, α, and the previous two time periods' returns decayed by two other constants, β and γ, and a normally distributed error term ε. If the returns-generating process is positively autocorrelated, the first step is more likely to be followed by another step in the same direction, reducing the likelihood of price crossing back over the opening print. The test in Table 15.3 used $\alpha = 0$, $\beta = 0.25$, $\gamma = 0.1$, and $\sigma = 0.5\%$ as inputs, and produced a significantly higher opening skew. This is slightly out of the scope of this chapter, but the AR model is only one of several returns-generating processes that could be considered. Heteroscedastic models and alternate distributions (e.g., mixture of normals) are capable of producing even more dramatic opening skews from random price paths.

Conclusions

In doing research or investigating the markets' movements, we will often find things that may not be what they appear to first glance. In all cases, a solid understanding of the what we would expect *if* the markets movements were completely random is a good baseline against which to compare any tendency we find. If we do not understand these "baseline", "what-if-it-were-all-random" assumptions, it's easy to be misled. This issue of the behavior of the opening skew is a good example of the problem. Many traders continue to believe that the opening skew cannot be the result of a random process and offer it as evidence of market inefficiency. However, the preceding tests and results would not have held any surprises for anyone with a formal education in mathematics and familiarity with stochastic processes. Feller (1951) did extensive work on random walks, dealing specifically with the probable timing of highs and lows, and many academic papers have followed (perhaps the most relevant is Acar and Toffel (1999)). Physicists and mathematicians are familiar with the well-known arcsine law of random walks, which gives a simple formula that describes the probability that the high or low of the session will occur at time t out of a session that is length T: (See Acar and Toffell for derivation and proof.)

$$f(t) = \frac{1}{\pi\sqrt{T-t}\sqrt{t}} \quad \forall\ 0 \le t \le T$$

The graph of this function looks very similar to what we have seen in both the random simulations and actual market data; this is a completely understood element of price behavior and random walks. The distribution of the opening print is completely consistent with random walk price action, which means that it is not evidence of market inefficiencies, nor does it necessarily offer *easy* opportunities for profits. There is good evidence that many traders, particularly futures traders, do make trades based on movements off the opening range, and that some profitable systems do incorporate the opening range, but it is still important to cultivate a deep understanding of price movements and the dynamics driving them.

Chapter 16
Quantitative Evidence of the Two Forces

Up to this point, the goal of this part has been twofold: One, to give fairly in-depth examples of the kind of thinking and quantitative analysis that can help to separate the wheat from the chaff, and valid trading ideas from worthless, random ideas. This is not always simple, as sometimes even properly defining the question is difficult, and results are rarely black and white. The second goal has been to dispel some myths about what works in the market. No moving average consistently provides statistically significant support. No crossing of moving averages or slope of moving averages provides a statistically significant trend indicator. What tendencies we do see around moving averages actually occur in giant zones around the moving average; we have seen no justification whatsoever for watching any specific moving average value. There is no point in noting that a market crosses the 100-day or 200-day moving average. No Fibonacci level provides any significant reference point—a random number is as good as any Fibonacci level. None of these things are any better than a coin flip!

Though this may be disheartening to some traders, I believe there is an important message here—it is better to know you don't know than to continue to waste your time and energy trading futile concepts. If you have been using these concepts in your trading, objectively consider your results. If they are performing well, meaning that you have substantial and consistent profits over a large sample size, then you have probably incorporated them into a framework that includes other inputs, and your positive results depend on many more elements. However, if you are struggling and are not pleased with your results, maybe it is time to reevaluate the tools you are using. Give up your preconceptions and your beliefs, and commit to finding what does work in the market. Struggling traders using futile concepts have a simple choice—let go of beliefs and preconceptions that or holding you back, or let go of your money. Let's now turn to some ideas that do have validity, that reveal significant truths about the nature of the market's movements.

Mean Reversion

Mean reversion is a term used in several different contexts to explain the markets' tendency to reverse after large movements in one direction. In its trivial form, traders say that price returns to a moving average. This is true, as Figure 16.31 shows, but it is not always a useful concept, because there are two ways to get to the average: price can move to the average or the average can move to price. Since traders are paid on price movement, the second case will usually result in trading losses. All of the points marked C in Figure 16.31 would have presented profitable mean-reversion trades, assuming that traders had some tool to identify the points where price had moved a significant distance from the moving average. They could simply have faded these moves by shorting above the average, buying below, and exiting the market when it came back to the moving average. This is the pattern that most traders have in mind when they speak of mean reversion, but they forget the possibilities of the sequence marked A to B. Here, the trader shorting at A would eventually have exited the trade when price did, in fact, revert to the average at point B, but the average was so far above the entry price that a substantial loss would have resulted.

Mean reversion exists in two slightly different contexts: mean reversion after a single large move (usually one bar on a chart) or mean reversion after a more extended move (usually multiple bars on a chart). In reality, these are the same concept on different time frames: what looks like a large multibar move will usually resolve into a single large bar on a higher time frame. A single large bar will usually include multibar trends on the lower time frame. The bar divisions and time frames that traders create are more or less arbitrary divisions; one of the skills discretionary traders work hard to develop is the ability to see beyond those divisions to perceive the flow of the market for what it really is.

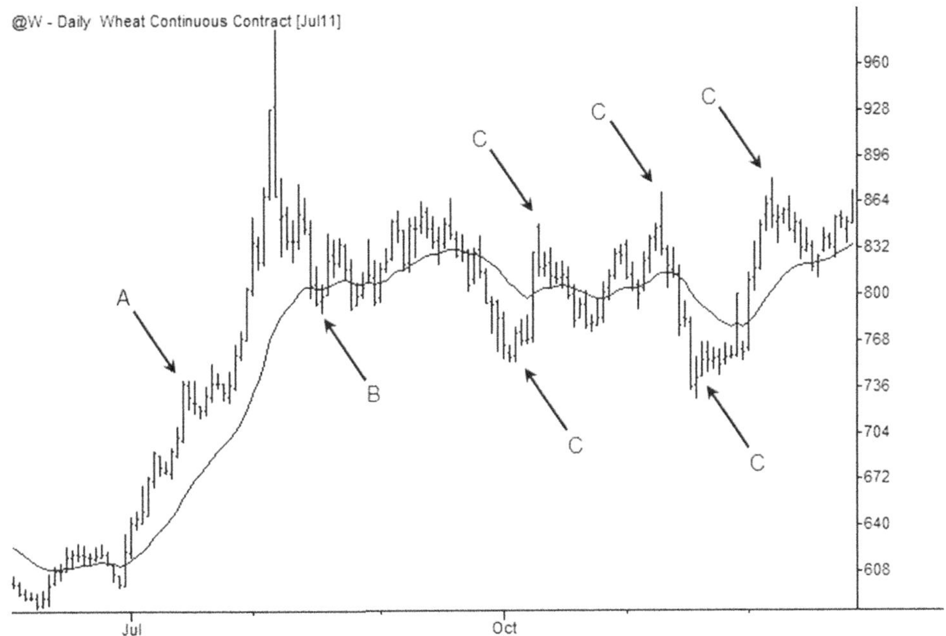

Figure 16.1 Ideal Mean Reversion Entries

Large Single Bars

Many traders assume that a strong close is a sign that the market will continue upward the next day, and that a very weak close is a sign of further impending weakness. This is logical, as strong buying or selling pressure from one session could be expected to spill over into the next. Unfortunately, as with so many things in the market that are logical, it is also wrong; the market works in some wonderfully counterintuitive ways. Figure 16.32 shows the Volatility Spike indicator plotted as a histogram below a daily chart of Apple Inc. stock. (This is a measure that normalizes each day's return as a standard deviation of the past 20 trading days. In some sense, you can think of it as a daily z-score, but I avoid using that term because of its association with normal distributions. The rules of thumb associated with standard deviations do not apply here, as 4 or 5 standard deviation measures on this tool are not uncommon in most markets.)

Figure 16.2 Volatility Spike Indicator Applied to Daily Bars of AAPL Days +/–3 standard deviations are marked.

A few things are apparent in Figure 16.2. First, remember that this is a close-to-close measure and it "knows" nothing about the highs and lows of the session. There was a trading day in May when AAPL traded down over 6 standard deviations, but recovered to close only –1.2 standard deviations on the day. Depending on what you are trying to accomplish, this can be a good or a bad thing, but it is important to realize that this is how the indicator behaves—it specifically measures close-to-close returns. Second, it responds quickly to changing volatility conditions. After a few large days, volatility has increased enough that it takes ever larger moves to register as large standard deviations on this indicator. On the other hand, after a few quiet days, volatility is compressed and a moderate move may register as a large standard deviation move. This is essentially a surprise indicator that measures how consistent a trading day is with the market's recent trading history. With this background in mind, take a look at Table 16.1, which shows a test that fades each move +/–3 standard deviations. Specifically, you would have bought the close of any day that closed down –3 standard deviations and have shorted any day that closed up +3 standard deviations.

Table 16.1 Fading +/−3 Standard Deviation Closes (Based on 20-Day Volatility Window)

	Equities—Buy			Futures—Buy			Forex—Buy		
Days	$\mu_{sig} - \mu_b$	Diff. Med.	%Up	$\mu_{sig} - \mu_b$	Diff. Med.	%Up	$\mu_{sig} - \mu_b$	Diff. Med.	%Up
1	11.3 **	8.3	51.7%	(12.1)	4.0	51.0%	5.9	(1.4)	50.0%
2	15.6 **	9.3	51.8%	(20.7)	2.5	52.7%	(0.9)	7.1	53.8%
3	(5.8)	(9.8)	49.5%	(36.8)*	(29.0)	47.3%	5.5	14.6	60.0%
4	(15.3)*	(9.1)	49.8%	(24.2)	(33.2)	45.9%	(4.1)	6.5	55.0%
5	(5.9)	(6.3)	50.3%	(31.2)	(26.8)	49.0%	14.3	7.4	55.0%
10	(34.2)**	(12.3)	50.7%	(20.8)	(35.1)	49.3%	(1.1)	7.5	53.8%
15	(46.2)**	(1.0)	51.8%	(34.4)	(81.8)	47.3%	(21.9)	22.2	57.5%
20	(63.5)**	15.5	52.9%	(29.7)	(89.0)	48.6%	(8.6)	28.6	62.5%
	Equities—Sell			Futures—Sell			Forex—Sell		
Days	$\mu_{sig} - \mu_b$	Diff. Med.	%Up	$\mu_{sig} - \mu_b$	Diff. Med.	%Up	$\mu_{sig} - \mu_b$	Diff. Med.	%Up
1	(10.5)**	(9.7)	47.8%	(3.2)	(10.4)	47.1%	(7.1)	(7.0)	44.6%
2	(26.8)**	(9.5)	48.9%	7.4	5.3	54.6%	(22.9)*	(16.6)	40.2%
3	(24.0)**	(12.8)	48.9%	20.1	21.5	55.3%	(19.2)	(12.4)	43.5%
4	(33.8)**	(14.1)	49.1%	19.3	16.2	54.9%	(18.0)	(17.8)	47.8%
5	(24.7)**	(8.5)	50.1%	30.8	2.9	54.9%	(6.2)	(4.0)	51.1%
10	(70.2)**	(11.2)	50.8%	27.4	(7.2)	54.3%	(8.8)	22.5	59.8%
15	(83.6)**	7.2	52.5%	29.7	(57.0)	49.8%	(28.2)	(12.4)	55.4%
20	(83.0)**	12.0	53.0%	12.8	(23.8)	53.9%	(22.4)	(3.2)	55.4%

Results for means and medians are in basis points, excess returns over the baseline for that asset class. %Up gives the number of days that closed higher than the entry price on the day following the signal entry. For comparison, the percent of one day Up closes in the Equity sample is 50.07%; in the Futures sample, 50.59%, and in Forex 51.0%.

* indicates difference of means are significant at the 0.05 level, and ** indicates they are significant at the 0.01 level.

Considering equities first, the evidence is clear. Based on these results, we see that large one-move days are more likely to be reversed than to continue in the same direction. In fact, 50.07 of the days in the entire equities universe close up from the previous day, but only 47.8 days close up after a registering a 3 or greater standard deviation close the previous day. If the previous day closed down more than 3 standard deviations, the current day has a 51.7 percent chance of closing up. These may not seem like large edges, but they are real and they are statistically significant ($z = 3.1$ for buys and $z = -4.7$ for sells). In addition to this edge to closing direction, there is a rather large, persistent, and statistically significant excess return for both buys and sells in equities. The sells are clear, underperforming out to the end of the test window, while the performance of the buys appears to be more complex. Regardless, there is a clear edge for the first and second day following the signal, and this is one of the most important aspects of market behavior in equities. If you take nothing else away from this chapter, realize that a stock is more likely to reverse than to continue after a large one-day move in either direction.

From this test, we see strong evidence of single-day mean reversion in equities, but it actually appears that futures are more likely to continue than to reverse (i.e., that a large single-day move is more likely to continue in the same direction tomorrow in futures). Though we do not see statistical significance in the test for futures (the lone * in the third day for Futures is an example of a significance test that should probably be ignored as it is likely to be the result of random chance), the patterns are suggestive of continuation. At the very least, it is clear that the behavior is not consistent with what we see in equities—this is an example of a quantifiable difference between price movements in different asset classes.

Our forex test may suffer on two fronts. First, the sample size is considerably smaller. There are 15,570 bars in the futures universe compared to 1,381,685 in equities, but also keep in mind that the equities universe is highly correlated, so statistical tests on that sample will not have the power we might normally expect from such a large sample. In general, forex markets tend to trade with more consistent volatility and fewer surprises. Table 16.2 compares some volatility measures for a small sample of equities, futures, and forex over a single year's trading. Note particularly the range (Max and Min) of volatilities covered by equities and futures; many of these markets have a 20 or 30 percent spread between their high and low values. Also interesting are the number of days that close greater than 3 or 4 standard deviations up or down on the day; it is not uncommon to see equities and futures put in 10 or more of these in a year. This chart was taken not too long after the massive earthquake and tsunami hit Japan, so it captures a period of exceptional volatility in the currency markets; even then, the currencies are tame by comparison to the other asset classes. It is difficult and potentially misleading to draw conclusions from the volatility spike test in Table 16.1 for forex, but it is fair to say that it looks more like equities than futures.

Table 16.2 Historical Volatility Ranges and Nσ Counts for 250 Trading Days

	Current	Max	Min	>5σ	>4σ	>3σ	>2σ	>1σ
Equities								
AAPL	18.2%	46.5%	7.2%	0	1	8	23	83
M	34.8%	62.3%	16.9%	0	3	7	15	85
LULU	33.8%	82.2%	26.9%	4	6	10	20	78
WFM	33.1%	55.2%	14.1%	2	2	6	17	77
XOM	19.4%	33.1%	5.2%	4	6	10	32	80
Futures								
Crude Oil	47.6%	48.1%	11.8%	1	3	8	19	93
Soybeans	20.7%	40.6%	10.9%	1	3	11	22	76
Coffee	28.4%	43.3%	14.3%	5	6	10	24	90
Forex								
EURUSD	12.1%	16.6%	7.2%	1	1	4	22	85
AUDUSD	12.3%	29.0%	7.3%	1	2	6	21	88
USDCAD	6.9%	19.8%	4.4%	1	1	4	18	90

Current is current (as of 5/18/11) 20-day annualized historical volatility. Max and Min are the highest and lowest values of 20-day historical volatility over the past year. The last five columns count the number of days that have absolute standard deviation spikes greater than 5, 4, 3, 2, and 1 standard deviation.

It might be instructive to add one more condition to this test. It seems likely that mean reversion could be the result of exhaustion or overextension. We also know that the standard deviation tool is blind to the day's range; if a market trades 12 standard deviations higher through the day, but sells off to close only 3 standard deviations higher, the only number this tool records is the 3 standard deviation close. In terms of market character, there is a big difference between a day that closes at the high of the day and one that might close up the same amount, but down significantly from a peak reached earlier in the session. The first example is more indicative of potential short-term exhaustion, while the second maybe may have pulled back and consolidated; at the very least, there was a significant amount of selling pressure on the second day. Table 16.3 repeats the 3 standard deviation test with two added criteria: for buys, the day has to have opened in the bottom of the day's range and has to have closed in the top 75 percent of that range; these criteria are flipped symmetrically for sells. It is not difficult to come up with other, possibly better, conditions to capture this tendency, but this is sufficient for an initial inquiry.

Table 16.3 Fading +/−3 Standard Deviation Closes, Close in Top 75 Percent of the Day's Range, and Open in Bottom 50 Percent of the Day's Range (For Buys)

	Equities—Buy			Futures—Buy			Forex—Buy		
Days	$\mu_{sig} - \mu_b$	Diff. Med.	%Up	$\mu_{sig} - \mu_b$	Diff. Med.	%Up	$\mu_{sig} - \mu_b$	Diff. Med.	%Up
1	25.7 **	19.2	53.8%	(9.7)	4.7	51.7%	14.0	(1.4)	50.0%
2	32.4 **	21.8	53.6%	(25.1)	(3.5)	51.3%	8.8	2.4	50.0%
3	11.1	2.6	50.9%	(34.9)*	(26.8)	47.6%	9.4	17.4	58.3%
4	1.2	3.2	51.1%	(21.5)	(21.8)	47.2%	14.6	15.1	56.7%
5	8.4	5.8	51.4%	(27.8)	(25.0)	49.1%	28.1	29.1	58.3%
10	(12.3)	9.2	52.1%	(16.7)	(35.1)	49.8%	13.7	14.3	56.7%
15	(25.6)*	13.3	52.4%	(24.1)	(80.0)	47.2%	(16.5)	27.1	56.7%
20	(47.7)**	37.3	53.9%	(19.8)	(90.2)	48.7%	(7.2)	42.6	63.3%
	Equities— Sell			Futures—Sell			Forex—Sell		
Days	$\mu_{sig} - \mu_b$	Diff. Med.	%Up	$\mu_{sig} - \mu_b$	Diff. Med.	%Up	$\mu_{sig} - \mu_b$	Diff. Med.	%Up
1	(18.3)**	(15.2)	46.4%	(9.9)	(13.0)	46.5%	(3.3)	(2.1)	48.2%
2	(33.8)**	(19.0)	47.6%	6.6	5.8	55.1%	(13.1)	(15.3)	39.8%
3	(28.6)**	(16.2)	48.5%	14.3	11.7	54.7%	(12.3)	(9.8)	47.0%
4	(41.6)**	(17.0)	48.7%	16.7	15.1	55.1%	(6.1)	(7.2)	50.6%
5	(30.1)**	(11.3)	49.8%	20.8	0.4	54.7%	3.6	0.7	53.0%
10	(67.5)**	(12.4)	50.7%	11.2	(11.6)	54.3%	16.9	25.1	62.7%
15	(67.2)**	10.6	52.8%	8.8	(69.8)	49.2%	(18.2)	(4.5)	57.8%
20	(75.7)**	7.7	52.7%	0.5	(32.8)	53.1%	(4.1)	29.2	59.0%

These results are interesting. With this one, simple addition, we have significantly incr eased the strength of the signal in equities, and now have more than a 3.6 percent edge over the baseline for both buys and sells. Forex and futures still fail significance tests, and should probably be disregarded. As a rule of thumb, be suspicious of effects that are small (less than 10 bp), especially when the mean and median do not seem to be in agreement (i.e., one is positive and one is negative). In addition, if the effect seems to be limited to one day in the series, it is probably noise; we are usually most interested in effects that show some degree of persistence. There could well be exceptions to each of these rules of thumb: some effects may be very small but still significant, and some may be extremely short term, perhaps limited to one or two days after the signal. Remember, these are crude tests of tendencies, not complete trading systems. It is very possible that one of these tests showing a slight edge, only a hint of a tendency, could be exploited with more conditions or in a discretionary framework. The mean/median rule is also only a guideline, as there could be valid trading signals in which all of the profitability is due to outliers, which would drag the mean but not the median.

The results seem to be clear: Equities are more likely to reverse than to continue after a large day, up or down, with a statistically and economically significant edge. In addition, adding some simple filters to assure the market closed near the high or low, perhaps to indicate exhaustion, strengthens the effect considerably. We see evidence of a more complex process at work in futures, and forex shows no tendency that is inconsistent with random action.

N-Day Runs

A fair coin has no memory of past flips. Though it may be counterintuitive, the probability of flipping a head is still 50 percent, regardless of whether the last flip was a head or a tail, or even if you have just flipped six heads in a row. It is important to build correct intuition about this idea because this is the source of many misperceptions about probabilities and games of chance. The probability of flipping eight heads in a row is 0.39 percent (the multiplicative rule of probability applies, so (1/2)8 = 0.0039), which is very small. Now, imagine that you have just flipped seven heads in a row; on the next flip, many people will be inclined to bet more on tails than heads, because they correctly realize the probability of eight heads in a row is very small. However, this is faulty intuition. The probability of the next flip being heads is 50 percent (assuming the coin is fair), regardless of past flips. One way to think about it is that you are already in a very unusual situation, having flipped seven heads in a row, but this does not affect the probability of the next flip. Imagine you find yourself at LaGuardia airport with the President of the United States and the Pope. If you pull a coin out of your pocket and flip the coin, what is the probability that it comes up heads? It is obvious that the airport situation does not impact the probability of the coin flip; it is simply an extremely improbable situation and has no bearing on the upcoming coin flip. Flipping after a long run of heads is, in terms of probabilities, no different. You are in an unlikely situation to begin with, but the next flip is still, literally, a coin flip.

Runs in Coin Flips

Formally, this is called a conditional probability, and is written Prob(A|B), which is read "the probability of A occurring, given that B has already occurred" or, more simply, "the probability of A, given B." Conditional probability is an important part of the branch of statistics called Bayesian statistics, which has many important applications to market situations. Consider an experiment: I generated 1,000,000 coin flips with a pseudo-random number generator, and found that 50.12 percent of the coins came up heads, which is normal variation to be expected. (We should be very suspicious to see exactly 50 percent heads or tails.) Next, I went back through the list of coin flips and counted the times that the next flip was the same as the preceding flip. I would expect this to be 50 percent since there are four ways that two coins can flip (HH TT HT TH) and two of those four fulfill the condition. In terms of notation, we could say let A be the condition "the next coin flip matches the previous flip" and could write Prob(A) = 0.50. In this experiment, A was true 50.1 percent of the time, in line with what we would expect based on theoretical probabilities.

Next, I counted the number of times the coin came up either heads or tails seven times in a row, in other words the number of N = 7 runs in the series, and found 7,835 of these runs in the 1,000,000 flips. Theoretically, the probability of an N = 7 run is 0.007813, so the results of this experiment match the theoretical probabilities quite well. Formally, let B be the event "I flipped seven heads or tails in a row"; then Prob(B) = 0.57 = 0.007813.

Now, here is where things get a little interesting. Go back in time and select all of those coins after either seven heads or seven tails in a row, in the moment before that eighth flip. This is an important moment at which many people make an intuitive error. Check yourself here. Would you be inclined to bet more on the run continuing or breaking? The question to ask is: are these special coins now, at this moment? Define another event, C, and let it be the event the next flip is the same as the previous flip (HH or TT). Let's select just those 7,835 potentially special coins and flip them, recording the number of times they match the previous flip. In this particular case, we would find that 50.05 of them come up the same as the previous flip, so there was no edge to betting either for or against the run continuing. It turns out the coin was fair, even on the improbable eighth flip. This is expected behavior for a fair, unbiased coin.

This has been a long example, but it is important. To review, A is the event "the next coin flip matches the previous flip," and we saw that Prob(A) ≈ 50 percent, both in theory and in our experiment. Condition B was the event "I flipped seven heads or tails in a row," and Prob(B) ≈ 0.78 percent, also verified in the experiment. Prob(A|B), the probability of A given that B has occurred, is ≈ 50 percent. This is actually a good definition of unrelated, or independent, events: if Prob(A) = Prob(A|B), then B has no influence on A. Advocates of the efficient markets hypothesis say that, even if you include all possible information into the set B, it will still not affect the probability of any market movement. If A is "the chance that my stock goes up today" and B is whatever you want it to be, whether that is technical patterns, news, fundamental information, market context, or what you had for breakfast, EMH tells us it is all equally relevant, which is to say, it is not relevant at all. Table 16.4presents several run lengths from the actual 1,000,000 random number experiment. In this table, the first column counts the number of occurrences of the run, Prob(B) obs is the percentage of the time we saw the run, which can be compared to Prob(B)theory, the theoretical probability of that run occurring calculated by (1/2)N, where N is the length of the run. The last column, Prob(A|B), is the probability that the next flip is the same as the previous flip, which, in these examples, is always very close to 50 percent. The results of this experiment match theoretical expectations very well.

Table 16.4 Conditional Probability Based on Run Results from 1,000,000 Random Coin Flips

N= Runs	Events	Prob(B)obs	Prob(B)theory	Prob(A|B)
2	249,777	25.0%	25.0%	50.1%
3	125,176	12.5%	12.5%	50.2%
4	62,861	6.3%	6.3%	50.0%
5	31,458	3.1%	3.1%	50.0%
6	15,738	1.6%	1.6%	49.8%
7	7,835	0.8%	0.8%	50.5%
8	3,957	0.4%	0.4%	50.1%

So we know what EMH says and see that it applies very well to randomly generated coin flips and numbers, but here is the question of the day: is the market a coin flip? (If so, I have wasted a lot of paper and your time reading this far.) One way to test this would be to repeat the coin flip experiment, but, instead of using a random number generator, to substitute the daily returns for the S&P 500 Cash index from 1/1/1980 to 5/17/2011 for the coin flipping process: if the daily return for the S&P 500 was positive, the coin flips heads; if it was negative, the coin flips tails. This results in 7,918 "coin flips," 52.99 percent of which are heads: Prob(Up) = 0.5299. The coin is not a fair coin, but is slightly weighted to come up heads, which is not evidence of a nonrandom process. It could well be a loaded coin but subsequent flips could be independent, and proof of this would be Prob(A) = Prob(A|B). Table 16.5 shows the results of this experiment.

Table 16.5 Conditional Probability Experiment Using S&P 500 Cash Returns, 1980–2011, Prob(A) = 52.99%

N= Runs	Events	Prob(B)obs	Prob(B)theory	Prob(A|B)
2	2,012	25.4%	25.0%	51.4%
3	1,035	13.1%	12.5%	45.9%
4	475	6.0%	6.3%	46.5%
5	221	2.8%	3.1%	47.5%
6	105	1.3%	1.6%	39.0%
7	41	0.5%	0.8%	51.2%
8	21	0.3%	0.4%	47.6%

Two things are apparent from this table. First, it seems like there are slightly fewer runs than we would expect theoretically from our loaded coin, but this is not true because Prob(Down) = 0.4670. Prob(Up) + Prob(Down) < 1, because the market was unchanged about 0.3 percent of all trading days, and these unchanged days will break some of the runs. However, the Prob(A|B) is extremely interesting. If weak form EMH were true, Prob(A) = Prob(A|B), so every entry in that column should be very close to 53 percent. The sample size may not be large enough to assure convergence (though at 7,918 it is not small) so a certain amount of variation above and below 53 percent is to be expected. However, the message of this table is clear—the S&P 500 is more likely to reverse direction after a run of closes in the same direction. This not a simple random coin; it is a coin that has some memory of its past steps. That is significant information. Contrary to the claims of the efficient markets hypothesis, Prob(A) ≠ Prob(A|B), at least for the S&P 500 Cash index.

Runs Tests on Market Data

It is common to see tests of runs in trading books and on blogs, but there is a common problem with many of these tests. Consider the following sequence of up and down closes: up, up, up, up, down. If we test for three-day runs, we would find two separate three-day runs in that series: days{1, 2, 3} and also days {2, 3, 4}. Looking at the day following those runs, we find that one of them closed up and the other closed down, so based on this tiny data set, we would say that three-day runs are followed by a reverse close 50 percent of the time. However, this is not what most people mean when they test three-day runs; usually they mean runs that are exactly three days. There is only a single exact three-day run in that series, and it is followed by a close in the same direction. It is important to specify the test condition precisely—all of the tests in this section for N length runs are based on exactly N length runs to avoid this problem. Table 16.6 and Table 16.7 show the results of the Pythia methodology applied to fading three-day and five-day runs (i.e., buying after exactly three consecutive closes down and shorting after exactly three consecutive upward closes) in our test universe.

Table 16.6 Fading Three-Day Runs

	Equities—Buy			Futures—Buy			Forex—Buy		
Days	$\mu_{sig} - \mu_b$	Diff. Med.	%Up	$\mu_{sig} - \mu_b$	Diff. Med.	%Up	$\mu_{sig} - \mu_b$	Diff. Med.	%Up
1	7.8 **	6.8	51.9%	4.1	1.9	52.2%	5.6 *	4.6	56.0%
2	7.0 **	13.8	52.9%	3.2	0.3	51.6%	9.0 *	9.6	58.2%
3	9.8 **	19.8	53.4%	4.3	(6.3)	50.6%	10.9 *	10.0	56.6%
4	16.2 **	27.7	54.3%	(1.1)	(14.0)	49.7%	4.8	7.5	55.6%
5	24.0 **	35.5	54.7%	2.5	(13.8)	50.4%	3.0	4.3	54.0%
10	24.9 **	54.2	55.5%	1.6	(20.6)	51.3%	2.2	4.8	54.8%
15	19.9 **	76.9	56.5%	(4.9)	(36.6)	51.2%	1.5	(2.5)	53.7%
20	20.5 **	89.2	57.0%	(4.4)	(57.9)	51.0%	(6.0)	(6.8)	55.2%
	Equities—Sell			Futures—Sell			Forex—Sell		
Days	$\mu_{sig} - \mu_b$	Diff. Med.	%Up	$\mu_{sig} - \mu_b$	Diff. Med.	%Up	$\mu_{sig} - \mu_b$	Diff. Med.	%Up
1	(3.5)**	(2.3)	49.6%	(1.1)	(3.5)	48.8%	(1.5)	(3.1)	48.2%
2	(10.1)**	(4.5)	50.0%	(3.9)	(2.4)	50.9%	(1.8)	(1.6)	51.4%
3	(16.1)**	(2.3)	50.4%	(2.5)	(0.8)	52.1%	1.2	5.1	54.4%
4	(20.0)**	(4.4)	50.4%	(1.1)	(1.9)	52.6%	0.9	3.0	54.0%
5	(25.7)**	(3.4)	50.8%	(0.2)	(4.2)	52.8%	(0.5)	5.1	54.1%
10	(34.9)**	7.1	52.4%	(4.8)	(13.4)	52.4%	(3.6)	6.1	55.3%
15	(49.3)**	17.8	53.4%	5.6	(22.7)	52.6%	2.4	9.7	56.4%
20	(59.6)**	30.0	54.2%	6.6	(27.1)	54.1%	1.0	(11.0)	54.6%

Table 16.7 Fading Five-Day Runs

	Equities—Buy			Futures—Buy			Forex—Buy		
Days	$\mu_{sig} - \mu_b$	Diff. Med.	%Up	$\mu_{sig} - \mu_b$	Diff. Med.	%Up	$\mu_{sig} - \mu_b$	Diff. Med.	%Up
1	18.4 **	8.1	52.0%	13.5 *	12.4	57.1%	(0.1)	3.6	53.9%
2	24.4 **	14.3	52.6%	3.2	4.3	53.1%	(8.8)	3.3	55.1%
3	39.2 **	19.6	53.1%	2.9	(3.0)	51.6%	(13.8)	(11.4)	48.5%
4	61.0 **	30.4	54.2%	(0.1)	(16.3)	48.6%	(31.7)*	(24.8)	42.5%
5	76.5 **	46.7	55.4%	3.5	(7.6)	51.0%	(30.4)*	(21.3)	46.7%
10	45.2 **	48.8	54.8%	15.5	(21.0)	53.3%	(22.8)	(17.7)	50.9%
15	47.6 **	70.9	56.0%	12.3	(46.7)	50.8%	(10.8)	12.8	56.9%
20	79.4 **	107.6	57.8%	30.5	(14.1)	54.7%	(9.4)	(4.7)	56.9%
	Equities—Sell			Futures—Sell			Forex—Sell		
Days	$\mu_{sig} - \mu_b$	Diff. Med.	%Up	$\mu_{sig} - \mu_b$	Diff. Med.	%Up	$\mu_{sig} - \mu_b$	Diff. Med.	%Up
1	(18.7)**	(3.9)	48.8%	1.2	(0.4)	50.2%	(1.9)	(2.1)	48.5%
2	(25.6)**	(8.4)	48.5%	8.2	7.0	53.8%	(2.0)	0.4	55.0%
3	(28.9)**	(12.9)	48.6%	16.8	13.0	54.3%	(3.1)	5.9	55.7%
4	(33.5)**	(13.2)	49.0%	12.4	17.1	54.6%	(3.8)	2.9	55.7%
5	(36.3)**	(11.3)	49.5%	14.8	19.6	55.9%	5.6	11.1	57.6%
10	(59.3)**	(5.3)	51.4%	15.9	2.3	55.0%	(7.0)	13.1	56.9%
15	(56.0)**	12.7	53.1%	(1.5)	(39.4)	51.2%	(2.1)	13.2	59.5%
20	(50.9)**	35.8	54.7%	9.6	(37.3)	52.8%	(4.6)	18.6	56.9%

These results confirm what we have seen in the previous section. Equities show clear and strong evidence of mean reversion, while futures and forex do not. These are, so far, the strongest results we have seen from any test and point to a very important structural feature in equities.

N-Day Channel Breakouts

Channel breakouts (also called Donchian channel breakouts) are commonly discussed in the technical analysis literature, partly because it is now well known that 20-day and 55-day channel breakouts were an important part of the systems used by the original Turtles (see Faith 2007). These are some of the simplest trading systems imaginable; you buy when the N-day high is exceeded and short when the N-day low is penetrated. Figure 16.3 shows a daily chart of Crude Oil futures with channels delineating the 20-day highs and lows marked. There is obvious logic to trading these breakouts: they will always get you into every trending trade because the market must violate an N-day high to go higher and an N-day low to go lower.

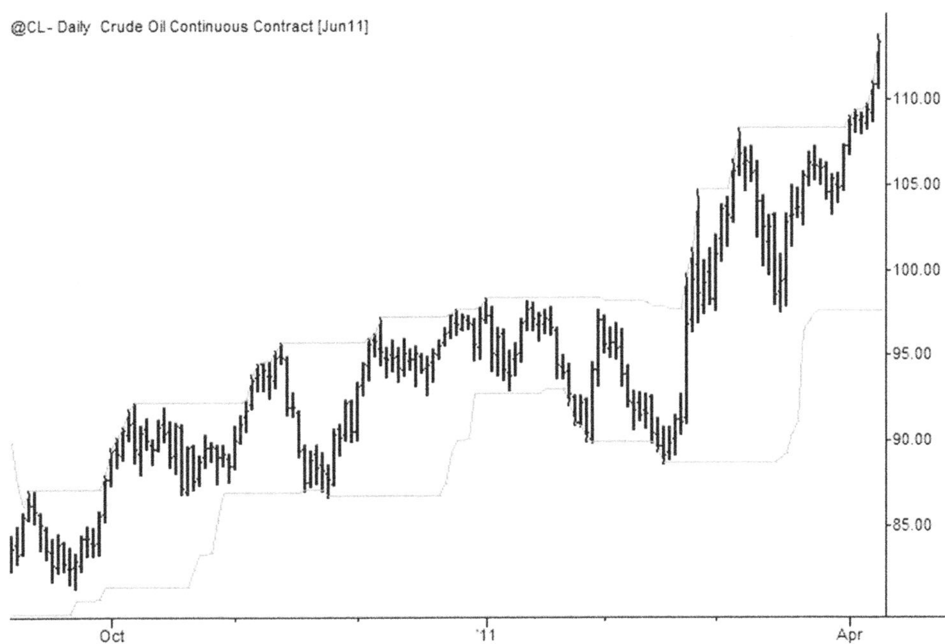

Figure 16.3 Daily Crude Oil Futures with 20-Day High/Low Channels

It is also well known that there was more to the Turtles' system than these simple channel breakouts, and that they are not a stand-alone trading system. In testing these channels, one thing we need to guard against is the situation where the market essentially presses against the channel and makes a higher high every day, as shown several times in Figure 16.8. If we do a naive test of the channels, it would have us entering a new trade on every one of those days, and, chances are, few traders would be prepared to trade like this because it is very difficult to manage position sizing in a system that could have 1, or 20, or more entries in the same direction. All of the following tests assume that we are entering on the close of the day that broke the channel, and not at the actual channel level, which would have given a more advantageous entry in many cases. Furthermore, they assume that entries in the same direction must be separated by five days. In other words, if we get a buy signal on a Monday, we cannot take any other buy signal before the following Monday. (We could, however, take a sell signal in the intervening period.)

Table 16.8 Trading 20-Day Channel Breakouts (Entry on Close, Five Days between Consecutive Entries)

	Equities—Buy			Futures—Buy			Forex—Buy		
Days	$\mu_{sig} - \mu_b$	Diff. Med.	%Up	$\mu_{sig} - \mu_b$	Diff. Med.	%Up	$\mu_{sig} - \mu_b$	Diff. Med.	%Up
1	(12.3)**	(6.0)	47.9%	7.2*	(0.1)	50.8%	0.6	(2.1)	49.2%
2	(24.3)**	(10.6)	48.0%	8.5	7.2	54.9%	4.0	(4.2)	49.7%
3	(30.1)**	(11.4)	48.6%	16.1*	8.9	55.4%	1.8	2.1	53.6%
4	(32.4)**	(12.9)	48.9%	10.8	8.5	55.7%	1.7	(1.2)	53.0%
5	(36.8)**	(11.3)	49.6%	12.4	4.5	54.9%	2.3	9.7	56.4%
10	(54.5)**	(8.0)	51.1%	15.3	(9.7)	53.7%	6.6	12.8	55.6%
15	(64.3)**	2.1	52.4%	17.7	(20.5)	52.9%	15.2	7.1	56.5%
20	(69.5)**	12.8	53.5%	15.5	(32.6)	53.0%	11.6	16.7	58.2%
	Equities—Sell			**Futures—Sell**			**Forex—Sell**		
Days	$\mu_{sig} - \mu_b$	Diff. Med.	%Up	$\mu_{sig} - \mu_b$	Diff. Med.	%Up	$\mu_{sig} - \mu_b$	Diff. Med.	%Up
1	7.8**	6.0	51.4%	(1.2)	2.4	52.3%	(2.8)	(0.3)	51.4%
2	12.0**	13.0	52.4%	1.5	(5.1)	50.5%	(4.5)	(4.2)	49.9%
3	16.0**	17.7	52.8%	2.2	(7.6)	50.4%	(4.7)	(7.9)	48.4%
4	18.5**	23.3	53.2%	(2.4)	(11.9)	50.2%	(11.4)	(6.6)	50.5%
5	35.4**	33.3	54.0%	(3.0)	(10.9)	51.0%	(7.2)	(9.6)	50.1%
10	30.6**	50.5	54.8%	(7.7)	(23.0)	51.6%	(8.4)	(9.5)	53.8%
15	35.8**	82.2	56.1%	(22.7)	(54.1)	49.5%	(15.2)	(2.5)	54.9%
20	57.3**	106.3	57.2%	(25.7)	(65.2)	50.1%	(26.1)	(16.4)	54.9%

You may have wondered what a test of breakout trades is doing in a section on mean reversion. The reason is simple: failed breakout trades are evidence of mean reversion. Table 16.8 is another strong affirmation of mean reversion in equities, showing negative returns for our buy signal and positive returns for shorts—the signal conditions were exactly wrong for this sample. It appears that there may be an exploitable opportunity by shorting new 20-day highs and buying new 20-day lows in stocks, fading the channel breakout. However, it would be a mistake to assume that you could apply the same system to futures and forex just because it works in equities. The futures sample seems to suggest an edge in going with the direction of the breakout. Positive returns for buys and negative returns for shorts, though probably not statistically significant (meaning that the trader actually trading these would see extreme variability in the results), suggest that fading the channel breakout in futures could be painful. This is also the first consistent signal we have seen in forex, as all of the returns on the sell side are negative. However, the small size of these returns, a few basis points at most, is a warning that this may not be an easily exploitable tendency.

Twenty-day channel breakouts are common, occurring on approximately 4 percent of all trading days; using a longer period for the breakout might result in more significant levels, so Table 16.9 shows the results of a 100-day channel breakout. At this point, futures and forex finally start to show something interesting, and we see that positioning with the direction of the breakout is clearly the correct trade in these markets. Particularly in forex, the signal size is small, but means and medians are consistently on the same side of zero, and the series appears to be flirting with statistical significance. Is this a stand-alone trading system? Probably not, but it is pretty strong evidence of an underlying tendency in the market. Note that mean reversion is still alive and well in equities in this test—this is perhaps the clearest evidence so far of different behavior between these asset classes.

Table 16.9 Trading 100-Day Channel Breakouts (Entry on Close, Five Days between Consecutive Entries)

	Equities—Buy			Futures—Buy			Forex—Buy		
Days	$\mu_{sig} - \mu_b$	Diff. Med.	%Up	$\mu_{sig} - \mu_b$	Diff. Med.	%Up	$\mu_{sig} - \mu_b$	Diff. Med.	%Up
1	(12.0)**	(6.2)	47.4%	10.1*	2.6	52.9%	0.5	2.1	51.9%
2	(24.2)**	(11.1)	47.3%	14.1	17.9	58.2%	10.8*	3.0	53.1%
3	(33.3)**	(12.6)	47.9%	23.7*	18.2	57.7%	4.8	9.9	57.0%
4	(39.1)**	(18.7)	47.8%	25.0*	21.1	59.2%	13.6*	18.6	58.5%
5	(46.7)**	(17.4)	48.3%	21.0	14.7	57.5%	14.2	29.0	60.9%
10	(77.1)**	(22.7)	49.2%	43.2*	22.2	56.1%	18.3	19.0	57.6%
15	(87.2)**	(18.2)	51.0%	59.6**	10.7	56.7%	29.7*	18.8	59.4%
20	(98.4)**	(15.0)	52.0%	73.3 **	0.3	57.3%	31.8 *	45.6	61.5%
	Equities—Sell			Futures—Sell			Forex—Sell		
Days	$\mu_{sig} - \mu_b$	Diff. Med.	%Up	$\mu_{sig} - \mu_b$	Diff. Med.	%Up	$\mu_{sig} - \mu_b$	Diff. Med.	%Up
1	4.1	2.1	50.4%	(10.1)	(3.5)	49.5%	(11.5)	(10.3)	44.7%
2	18.7**	12.1	51.7%	(4.8)	(2.2)	51.0%	(15.1)	(4.2)	49.3%
3	25.5**	26.1	53.1%	(6.4)	(13.7)	48.7%	(21.8)	(15.4)	45.4%
4	29.9**	28.2	52.8%	(26.9)*	(21.7)	48.2%	(27.6)	(16.7)	46.1%
5	74.7**	50.9	54.6%	(26.6)	(19.1)	49.2%	(28.2)	(15.5)	47.4%
10	79.5**	81.9	55.9%	(52.5)**	(46.7)	47.7%	(46.8)*	(40.1)	42.8%
15	93.8**	132.9	57.2%	(87.8)**	(85.3)	45.5%	(79.4)**	(49.6)	44.7%
20	133.1**	173.3	58.5%	(115.6)**	(107.7)	46.5%	(85.5)**	(59.7)	48.0%

Table 16.10 shows one last channel breakout test of a 260-day channel breakout, approximately a full calendar year. Stock traders, in particular, like to buy stocks that are near 52-week highs; many stock traders approach the market with a focus on fundamental factors (fundamental in this concept meaning balance sheet, income statement, competitive position, etc.) and add one or two elementary technical tools to their decision process. Two of the most common basic technical tools used by these traders are moving averages and breakouts to 52-week highs, the idea being that a stock at 52-week highs is experiencing unusual buying pressure and interest. Do these traders realize that, by entering on breakouts to 52-week highs, they are actually trading against one of the strongest statistical tendencies in the market? Table 16.35 shows that, in this sample, stocks that broke to 52-week highs were down, on average, 1 percent two weeks (20 trading days) later. Furthermore, going long a stock that has just broken to 52-week highs will usually result in a losing trade the next day, as only 47 percent of them close higher the following day. Stock traders who use this as a filter are putting themselves on the wrong side of the market before they even begin.

Table 16.10 Trading 260-Day (~52 Week) Channel Breakouts (Entry on Close, Five Days between Consecutive Entries)

	Equities—Buy			Futures—Buy			Forex—Buy		
Days	$\mu_{sig} - \mu_b$	Diff. Med.	%Up	$\mu_{sig} - \mu_b$	Diff. Med.	%Up	$\mu_{sig} - \mu_b$	Diff. Med.	%Up
1	(10.9)**	(6.4)	47.0%	4.8	2.1	52.1%	4.2	3.7	55.4%
2	(22.6)**	(10.0)	47.4%	13.8	20.3	59.0%	6.6	5.3	53.1%
3	(33.0)**	(10.0)	48.1%	16.4	14.3	57.9%	2.4	13.9	58.5%
4	(41.7)**	(17.0)	47.8%	17.9	19.7	59.0%	12.9	28.8	59.8%
5	(50.4)**	(15.8)	48.3%	14.8	13.6	56.9%	14.2	33.2	65.6%
10	(79.6)**	(22.7)	49.3%	56.9 **	44.7	58.4%	10.2	20.1	55.8%
15	(90.9)**	(19.7)	51.0%	72.4 **	23.8	57.9%	18.6	(2.3)	56.3%
20	(102.4)**	(17.2)	51.7%	101.7 **	11.9	57.5%	20.4	14.6	59.4%
	Equities—Sell			Futures—Sell			Forex—Sell		
Days	$\mu_{sig} - \mu_b$	Diff. Med.	%Up	$\mu_{sig} - \mu_b$	Diff. Med.	%Up	$\mu_{sig} - \mu_b$	Diff. Med.	%Up
1	1.7	(2.3)	49.5%	(3.6)	(1.0)	50.9%	(8.9)	(6.9)	48.5%
2	23.0 *	3.8	50.6%	(3.2)	(4.6)	50.7%	(24.1)	(27.7)	42.6%
3	37.5 **	22.8	52.2%	(1.5)	(13.7)	49.1%	(51.2)*	(30.9)	38.2%
4	54.7 **	27.0	52.4%	(14.7)	(19.4)	48.8%	(52.9)	(26.8)	41.2%
5	122.5 **	57.9	53.9%	(7.3)	(17.6)	49.1%	(40.1)	(19.1)	44.1%
10	122.7 **	92.7	54.8%	(23.3)	(35.1)	49.9%	(57.5)	(28.7)	44.1%
15	151.1 **	166.0	56.7%	(68.2)*	(67.7)	47.0%	(103.9)*	(34.2)	47.1%
20	233.6 **	234.2	58.9%	(68.2)*	(72.3)	49.9%	(71.0)	(11.2)	54.4%

Channels and Bands

Most traders are familiar with Bollinger bands, which plot bands a multiple of the standard deviation of price above and below a moving average. I prefer to use modified Keltner channels, which are discussed in considerable detail in Chapter 8, but both of these are adaptive indicators. They automatically adjust to the market's current volatility conditions, which is preferable to the static percentage bands that some traders use. I use slightly modified Keltner channels set 2.25 ATRs above and below a 20-period exponential moving average (the standard calculation uses a simple moving average) that contain about 85 percent of market activity across a wide range of asset classes and time frames. Figure 16.4 shows an example of these bands applied to daily bars of the Dow Jones Japan Index.

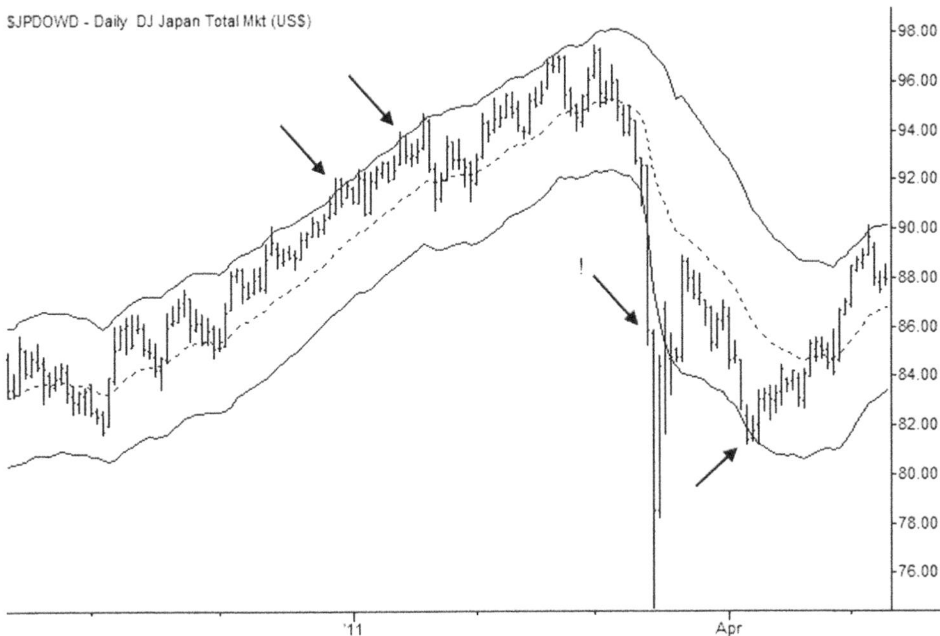

Figure 16.4 Closes Outside the Keltner Channels Indicate Potentially Overextended Market

A market's relationship to the bands is one way to quantify potential overextension and to point out markets that could be due for reversion to the mean. Table 16.11 shows the results of a test that fades moves beyond the Keltner channels. Specifically, it buys a close below the channels, provided that the previous low was above the channel. This condition prevents triggering multiple entries on every day while the market is extended in a strong push outside the channel. Without this condition, such a push could potentially result in a winning trade as the test system basically scales in with a separate entry at every bar. With this condition, such an extended push becomes what it would most likely be for the mean-reversion trader: a loss. (Another way to accomplish the same goal would be to require a time period, say 10 trading days, in between entries in the same direction. This is probably not as good a solution, as that time window is an arbitrary choice, though that test actually shows a stronger edge over a considerably larger number of events.)

Table 16.11 tells a story that should be familiar by now: strong evidence of mean reversion in equities, and a more confusing result in the other two markets. This test shows a strong one-day tendency in futures, with a 60.3 percent chance of a close up on that day, compared to 50.6 percent of days that close up in the futures baseline. Similarly, the sell signal in futures shows a strong one-day probability of a down close, but this is followed by a series of outperforming days that erase the edge. It is possible that this system could be traded with different parameters or additional qualifying conditions in futures. In forex, we actually see strong evidence of continuation, suggesting that breaks below the channel should be shorted and breaks above bought—precisely the opposite of equities. The message should be clear by now, and if there was some way to write it in large, flashing neon letters I would: there are significant differences in the ways that equities, futures, and currencies trade.

Table 16.11 Fading Moves Outside Keltner Channel; Previous Bar Must Have Been Inside Channel

	Equities—Buy			Futures—Buy			Forex—Buy		
Days	$\mu_{sig} - \mu_b$	Diff. Med.	%Up	$\mu_{sig} - \mu_b$	Diff. Med.	%Up	$\mu_{sig} - \mu_b$	Diff. Med.	%Up
1	24.4 **	19.3	53.7%	12.2	18.8	60.3%	(12.7)	(10.3)	45.7%
2	27.9 **	22.6	53.6%	15.6	13.3	57.7%	(10.3)	3.1	55.4%
3	23.8 **	27.0	53.6%	12.1	3.6	53.2%	(5.7)	0.2	52.2%
4	23.0 **	29.9	53.2%	7.6	(2.5)	52.1%	(27.6)	(12.6)	46.7%
5	33.0 **	38.6	53.9%	0.2	2.0	53.4%	(11.4)	(10.6)	50.0%
10	20.8 *	40.2	54.1%	(45.4)	(27.1)	50.5%	(30.7)	(8.9)	53.3%
15	43.0 **	91.1	56.4%	(14.4)	(19.6)	52.9%	(15.0)	18.6	58.7%
20	47.2 **	113.8	57.3%	(27.8)	(54.2)	51.6%	(22.7)	29.4	58.7%
	Equities—Sell			Futures—Sell			Forex—Sell		
Days	$\mu_{sig} - \mu_b$	Diff. Med.	%Up	$\mu_{sig} - \mu_b$	Diff. Med.	%Up	$\mu_{sig} - \mu_b$	Diff. Med.	%Up
1	(18.9)**	(14.7)	45.9%	(1.1)	(3.5)	47.7%	6.9	(1.2)	50.3%
2	(29.1)**	(18.5)	46.8%	22.9 *	4.9	54.8%	15.4	2.6	54.5%
3	(38.6)**	(22.5)	47.1%	31.7 *	9.3	55.5%	13.0	2.0	51.7%
4	(37.3)**	(21.5)	48.2%	20.8	4.7	54.4%	10.8	8.0	56.6%
5	(41.8)**	(16.7)	49.1%	13.0	(0.4)	54.6%	19.8	30.9	62.8%
10	(63.3)**	(22.7)	50.0%	0.4	(22.4)	51.6%	54.8 **	67.0	66.2%
15	(73.5)**	(13.2)	51.3%	(3.3)	(55.9)	49.3%	72.1 **	70.9	68.3%
20	(65.7)**	7.7	53.1%	2.1	(36.5)	52.8%	54.4 *	42.4	62.8%

Using Overbought/Oversold Indicators

There are many technical indicators that are designed to highlight overbought and oversold levels, but they are difficult to apply in a systematic manner. Tom DeMark (1997) has done extensive work quantifying overbought and oversold patterns in indicators. If you are interested in pursuing this topic, his work might provide a good departure point. Though he has also developed a set of custom, specialized oscillators, most of his concepts can be applied to standard indicators as well. One common indicator is the Relative Strength Index (RSI) created by J. Welles Wilder (1978) to measure the strength or weakness of a market based on the ratio of up and down closes in an evaluation period. The name, like those of many technical indicators, is confusing because it has nothing to do with relative strength, nor is it an index, but, regardless, it does have a statistically verifiable edge. Figure 16.5 shows a standard RSI on a daily stock chart with trades marked according to a simple trading plan: short when the RSI goes above 70, the top band, and buy when it goes below the lower band at 30. Most traders do not use it in such a simple way, but more often combine it with other patterns or other tools to build a complete trading system.

Figure 16.5 Standard 14-Period RSI Applied to Daily LULU

Table 16.12 shows the results of a simple, naive test of the basic RSI, and, perhaps surprisingly, it does show an edge in all asset classes. Once again, equities show clear evidence of mean reversion; it looks like the RSI could actually give us a pretty good head start trading this condition, based on the size and persistent statistical significance of the excess returns. Also once again, futures and forex refuse to play along, showing slight tendencies that are basically indistinguishable from noise.

Table 16.12 Standard 14-Period RSI Overbought/Oversold at 70/30

	Equities—Buy			Futures—Buy			Forex—Buy		
Days	$\mu_{sig} - \mu_b$	Diff. Med.	%Up	$\mu_{sig} - \mu_b$	Diff. Med.	%Up	$\mu_{sig} - \mu_b$	Diff. Med.	%Up
1	15.8 **	14.3	52.8%	(13.7)	4.7	52.9%	(18.7)**	0.6	51.7%
2	32.2 **	28.8	53.9%	(8.4)	16.5	55.8%	(21.5)*	(3.0)	50.3%
3	38.8 **	42.6	54.9%	(11.6)	(5.0)	50.5%	(20.3)	(14.4)	45.5%
4	42.4 **	46.8	54.8%	(20.6)	4.4	54.8%	(26.7)	(15.0)	46.9%
5	53.8 **	57.6	55.6%	(20.0)	(24.0)	48.8%	(26.4)	(9.7)	50.3%
10	64.9 **	81.2	56.3%	(53.5)*	(31.9)	50.3%	(47.3)*	(38.0)	45.5%
15	89.9 **	137.0	58.4%	(30.0)	(33.3)	52.2%	(30.9)	(1.6)	55.9%
20	98.9 **	150.6	58.5%	(21.8)	(15.8)	54.3%	(32.5)	(20.0)	53.1%
	Equities—Sell			Futures—Sell			Forex—Sell		
Days	$\mu_{sig} - \mu_b$	Diff. Med.	%Up	$\mu_{sig} - \mu_b$	Diff. Med.	%Up	$\mu_{sig} - \mu_b$	Diff. Med.	%Up
1	(16.1)**	(10.4)	46.7%	3.0	(3.5)	49.1%	1.1	(2.1)	48.9%
2	(29.6)**	(16.6)	46.9%	14.6	10.3	54.7%	8.5	0.2	52.2%
3	(38.5)**	(19.8)	47.5%	13.1	9.5	54.0%	1.4	9.6	56.9%
4	(40.3)**	(21.2)	47.8%	14.5	11.9	55.7%	3.4	9.6	57.6%
5	(47.5)**	(19.4)	48.6%	15.0	7.1	55.3%	10.5	26.5	56.9%
10	(63.5)**	(19.8)	50.1%	11.7	(15.2)	52.0%	24.0 *	31.3	60.5%
15	(72.9)**	(8.6)	51.8%	23.7	(64.8)	49.0%	28.0	21.6	60.9%
20	(76.4)**	4.9	53.3%	33.9	(47.8)	52.6%	28.4	32.3	62.0%

Momentum

Momentum is essentially the opposite of mean reversion: the tendency for markets to continue in the same direction after a large move; some of the mean-reversion tests showed tendencies for momentum in futures and forex. In the interest of clarifying definitions, losing mean-reversion trades usually occur because momentum is dominating price action at that point, and momentum trades fail via mean reversion. In some sense, this is not a meaningful statement, and is akin to saying that when you buy something and lose money it is because it went down—true, but not really helpful. In this case, there is some actual value in the statement, because if we can identify environments where momentum or mean reversion are more likely, we then know the correct trading patterns to apply in each environment. Most trading losses come from incorrectly identifying the emerging volatility environment; much of the job of trading is building a discretionary tool set that will aid in that analysis. Figure 16.6 shows the two specific environments that tend to favor range expansion over mean reversion: volatility compression and simple pullbacks.

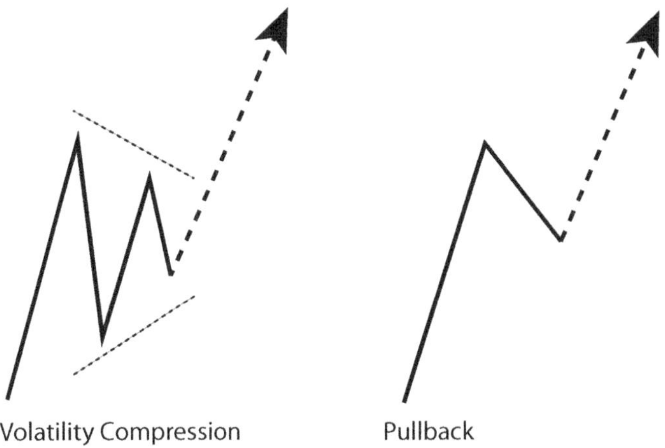

Figure 16.6 Volatility Compression and Simple Pullbacks Are Conditions That Tend to Set Up Range Expansion

Volatility Compression

There is a natural ebb and flow to the level of volatility in most markets—volatility is somewhat more predictable than price. This is captured in many of the academic models (GARCH, EGARCH, etc.), which seek to model the predictable elements of changing volatility levels within the framework of an otherwise random returns–generating process. We have not dealt extensively with volatility per se in this book, but an awareness of volatility and the most likely emerging volatility conditions supports many of the trading decisions and patterns in our work. For instance, there are few recurring, visible cycles in prices, because they are immediately erased by arbitrage as soon as they emerge. Once it becomes obvious, say, that a commodity will increase and decrease in price at certain times of the year, large players will trade in anticipation of this, buying and selling before the movement. Their selling activity will move prices, eventually erasing the cycle altogether. However, there is no such arbitrage mechanism to dampen swings or cycles in volatility. Traders can trade volatility in a pure form via nondirectional option spreads and other over-the-counter (OTC) derivatives, but trades in those instruments do not have a direct impact on the volatility of the underlying except in a few isolated cases.

We saw in earlier tests that single large days were likely to fail and to reverse back in the previous direction. The results were clearest in equities, but there was also evidence of this force at work in futures and, to a lesser extent, forex. Mean reversion is essentially a type of exhaustion: buyers or sellers have driven the price in one direction, and eventually they run out of steam. At that point, the market reverses and moves back into the vacuum. However, something interesting happens if volatility is compressed before the large move—it is more likely to continue in the same direction than to reverse. Volatility compression is a filter that can identify when a market is poised for range expansion.

There are many ways to measure volatility compression, and some are more successful than others in certain contexts. They key question is: what is a low level of volatility? For some markets it might be 3 percent annualized historical volatility, for others it might be 10 percent, and for still others it might be 20 percent, so it is not possible to use the same fixed levels across different markets. One possibility is to use a percentile rank of a volatility measure; for instance, flagging a market's volatility as compressed when a historical volatility measure is in the bottom 20th percentile of its historical range. Another good possibility is to use a ratio of volatilities measured on different time frames. Historical volatility measured over a short time period (5 to 20 days) might be compared to a longer-term measure (50 to 260 days), and that ratio used as an indicator of volatility compression. The idea is to always have a measure that adapts automatically to each market. Figure 16.7 shows an example of this concept: the middle panel on the chart has both 10-day (2-week) and 60-day (1-quarter) historical volatility measures; the bottom panel shows the ratio of the two. Spots where the volatility ratio was very low are marked on the chart. Though nothing works all the time (the two trades marked with asterisks would probably have been losing range expansion trades), notice how many of these spots led to fairly clean 3- to 5-day price movements. If we are aware of volatility compression, we can approach the market with a mind-set that favors continuation, range expansion, rather than reversal at these times.

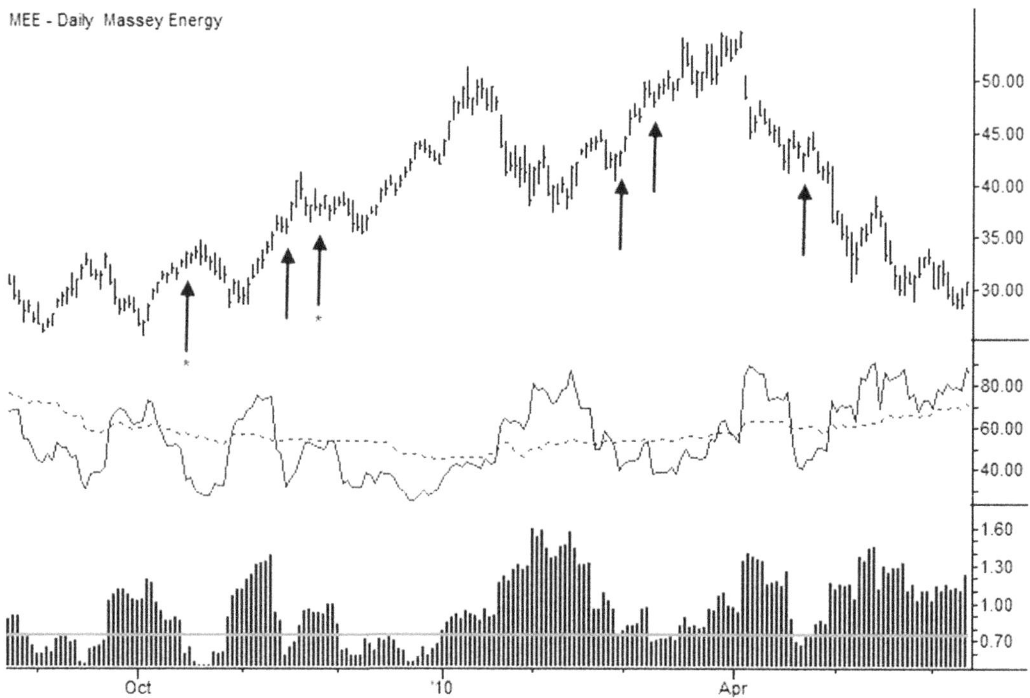

Figure 16.7 Trading 10- and 50-Day Historical Volatilities on Daily Massey Energy (NYSE: MEE), with the Ratio of the Volatilities in the Bottom Panel

Table 16.13 shows a quantitative test of a range expansion tendency, structured a bit differently, and using the ratio of 5-day to 40-day Average True Ranges as the measure of volatility compression. (Note that this is a completely different concept: measuring volatility by the range of the bars rather than by standard deviation of returns, which is a close-to-close measure.) A long trade was entered when:

- The ratio of 5-day to 40-day historical volatilities was less than 0.5 on the previous day.
- The current day's true range is greater or equal to the 5-day historical volatility.
- Today's close is in the upper half of today's range and above yesterday's close.

There are three distinct parts to this criterion set: the setup condition indicating compressed volatility; the trigger indicating that the current day's move was at least as large as the prevailing short-term volatility (in many cases, it was much larger on the trigger days); and a filter that forced the market to close strong on the day. This is an example of a test that moves us much closer to a condition that could be traded in practice. Criteria were reversed for shorts.

Table 16.13 Volatility Compression Breakout Test
(Ratio of 5-day to 40-day ATR < 0.5. Current day's range is ≥ 5-day ATR and current day closes in top 50 percent of day's range.)

	Equities—Buy			Futures—Buy		
Days	$\mu_{sig} - \mu_b$	Diff. Med.	%Up	$\mu_{sig} - \mu_b$	Diff. Med.	%Up
1	45.1 **	22.1	55.2%	53.8	3.3	51.4%
2	74.1 **	28.5	56.0%	69.6	30.8	56.8%
3	72.1 **	19.1	54.1%	91.8 *	53.6	62.2%
4	56.1 **	13.2	52.7%	128.2 **	78.7	64.9%
5	28.7 *	14.3	52.7%	89.5 *	26.6	73.0%
10	(70.5)**	(22.7)	49.7%	28.1	(10.7)	59.5%
15	(108.6)**	(18.5)	50.9%	(18.0)	(43.2)	51.4%
20	(130.0)**	(68.5)	48.6%	(58.5)	(7.2)	56.8%
	Equities—Sell			Futures—Sell		
Days	$\mu_{sig} - \mu_b$	Diff. Med.	%Up	$\mu_{sig} - \mu_b$	Diff. Med.	%Up
1	(4.3)	(0.1)	50.2%	(37.7)	(16.8)	43.8%
2	(22.5)*	(4.5)	49.7%	(39.5)	(7.5)	50.0%
3	(27.5)*	(10.9)	49.3%	2.1	10.7	58.3%
4	(42.8)**	(15.2)	48.6%	(15.0)	4.9	54.2%
5	(50.8)**	(17.2)	49.1%	(6.1)	21.4	56.3%
10	(120.8)**	(46.0)	48.8%	(28.0)	(111.3)	37.5%
15	(123.8)**	(71.7)	47.8%	(105.2)	(99.6)	41.7%
20	(76.2)*	(57.5)	49.4%	(119.2)	(122.3)	45.8%

First of all, note that forex is excluded from this test. The reason is that volatility fluctuates differently in forex, and these conditions produced only five long trades and two short trades for forex. It would be extremely misleading to draw conclusions from such a small sample; volatility compression is alive and well in forex, but this particular way to quantify it does not work very well. Leaving that aside for now, this test is one of the most convincing we have seen so far. Means and medians are consistently on the correct side of zero, which suggests that there is a real, underlying tendency driving this trade. Two factors complicate this analysis. First, sample sizes are small across the board, as this setup occurs approximately once in every 500 trading days. Second, it is by definition a volatile trade, with a wide dispersion of returns.

Up to this point, every test on equities has shown a clear tendency for mean reversion—based on those past tests, it seems as though you could actually trade equities simply by fading large moves. However, the addition of a very simple filter has completely changed the results, and we have now identified a subset of those large days that are more likely to continue in the same direction. Furthermore, this filter condition seems to strengthen the tendency for continuation in futures as well. Can we use this information to filter out profitable breakout trades? Could we also use it to increase the probability of success of mean reversion trades, by not taking them in times of volatility compression? The answer to both questions is a resounding yes.

Pullbacks

The other condition that can set a market up for a range expansion move is a pullback after a sharp directional move. What usually happens is the large move exhausts itself, mean reversion takes over, and part of the move is reversed while the market reaches an equilibrium point. After a period of relative rest, the original movement reasserts itself and the market makes another thrust in the initial direction. (We looked at this structural tendency in some detail in the section on Fibonacci retracements, and it was one of the most important trading patterns from earlier sections of this work.) The concept of impulse, retracement, impulse is valid—it actually is one of the most important patterns in the market.

We also saw earlier in this chapter that expecting moving averages to provide support and resistance is not likely to be a path to profitable trading. However, there is more to the story. A moving average does mark a position of relative equilibrium and balance, but the key question is "relative to what?" The answer—relative to the market's excursions from that particular average—implies that some way must be found to standardize those swings and the distances from the average. Fortunately, both Keltner channels and Bollinger bands present an ideal way to do this. They adapt to the volatility of the underlying market, and so, when properly calibrated, they mark significant extensions in all markets and all time frames. Figure 16.8 shows four short entries according to the following criteria:

- Shorts are allowed after the market closes below the lower Keltner channel.
- The entry trigger is a touch of the 20-period exponential moving average.
- Only one entry is allowed per touch of the channel; once a short entry has been taken, price must again close outside the lower channel to set up another potential short.
- Rules are symmetrical to the buy side.

Figure 16.8 Four Short Entries for a Simple System That Trades at the EMA After the Keltner Channel Has Been Broken

Table 16.14 shows the results of applying this test to the full test universe, with one small modification: the entry was made at the previous bar's moving average, to avoid the situation where a large close pulls the average into the bar. This entry value would be known in advance, and, from a practical perspective, a trader could be bidding or offering at that level for each bar. The results are nothing short of astounding: clear edges for buys and sells for all asset classes, most of which also show statistical significance. This is not an infrequent signal, occurring on about 1 percent of all trading days, so the sample size is certainly adequate. This is an important element of market structure: after a market makes a sharp move, in this case quantified by penetrating the channel, and then pulls back, in this case to the moving average, a move in the previous direction is likely. This is the very essence of trend trading. We could continue and quantify this pattern many more ways, but this simple test serves to illustrate the point.

Table 16.14 Keltner Pullback Entry on Previous Bar's EMA

	Equities—Buy			Futures—Buy			Forex—Buy		
Days	$\mu_{sig} - \mu_b$	Diff. Med.	%Up	$\mu_{sig} - \mu_b$	Diff. Med.	%Up	$\mu_{sig} - \mu_b$	Diff. Med.	%Up
1	50.1 **	36.3	57.3%	0.7	0.7	51.3%	23.0 **	35.7	68.6%
2	58.1 **	47.1	57.9%	5.6	(2.8)	51.0%	24.8 **	31.3	64.7%
3	63.7 **	54.1	58.0%	2.9	(11.2)	49.6%	37.8 **	43.5	65.4%
4	71.6 **	66.7	58.6%	12.8	(7.2)	51.3%	28.6 **	20.6	59.0%
5	73.3 **	75.6	58.8%	15.0	(23.6)	49.4%	24.2 *	17.9	59.0%
10	74.3 **	83.2	58.4%	18.7	6.6	54.0%	29.9	28.4	59.6%
15	53.0 **	99.7	58.4%	16.9	(7.6)	54.8%	15.0	0.3	55.8%
20	45.8 **	115.2	58.5%	26.5	(3.6)	54.8%	12.3	(4.9)	53.8%
	Equities—Sell			Futures—Sell			Forex—Sell		
Days	µsig - µb	Diff. Med.	%Up	µsig – µb	Diff. Med.	%Up	µsig – µb	Diff. Med.	%Up
1	(53.3)**	(14.3)	47.9%	(59.0)**	(30.4)	40.4%	(23.3)*	(6.5)	47.3%
2	(56.5)**	(14.5)	48.7%	(54.7)**	(25.1)	46.4%	(8.2)	(5.9)	49.5%
3	(65.7)**	(21.4)	48.5%	(45.5)**	(33.1)	44.9%	(8.3)	1.8	50.5%
4	(63.7)**	(27.9)	48.3%	(30.9)	(17.5)	48.6%	(4.0)	(2.5)	51.6%
5	(81.0)**	(43.0)	47.2%	(40.0)*	(43.0)	46.7%	(5.2)	(6.6)	50.5%
10	(96.3)**	(28.1)	49.7%	(63.5)*	(69.4)	46.9%	(7.3)	(3.9)	55.9%
15	(94.7)**	1.3	51.8%	(76.6)*	(97.3)	44.4%	(44.1)	22.1	55.9%
20	(70.2)**	43.8	53.9%	(86.4)*	(105.3)	48.6%	(21.9)	(27.5)	51.6%

One last point needs to be made: Is there an inconsistency between this test, which shows a strong edge for entering pullbacks at a moving average, and the previous work that finds moving averages essentially meaningless? No, there is not. The moving average, in this case, is only a rough reference point, and the results are unchanged across a wide range of parameters. It is possible to execute at a fairly wide band above or below the average, or even to randomize the average with an offset on every bar and the results are essentially unchanged.

The operative concept is that the market makes a sharp move and then retraces against that move, at which point a trade is entered. The bands and moving average are just one way to add structure to the market. This should not be taken as a successful test of a moving average; it is a successful test of a pullback tendency.

Summary

This has been a long chapter with a lot of information, but the point is simple: It is very important to understand how markets move and how they behave—quantitative testing is the only way to effectively do this. It is vitally important to have an objective system for evaluating price patterns, because even subtle biases can dramatically skew the results of any study. If you are picking out patterns by hand, you will unavoidably make some choices that compromise your results, and we all have poor intuition about probabilities and patterns. Verify everything before you trust it in the market.

We saw no evidence for the claims that Fibonacci ratios are important, and no evidence to support the idea that moving averages act as support and resistance or that some averages are somehow special. There is a clear tendency for the open to cluster near the high or low of the session, but exploiting that tendency may not be easy, as it is consistent with randomly generated price paths. However interesting it was to review these common practice technical patterns and to find no verifiable edge, what we have found that does work is far more important:

- Mean reversion is the tendency of markets to reverse after large movements. This is most prevalent in equities, and in all asset classes after a period of expanded volatility.
- Range expansion is the tendency for a directional move to continue or to spawn other moves in the same direction. These trades can be picked out through volatility filters, as many good trades follow periods of compressed volatility, or by exploiting the structure of impulse, retracement, impulse that characterizes most trending patterns in markets.

There is a common thread tying both of these together: Markets tend to work in mean reversion mode after a period of expanded volatility, and in range expansion mode after a period of contracted volatility. This is a price-pattern expression of an underlying cycle in volatility. Cueing in to this cycle, and being able to predict the most likely emerging volatility regime, is perhaps the most important skill for the discretionary trader.

Keep in mind that the tests in this chapter are not tests of complete trading systems—they are simple, almost crude, high-level tests of overarching market tendencies. A conscious effort was made to use no more than three conditions in each test and not to modify those conditions for different asset classes. (For instance, it is possible to structure a volatility compression breakout on forex, but the criteria need to be adapted to the volatility profile of that asset class.) It is entirely possible that, with additional filters, perhaps combining some of these concepts, or with the addition of some discretionary criteria, we could filter out more of the winning signals from the noise and greatly increase the edge of these tendencies.

This is the statistical backdrop for the trading patterns earlier in this book, which have already expanded on this work and have put these forces in the context of real market structure. We looked at many tools and patterns that can help the trader differentiate between the two volatility regimes; as discretionary traders, our work includes a large subjective component, but it must rest on a solid foundation of statistically significant market behavior. In the best case, discretionary trading techniques are an ideal fusion of reason and intuition—right-brain and left-brain thinking—that tap into the most powerful analytical and decision-making abilities of the human trader, but everything depends on a deep understanding of the true tendencies and forces behind market action. This work begins here.

Afterword

No book can make you a trader. No trading course can make you a trader. No teacher can make you into a trader. In fact, nothing in the world, other than your own hard work and dedication, can lead you to trading success. My goal in this book, in the online course at MarketLife.com this book supports, and in my first book, *The Art and Science of Technical Analysis,* has been to provide with information, perspectives, and a framework that can give you the best chance of success, but now the hard begins—and that hard work must be your own.

Most people who trade find the markets endlessly fascinating. You will face challenges from within and without, and you may find success, at first, is elusive. Persevere. Though few pursuits in modern life are as challenging as learning to manage risk and extract opportunities from the markets, the rewards may go beyond your wildest dreams.

As I said that beginning of this book, I thank you, each of my readers, for letting me be some small part of your journey, and I do wish you success in this, and in all your endeavors.

Bibliography

Acar, Emmanuel, and Robert Toffel. "Highs and Lows: Times of the Day in the Currency CME Market." In *Financial Markets Tick by Tick*, edited by Pierre Lequeux. New York: John Wiley & Sons, 1999.

Brock, William, Joseph Lakonishok, and Blake LeBaron. "Simple Technical Trading Rules and the Stochastic Properties of Stock Returns." *Journal of Finance* 47, issue 5 (December 1992): 1731–1764.

Bruguier, Antoine Jean, Steven R. Quartz, and Peter L. Bossaerts. "Exploring the Nature of 'Trader Intuition.'" *Journal of Finance* 65, issue 5 (October 2010): 1703–1723; Swiss Finance Institute Research Paper No. 10-02. Available at SSRN: ssrn.com/abstract-1530263.

Campbell, John Y., Andrew W. Lo, and A. Craig MacKinlay. *The Econometrics of Financial Markets.* Princeton, NJ: Princeton University Press, 1996.

Conover, W. J. *Practical Nonparametric Statistics.* New York: John Wiley & Sons, 1998.

Crabel, Toby. *Day Trading with Short Term Price Patterns and Opening Range Breakout.* Greenville, SC: Trader's Press, 1990.

Csíkszentmihályi , Mihály. *Finding Flow.* New York: HarperCollins, 1997.

Csíkszentmihályi, M., S. Abuhamdeh, and J. Nakamura. "Flow." In *Handbook of Competence and Motivation*, edited by A. Elliot, 598–698. New York: Guilford Press, 2005.

DeMark, Thomas R. *New Market Timing Techniques: Innovative Studies in Market Rhythm & Price Exhaustion.* New York: John Wiley & Sons, 1997.

Dimson, Elroy, Paul Marsh, and Mike Staunton. *Triumph of the Optimists: 101 Years of Global Investment Returns.* Princeton, NJ: Princeton University Press, 2002.

Douglas, Mark. *Trading in the Zone: Master the Market with Confidence, Discipline and a Winning Attitude.* Upper Saddle River, NJ: Prentice Hall Press, 2001.

Drummond, Charles. *Charles Drummond on Advanced P&L.* Self-published, 1980.

Edwards, Robert D., and John Magee. *Technical Analysis of Stock Trends*, 4th ed. Springfield, MA: J. Magee, 1964 (orig. pub. 1948).

Ehlers, John F. *Cybernetic Analysis for Stocks and Futures: Cutting-Edge DSP Technology to Improve Your Trading.* Hoboken, NJ: John Wiley & Sons, 2004.

Elder, Alexander. *Trading for a Living: Psychology, Trading Tactics, Money Management.* New York: John Wiley & Sons, 1993.

Faith, Curtis. *Way of the Turtle: The Secret Methods That Turned Ordinary People into Legendary Traders.* New York: McGraw-Hill, 2007.

Fama, Eugene F., and Kenneth R. French. "The Capital Asset Pricing Model: Theory and Evidence." *Journal of Economic Perspectives* 18, no. 3 (Summer 2004): 24–46.

Feller, William. *An Introduction to Probability Theory and Its Applications.* New York: John Wiley & Sons, 1951.

Fisher, Mark B. *The Logical Trader: Applying a Method to the Madness.* Hoboken, NJ: John Wiley & Sons, 2002.

Grimes, Adam H. *The Art and Science of Technical Analysis: Market Structure, Price Action, and Trading Strategies.* Hoboken, NJ: John Wiley & Sons, 2012.

Grossman, S., and J. Stiglitz. "On the Impossibility of Informationally Efficient Markets." *American Economic Review* 70 (1980): 393–408.

Harris, Larry. *Trading and Exchanges: Market Microstructure for Practitioners.* New York: Oxford University Press, 2002.

Hintze, Jerry L., and Ray D. Nelson. "Violin Plots: A Box Plot-Density Trace Synergism." *American Statistician* 52, no. 2 (1998): 181–184.

Jung, C. G. *Psychology and Alchemy.* Vol. 12 of *Collected Works of C. G. Jung*. Princeton, NJ: Princeton University Press, 1980.

Kelly, J. L., Jr. "A New Interpretation of Information Rate." *Bell System Technical Journal* 35 (1956): 917–926.

Kirkpatrick, Charles D., II. *Technical Analysis: The Complete Resource for Financial Market Technicians.* Upper Saddle River, NJ: FT Press, 2006.

Langer, E. J. "The Illusion of Control." *Journal of Personality and Social Psychology* 32, no. 2 (1975): 311–328.

Lo, Andrew. "Reconciling Efficient Markets with Behavioral Finance: The Adaptive Markets Hypothesis." *Journal of Investment Consulting*, forthcoming.

Lo, Andrew W., and A. Craig MacKinlay. *A Non-Random Walk Down Wall Street.* Princeton, NJ: Princeton University Press, 1999.

Lucas, Robert E., Jr. "Asset Prices in an Exchange Economy." *Econometrica* 46, no. 6 (1978): 1429–1445.

Macnamara, Brook N., David Z. Hambrick, and Frederick L. Oswald. "Deliberate Practice and Performance in Music, Games, Sports, Education, and Professions: A Meta-Analysis." *Pyschological Science* Vol 25, Issue 8 (2014), pp. 1608–1618.

Malkiel, Burton G. "The Efficient Market Hypothesis and Its Critics." *Journal of Economic Perspectives* 17, no. 1 (2003): 59–82.

Mandelbrot, Benoît, and Richard L. Hudson. *The Misbehavior of Markets: A Fractal View of Financial Turbulence.* New York: Basic Books, 2006.

Mauboussin, Michael J. "Untangling Skill and Luck: How to Think about Outcomes—Past, Present and Future." *Maboussin on Strategy*, Legg Mason Capital Management, July 2010.

Miles, Jeremy, and Mark Shevlin. *Applying Regression and Correlation: A Guide for Students and Researchers.* Thousand Oaks, CA: Sage Publications, 2000.

Niederhoffer, Victor. *The Education of a Speculator.* New York: John Wiley & Sons, 1998.

Plummer, Tony. *Forecasting Financial Markets: The Psychology of Successful Investing*, 6th ed. London: Kogan Page, 2010.

Raschke, Linda Bradford, and Laurence A. Conners. *Street Smarts: High Probability Short-Term Trading Strategies.* Jersey City, NJ: M. Gordon Publishing Group, 1996.

Schabacker, Richard Wallace. *Technical Analysis and Stock Market Profits.* New York: Forbes Publishing Co., 1932.

Schabacker, Richard Wallace. *Stock Market Profits.* New York: Forbes Publishing Co., 1934.

Schwager, Jack D. *Market Wizards: Interviews with Top Traders.* New York: HarperCollins, 1992.

Snedecor, George W., and William G. Cochran. *Statistical Methods*, 8th ed. Ames: Iowa State University Press, 1989.

Soros, George. *The Alchemy of Finance: Reading the Mind of the Market.* New York: John Wiley & Sons, 1994.

Sperandeo, Victor. *Trader Vic: Methods of a Wall Street Master.* New York: John Wiley & Sons, 1993.

Sperandeo, Victor. *Trader Vic II: Principles of Professional Speculation.* New York: John Wiley & Sons, 1998.

Steenbarger, Brett. *Enhancing Trader Performance: Proven Strategies From the Cutting Edge of Trading Psychology.* New York: John Wiley & Sons, 2008.

Taleb, Nassim. *Fooled by Randomness: The Hidden Role of Chance in Life and in the Markets.* New York: Random House, 2008.

Tsay, Ruey S. *Analysis of Financial Time Series.* Hoboken, NJ: John Wiley & Sons, 2005.

Vince, Ralph. *The Leverage Space Trading Model: Reconciling Portfolio Management Strategies and Economic Theory.* Hoboken, NJ: John Wiley & Sons, 2009.

Waitzkin, Josh. *The Art of Learning: An Inner Journey to Optimal Performance.* New York: Free Press, 2008.

Wasserman, Larry. *All of Nonparametric Statistics.* New York: Springer, 2010.

Wilder, J. Welles, Jr. *New Concepts in Technical Trading Systems.* McLeansville, NC: Trend Research, 1978.

About the Author

Adam Grimes has over two decades experience as a trader and system developer. He's worked for small firms and big firms, from the farmlands of the Ohio Valley to the trading floors of the New York Mercantile Exchange. He is Managing Partner and CIO for Waverly Advisors, LLC, a New York-based research and advisory firm for which he writes daily market commentary . He blogs regularly at adamhgrimes.com, and is also a contributing author for many publications on quantitative finance and trading, and is much in demand as a speaker and lecturer.

In addition to being a trader, Adam also has deep training in classical music (piano and composition) and classical French cooking. His perspective is both deeply quantitative and practical, and he has done extensive personal work developing his skills as a teacher, coach, and mentor. He is fascinated by the limits of human knowledge and peak performance—specifically, how do we get there and stay there, and how to teach others to do the same?

Adam's relentless focus on trading excellence and self-development through financial markets has created a unique body of work that has helped many traders move along the path to trading success.

You can find much more of Adam's work and teaching on his website, MarketLife.com.

Index

A

B

C

L

M

N

O

P

Made in the USA
Monee, IL
25 September 2023